INTRODUCTION TO
INTERNATIONAL RELATIONS THEORIES

INTRODUCTION TO
INTERNATIONAL RELATIONS THEORIES

PETER **LAWLER**

Great Clarendon Street, Oxford, OX2 6DP,
United Kingdom

Oxford University Press is a department of the University of Oxford.
It furthers the University's objective of excellence in research, scholarship,
and education by publishing worldwide. Oxford is a registered trade mark of
Oxford University Press in the UK and in certain other countries

© Oxford University Press 2024

The moral rights of the author have been asserted

All rights reserved. No part of this publication may be reproduced, stored in
a retrieval system, or transmitted, in any form or by any means, without the
prior permission in writing of Oxford University Press, or as expressly permitted
by law, by licence or under terms agreed with the appropriate reprographics
rights organization. Enquiries concerning reproduction outside the scope of the
above should be sent to the Rights Department, Oxford University Press, at the
address above

You must not circulate this work in any other form
and you must impose this same condition on any acquirer

Published in the United States of America by Oxford University Press
198 Madison Avenue, New York, NY 10016, United States of America

British Library Cataloguing in Publication Data
Data available

Library of Congress Control Number: 2023942291

ISBN 978–0–19–878489–0

Printed in the UK by
Bell & Bain Ltd., Glasgow

Links to third party websites are provided by Oxford in good faith and
for information only. Oxford disclaims any responsibility for the materials
contained in any third party website referenced in this work.

In memory of Professor Andrew Linklater (1949–2023)
Scholar, mentor, and dear friend.

PREFACE

Over the last few decades, the range of theoretical perspectives within the international relations (IR) academic discipline has evolved rapidly and dramatically. This theoretical development has followed many novel paths but there are some that have become especially prominent. Among the more recent of these are theoretical explorations around what is often referred to as the politics of identity, particularly the significance of gender, culture, and race. An increasingly common complaint is that for too long the conduct, analysis, and teaching of international politics has been dominated by a particular group of people: white men of Western origin. Thankfully, this is now changing, although whether it is changing fast enough remains, however, a matter of debate.

This presents something of a dilemma for me as the author of this text, because I am male, white, and a product of the West, just like most of the people who taught me when I was an undergraduate and graduate student of IR. Over the four decades or so of my academic career, however, I have witnessed the increasing diversification of my student audience and in the latter half of my career especially, the diversification of my colleagues as well. Personally, I have found this to be a long overdue, very welcome, and intensely stimulating development. It has required me to think very hard not only about what I teach but how I teach it. Nonetheless, much as I might try to appreciate and learn from the variety of perspectives and outlooks that accompanies such diversification, I cannot step entirely out of my own skin, so to speak.

A highlight of the latter part of my teaching career was a decade spent teaching a very large introductory IR course at the University of Manchester, in the North-West of England. The students came from more than 50 different countries across the world. Student feedback consistently told me that the course was a success. Nonetheless, I was increasingly mindful of the fact that the background and experiences of many, perhaps most, of my students was very different from my own and I often wondered what they made of the ageing, increasingly grey-haired Western man at the front of their lecture theatre. Similarly, I am very aware that the readers of this textbook are also likely to be from a wide range of backgrounds and experiences. It seems only fair then to put my own identity cards on the table and tell you, the readers, a bit about myself. What you choose to do with this information is entirely up to you.

I am the son of Irish Catholic immigrants to the United Kingdom. I didn't start my university education until my mid-twenties, preferring instead to go travelling and experience the world. I undertook my first two degrees in the UK and then emigrated to Melbourne, Australia where I undertook my PhD, started my academic teaching and research career, and took up Australian citizenship, alongside my Irish and British citizenships. Some 15 years later I returned to the UK to take up a position at the University of Manchester where I remained until I retired in 2019. Along the way, I accepted short-term invitations to teach in Ireland, Spain, Russia, Canada, India, and Belgium. I cannot say I have taught students from every country in the world, but I think I have encountered students from most of them. I once attempted to estimate how many students, at all levels from first year undergraduates through to PhD candidates, I had taught. This proved rather difficult, but a conservative guess is that it is many thousands.

Teaching has been a sometimes challenging but ultimately richly rewarding experience for me and it provides the bedrock of this textbook. I now live in West London with my Iraqi wife who was raised in the Middle East and now works as an international development consultant, specialising in media development in the Middle East and North Africa. Her life experiences are also very different to my own and this further encourages me to look beyond my own horizons when endeavouring to understand contemporary world politics. In the end, I am, like you the readers, also a student as much as a teacher of IR.

ACKNOWLEDGEMENTS

Much of this textbook was drafted during the Covid-19 pandemic. This meant that the process of writing was often a more solitary process than I had anticipated. Nonetheless, writing a textbook can never be an entirely solitary enterprise. So, I must first express my profound appreciation to the editorial team at Oxford University Press, especially Stephanie Southall-Paddock and Sarah Iles. Stephanie guided me firmly but always fairly through the foundational stages of drafting the manuscript and I dread to think how it might have gone without her looking over my shoulder. The finalising of the textbook was carried out under the watchful eyes of Sarah, whose sheer depth of experience was both reassuring and of immense practical value. They are also nice people, which certainly helps!

All the chapters were reviewed by a wide panel of anonymous reviewers, and I wish to thank them all sincerely for their invaluable and very constructive feedback. Two of the chapters—'Feminisms, Gender, and International Politics' and 'Postcolonialism'—were further closely reviewed by invited external readers, Clara Eroukhmanoff and Meera Sabaratnam respectively. I am very grateful for their robust, constructive, and immensely useful feedback from which I learned a great deal. I have endeavoured to take it all fully on board, hopefully to their satisfaction.

Inevitably, this textbook draws very heavily on the work of a wide range of IR scholars from across the world. Although I have yet to meet many of them, over the decades I have come to know quite a few, and some became colleagues and friends. A few of them were once students of mine who have gone on to become leading lights of key IR theoretical perspectives. Whether we always agreed on matters theoretical or not, I have benefited immeasurably from intellectual interaction with them all. There is a group of scholars whose influence on my thinking and teaching has been especially significant, whether I have ever openly admitted this to them or not. Many of their names rightly pop up throughout this book and I owe them explicit acknowledgement here. These include Richard Devetak, Chris Reus-Smit, Véronique Pin-Fat, Emmanuel-Pierre Guittet, Maja Zehfuss, Elizabeth Dauphinee, Paul Cammack, Cristina Masters, Robyn Eckersley, Maria Stern, David Campbell, Rob Walker, Roland Bleiker, Jenny Edkins, Natalie Bormann, Matthew Paterson, Stuart Shields, Felix Ciuta, and Annika Bergman-Rosamond.

Just after I completed this manuscript and at the end of a delayed honeymoon in Australia, I learned of the death of Professor Andrew Linklater (to whom this textbook is dedicated). I knew Andy from my very first day as a tutor (Graduate Teaching Assistant) on one of his courses at Monash University, Melbourne some 40 years ago. Andy not only inspired me intellectually, but also became an invaluable mentor and dear friend. I miss him terribly.

Finally, the writing of this textbook happily coincided with me falling in love and getting married. Consequently, my fabulous wife, Dr Aida Al-Kaisy, had to not only wrestle with advancing her own career and completing her PhD, but also putting up with the tedium of me working on this textbook. For her love, patience, and support I am eternally grateful. I was also very lucky to meet Aida's father, Farouk Al-Kaisy, a lovely cerebral and open-minded polymath. Sadly, Farouk passed away while this book was being completed. I like to think he would have read it and told me honestly what he thought!

FOREWORD

About this book

This textbook is in large part the product of my nearly four decades of teaching about various dimensions of international and global politics, mostly in the UK and Australia but also Canada, Spain, Switzerland, Russia, Belgium, and India. I have taught at all levels from first year undergraduates through to MA and PhD students, at universities large and small, and to students from all over the world. Over the same period, the discipline commonly known as International Relations or simply 'IR' has undergone dramatic change. An obvious reason is that the practice of international or global politics—the primary focus of the IR discipline—has changed because of such developments as the end of the Cold War, the 9/11 terrorist attacks on the US, the increasing global prominence of questions about the significance of gender in international politics or the legacies of colonialism and imperialism, and the widespread recognition of a global environmental crisis. Several new sub-disciplines have also emerged, such as International Political Economy and Security Studies and some would say that these have gone on to become distinct stand-alone disciplines.

The most dramatic change, however, is surely in the realm of IR theory. When I started out as a student in the mid 1970s, the IR theoretical menu was very limited. Now, it offers far richer pickings. There are a lot more theoretical perspectives in today's IR discipline and they in turn draw upon a much wider range of other disciplines, across the social sciences and humanities. In combination, they offer up a far more complex and rich picture of the world than ever before. This is good news for you, the budding IR student but, of course, it also means that there's a lot more theoretical ground to cover.

This book focuses on the key theoretical perspectives found within the IR discipline today. These are examined in roughly the order in which they emerged historically since the modern IR discipline was established just over a century ago. This is intended to help you grasp how the IR discipline has evolved and how that evolution seemingly intersects with key historical moments and eras. It is important to note, however, that this structure is not intended to suggest that IR theory has 'progressed' in some indisputable cumulative sense, or that older IR theoretical perspectives have become redundant or should be disregarded simply because of their vintage. All the perspectives covered in this textbook—new and old—are alive and well.

Additionally, answers to questions along the lines of 'why do theories emerge when they do?' are themselves matters of debate. This textbook encourages you to think about the relationship between history and the evolution of our theoretical understanding of our world: do theories emerge out of the blue, so to speak; does history generate theory in some way; or do new interpretations of international politics themselves somehow influence history's path? These are large and difficult questions, and this book does not attempt to offer definitive answers. If, however, it gets you thinking about these questions and wanting to carry on thinking about them (along with the many other questions that will arise as you delve further into the world of IR theories), then it will have achieved one of its objectives.

The key aim of this book is to help you interpret and assess the various IR perspectives it examines. What it will not tell you is which theoretical lenses you should choose to look at the world around you. That is for you as a student of IR to decide.

Who is this textbook for?

This textbook is aimed primarily at those with little or no knowledge of the IR discipline and, more specifically, the various theoretical perspectives that make up that discipline today. It may also serve as a refresher text for those who are returning to the study of IR or wanting a quick introductory reminder of the key themes and features of key IR theories.

It is not a book about international or world politics in all their historical and empirical dimensions, although it does contain frequent reference throughout to key actors, processes, and historical episodes of international politics. The purpose of such references, however, is primarily to help you to better understand what specific theories focus on and possible reasons why, how the different theoretical perspectives can be distinguished from each other, and the historical contexts in which they emerge, become more influential, or fall out of favour.

Covering every aspect of the various IR theoretical perspectives available to the IR student today, especially when all the variations found within them are included, would take a larger and more complex book than this one. From the outset, the intention behind this book has been to provide a comprehensive introductory text that covers all the key theoretical perspectives in the contemporary IR discipline, without pretending that it could ever be the last word. The writing of an introductory and accessible text covering IR theory today entails some unavoidable costs: detail must be left out, complex arguments must be simplified for heuristic purposes, and so on. Therefore, this book can only offer a first step. Hopefully, it is a sufficiently robust step from which you can go on to delve deeper into any or all the theoretical perspectives it covers. if you want to develop a more advanced understanding of the range of IR theories and perspectives available to you, you will eventually have to (and hopefully will want to) go beyond what is covered here. Indeed, one of the book's objectives is to encourage you to do just that.

How to use this book

As noted earlier, the book is structured as a linear historical account to help you understand how and why theoretical perspectives emerge and why their subsequent influence fluctuates. This suggests one obvious way to read it: from beginning to end. Of course, it does not have to be the only way.

Introductory courses on IR theory or IR more generally vary widely between universities and colleges. Some will introduce IR theories in a similar order to this book, but others might focus on a smaller range of theories or introduce the theories in a different sequence. Such variations may reflect where those institutions are located, the intellectual and theoretical preferences of the lecturer or professor, the length of the course, or because the course is designed to highlight a particular theme, such as security, the impact of colonialism, or gender. In such cases you may want to, or be advised to start with a specific chapter, or dip in and out as the course proceeds. Each of the chapters is intended to stand on its own, although most will also cross-refer the reader to other chapters if this is needed for purposes of clarity.

However, as you approach the book, you are advised to read Chapter 1 'Making Sense of Today's World' first as this provides a first guide to the world of IR theory, as well as some key theoretical debates and useful terms to help you on your way. It also offers brief summaries of all the theories covered to give you an initial sense of their range and variation. There's no denying that some can seem more challenging than others on first sight. If you persevere, however, getting to know the full range of IR theoretical perspectives will reward you by enabling you to think quite differently and more insightfully about world politics today.

Gain a deeper understanding of IR theories

Through a series of 'Conversations with . . .' videos, get a deeper understanding of the key IR theories by watching the author interview academics to get a range of perspectives and views on IR theories and approaches.

Resources for lecturers

www.oup.com/he/lawler1e
Adopting lecturers can access the following online resources:

For registered lecturers

- Use the adaptable PowerPoint slides as the basis for a lecture presentation, or as hand-outs in class
- Save time preparing assessments and seminars with a bank of questions

BRIEF CONTENTS

1 MAKING SENSE OF TODAY'S WORLD   1

2 THE LIBERAL 'IDEALIST' ORIGINS OF THE INTERNATIONAL RELATIONS DISCIPLINE   22

3 CLASSICAL REALISM AND NEOREALISM   63

4 THE ENGLISH SCHOOL OF INTERNATIONAL RELATIONS   105

5 MARXISM AND INTERNATIONAL RELATIONS   149

6 CRITICAL INTERNATIONAL THEORY   188

7 POSTSTRUCTURALISM AND INTERNATIONAL RELATIONS   231

8 CONSTRUCTIVISM AND INTERNATIONAL RELATIONS   277

9 POSTCOLONIALISM AND INTERNATIONAL RELATIONS   321

10 FEMINISMS, GENDER, AND INTERNATIONAL RELATIONS   373

11 GREEN PERSPECTIVES AND INTERNATIONAL RELATIONS   425

12 CONCLUSION   472

Bibliography   487

Subject Index   507

FULL CONTENTS

1 MAKING SENSE OF TODAY'S WORLD — 1

  1.1 INTRODUCTION — 1
    The importance of historical context — 3
    You know more about theories than you probably think — 5

  1.2 WHAT'S IN A NAME—INTERNATIONAL RELATIONS, INTERNATIONAL POLITICS, WORLD POLITICS? — 6
    International Relations (IR) — 6
    International Politics — 6
    World Politics or Global Politics — 6

  1.3 WHAT ARE IR THEORIES? — 7
    Three key terms: ontology; epistemology; and methodology — 8
    Mainstream versus critical theories — 10

  1.4 AN OUTLINE OF THE IR THEORIES COVERED IN THIS BOOK — 12
    Liberalism (CHAPTER 2) — 12
    Realism (CHAPTER 3) — 13
    The English School (CHAPTER 4) — 14
    Marxism (CHAPTER 5) — 14
    Critical IR Theory (CHAPTER 6) — 15
    Poststructuralism (CHAPTER 7) — 16
    Constructivism (CHAPTER 8) — 17
    Postcolonialism (CHAPTER 9) — 17
    Feminisms and Gender (CHAPTER 10) — 18
    Green perspectives (CHAPTER 11) — 19

  1.5 CONCLUSION — 20

2 THE LIBERAL 'IDEALIST' ORIGINS OF THE INTERNATIONAL RELATIONS DISCIPLINE — 22

  2.1 INTRODUCTION — 22

  2.2 WHAT IS LIBERALISM? — 23
    The core tenets of liberalism — 24

  2.3 LIBERALISM AND INTERNATIONAL POLITICS—THE FOUNDATIONAL PHASE — 26

	Immanuel Kant and 'inside-out' international reformism	27
	The liberal origins of the IR discipline	30
	Applying liberal 'idealism' to International Politics: Woodrow Wilson and the League of Nations	32
2.4	CHALLENGING THE COMMON STORY OF THE IR DISCIPLINE'S ORIGINS	37
	Was early liberal thinking on IR actually 'idealist'?	37
	Imperialism, racism, and the establishment of the IR discipline	38
2.5	THE 'IDEALIST' LEGACY IN IR TODAY—THE CONTINUING DEVELOPMENT OF THE LIBERAL APPROACH TO IR	40
	Liberalism and the institutionalization of international politics	41
	The development of liberal IR thinking after 1945—history and theory	45
	Complex interdependence	47
	The end of the Cold War—the triumph of the liberal West?	48
2.6	CONTEMPORARY LIBERAL IR AND IMPERIALISM	51
2.7	KANT REVISITED: ALEX BELLAMY'S WORLD PEACE (AND HOW WE CAN ACHIEVE IT)	54
2.8	CONCLUSION	56
	IR THEORY TODAY HUNGARY: POST-COLD WAR LIBERAL TRIUMPHALISM REVISITED	59

3 CLASSICAL REALISM AND NEOREALISM

		63
3.1	INTRODUCTION	63
3.2	WHAT IS REALISM?	64
	Why is it called realism?	65
3.3	REALISM AND INTERNATIONAL POLITICS	66
	The early sources of realism	67
3.4	THE EMERGENCE OF CONTEMPORARY CLASSICAL REALISM	71
	E.H. Carr and the neglect of power	72
	Hans Morgenthau and the 'six principles of political realism'	74
3.5	THE CORE ASSUMPTIONS OF CLASSICAL REALISM	78
3.6	FROM CLASSICAL REALISM TO NEOREALISM	82
	Man, the State and War	83
	Waltz's theory of international politics	84
	Neorealism and 'great powers'	86
	Defensive or offensive neorealism?	87
3.7	LIBERALISM ANSWERS BACK—NEOLIBERALISM, NEOREALISM, AND THE 'NEO-NEO' DEBATE	88
	Relative versus absolute gains	89
	Neoliberal institutionalism's challenge to neorealism: 'cooperation under anarchy'	90
	The neorealist response	91
3.8	NEOCLASSICAL REALISM—BRIDGING THE CLASSICAL REALIST-NEOREALIST DIVIDE	94

FULL CONTENTS **xix**

3.9	REALISM AND NUCLEAR WEAPONS	95
	Morgenthau on nuclear weapons	95
	Waltz on nuclear weapons	96
	Three realist positions on nuclear weapons: exclusion, participation, or renunciation	97
3.10	CONCLUSION	98
	IR THEORY TODAY REALISM AND THE WAR IN AFGHANISTAN	101

4 THE ENGLISH SCHOOL OF INTERNATIONAL RELATIONS · 105

4.1	INTRODUCTION	105
4.2	WHAT IS THE ENGLISH SCHOOL?	106
	The anarchical society of states	107
	Pluralists and Solidarists	111
4.3	THE FIRST PHASE: THE ORIGINS OF THE ENGLISH SCHOOL	112
	Martin Wight: the 'Three Traditions' of thinking about international relations	113
	Hedley Bull and the anarchical society of states	118
4.4	THE SECOND PHASE: ORDER VS JUSTICE	125
	Hedley Bull and the 'Revolt against Western dominance'	126
	The ascendancy of solidarism in the post-Cold War era	129
	Pluralist scepticism about the prospects and virtues of greater solidarism	136
4.5	THE THIRD PHASE: FROM INTERNATIONAL SOCIETY TO WORLD SOCIETY?	138
	Barry Buzan's reappraisal of the English School	138
	Feminism and the English School	142
4.6	CONCLUSION	144
	IR THEORY TODAY ARE TODAY'S 'GREAT POWERS' BEHAVING 'RESPONSIBLY'?	146

5 MARXISM AND INTERNATIONAL RELATIONS · 149

5.1	INTRODUCTION	149
5.2	WHAT IS MARXISM?	150
	Marxism: key themes	152
5.3	MARXISM AND IR	159
	Marxism and imperialism	160
	From imperialism to dependency theory	162
	World Systems Theory	168
5.4	MARXISM AND IPE/GPE	169
	Marxism and Globalization	170
	Neo-Gramscianism and the concept of hegemony	175
	Challenging the 'Washington consensus'	178
5.5	CONCLUSION	180
	IR THEORY TODAY 'VACCINE APARTHEID': CORONAVIRUS VACCINATIONS AND GLOBAL INEQUALITY	183

xx FULL CONTENTS

6 CRITICAL INTERNATIONAL THEORY 188

6.1	INTRODUCTION	188
6.2	WHAT IS CRITICAL THEORY?	189
	The origins of Critical Theory	190
	Was there a distinctive 'Young' Marx?	193
	Are the social sciences (such as IR) 'scientific'?	194
	Traditional versus critical theory	195
	Jürgen Habermas: knowledge and human interests	198
	Critical theory and emancipation	200
6.3	CRITICAL THEORY AND IR	201
	Richard Ashley—realism and human interests	201
	Robert Cox: traditional IR theory versus Critical International Theory	204
6.4	APPLYING CRITICAL INTERNATIONAL THEORY	208
	Material power, ideology, and institutions—Neo-Gramscianism and world order	209
	The Frankfurt School's Critical Theory and IR	215
	Inclusion, Exclusion, and 'The Transformation of Community'	219
	Critical Theory and Security	222
6.5	FROM CRITICAL INTERNATIONAL THEORY TO CRITICAL IR THEORIES	224
6.6	CONCLUSION	225
	IR THEORY TODAY CRITICAL INTERNATIONAL THEORY AND THE GLOBAL ENVIRONMENTAL MOVEMENT	227

7 POSTSTRUCTURALISM AND INTERNATIONAL RELATIONS 231

7.1	INTRODUCTION	231
7.2	WHAT IS POSTSTRUCTURALISM?	232
	What is 'post' about poststructuralism?	233
7.3	POSTSTRUCTURALISM: KEY SOURCES AND THEMES	236
	Jacques Derrida and deconstruction	236
	Michel Foucault: Power and knowledge	240
	Summary of key themes in poststructuralism	246
7.4	POSTSTRUCTURALISM AND IR	248
	Representation and IR: Baudrillard's 'The Gulf War Did Not Take Place'	248
	Mapping the World	251
	Problematizing the discipline of IR	255
	Problematizing the Sovereign State	257
	Representing the non-Western 'other' in the liberal media and entertainment industries	267
7.5	POSTSTRUCTURALISM AND OTHER CRITICAL APPROACHES TO IR	268
7.6	CONCLUSION	270
	IR THEORY TODAY 'BREXIT': THE UNITED KINGDOM LEAVES THE EUROPEAN UNION (EU)	272

8 CONSTRUCTIVISM AND INTERNATIONAL RELATIONS — 277

8.1 INTRODUCTION — 277

8.2 WHAT IS CONSTRUCTIVISM? — 278
Why did constructivism emerge? — 278
The essence of constructivism — 282

8.3 LOCATING CONSTRUCTIVISM ON THE SPECTRUM OF IR THEORIES — 286
Agency and Structure — 290
Conventional and critical constructivism — 292
Constructivism and the 'middle ground' of the IR theory spectrum — 296

8.4 THE IMPORTANCE OF IDENTITY — 297
'Systemic' constructivism and 'unit-level' constructivism — 301

8.5 THE IMPORTANCE OF NORMS — 305
Norms, normativity, and constructivism — 307
Constructivism and the nuclear weapons debate — 310

8.6 CONCLUSION — 313
IR THEORY TODAY CONSTRUCTING THE COVID-19 PANDEMIC — 316

9 POSTCOLONIALISM AND INTERNATIONAL RELATIONS — 321

9.1 INTRODUCTION — 321

9.2 WHAT IS POSTCOLONIALISM? — 322

9.3 KEY ASPECTS OF EUROPEAN COLONIALISM — 324
The challenge of remembering difficult histories — 325
The expansion of European colonialism — 326
Colonialism, race, and racism — 328

9.4 RESISTING COLONIALISM — 331
Early Resistance — 331
The anticolonial struggles of the twentieth century — 334

9.5 KEY SOURCES OF CONTEMPORARY POSTCOLONIAL THOUGHT — 339
Frantz Fanon — 339
Edward Said and Orientalism — 342
Subaltern Studies—excavating unheard voices from below — 343
Homi K. Bhabha and 'hybridity' — 345

9.6 POSTCOLONIALISM AND THE IR DISCIPLINE — 347
Postcolonialism and the Cold War — 348
Postcolonialism and international law — 349
Postcolonialism and the state — 352
Postcolonialism and human rights — 354

9.7 EUROCENTRISM AND RACISM IN THE IR DISCIPLINE? — 358
Race, racism, and IR theory — 360

xxii FULL CONTENTS

9.8	DECOLONIAL APPROACHES	363
9.9	CONCLUSION	368
	IR THEORY TODAY VOLUNTOURISM	370

10 FEMINISMS, GENDER, AND INTERNATIONAL RELATIONS — 373

10.1	INTRODUCTION	373
10.2	WHAT ARE FEMINISMS?	375
	The fight for women's suffrage	376
	The evolution of contemporary feminisms	378
10.3	FEMINISMS, GENDER, AND INTERNATIONAL POLITICS	386
	Why did feminist perspectives take so long to emerge in the IR discipline?	386
	Early feminist analyses of the international: women, peace, and development	388
	'Add women and stir'?	395
	Postpositivist IR feminisms	399
10.4	KEY THEMES IN CONTEMPORARY FEMINIST AND GENDER IR PERSPECTIVES	405
	Gender and Security	406
10.5	GENDER AND THE 'QUEERING' OF THE IR DISCIPLINE	412
	Men and masculinities	413
	LGBT perspectives, Queer Theory, and IR	414
10.6	CONCLUSION	418
	IR THEORY TODAY THE SARAH EVERARD MURDER AND GLOBAL VIOLENCE AGAINST WOMEN	420

11 GREEN PERSPECTIVES AND INTERNATIONAL RELATIONS — 425

11.1	INTRODUCTION	425
11.2	WHAT IS GREEN THEORY?	426
	Environmentalism versus ecologism	427
	Anthropocentrism or ecocentrism?	429
11.3	THE EMERGENCE OF GREEN POLITICAL THINKING	432
	Early antecedents	432
	The growth of environmental awareness	437
11.4	THE ARRIVAL OF GREEN POLITICAL THEORY	438
	The impact of green political success	441
11.5	GREEN PERSPECTIVES AND INTERNATIONAL POLITICS I—LOOKING THROUGH STATE-CENTRIC LENSES	442
	Garrett Hardin and the 'The Tragedy of the Commons' (1968)	444
	The *Limits to Growth* debate (1970s)	447
	The evolution of 'global environmental governance'—from Rio 1992 to COP26	448

FULL CONTENTS **xxiii**

11.6 GREEN PERSPECTIVES AND INTERNATIONAL POLITICS II—
CRITICAL GREEN IR PERSPECTIVES 451

Green international political economy 453

Environmental justice 455

Towards an alternative ecological world order? 458

11.7 IR IN THE 'ANTHROPOCENE' 462

11.8 CONCLUSION 465

IR THEORY TODAY ANALYSING CARBON DIOXIDE (CO_2) EMISSIONS 468

12 CONCLUSION 472

12.1 IR THEORY AND HISTORY—A REVIEW 472

The First World War and after 473

The Cold War 474

Détente, the revival of liberal IR and the shift from 'East–West' to 'North–South' 475

The Second Cold War and after 476

The post-Cold War era 477

The twenty-first century—from 9/11 to the Anthropocene 479

12.2 SUMMARIZING BROAD THEORETICAL TRENDS OVER THE LIFE
OF THE IR DISCIPLINE 482

From simplicity to complexity 482

From explanation to understanding 482

Decentring the state and the international system of states 483

The growing recognition of the coloniality of the IR discipline 484

12.3 CONCLUDING THOUGHTS: DISCIPLINE, INTERDISCIPLINE,
OR ANTI-DISCIPLINE? 485

Discipline 485

Interdiscipline 486

Anti-discipline 486

Bibliography 487

Index 507

'PRAISE FOR INTERNATIONAL RELATIONS THEORIES'

- This masterful textbook sets a new benchmark for introductions to International Relations theory. Lawler combines a comprehensive and insightful engagement with a broad spectrum of theories with a strong pedagogical sensibility. He works out from students lived experiences to introduce not only the importance of theory but also the nuances of particular theories, paying close attention to the historical contexts in which they emerged. In doing so, Lawler has crafted a work that will build student understanding *and* prompt established scholars to think afresh about the theories they teach, employ, and debate. It is an introduction without peers. – **Professor Christian Reus-Smit, The University of Queensland, Australia**

- An accessible yet comprehensive IR theory textbook that guides students in understanding what theory is, what it is used for (and how), what the landscape of IR theory looks like, and how we can theorise specific events, issues, and processes that are shaping our world today. – **Dr Imad El-Anis, Nottingham Trent University**

- A very accessible and comprehensive account of IR theory that is well situated within both its historical context and wider political and social debate. – **Dr Ed Stoddard, University of Portsmouth**

- A comprehensive introduction to international relations theories, which provides readers not only with "real world" examples but also asks them important and challenging questions. – **Dr Matthew Jones, University of Greenwich**

CHAPTER 1

MAKING SENSE OF TODAY'S WORLD

LEARNING OBJECTIVES

- Recognize how your own life experience means you know more than you think about IR theory

- Discover the key questions and issues in international politics today and appreciate the vital role of theory in helping you to make sense of them

- Understand the importance of the relationship between historical context and theories

- Acquire a firm understanding of the meaning and relevance of key theoretical terms

- Summarize all the IR theories covered in this book

1.1 INTRODUCTION

A quick look at the news and social media, shows that there is a lot going on in global politics today. How can we make sense of our politically complex world, a world which, arguably, sends out very mixed messages?

For example, it would not be difficult to paint a rather pessimistic picture of today's world. It is not hard to find considerable evidence of division, competition, conflict, and actual or potential outbreaks of armed violence. It can seem like the world is driven primarily by a relentless struggle for power between selfish sovereign states. Moreover, most states maintain standing armies, and some possess immense military power and spend vast sums maintaining it. It is a world that is marked also by the sometimes-violent clash of differences between political ideologies, religious beliefs, or the various ways people identify either as groups or individuals. You might want to pause at this point and think of examples of this in today's world. A look across the history of the world might also tempt you to think that it has always been like this and, thus, likely to remain so.

Yet, there are also things going on in the world today that could be seen to create a more optimistic global picture. There is considerable evidence, both historically and presently, of peaceful interaction and cooperation across political, social, and cultural boundaries. People may be divided by political borders or social, economic, and cultural differences, but in many regions of the world they have coexisted peacefully and continue to do so. We know that states, concerned groups, and individuals respond supportively to such things as natural disasters, famines, or the needs of victims of violent conflict. Again, a pause for reflection on the world around you might be useful here. Such actions suggest that humans have a demonstrable capacity to identify with distant and different others and possess some shared sense of belonging to a single human community despite all our evident differences. Pressures to cooperate further (and more urgently) are emerging because of the widespread recognition of threats to the whole human community and the planet on which it resides, such as the impact of the COVID-19 global pandemic, and the ongoing climate crisis.

Considering these two images of the contemporary world, one pessimistic the other more optimistic, which of them makes more sense to you? Perhaps, you think both represent different, perhaps contradictory aspects of the world today. Or do either or both fail to fully convince you? It could be argued, for example, that both images are rather simplistic, and the world is more complex than either of them suggests. Each could be criticized for underplaying key dimensions of contemporary global politics. The more pessimistic image is largely centred on relations between states and the ever-present possibility of conflict whereas the second image emphasizes cooperation, not only between states but also between peoples. It places more emphasis on the idea of the world as a single community, rather than on the individual states within which people reside. In other words, each image offers a different broad-brush view of the world and both rest on underlying key assumptions about such things as which actors and what processes matter most in world politics. Let us explore these underlying assumptions a bit further.

One key factor to consider is who the key actors on the contemporary world stage are. We might focus on the nearly 200 sovereign states that make up the contemporary international political order, as the first image seems to do. Or we might see the influence of international or regional organizations (the UN, EU, NATO, African Union, World Bank, and so on), or multinational corporations (MNCs—such as Apple, Amazon, Microsoft, Ford, or Samsung) as central to the analysis of contemporary world politics. Non-Governmental Organizations (NGOs) arguably also play a significant role, be they large ones such as Amnesty International, the Red Cross, Human Rights Watch, Greenpeace, and the World Economic Forum, or the many millions of smaller organizations found worldwide.

Also vying for our attention are the various ways in which people around the world identify with or distinguish themselves from others based on such things as national identity, ethnicity, religion, culture, race, sexual orientation, and gender. The politics of personal and collective identity have long played out within states, as illustrated by the history of class conflict, the long-running civil rights movements in the US and elsewhere, or the struggles by indigenous peoples in various countries around the world for greater political and social justice. More recent developments such as Black Lives Matter, #metoo, or campaigns around LBTQA+ rights, remind us also that identity politics can transcend political boundaries and acquire a truly global reach. Identity can both divide and unite people in complex and often tension-riddled ways. How does this fit into the depiction and analysis of contemporary world politics?

Just as the emphasis placed on the roles and influence of different key actors can generate different images of world politics, so too can assumptions about the key processes or issue areas that drive international politics. The pessimistic image rests upon a central focus on the competition for power and influence between states and such things as the difference between their relative military capabilities. It takes as a given that the risk of war remains an ever-present possibility and it depicts the differences between nations and peoples predominantly as potential sources of tension and conflict. It suggests also that the fundamental character of international politics is unlikely to change much.

In contrast, the more optimistic image of the world shifts our focus away from a preoccupation with relations between states. It places greater emphasis on cooperative processes that bind not only states but also peoples, despite their political, social, and cultural differences. Such processes include economic and trade relations, shared appreciation of the benefits of cooperation and peaceful competition, tourism, and even shared interests in cultural products such as music, film, and art. It gives weight to a shared sense of identity as members of a single human community, and even a shared sense of moral responsibility towards the plight of perhaps distant others. It depicts a world with inherent capacities to bring about positive change.

Although the two images of the world today are simplifications for illustrative purposes, each does reflect the key assumptions of some of the theories examined in this textbook. Similarly, both images could be questioned in various ways with the help of other theoretical perspectives that we will also be looking at. Different theories can generate contrasting images of today's world while also providing you with an intellectual toolbox to scrutinize contrasting depictions of the contemporary world. The challenge for you, the student of world politics, is to assess their relative merits.

The importance of historical context

A key question this textbook encourages you to consider is why the different theories of international relations emerge when they do and, furthermore, why they seem to fall in and out of favour. The historical context seemingly plays a significant part here. For example, if you were studying international politics 40 to 50 years ago, then the Cold War between the superpowers, the United States and The Soviet Union, would have figured very prominently. Between 1946 (just after the Second World War), and 1989 when the Berlin Wall came down signalling the Cold War's end, the world was very much organized around an 'East–West' rivalry between two competing blocs of states, a Western bloc led by the United States and an Eastern bloc led by the communist Soviet Union. This was widely referred to as a 'bipolar world' because of the prominence of the two blocs. A key issue during the Cold War era, not only in scholarly circles but also in public debate, was the nuclear arms race that developed between the two superpowers, as well as their support for opposing sides in various regional conflicts in SE Asia, the Middle East, and elsewhere. Perhaps not surprisingly, then, the dominant IR theory for much of this period was realism (Chapter 3), one of the key sources for the more pessimistic image presented at the beginning of this chapter. Realism emphasizes the rivalry between great powers throughout the history of the international system and the perpetual risk of conflict. Many realists also saw a bipolar world as comparatively stable since the two blocs effectively balanced each other out.

In the latter half of the Cold War, from the 1960s onwards, tensions between the Global North (the industrialized capitalist states) and the Global South (comprised mostly of newly independent former colonies) also gathered pace. These tensions centred on issues such as economic inequality and exploitation and uneven social and economic development, which many in the Global South perceived as the historical legacies of European colonialism. This was the period when the influence of Marxism (Chapter 5) begins to rise in the scholarly analysis of international politics. This was because Marxism is centred around the analysis of the historical role of the growth of a capitalist world economy and raises a series of critical questions about global economic exploitation and social injustice.

If we jump forward to the end of the Cold War, we enter a period when there was a widespread sense of triumph in the West because of the collapse of the Soviet-led communist bloc, widely seen as the West's principal ideological and political rival. Former members of the Soviet bloc began to realign politically and join key institutions of the West, such as NATO and the EU. This was also a time when liberal thinking on international politics, a key source of our more optimistic image, became more prominent. Liberal perspectives on international politics (Chapter 2) emphasize the virtues of cooperation and the capacity of the international system to change, as suggested by the end of the Cold War.

As the twentieth century turned into the twenty-first, other issues such as the impact of globalization, the rise of new global powers such as China and India, the emergence of so-called 'new wars' (ones that don't fit neatly into traditional depictions of war as predominantly between states and their military forces), greater public awareness and scholarly interest in the political, social, and cultural legacies of imperialism and colonialism, and the global politics of gender, now command much greater attention from scholars of world politics. This has been reflected in the emergence of a host of new theoretical perspectives, most of which in various ways question the capacity of earlier theories to adequately address the complexity of today's world.

The Cold War is now long gone (as is the Soviet Union), although tensions between post-Soviet Russia and the US clearly remain. The nuclear weapons that were such a prominent feature of Cold War politics have been reduced in number, but they are still sufficient to pose a threat to humanity's survival should they ever be used. Indeed, the risk of nuclear conflict returned to the international news headlines soon after Russia's invasion of Ukraine in February 2022.

Global inequality and injustice evidently also remain with us with considerable evidence to show that transnational crises such as the covid pandemic, the environmental crisis, or economic and supply problems stemming from the Russia–Ukraine conflict impacted disproportionally upon the poorer regions of the world.

Finally, the emergence of new forms of news gathering and reporting coupled with the growth of transnational social media has altered how we find out about what is going on worldwide. The speed with which information circulates has accelerated significantly. At the same time the quality of the information available to us has itself become a matter of worldwide debate. How do we distinguish, for example, between so-called 'fake news' and accurate information?

None of this is intended to suggest that there is always a straightforward and obvious connection between specific historical contexts and the emergence of theoretical perspectives. Theoretical perspectives do emerge and develop also for predominantly intellectual reasons, because of scholarly debate and disagreement for example. Yet, even then the shadow cast by specific historical contexts can still be detected, as this book will illustrate throughout its survey of the range of theories of international politics.

You know more about theories than you probably think

You might still be wondering why you need theory to understand world politics. Are not the facts enough? The short answer is no, they are not. On their own most facts about international politics (assuming we could agree on what the significant ones are) can do very little for you. As soon as you do something with the facts (such as naming something as a 'fact' or choosing what you think are the key facts and then drawing some conclusions from them) you are stepping down the theory road. We will discuss what theory is, and how it can be applied to global politics throughout this textbook. But for now, it is worth remembering that you have almost certainly already been engaged in some form of theorizing which has been shaping your view of the world for most of your life, whether you realized it or not.

Let's look at this a bit more closely. When we say that you are doing something with the facts, what we mean is that you are interpreting the world in a way that makes sense to you. In other words, what you might view as simply the facts of the case or a commonsensical interpretation of the world around you unavoidably rests on several key conceptual assumptions about that world, such as who the key actors are, what kinds of events are the most significant, or what processes matter most. You may have consciously acquired these, or you may have absorbed them from your own social setting—your family, friends, your cultural affiliations, your social class, where you have lived and were educated, and so on (Baylis, Smith, and Owens, 2020: 8). These underlying conceptual assumptions help you to mentally construct a *worldview*, knowingly or unknowingly, within which you organize and assess the supposed facts of any matter. Indeed, you may soon discover that how you see the world bears a clear resemblance to one or more of the theories covered in this textbook.

So far, then, we have discussed the sorts of global issues and questions that you may be exploring and talked a little bit about what role theory will have in the way you approach answering those wider questions. What we will do in the rest of this chapter is explore the general idea of theories of international relations a bit further and then briefly summarize the theories which are covered in this textbook.

1.2 WHAT'S IN A NAME—INTERNATIONAL RELATIONS, INTERNATIONAL POLITICS, WORLD POLITICS?

You may have noticed already in this chapter that reference has already been made to international relations, international politics, and world or global politics. Do these all mean the same thing, or do they each refer to different types of events or issues? Let's go through each one in turn, starting with international relations.

International Relations (IR)

This is a rather old–fashioned name that captures what most early studies of international politics were focused on: relations between nation-states. It is commonly referred to by the acronym 'IR'. It conjures up an image of global politics as largely about relations between 'nations' (by which these days is largely meant sovereign states) in which such things as the art of diplomacy and defence of the national realm matter most. In other words, it is a *state-centric* label; the state lies at its heart. Yet it is used in the title of some textbooks that cover much more than this. This is because it is the label most used still by IR scholars, including those who would intellectually question it, to locate themselves quickly within the wider scholarly world.

International Politics

This is a disarmingly straightforward label that seemingly gets across clearly what the field of enquiry is about. Like IR, it implies a state-centric perspective and suggests that the discipline is or should be confined primarily to the political dimensions of relations between states. There are some perspectives that do start from that basic premise, such as classical realism (see Chapter 3), but there also many others that for various reasons see it as too narrow. It very much depends on what you understand by the term politics. Does the term refer to the formal institutionalized aspects of international political relations—diplomacy, foreign and security policy, international institutions, and organizations, and so on? Or, should it also embrace relations (formal and informal) between peoples, individuals, and a whole range of different social groups that operate not only within but also across international political boundaries? It also implies that politics is a distinctive realm, but can international politics be neatly separated out from, say, international economics or transnational social, cultural, or religious connections?

World Politics or Global Politics

These are increasingly common labels for the subject reflecting the view that international politics might indeed be about much more than relations between states. These alternative labels began to emerge in the titles of some IR textbooks in the 1960s, but their wider usage today reflects the emergence of newer theoretical perspectives that actively seek to push the discipline well beyond the study of relations between states. Many of these newer perspectives emphasize such things as the importance of the complex intersection of politics and economics (as reflected in processes such as globalization, for example), the need to include such factors as gender, race, and class into the analysis of international politics, and the growing salience of the global environment (see Chapters 5–11). In various ways these all offer profound challenges to the depiction of international relations as largely about relations between states, even if many of the newer perspectives recognize (and strongly criticize) the fact that sovereign states remain the dominant actors in the world.

For all the differences that the various names imply, they are often also used interchangeably. There are no hard and fast rules about what they mean or should mean. In other words, the meaning and ambit of IR as an academic discipline is itself a matter of ongoing debate. Nonetheless, the discipline, including the now very diverse variety of perspectives contained within it, is still widely referred to by scholars and students alike simply as IR.

1.3 **WHAT ARE IR THEORIES?**

As noted earlier, the act of theorizing is, arguably, very much a part of our daily lives even if we are not consciously aware of it. In the academic world, however, there have been long-running debates about what more precisely constitutes theoretical knowledge and what is its primary purpose. As you work your way through the theories in this textbook it should become apparent that the IR discipline is no exception here. IR theories vary not only in their depictions of the world, but also in their understanding of what it means to theorize about that world. An honest answer to the question 'what is IR theory?' is that it is very much a matter of debate and your theoretical perspective. That is why the title of this textbook refers to *theories* of international relations.

If you look back at the discussion of the different names used to refer to what is commonly called IR, it is apparent that each implies a somewhat different understanding of what IR theory should be concerned with. As we saw, International Relations or International Politics are *state-centric* terms which suggests a quite narrow field of enquiry: political relations between states. Furthermore, they imply a distinction between what goes on *between* states and what goes on *within* them (the latter being the focus of much of the Political Science discipline). This distinction is often referred to as a distinction between international politics and domestic politics, or between inside and outside the state. What is seen to matter above all is how the states interact, with comparatively little focus on their internal workings.

World Politics or Global Politics are much broader terms that invoke a much more expansive range of concerns. Many of the IR scholars who prefer these labels to describe their work in various ways challenge the drawing of a firm boundary between inside and outside of the state. This is because they look at processes and relations that often operate across the boundaries of states.

If you think of how actors such as globally focused NGOs, various international organizations, social movements, or international terrorist groups operate, they clearly are not contained within the boundaries of states. Similarly, if you look at the intersection of politics and economics at a global level, it is also apparent that it entails a whole range of other actors, such as MNCs and international financial organizations like the World Bank or WTO, as well as states. It is reflected in various processes that traverse formal political boundaries, such as trade, the movement of money, environmental crises, and the transnational flow of migrants looking for work and a better, more secure life. Additionally, many people identify with or mark themselves out from others around the world based on such things as national identity, class, gender orientation, religion, or race. These are allegiances which, again, do not conform tidily to the political boundaries of states.

This not to say that relations between states can or should be ignored. States and the relations between them are key components of contemporary world politics and few IR scholars dispute this. In various ways, however, non-state-centric theoretical perspectives ask just how important are states and their relations? Has their significance changed over time? What might be being ignored or insufficiently analysed if they remain the primary focus of our study of world politics?

Three key terms: ontology; epistemology; and methodology

As we have already noted, the meaning and purpose of theory is a matter of debate. There are, however, three key terms that can help you to distinguish between the various IR theories covered in this textbook: ontology, epistemology, and methodology.

Ontology

Ontology is a philosophical term which refers to the study of what exists in the world. It explores such questions as:

- What kinds of entities constitute 'reality'?
- How might we classify and explain them?
- Are there components of reality that exist independently of our minds and our language, or do we create them mentally in some way?

IR theories can usefully be differentiated by their ontological assumptions about what really exists in the world, and on which of these we should focus. We have seen already that some theories of IR focus primarily on states and relations between them as the key entities to investigate in IR. Other theories identify a whole range of other actors, processes, and experiences that exist and need to be studied to develop a fuller understanding of world politics. Some of the newer theories of IR go further in challenging the ontological assumptions of the more established theories. They do this by questioning the claim that we can know definitively that things exist outside of our attempts to capture them in theoretical or everyday language. In other words, language brings things into being and what supposedly exists in the world becomes a matter of interpretation.

We can illustrate this ontological dispute with reference to the state and international system of states. In contrast to the most long-established IR theories that treat states and the international system of states as objects that exist independently of our ideas or beliefs about them, some of the newer IR theories (notably poststructuralism discussed in Chapter 7), argue that they should be understood as constructed within the dominant and most influential theories of international politics. This dominance had led to the widespread assumption that what states are, and how they can or should act is taken too much for granted rather than being subjected to critical scrutiny. This is a much-disputed area of scholarly debate, but its impact on the IR discipline will become clearer as you deepen your knowledge of IR theories.

Epistemology

Epistemology is concerned with how knowledge is acquired. For example, if you are thinking about epistemology you might ask:

- What is knowledge?
- What can be known about the world?
- How do we judge between competing knowledge claims?
- What influences our acquisition of knowledge?

There are some key epistemological distinctions between the various theories examined in this textbook. Key epistemological debates between different IR theoretical perspectives include:

- Whether IR theories should try to produce a definitive and authoritative *explanation* of international politics, or, more modestly, aim for an *understanding* of the world, i.e., a compelling *interpretation* of how the world, or key aspects of it, seemingly works.

- Should the IR theorist endeavour to stand outside of the world they are attempting to explain or understand to offer as objective a viewpoint as possible? Some IR theories, notably the longer established perspectives such as realism and liberalism, hold to this view or something close to it. In contrast, many of the newer IR theories depict theory as actively contributing to the making or constitution of the world. They argue that because theorists are inescapably a part of the world they are theorizing, the social and political settings in which the theorist is situated and the assumptions the theorist holds are likely to influence their theoretical findings.

- Are there solid foundations for our knowledge claims? In other words, can we make theoretical claims about international politics that can ultimately be shown incontrovertibly to be true or false? Or do all our theoretical postulates about the world unavoidably rest on contestable premises, assumptions, or biases?

- Is a general 'explain-all' theory of international or world politics possible? Some IR perspectives seemingly offer a general theory of international politics whereas others argue that it is neither possible nor desirable because of what it is likely to exclude (intentionally or otherwise), fail to see, or simply ignore.

INTRODUCTION TO INTERNATIONAL RELATIONS THEORIES

These are very short summaries of some very complex debates. We will be revisiting these debates at various points throughout the discussions of specific IR theories.

Methodology

Methodology refers to how we go about gaining knowledge of what is in the world. For example:

- What research methods and techniques do we use to gather evidence to help us both formulate and assess theoretical claims?

The answer depends very much on the types of research questions you are seeking to answer. In the social sciences generally, a distinction is usually drawn between quantitative and qualitative data. Quantitative data derives from sources such as surveys, questionnaires, or the results of various systematic observational activities, that produce results that can be measured numerically. Statistical methods are used to produce findings that can be generalized to apply to wider groups than the research sample (studies of people's voting intentions is a common example of this). The use of quantitative data is often depicted as being somehow more scientific or objective.

Qualitative research is carried out using a wider range of methodologies, that include such things as semi-structured or structured interviews, participant observations (where a researcher endeavours to immerse themselves in a specific social setting to better understand it), and the analysis of documents, the historical record, other scholarly writings, or even literature and film. For some theorists a key focus is the language of theory itself and how it works to construct a particular account of the world. In the case of IR, much of the earliest work relied very much on interpretations of the historical record of how states have acted over the centuries or on the written recollections of key practitioners, such as diplomats, prominent military figures, and so on. Within the contemporary IR discipline, the study of history remains a key feature but examples of pretty much the whole range of both qualitative and quantitative methodologies can now also be found.

As you work your way through the different IR theories covered in the chapters of this textbook you will see that these differences between understandings of what exists in the world, how we acquire knowledge of that world, and what methods we use to gain that knowledge, frequently come into the picture.

Mainstream versus critical theories

Prior to briefly reviewing the theories examined in this text, it is useful to identify a broad and commonly used binary distinction between them. At various points throughout this textbook reference is made to 'mainstream' or 'orthodox' theories on the one hand, and 'critical' theories on the other. The mainstream is usually seen to be comprised of liberalism and realism (discussed in Chapters 2 and 3). The critical theories draw upon some, or all the ontological, epistemological, and methodological debates outlined in Section 1.2

to criticize the longer-standing mainstream theories (especially Chapters 6, 7, 9, 10). However, some theoretical perspectives, such as the English School and Constructivism (Chapters 4 and 8) are widely depicted as straddling the mainstream–critical divide.

At the centre of the broad distinction between mainstream and critical IR theories lies an epistemological debate concerning the theorizing of social phenomena, in contrast to theoretical claims about the natural world. This debate developed in some branches of the social sciences many decades ago, but it developed quite dramatically in the IR field in the early 1980s when Critical IR Theory (the subject of Chapter 6) emerged. This new theoretical approach criticized earlier IR theorizing for being 'positivist' and argued for a non-positivist or post-positivist mode of theoretical enquiry.

Positivism and Post-positivism

What is at stake in the positivist and post-positivist debate is the status of research in the social sciences, a family of academic disciplines focused on the analysis of the social world and within which IR is usually located. Let us briefly examine the two terms positivism and post-positivism.

Positivism

The term Positivism emerged in the nineteenth century when the modern discipline of sociology was being established. Positivism is a philosophical theory of *social* scientific research that states that valid knowledge about the social world is only that which is gained through the acquisition of empirical information, which is then assessed through the scientific method. In essence it sees the natural sciences as providing a benchmark which research about social phenomena should try and emulate.

Positivism requires a commitment to objectivity, in other words a clear separation between facts about social world and values (the personal preferences, political beliefs, and prejudices of the researcher). Furthermore, the truth of our knowledge claims about the social world can only be established by testing our theoretical claims against neutral facts. These facts should be established 'by a careful, unprejudiced use of the senses' (Chalmers, 2013: 2). In other words, facts are the products of observation and not of abstract speculation or mere opinion. The overall aim is to provide an objective and definitive *explanation* of the social phenomena (such as some aspect of relations between states) that is demonstrably true. This very much corresponds with what Alan Chalmers calls a 'commonsense view of science'.

It is a matter of ongoing debate as to whether the social sciences have or ever could produce work that could be deemed to be truly scientific. Indeed, these days even within the natural sciences there is much debate about what scientific research entails and in many areas, such as quantum physics, the idea there is a single universal model of science has long been challenged. Nonetheless, the positivist model of social scientific research exercised a powerful hold over the social sciences, especially in their formative years. This is reflected in the fact that the various disciplines that make up the social sciences are still referred to as social *sciences*, even if many social science scholars, perhaps most, today do not see themselves as engaging in 'scientific' research.

Whether or not any of the IR theories covered in this book are strictly positivist is debatable, but the longer established theoretical schools, such as realism and liberalism, are widely seen as more committed to a positivistic depiction of theory.

Post-positivism

Post-positivism is a term used to refer to those theories in the social sciences that for various reasons reject the positivist model of social scientific research. Above all post-positivist theories question the possibility or indeed the desirability of truly objective knowledge claims about social phenomena. Again, this is a theme that will be explored throughout this book.

The newer IR theories such as Critical Theory, the various kinds of feminism and gender-focused IR theories, constructivism, poststructuralism, and postcolonialism are commonly described as post-positivist. The reason for this is that these newer theories are either critical of what they see as positivist theorizing, or they are themselves divided between those who adopt a more positivistic view of theory and those who regard themselves as post-positivist. The English School (examined in Chapter 4) and constructivism (discussed in Chapter 8) are examples of perspectives with both positivistic and more overtly post-positivist branches.

Again, this distinction will become much more evident as you get to know the individual IR theoretical perspectives better.

1.4 AN OUTLINE OF THE IR THEORIES COVERED IN THIS BOOK

So far, we have seen that there are a variety of understandings of the nature and purpose of theory, and these are all reflected in the similarities and differences between the different IR theories found in the contemporary IR discipline. This can be illustrated in a brief introductory survey of the theories covered in this book. These are, however, very brief summaries of often quite complex theoretical perspectives, many of which contain distinctive strands within them. The intention at this stage is simply to give you a preliminary sense of the variety of theoretical perspectives covered in this book. To develop a more in-depth understanding you will of course need to read the specific chapters dedicated to each of the theoretical perspectives.

Liberalism (Chapter 2)

Liberalism as a political philosophy emerged in Europe during the Enlightenment era. It is widely seen to have heavily influenced IR thinking when the discipline emerged in the aftermath of the First World War. It is also sometimes referred to as liberal internationalism or 'idealism' (although that label has been widely questioned in recent years). As with liberal political philosophy more generally the key *ontological* category for liberal

IR theory is the individual. Liberalism is particularly noted for its emphasis on individual rights and freedoms, the benefits of liberal democracy and the virtues of free trade. These are reflected in liberal IR theoretical perspectives, which are generally progressive in that they see the international system as amenable to reform, notably through the worldwide spread of democracy, free trade, and the advancement of universal human rights. Although much liberal IR thinking is state-centric, it views the state as ultimately comprised of individuals and other actors. Liberals tend to emphasize the benefits of international cooperation through the development of international institutions and a rule-governed international order which regulates both economic and political relations. Liberal IR theorists emphasize the *interdependence* of states and the significance of relations not only between states, but also between states and a host of other actors.

The influence of liberalism is evident in the foreign policies of most Western states—their criticisms of other states for breaches of human rights, for example—although this often sits in tension with other aspects of Western foreign policies which reflect a more realist outlook. In recent years, scholars from some of the critical perspectives, such as postcolonialism (which we will touch upon later in this chapter and discuss in detail in Chapter 9), have highlighted the long historical association of liberalism with colonialism and imperialism. In so doing they question the supposed progressivism of much liberal IR thought.

Realism (Chapter 3)

Probably the most well-known of the IR theoretical perspectives, realism was particularly influential during the Cold War era and remains a prominent perspective in the contemporary IR discipline. Some realists claim an intellectual lineage that can be traced back to antiquity and this forms the basis for the claim that realism reflects a timeless wisdom about international politics.

There are several distinct strands within realism, but they generally share a strongly state-centric view of the world which emphasizes the sovereignty of states who are seen moreover to interact within an anarchic international system. Realists use the term *anarchy* in its strict sense, i.e., it is a system without government in that there is no global actor or authority above the state.

In contrast to liberalism, realists emphasize competition rather than cooperation as the hallmark of international relations and thus the perpetual risk of conflict. For realists, International Politics is primarily a struggle for power between sovereign states looking to protect their selfish national interests. However, realists do vary in their explanation of the propensity for conflict in international politics.

For some varieties of Realism, conflict in international politics is a product of selfish human nature, whereas for others, notably the neorealist strand that emerged in the early 1980s, the key explanation lies in the anarchical structure of the international system. Realists see order in the international system as primarily the product of a balance of power which entails states acting, through such processes as forming alliances, to prevent any one state dominating the system entirely. Realism does not deny the possibility of cooperation or the creation of rules for the game of power politics. However, these generally are seen to reflect the interests of the most powerful states, the great powers in history such as the two superpowers in the Cold War.

Realists are often depicted as offering a pessimistic view of international politics in which the prospects of significant change or reform are seen as poor to non-existent unless the structure of the international system changes dramatically. This is something which most realists see as unlikely to happen in the foreseeable future.

The English School (Chapter 4)

The origins of the English School lie in debates between IR scholars (not all of whom were English) at several English universities from the late 1950s onwards. The English School, especially in its earlier years, has evident commonalities with both realism and liberalism. Like realism, it is state-centric and many English school scholars are sceptical about the prospects of significant change in the international system.

The unique dimension of the English School is an emphasis on the existence of what they call an *anarchical society of states*. As the name suggests, this echoes realism's emphasis on the anarchical structure of the international system but it also reflects a belief in the capacity of states, just like individuals, to develop sustainable social relations over time that add up to something that can meaningfully be called an international society. This is grounded in liberal political and legal thinking.

The English School argues that history shows that international order does not arrive solely from a balance of power but from the interests of all states in creating a stable international order within which to pursue their national interests. The English School sees such things as long-standing diplomatic practice, the development of international law, the roles and responsibilities of great powers, and even the resort to war as historically evolved, institutionalized aspects of international politics that underpin their claim that an international society exists.

Since the 1980s, the English school has tended to divide into two distinct strands, known as pluralism and solidarism. The pluralists generally work with the earlier depiction of an international society which, while emphasizing the social dimensions of international order, is sceptical about the prospects for significant change. In this sense they could be said to lean towards a realist perspective. The solidarists adopt a more progressive view that emphasizes the continuing development of international society and its capacity to embrace demands for greater international social justice, reflecting the influence of liberalism as well as Critical Theory.

Marxism (Chapter 5)

Although Marxism is undoubtedly a very significant and influential long-standing strand of Western political thought, its influence within the IR discipline was limited until comparatively recently. This is arguably because Marxism sees states and relations between them as determined primarily by the development of the international capitalist economic system.

For Marxists, social classes, not individuals or states are the primary *ontological* category. Marxism's influence within the IR discipline has grown since the 1960s and 1970s, alongside increased concern with the injustices of political and economic relations between the Global South and the industrialized Global North following the independence of former colonial states.

Marxism brings to IR an overriding concern with the question of human social and economic inequality, how it came about, and how it is sustained globally. Like liberalism, Marxism is a progressive political philosophy in arguing for both the possibility and necessity of change at the international level. However, it radically parts company with liberalism when it comes to how such change might come about. What liberals see as a pathway to a fairer, safer world in which individual freedom is enhanced—a global, market-based capitalist economy—is for Marxists the principal barrier to realizing a more just and equitable world. The realization of true emancipation (or liberation) for all humans is not to be achieved through the reform of the global capitalist system, but through its eventual elimination and replacement with a radically different system.

From a Marxist point of view, both liberalism and realism mask the underlying economic forces at work in world politics and in so doing help to sustain global inequality and exploitation. Marxists have been particularly prominent in challenging orthodox, liberal understandings of *Globalization*. Whereas liberal IR theories tend to depict globalization as a relatively new and largely positive development, Marxists argue that globalization is the outcome of a long historical process of capitalist expansion. They depict globalization as an ideological construction intended to legitimize and make virtue of the continuing global expansion of capitalism.

Critical IR Theory (Chapter 6)

The quite sudden emergence of Critical Theory (capital C and capital T) in the IR discipline in the early 1980s marked a watershed in the discipline's development. It signalled the beginning of the rapid emergence of a range of critical theories (small c, small t) of IR that challenge the theoretical mainstream of the IR discipline. Although its roots lie in a branch of Marxist thinking known as the Frankfurt School, Critical Theory rejects what it sees as the economic determinism of orthodox Marxism and places comparatively greater emphasis on the political and cultural superstructure that sustains capitalism.

Critical Theory rejects positivism, particularly the view that theorists of the social world can and should endeavour to stand apart from that world to assess it objectively. Critical Theory sees all theorists as products of the social world they are studying. This is seen to inescapably influence their work, whether they admit this or not. Knowledge and politics are thus intimately connected. Critical IR Theory is thus most noted for its *epistemological* critique of the IR discipline's mainstream, comprised primarily of liberalism and realism.

Critical IR Theory depicts theories such as realism and liberalism as examples of merely 'problem solving' theories which only examine the surface features of international politics and fail to uncover the historical processes which led to the formation of the contemporary international system. Critical IR Theory views problem-solving theories as effectively upholding the present international order and thus the interests of those who benefit most from it. Although there are some distinct strands within Critical IR Theory, they share a *normative* (value-driven) conception of theory as acting as a force for change in world politics. Critical IR theorists explore the processes that might lead to universal human emancipation from what they see as unjustifiable constraints upon humans in realizing their full potential. Some Critical IR theorists focus mainly on critiquing the different forms of hegemonic (i.e., dominant) power in global politics, while others argue for the development of more inclusive forms of community and democratic accountability that extend beyond the boundaries of the territorial sovereign state.

Poststructuralism (Chapter 7)

Poststructuralist IR theory emerged only a few years after Critical Theory. It is sometimes (inaccurately) referred to as postmodernism. In contrast to Critical Theory, poststructuralism does not present itself as an alternative theoretical perspective of IR. Instead, its advocates present it as more like an interpretive standpoint, or ethos.

Poststructuralist IR scholarship is certainly highly theoretical, but there is no singular poststructuralist theory of IR. Indeed, most poststructuralist IR theorists are highly resistant to the idea that anything like a general theory of IR is either possible or desirable. Given this, it is perhaps not surprising that poststructuralism's arrival in the IR discipline initially created an extraordinary amount of hostility from most quarters. Many scholars viewed it as offering sweeping criticism of most preceding IR theoretical perspectives while offering nothing substantial in their place. Much of this critical reaction has subsided and poststructuralism has subsequently become an influential body of theoretical IR scholarship.

Summarizing poststructuralism is not easy because it draws from a diverse range of theoretical sources (many of which seemingly have little to do with the traditional concerns of the established discipline of IR) and there is no tidy theoretical endpoint to arrive at. It seeks to problematize all theoretical perspectives on international politics that claim to know or understand IR in some decisive and authoritative sense (what poststructuralists call 'metanarratives'), seeing them as always incomplete. It seeks to show how different representations of IR or world politics emerge historically and are sustained, thereby excluding or marginalizing alternative representations and interpretations of international and global politics and therefore other possible forms of international and global social life. For these reasons poststructuralism also challenges the ontology of mainstream IR theories, the entities that they prioritize, such as the sovereign state, and how these are understood.

Constructivism (Chapter 8)

Constructivism emerged during the late 1980s, a time of theoretical upheaval in the IR discipline. The core argument of the constructivist perspective is that the reality of the world we find ourselves in is socially constructed rather than simply given. In other words, it sees a more significant role for human agency in international politics.

For constructivists, many facts about the world are *social* facts; they are dependent upon human agreement as to their significance and value. What this means is that what mainstream IR theories take as the inherent features of the anarchical international system are in fact socially constructed: they emerge out of the ongoing social practices and interactions of states (whose actions are of course determined by human policy makers). Thus, constructivists question the ontological assumptions of mainstream IR theories, notably their understanding of the state as an actor.

Constructivists are interested in how ideas and perceptions influence the concrete practices of international politics, through the creation of shared norms or rules of international conduct for example, or how states construct and sustain a sense of their own identity and perceive the identity of other states.

Locating constructivism within the spectrum of IR theories, however, is itself a matter of debate. In seeing the world as socially constructed in language and ideas, constructivism seems to have quite a lot in common with critical IR theories. However, some depict constructivism as occupying a middle ground between mainstream and critical IR theories. This is because although constructivists criticize mainstream IR theories for failing to adequately consider why key actors can change their perceptions of how the world works and what their key interests are, they remain epistemologically committed to the idea that IR theory should produce rigorous and testable explanations of international politics.

Other constructivists see themselves as more aligned with the critical end of the IR theory spectrum and adopt a more interpretive approach to theoretical enquiry. For these constructivists the objective is to try and understand how actors interpret their world and the reasons why such interpretations can change.

Postcolonialism (Chapter 9)

Postcolonial IR theorizing emerged within the IR discipline from the 1990s onwards and its influence continues to grow rapidly. The term postcolonialism is intended to indicate that although the colonialization of territories may have been largely formally eradicated, many of its features remain with us.

Postcolonial perspectives focus on the histories of European colonialism and the process of decolonization viewed from the perspectives of those who were colonized, as well as the legacies of colonialism and decolonization in the contemporary era. In various ways, they depict the present as a period that may be *after* colonialism, yet within which social relations at all levels of human interaction—from the domestic to the global—continue to exhibit the impact of the colonial era.

As with poststructuralism, postcolonial IR perspectives do not constitute a single theory but a diverse body of scholarship. In various ways this challenges *Eurocentrism*, i.e., the dominance within most IR perspectives of ideas, theoretical assumptions, and values of Western, mostly European origin. From a postcolonial perspective this has resulted in non-Eurocentric forms of knowledge, value systems, and historical experiences being widely treated as inferior, insignificant, or simply ignored. In contrast, postcolonialism draws upon the experiences, perspectives, and values of those who were colonized, and those whose lives continue to be shaped significantly by colonialist attitudes (such as migrants and their descendants from the Global South living in the West). These are used to develop critical interpretations of contemporary global politics from non-Western points of view and experiences.

In effect, postcolonial perspectives seek to confront the West both politically and intellectually with the consequences of its imperial and colonial history. In so doing, postcolonialism invites us to think very differently about international politics.

Postcolonialist IR has led to greater attention being paid to the significance of race and racism in the theory and practice of IR, issues that have hitherto been largely ignored. Some IR postcolonialist scholars are also unearthing the largely forgotten yet significant contributions of Black IR scholars since the earliest days of the discipline. An important recent development is decolonial scholarship, which explores how we can expose and remove the often-hidden colonial assumptions and prejudices from the theorizing and teaching of world politics.

Feminisms and Gender (Chapter 10)

Feminist perspectives and acknowledgement of the importance of gender began to gain prominence in the IR discipline in the late 1980s and early 1990s, although feminism's roots can be traced back much further. The term feminism is often used today as a rather generalized label, which masks the fact that contemporary feminist thinking ranges across a wide range of diverse theoretical perspectives which are also reflected in contemporary feminist IR scholarship.

Despite their differences, all feminist IR perspectives start from a simple premise: in international politics, as in any other political arena, gender matters. Therefore, feminist and gender-focused IR scholarship is generally critical of mainstream IR scholarship which throughout most of its history paid little attention to gender and is seen to therefore offer only a partial account of world politics as seen through distinctly masculinist lenses.

Some IR feminists, notably liberal feminists, are primarily concerned with the historical absence of women in international power as well as the mainstream theorizing of international politics. However, much contemporary IR feminism shares common ground with critical IR perspectives and intersects extensively with Critical Theory, poststructuralism, and postcolonialism. A key outcome of this is greater attention to *intersectionality*, i.e. the complex relationships between gender, class, and race and how these play out globally.

Feminist IR now addresses all aspects of the discipline including its long-standing core concerns such as the state, foreign policy, security, and the global economy. Much of it is marked by methodological innovation, such as the use of the personal everyday experiences and stories of women worldwide to develop alternative accounts of international politics.

Feminism's roots lie in the analysis of, and resistance to, the historical subordination of women to the interests and power of men. However, the very categories of man and woman and the related concepts of masculinity and femininity have themselves become the subjects of heated debate. This has become increasingly reflected within gender-focused IR scholarship. There has been a decisive shift away from focusing primarily on women's subordination to men towards a greater recognition of the complexities of the global politics of people's diverse gender and sexual orientations. Most recently, a distinctive stream of gender theorizing known as Queer IR Theory has emerged. This is centred around the analysis of the fluidity of sex and gender identities and exploration of the complex global politics around the rights of LGBTQI+ people.

Green perspectives (Chapter 11)

Environmental issues have periodically attracted the attention of IR scholars since 1945, but it is only relatively recently that distinctly 'green' IR perspectives have emerged.

Many green IR theorists argue that there is not merely a series of environmental problems and challenges to confront at all levels of human society but an environmental *crisis* of global proportions. Most argue also that international multilateral environmental agreements to date have been insufficient to significantly reduce the risk of global environmental catastrophe.

Green IR perspectives vary widely in their scope. They can be distinguished by their underlying philosophical understanding of the relationship between humans and the non-human natural world. Some green perspectives argue that we should adapt our existing political and economic systems, perhaps quite substantially, but they generally still view the natural world through the lenses of the needs and interests of the human species. In other words, they are *anthropocentric*. Others adopt an *ecocentric* standpoint in that they depict the natural world as a complex bio-organic system of which the human species is just one constituent part.

These two broad green standpoints have radically different implications for the future of world politics. Anthropocentric perspectives are broadly focused on the modification of human behaviour to ensure that the natural world can be sufficiently sustained for it to still function as a source of raw materials, a depository for our waste, or a place for human recreation. For those adopting an ecocentric standpoint, however, this is an inadequate even dangerous outlook.

Much of green IR scholarship thus revolves around the question of whether the current international system can be sufficiently 'greened'. For some green IR scholars, the human impact on the global environment is so great that it warrants the declaration of a new geological era: the Anthropocene (from *anthropo*, for 'man' and *cene* for 'new').

They go on to suggest that this requires us to abandon the concept of international politics entirely in favour of a genuinely planetary perspective. Their critics argue, however, that the concept of the Anthropocene is anchored in Western points of view and fails to recognize the diversity of human communities and their relationships with the environment; not all are equally to blame. Others argue that the main culprit is a carbon-hungry, high-consumption capitalist world economy and it is this we need to change.

1.5 **CONCLUSION**

By learning about different international relations theories, you will develop an intellectual toolbox to critically assess not only your own conceptual assumptions, but also those of others. You will learn to engage critically with the various theoretical perspectives available to you. Some theoretical perspectives suggest that we can develop a general theory of international politics (such as liberalism, realism, neorealism, and Marxism), while others (such as poststructuralism and postcolonialism) question whether this is either possible or desirable. There is a wide and varied theoretical menu for you to consider as a student of international politics. You may find one theoretical perspective particularly compelling or find yourself drawn to certain aspects of a range of theories.

Theories can also have practical consequences. Each of the theories examined in this textbook shines a distinctive light on global issues and events. Some (such as realism and neorealism) suggest that the world as it is unlikely to fundamentally change and thus the future will not be very dissimilar to the present or past, whether we like it or not. Others question this pessimistic claim, some moderately (such as liberalism, or the English School), and others much more stringently so (such as Marxism, Critical IR Theory, postcolonialism, feminism, or Green Theory). In so doing they depict the world more dynamically, pointing us towards different answers to the questions that concern us or crises that challenge us, different ways in which we might practise international politics. This suggests a range of possible futures for the global community. The future need not be like the present or past.

Although the key themes of each of the IR theories may be relatively simple to grasp, most (if not all) of the theoretical perspectives covered contain various distinctive strands within them. For example, realism is commonly subdivided into classical realism, neorealism, and neoclassical realism (these are explored more fully in Chapter 3). There is much that binds these different strands, but there also significant differences between them. To fully grasp these similarities and differences will require further and wider reading. Additionally, many of the theories examined, especially some of the newer critical theories, rest upon quite complex theoretical or philosophical conceptual assumptions. This textbook will give you a firm understanding of these, but a fuller understanding will also require further reading. You should see this book as the beginning of your theoretical journey, not as all you need to know.

Finally, as we noted earlier, a key emphasis of this book is on the historical context within which theories emerge or fall out of favour. You may be surprised at how knowledge of key historical contexts—such as the 1960s, decolonization, the beginning and end of the Cold War, the 9/11 terrorist attacks on the US in 2001, and their aftermath, or the impact of growing concern about global climate change in the twenty-first century—can help you understand theoretical perspectives and their influence.

It is not the intention of this book to tell you which of the IR theories is the right one or the best. Ultimately, that is for you to decide. The important thing is to keep an open mind and don't be afraid to question the claims of different key theoretical perspectives on IR. Do not worry if some theories prove harder to grasp initially than others. With further reading or discussion with both your lecturers and fellow students and, importantly, allowing yourself time to think, you may be surprised at how quickly you can grasp the key theoretical debates in IR. Be patient—you will get there!

CHAPTER 2

THE LIBERAL 'IDEALIST' ORIGINS OF THE INTERNATIONAL RELATIONS DISCIPLINE

LEARNING OBJECTIVES

- Describe the common story of liberalism's role in the founding of the modern IR discipline and recent challenges to it
- Understand the political legacy of using labels such as 'idealism'
- Remember the key phases in the development of liberal approaches to the analysis of international politics and assess their relationship with history
- Identify the contribution of liberalism to the institutions and practices of contemporary international politics
- Analyse the extent to which liberal IR perspectives have imperialist and colonialist undertones

2.1 INTRODUCTION

Even though thinking about international relations, international politics, or world politics can be traced back to antiquity, liberalism was central to the formal establishment of international relations (IR) as a distinct academic discipline in a few mostly Western states in the immediate aftermath of the First World War (1914–1918).

2 THE LIBERAL 'IDEALIST' ORIGINS OF THE INTERNATIONAL RELATIONS DISCIPLINE

The much-repeated common story of the IR discipline's emergence depicts its founders as predominantly liberals who believed that to avoid a world war reoccurring there needed to be a dedicated field of scholarly enquiry devoted to explaining and understanding international politics. The key motivation of the discipline's founders is widely presented as the creation of a less war-prone, stable, and peaceful international order built around core liberal values. Because of the reformist inclinations of its founders, the broad theoretical and philosophical tone of the foundational phase of the discipline has also been described as 'idealist' or 'liberal idealism'. In this chapter, however, we question the utility of these loaded labels and suggest it is both more accurate and fairer to simply use the term liberalism.

Recently, however, that common story of the establishment of the IR discipline, and the liberalism underpinning it, has been subjected to increasing critical scrutiny, especially regarding what it leaves out. For many critics, the standardized account of the IR discipline's origins fails to acknowledge the colonialist and often overtly racist dimensions of the discipline founders' vision of a future international order. Although it is improbable that any contemporary liberal IR scholars would openly subscribe to these aspects of the views of the discipline's founding figures, as we shall see the relationship between Western liberal thinking and colonialist attitudes remains a matter of debate today.

The history of liberalism as a political philosophy goes back to the eighteenth century, so in this chapter we start by briefly outlining the key themes in liberal thought that have emerged since then. We'll go on to consider the implications of liberal thought for thinking about international politics, focusing particularly on the influence of the eighteenth-century liberal philosopher, Immanuel Kant.

We'll then consider the foundational era of the modern IR discipline, and the key historical phases of liberal thinking about IR during the twentieth and twenty-first century. This account will show that liberalism's influence has fluctuated through changing historical contexts as well as liberalism's relationship with realist IR perspectives (which are the subject of Chapter 3). Indeed, the history of the IR discipline was for a long time very much dominated by the contestation between liberalism and realism. This has been less the case in the last three decades or so, as new theoretical perspectives gained increasing prominence.

Nonetheless, the influence of liberal thinking on both the theory and practice of international politics remains very substantial. Indeed, a wide range of scholars depict the contemporary international order—the key institutions and practices of international politics—as still reflecting liberal values. For how long this will remain the case and whether this is a good or bad thing are, however, matters of considerable debate, especially outside of the West.

2.2 **WHAT IS LIBERALISM?**

Liberal thinking about IR is so called because of its relationship to a very prominent current of Western political philosophy whose origins long predate the establishment of the modern IR discipline: liberalism. The only other IR perspective that connects so directly to a long-established current of Western political thinking is Marxism (the subject of Chapter 5). Therefore, to begin our discussion about liberalism and IR, we must first define liberalism.

The core tenets of liberalism

Contemporary liberalism is a *progressive* political philosophy; it believes in the possibility of social and political reforms that will enhance individual liberty or freedom (note how the name 'liberal' is derived from 'liberty'). Liberalism's origins lie in what is commonly referred to as the Enlightenment. This was a period in Western history, from the mid-seventeenth century and through the eighteenth century, which saw rapid and often sweeping developments in the scientific, political, and cultural spheres. These changes centred around the idea that the human capacity for rational thought should prevail over earlier religiously inspired modes of thinking. It was during the Enlightenment that the idea emerged that, individually and collectively, humans could shape their own destinies through the application of reason and thereby transform their lives and the societies in which they lived. Although the label liberalism did not come into widespread use until the mid-nineteenth century, liberal thinking was very much a product of the Enlightenment.

Liberalism today is a broad body of diverse ideas and practices, and liberals can disagree as much as agree about the finer points of social and political life. Nonetheless, we can identify some core values which most liberals would agree upon. As a basic summary, liberalism can be defined as a combination of the following ideas:

- individual freedom (or individualism)
- free markets/free trade
- democracy

Individualism

To put it formally, for liberals the individual has *ontological primacy*. In other words, the individual is the more important category of *being*, compared to, say, social class, society, or the state. Although many liberals see a significant role for the state in assisting those who are disadvantaged in some way or believe that individuals have extensive social responsibilities to their wider communities, this is always ultimately subordinate to the enhancement of individual liberty.

Free Trade

Liberalism is characterized by a belief in the virtues of free trade and the operation of market forces, even if liberals disagree as to precisely how free trade should be or to what extent markets should be allowed to operate unhindered. Liberalism is therefore very strongly associated with the capitalist economic system. It has often been said that you can have capitalism without liberalism (think here of contemporary China, Vietnam, or Russia, for example), but you can't have liberalism without capitalism. Historically, liberals have disagreed over the extent to which capitalism can and should be regulated to protect vulnerable individuals and groups of individuals from the impact of capitalist market forces. This is reflected in the varying approaches adopted by liberal states towards such things as welfare and social services, the regulation of the financial system, the levels and forms of taxation, worker's rights, unemployment benefits, and so on.

Democracy

Thirdly, liberalism is indelibly associated with democracy, which, for liberals, means the right of individuals to decide through a free and fair electoral process who should govern them. The history of liberalism is also a story (and a sometimes violent story) of the expansion of suffrage—the right to vote—over the last two centuries, from a limited section of the white male population (such as property owners) through to the universal suffrage now found, in principle at least, in all contemporary liberal states.

Liberalism is arguably the most influential of Western political philosophies and can be said to be the key source of the values that govern most Western societies today. Like many political philosophies, it has many strands, each of which is characterized by greater or less emphasis on one or more core liberal values.

You can get a sense of the varying emphases within liberal political thought by comparing different Western states, as well as the political values of the many mainstream political parties within them. These values have evolved since the Enlightenment and many contemporary liberal states show how the modern liberal state has sometimes taken on board ideas and values associated with the rival conservative and socialist traditions of Western political thinking. This can be illustrated by comparing attitudes towards, say, the provision of public health and welfare services in the United States and most contemporary Western European states. Similarly, there are evident variations between Western European member states of the EU, such as France, the Netherlands, Germany, or Sweden and some of newer Eastern European member states, such as Hungary and Poland. Although after the end of the Cold War in 1989 the Eastern European states abandoned communism in favour of liberal ideas about democracy and free trade, their populations generally hold more conservative attitudes about such things as individual sexuality, the role of the church in society, and so on.

Over the last three decades a variety of liberal economic thinking commonly referred to as *neoliberalism* has emerged. This is characterized by a greater emphasis on individual responsibilities, a declining role for the state as a provider of welfare in favour of private, market-based provision of core social services, and the rolling back of regulatory restrictions on economic activity more generally in favour of a greater role for market forces. Neoliberalism has been contested from both the right and left of the Western political spectrum. This is principally because it is seen (especially from the political Left) to have increased social and economic inequality, or (from the political Right) to have promoted excessive individualism at the expense of traditional values centred around duty to the wider national community. Nonetheless, many would argue that the historical differences between Western Liberal states are eroding in favour of a shared neoliberal model.

2.3 LIBERALISM AND INTERNATIONAL POLITICS—THE FOUNDATIONAL PHASE

It is important to emphasize that liberalism presents itself as a *universalist* political philosophy, i.e., one that is deemed to be appropriate for all humans, regardless of where they are located. This immediately connects liberalism with a distinctive vision of international politics. In principle at least, liberalism invokes a cosmopolitan image of the world as comprised of a single human community. Liberalism is the key source of the modern idea of universal human rights. These rights are, in principle at least, supposedly attached to all of us by virtue of our shared rationality and humanity, as illustrated in the famous second sentence of the American Declaration of Independence: 'We hold these truths to be self-evident, that all men are created equal, that they are endowed by their Creator with certain unalienable Rights, that among these are Life, Liberty and the pursuit of Happiness'.

The reference in the American Declaration of Independence to 'men' being created equal reminds us that the historical record shows that until recently many if not most liberal states were highly reticent, in both their internal social relations as well as their external relations, in recognizing fully the universality of human rights and the inherent equality of all humans. The history of the modern liberal state is marked by sustained and sometimes violent political challenges to discrimination based on gender, race, and sexual orientation. This has been accompanied also by the historical evidence of the sometimes highly discriminatory international outlook of liberal states, as expressed most vividly in the colonialism and imperialism practised by Western, liberal states until the mid-twentieth century, which we will be discussing later in this chapter and more extensively in Chapter 9. Although much has changed for the better, especially since the latter half of the twentieth century, numerous critics identify significant elements of racial and gendered discrimination still permeating the internal and external policies of liberal states today. We will be examining some of these criticisms more closely further on in this chapter as well as in later chapters of this textbook.

In its evolution between the seventeenth and twentieth centuries, liberalism thus identified itself as a universalist, individualist, and reformist political philosophy in abstract terms at least. These core features of classical liberalism have figured prominently in liberal thinking on international politics since the early twentieth century when the discipline of IR was being established. A close, critical reading of foundational liberal thinking, as well as the historical record, shows, however, that early liberal IR often operated with a much narrower and racialized understanding of the universal individual, a point we will be returning to in Section 2.4 of this chapter.

International politics presents an evident immediate challenge even to the abstract liberal vision of a universal community of humankind. This is because of the long history of armed conflict between states since the emergence of the modern state system in the seventeenth century. As we shall see in Chapter 3 on realism, there is a long alternative tradition of depicting international politics as a unique realm, markedly distinct from politics inside sovereign states (which are often referred to as *domestic politics*). For many observers, one of the key features of international politics, perhaps tragically, is how little has changed over the centuries, in stark contrast to the profound changes that have taken place within states, especially those in the Western world. Nonetheless, liberals promote the possibility, indeed the necessity, of reforming the international system as a means of mitigating and perhaps eventually eliminating the risks of large-scale armed conflict. This reformist zeal became very visible in the early twentieth century and especially after the First World War. That war not only illustrated the horrific consequences of the increasing industrialization of war, for many liberals it also exposed the lack of international institutional mechanisms that might reduce or even eradicate the impetus to resort to war to resolve disputes between states.

Immanuel Kant and 'inside-out' international reformism

The earliest signs of liberalism's international reformism can be traced back to the eighteenth century, most notably in the work of the philosopher, Immanuel Kant (see Key thinkers 2.1). Kant's most notable publication on international politics was a short pamphlet entitled *Perpetual Peace: A Philosophical Sketch*, published in 1795. This explored the conditions for the possibility of ending wars and creating a lasting peace.

In *Perpetual Peace*, we find an example of an 'inside-out' approach to reform of the international system, meaning that the key to reducing and eventually eradicating the risk of states resorting to war is seen to lie in reform of the states themselves. By starting with reform *inside* states, Kant argued, humanity might progress to reforming the *outside*, i.e., the system of states.

KEY THINKER 2.1 IMMANUEL KANT

Kant (1724–1804) is seen by many as one of the foremost thinkers of the Enlightenment and perhaps one of the greatest and most influential of Western philosophers. Kant was noted for his often-complex, voluminous writings on epistemology (the theory of knowledge), ethics, aesthetics, anthropology, and astronomy. He spent his whole life in Konigsberg, Prussia (today Kaliningrad, Russia) yet was clearly interested in both politics and the wider world.

Kant's political philosophy centred on an account of a just and rational society in which all individuals should be free to pursue their own happiness as they wish if this did not impinge upon the freedom of others. This clearly informed Kant's work on international politics, which was only a small part of his output, but it has been highly influential nonetheless in the evolution of the liberal perspective on IR. For Kant, the elimination of war could only come about when relations between states broadly reflected relations between individuals in a just society.

> Kant is famously seen as a key proponent of the moral philosophy of cosmopolitanism, which holds that all persons are of equal moral standing and thus equally possessed of basic rights that should not be violated by others. Kant was also writing when ideas about race and the supposed differences between races were developing rapidly in European intellectual circles in tandem with the expansion of European colonialism. Although Kant explicitly condemned colonialism on moral grounds, his criticism was still cast in terms that emphasized the superiority of the white European colonizers over those they colonized (Allais, 2016: 20). In recent years several scholars have raised questions about the tensions between Kant's cosmopolitan moral philosophy and his depictions of non-white peoples that were unequivocally racist (Hill Jr and Boxill, 2001; Kleingeld, 2007; Allais, 2016; Mills, 2017: 91–113).

In *Perpetual Peace* Kant argued that 'republics' were less likely to go to war. By a republic, Kant meant a state in which the rulers were not selected purely by birth right—as in a monarchy—but were more meaningfully representative of the people. In other words, the prospect of an international system that is less prone to war (and may even learn to abandon preparation for war entirely) depended in large part upon states first reforming themselves within.

But why are republics more inclined towards peaceful interaction with other states? First, argued Kant, it is completely rational that most people are less bellicose than their rulers, because they bear the real economic and social costs of waging war. In contrast, despotic rulers are unlikely to suffer personal harm or lose their privileged lifestyle.

Monument to the philosopher Immanuel Kant

2 THE LIBERAL 'IDEALIST' ORIGINS OF THE INTERNATIONAL RELATIONS DISCIPLINE

Thus, in a republic in which some degree of popular consent is required prior to going to war the populace is more likely to constrain the aggressive tendencies of their leaders.

Secondly, Kant claimed that only a republic could ensure the development of a good moral culture in which individuals learn to heed the voice of reason (something Kant believed all humans can do—a key aspect of his wider moral philosophy) and learn from experience that war can lead only to suffering.

Thirdly, individual moral development should lead us, Kant believed, to see ourselves as part of a global community of humankind. Even if we are individuals living inside bounded communities such as sovereign states, we are nonetheless also members of a single universal moral community and therefore any worthwhile moral principles should apply to all of humanity, regardless of individual circumstances or location. Such a cosmopolitan moral outlook has been highly influential in liberal political thought.

Finally, Kant argued that the more publics within states became like-minded and saw themselves as part of a wider human community, the better relations between states would be and we might even eventually eliminate the need for standing armies. For Kant, even if the genuinely universally peaceful human community seems an impossible ideal, reason surely tells us we should nonetheless strive to realize it.

Kant's *Perpetual Peace* was centred around several key arguments:

- A belief in a universal, human rational self-interest (universalism)

- That there is a 'harmony of interests' binding all people, despite our many apparent differences. Our shared human capacity to reason compels us to seek perpetual peace, no matter how improbable it might appear (cosmopolitanism)

- The hopes of world peace lie first in the establishment of republican and responsible governments in all states (what many subsequent liberals read as a call to promote democracy worldwide)

- The rule of law can and should prevail globally (legalism)

- Free trade is the best foundation for peaceful relations between states (global capitalism)

- There should be an international 'federation' of states (international institutionalism).

As we will see in Section 2.4, similar ideas can be found in the arguments of the so-called idealists of the early twentieth century and they are still prominent, albeit in more contemporary forms, in liberal thinking about IR today (as is discussed in Section 2.5).

In the evolution of liberal IR thinking from Kant onwards we can see a consistent core perspective develop. This can be captured in the following simple formula:

$$\text{democracy} + \text{free trade} + \text{international law} +$$
$$\text{international institutions} = \text{international peace and progress}$$

Kant's *Perpetual Peace* was a clear precursor to the more modern argument that democracies don't go to war with each other, often referred to as the democratic peace theory (Doyle, 1983 and Levy, 1988). From this inside-out viewpoint, the spread of democracy is central to the elimination of war between states. Although some question its accuracy (for example, Layne, 1994, and Spiro, 1994), this line of argument remains highly influential today in liberal thinking about international politics. During the Cold War, for example, much of the Western political rhetoric surrounding the confrontation with the Soviet Union referred to the undemocratic nature of the communist political systems in the Soviet Union and its key allies. They were widely depicted as the enemies of individual freedom, a core liberal value and something many liberals would argue all humans should surely aspire to achieve. Not surprisingly, the end of the Cold War, the subsequent collapse of the Soviet Union, and the transformation of its former communist allies in Eastern Europe into democracies was greeted as something of a triumph throughout the liberal West. Democracy, it seemed, had won.

As we will discuss further in Section 2.6, this kind of argument has become increasingly controversial in the post-Cold War era. This is because of the prominence of democratization as a key rationale for Western military interventions in non-Western states (such as Afghanistan, Iraq, and Libya). Such interventions have deposed authoritarian leaders, who often had poor human rights records when judged by the standards of the UN's Universal Declaration of Human Rights. However, they also came with considerable costs in terms of human lives, the destruction of vital infrastructure, and the creation of often violent and endless political and social instability.

THINK CRITICALLY 2.1 ARE DEMOCRATIC STATES INHERENTLY MORE PEACEFUL THAN STATES WITH OTHER POLITICAL SYSTEMS? WHY/WHY NOT?

To help you answer this question, consider the following:
- The 'inside-out' approach to understanding international politics
- Kant's claim that 'republican' states are less likely to resolve disputes through war
- The claim that today's democracies will not go to war with each other (but they might go to war with what they perceive to be undemocratic states).

The liberal origins of the IR discipline

The influence of Kant, and other classical liberal thinkers, was very evident in the efforts of the so-called idealists after the First World War and during the inter-war years—the period between the end of the First World War and the beginning of the Second World War—to promote the reform of international relations through the establishment of a new academic discipline.

Although Western scholarly reference to 'international relations' began to appear prior to and during the First World War, the emergence of the modern academic IR discipline can be dated quite precisely, with the creation of several 'Chairs' (professorships), think tanks, and Departments of International Relations at universities in the UK, Switzerland, and the US in the immediate aftermath of the war. The reasoning behind the establishment of a new IR discipline was very evidently reformist in tone and ostensibly driven by broadly liberal values.

The common story of the IR discipline's establishment, as told in innumerable textbooks, presents the key impetus to establish a discipline centred on the academic study of international politics as practical. It was a response to the horrors and questionable necessity of the First World War. The outbreak of war was greeted with widespread public enthusiasm, encouraged by governments on both sides keen to lift nationalist sentiment and thereby generate public support. By the war's end however public attitudes on both sides had changed due to the enormous human and economic costs of the war. The First World War was the first example of industrialized total war, involving whole populations and, especially with the emergence of military air power, few could escape its effects. In many respects, the war stood in stark contrast to the sense of progress in the Western world, stimulated in part by the rapid industrial development that had proceeded it. With the invention of telegraph communications and the growth of print media, public awareness of war's destructive effects increased, and public opinion could no longer be ignored. As the extent of the destructiveness of modern warfare became apparent, public opinion swung decisively against war. The question thus arose: how to prevent such wars happening again?

One part of the answer was seen to lie in the establishment of research and education programmes, with the explicit purpose of controlling and reforming the conduct of international relations as well as educating the public. The drive to establish a formal academic discipline emerges directly out of the Paris Peace Conference (also known as the Versailles Peace Conference—see Key event 2.1) during 1919, where the French, British, and American representatives agreed to set up private institutions to promote a better understanding of international issues.

In the UK, for example, the Royal Institute of International Affairs was established ostensibly to 'advance the sciences of international politics, economics and jurisprudence (and) to encourage and facilitate the scientific study of international questions'. The World's first university department of international politics was set up, perhaps surprisingly, in the small Welsh coastal town of Aberystwyth at the then University College, Wales. There the Welsh Liberal politician and philanthropist David Davies funded the establishment of the first Chair in International Politics—the Woodrow Wilson Chair. This had the explicit purpose of developing 'political science in its application to IR with special reference to the best means of promoting peace between nations'. The professorship was named after the President of the United States, Woodrow Wilson, who was very prominent during the Versailles Peace conference and is generally recognized as the key figure behind the establishment of the League of Nations.

In the US, the Council of Foreign Relations was established in New York and its stated mission was to 'develop by scientific and impartial study, a better understanding of international problems, and an intelligent American foreign policy'. In 1927, the *Institut Universitaire des Hautes Études Internationales* (now the Graduate Institute of International Studies) was established in Geneva as the world's first postgraduate university dedicated solely to the study of international politics. The Institute was intended to work closely with both the League of Nations and the also recently established International Labour Organisation.

KEY EVENT 2.1 THE VERSAILLES PEACE CONFERENCE

The conference (also known as the Paris Peace Conference) was convened in January 1919, at Versailles, just outside Paris. It was intended to establish the terms of the peace after the end of the First World War. Delegates from 32 states participated, but the conference was dominated by the United Kingdom, the United States, and France.

Initially, the 'Big Three' differed significantly in their objectives, notably over the terms of the armistice with defeated Germany and the degree to which Germany should be punished. Germany was not allowed to participate or negotiate the terms of any settlement. The principal outcome of the complex negotiations over five months was the Treaty of Versailles. The Treaty established the League of Nations (which Germany was not allowed to join), required Germany to take responsibility for starting the war—the so-called 'Guilt Clause'—and to effectively demilitarize as well as accept highly punitive economic reparations.

Many historians argue that the harshness of the treaty, notably the huge reparations imposed on Germany and the Guilt Clause, fostered bitter resentment in Germany and contributed to political instability, the resurgence of militarism, and, ultimately, Adolf Hitler's ascent to power.

In these brief and often repeated stories of the discipline's origins, we can already see some of the key themes of liberal thinking on international politics that underpinned the discipline's early years: a belief in progress through the application of reason and knowledge; a *normative* (i.e., value driven) commitment to the possibility and necessity of reforming international relations in pursuit of peace; and the virtues of public and private internationally focused research and teaching institutions. They also show that the emerging IR discipline was very much a Western creation something that in recent years has attracted an increasing amount of critical commentary, much of it influenced by postcolonialist IR perspectives (which are the subject of Chapter 9). The general thrust of recent challenges to the common story of the IR discipline's origins is that it obscures the preoccupation of many of the discipline's founding figures with empire and race. We will return to this issue later in Section 2.4, but it is also discussed more fully in Section 9.8 of Chapter 9.

Applying liberal 'idealism' to International Politics: Woodrow Wilson and the League of Nations

In the aftermath of the first World War, some liberals, most notably Woodrow Wilson (Key thinker 2.2), wanted to take Kant's claim that the international system could make substantial progress towards the elimination of war through the creation of an international federation of states. What they sought to establish was a rules-based international order centred around the creation of an international institution comprised of representatives of all the world's sovereign states.

KEY THINKER 2.2 WOODROW WILSON

Wilson (1856–1924) was a noted academic prior to becoming the 28th President of the United States. One of the first recipients of a PhD in political science (and the only US President to have received one), Wilson went on to become President of Princeton University prior to entering politics.

A prominent advocate of an *internationalist* US foreign policy underpinned by evidently liberal values, Wilson led the United States into the First World War. Wilson's internationalism contrasted with the longstanding and highly influential *isolationist* viewpoint held by an influential group in the US Congress who were supported by a large portion of the American public. A mixture of progressives and conservatives, the isolationists argued that the US should avoid getting overly entangled in international political affairs. Their viewpoint was reinforced by the widespread public perception that the US's participation in the First World War was driven predominantly by the interests of US bankers and arms manufacturers and entailed too great a sacrifice of American lives.

Although Wilson was the leading advocate of the creation of a League of Nations, for which he received the Nobel Peace Prize in 1919, the isolationists in the US Congress successfully blocked US membership in the League, fearing its 'collective security' clause. This would require the US to participate in any military response to an attack on any other member state of the League and potentially obligated the US to become perpetually entangled in international conflicts.

In recent years, several IR scholars have identified distinctly racist undertones to the liberal worldview promoted by Wilson and many of his contemporaries, which, they argue, the IR discipline has ignored or forgotten (we discuss this further later in this chapter and in Chapter 9). President Wilson was an active supporter of racial segregation in the US, notably in the federal civil service, which now casts a significant shadow over his reputation as a liberal progressive in both domestic and international politics.

Ten months prior to the Armistice with Germany that ended the First World War, Wilson delivered a speech to the US Congress, which became known as the '14 Points Speech'. The key points of the speech were:

- Diplomacy should be more transparent and publicly accountable (although Wilson later came to recognize that some secrecy was inevitable and perhaps necessary)
- Absolute freedom of navigation on the seas
- Free trade wherever possible
- Arms reduction to the minimal level consistent with domestic defence
- The establishment of a League of Nations
- An impartial settlement of all disputes about the sovereignty of colonized territories, in which the interests of Indigenous populations would carry equal weight to that of the governments claiming sovereignty (although what Wilson meant by this remains a matter of debate).

Such themes reflected the liberal worldview that figured so prominently in the arguments for the establishment of the new academic discipline of IR. They also led to the coining of the term 'Wilsonian Internationalism' (or 'Wilsonianism') to capture his international reformism. It was the overt intentions of Wilson and other prominent Western liberals to reform the international system that led to many of their critics to describe them disparagingly as 'idealists' (see Key concept 2.1).

KEY CONCEPT 2.1 IDEALISM IN IR

Idealism is a formal term that can be used to describe philosophical standpoints which argue that reality is largely a mental or conceptual construction (i.e., reality is what we *think* it is) or that human ideas can and do significantly shape our world. Kant is one of the most famous of idealist philosophers in both formal philosophical meanings of the term. This contrasts with various kinds of philosophical realism, which argue that reality exists outside of and independently of the human mind. The debate between idealism and realism in philosophy is complex and ongoing.

In more everyday language, as well as in politics, however, referring to someone as an idealist tends to suggest that person is primarily driven by high ideals and values, but perhaps at the expense of ignoring supposed concrete realities. Political idealism is thus frequently associated with a preoccupation with how the world *should be*, rather than how the world *is*, and a faith in the transformative power of ideas.

This is often presented in negative terms; an idealist is often portrayed as someone who is naïve about, or out of touch with the 'real' world. This negative connotation of idealism implicitly and sometimes explicitly threaded through much of the criticism that the foundational liberal phase of IR thinking attracted.

In recent years several IR scholars have questioned the extent to which there was really a debate between idealism and realism in the early years of the IR discipline. However, since E.H. Carr's famous attack on the liberal thinkers of the interwar years, whom he described as 'utopians' (We discuss E.H. Carr in Chapter 3, Section 3.4), a supposed debate between idealists and realists has become part of the common story of the evolution of the IR discipline.

It was his advocacy of the establishment of a new international organization—the League of Nations—for which Wilson is perhaps best remembered. Underpinning the proposed League was the principle of *collective security* (see Key concept 2.2). This was intended to inhibit states from engaging in aggressive actions towards other states because an attack on any member of the League would be viewed as an attack on all members and would thus risk a collective response. The assumption is that the risk of retaliation by a large and therefore overwhelmingly superior group of states (ideally, most if not all other states) will deter any individual state from resorting to war against any other.

KEY CONCEPT 2.2 COLLECTIVE SECURITY

Collective security is a model of international security that fundamentally rests on the assumption that there is a sufficient harmony of interests among states, despite their myriad differences, to enable them to recognize their mutual interest in a rule-governed international security order. Considered from a Liberal perspective, adherence to the principle of collective security, ultimately by all states, might provide a building block towards an international system governed, in part at least, by some shared rules and norms.

Collective security is more ambitious and wide-ranging than *collective defence* agreements (as illustrated, until recently at least, by Article 5 of the 1949 North Atlantic Treaty), wherein a select group of states enter a pact to defend each other should any be attacked. Whereas collective defence pacts are usually intended to address a limited range of threat scenarios, collective security seeks to prevent all resort to aggression, requiring states to uphold universal norms of conduct and pursue the non-military resolution of conflict.

When Wilson travelled to Europe to take part in the Versailles peace conference in 1919, he attracted significant public attention and expressions of approval. However, though the leading victorious European states signed up to the League, their subsequent commitment to the values underpinning it was questionable at best. Additionally, Wilson failed to persuade the US Congress to agree to US membership of the League. Given the rapidly growing prominence and influence of the US in international politics, this severely limited the League's prospects for success from the outset.

The League of Nations and the principle of collective security proved to be mostly ineffective. Although at its peak in 1934 the League had 58 member states, its membership fluctuated considerably during its 26 years of existence. Of the 42 states who joined the League when it was established, only 23 of them were still there when it was dissolved. The US never joined, and Germany and the Soviet Union were initially excluded. The Soviet Union was subsequently admitted in 1934 only to be expelled in 1939 for invading Finland. A further 16 states joined but later left. Germany was admitted in 1926 but Hitler withdrew from the League when he came to power in 1933, as did Japan in the same year. The two main European powers—Britain and France—stayed in the League but were reluctant to use either economic sanctions or military force to support the League's decisions.

There were some small successes, but the starkest indication of the League's weakness was the failure to enact the principle of collective security. In large part this was because the definition of aggression was left for member states to agree among themselves, which they consistently failed to do. The League failed to stop Imperial Japan from invading Manchuria in 1931, or fascist Italy invading Abyssinia (now Ethiopia) in 1936, or to constrain the rise of Hitler's Germany and its open ambition to subjugate most of Europe to its rule. With the outbreak of the Second World War in 1939, the League had effectively ceased to function, and it was formally dissolved in 1946 to be immediately succeeded by the establishment of the United Nations.

The ineffectiveness of the League of Nations was one of the key issues which critics of the liberal view of international politics used to question the general plausibility of liberal international reformism. It was during the lead up to Second World War that academic criticism of the liberal perspective in international politics began to gather pace. The critical reaction to liberal international reformism and progressivism was, arguably, very much a product of the failure of states to substantially reform the conduct of international politics during the inter-war period, despite evident public enthusiasm for change. Historians continue to argue over who or what was to blame, but key factors were the legacy of the 1919 Versailles Treaty, which many see as having imposed excessively harsh punishment on Germany (thus contributing to the rise of Hitler and Nazi fascism), the continuing influence of isolationism in US politics, and the failure of the League of Nations to live up to its promise.

Scholars on both sides of the Atlantic were developing a realist retort to liberal progressivism. The British historian E.H. Carr's *The Twenty Years Crisis,* written in 1939 just prior to the outbreak of the Second World War, is one of the most cited sources of criticism of the foundational phase of IR scholarship as idealist (or 'utopian', as he preferred to call it). Carr is also commonly identified as one of the founding figures of the IR perspective known as realism. He did not, however, systematically analyse the work of specific supposedly idealist writers; Carr was more concerned with examining, angrily, how, despite all the promise of the international reformism promoted during and after the Versailles Peace Treaty, the world had returned to the brink of war only 20 years later. He was, however, certainly a critic of liberal universalism and argued for a much more systematic and rigorous study of international politics which took greater account of the complex reality of international politics, especially the role of power.

This emphasis on the distinction between idealism and realism became very widespread, especially after 1945, and arguably led to oversimplification and a caricaturing of positions. Indeed, many IR textbooks today still label the early phase of IR scholarship as idealist and often go on to depict the tension between liberal idealism and the emerging realist retort as the first of a series of 'great debates' that mark the evolution of the discipline. The principal objection to the liberal approach to international politics was its perceived failure to adequately address the supposed realities of power in international politics. Yet, as we discuss in the next section, more recent scholarship questions whether such a debate really occurred and argues, moreover, that while the so-called idealists were certainly progressive and reformist thinkers, they also had a thoroughly realistic grasp of international politics. Importantly, they were also in tune with widespread public sentiment. Was liberal idealism fundamentally flawed as a set of ideas and policies then, or was it more a victim of a combination of events and the failure of key states at the time to change long-established outlooks?

Whatever the case, the failure of the League and the subsequent descent of the international system into another world war did considerable damage to the foundational liberal perspective that marked the establishment of the discipline of IR. Nonetheless, as we discuss in Section 2.5, the so-called idealists left a considerable intellectual legacy and undoubtedly accurately foresaw some key features of the future development of the international system.

2.4 **CHALLENGING THE COMMON STORY OF THE IR DISCIPLINE'S ORIGINS**

The introduction to this chapter flagged up two lines of criticism of the common story of the liberal origins of the modern IR discipline. The first is that the standard depiction of the foundational phase of the IR discipline as 'idealist' is questionable. The second and more profound criticism is that the common story fails to address the racist and imperial sentiments underpinning the IR discipline's establishment.

Let us now examine these two criticisms more closely, starting with the challenge to the label idealism.

Was early liberal thinking on IR actually 'idealist'?

Who were these so-called idealists and was the criticism of them justified? In the early IR literature that appeared after the establishment of the discipline, the term idealism was rarely used. Where it was used in either academic literature or public debate there was little evident consensus as to the precise meaning of the term (Ashworth, 2006). One analysis of the origins of the discipline argues that what evidence there was of idealism in the 1920s was largely to be found in popular tracts written by political activists and there was little evidence of any idealism in the early IR textbooks (Olsen and Groom, 1991: 69). That there was a lot of populist political writing about the need for international reform was hardly surprising, given that the public mood across much of the Western world in the aftermath of the First World War was decisively anti-war (as Kant had suggested it would be).

In recent years, several scholars have questioned the common depiction of the founding figures of the IR discipline as idealists or utopians. Lucian Ashworth argues, for example, that the key figures associated with idealism in the 1920s and 1930s—such as Norman Angell, Leonard Woolf, Phillip Noel-Baker, H. N. Brailsford and David Mitrany—were certainly reformist-minded progressives, but their main concern was with gradual reform rather than visionary, utopian projects. In other words, the so-called idealists were certainly progressive thinkers who believed that the international system could and needed to be reformed. Whether they were 'idealists' in the common sense of the term is, however, a matter of debate (Ashworth, 2006: 301–304). They generally endeavoured to base their arguments on perceptions of significant changes already underway in the international system and the global economy, or the very real risks and costs associated with the increasing industrialization and modernization of weaponry and warfare, as the First World War had so painfully shown.

Norman Angell was concerned, for example, with managing a rapidly changing world economy (which he saw as moving towards what we now call globalization). David Mitrany was one of the early proponents, along with Leonard Woolf, of greater institutionalized cooperation among states to reduce antagonism and thus the risk of war. Indeed, Mitrany's work on the peaceful benefits of institutionalized functional cooperation, first developed in the 1920s and 1930s, was highly influential in the early stages of European integration after 1945 which ultimately led to the creation of today's European Union (EU). Another prominent Liberal, Noel Baker, was a strong advocate of the League of Nations, while recognizing its many flaws, as well as the need to strengthen international law. The arguments of Angell, Mitrany, Woolf, and Baker shifted throughout the period between the First and Second World War, suggesting that they were certainly mindful of changing international realities. Indeed, it was the changing reality of international politics that they believed needed addressing urgently (Ashworth, 2006; 301–302).

Whatever the perceived weaknesses of the arguments of these founding figures of IR were at the time, subsequent developments suggest that their arguments were rather prescient. The world since then has seen significant changes in economic relations between states and the rapid institutionalization of international relations. Formal and informal cooperation between many if not most states has deepened significantly, illustrated most starkly by the evolution of today's EU with its 27 member states.

Imperialism, racism, and the establishment of the IR discipline

The common story of the establishment of the IR discipline has also been challenged in recent years around the questions of colonialism and racism. Several scholars argue that the widespread depiction of the origins of the IR discipline inadequately considers or omits entirely the colonialist and racialized worldviews of many of its founding figures.

In reference to the establishment of the IR discipline in the UK, critics sometime refer to the common story as the 'Aberystwyth narrative'. This is because, as we have already noted, it depicts the IR discipline's origins as primarily a reaction to the First World War as illustrated by such events as the establishment of the world's first university department of International Politics at Aberystwyth. Recent scholarship, however, offers an alternative starting point prior to the war: the founding of the oldest British international affairs journal, *The Round Table,* in 1910.

The journal came out of the Round Table society whose roots lay in the newly created British dominion of South Africa. The Round Table movement's purpose was to explore 'the organic union of the British Empire' (in essence a more federated model of the Empire) which might lay the groundwork for some form of world government (Davis, Thakur, and Vale, 2020: 2–3). The Society brought together some of the key figures in the eventual establishment of a formal IR discipline, including the historian Alfred Zimmerman who was the inaugural Woodrow Wilson professor at Aberystwyth, Lionel Curtis, the founder of Chatham House (the home of the Royal Institute of International Affairs) and Philip Kerr, the first editor of *The Round Table* journal. In thus taking the origins of the IR discipline back just a few years, the liberal underpinnings of the common story of the IR discipline's beginnings are shown to have been underpinned by imperial ambitions.

IR has also frequently been depicted as 'an American social science' (Hoffman, 1977). In fact, there was significant intellectual interchange between British and American scholars and political figures during the foundational years of the IR discipline and a shared concern about race and empire. The Round Table's founders all spent time in the US and were interested in its racial politics just as American liberal scholars sought to draw from Britain's imperial experience of managing race relations in its colonies, such as South Africa (Davis, Thakur, and Vale, 2020: 5). It is worth noting here that the first US academic journal covering international relations was called the *Journal of Race Development,* first published in 1910. After briefly being renamed as the *Journal of International Relations*, it was merged into the *Foreign Affairs* magazine founded by the US Council of Foreign Relations in 1922 and which remains a highly influential publication today. Scholars such as Robert Vitalis and Jessica Blatt have shown how the question of race relations within and between states was central to the early development of political science and IR in the US (Vitalis, 2015; Blatt, 2018).

Several international historians and IR scholars have also argued that some of the most prominent figures behind the establishment of the League of Nations, such as President Woodrow Wilson and the South African statesman Jan Smuts, overtly held white supremacist views (Krishna, 2001; Mazower, 2006 and 2009; Hobson, 2012; Seth 2013; Vitalis, 2015; Davis, Thakur, and Vale, 2020). Their ostensibly liberal progressive international outlook, was, these critics argue, underpinned by a preoccupation with the future management of the colonized world and the preservation of the global supremacy of the white race. Although they conceded, in principle at least, that at some point colonized territories should receive their independence they were much more circumspect about when this should eventuate.

In the case of Woodrow Wilson, his openly proclaimed and seemingly unequivocal commitment to the moral principle of 'self-determination' for colonized peoples, as suggested in his '14 Points speech' to Congress, sat uncomfortably with his support for the maintenance of racial segregation within the United States. Like many other prominent white liberal men of the time, Wilson's commitment to the principle of self-determination was ultimately premised upon a paternalistic view of non-Western peoples as needing the support of the supposedly more civilized Western states to prepare them for eventual independence. In other words, the abstract commitment to the ending of colonial rule rested upon a worldview which classified the peoples of the world according to a graduated scale of levels of development, with the white Western nations at its top (Milne, 2015; Vitalis, 2015; Henderson, 2017). Such views could also be found in some of the earliest IR textbooks (Henderson, 2017).

What these critical challenges to the common story or the 'Aberystwyth narrative' add up to is a rather different story about the IR discipline's birth. In contrast to the claim that the IR discipline began with the efforts of liberal 'idealists' on both sides of the Atlantic to promote the scientific study of international affairs in the aftermath of a devastating world war, 'they argue that the "birth of the discipline" not only precedes WWI, but also that it emerged out of discussions about race and empire, not peace and war' (Davis, Thakur, and Vale, 2020: 4). This is not to say that the common story of the origins of the discipline is entirely false, rather that it has become sanitized over time.

Why has the criticism of the racist underpinnings of liberal IR thinking in the early twentieth century only emerged relatively recently? After all, as the historian of US foreign policy, David Milne, notes, 'Wilson's impact on international affairs was profound; few nations were unaffected by his words and actions, while adherents to his diplomatic vision, Wilsonianism, remain an influential force today' (Milne, 2015: 1). It seems that Wilson's ideas and often soaring rhetoric about the need for reform of international politics somehow became detached from his personal views and prejudices and effectively acquired a life of their own.

Certainly, liberalism's influence in the IR discipline declined after the onset of the Second World War in 1939 and the subsequent collapse of the League of Nations. The world after the war's end in 1945 was also markedly different. The central preoccupation of IR scholars rapidly became the emerging Cold War between the United States and the Soviet Union, and realism became the dominant theoretical orientation within the IR discipline. Several IR scholars argue that the IR discipline seemingly underwent a process of 'whitewashing' the story of its founding years (Krishna, 2001; Hobson 2012; Vitalis, 2015; Sabaratnam, 2020). In its place emerged the now common story of the IR discipline's origins centred around the core ideas of liberal international reformism yet stripped of the racist prejudices and imperial ambitions of some of the discipline's leading founding figures (we discuss this further in Chapter 9).

2.5 THE 'IDEALIST' LEGACY IN IR TODAY—THE CONTINUING DEVELOPMENT OF THE LIBERAL APPROACH TO IR

The dominance of liberalism in the new discipline of IR was rather short-lived. After the end of the Second World War it was rapidly supplanted by a rather different theoretical perspective, realism, the subject of the next chapter in this textbook. There is a widespread consensus that realism came to dominate the IR discipline for several decades after 1945, this dominance very much coinciding with the development of a Cold War between the US and the Soviet Union. Nonetheless, Liberal thinking about international politics did not simply disappear and many core Kantian and Wilsonian themes remained highly influential. They are not only alive and well today in contemporary liberal IR scholarship (especially in the West), but also in the conduct of international politics itself.

Despite the dominance of realism in both scholarly and diplomatic circles, liberal thinking about IR underwent a series of revivals in the post-1945 era. These can be roughly divided into two broad and interconnected strands:

- normatively driven arguments about how international politics *ought* to be conducted

- empirically driven arguments, centred on claims about the changing concrete reality of international politics—how the world *is*.

Whereas the normative strand of liberal IR thought can be traced more directly back to the overtly progressive and reformist sentiments of the foundational era of the discipline (the supposed idealism of the discipline's founders as discussed in Sections 2.3 and 2.4), the more empirical strand was very much an attempt to shed the idealist image of the liberal perspective on IR and demonstrate its practical relevance to understanding and responding effectively to a rapidly changing world. In many respects, it can be understood in part as a response to the criticism of E. H. Carr and others that the foundational liberal idealists were too preoccupied with how the world *ought* to be. It was also influenced by the growing prominence of the idea that the discipline of IR needed to be more rigorous, scientific, and objective, in reflection of broad trends within the social sciences, especially in the US, during the 1950s and 1960s (which are discussed in Chapter 1).

Liberalism and the institutionalization of international politics

We have already seen that the creation of international institutions was a key component of liberal IR thought, as exemplified by the establishment of the League of Nations. The institutionalization of international politics has remained a central tenant of liberal IR thinking today.

The UN System

A prominent empirical example of the liberal legacy is the establishment of the United Nations (UN). Not only has it not suffered the fate of its predecessor, the League of Nations, but it has also had an undoubtedly significant impact upon international politics, particularly regarding the further development of international organization and the international legal framework as well. Most states are members and rare is the state that voluntarily opts to leave the organization. Under its auspices, there has been a proliferation of related international organizations. The UN has been central to the development of human rights conventions, as well as the development of a range of legal constraints upon war and its conduct. Although the UN charter reveals the influence of broadly Western liberal values, during the Cold War the General Assembly of the UN also evolved into a key site for questioning and challenging many aspects of the West's historical dominance of the international system.

The UN's many inadequacies, not least a frequent incapacity to act upon or control moments of crisis in the international system, have been frequently pointed out. A liberal might well argue, however, that the UN's failings are in part at least a consequence of conceding too much to the supposed realities of international power politics that, as we will see in Chapter 3, realists emphasize in their theoretical challenges to the liberal worldview. As it stands, the UN can only do what its member states permit it to do and as sovereign states they are generally inclined to not grant the UN too much power over themselves. A realist would also probably point out that the UN has succeeded where the League of Nations failed because, unlike the League, its leading member states—as represented by the permanent members of the UN Security Council—have a right of veto. As with the League of Nations, the principle of collective security is woven into the UN Charter. However, critics have pointed out that the effectiveness of the UN's commitment to collective security is fatally undermined by the fact that the permanent members' power of veto enables them to prevent the UN from invoking the collective security principal should they deem it to be against their own interests.

From a realist point of view, this demonstrates a significant concession to the brute reality that if the most powerful states don't want the UN to act because it does not suit their national interests, they can simply prevent it from so doing. In other words, the UN has succeeded where the League failed because the limits to its authority were clearly established from the outset. Nonetheless, The Security Council's resolutions do have substantive authority. Even if states fail to comply with them, they can act as embodiments of principles that set important benchmarks for judging the conduct of states or the claims they make within a dispute. One example of this is resolution 242 of 1967. This required Israel to withdraw from territories, which included the Sinai Desert taken from Egypt, the Golan Heights taken from Syria and the West Bank taken from Jordan during the 1967 Six Day War with its neighbouring Arab states. The resolution introduced the concept of 'land for peace', wherein Israel would give up occupied territory in exchange for peace agreements with its neighbours. It certainly cannot be said that the resolution has been fully implemented; although Israel returned the Sinai Peninsula to Egypt, it continues, controversially, to effectively control the West Bank and has retained occupation of the Golan Heights.

From a liberal perspective the significance of such resolutions arises not just from whether they achieve their objectives or not, but also in the fact they set benchmarks and can form the basis for future negotiations between parties to a conflict. Although the Palestinian Liberation Organization originally rejected Resolution 242 outright, it did form the basis for subsequent peace treaties between Israel and Egypt and Israel and Jordan as well as the 1993 and 1995 Oslo Accords between Israel and the Palestinians. The long-hoped for resolution of the Israel–Palestine conflict seems a long way off still, but the key point from a liberal perspective is the role that international norms, rules, and institutions can and do play in the process.

The UN is now only one of a vast network of international political and economic organizations. When coupled with the extent of complex formal and informal cooperation between states as well as the prominence of human rights in today's world, this arguably demonstrates the extent to which international politics has become increasingly institutionalized and rule-governed in the decades after the Second World War. Some observers go so far as to claim that we all now live within a liberal international order.

The Bretton Woods System

Central to the claim that the international system created in the post-1945 era is essentially liberal in form, has been the institutionalization of management of the international economy, initially through the establishment of the Bretton Woods System (Key event 2.2).

Underpinning the design of the Bretton Woods system was the belief that a liberal international economic order would provide the best prospects for lasting peace. The two Bretton Woods Institutions—the World Bank and IMF—became the key pillars of the management and regulation of the international capitalist system and remain powerful players in the contemporary world economy. Although there is considerable debate these

United Nations Headquarters in New York City

KEY EVENT 2.2 THE ESTABLISHMENT OF THE BRETTON WOODS SYSTEM

The Bretton Woods system of international monetary and financial management was the product of an agreement drawn up between 44 allied states in July 1944, towards the end of the Second World War. The intention was to plan for the recovery of the international economic system after the war. The Bretton Woods Agreement established a set of rules, procedures, and institutions (what liberal IR theory calls an 'international regime') to manage monetary exchange between states.

The system centred on the US dollar acting as a reserve currency, whose value was backed up by the US's gold reserves (which at the time amounted to two thirds of the world's gold supply), and the introduction of fixed exchange rates set in reference to the US dollar which was seen to be 'as good as gold'. The agreement also established two international institutions: the International Monetary Fund (IMF) and the International Bank for Reconstruction and Development which later became the World Bank. Although the fixed rate exchange system was abandoned in 1971 after the US terminated the convertibility of the US dollar into gold, thereby bringing an end to the Bretton Woods System, the two key Bretton Woods institutions remain significant and powerful participants in the management of the global economy.

The global financial crisis of 2008 led to a debate about reforming the global financial architecture. Additionally, there have been shifts in the policies of the IMF and World Bank which some see as evidence of a stepping away from a primary focus on global market stability towards a greater emphasis on unemployment and inequality as issues that need to play a more prominent role in their policies. The significance of this shift is, however, a matter of considerable debate.

days about whether there is a need for a new international financial management system to replace the Bretton Woods institutional architecture, from a liberal perspective Bretton Woods reinforces both the possibility and continuing necessity of extensive international institutionalized cooperation and negotiated management of the global economy.

If management of the world economy can be seen as further evidence of the essentially liberal character of the contemporary international order, it is also open to critique from a range of more critical perspectives, such as Marxism (the subject of Chapter 5). In many ways, these critical perspectives reinforce the claim that the international order is essentially liberal in character because they depict the prevailing international political and economic order as reflecting the entrenched dominance of the liberal capitalist West, to the political and economic disadvantage of the Global South (we discuss this further in Chapters 5 and 9). However, the continuing rise in the strength and influence of several non-Western powers, such as China and India, raises a range of questions not only about the future robustness of that liberal international political and economic order, but also the principles that underpin it.

The European integration project

In the post-1945 era, Europe has provided further evidence supporting the liberal case for the possibility of significant international reform. In the early 1950s the European integration project commenced with the establishment of the European Coal and Steel Community (ECSC) between 6 European states who, only a decade before had been at war. The ECSC was the beginning of a process of widening and deepening cooperation between an expanding number of European states that culminated in the development of today's EU of 27 states. The EU's membership is of course limited; it is confined to the European region and is comprised entirely of developed states. Yet from a liberal point of view, it lends credence to Kant's view in *Perpetual Peace* that like-minded states can develop close cooperative relationships and ultimately renounce the use of war amongst themselves, thereby setting an example to other groups of states.

In recent years this positive Liberal reading of the EU has come under challenge from several quarters. These would include Brexit (the departure of the UK from the EU in 2020), and the growth of public resistance to deepening European integration (Euroscepticism) in several EU member states, including some of the EU's founding members, such as France and Italy. Additionally, there is evident public resistance within some of the EU's newer, formerly communist, member states (such as Poland and Hungary) to some key aspects of the social liberalism that threads through the EU's political and normative foundations, such as abortion, same-sex marriage, and LGBTQI+ rights more generally. In combination, such developments raise questions about the limits to and robustness of a liberal international order, even when it is developing at a regional level among comparatively similar states.

NATO

Also interesting from a liberal perspective is the evolving role of The North Atlantic Treaty Organization (NATO), established at the beginning of the Cold War by a

2 THE LIBERAL 'IDEALIST' ORIGINS OF THE INTERNATIONAL RELATIONS DISCIPLINE

group of Western allies—Canada, the US, the UK, and most West European states—to counter the perceived threat posed by the Soviet Union and its East European allied states. It is perhaps the most prominent example of a system of *collective defence* based around a shared understanding of the key security threat among its members. With the end of the Cold War in 1989 and NATO's subsequent expansion from 12 to 30 member states, however, it is arguable that NATO is moving closer to a *collective security* arrangement in reflection of changing perceptions as to what the contemporary threats to its members' security are in today's post-Cold War world (see Key concept 2.2). NATO's 'Article 5', which triggers the enactment of the collective defence principle, was in fact first used after the 9/11 terrorist attacks on the US, which was more than a decade after the end of the Cold War. Since then, NATO has been engaged in a range of ongoing counter-terrorism actions, including the development of joint intelligence, surveillance, and reconnaissance capabilities that reach well beyond the borders of its member states.

In the post-Cold War era, NATO has shifted from an organization intended primarily to deter attacks on the territorial integrity of its member states by a defined enemy (a collective defence agreement) towards one that seeks to protect and uphold the values shared by its member states or, indeed, the wider international community. This is more suggestive of a collective security arrangement such as that envisioned by the proponents of the League of Nations. However, the fact that its membership is selective and is essentially confined to Europe and North America arguably induces competition as well as cooperation when viewed from a global perspective.

The development of liberal IR thinking after 1945—history and theory

The modern history of liberal thinking about IR alerts us to the relationship between theory and history, something we discuss throughout this book. As we have seen, the modern IR discipline emerged in a distinctly liberal form and predominantly in the West during a key historical moment: the aftermath of the First World War. Similarly, the subsequent development of liberal IR thinking, as well as many other perspectives, can also be connected to key historical periods and events in international politics. Indeed, the varying influence of both liberalism and realism, the two key theories of mainstream or orthodox IR theory, very much reflected the fluctuations of international politics during the Cold War.

In the case of the revival of liberal scholarship, several historical developments are of note. We have already identified four of these:

- the establishment of the UN
- the creation of the Bretton Woods system
- the European integration project
- NATO.

All these historical developments emerged out of changes brought about by the Second World War. The design of the UN, especially the creation of five permanent members of the UN Security Council with veto rights, arguably reflected the influence of realist thinking and its insistence on the importance of power. Nonetheless, the establishment of the UN and other post-1945 international institutions such as those set up as part of the Bretton Woods system, all served to underscore the liberal emphasis on the practical utility and substantive impact of increasingly institutionalized *cooperation* at a global level. The value of cooperation at a regional level, especially a region of the world that had hitherto been marked by a history of war, is also illustrated by the European integration project. Although today the EU attracts attention sometimes because of its weaknesses as much its strengths, it can also be viewed as a remarkable liberal peace project. This has significantly transformed relations between an expanding group of states who had a long history of frequently being at war with each other, or, more recently, had been on opposite sides during the Cold War. The idea of war between the European states surely seems almost inconceivable today.

A further historical moment of significance for the development of liberal IR theory emerged in the late 1960s and early 1970s when there was an easing of the Cold War into a decade of *détente* (relaxation) in superpower relations (see Key events 2.3). There was a marked increase in diplomatic activity between the Soviet Union and the USA (referred to at the time as 'shuttle diplomacy'), which started to produce some significant outcomes, not least a series of landmark nuclear arms control agreements.

It would be a mistake to overstate the significance of détente. After all, this was also a period marked by wars in S.E. Asia (notably the Vietnam War) in which the superpowers were supporting the opposing sides, just as they did in the 1973 Arab-Israeli war (the 'Yom Kippur' war). Nonetheless, a lessening of the preoccupation with the Cold War between the superpowers, that had marked the IR discipline since 1945 and helped to cement the dominance of realism and its focus on 'power politics', did help to create a more open and exploratory intellectual environment within the IR scholarly community. It was in this context that some scholars shifted their attention away from superpower rivalry to other dimensions of international politics.

KEY EVENT 2.3 DÉTENTE

Détente (from the French for relaxation) refers to a period during the Cold War when relations between the United States and the Soviet Union eased significantly. Though the precise dates of the period of *détente* are a matter of debate, it is generally agreed that it commenced in 1969 and that by 1979, when the Soviet Union invaded Afghanistan, the Cold War had most definitely flared up again.

Between 1969 and 1974 the superpowers engaged in a series of bilateral summits that resulted in several landmark agreements, including the Strategic Arms Limitations Treaty of 1972 (SALT I) which temporarily capped the number of strategic nuclear weapons each side could deploy. This was immediately followed by the commencement of talks on a further arms control treaty (SALT II). Additionally, in the same year the superpowers signed the Anti-Ballistic Missile Treaty (ABM treaty) which limited the number of missiles that either side could deploy to defend against an incoming nuclear missile attack. The intention was to preserve the risk of **mutually assured destruction** (MAD) as the basis for deterring each side from initiating a nuclear missile exchange.

There has been considerable debate as to the significance of *détente*. Some see it as a lull within a single ongoing Cold War whereas others see it as period when the Cold War declined sufficiently to consider the return to Cold War after 1979 as a distinctive 'Second Cold War' (Halliday, 1983).

Complex interdependence

During the late 1960s and early 1970s several liberal IR scholars began to depict international politics as a complex system of multiple actors and not just sovereign states. One of the earliest and more radical versions of this argument can be found in the work of the Australian former diplomat and scholar, John Burton. In contrast to realist depictions of international politics as primarily concerned with relations between sovereign states (i.e., an exclusively *state-centric* approach), Burton suggested that it could also be understood as a series of cobwebs of *transactions* between multiple types of actors (Burton, 1972: 43).

A more modest and more influential version of this line of argument can be found in the work of the liberal American Scholars, Robert Keohane and Joseph Nye. For Keohane and Nye the international system since 1945 had been undergoing significant change. In their book *Power and Interdependence*, first published in 1977, Keohane and Nye argued that although *inter-state* relations (relations between sovereign states) remained highly significant, international politics was increasingly characterized by the emergence of a wide range of formal and informal *trans-governmental* (relations between national governments or sub-sections of national governments) and *transnational* relations (formal and informal relations between a variety of actors that cut across national boundaries). Consequently, international politics increasingly consisted of multiple issues, with no clear or consistent hierarchy among them. Issues were arising from both domestic and international policy arenas, generated different coalitions of actors, and involved different degrees of conflict. States were therefore increasingly finding themselves in a condition Keohane and Nye called *complex interdependence*. Importantly, they claimed that military force was not used where complex interdependence prevailed. In contrast to realism's preoccupation with states and how they survive in a dangerous world marked by the ever-present threat of war, Keohane and Nye argued that for most states it was not in fact the 'high' politics of security and survival, but the 'low' politics of trade and economic interaction that increasingly mattered most (Keohane and Nye, 1989).

Keohane and Nye's pioneering work contributed to a rapid growth in a liberal IR scholarship that emphasized the breaking down of the division between domestic and international politics and policy making. The sovereign state was depicted less as a single actor and more as a combination of actual and potential international actors. Liberals emphasized the need for a greater focus on formal and informal cooperation between these diverse international actors. It was during this period that scholarly interest in the *international political economy* (IPE) also rapidly developed, pioneered in the work of the British IR scholar Susan Strange and the US IR scholar Robert Gilpin. They reflected the increasingly widespread view that to understand IR fully, you needed to look at the intersection of political and economic relations between an array of actors, which included but were not confined to sovereign states. IPE has subsequently grown into a major scholarly field, overlapping extensively with IR but with its own distinctive schools of thought and key issue areas. It remains a key arena for liberal scholarship today.

Keohane and Nye's analysis of international politics was centred around a series of empirical claims about how they believed the world was—not explicitly normative arguments about how they wanted it to be. Nonetheless, Keohane and Nye's underlying liberal, progressive orientation was clear enough; after all, they were making a case for foreign policy, especially US foreign policy, needing to adapt to a changing and increasingly complex international environment. Here we can see connections with the pioneering work of many of the liberal scholars that founded the discipline of IR. They all share an emphasis on the need for states to more effectively engage with an increasingly complex world and develop foreign policies that better reflect significant changes underway. Kant's legacy can be seen threading through the work of Burton, Keohane, Nye, and others. They were all claiming that if states recognized more fully the changing world around them and responded to it intelligently (or, as Kant might say, rationally), a more cooperative and productive future in which war was increasingly irrelevant beckoned.

The end of the Cold War—the triumph of the liberal West?

The period of *détente* between the superpowers was short-lived. By the late 1970s, the relationship between the superpowers had soured and the Cold War between them seemed to have fully returned. Reinforcing the relationship between theory and history, this coincided with a significant restatement of realism, liberal IR's principal theoretical rival, that came to be known as *neorealism* (which is discussed in Chapter 3, Section 3.6). This second phase of the Cold War, proved also to be relatively brief. By the late 1980s, remarkable changes were underway, especially in the communist bloc of states. These culminated in the fall of the Berlin Wall in 1989, the collapse of communist regimes in Eastern Europe, and ultimately the dissolution of the Soviet Union. For many observers, a 'New World Order' was emerging. The principal rival to the liberal West, the Soviet-led bloc of communist states had effectively disappeared and the surviving major communist power, China, was participating increasingly fully in the global capitalist system.

Not surprisingly, liberal commentators, government leaders, and many scholars throughout the West hailed the opportunity this historic moment presented for the realization of a liberal world order that more fully reflected the values espoused in the writings of those foundational IR scholars. One of the most famous examples of such liberal triumphalism was Francis Fukuyama's claim that the defeat of the Soviet bloc marked the 'end of history' (Fukuyama, 1989 and 1992). Fukuyama was not suggesting that history itself had ended, but rather that the history of humanity's ideological development had reached its end. Liberalism's triumph over the Soviet communist alternative, he argued, had proven that liberal democracy was economically, politically, and ethically superior to all other actual or possible systems. It was, Fukuyama claimed, the 'final form of government' (Fukuyama, 1992: xi). Fukuyama's claim has been roundly criticised, not least because it didn't address the inequities of the liberal capitalist system, and the often-brutal history of colonial and imperial exploitation that underpinned the development of the liberal West. Additionally, the rise of non-democratic China in the post-Cold War era seemingly presents a challenge to Fukuyama's thesis. Whether or not Fukuyama's thesis is seen to be conclusive, the idea that liberal democracies are inherently superior remains powerfully influential within Western political thought and practice.

THINK CRITICALLY 2.2

- Francis Fukuyama and others claim that the collapse of the Soviet bloc at the end of the Cold War demonstrated the inherent superiority of liberal democracy. Do you agree? Why/Why not?
- Assess what other explanations there might be for the collapse of the Soviet bloc at this time.

To help you answer this question, consider the following (the first two might require some quick historical research):

- Do you think it was the intention of the Soviet Union's leader at the time, Mikhail Gorbachev, to abandon communism in favour of Western Liberalism or to reform Soviet communism to ensure its survival?
- What was the condition of the Soviet economy at the time?
- What do you think the subsequent history of post-Soviet Russia, other countries that were once part of the Soviet Union, or former member states of the Soviet Bloc tells us about the longer-term influence of liberal democracy and values?

Hint: Consider the Russia–Ukraine conflict here

Issues such as human rights, democratization, global social and economic justice, and ensuring the rule of international law visibly climbed up the international agenda in the post-Cold War world and many Western states shifted their focus from confronting the communist bloc to wider questions of international reform.

The notion that the end of the Cold War presented a unique historical opportunity to finally realize the vision of Woodrow Wilson and other liberals is succinctly captured in a 1993 article by Charles Kegley, entitled 'The Neoidealist Moment in International Studies? Realist Myths and the New International Realities' (Kegley, 1993). The paper was based on a speech by Kegley in his role as the then President of the International Studies Association, the leading professional association for IR academics. The 'new international realities', Kegley argued, 'have created a hospitable home for the reconstruction of realism inspired by Wilsonian Idealism'. Realists had criticized the founders of the discipline as idealists, but Kegley claimed that with the end of the Cold War, it was time for realists to reconsider their previous dismissal of the progressivism espoused by the so-called idealists and recognize that even before the Cold War ended, the foundational liberal vision was coming into being.

On what basis could Kegley make this claim? Citing numerous other leading Liberal IR scholars along the way, Kegley itemized several developments that had been underway for some time which, he claimed, echoed the key themes of Woodrow Wilson's famous '14 points speech' of 1919 (as we discussed in Section 2.3). These developments as seen by Kegley in the early 1990s were as follows:

- the worldwide demand for democracy (as evidenced particularly by the collapse of the Soviet-led bloc)
- the growing emphasis on 'the economic underpinnings of world politics', i.e., the politics of international trade
- the growing support for, adherence to, and advocacy of international law
- the importance of international organizations for the preservation of peace, especially with the revivifying of the UN in the aftermath of the Cold War
- the growth in arms control and especially the reduction of deployed nuclear arsenals
- the significance of the 'power of the people'. The collapse of the former communist bloc of East European states showed how governments had relinquished their authority, mostly peacefully, in response to public pressure for change
- The collapse of communist regimes, including the Soviet Union, mostly without significant violence which showed that the goals of states are not fixed but can change significantly
- A reinvigoration of concerns about human rights abuses and a renewed willingness within the international community to do something about them.

Kegley was primarily highlighting developments that seemingly underscored the political virtues of liberalism. It is important to emphasize also liberalism's strong association with the promotion of a capitalist international economic order. The liberal emphasis on individual freedom corresponds with a belief in the virtues of free markets because they are seen ultimately to promote greater freedom of individual choice. At the global level, liberals generally advocate, in principle at least, free trade between states. Liberal states disagree, however, on the extent to which global trade should be regulated to ensure international economic stability (this was a key issue in the disagreement between the UK and the EU that led to 'Brexit', Britain's exit from the EU). Additionally, some liberal states, such as the US, also use tariffs on imports to protect vulnerable domestic industries or in response to domestic political pressures.

Nonetheless the close association between liberalism and capitalism has generated critical challenges from outside the mainstream of IR debate. For example, around the same time as Keohane and Nye were introducing the concept of complex interdependence, scholars drawing upon Marxist political theory were engaging critically with the discipline of IR, particularly its liberal wing (as discussed in Chapter 5). They were focusing particularly on another major development in international politics since 1945: decolonization. As the former European empires collapsed during the twentieth century and especially after 1945, the number of independent sovereign states had expanded dramatically.

Marxist scholars argued that liberal scholars such as Keohane and Nye were overly focused on relations between the developed, industrialized, and mostly Western states, a point that Keohane and Nye conceded in a later edition of their path-breaking book (Keohane and Nye, 1989). In so doing, they were failing to reflect the world as seen from the point of view of what was now most states in the developing world. In contrast to Keohane and Nye's liberal depiction of a world of increasingly interdependent states, scholars such as Andre Gunder Frank (1967) drew upon Marxism and the experiences of Latin American states to highlight the relationship of *dependency* between the industrialized states of the Global North and the post-colonial states of the Global South.

Other scholars, such as Immanuel Wallerstein (1974a), also drew from Marxism to depict the world as comprised of three regions—core, periphery, and semi-periphery—depending on the level of development of the states within them. As a counterpoint to the benign liberal image of a world characterized by increasing cooperation between developed states within a global Liberal capitalist economic order, these alternative perspectives highlighted the exploitative relationship between the developed states of the West and developing states in the Global South, which was very much tied to the historical expansion of the global capitalist system. Decolonization may have granted many former colonies formal independence, but this had not ended the economic exploitation that had underpinned the colonial era. We examine Marxist approaches to IR in further detail in Chapter 5, but the general theme of a long historical connection between liberalism and the West's imperial and colonial past continues to haunt liberal IR theory and practice, which we will now explore further.

2.6 CONTEMPORARY LIBERAL IR AND IMPERIALISM

In Section 2.4 it was noted that some recent IR scholarship has argued that the foundational liberal idealist phase of the IR discipline was driven in part by a desire to sustain Western imperial interests and the dominance of the White race. We have also seen that during the 1960s and 1970s, Marxist scholars were highlighting the inequity and injustice of the global liberal-capitalist international economic order.

In the post-Cold War era, questions about a continuing imperial and colonial dimension to Western foreign and security policies emerged again within debates around the issue of *humanitarian intervention*. The period since the end of the Cold War has seen a marked increase in armed interventions by coalitions of mostly Western states in the name of universal humanitarian values. These values—human rights, democratic accountability, respect for the rule of law and so on—are largely derived from the long history of liberal thought.

One of the most significant outcomes of the collapse of communism, was the break-up of the formerly communist Yugoslavia. This was followed by the outbreak of armed conflict, firstly in Bosnia and subsequently in Kosovo, between the constituent ethnic communities of the former Yugoslavia—Serbs, Croats, Muslims in Bosnia, and Albanian Muslims in Kosovo. These conflicts were marked by what became known as *ethnic cleansing*. The widespread demand that something should be done to stop the killing led to interventions by Western-led coalitions, some of which were supported by UN resolutions. Although these succeeded in stopping armed violence, questions remain as to whether the conflicts underpinning the violence have been resolved, or merely frozen.

The interventions in ex-Yugoslavia took place at the margins of Western Europe. Subsequent Western-led interventions in the early twenty-first century outside the West, notably in the Muslim world in countries such as Afghanistan, Iraq (as part of the US-led 'War on Terror'), and Libya, generated even greater controversy and public disquiet across the world, including within the intervening states themselves. In the cases of Iraq, and Libya the interventions have been followed by long-term political and social instability which is still ongoing. In Afghanistan, the Taliban returned to power in 2021, thereby entirely negating the aims of the Western intervention. At the heart of much of the criticism is public and scholarly unease not only with the interventions themselves, but also with the imperial and colonial undertones of post-intervention liberal peace building operations (Orford, 1999; Whitman, 2005; Bulley, 2009; Pugh, 2013; Bellamy and Wheeler, 2020).

For their many critics, key aspects of the contemporary interventions uncomfortably recall the colonial era, from the sixteenth century through to the mid-twentieth century, when European states set out to discover new sources of wealth and subsequently forcefully extended their control over vast swathes of the world. The European states frequently endeavoured to legitimate the extension of their empires and the often-violent imposition of direct colonial control over overseas territories through reference to a 'civilizing mission' centred around the export of liberal values (this is discussed further in Chapter 9).

History has shown how the supposedly civilizing missions of European states such as Great Britain, France, Spain, the Netherlands, Belgium, Portugal, Italy, and Germany were carried out at enormous human cost, overwhelmingly to those people who were violently incorporated into the European empires. Although every 4 July the US celebrates its birth out of an anti-colonial struggle against the British, the history of its subsequent development was marked by the exploitation and mistreatment of its Indigenous peoples and reliance on the importation of slaves from the Global South. The US's relationship with states in Latin America and South America also became indelibly associated with what many call *neo-imperialism* or *neo-colonialism*. These terms are intended to capture the idea that although the European empires and formal colonial rule may have almost entirely disappeared, many of the exploitative dimensions of imperialism and colonialism remain (we explore this more extensively in Chapter 5 and Chapter 9).

In the post-Cold War era there have been a few cases where international armed interventions and their aftermath could be judged as successes, such as the UN approved, Australian-led international intervention in East Timor in 1999, or the British-led international intervention in Sierra Leone in 2000. By and large, however, the enthusiasm of Western liberal states for armed humanitarian missions has waned markedly in recent years. This is no doubt in large part because of the belated recognition by the intervening states of the sheer challenge of succeeding according to their own terms in a meaningful sense, as well as the perceived human and economic costs of such interventions (Paris, 2010). Arguably, it is also a consequence of the widespread criticism of such armed humanitarian interventions. Marxist scholars were some of the first to highlight contemporary forms of imperialism and colonialism but the spate of increasingly controversial interventions in the post-cold War era has generated highly critical scholarship from a wide range of theoretical and political viewpoints.

How might liberal scholars respond to the claim that the West is endeavouring to create an international order that works primarily to serve the liberal West's interests and values? Some, such as Roland Paris, acknowledge that in the early years following the end of the Cold War in 1989, interventions were often defended with 'rosy pro-Liberalisation' rhetoric (Paris, 2010: 338). Paris goes on to note that, even if well intended, many of the post-Cold War interventions have been clearly unsuccessful in achieving their aim because they were deficient in many ways. They were often poorly planned, poorly executed, and, perhaps most significantly, showed insufficient awareness of the political complexities and cultural dynamics of the conflict or crisis that the intervention was intended to resolve (on the problems surrounding the idea of a 'Liberal peace', see also Richmond, 2006 and Pugh, 2013). Paris argues, nonetheless, that critics of 'Liberal peace building' tend to conflate the detection of 'echoes of colonialism' with a complete equivalence between colonialism and Liberal peace building (Paris, 2010: 348–350). Additionally, liberal scholars could point out that in recent years there has been a move towards asking non-Western coalitions of states or regional organizations to intervene in conflicts in their own regions on behalf of or with the explicit approval of the UN (such as ECOWAS and the AU in Africa for example). Liberals could also point out that although the international human rights regime is of Western origin and undoubtedly reflects core liberal values, most states in the world have signed up to it, not least through their membership of the UN. Additionally, there are many political struggles outside of the West in which appeals are made to the concept of human rights to attract international attention or support from the international community.

The debates around humanitarian intervention highlight what is at stake in contemporary debates about liberalism and international politics. This is Liberalism's underlying universalism—the view that Liberalism reflects values and principles that all rational humans should uphold, regardless of their specific circumstances. A key issue is the extent to which Western-led interventions are aimed primarily at transforming those states in ways that conform to Western notions of statehood: representative forms of government; liberal capitalist models of economic development; and so on. In other words, are liberal peace operations effectively in the business of imposing the values and institutions of Western developed states upon the non-West as the price to be paid for receiving the West's help? Of course, many contemporary liberals in the West would recoil at the idea that they are in any way intentionally imperialist. Nonetheless, when we examine some of the newer critical theories of IR, notably poststructuralism (Chapter 7) and postcolonialism (Chapter 9), we will see that a common theme is a questioning of the universalist assumptions underpinning Western liberal IR scholarship (and Western mainstream IR thinking more generally), especially when they are deployed to legitimize the use of force outside of the West.

Even if the world does displays signs of greater cooperation and integration as well as the spreading of democracy, the post-colonial era has also seen increasing resistance to what is widely perceived as a presumptive arrogance on the part of the liberal Western world. Most of the world's states lie in the Global South and for all their evident differences many share a history of a struggle against Western imperial and colonial dominance and a subsequent struggle to achieve greater equality within a still Western-dominated world order. Thus, the contemporary world undoubtedly presents a range of challenges to contemporary liberal international progressivism.

It must be noted here that much of contemporary liberal IR scholarship does exhibit greater sensitivity to the *politics of identity*, i.e., people's senses of belonging, be it to specific nation, state, religion, ethnicity, or complex mixes of all such allegiances. Nonetheless, the liberal worldview ultimately rests upon the assumption that for all our differences we belong to a universal community of humankind. Despite his recognition of the multiple shortcomings of liberal peace operations, Paris (2010) argues that there is no alternative to liberal values as the basis for post-conflict peace building, even if the practice of liberal peacebuilding needs critique and reform. Some scholars argue that the future viability of liberal peacebuilding requires greater 'hybridity', a blending of Western and non-Western values and procedures. The challenge is to develop post-conflict strategies that try to reconcile those broadly liberal values impelling external intervention with more 'bottom-up' and locally owned initiatives for long-term post-conflict recovery, even if some of these may not accord fully with liberal values (Mac Ginty, 2010; Richmond and Mitchell, 2011).

2.7 **KANT REVISITED: ALEX BELLAMY'S** *WORLD PEACE (AND HOW WE CAN ACHIEVE IT)*

At the beginning of Section 2.5 it was noted that liberal IR thinking has developed along two broad but interconnected strands One is more normative in orientation, drawing upon liberal values to explore how the world *should* be. This is the side of liberal IR that critics often still like to describe as 'idealist'.

The other strand, exemplified by the work of Keohane and Nye that we discussed in Section 2.5, is less overtly normative. It endeavours to focus more on the evolving processes of international politics, on how the world *is* evolving as liberal IR scholars see it. We explore this strand of liberal IR scholarship further in Chapter 3 on realism. This

2 THE LIBERAL 'IDEALIST' ORIGINS OF THE INTERNATIONAL RELATIONS DISCIPLINE **55**

is because its development has been very much influenced by the emergence of a new school of realist thought, which has come to be known as neorealism. The response of liberal scholars to neorealism has in turn been characterized as neoliberalism (not to be confused with the neoliberalism discussed in Section 2.1). The debate between neorealism and neoliberalism in IR is often referred to as the 'neo-neo debate' and it is discussed more extensively in Chapter 3.

In this section we look at an example of recent liberal IR scholarship that is more overtly normative in orientation: Alex Bellamy's 2019 book *World Peace (and How We Can Achieve It)*. Although the book draws directly on the work of Kant, Bellamy does not see Kant as a utopian or an idealist, but rather as promoter of the gradual reform of the international system from the ground upwards (Bellamy, 2019: 36). Additionally, Bellamy seeks to update Kant by utilizing a comprehensive understanding of violence and war and therefore a more fleshed out conception of peace that considers the problems of violent discrimination against people because of their gender or race. In effect, Bellamy wants to reconcile liberal universalism with a sensitivity to the multiple differences between peoples. To do this he returns to Kant's *Perpetual Peace* and its focus on finding a pathway to the elimination of war (Bellamy, 2019).

Bellamy challenges the widespread view, especially among US liberal IR scholars, that the post-1945 era saw the establishment of a peaceful liberal rules-based order which is now in decline. In contrast, Bellamy claims that a rules-based international order remains still only a good idea. The post-1945 order has never been truly liberal in his view because human rights are often seen as secondary to state sovereignty or the interests of dominant powers, and states, including the Cold War superpowers, have routinely violated international law when it suited them to do so (Bellamy, 2019: 6).

Bellamy's starting point is 'the basic fact that humans are divided into different political groups that have contending interest and values' (Bellamy, 2019: 11). In other words, plans for reform of the international system must, Bellamy argues, face up to the world as they find it, not as they might like it to be. Bellamy then goes on to suggest a model for achieving world peace that steps back from the assumption that achieving lasting world peace ultimately requires the universal wholesale adoption of Western values and norms. There is, Bellamy acknowledges, no universal moral consensus: 'world peace must involve living with a degree of moral plurality'. Nonetheless Bellamy also believes that there are visions of pathways to a peaceful world that are 'compromises between different value sets, identities, histories and interests based on overlapping points of consensus between different communities' (Bellamy, 2019: 19). Bellamy takes from Kant the idea that for all their evident differences, most humans do have a sense of themselves as part of a single community of all humankind. Bellamy's vision of the possibility for lasting world peace rests also on the establishment of strong and legitimate states that can protect the rights and livelihoods of their people. Here we can see the Kantian emphasis on the importance of the right kind of state for world peace (as we discussed in Section 2.3).

Bellamy does not insist that all states should be modelled on Western liberal democracies, but he does believe that all states should fulfil some minimum conditions: they should be accountable to their people in some meaningful way (this is similar to what

Kant meant by 'republics'), they should uphold a basic set of human rights for their people, and, something not considered by Kant, they should promote gender equality.

Bellamy goes on to propose a set of principles, again drawn in modified form from Kant, that all states need to adopt to realize a peaceful world. These include:

- Upholding international law relating to the use of force and conduct of armed conflict

- contributing a fair share to the full and prompt implementation of UN decisions

- not selling arms to those who might use them in violation of international law

- working with neighbouring states to create local security communities

- offering all individuals, no matter where they are from, a 'universal right of hospitality' (there should be a free flow of goods, service, people, and ideas between states)

- holding individuals involved in acts of genocide, war crimes, crimes against humanity, and aggression criminally accountable.

Like Kant, Bellamy is proposing a model for a peaceful world that works on the assumption that sovereign states are here to stay. However, despite their differences, it is envisioned that all states will nonetheless share some common basic attributes, sufficient for them to accept submission to a set of international rules concerning the resort to armed force and the punishment of those who do so illegitimately. On the one hand, Bellamy is stepping back from grandiose liberal visions of a world of states made entirely in liberalism's own image and clearly wishes to respect difference and diversity in beliefs, values, and ways of life. Bellamy clearly wants to consider what divides humanity as well as what binds it. On the other hand, he retains a core liberal belief in a universal community of humankind that for all its differences and disagreements has sufficient in common (what Kant called a 'harmony of interests') to construct a stable and peaceful rule-governed international order.

Bellamy presents us with a revised and updated liberal vision of a preferable world that openly draws substantially from Kant's *Perpetual Peace*. The influence of other contemporary IR theoretical perspectives can also be detected, notably in the stepping back from many of liberalism's universalizing assumptions. Perhaps, after reading some of the other chapters in this textbook you might return to Bellamy's argument and scrutinize it considering what you have learned. For example, do you think it takes sufficient account of the various criticisms of liberal IR thought that have been discussed in this chapter? Is Bellamy's revised Kantian vision of an achievable peaceful world viable in your view? If not, why not?

2.8 CONCLUSION

We have recently passed the 100th anniversary of the establishment of the discipline of IR. The foundational, 'Idealist' phase of that new discipline was strongly connected with the political philosophy of liberalism. An emphasis on the distinction between idealism

2 THE LIBERAL 'IDEALIST' ORIGINS OF THE INTERNATIONAL RELATIONS DISCIPLINE

and the realism that emerged shortly afterwards became very widespread after 1945. Did this lead to oversimplification and the caricaturing of theoretical positions? Critics, notably realists, accused early IR thinkers of being overly idealist and naïve, especially about the role of power in international politics. More recent scholarship questions this and argues that the idealists were certainly progressive and reformist thinkers, but they also had a realistic grasp of how international politics worked and, importantly, were in tune with public sentiment at the time.

We have also seen that many contemporary critics of liberal IR perspectives also highlight the historical connections between liberalism, imperialism, and colonialism as well as detecting ongoing colonialist attitudes in liberal thinking about international politics today, not least in the foreign and security policies of many Western states.

Although the influence of liberalism within the discipline has varied significantly, there can be little doubt that it continues to form a major part of the discipline's mainstream. Indeed, some now argue it has surpassed realism as the dominant mainstream Western IR perspective (Sterling-Folker, 2015: 44–45). Additionally, liberal values and policies can be found threaded, to a greater or lesser extent, through the foreign policies of many states today, principally, but by no means only, in the West. Core liberal principles form a significant part of everyday public and official discourse about international politics. Liberals can plausibly claim that there is much about the contemporary world order that suggests that liberal values and policies do have some currency outside their Western origins. At the same time, they also continue to attract new forms of criticism because of their association with developments such as globalization and, especially in the post-Cold War era, predominantly Western-led interventions, ostensibly in the name of distinctly liberal humanitarian values.

Liberal IR thinking is now frequently accused of being insufficiently tuned in to the important political, social, and cultural differences within the global human community. Yet, to confuse matters, concepts of distinctly liberal origin—such as the idea of universal human rights—are also deployed to defend the preservation of key differences between the many communities, variously defined, that make up the human community today.

This chapter offered only a brief introduction to the large and diverse body of liberal IR scholarship that exists today and we will be returning to liberalism throughout the rest of this book. In Chapter 3, we examine the response of some liberal IR scholars to the emergence of neorealism in the late 1970s, which generated what is now commonly known as the 'neo-neo' debate.

SUMMARIZING THE LIBERAL 'IDEALIST' ORIGINS OF THE DISCIPLINE

- The history of liberalism goes back to the Enlightenment era of the seventeenth and eighteenth centuries
- Much of liberal IR thinking reflects the influence of the Enlightenment philosopher, Immanuel Kant, notably his 1795 pamphlet *Perpetual Peace*

- Although scholarly writing on international politics can be traced back to antiquity and from all over the world, the modern IR academic discipline only emerged, primarily in the West, in the aftermath of the First World War

- Most of the foundational IR literature was overtly liberal in political and philosophical orientation and explored the prospects for the progressive reform of the international system, ostensibly in reaction to the horrors and costs of the First World War

- More recent scholarship has challenged the common story of the IR discipline's emergence and argues that early liberal IR thinking was motivated also by the desire to preserve Western imperialism and the global domination of the white race

- The foundational phase of IR is widely described as 'idealist', particularly in its failure to confront the realities of power politics in the international system, illustrated especially by the failure of the League of Nations

- Recent scholarship has questioned the depiction of early liberal IR scholarship as idealist, arguing that many of the discipline's founding contributors were very mindful of international realities

- Although realism came to dominate the IR discipline during much of the Cold War, the liberal IR perspective continued to evolve and influence international politics

- Evidence of liberalism's practical impact on international politics since 1945 includes the establishment of the UN, the Bretton Woods system, the growth of international organizations, the European integration project, and the emergence of human rights as an issue in international politics

- In the 1960s and 1970s, during a *détente* between the superpowers, liberal scholars began depicting the international system as characterized by 'complex interdependence', wherein states were increasingly more concerned about the 'low' politics of trade and cooperation and less about the 'high' politics of security and survival

- At the same time Marxist critics challenged the liberal depiction of the international economic order, arguing that it was overly focused on relations between developed states and fails to acknowledge the exploitative relationship between the liberal West and the Global South

- The end of the Cold War led to a revival in liberal reformism in both theory and practice, as evidenced most notably by the rapid increase in predominantly Western-led 'humanitarian interventions'

- The very mixed consequences of those interventions, notably those occurring outside of the West, has spawned a lot of critical scholarship. Much this emphasizes liberalism's continuing links with the colonial and imperial era

- More than 100 years after the establishment of the IR discipline, liberal IR perspectives continue to form a major part of its mainstream. The evolution of the modern liberal IR perspective also suggests that there is a significant relationship between theory development and historical context.

IR THEORY TODAY HUNGARY: POST-COLD WAR LIBERAL TRIUMPHALISM REVISITED

In this and other chapters we explore various criticisms of Western liberalism, regarding both its universalizing assumptions and its relationship to the Global South. But what about Liberalism's fortunes closer to its European origins?

At the end of the Cold War all the communist governments in East-Central Europe collapsed, to be replaced by democratically elected governments. Such changes were, initially at least, widely seen to confirm their transformation from authoritarian communist states to liberal democracies. Most of the post-communist states joined or hope to join NATO, the EU, or both.

Given that seemingly historical transformation, consider the following recent events in Hungary (a member of both the EU and NATO):

- In a 2014 speech, the Hungarian Prime Minister, Viktor Orbán explicitly proposed that Hungary 'abandon Liberal methods and principles of organising a society, as well as the Liberal way to look at the world' (Orbán, 2014)

- In a 2016 speech, Orbán described the arrival of asylum seekers in Europe as a 'poison', claiming that 'Hungary does not need a single migrant for the economy to work', and that 'every single migrant poses a public security and terror risk' (*The Guardian* 27 July 2016)

- In December 2019, an independent investigation of press freedom in Hungary concluded that 'since 2010 the Hungarian government has systematically dismantled media independence, freedom and pluralism, distorted the media market . . . achieving a degree of media control unprecedented in an EU member state' (European Federation of Journalists, 2019)

- In 2020, the Hungarian Parliament passed legislation prohibiting the legal recognition of transgender and intersex people, banning LGBT content in schools or on children's television, and prohibiting same-sex couples from adopting children. It also called on the government not to ratify the Council of Europe Convention on preventing violence against women and domestic violence, despite initially signing it in 2014

- In its October 2020 Rule of Law report, the EU raised concerns about the lack of independence of the Hungarian judiciary, the intimidation of independent Hungarian media, and the impact of weakened independent institutions on democratic checks and balances in Hungary

- In the April 2022 general election, Orbán easily won a fifth term as Prime Minister with his Fidesz party gaining a substantially increased parliamentary majority.

QUESTIONS

Drawing upon what you have learned from this chapter (particularly the work of Francis Fukuyama and Charles Kegley in Section 2.4 of this chapter) and your own research:

1. What would be a liberal IR perspective on recent developments in Hungary?

2. Would you describe some or all the other former East-Central European communist states as liberal democracies today? Why/why not? (Hint: they all hold democratic elections, but consider also recent illiberal trends in Poland, the Czech Republic, and Slovakia around issues such as LGBTQi+ rights, migrants, and refugees)

3. What wider implications, if any, can you draw from recent developments in East-Central Europe, regarding the global influence of Western liberalism in the future. In your view, is it rising or declining? (Hint: consider illiberal trends in Russia and the other 14 independent states that emerged from the break-up of the Soviet Union. For example, what are the implications of the 2022 Russian invasion of Ukraine for the prospects of liberalism outside the West?)

TWISTING THE LENS

Look at Chapter 10 on feminism, gender, and International Relations

- What additional insights, if any, do you think a gender-focused perspective brings to the analysis of developments in Hungary and other East-Central European states (Hint: anti-feminist and anti-LGBTQi+ politics and policies can also be found across the globe including within the West)

USEFUL REFERENCE

Lorenz, Astrid and Anders, Lisa H. eds (2021), *Illiberal Trends and anti-EU Politics in East Central Europe*, (Cham, Switzerland: Palgrave-Macmillan/Springer Nature) This is an Open Access book and is freely available online.

USEFUL RESOURCES YOU CAN FIND ONLINE

Amnesty International, 'Hungary 2022'. amnesty.org

Human Rights Watch (2023), 'Hungary Events of 2022' *in Human Rights Watch World Report 2023*

Markowski, Radoslaw (2015), 'The State of Democracy in Central and Eastern Europe', *SciencesPo—Centre de Recherches Internationales. Sciencespo.fr*

Orbán, Viktor (2014), 'Speech at the XXV. Bálványos Free Summer University and Camp', available at: https://budapestbeacon.com/full-text-of-viktor-orbans-speech-at-baile-tusnad-tusnadfurdo-of-26-july-2014/

Rankin, Jennifer (2021), 'Hungary Passes Law Banning LGBT Content in Schools or Kids' TV', *The Guardian*, 15 June.

QUESTIONS

1. What is Kant's legacy in liberal thinking about international politics today?

2. Why is the foundational phase of the modern IR discipline frequently described as 'idealist'?

3. Do you think the contemporary international system can be described as essentially a liberal system? What criteria or empirical evidence would you use to make your judgement?

2 THE LIBERAL 'IDEALIST' ORIGINS OF THE INTERNATIONAL RELATIONS DISCIPLINE

4. Does the contemporary international system display the features of 'complex interdependence', as suggested by Keohane and Nye?

5. Do you think the foreign policies of Western states consistently demonstrate the influence of liberal values? If not, why not?

6. In what ways, if any, might contemporary liberal IR perspectives display the legacies of colonialism and imperialism?

FURTHER READING

ADDITIONAL INTRODUCTORY READING

Dunne, T. (2020), 'Liberal Internationalism' in J. Baylis, S. Smith, and P. Owens, *The Globalization of World Politics: an Introduction to International Relations*, 8th edn (Oxford: Oxford University Press).
An accessible introductory survey of the key ideas underpinning and the controversies surrounding liberal IR thought, notably its reformist aspirations.

Russett, B (2021), 'Liberalism' in T. Dunne, M. Kurki, and S. Smith, *International Relations Theories: Discipline and Diversity*, 5th edn (Oxford: Oxford University Press).
A more advanced introduction to liberal IR theory written by a noted American liberal IR scholar.

Sterling-Folker, J. (2021), 'Neoliberalism', in T. Dunne, M. Kurki, and S. Smith, *International Relations Theories: Discipline and Diversity*, 5th edn (Oxford: Oxford University Press).
A succinct introduction to the liberal response to the emergence of neorealism in the late 1970s, which is discussed in Chapter 3 of this book.

MORE IN-DEPTH READING

Ashworth, L. M. (2006), 'Where Are the Idealists in Interwar International Relations?' *Review of International Studies*, 32/291–308.
Ashworth challenges the common and often derogatory depiction of prominent interwar liberal scholars as 'idealists' or 'utopians', arguing that such labels are misleading and anachronistic.

Bellamy, A. J. (2019), *World Peace (and How We Can Achieve It)* (Oxford: Oxford University Press).
A leading Australian IR scholar presents a set of principles for achieving a peaceful international order that is directly inspired by Kant's Perpetual Peace, yet also endeavours to take account of contemporary concerns about liberalism's universalist assumptions.

Burton, John W. (1972), *World Society* (Cambridge: Cambridge University Press).
This book by a legendary Australian diplomat and IR scholar provides an early example of a depiction of international politics as far more multi-layered and complex than merely the interaction of sovereign states.

Carr, E.H. (1939), *The Twenty Years Crisis 1919–1939* (London: Palgrave Macmillan).
Written in 1939 by a renowned British historian, this book is one of the key sources of the criticism of interwar liberal IR thinking as 'utopian'. Carr posits an alternative realist theory of IR as a counterpoint, but goes on to suggest that both utopian and realist thinking are necessary components of the analysis of international politics

Davis, A. E., Thakur, V., and Vale, P. (2020), *The Imperial Discipline: Race and the Founding of International Relations* (London: Pluto Press).
This book examines the role of the Round Table network of British imperialists in the founding of the IR Discipline. In so doing it challenges the common story, or 'Aberystwyth narrative' about the

discipline's origins and highlights the preoccupation of some of the discipline's key figures with empire and race.

Doyle, M. (2012), *Liberal Peace: Selected Essays* (Abingdon, Oxon: Routledge).

A collection of essays by a leading liberal IR scholar, which examines such things as Kant's legacy in contemporary liberal IR theory and practice and debates around the concept of a 'Liberal peace'.

Fukuyama, F. (1992), *The End of History and the Last Man* (Harmondsworth: Penguin).

Based on an essay first published in 1989, this is perhaps the best known and most controversial statement of the superiority of liberal democracy over all actual and potential rival political systems.

Kegley, C. (1993), 'The Neoidealist Moment in International Studies? Realist Myths and New International Realities', *International Studies Quarterly*, 37/2: 131–146.

A 1993 speech by the then President of the International Studies Association (ISA) which outlines the opportunities presented by the end of the Cold War for moving the international system in a distinctly more liberal direction.

Keohane, R. O. and Nye, J. S. (1989*), Power and Interdependence*, 2nd edn (Glenview, IL; Scott, Foresman and Company).

This is the second edition of the pathbreaking book, first published in the mid-1970s, written by two leading American Liberal IR scholars, and noted particularly for the concept of 'complex interdependence'. In addition to the original text, this edition contains reflections on its validity by the authors two decades later.

Mazower, M. (2009), *No Enchanted Palace: The End of Empire and the Ideological Origins of the United Nations* (Princeton, NJ: Princeton University Press).

A noted British historian examines the controversial relationship between liberal internationalism and European imperialism. It examines the roles played by some of the leading liberal IR thinkers and political figures of the interwar years in endeavouring to reconcile liberal values with the preservation of Western dominance.

Olsen, W. C. and Groom, A.J.R. (1992), *International Relations Then & Now: Origins and Trends in Interpretation* (London: Routledge).

Part One of this book tells the story of the roots and emergence of the IR discipline and tracks the development of IR theories in the discipline's formative years. Chapters 4 and 5 are particularly useful for understanding the influence of liberal thought within the discipline during the interwar years.

Sterling-Folker, J. (2015), 'All Hail to the Chief: Liberal IR Theory in the New World Order', *International Studies Perspectives*, 16, 40–49.

A critical examination of what the author sees as a lack of analytical diversity and innovation within liberal IR scholarship compared to other prominent IR theoretical perspectives.

Vitalis, R. (2015), *White Order, Black Power Politics: The Birth of American International Relations* (Ithaca, NY: Cornell University Press).

An examination of the racial politics surrounding the birth of the IR discipline in the US, highlighting the largely ignored or forgotten contributions of Black US scholars to early debates about international relations.

USEFUL ONLINE RESOURCES

Immanuel Kant's *Perpetual Peace: A Philosophical Essay* is widely recognized as an early and highly influential sources of liberal IR thinking. Free legal copies are available online.

You can find out more about the League of Nations and the causes of its demise from the *1914–1918-online International Encyclopaedia of the First World War*.

CHAPTER 3

CLASSICAL REALISM AND NEOREALISM

LEARNING OBJECTIVES

- Identify the historical roots of the modern realist perspective on international politics
- Recognize the relationship between contemporary history and the key phases in the development of the varieties of realism since 1945
- Describe the key themes in classical realism
- Explain the distinction between classical realism and neorealism
- Evaluate the key issues in the debate between neorealism and the liberal response to it—the 'neo-neo' debate.

3.1 INTRODUCTION

This chapter examines the family of realist theories, which came to dominate the IR field after 1945 and remain highly influential today, not only in academic circles but in the foreign policy arena as well. Although realism's dominance in the field has arguably faded in the post-Cold War era, alongside liberalism it remains a key component of the mainstream of IR theory. After looking at the meaning of the term 'realism', the chapter examines the claim by many realists that the modern realist perspective expresses a timeless body of theoretical wisdom that can be traced back to the classical Greek era.

In tracing the most cited examples of early realist wisdom, the key claims that still bind most contemporary realists will be discussed. After exploring these themes further in the context of contemporary realism, we go on to examine the subsequent emergence of neorealism in the late 1970s and the controversial claim by its founder, Kenneth Waltz, to have put realism on a more solid theoretical footing.

The chapter then examines how neorealism's emergence generated a liberal response in the form of neoliberalism, producing the 'neo-neo' debate. The chapter then goes on to examine the most recent strand of realism—neoclassical realism. We conclude with an examination of different realist interpretations of the impact of the creation of nuclear weapons on international politics.

3.2 WHAT IS REALISM?

To begin our discussion about realism, we must first define what it is. The term realism is used in philosophy to denote that something exists, i.e., that it is real, and that its existence is seen to be independent of what we say or think about it. The term realism is also found in the arts to refer to the representation of subject matter—through painting, sculpture, literature, and so on—in as truthful or as least distorted form as is possible. The precise meanings and implications of these usages are, however, matters of considerable debate.

In IR, realism is used more narrowly to refer to a distinct group of closely related theoretical perspectives on international politics. We started in Chapter 2 by looking at the political philosophy of liberalism, which underpinned the liberal perspective on international politics. Realism is somewhat different. Although some realists have depicted realism as a perspective of relevance to all aspects of politics, most contemporary realists in IR treat it as a theoretical perspective on *international* politics only. It is sometimes referred to as 'power politics', because of its emphasis on the centrality of power or (somewhat inaccurately) as *realpolitik*, a name of nineteenth-century German origin.

Most realist IR scholarship falls within one of three broad strands of realist thought:

- **Classical realism**—this label is now widely used to refer to realist scholarship prior to the emergence of neorealism in the late 1970s and is perhaps most famously associated with the work of Hans Morgenthau

- **Neorealism**—this refers to a theoretically distinctive variant of realism first proposed by the American scholar Kenneth Waltz in 1979 and subsequently developed by a range of scholars, such as Robert Gilpin, Stephen Walt, and John Mearsheimer. It is also frequently referred to as **Structural Realism**

- **Neoclassical realism**—this is the most recent strand of realism, which endeavours to marry the classical and neorealist strands as illustrated by the work of Gideon Rose, Randolph Schweller, Fareed Zakaria, and others.

We will be looking at all these strands in this chapter, but at this point it is important to note that all the varieties of realism continue to be represented in contemporary realist IR scholarship.

What binds most realists is the view that international politics is a distinct realm of politics which requires a distinct body of theory to understand or explain it. This distinctiveness stems from the observation that the equivalent of what is usually called government inside sovereign states is absent in international politics. For all realists, the international system is therefore an anarchy. In everyday speech, to suggest there is anarchy implies chaos and disorder. Realists, however, use the term in its strict sense, derived from the Greek *anarchia*, to mean quite simply 'without rulers'. For realists, the key feature of international politics is that there is no authority above the sovereign state.

The bulk of the realist perspective flows from this core premise. In a world without a central government or something similar, the *relative power* of the main actors—which, for all realists, are sovereign states—becomes the crucial factor. It is also a world in which the risk of conflict breaking out is always present which makes simply preserving a semblance of international order and stability more challenging. This is why realists are generally noted for being pessimistic about the prospects of significant change or progress in international politics. Some argue that realism offers a 'tragic' view of international politics (Lebow, 2003; Williams, 2005), again in marked contrast to the greater optimism of liberal IR perspectives we discussed in Chapter 2.

Why might realism be a tragic view of IR? This is because in contrast to the liberal view that international politics can and does change in positive ways, realists tend to see any order or stability that exists in international politics as inherently fragile and thus always liable to collapse into conflict or war. Furthermore, they recognize that states may adopt morally questionable tactics (such as resorting to war) to protect what they perceive to be their vital interests or to ensure their survival. In contrast to the *progressive* view of history underpinning liberal IR perspectives, realists tend to adopt a *cyclical* view of history; the history of international politics is one of 'recurrence and repetition' (Wight, 1960: 43). For realists, the international system has shown little sign of fundamental change over the centuries.

International anarchy, the central importance of power, and the limited prospects for change in the international system are all recurring themes that you need to bear in mind as we explore realism further. Although it is a simplification, a quick initial summation of the realist perspective can be expressed as three Ss:

- Statism—The primary focus of realism is on the interaction of sovereign states in an anarchical system of states

- Survival—states are seen as primarily concerned with ensuring their survival

- Self-reliance—because of the lack of any higher authority, states must decide largely for themselves what they need to do and how they go about it.

Why is it called realism?

Before we look at realism in detail, we need also to consider its name. Certainly, modern realism emerged in reaction to perceived idealism or utopianism in the work of the liberal-minded thinkers who established the discipline of international relations in the wake of the First World War (as discussed in Chapter 2). In this sense, realists claimed to offer a more plausible and more realistic account of how international politics actually works. The name realism also highlights an important *ontological* claim (about what exists in the world); it depicts a world that exists independently from the ideas or beliefs of the observer; the world being observed is therefore real and not imagined. This leads on to an *epistemological* perspective (on how we acquire knowledge) that claims that the world 'out there' can be observed objectively (or we should at least endeavour to be as objective as possible) and through such observation we can come to understand definitively how it works (if you need a reminder of these terms, go back to Section 1.3 in Chapter 1).

As we shall see, the idea that we can best understand the international politics system through dispassionately observing it can be presented to varying degrees of formality within the realist family of IR theories. Classical realism tends to see observation in a comparatively loose sense as entailing the study of the history of how states have behaved and are currently conducting their external relations. Neorealism adopts a more formal stance, inspired by the idea of IR as a social *science*. It takes from the natural sciences a depiction of observation as part of a process wherein theoretical hypotheses about how the world works are carefully tested against empirical evidence of what states have done or are doing to generate authoritative explanations (we discuss the idea of IR as a social science further in Chapter 1). In later chapters we will see that many critical perspectives challenge the idea that the observer (i.e., the IR scholar) can simply stand apart from the world they are observing and they also question the suitability of the natural sciences as an appropriate model for studying social phenomena, such as international politics (this theme is explored further in Chapter 1, Section 1.3 and Chapter 6, Section 6.2).

Whether or not realist IR perspectives are in themselves realistic in the everyday sense of the term, is ultimately for you to decide. As we will see throughout this textbook, many kinds of critics have emerged to claim that realist perspectives offer flawed and overly simplistic accounts of the complexities of contemporary international politics. Additionally, although the history of realist IR perspectives shows that they are very much intellectual products of the West, and the US in particular (where they remain very influential within IR scholarly circles), their influence or the prominence of ideas that are broadly compatible with realism can readily be seen threading through foreign policy thinking and practice worldwide. Whatever your assessment of realist perspectives, however, they have been and continue to be highly influential in both the academic study and the practice of international politics. For these reasons alone, they cannot be ignored.

3.3 **REALISM AND INTERNATIONAL POLITICS**

What is now commonly referred to as classical realism dominated the IR discipline after 1945 and throughout most of the Cold War (1945–1989). It seems, therefore, to be a twentieth-century perspective. Many realists claim, however, that classical realism's intellectual origins can be traced back to antiquity. The fifth-century Greek historian Thucydides provides one of the many sources that classical realists cite in support of the claim that realism reflects timeless wisdom about international politics. A prominent realist, Robert Gilpin, has even suggested that it was questionable whether students of international politics today knew anything that Thucydides and his fifth-century compatriots did not know already about the behaviour of states (Gilpin, 1981: 227). Richard

Ned Lebow echoes Gilpin in claiming that 'classical realism has displayed a fundamental unity of thought across nearly 2500 years' (Lebow, 2020: 33).

What Gilpin and Lebow are claiming is that although the kinds of political communities that existed in the world many centuries ago differed significantly from the sovereign states of the contemporary world, the writings of their prominent scholars and historians suggest that their understanding of the relations between their political communities were directly comparable to how realists understand relations between modern states today.

The early sources of realism

Let us look at some of the key historical sources to which classical realists commonly refer, to see how the key themes of contemporary realism are drawn from them.

Thucydides and the Peloponnesian War

Thucydides (see Key thinker 3.1) is often cited as one of the earliest exponents of what is now called realism. His book, *History of the Peloponnesian War*, is long and complex, but some passages particularly stand out when it comes to detecting distinctly realist themes in Thucydides' account.

KEY THINKER 3.1 THUCYDIDES

Thucydides (c.460–400 BCE) was an Athenian general and historian, widely recognized as one of the greatest historians of the ancient world. His *The Peloponnesian War* (also referred to as *The History of the Peloponnesian War*) examines the conflict between the city-states of Sparta and Athens (431–403 BCE). It is widely seen as one of the earliest examples of contemporary historical writing that endeavoured to offer a balanced definitive analysis based upon research methods still in use today, such as his own experience, the cross-examination of eyewitness statements, and the interpretation of speeches.

In contrast to his predecessors, such as Homer, Thucydides did not claim to have been inspired by the gods or endeavour to explain events through reference to the gods; he preferred instead to draw upon the evidence available to assess the human causes of events. His writing style was also unusually direct for the time and is especially known for its highly detailed accounts of events and their social and political effects.

Little is known about Thucydides' life other than what he tells of it in *History of the Peloponnesian War*. Although Thucydides lived through the whole war, his account seems to have been an unfinished work as it ends mid-sentence and some years before the war ended. It also seems to have taken until the first century BCE, for his status as a great historian to become widely recognized.

Perhaps the most famous of these is his account of the 'Melian Dialogues', which took place on the island of Melos during the Peloponnesian War between the city-states of Athens and Sparta. Melos had maintained a neutral standpoint during the war. However, the Athenians saw small independent states like Melos as a risk because they might at some point side with their enemies. They sent a significant naval and military force to confront the Melians. As their forces waited offshore, Athenian delegates met with the Melian leaders and argued that if they agreed to become part of the Athenian empire then the Melian people would not be harmed, and their possessions would be safe. The Melians rejected the offer, claiming that they were entitled to remain neutral, and no state had a right to engage in an unprovoked attack.

It is during this dialogue between the Athenians and the Melians that a core realist theme arguably emerges. The Athenians argue that they are not going to deliver a speech about the rights and wrongs of their forcing Melos to submit to their will. They also argue that there is little point in the Melians appealing to notions of what is right or the fact that they have never threatened Athens. Rather, the Athenians argued, it is best that the Melians recognize what they can realistically achieve. It is here that they use a line that is seen as consummately realist: 'the dominant exact what they can and the weak concede what they must' (Thucydides, 2009: 302). On face value, this seems to suggest that might equals right.

The Athenians went on to argue that allowing Melos to remain neutral would make Athens appear weak in their enemies' eyes and might embolden other small states to resist Athens. According to Thucydides, the Melians retorted that it would be shameful for them to surrender without a fight. The Athenians countered by arguing that the Melians had no chance of victory and there would be no shame in surrendering to a superior power. The Athenians then withdrew from the dialogue to leave the Melians to think their offer over. As they departed, they warned the Melians not to put their faith in an unknowable future rather than facing up to the reality that confronted them. Nonetheless, the Melians rejected Athens's terms, saying that they preferred to put their hopes in the hands of the Gods, fortune, or others coming to their aid. The Athenians returned to attack and capture Melos, slaughtering all captured men, and putting all the women and children into slavery.

Many realists see in this dialogue an example of the dangers of a comparatively weak state putting its faith in abstract ideals of justice and fairness, when the brute reality is simply that of highly unequal power. However, some scholars, including other realists, question such a straightforward reading. For example, Lebow argues that the Athenians' treatment of the Melians was in fact a departure from long-standing Athenian tradition in which wise leadership and a clear moral compass had traditionally earned Athens loyalty and respect from its allies (Lebow, 2003: 125–126). In other words, Lebow reads Thucydides as criticizing the Athenians, not because they sought to enhance their power but because in pursuit of it, they had abandoned principles of dialogue, respect for moral codes, and established diplomatic conventions. Although this sealed the fate of the Melians, in the longer term it would also lead to Athens' downfall. On this reading, the Melian dialogue could be seen to offer a warning that the exercise of brute power alone may not actually serve the longer-term interests of a state.

Machiavelli, morality, and international politics

For a second commonly cited example of realist thinking, we jump nearly 2,000 years to Renaissance Italy. At that time, the north of what we now call Italy consisted of several small, prosperous independent city-states. As was the case with city-states of Ancient Greece, this was rather like a mini-international system, marked by both collaboration and conflict within and between the small states.

Niccolo Machiavelli (1469–1527) was a diplomat, historian, and philosopher who lived in one of the most prominent of the city-states, the Florentine Republic centred around the city of Florence. His most famous publication was a controversial, short yet highly influential book, *The Prince*, written in 1513.

In *The Prince*, Machiavelli offers advice, 'in plain language', on how to acquire and maintain political power. It is Machiavelli's advice on the character and conduct required of a prince, if they are to rule successfully, that is perhaps the most controversial and certainly the most noted part of the book. Machiavelli advises a prince to avoid making themselves hated or despised, since the goodwill of the people is a vital source of security. Princes should also undertake great projects to enhance their standing and choose advisors wisely. However, he also advises that it is sometimes better to be cruel rather than merciful, better to be feared rather than loved, and that promises must sometimes be broken if the vital interests of the state are at stake. Indeed, for Machiavelli almost

Machiavelli statue in Florence, Italy

any action by a ruler is justifiable if it ultimately enhances the stability and prospects of the state (Machiavelli, 1975). Although Machiavelli does not use the phrase himself, *The Prince* is seen by many as an early example of advocating 'Reason of State' as a principle that gives legitimacy to otherwise morally questionable actions (you may also come across this principle in its French form—*Raison D'État*).

For many scholars, *The Prince* offers one of the earliest examples of an attempt to offer an account of politics as it is actually practised rather than as it should ideally be conducted, in other words a realist rather than an idealist account. Machiavelli suggests that when vital state interests are at stake (what we today would call the *national interest*), ordinary standards of morality must be set aside.

There is some debate as to whether Machiavelli is promoting immorality or amorality in politics here. Certainly, he was not an advocate of cruelty or dishonesty for their own sakes. Nonetheless, he does seem to suggest there are two moralities:

- one for everyday life
- one for guiding the pursuit and maintenance of national power and interest (which may appear immoral by everyday standards).

Certainly, Machiavelli's advice on princely rule in *The Prince* led to the emergence of the term 'Machiavellian' to describe a particularly hard-headed, devious, and duplicitous approach to politics. The precise intentions behind *The Prince* remain a matter of scholarly debate. Nonetheless, at face value, Machiavelli's focus on how a prince should negotiate the brute reality of politics, and not be constrained by ordinary morality in the exercise of their power resonates with the claims made by contemporary realists about the pursuit of the national interest in an anarchical international system.

Thomas Hobbes and 'the state of nature'

A third commonly cited source of early realist thinking is found in the work of Thomas Hobbes. He was a seventeenth-century English political philosopher whose most famous work was *The Leviathan*, written during the English Civil War of 1642–1651. Hobbes is seen as one of the early exponents of what came to be known as liberalism and, in particular, the idea that viable political communities relied upon a 'social contract' between those who rule (a 'sovereign authority') and those who are subordinate to such rule, in order to avoid a descent into violent disorder.

Hobbes builds his argument around a thought experiment to imagine what life would be like in the absence of political communities or sovereign authority over them. Without a sovereign power, argues Hobbes, Men (as was the case with most philosophers of his era, Hobbes had a male-centred view of the world) would effectively be living in a 'state of nature'. Although Hobbes saw men as inherently equal, conditions of scarcity meant that not everyone could get what they wanted or what they believed they deserved. Hobbes also emphasized the competitive and glory-seeking aspects of human nature, which meant that the risk of conflict was ever-present. Without a sovereign authority (or 'common power'), to constrain these basic human desires, Hobbes suggested that life would become intolerable:

> During the time men live without a common power to keep them all in awe, they are in that condition which is called war . . . and such a war as is of every man, against every man . . . and the life of man (would be) . . . solitary, poor, nasty, brutish, and short. (Hobbes, 2005: 391–392)

Hobbes made no pretence that such a state of nature actually existed, nor was he specifically writing about international politics. His influence on realist IR thought is therefore somewhat indirect.

Nonetheless, what realists see in Hobbes' notion of the state of nature is something that seems comparable to international anarchy: the consequences of the absence of a sovereign authority. Of course, the analogy is not perfect, and no realist would claim that it is. War is, for realists, an ever-present risk in a world without government, but international politics has historically also displayed periods of stability even if it has rarely been entirely peaceful. The possibility of a war of all against all, that is suggested by Hobbes imaginary state of nature, is relatively slight, although the two world wars of the twentieth century remind us that is not entirely implausible. Hobbes' state of nature also refers to how life might be between nominally equal men, whereas the international system is comprised of highly unequal states.

Despite its weaknesses, Hobbes' account of a state of nature is seen by many classical realists to provide useful insight into the nature of politics in an anarchical international system. Some notable classical realists not only emphasize the perpetual risk of a descent into war, but also follow Hobbes in emphasizing the influence of a selfish and largely unchanging human nature in international politics. For this reason, you may sometimes see realism referred to as depicting a 'Hobbesian' world.

From our brief look at Thucydides, Machiavelli, and Hobbes we can already identify some central and interlinking themes that are also found in contemporary realist scholarship on international politics:

- the importance of power and how it is used
- the central role of ensuring the survival of the state and the pursuit of its vital interests (i.e., the national interest)
- the implications of an anarchical international system.

3.4 **THE EMERGENCE OF CONTEMPORARY CLASSICAL REALISM**

Although realism claims long historical roots, it came to prominence as an IR perspective in the mid-twentieth century. We see in Chapter 2 how the liberalism that underpinned the establishment of the modern IR discipline after the First World War attracted considerable criticism, especially as the world drew closer to the Second World War. During that war and in its immediate aftermath, some scholars, especially in the US, were promoting a distinctive account of IR, which emphasized the importance of *power* in international politics. One of the most prominent early voices arguing this was a British historian, E.H. Carr, in his book *The Twenty Years Crisis, 1919–1939*.

E.H. Carr and the neglect of power

E.H. Carr (see Key thinker 3.2) published *The Twenty Years Crisis* in 1939, literally as the Second World War was breaking out. In it, Carr famously attacks what he called the utopianism of the foundational liberal scholars of IR:

> Like other infant sciences, the science of international politics has been markedly and frankly utopian. It has been in the initial stage in which wishing prevails over the thinking, generalization over observation, and in which little attempt is made at a critical analysis of existing facts or available means. (Carr, [1939] 2016: 8)

In contrast Carr argued for a realist approach. Realism, he claimed,

> tends to emphasise the irresistible strength of existing forces and the inevitable character of existing tendencies and to insist that the highest wisdom lies in accepting, and adapting oneself to these forces and these tendencies. (Carr, 2016: 10)

In the second edition of *The Twenty Years Crisis*, Carr states what motivated him to write the book in the first place. It was because, in his view, the most glaring defect of 'nearly all thinking, both academic and popular, about international politics in English-speaking countries from 1919–1939' was 'the almost total neglect of power' (Carr, 2016: cxxi). Indeed, for Carr, 'international politics are always power politics; for it is impossible to eliminate power from them' (Carr, 2016: 130). Although Carr recognized that in their foreign policy pronouncements states often appealed to abstract principles or ideals, he argued that these principles were largely masks for the selfish interests of those states.

KEY THINKER 3.2 E.H. CARR

E.H. Carr (1892–1982) was an English historian, diplomat, and journalist. Although known in the IR field primarily for his book *The Twenty Years Crisis*, in history circles he is also noted for his monumental 14 volume history of the Soviet Union on which he was still working at the time of his death, as well as his writing on historical methods.

As a diplomat, Carr was a member of the British delegation at the Paris Peace Conference in 1919 and later worked in the Foreign Office section devoted to relations with the newly established League of Nations. Carr was initially a supporter of the League but by the mid-1930s he had become highly critical of it. Nonetheless, Carr was appointed, controversially, to the Woodrow Wilson chair in international politics at the University College of Wales, Aberystwyth, which is named in honour of one of the League's

> most passionate supporters. It was while he was the Woodrow Wilson professor that he wrote the *Twenty Years Crisis*.
>
> From the late 1930s onwards, Carr's political leanings, by his own admission, also began to shift in a distinctly Marxist direction and in his later writings he depicted international politics as primarily a struggle between 'have' and 'have not' nations. In spite of his reputation as one of the founding figures of modern realism, it is a matter of debate as to whether Carr was a realist in the sense with which the label is generally understood today.

As is noted in Chapter 2, Carr has also been subsequently criticized for both exaggerating and caricaturing what he called the utopianism of the liberal IR thinkers that had been dominant in the IR field during the inter-war years. In the *Twenty Years Crisis*, Carr made several claims which were to be echoed in subsequent realist scholarship. Above all, he depicted international politics as a struggle for power. There was little evidence, in Carr's view, of the idea of a 'harmony of interests' binding all peoples, as Woodrow Wilson had famously claimed. For Carr, international politics was more plausibly understood as a *conflict* of interests. The collapse of the League of Nations only served to reinforce his view that claims by states to be upholding universal moral or legal principles simply masked the selfish national interests of dominant powers. When push came to shove, the dominant powers would only support the reform of international politics if it suited their own interests. What really mattered was the *balance of power* between states.

Given such observations it is not hard to see why Carr is frequently cited as one of the key figures who pushed realism to the intellectual foreground of the discipline. If you read the whole of *The Twenty Years Crisis*, however, it becomes clear that Carr's view of international politics cannot simply be reduced to realism. Carr declares that he was not a pure realist. 'Pure realism', he claimed, 'can offer nothing than a naked struggle for power'. For Carr, there was a place for what he called utopianism, but it should not be at the expense of ignoring the world as it existed, especially the centrality of power. The challenge was, he said, to find the right 'combination of utopia and reality'.

Carr did not discount the role of law and morality in international politics; indeed he addresses the importance of both in the conclusion to *The Twenty Years Crisis*. Nonetheless, in his view they would always be constrained by the play of power politics. Carr rejected what he saw as a liberal presumption that there was a natural harmony of interests between states that could be maintained simply through good will. For Carr, reconciliation between sovereign states would require hard work and inevitable sacrifices. Yet Carr also believed that insight into how states might reconcile their competing interests could be drawn from studying the reconciliation of social classes within states. Carr seems to echo a liberal inside-out view of international reform (which is discussed in Chapter 2) when he goes on to suggest that states that had learned how to reconcile competing social, political, and economic differences within themselves, without simply resorting to the exercise of naked power, were better placed to bring about a more peaceful international order. To further confuse matters, when Carr explores the prospects for a new international order in the closing pages of his book, it is clear that he sees economic inequality both within and between states as a key obstacle to a more peaceful world.

His analysis here echoes some of the key themes that would emerge some decades later in Marxist IR perspectives (the subject of Chapter 5).

Carr was also noted for his advocacy of a more 'scientific' study of international politics. Carr used the term science rather loosely, but what he was driving at was the idea that the study of international politics needed to adopt a more sober, objective analysis of the facts on the ground and put aside approaches that, in his view, were excessively driven by the desire to explore how the world could be made to reflect an ideal image of a preferred world.

Carr's path-breaking work was rapidly followed by that of other scholars developing the realist approach to analysing international politics. In contrast to the focus of the early liberal scholars on reforming the conduct of international politics through the development of international institutions or cooperative economic relations between states, the emerging realist scholars were interested in such things as analysing the nature of international power politics, the role of military strategy, diplomatic practice, and the making of foreign policy.

The study of international history, in particular the causes of war and the role of diplomacy, was seen as a key source of evidence about the distinctive nature of international politics. Whereas the liberal perspective was forward looking, in key respects classical realism tends to look back. It seeks to learn from history, and to look over the shoulders of noted statesmen and diplomats for insight into how states have dealt best with an anarchical international system. The emphasis on the lessons of history and the value of drawing upon the experiences of noted statesmen was central to the work of another founder of the classical realist perspective: Hans Morgenthau.

Hans Morgenthau and the 'six principles of political realism'

Hans Morgenthau (introduced to you in Key thinker 3.3) was the author of what was arguably the first modern IR textbook: *Politics Among Nations: The Struggle for Power and Peace*, first published in 1948.

Like Carr, Morgenthau argues that liberalism took a naïve and too benign view of international politics. Morgenthau also agrees with Carr on the need to focus on the real and observable phenomena of international politics and not abstract ideals or principles. Although Morgenthau also did not entirely discount the role of morality in international politics, he shares with all realists a rejection of *moralism*, i.e., abstract moral arguments that do not take account of political realities.

KEY THINKER 3.3 HANS J. MORGENTHAU

Hans Morgenthau (1904–1980) was a German-American historian and IR scholar. After completing a doctorate in international law, Morgenthau went on to practise and teach law in Germany, prior to emigrating to the US in 1937 because of the rise of Hitler. He became a US citizen in 1943.

Although Morgenthau is widely viewed as one of the founding fathers of the modern realist perspective on international politics, noted for its emphasis on the role of power and scepticism about the role of ethics in international politics, there was a strongly moral dimension to his own account of realism and in much of his writing.

Like most realists, Morgenthau was critical of crusading moralism in foreign policy but maintained, nonetheless, that there was a moral dimension to the exercise of power. A vehement critic of the Soviet Union, he was also a prominent supporter of US Democrat presidents and acted as a consultant to the Kennedy administration. Initially appointed as an advisor to the Johnson administration after Kennedy's assassination, Morgenthau was subsequently dismissed because of his vocal and public criticism of US anti-commmunist interventions in S.E. Asia.

In his later work Morgenthau became increasingly critical of US policy on nuclear weapons and an advocate for greater regulation of the nuclear arms race. Indeed, Joel Rosenthal has described Morgenthau as a 'righteous realist' concerned not just with the role of power in international politics, but also with the responsible exercise of it, especially by a superpower such as the US (Rosenthal, 1991).

In spite of his status as a leading realist scholar, Morgenthau also saw the possibility of a world beyond a system of states. Indeed in his later work he came to the view that the arrival of nuclear weapons might make the pursuit of a very different international order a necessity (we examine realist perspectives on nuclear weapons further in Section 3.6).

Like Hobbes, Morgenthau starts from a very particular view of human nature. Morgenthau depicts human nature as unchanging and characterized by selfishness and a desire to dominate. At the same time, humans are also rational beings who aim to minimize risks and maximize benefits, which constrains their lust for power. Thus, sovereign states, which are of course created by humans, can also be understood as rational actors. They may well pursue power relentlessly, but if they want to have an intelligent foreign policy, then they will pursue their interests fully mindful of the realities of power in an anarchical international system.

Morgenthau's objective was to present realism as a fully developed theory of international politics, which also provided a guide for the making of good foreign policy. The basis of such a theory is first proposed in the 1954 expanded second edition of *Politics Among Nations* as 'six principles of political realism' (Morgenthau, 1978: 4–15). Although not all contemporary realists would agree fully with Morgenthau's rather distinctive viewpoint, his six principles do capture many of the key themes that can be found across the spectrum of classical realist thinking on IR.

Morgenthau's Six Principles are:

1. *Politics is governed by objective laws which have their roots in human nature*

   Given that human nature remained constant throughout history, Morgenthau argues that we can develop an objective and rational understanding of how statesmen have acted and are likely to act. This is achieved 'through an examination of the political acts performed and the . . . consequences of these acts', which enables us to ascertain what the political objectives might have been. Through the study of the history of international politics we can effectively look over the shoulders of statesmen and learn from how they responded to 'a certain foreign policy problem under certain circumstances'.

2. *The key to understanding international politics is the concept of interest defined in terms of power*

This is perhaps Morgenthau's most well-known principle. He is arguing, like all realists, that all rational political decision makers 'think and act in terms of interests defined as power'. History shows, Morgenthau argues, that regardless of their personal motives or ideological outlook there has been a remarkable continuity in the way statesmen respond to the challenges confronting them. This is because they are all guided by the pursuit of the national interest and the realities of power. Of course, some foreign policy decisions are driven by the personal prejudices or ideological leanings of individual statesmen, but for Morgenthau such decisions are fundamentally irrational and risk failing to consider the realities of power politics.

For Morgenthau only a rational foreign policy, based on a sober analysis of the interests at stake and the prevailing balance of power in the international system, is a good foreign policy. What is clear here, is that Morgenthau is interested in not only how international politics has been practised historically, but also how it should be practised in the future. This is what, in his view, makes realism both a proper and practical theory of international politics and foreign policy.

3. *State power will vary according to time and place but the concept of interest is universally valid*

Morgenthau argues that although 'interest defined as power' is a universal feature of politics, the precise meanings of interests and power do vary according to specific political and cultural circumstances. In other words, the national interest of a state may be defined differently in different states. Similarly, power can take many forms, ranging from the use of violence—in the form of war, for example—to the exercise of political influence (what these days is often referred to as 'soft power').

4. *Political realism is aware of the moral significance of political action*

Realism does not deny that morality matters in international politics, but there is always a tension between the demands of morality and successful political action. Moral principles, Morgenthau says, 'must be filtered through the concrete circumstances of time and place'. This is an important point, as realism is often accused of promoting amoralism (the complete disregard of morality) or even immorality in foreign policy. Like most realists, however, Morgenthau argues that basing foreign policy solely on moral principles, without taking regard of political circumstances and what is actually achievable, is naïve and irresponsible. An individual may choose to sacrifice themselves in the name of a moral principle, but a state has no right to do this if it risks national survival. What Morgenthau seems to be saying is that it may even be immoral for a state to put its population at risk, solely in the name of a moral principle. For Morgenthau, as with many other realists, states should be prudent in their foreign policy and carefully weigh up moral principles with political consequences.

5. *Political realism refuses to identify the moral aspirations of a particular nation with the moral laws that govern the universe*

   States may claim that the moral principles that guide their foreign policy are, or should be, applicable to all of humankind, but for Morgenthau this is a dangerous basis for making foreign policy. It can lead to disastrous moral crusades or ideologically driven confrontation. Instead, Morgenthau argues that all states should recognize that other states are also pursuing their vital interests, which may be guided in part by moral values different from their own. We may judge the actions of other states by our own moral principles, but our political decisions should be guided above all by prudence. Even if we believe our values are superior to those of others, it is another matter altogether to also believe we should blindly act upon those values, to do so in a fragile and anarchical international system can lead to disastrous foreign policy decisions.

6. *Intellectually, the political sphere needs to be understood as autonomous from other spheres of human activity*

   Morgenthau's final principle reiterates his belief that politics should be analysed as a distinctive area of human activity to be distinguished from other realms, such as economics, law, or ethics. This distinction is based primarily on the second principle, that politics is uniquely about interest defined as power. Nonetheless, Morgenthau recognizes the value of other spheres in helping to a construct a full picture of human nature. The key point here is that if we accept that politics is fundamentally about the pursuit of power, then political analysis and policy should not be primarily driven by guidelines derived from other spheres of human activity. It is the pursuit of power that defines politics and international politics and any theory of IR must start from that premise.

Morgenthau's six principles undoubtedly contain inconsistencies and repetitions. Many contemporary realists would not agree with Morgenthau's emphasis on an unchanging human nature (the first principle) or the absolute separation of politics from other spheres of human thought and action (the sixth principle). Nonetheless, the principles do highlight several themes found across the contemporary spectrum of realist thought. They are repeated, with some variations throughout much classical realist scholarship, just as they can also be detected in some of the historical sources of realist thinking that we looked at earlier in this chapter.

THINK CRITICALLY 3.1 HUMAN NATURE

Hans Morgenthau was noted for his emphasis on the constancy of human nature as a determinant of international politics. In everyday speech or debate it is also common to hear people refer to human nature as either essentially good (or kind or decent) or essentially bad (or evil, or selfish).

- What do you understand by the concept of 'human nature'?
- Do you think it is plausible to speak of all humans sharing a similar 'good' or 'bad' human nature? If not, why not? If so, how would you demonstrate this?

Consider the following thinking points to help you:

- Philosophers dispute the meaning of the term 'human nature'. It has often been traditionally associated with claims such as humans are 'rational animals' or 'political animals', but some argue these are merely slogans with no demonstrable substantial content.

- If human nature is inherently 'good' or 'kind', how do we explain the existence of 'bad' or 'unkind' people, and vice versa?

- What, if anything, do you think distinguishes the human species from all other species?

3.5 **THE CORE ASSUMPTIONS OF CLASSICAL REALISM**

We shall now pull together the themes that have emerged in our survey of some historical sources of realist thought and the work of two of the key figures—Carr and Morgenthau—behind the emergence of realism as the dominant IR perspective after 1945. As is the case with most perspectives in both IR and the study of politics more generally, different realist scholars will place different emphases on specific assumptions, just as some will disagree about the precise implications arising from each of the key assumptions. Nonetheless, the following assumptions very much set the tone of most classical realist scholarship:

- *The international system is anarchical. It is thus a 'self-help' system.*

For realists, anarchy is the most significant feature of the international system. In the absence of a superior authority to regulate their behaviour or take on some of the key tasks confronting them (such as providing security), states are effectively on their own. Above all, states are *sovereign* powers; they are ultimately answerable to no one but themselves.

- *The main actors in the international system are sovereign states.*

Realism is a *state-centric* perspective. Although many contemporary realists acknowledge that there are other significant actors on the world stage (such as international organizations, religious authorities, large private corporations, and so on), they are of much less significance compared to sovereign states. For realists, international organizations, such as the UN for example, only work to the extent that their member states see it as in their interests for them to work.

It is important to note, however, that although both the two most cited founding figures, Carr and Morgenthau, place sovereign states at the centre of their analyses: both viewed the state as a flawed and even anachronistic institution and neither discounted the possibility of a post-state-centric world order ultimately emerging. The key point is that realism generally depicts the reform of the international states system as very difficult to achieve and thus the prospects for any radical transformation of the system as dim.

- *States are inherently self-interested*

For some classical realists, such as Morgenthau, this is a product of an unchanging selfish human nature. However, not all realists emphasize human nature to the same extent. Some see the selfishness of states as a consequence of the anarchical international system itself, which induces states to put their own interests and preservation above all else. This is particularly the case with neorealists, who we will be looking at later in this chapter. Realists accept that states will often cooperate with other states and in so doing put some of their interests aside, but such cooperation will always be limited and will only prevail as long as the states involved see it as in their own interests to cooperate, i.e., that they will gain from it. However, even if there is seemingly a strong mutual interest in cooperating, this does not mean states will therefore cooperate. One famous illustration of this is provided by the metaphor of the Stag Hunt (which is summarized in Key concept 3.1).

KEY CONCEPT 3.1 THE STAG HUNT

The 'Stag Hunt' is a political metaphor, first found in Rousseau's *Discourse on the Origins of Inequality* (1755). Rousseau wanted to demonstrate what happens if there is a weak or non-existent sense of a social contract between people. Since then it has been used by the realist Kenneth Waltz in his 1959 book, *Man, The State and War* to illustrate some of the consequences of an anarchic, self-help international system.

A group of primitive hunters from different villages gather on a piece of common land knowing that if they cooperate and form a circle they might capture a stag, which will feed all of them and their dependants. But if one should defect from the circle to catch a much smaller hare that happens to run by, which would feed only that hunter and his dependants, then the stag could escape and everyone else will lose.

The dilemma for all the hunters is that no one can know if they will succeed in catching a stag through cooperation, nor can they be absolutely certain that another of the hunters will not break the circle to catch a hare and thereby let the stag escape. This is intended to illustrate the weak incentive for states to cooperate in an anarchical system, and the stronger incentive to act in a self-interested and selfish manner.

- *The principle concern of states is the acquisition of power and ensuring their survival—the preservation of national security*

In an anarchical international system, states are preoccupied with preserving their own security. Given that all states are endeavouring to do this, principally through the acquisition and maintenance of sufficient military power, this creates a *security dilemma* in which the efforts of one state to ensure their security, primarily through military means, can be interpreted as a potential threat by other states who will respond by endeavouring to further enhance their own security. This was starkly illustrated during the Cold War by the nuclear arms race between the two superpowers, the USA and the Soviet Union.

On this point, realists take different views. We have seen that Morgenthau saw the invention of nuclear weapons as posing a real challenge for realism. For a state to engage in nuclear war would be utterly irrational as it could not result in the defence of a state's national interest, but only in the destruction of that state along with many if not most others. For Morgenthau the invention of nuclear weapons provided a compelling incentive to consider moving beyond the sovereign state as the principle actor in international order. Other realists, such as Kenneth Waltz, depict the invention of nuclear weapons as part of the international reality within which states find themselves (we return to this issue in Section 3.6).

- *The primary influence on a state's foreign policy is (or should be) the 'national interest'*

Whether it is a product of human nature, the anarchical international system, or a combination of both, realism emphasizes the centrality of the national interest in the making of foreign policy (see Think critically 3.2). Although realists generally discount the role of morality in international politics, for some realists, putting the national interest (not least the security and welfare of the state's inhabitants) first is a moral requirement of states in a dangerous world. States may refer to universal ideals and principles in their foreign policy rhetoric, but realism is inherently sceptical about such claims, seeing national self-interest lying behind them. It is important to emphasize, however, that realist scepticism is not the same as outright dismissal of the relevance of morality. Both Carr and Morgenthau saw a role for morality in international politics, but emphasized the challenges of reconciling morality with competing interests and values in an anarchic international order.

For Carr, international economic injustice and, for Morgenthau, the proliferation of nuclear weapons raised important moral issues that should influence the making of national foreign and security policies. In his study of five leading American classical realist theorists—Hans Morgenthau, George Kennan, Reinhold Niebuhr, Walter Lippman, and Dean Acheson—Joel Rosenthal describes them as 'righteous realists' (Rosenthal, 1991). This is because values were central to their arguments. They all depicted the US as a dominant power but one with a repository of values which should inform its foreign policy. In this they shared more with American liberal IR scholars than might at first appear to be the case. What they all rejected, however, was moralism in international politics. By moralism they were referring to states acting primarily on moral principle without sufficient regard to what was actually possible given the realities of power politics in the international system and the limited degree of moral consensus between states.

- *International order arises largely from the balance of power, but war is an everpresent possibility*

Although it is anarchic and its principle actors are inherently selfish, the international system has displayed extended periods of relative stability and a semblance of order. For realists, this arises primarily from a *balance of power* brought about by states allying with other states to counteract dangerously powerful states and ensure their own survival.

Realists do not agree, however, on whether such balancing is the product of explicit policy decisions by states, a naturally occurring phenomenon, or simply a fortuitous outcome. Since balances can break down, even during periods of stability, war is an ever-present possibility in an anarchic international system. This is captured by the old

Latin adage *si vis pacem, para bellum*—if you want peace, prepare for war. For realists, it is unsurprising that most states still maintain and develop their military capabilities (Costa Rica is an interesting exception to this) even during extended periods of international stability and peace.

- *The possibility of reform of the international system is very limited or non-existent*

Realists see the history of international politics as cyclical; there are periodic variations in the level of stability and order, as well as in the balance of power. However, they generally see little evidence of substantial change in the fundamental principles that govern relations between states. As we saw in Chapter 2, liberal IR thinking tends to express a progressive view of history: reform of the international system is possible and even if it is difficult to achieve, we should try to make the system better. In contrast, realism draws upon more than 2,000 years of history to show how the behaviour of states has changed little. Not surprisingly, then, realists generally offer a pessimistic view of international politics, when it comes to the prospects for change. Again, it must be emphasized that for some of the most prominent classical realists their pessimism was not intended be read as an outright denial of both the necessity of and possibility for international reform.

- *IR requires its own, unique theoretical tools*

All the assumptions listed above add up to an account of international politics that emphasizes its distinctiveness from domestic politics (politics inside states). Although a few realists, including Morgenthau, at times seem to see realism as a perspective on politics more generally, most realists emphasize the uniqueness of the international sphere. For this reason, they believe we need to develop theoretical tools that reflect and build upon this distinctiveness.

THINK CRITICALLY 3.2 THE 'NATIONAL INTEREST'

1. Realists commonly refer to the 'national interest' as a primary driver of states' relations with each other. Many national leaders also defend their policy decisions in reference to the national interest. But how and by whom is the national interest defined?

To answer this question, consider the following prompts:

- Can it be said, in an objective sense, that all states have certain national interests in common by virtue of being sovereign states, such as defending their territorial integrity, or maintaining control of their borders?

- Or, is defining the national interest a highly political process? Does it refer to the interests of national elites or a dominant class, as a Marxist might argue?

2. Thinking of your own country, do you think there is a public consensus as to what the national interest is?

It must be stressed that this summary of the core assumptions of classical realism is drawn from what is now a vast body of scholarship. Classical realists are a diverse body of scholars who vary significantly in the emphasis they put on these core assumptions or how they interpret them (such as how balances of power emerge, for example). Although realism is generally state-centric in outlook, some of the most noted realists, such as Hans Morgenthau, John Herz, and the French realist Raymond Aron were also highly critical of the state while recognizing their dominance as actors in international politics (Rösch and Lebow, 2018).

Classical realism traces its idea back to antiquity and is a perspective most commonly associated with the Cold War, yet classical realism has also seen something of a revival in the post-Cold War era and continues to be seen by many contemporary IR scholars, old and young, as providing valuable and practical insight into contemporary international politics (this is illustrated, for example, by the collection of essays in Orsi, Avgustin, and Nurnus, 2018).

3.6 **FROM CLASSICAL REALISM TO NEOREALISM**

We note in Chapter 2 that liberalism continued to develop as an IR perspective in the post-1945 period, in spite of realism's rise to theoretical dominance during the same period. During the 1970s, relations between the US and the USSR moved into a period of *détente* (relaxation of tensions) resulting in a distinct waning of the Cold War, even if it did not disappear entirely (see Key event 2.4 in Chapter 2). During this period, some IR scholars were shifting their attention away from superpower relations to reflect on the development of the wider international system. As is also noted in Chapter 2, liberal IR scholars, especially in the US, were emphasizing what they saw as the increasingly complex and cooperative nature of relations between developed states. This led to the development of the concept of *complex interdependence*, which was intended to suggest that realism did not really capture the growing complexity of relations between states, or sufficiently take into account the importance of such things as international institutions and non-state actors. However, as relations between the superpowers became decidedly cooler again in the late 1970s leading to what some scholars called the Second Cold War, a new variety of realism emerged. This soon came to be referred to as *neorealism*.

The US scholar who led this revision of realism was Kenneth Waltz, who in 1979 published a landmark book, entitled *Theory of International Politics*. Waltz's intention was to reformulate realism to 'remedy the defects of present theories' (Waltz, 1979: 1). In so doing, Waltz clearly wants to challenge both earlier forms of realism as well as revived liberal thinking.

In *Theory of International Politics*, Waltz sets out the distinctive features of his proposed theory of international politics. It is important to note that Waltz explicitly does not want to develop a theory of foreign policy, unlike much of classical realism which blends the analysis of international politics with providing guidance to foreign policy makers. What Waltz wants to do is simply to provide a robust explanation of why the international system is like it is and, thus, why it is unlikely to change very much.

Man, the State and War

The origins of Waltz's neorealism lie in an earlier book, *Man, the State and War*, published in 1959. In it, Waltz identified three possible levels of analysis for explaining why wars occur in the international system—what he called 'three images of analysis':

- The first image—the level of the individual
- The second image—the level of states
- The third image—the level of the international system

Let us look at these images in more detail.

The first image tries to explain international politics at the level of individuals. This would correspond with the emphasis on human nature in much of classical realism, for example, or an emphasis on the character of individual leaders (think here of how leaders such as Brazil's former president Jair Bolsanaro, the former US President Donald Trump, Russia's Vladimir Putin, or Kim Jong Un of North Korea are often presented in the press).

In contrast, the second image attempts to explain war at the level of states—the 'inside-out' perspective favoured by many liberals. Indeed, many theorists from a variety of political perspectives over the years have suggested that it is the internal nature of states that makes them more or less prone to engage in war. For example, Lenin, leader of the Russian Revolution and a prominent Marxist theoretician, argued in a famous essay, *Imperialism, The Highest Stage of Capitalism*, that the imperialist ambitions of capitalist states were a primary cause of war. In contrast, during the Cold War it was commonplace in the West to depict communist states as inherently more warlike. More recently, as we note in Chapter 2, many academics and political commentators have remarked critically on the propensity of liberal states since the end of the Cold War to engage in warfare in the name of liberal or humanitarian values.

Waltz argued that while the first two images could tell us something about why specific wars occurred, they could not adequately explain why war has always been an ever-present possibility throughout the international system's existence. For this reason, Waltz argued for the necessity of a third image, which places the causes of war at the level of the international system itself. It is the anarchical nature of the international system that leads Waltz to conclude that 'wars occur because there is nothing to prevent them' (Waltz, 1959: 232). Without any superior authority to constrain states effectively, all states must operate on the assumption that other states might resort to war and therefore always prepare for this possibility. It is only at this third image level, Waltz argues, that we can see the consistent underlying cause of the perennial risk of war in international politics.

Waltz's theory of international politics

Man, the State and War, was focused specifically on the causes of war. Twenty years later, in his *Theory of International Politics*, Waltz took the third image further to develop a general theory of international politics.

For Waltz, other theories of international politics, including earlier forms of realism, tend to be 'reductionist' (Waltz, 1979: 18–37). By this, he means they try to explain the *whole*—the international system—through reference to features of its *parts* or units—states or individuals—that make up the whole. In other words, they operate with either of the first two images that Waltz identified in *Man, the State and War*. What Waltz wants to develop is a systemic theory which is not reductionist. Waltz's criticisms of both liberal and some classical realist efforts to explain international politics can be boiled down to a critique of *inside-out* approaches to understanding international politics. These start from inside the unit level (individual humans, or states), to explain the bigger system outside (the international system). In contrast, Waltz presents an *outside-in* approach: you start from the system itself to explain the behaviour of the units, i.e., states. Thus, for Waltz, *structure* (of the international system) takes precedence over *agency* (the actions of states or individuals). This is why neorealism is also frequently referred to as 'structural realism'.

Let's just pause here for a moment and ask the question why does Waltz want a systemic theory that focuses on the structure of the international system? This is because he wants to be able to explain how the international system itself is reproduced and is resistant to fundamental change. Importantly, Waltz also argues that what we need to achieve this is a *parsimonious* theory. By this, he means a simple explanation that only focuses on what is necessary to explain the phenomenon under investigation. As we have seen, classical realists have long argued that the international system has not changed fundamentally, in stark contrast to domestic political systems, which is why, in their view, the insights gleaned from Thucydides and others are still relevant today. What Waltz is claiming is that they have not provided a robust, parsimonious theory to properly explain this. In contrast to classical realism's somewhat looser epistemological commitment to dispassionate, objective enquiry, based primarily on historical analysis, Waltz is proposing a more formalized model of enquiry. (If you need a reminder of what these terms, such as epistemology, mean, read through Section 1.3 of Chapter 1.)

The three elements of Waltz's theory of international politics

Waltz's neorealist theory of international politics has three key elements:

1. The ordering principle of a system—is it hierarchic or anarchic?
2. The nature of the units (i.e., states) within the system
3. The distribution of capabilities.

Hierarchy or anarchy?

A system's ordering principle is, for Waltz, the analytical starting point. Political systems inside states are *hierarchical*. The constituent units in such systems (the individuals) interact within a complex set of rules and procedures backed up by a legal system (courts, a police force, and so on) with a capacity to punish non-compliance. If the rules or legal procedures are breached, then wrongdoers risk enforceable punishment in the name of the state that rules over the individuals who comprise it. Although law-breakers can sometimes get away with it and wrongdoers can go unpunished, this does not undermine the underlying point that the system is, in principle at least, hierarchical: there are rulers, rules, and the ruled.

Of course, in some states life can be more precarious than others, or people can be discontented with some aspects of the system within which they live. However, such discontent can be the basis for political protest and action aimed at reforming a troubled or failing domestic political system. After all, history provides ample evidence of domestic political systems changing fundamentally, either slowly or quickly, as a consequence of political action by individuals or groups of individuals. The key point, however, is that within a hierarchical political system the interacting units (people) can become *functionally specialized*. There is a functional division of labour; people fulfil distinctive roles such as factory workers, professors, lawyers, doctors, members of police forces, and so on.

The units within a system—the uniqueness of states

In the international system, by contrast, there is no higher authority above states, which are the key acting units in that system. Because the ordering principle, or structure, of the international system is anarchical, the constituent states are not functionally differentiated. In other words, unlike individual citizens within states who carry out different roles, states all fulfil similar functions to each other. Waltz argues that the anarchical structure of the international system does not directly cause states to behave in particular ways, but it does significantly constrain state behaviour:

> Structures limit and mould agents . . . and point them in ways that tend towards a common quality of outcomes even if the efforts of and aims of agents vary . . . (Waltz, 1979: 74)

What Waltz is saying here is that the behaviour of states is indirectly shaped by the anarchical international structure so that their behaviour will fall within a narrow range of action, even if the explicit intentions of individual states may seemingly differ significantly.

How does the international structure help to constrain the behaviour of states? Waltz identifies two key mechanisms: *socialization* and *competition*. First, all states are socialized into similar behaviour to ensure their survival. They will tend to pursue the same goals by the same means, in particular securing themselves against external threats. A state that does not conform to the necessity to protect itself, risks disaster. Second, all states will tend to compete in the effort to be successful. Therefore, the only significant thing that distinguishes states, Waltz proposes, is their *relative capability*. By this Waltz means that the capacity of states to pursue and achieve their objectives (i.e., what they perceive to be their national interests), varies according to where they are placed in the international system, in other words, their relative power. A powerful state is going to have a greater capacity to pursue its core objectives than a weaker or smaller state. Waltz goes on to argue that a clear hypothesis can be drawn from these preliminary observations: unless the ordering principle of the international system changes from anarchy to hierarchy, the system will tend to reproduce itself. This is why the international system is resistant to significant change.

The distribution of capabilities

If we return to the three images Waltz referred to in his *Man, the State and War*, we can see how Waltz claims to have produced a simple explanatory theory of international politics. You don't need to take into consideration whether human nature is good or bad (the first image) or to know much about the internal qualities of states, such as the prevailing political ideology (the second image), because it is the structure of the international system itself that is the primary determinant of state behaviour. States that are led by very different kinds of leaders or appear to be very distinctive internally will tend, nonetheless, to act in markedly similar fashion. What variations do exist in the behaviour of states are determined largely by their *relative power* within the international system. There may be changes in the *distribution of capabilities*—the relative power of states can rise and fall—within the international system, but the system remains fundamentally the same.

For Waltz and other neorealists, both the history of international politics and the contemporary behaviour of states provide sufficient evidence to confirm neorealism's core hypothesis. Beyond this, there are some important disagreements among neorealists. Let us examine some of these more closely.

Neorealism and 'great powers'

For neorealists, great powers (the most powerful states on the world stage) are the states that really matter in international politics and, importantly, they fear each other. As with all states, the relative capabilities (and thus the distribution of power) among great powers can, of course, vary over time. For various reasons, states can become stronger or weaker, as a consequence of war, changing economic circumstances, and so on.

Such shifts in the balance of power, however, do not mean that the underlying anarchical system has changed. Waltz argues that a bipolar international system in which there are two dominant powers balancing each other is the most stable. This is because weaker states will tend to align with either one of the two dominant powers. This was the type of system operating during the Cold War, when the USA and the USSR were the two dominant *superpowers* (a term that emerged to reflect the enormous impact of the possession of large amounts of nuclear weaponry) and many other comparatively weaker states aligned with either of them.

In contrast to the more stable bipolar system, a unipolar system, in which there is only a single unbalanced dominant power can, Waltz claims, encourage recklessness. Thus, the collapse of the Soviet Union at the end of the Cold War was not necessarily something to be entirely welcomed from a neorealist perspective. It left the US as an unbalanced, sole superpower and Waltz has questioned whether this might induce the US to adopt riskier foreign policy strategies.

Not all neorealists agree with Waltz on this point. Some, such as Robert Gilpin and Stephen Krasner, argue that a stable system is still possible with a single dominant power—a *hegemon*—an approach known as Hegemonic Stability Theory (Key concept 3.2). Others think a multipolar system, in which there are a number of exceptionally powerful states, can also be stable and less war prone (Mearsheimer, 2020: 59). Great power multipolarity, John Mearsheimer argues, makes balancing more complex and thus induces caution. It also means that dominant powers have to take into consideration more than one potential opponent. In other words, greater complexity can reduce the likelihood of war between powerful states.

>>> KEY CONCEPT 3.2 HEGEMONIC STABILITY THEORY

Hegemonic Stability Theory (HST) arose from efforts to reconcile the realities of power politics in the international system with the need to maintain a stable international free market economy. It is an idea already implicit in commonplace references to the period prior to the Second World War as *Pax Britannica* (the British peace) and the period after as *Pax Americana* (the American peace). Such labels suggest that international stability in these eras depended heavily on the dominant influence of either imperial Britain or the US as a newly emergent superpower.

Charles Kindleberger is usually seen as the key early proponent of HST as a theoretical model. In a landmark study, *The World In Depression, 1929–39*, published in 1973, he argues that a key factor in the Great Depression that hit the world economy in the period between the world wars was the absence of a dominant, or hegemonic, national economy.

HST has subsequently been adopted by a number of prominent neorealists who argue that the anarchical international system is more likely to remain stable if there is a dominant world power, or hegemon. If there is a hegemon, then international institutions are more likely to function effectively and states are more likely to adhere to international regulations because the hegemon can either offer inducements for states to cooperate, or threaten them with sanctions if they do not.

Neoliberals (who are examined further in Section 3.5 below) agree that responsibly exercised hegemonic power can lead to the creation of stable international institutions, but go on to argue that these institutions can take on a life of their own even if the power of the hegemon declines. This is because the states participating in those institutions have learned to appreciate their benefits; in other words there can be institution-based international stability 'after Hegemony' (Keohane, 1984).

Defensive or offensive neorealism?

A notable debate that developed within neorealist scholarship is between *defensive* and *offensive* versions of neorealism. In common with all realists, neorealists agree that the anarchical international system creates strong incentives for states to acquire power. The key question this debate addresses is how much power is enough?

Defensive neorealism

Waltz makes the case for what came to be known as *defensive realism*. He argues that though all states seek power, it would be foolish for them to maximize or over-expand their power. This can lead to dangerous and destabilizing attempts at balancing by other states, the costs of which may outweigh any perceived benefits. States should, therefore, pursue appropriate levels of power to ensure international order and secure their own interests yet also avoid war.

Offensive neorealism

Another prominent neorealist, John Mearsheimer, posits a version of neorealism that he describes as *offensive realism*. Mearsheimer argues that powerful states will tend to seek dominance (hegemony) and this is both achievable and preferable from their point of view. True dominance is the most assured way of ensuring a state's survival. States want to be 'the biggest, baddest dudes on the block' although no state can be a truly global hegemon (Mearsheimer in Kriesler, 2002). The US is certainly the hegemon in the Western Hemisphere and tolerates no rivals, Mearsheimer argues, but it cannot enforce its dominance in all other regions, due to competitor regional hegemons and the risk of major war (Mearsheimer, 2002).

Both types of neorealist have become particularly interested in the rise of China over the last couple of decades. Does China seek only regional hegemony, as defensive realists would argue? Or are offensive realists right to think that China might seek to confront the US at a global level, perhaps to generate a new bipolar system, similar to that which existed during the Cold War? Within neorealism there are disagreements about this as well as a range of other key international issues. But what neorealists do agree on is that the anarchical international system induces great powers to compete among themselves in a relentless pursuit of power. The distribution of power and capability may shift, but the game remains essentially the same.

The impact of Waltz's restatement of realism on the discipline has been dramatic. It not only generated a great deal of criticism from a variety of perspectives but also helped to stimulate the emergence of many of the newer perspectives such as Critical Theory (discussed in Chapter 6) and Constructivism (which we examine in Chapter 9). In this chapter we will focus on the response to neorealism that emerged from within realism's primary theoretical rival within the mainstream of IR theory: liberalism.

3.7 LIBERALISM ANSWERS BACK— NEOLIBERALISM, NEOREALISM, AND THE 'NEO-NEO' DEBATE

Within a few years of neorealism emerging, a number of leading liberal scholars developed a response to it. This rapidly became known as *neoliberalism*. It is important to note that the term neoliberalism when used as a label to describe a variety of liberal thinking about IR should not be confused with the use of neoliberalism to describe the economic policies that began to emerge in liberal capitalist states from the late 1980s and early 1990s onwards.

The neoliberalism we are examining here builds upon the idea of *complex interdependence* that we examine in Chapter 2. Recall here that during the 1970s liberal scholars had begun to challenge classical realism's pessimistic account of international politics by emphasizing evidence that suggested that the international system was becoming increasingly complex, even if formally it was still anarchical. They argued that states were cooperating to greater and greater levels, other types of international actor were becoming increasingly important, and the number of international institutions had proliferated markedly during the twentieth century. In other words, the international system was changing in significant ways that classical realism could not adequately capture or explain.

Neoliberalism entails something of a stepping back from earlier liberal ideas of complex interdependence, which for some liberals signalled the possibility of the eventual transcendence of a state-centric international system or even the end of international anarchy. Neoliberals broadly concur with neorealism on the significance of anarchy in the international system and that states remained the key actors. They also agree that the discipline needs more rigorous and parsimonious theories. Some neoliberals also agree with some neorealists about the key role that a dominant power (a hegemon), such as the US in the current international system, can play in maintaining international order and stability. For neoliberals, however, hegemonic powers can be more selfless and other-regarding than neorealism concedes (see Key concept 3.7).

A key area of disagreement between neoliberals and neorealists concerns the significance of non-state actors and the importance of international regimes, institutions, and conventions—an issue we will return to shortly. Neoliberals also question neorealism's scepticism about the prospects for system change. In other words, they retain liberalism's progressive view of history, albeit in a more cautious form.

Relative versus absolute gains

Much of the debate between neorealism and neoliberalism stems from disagreement about the motivations behind state behaviour. Neorealism argues that states are predominantly driven by the pursuit of *relative* gains: how do they benefit compared to others? In contrast, neoliberals claim that states are also driven by *absolute* gains: how do they benefit, regardless of others? Neoliberals argue that states are not entirely preoccupied by where they stand within the international distribution of power and capabilities as neorealism suggests; sometimes states act simply for themselves and are thus capable of seeing that other states gains are not always to be viewed with concern or as a threat.

The neorealist emphasis on relative gains underpins their depiction of the international system as predominantly conflictual. The neoliberal understanding, however, allows for a greater role for cooperative behaviour by states. Such cooperation is enhanced by the growing institutionalization of the international system. Indeed, so central are institutions to the neoliberal position that it is often referred to as 'neoliberal institutionalism', a name originally coined by one of the leading contemporary liberal IR scholars Robert Keohane.

Neoliberal institutionalism's challenge to neorealism: 'cooperation under anarchy'

The liberal IR scholar Robert Keohane was one of the noted proponents of the idea of 'complex interdependence' back in the 1970s (as we discuss in Chapter 2) and neoliberal institutionalism builds upon that earlier work. Keohane expresses neoliberal institutionalism's response to Waltz's neorealism thus: 'state actions depend to a considerable degree on prevailing institutional arrangements'. In other words how states act depends very much on the degree to which the environment within which they operate has become institutionalized.

For neoliberals, the historical evidence shows that states operate within an increasingly *institutionalized* environment. As we note in Chapter 2, liberal IR thinkers have long argued that international institutions can and do transform international politics. Neoliberal institutionalism endeavours to develop a more measured and systematic understanding of the role and impact of institutions than was the case with earlier liberal explorations. Keohane describes international institutions as 'persistent and connected sets of rules (formal and informal) that prescribe behavioural, constrain activity and shape expectations'. They can be formal creations of governments (like many international governmental organizations such as the EU, NATO, the UN, the OECD, and so on) or they can take the form of international *regimes*—formal and informal management systems that regulate and facilitate a host of complex international and transnational activities. They can also be comprised of informal conventions, or simply habitual ways of interaction between states.

International institutions are important, neoliberal institutionalists argue because they affect:

- The flow of information and opportunities to negotiate
- The ability of governments to monitor each other's compliance with rules and agreements
- The expectations of states about the solidity of international agreements
- The incentives facing states and the understandings that state leaders have about their roles.

However, in a significant concession to neorealism, neoliberals concede that institutions will only work if the states involved have some mutual interests. In other words, they must all potentially gain from cooperation, even if these gains may be quite unevenly distributed (remember, liberals are less convinced that states are predominantly motivated by relative gains). Much of the research by neoliberal scholars is therefore focused on institutional design, the processes of negotiation and bargaining and how the compliance of states with increasingly complex and wide-range regulatory regimes is maintained, in spite of the international anarchy (Keohane, 1989: 1–20. See also Ruggie, 1992).

The neoliberal perspective is captured succinctly by the phrase 'cooperation under anarchy', the title of a collection of essays by leading neoliberal scholars, published in the mid-1980s, that examines the prospects for cooperation in rather dry, technical terms

(Oye, 1986). It is clear that neoliberalism is distinctly closer to the realist position than earlier liberal scholarship and the overtly normative and reformist language of other liberal scholars is largely absent. Nonetheless, neoliberals continue to offer a moderately progressive vision of the possible future of the international system, in keeping with the long history of the liberal political tradition.

In spite of the fact that neoliberals and neorealists share a lot of common ground, neoliberal scholars often prefer to speak of developing a theory of *world* politics or *global* politics rather than the more limited vision of international politics of the neorealists (i.e., focusing exclusively on relations between states). The progressive intentions of neoliberalism are, however, couched in cautious terms. Keohane argues that the improvements in international politics gained from greater institutionalization are more likely to be incremental than sudden, building on the knowledge and experience created by successful cooperation (Keohane, 1984: 257).

The neorealist response

How do neorealists respond to the claims made for the significance of institutions by neoliberals? In an article entitled 'The False Promise of International Institutions', the neorealist John Mearsheimer argues that the liberal emphasis on the significance of institutions largely ignores security issues, where claims about the benefits of institutionalization would be much harder to substantiate, and focuses predominantly on economic issues. The area of security is, however, much less transparent because states value their security issues so highly. Therefore, such things as ensuring states always comply with agreements, do not cheat, or suddenly defect from an agreement or alliance are much harder to anticipate or prevent (Mearsheimer, 1994–95: 11 and 15). Some neoliberals have conceded that institutional arrangements in the realm of security are indeed much less substantial or effective than in economic relations between states. They claim, nonetheless, that greater economic cooperation does contribute to global stability, which in turn enhances security for cooperating states.

A central theme in Mearsheimer's critique of neoliberal institutionalism is that states are much more concerned about relative gains than neoliberals recognize (Mearsheimer, 1994–95: 19–20). A state's concern for relative gains will always inhibit cooperation, from a neorealist point of view. In issue areas such as national security, where states care deeply about such things as who has the best or most weapons, there is little incentive to cooperate significantly because states can never be sure of the intentions of other rival states. Mearsheimer also thinks that relative gains matter more in the economic realm that neoliberalism assumes, because 'the relative size of a state's economy has profound consequences for its standing in the international balance of military power' (Mearsheimer, 1994–95: 20).

In Mearsheimer's view, neoliberal institutionalists have failed to prove that existing levels of cooperation would not have existed without institutions (Mearsheimer, 1994–95: 24). Neorealists do not deny that some states, especially those with closely aligned interests, may see real benefits through greater cooperation. However, we need to recall here that throughout its history realist thought has always regarded changes in state behaviour as impermanent. Changes in the distribution of power or the national perception of threats emanating from the international system can result in states quickly abandoning formal or informal agreements, as well as other forms of cooperative commitments. Underpinning neorealist scepticism about neoliberalism's progressive vision of a world of increasing cooperation and institutionalization, leading to a lower risk of war and thus a more peaceful world, is their insistence that the anarchical structure of the international system is the primary determinant of state behaviour. Any changes in the behaviour of states are likely to be relatively minor and always liable to be reversed.

Neorealism and the European integration project

To better understand the neorealist viewpoint we can examine the emergence of the European Union (EU) through neorealist lenses. From a liberal perspective, the European integration project that led to the creation of the EU is a powerful demonstration of the capacity of states to transform their relations with each other and go so far as to surrender some of their national sovereignty to a higher authority in the name of greater cooperation and the preservation of peace between them. The EU is therefore seen to offer evidence of the capacity of a significant region within the international system to transform itself and, in so doing, offer a model for other parts of the international system to follow.

A neorealist would concede that there is indeed a high degree of cooperation between the member states of the EU. Yet they would question its true significance for the theorizing of international politics more generally. For example, a neorealist would note that European integration began during the early part of the Cold War when all the Western states were united in their desire to counter the power of the soviet-led communist bloc, which bordered Western Europe. There was a high degree of mutual self-interest, underpinned by a shared perception of threat. This resulted in a willingness of European states to align with each other and the US. Furthermore, European integration developed further and expanded its membership as the Cold War progressed, but this was under the protective umbrella provided by US nuclear deterrence. In other words, the US was a 'security-giver' and the EU members were 'security-takers'. The US generally supported European integration because it fitted with its own interest in countering or balancing Soviet power. The EU provided a bastion against Soviet influence in communist Eastern Europe (Mearsheimer, 1990).

A liberal might respond by saying that with the end of the Cold War, the EU actually expanded further as former communist states applied to join it. However, a neorealist could also note that since the end of the Cold War, European integration has also begun to show signs of crisis. Perhaps most starkly, the United Kingdom, a key member state, left the EU in 2021 after more than four decades of membership. Many of the newer formerly communist member states in East-Central Europe are openly expressing resentment at the EU requirements that their domestic social polices comply with EU standards. Additionally, since the end of the Cold War, hostility to the further deepening of European integration or even the project of integration itself (Euroscepticism) has become increasingly visible, even within some of the founding and most 'Europhile' (strongly pro-EU) member states, such as Germany, Italy, and France (Kaeding, Pollack, and Schmidt, 2019; Henley, 2020). It is not necessarily the case that Eurosceptics want their state to leave the EU completely, but they generally want the EU to become a looser organization which will help to restore what they see as the loss of their national sovereignty (Mudde, 2019).

A key driver behind such Euroscepticism is widespread public hostility to the 'free movement of people', a central principle of European integration (Mudde, 2019). From a neorealist point of view, this suggests that European integration was indeed more a product of a mutually beneficial alignment of national self-interests in the specific historical context of the bipolar Cold War world than an indication of a fundamental transformation of international politics. With the collapse of the Soviet bloc, a key incentive for European states to integrate disappeared. This is not to say they will not continue to cooperate extensively. As we have noted, neorealism does not question the utility of cooperation, if it is seen to be beneficial to all of the national interests of the cooperating states. What it does question is the assumption that such cooperation is indicative of a fundamental, systemic change in relations between states (Mearsheimer, 1990).

KEY EVENT 3.1 NEOREALISM AND THE END OF THE COLD WAR

Liberal IR theorists reacted positively to the end of the Cold War in 1990. Many saw it as heralding a 'New World Order', presenting new opportunities for reform of the international system and the further development of a liberal international order (see the discussion in Chapter 2).

Realists and neorealists were generally much more circumspect. In 1990 the neorealist John Mearsheimer published an article in *The Atlantic Monthly* entitled 'Why We Will Soon Miss the Cold War'. Mearsheimer acknowledged that many aspects of the Cold War would not be missed, such as the wars in Korea and Vietnam, the Cuban Missile Crisis, or the at times hysterical pursuit of suspected communists within the US (the so-called McCarthy Era). What would be missed, Mearsheimer argued, was the stability that a bipolar international system brought to international politics, the 'order that the Cold War gave to the anarchy of international politics' (Mearsheimer, 1990: 35).

Mearsheimer was particularly concerned about the impact of the Cold War's end on stability and cooperation in Europe. In his view Europe would revert to a less stable multipolar system marked by increasing rivalry between regional great powers. In contrast to the liberal view that in a post-Cold War world, states would be more interested in economic prosperity and pursue greater interdependence, Mearsheimer argued that a multipolar regional order in Europe would push security up not down the national agendas of states. States, he argues, would then become increasingly more concerned about relative rather than absolute gains. Additionally, Mearsheimer foresaw a return to hypernationalist politics, especially in Eastern Europe.

Mearsheimer concluded that if the Cold War was truly over 'the stability of the past 45 years is not likely to be seen again in the coming decades' (Mearsheimer, 1990: 50).

USEFUL REFERENCE:

Mearsheimer, John, J. (1990) 'Why We Will Soon Miss the Cold War', *The Atlantic Monthly*, 266(2), 35–50.

3.8 NEOCLASSICAL REALISM—BRIDGING THE CLASSICAL REALIST-NEOREALIST DIVIDE

In recent years, a hybrid variety of realism referred to as neoclassical realism has emerged, which draws from both classical and neorealist thought. It was noted in Section 3.6 that Waltz's reformulation of realism was explicitly and solely aimed at developing a theory of international politics, not an attempt to understand the making of national foreign policy. Waltz argued that the making of foreign policy was too complex to be captured by the kind of parsimonious theory he was aiming to develop. This marked a clear break from the classical realist tradition which did not draw such a clear distinction between the analysis of foreign policy and that of the international system more generally.

Neoclassical realists want to bring neorealism into the analysis of foreign policy. They start from the neorealist assumption that a state's relative power in the anarchical international system is what matters most. However, they argue that neorealism over-emphasizes the direct influence of the international system on the concrete foreign policies of states. They argue that foreign policy makers in fact often struggle to interpret or 'read' the international system and how they fit within it: for foreign policy makers 'anarchy is murky' (Rose, 1998: 154, Table 1). This is especially the case when the power of specific states rises or falls. What is needed, then, is a better understanding of how policy makers *interpret* or misinterpret the external environment. In some respects, this marks a return to Morgenthau's interest in looking over the shoulders of statesmen in order to understand how and why states behave the way they do at specific historical moments. However, neoclassical realists follow Waltz in rejecting Morgenthau's references to human nature as a basis for explaining the international system.

Like neorealism, neoclassical realism emphasizes the significance of the international anarchy as an external determinant of state behaviour and, thus, the importance of the prevailing balance of power. Yet, neoclassical realist scholars also see Waltz's neorealism as too narrowly focused. In common with much classical realism (and what Waltz described as 'second image' analysis that we discussed at the beginning of Section 3.6), neoclassical realists also see unit-level variables—factors within individual states—as important. They question therefore Waltz's famous insistence that the interests of all states are pretty much alike. Put differently, whereas neorealists argue from a predominantly *outside-in* point of view—the anarchical system determines state behaviour from the outside—neoclassical realists also attach importance to the differences between specific states. They recognize that there are also significant *inside-out* determinants of state behaviour.

Neoclassical realism endeavours then to explore the interaction between the internal characteristics of states and the anarchical international system. According to the neoclassical realist Randall Schweller, the interests of states, including their security interests, do vary in important ways. This is a consequence of such things as the differing perceptions of the international system, differences in the relationship between society and state which can affect the capacity of states to translate national resources into state power, and differences in the prevailing senses of their national identity (Schweller, 1996;

Schweller, 2008, especially Chapter 2). This emphasis on perception found in neoclassical realism—on how the international system is viewed from within specific states and what influences that perception—is developed considerably further and also rather differently in other theories of international politics, notably constructivism (the subject of Chapter 8).

We can explore further the differences between varieties of realism by looking at an issue area that has long attracted the attention of realists because of their emphasis on the importance of national security: nuclear weapons.

3.9 REALISM AND NUCLEAR WEAPONS

Hopefully by now you are starting to understand that there are a variety of realist perspectives that share some core theoretical assumptions but also diverge significantly in key respects. One issue area that brings out the differences within realism, broadly defined, is nuclear weapons. There are only five legally recognized nuclear weapons states (NWSs) and they are also the permanent members of the UN Security Council. The declared position of the UN, and the vast majority of its members, is that there should no further proliferation of nuclear weapons and all states, inculding the NWSs, should pursue the eventual elimination of all nuclear weapons. The cornerstone of the global nuclear non-proliferation regime is the 1970 Nuclear non-Proliferation Treaty (NPT). Other states are known to possess nuclear weapons—notably Israel, India, and Pakistan—but they are also three of only five states who have not signed or have withdrawn from the NPT (the other two being North Korea and South Sudan).

Nuclear weapons have only been used twice, by the US against the Japanese cities of Hiroshima and Nagasaki in 1945. Since then, *horizontal proliferation* (an increase in the number of states possessing nuclear weapons) has been far slower than many initially predicted. Since the end of the Cold War, the number of nuclear weapons deployed—*vertical proliferation*—by the major powers has also declined significantly. Nonetheless, there are still sufficient numbers deployed or easily readied for use to enable humankind to obliterate itself ('omnicide'). In spite of their obligations as signatories to the NPT to work towards total nuclear disarmament, the NWSs have also shown little interest in giving up their nuclear arsenals. Additionally, states such as North Korea and Iran are seen as actively pursuing the development of a nuclear weapons capability in overt contravention of the principle of non-proliferation.

Morgenthau on nuclear weapons

How have realists addressed the issue of nuclear weapons? In his earlier work the classical realist Hans Morgenthau seemed to accept that the emergence of nuclear weapons might be compatible with the conduct of international politics. Initially, he took the view that nuclear weapons could be used selectively in certain war scenarios (what is known as limited nuclear warfare). Within a few years, however, Morgenthau changed his mind and argued that nuclear warfare could no longer be viewed as a rational 'instrument of policy' and the only useful purpose of nuclear weapons was to act as a deterrent. He advocated the reduction of nuclear stockpiles to the minimum required to deter a potential threat to national survival. In his later work, Morgenthau's position shifted even further and he came to the view that any use of nuclear weapons to defend a nation's interests was fundamentally irrational:

> If a nation cannot resort to nuclear weapons without risking its own destruction, how can it support its interests in a world of sovereign nations which is ruled by violence as the last resort? (Morgenthau, 1962: 174)

An all-out nuclear exchange between the superpowers would be so destructive that, in his view, it would destroy the meaning of life itself. Indeed, Morgenthau now depicted the invention and deployment of nuclear weapons as an historic game changer. It was so significant a development that it raised questions about the future sustainability of the international system of states in its present form (Morgenthau, 1961). Indeed, the impact of nuclear weapons was sufficient to eventually lead Morgenthau, one of the founding figures of modern realism, to the view that 'the realistic and utopian approaches to politics in general, and to international relations in particular, merge' (Morgenthau cited in Nobel, 1995: 84).

Waltz on nuclear weapons

Some 20 years later, neorealism's founder, Kenneth Waltz, took a very different view. Waltz argued during the height of the Cold War that horizontal proliferation was never likely to be fast but some proliferation might even be a good thing: 'more may be better' (part of the title of Waltz, 1981).

Waltz argued that the stability of the Cold War era was down to two things: bipolarity and nuclear weapons. The bipolar balance was, in his view, the most stable structure of an anarchic international system. In the absence of a fool-proof counter-attack capacity (and no one has yet devised one), nuclear weapons vastly increased the costs of the superpowers going to war with each other because of the risk of Mutually Assured Destruction (MAD). Waltz argues that the emergence of some more nuclear armed states is not likely to destabilize the world because the same factors that constrained the superpowers will operate to constrain new nuclear powers, including the continuing presence of the two overwhelmingly superior nuclear powers. Indeed, the resort to conventional war may become less likely because of the risk of escalation to the nuclear threshold. Waltz argued that

> it is not likely that nuclear weapons will spread with a speed that exceeds the ability of their new owners to adjust to them. The spread of nuclear weapons is something that we have worried too much about and tried too hard to stop. (Waltz, 1981: 34)

In other words, more nuclear weapons might actually make make the world safer.

3 CLASSICAL REALISM AND NEOREALISM   **97**

Of course, Morgenthau and Waltz made their arguments during the Cold War, when fear of a nuclear conflict was much more heightened than it is today. Nonetheless, Waltz maintained his view even after the end of the Cold War.

In making his argument for allowing nuclear proliferation Waltz also noted that

> Many Westerners who write fearfully about a future in which Third World countries have nuclear weapons seem to view their people in the once familiar imperial manner as 'lesser breeds without the law'. As is usual with ethnocentric views, speculation takes the place of evidence. (Waltz, 1981: 13)

More recently, others have drawn upon postcolonial perspectives to make similar observations. For example, Hugh Gusterson has argued that arguments against permitting so-called Third World states to possess nuclear weapons are often couched in racialized terms which depict developing countries as too poor, too unstable, or lacking sufficient technical and political maturity (Gusterson, 1999. We discuss the significance of race in international politcs extensively in Chapter 9). The NPT is effectively, Gusterson suggests, a form of 'nuclear apartheid' based upon a double standard wherein the world's major powers keep their nuclear arsenals while insisting that other states, especially those in the Global South, be prohibited from acquiring their own nuclear weapons.

Three realist positions on nuclear weapons: exclusion, participation, or renunciation

Gusterson concludes that there are broadly three ways in which we can address the question of nuclear weapons without using the racialized double standard that he believes operates today. All of the three ways identified by Gusterson can be connected to different forms of realist argument.

Exclusion

The first way Gusterson calls 'exclusion', which entails declaring that possessing nuclear weapons simply reflects the realities of power. The NWSs can simply exclude weaker states from joining the nuclear club. This echoes Thucydides's recounting of the Athenian justification for subjugating Melos in the Melian Dialogue (discussed in Section 3.3 above). It reflects a brutish appreciation of the power of the strong over the weak:

> It involves the candid declaration that, while nuclear weapons may be no more dangerous in the hands of Muslims or Hindus than in those of Christians, they are a prerogative of power, and the powerful have no intention of allowing the powerless to acquire them. This is a position that, in its rejection of easy racism and phony moralism, is at least honorable in its frankness. (Gusterson, 1999: 133)

Participation

The second way of viewing nuclear weapons suggested by Gusterson is that of 'participation'. This follows Waltz's argument that we discussed earlier: nuclear proliferation may actually prove beneficial to the security interests of a number of states and may therefore make the world more rather than less stable and lower the risk of large scale war.

Renunciation

The third way (and Gusterson's preferred approach) of viewing nuclear weapons is 're-nunciation': no state should possess them. Although Gusterson gets to it by a somewhat different route, this is compatible with the view that Morgenthau eventually adopted.

The renunciation of all nuclear weapons also became the view of George Kennan, a former US ambassador to the Soviet Union and one of the most influential figures in US foreign and security policy during the Cold War. He is best known for designing the US Cold War policy known as 'containment', whereby the US would work to always surround the Soviet Union and its allies with preponderant US military power. Kennan's outlook on international politics was thoroughly realist and Morgenthau's shadow argu-ably hangs over Kennan's observation that he saw

> the danger not in the number or quality of the weapons or in the intentions of those who hold them but in the very existence of weapons of this nature, regardless of whose hands they are in . . . the nuclear weapons we hold in our hands are as much a danger to us as those that repose in the hands of our supposed adversaries . . . I see no solution to the problem other than the complete elimination of these and all other weapons of mass destruction from national arsenals. (Kennan, 1981: 54)

From this survey of the different views taken by realists regarding the issue of nuclear weapons, it should be clear that although realists share a number of key theoretical as-sumptions they can arrive nonetheless at very different conclusions about a key issue in international politics.

3.10 CONCLUSION

Although neorealism grabbed the theoretical headlines when it emerged in the late 1970s, classical realism remains alive and well. Today, you can find IR scholars draw-ing from the full spectrum of realist thinking: classical realists; defensive neorealists; offensive neorealists; and, more recently, neoclassical realists. There are significant disa-greements between them, but the precise boundaries between the different varieties of realism are also quite blurred. Treating the realist tradition as a single perspective risks caricaturing it and papering over important theoretical differences within.

Nonetheless, there is little doubt also that all realists share some common assumptions:

- the international system is anarchic and this is its most significant feature
- states are the most important actors in that system
- the pursuit of power is a primary determinant of the behaviour of those states
- the prospects of fundamental and sustainable change in the functioning of the international system are, at best, poor.

It is important to emphasize that realists do not celebrate the resistance of the international system to change, just as they do not celebrate the perpetual risk of war and the consequent need for all states to prepare for it. Indeed, some prominent realists and neorealists are noted for their opposition to war, unless what they perceive to be vital national interests are at stake. Morgenthau was a prominent critic of the US's war with Vietnam during the Cold War and the neorealists John Mearsheimer and Stephen Walt have vociferously questioned the US-led Invasion of Iraq in 2003 (Mearsheimer and Walt, 2003).

Realism is also undoubtedly a state-centric perspective. It is worth noting, however, that some of the most well-known classical realists—such as E.H. Carr, Hans Morgenthau, and John Herz—also recognized and regretted the limitations upon addressing some of humanity's most pressing problems that came with the continuing dominance of sovereign states within an anarchical state system.

What realists do claim, from Thucydides through to Waltz, is that it is more dangerous simply to ignore the perennial features of the international system. In this respect, realists are generally conservative with a small 'c', when it comes to practical questions about foreign and security policy. Individual realist scholars may or may not embrace conservatism as a general political philosophy (many certainly do not), but they all favour caution and prudence in foreign policy. This is because bold foreign policy moves that do not clearly serve the national interest and fail to take account of the prevailing international distribution of power can, in their view, have very dangerous and often unintended consequences.

SUMMARIZING REALISM AND NEOREALISM

- Realists claim that realism's core assumptions can be traced back to antiquity and thus represent 'timeless wisdom'
- Thucydides in the fourth century BCE, Niccolo Machiavelli, in the fourteenth century and Thomas Hobbes in the seventeenth century are commonly identified as early proponents of realist thought
- A simple summary of realism is provided by three 'Ss': Statism, Survival, and Self-reliance
- E.H. Carr and Hans Morgenthau are widely regarded as key figures in the emergence of the modern realist perspective after 1945. The extent to which either fully embraced some of the commonly held assumptions about the realist perspective is, however, a matter of debate
- Kenneth Waltz's reformulation of realism in 1979 came to be known as neorealism. Since then, earlier realist thought is commonly referred to as 'classical realism'
- Neorealism criticizes other IR perspectives (including some classical realism) as 'reductionist' because they endeavour to explain the functioning of the whole international system through reference primarily to its parts—such as individual human nature or the internal features of states

- Waltz's neorealism is also referred to as structural realism because it sees the anarchic structure of the international system as significantly constraining state behaviour

- Neorealism argues that unless the structure of the international system changes from anarchy to some kind of hierarchy, the behaviour of states is unlikely to change substantially over time. What does change is the distribution of power within the overall anarchical system

- More recently, some scholars have attempted to bridge the two strands of realist thought in the form of neoclassical realism

- Neoclassical realists argue that neorealism understates the influence of domestic factors in the making of the foreign policies of states

- A number of liberal scholars have responded to the emergence of neorealism by reformulating liberal IR theory into a 'neoliberal' perspective. The debate between the two rival schools has come to be known as the 'neo-neo' debate

- While making some concessions to Waltz's neorealism, neoliberalism maintains that states will cooperate more extensively and international institutions matter more than neorealism claims

- Neorealists argue that the foreign policies of states are primarily driven by calculations of 'relative gains' (how do we benefit compared to our rivals?), whereas neoliberals claim that states are increasingly driven by 'absolute gains' (as long as we benefit it does not necessarily matter that others many benefit more than us)

- Realists and neorealists do not dispute the fact that states may cooperate. What they question, especially neorealists, is whether such cooperation indicates a fundamental transformation of relations between states or merely reflects a period or issue area where the national self-interests of states may coincide

- Although realists and neorealists accept that war will remain an ever-present possibility in an anarchical system of states, many are also noted opponents of going to war for any reasons other than defence of vital national interests.

QUESTIONS

1. How would you briefly summarize the realist perspective?

2. Why did realism become prominent during the early years of the Cold War?

3. Explain, with examples, what the neorealist Kenneth Waltz mean when he describes other theories (including some forms of classical realism) as 'reductionist'?

4. How does neorealism explain the international system's resistance to significant change?

5. Why do neoclassical realists see neorealism as too 'parsimonious' to explain the concrete foreign policies of states?

6. What, if anything, do you think is missing from either classical realism or neorealism?

IR THEORY TODAY REALISM AND THE WAR IN AFGHANISTAN

It is more than 20 years since the US-led 'Operation Enduring Freedom' was launched in October 2001. The operation commenced with a US/UK bombing campaign targetting al-Qaida, followed by the deployment of ground troops inside Afghanistan. The operation was the beginning of the US's 'War on Terror' in response to the '9/11' terrorist attacks on targets in the US in September 2001. These were carried out by the terrorist group al-Qaida which was then based inside Afghanistan. Al-Qaida were largely chased out of Afghanistan and by December 2001 the Taliban Islamic regime that had been in power since 1996 had collapsed. Yet nearly 20 years later, on 16 August 2021, the Taliban entered Kabul, the capital of Afghanistan and began to establish a new government.

In 2002, President Bush called for the reconstruction of Afghanistan and an interim administration was established. In 2003, the US Secretary of State, Donald Rumsfeld declared that 'major combat' in Afghanistan was over and NATO assumed command of International Security Forces in Afghanistan (ISAF), which by 2006 had grown to 65,000 troops from 42 countries. By 2004 Afghanistan had a new constitution which was followed by Presidential elections in 2005 and Parliamentary elections in 2006 in which nearly half of those who voted were women.

By 2006, however, the Taliban had regrouped and launched an offensive against the new Afghan government, capturing large swathes of Afghan territory. The initial military response by the US and its NATO allies failed to stop the Taliban's advances. When

Old Taliban tanks and guns on the outskirts of Kabul city, Afghanistan

US president Barack Obama came into office in 2009 he initiated a short-term 'surge' of US troop reinforcements. At its peak in 2011 this resulted in more than 100,000 US troops being stationed there. However, the deaths and casualities of US troops as well as US-trained Afghani armed forces also rose dramatically.

The intention of the 'surge' was to create the conditions for Afghani forces to increasingly take over the fight against the Taliban. Recognizing that US public opinion was turning against continuing US involvement, Obama also foreshadowed the eventual drawdown of the American military presence. By 2015 only about 10,000 US troops remained although 350,000 Afghan soliders and police had by now been trained, armed, and deployed. However, a series of successful Taliban offensives exposed the weaknesses of the Afghani forces and further increased the territory under Taliban control.

When President Donald Trump assumed office in 2017 he initially increased US forces, although his opposition to continuing the war was well known. Trump also initiated negotiations with the Taliban in 2018 but this failed to produce any concrete results. In April 2021 Trump's successor, Joe Biden, announced the complete withdrawal of US forces (and also NATO forces) from Afghanistan by September 2021, which was effectively completed by July 2021. Afghani forces subsequently offered little resistance to rapid advances by Taliban forces who, within only a few weeks, regained complete control in Afghanistan and remain in power today.

It has been estimated that more than 170,000 lives were lost during nearly two decades of conflict in Afghanistan. A Brown University study in 2019 estimated that the War in Afghanistan between 2001 and 2020 had cost the US about $978 billion.

QUESTIONS

Drawing upon this chapter and your own research:

1. From a realist perspective, do you think that the US was justified in leading the invasion of Afghanistan in 2001?

3. From a realist perspective, do you think there were alternative responses to the 9/11 terrorist attacks the US could have adopted other than invading Afghanistan?

4. Take a look at the 2009 letter to President Obama signed by a number of prominent US realists such as John Mearsheimer and Stephen Walt (see Smith, 2009, below). What are the main concerns they raise about continuing US involvement in Afghanistan? Do you agree or disagree with them? Explain your reasons.

TWISTING THE LENS

1. Take a look at Chapter 10 on Feminisms and gender. How might feminist/gender-focused viewpoints cast a distinctive light on the war in Afghanistan?

(Hint: think about the changing roles of women in Afghanistan prior to and after the 2001 invasion and their prospects under the new Taliban regime)

2. Take a look at Chapter 9 on Postcolonialism. In what ways, if any, do you think postcolonialism can offer valuable insights on the war in Afghanistan?

USEFUL REFERENCES

Malkasian, Carter (2020), 'How the Good War Went Bad', *Foreign Affairs*, 99 (2): 77–91.

USEFUL RESOURCES YOU CAN FIND ONLINE

Cordesman, Anthony H. (2010), 'Realism in Afghanistan: Rethinking an Uncertain Case for the War', *Center for Strategic and International Studies*, Commentary, 16 June.
Council for Foreign Relations Timeline: The US War in Afghanistan 1999–2021.
Mearsheimer, John J. (2001), 'Guns Won't Win the Afghan War', *The New York Times*, 4 November.
Smith, Ben (2009), 'Realists Warn on Afghan War', *Politico*, 15 September.

FURTHER READING

ADDITIONAL INTRODUCTORY READING

Donnelly, J. (2000), *Realism and International Relations* (Cambridge: Cambridge University Press).
A very comprehensive yet accessible and student-focused introduction to the full range of realist thought.
Dunne, T. and Schmidt, B. C. (2020), 'Realism' in J. Baylis, S. Smith, and P. Owens, *The Globalization of World Politics: An Introduction to International Relations*, 8th Edition (Oxford: Oxford University Press).
A highly accessible and brief introductory survey of the main varieties of realist thought.
Lebow, R. N. (2020) 'Classical Realism' in T. Dunne, M. Kurki, and S. Smith, *International Relations Theories: Discipline and Diversity* (Oxford: Oxford University Press).
Mearsheimer, J. J. (2020) 'Structural Realism' in T. Dunne, M. Kurki, and S. Smith, *International Relations Theories: Discipline and Diversity* (Oxford: Oxford University Press).
These two chapters, by two leading US realist scholars representing both the classical realist and neorealist perspectives, collectively offer a more advanced introduction to realist IR theories.
Sterling-Folker, J. (2021), 'Neoliberalism', in T. Dunne, M. Kurki, and S. Smith, *International Relations Theories: Discipline and Diversity*, 5th edn (Oxford: Oxford University Press).
A succinct introduction to the response of some leading Liberal IR scholars to the emergence of neorealism in the late 1970s.

MORE IN-DEPTH READING

Bell, D. (2017), 'Political Realism and International Relations', *Philosophy Compass*, 12/2, 12 pp. Available at: https://compass.onlinelibrary.wiley.com/doi/abs/10.1111/phc3.12403.
An examination of Realist IR thought through the lenses of political theory, focusing particularly on the realist criticism of moralism in foreign policy and realist contributions to debates about global justice.
Gilpin, R. (1981), *War and Change in International Politics* (Cambridge: Cambridge University Press).
An influential example of realist thinking which is centred around the role of a hegemonic power, such as the US, in maintaining international stability.
Lobell, S. E., Ripsman, N. M., and Taliaferro, J. W. (eds) (2009), *Neoclassical Realism, the State, and Foreign Policy* (Cambridge: Cambridge University Press).
A systematic survey of the neoclassical realist approach which assesses its relevance to the analysis, making, and conduct of foreign policy.

Mearsheimer, J. J. (2014), *The Tragedy of Great Power Politics* (New York: W.W. Norton).
Written by one of the leading contemporary neorealist scholars and first published in 2001. Mearsheimer deploys his version of neorealism—'offensive realism'—to examine the behaviour of great powers in the international system.

Mearsheimer, J. J. and Walt, S. M. (2003), 'An Unnecessary War', *Foreign Policy*, (Jan/Feb), pp. 51–59.
A highly readable example of a neorealist critique of the decision by the US to invade Iraq, by two of the leading contemporary neorealists.

Morgenthau, H. J. (1961), 'Death in the Nuclear Age', *Commentary*, Vol. 32, p. 231.
A brief philosophical commentary on the deadly significance of nuclear weapons by the legendary realist scholar.

Morgenthau, H. J. (1993), *Politics Among Nations: The Struggle for Power and Peace*, 7th edn (New York: McGraw-Hill).
Perhaps the most famous of realist texts, which from the 2nd edition onwards opens with the widely cited 'Six Principles of Political Realism'.

Morgenthau, H. J. (2012), *The Concept of the Political*, edited by H. Behr and F. Rösch, translated by M. Vidal (Basingstoke: Palgrave Macmillan).
Although first published in French in 1933, this early work by Morgenthau is now seen by leading Realist scholars as providing vital insight into Morgethau's understanding of the connection between domestic and international politics and the meaning of 'the National Interest'.

Rose, G. (1998), 'Neoclassical Realism and Theories of Foreign Policy', *World Politics*, Vol. 51, pp. 144–172.
This article reviews 5 books by leading realist writers and is noted particularly for coining the label 'neoclassical realism' to describe these works because they are seen to bridge classical realism and neorealism.

Rosenthal, J. H. (1991), *Righteous Realists: Political Realism, Responsible Power, and American Culture in the Nuclear Age* (Baton Rouge: Louisiana University Press).
Rosenthal examines the work of some key founders of modern realism to show how moral concerns threaded through their analyses of international politics.

Waltz, K. N. (1959), *Man, the State, and War: A Theoretical Analysis* (New York: Columbia University Press).
A seminal realist text, in which Waltz outlines his three-images analysis of international politics. His 'third image' lays the groundwork for his subsequent development of neorealism.

Waltz, K. N. (1979), *Theory of International Politics* (Reading, MA: Addison-Wesley Publishing Co.).
One of the most influential (and criticized) of all IR theory texts. It is the first book to outline a revised realist theory of IR which subsequently came to be known as neorealism.

Waltz, K. N. (1981), 'The Spread of Nuclear Weapons: More May Be Better', *The Adelphi Papers*, No. 171 (London: IISS).
In this controversial paper Waltz applies neorealist thinking to the question of nuclear weapons.

Williams, M. C. (ed) (2005), *Realism Reconsidered: The Legacy of Hans Morgenthau in International Relations* (Oxford: Oxford University Press).
A series of essays by leading British and American IR scholars reflecting on Morgethau's intellectual legacy and the relevance of his work to the analysis of contemporary international politics.

CHAPTER 4

THE ENGLISH SCHOOL OF INTERNATIONAL RELATIONS

LEARNING OBJECTIVES

- Identify the origins and key developmental phases of the English School
- Evaluate the significance of the work of Martin Wight and Hedley Bull in the establishment and development of the English School
- Understand the meaning and significance of the core English School claim that we live in an 'anarchical society of states'
- Analyse the pluralist and solidarist wings of English School thought in relation to the tension between the pursuit of international order and international justice
- Identify synergies between the English School and other IR theoretical approaches
- Explain the key aspects of Barry Buzan's reappraisal of the English school.

4.1 INTRODUCTION

The origins of the English School lie in debates among IR scholars (only some of whom were English) in a few English universities in the 1950s and 1960s. The intellectual influence of the English School is now considerable and extends well beyond England. Nonetheless, because of the historical dominance of US-centred theoretical debates in the IR field, for a long time it was one of the less visible streams of mainstream thought, especially to US audiences. Additionally, the English School's theoretical location, at least in its formative years, somewhere between realism and liberalism has meant that it has been resistant to precise classification. This undoubtedly forms part of its ongoing appeal to an eclectic range of IR scholars.

The English School is a theoretical perspective that clearly resonates with core themes in both classical realist and liberal IR scholarship, yet at the same time it also offers a basis for critiquing both. The early output of the key figures of the English School could be viewed as offering a rather old-fashioned theoretical take on international politics by today's standards and a number of the school's core assumptions have indeed been subjected to robust scrutiny from newer critical IR theoretical perspectives. Nonetheless, many contemporary English School scholars have confronted such criticisms head on while also identifying actual and potential synergies between the English School and other IR theories, notably Critical Theory.

This chapter starts by outlining two key features of the English School: the key conceptual claim that states are located within an *anarchical society of states*, and the emergence of two distinctive strands within the English School: pluralism and solidarism. We go on then to look at three broad phases of the development of the English School and identify their distinctive contributions to the evolution of the English School into the diverse body of thought that it is today.

4.2 **WHAT IS THE ENGLISH SCHOOL?**

Realism and neorealism, especially neorealism, have exerted a much more visible influence on IR scholarship in the US than in the UK, or indeed elsewhere in the English-speaking world. Part of the explanation for this is that for many years the teaching of IR in the UK (and to a certain extent also Australia and Canada) reflected the influence of a distinctive perspective, originally known as rationalism but now commonly referred to as the English School.

Cornelia Navari (2014: 207) has usefully described the methodology of the founding figures of the English School as a form of 'participant observation', wherein the scholar observes those who make foreign policy and tries to discern the intentions underpinning their foreign policy choices. This does suggest some affinities with classical realism, notably the work of Hans Morgenthau who also depicted the study of international politics as akin to looking over the shoulders of statesmen throughout history (see the discussion of Morgenthau in Chapter 3, Section 3.4). More generally, however, the tone and style of the English School distinguishes it from much of the US-dominated IR theoretical mainstream. These differences should become clearer as you work through this chapter.

Before going into the evolution and theoretical development of the English School we will first outline two of its key features:

- The first is the claim that there exists an anarchical society of states, also referred to as a society of states, or international society. This is the English School's defining claim, which still forms its conceptual heart.

- The second key feature is the evolution of two distinct wings to the English School: pluralism and solidarism. These are distinguished by their different interpretations of the purpose of an international society of states.

We start with a brief overview of the concept of an anarchical society of states, which we will be exploring further throughout this chapter.

The anarchical society of states

Like realists, the founding figures of the English School were thoroughly state-centric. However, whereas realism's central focus is on states within what is seen to be a largely unchanging international *system* of states, the English School emphasizes the historical evolution of certain features of that international system. In combination, these features are seen to constitute an international society or, more precisely, an 'anarchical society of states'. Indeed the title of probably the best known of the foundational texts of the English School, written by the Australian Scholar Hedley Bull, is *The Anarchical Society*, first published in 1977.

The crucial word here is society. Why is this? Barry Buzan, who has been a central figure in the third phase of the English School's development (we examine this phase in Section 4.5), offers a succinct explanation:

> The basic idea of international society is quite simple: just as human beings as individuals live in societies which they both shape and are shaped by, so also states live in an international society which they shape and are shaped by. (Buzan, 2014: 13)

Of course, states and human individuals are not the same, and neither, therefore, are the societies in which they are situated. For this reason, the English School has always depicted the international society of states as a unique form of society. It is, after all, a society with a small number of members—there are currently around 200 sovereign states—each of which also contains at least one national society (and sometimes more than one group of people who regard themselves as part of a distinct national society) within its borders.

This leads to a clear distinction between the realist understanding and the English School understanding of international anarchy. The strict meaning of international anarchy is that there is an absence of power above the sovereign state, and both realists and the English School agree on this. From a realist perspective, however, the idea of an international anarchy is antithetical to any notion of a society, as is commonly understood by the term. This reflects the widespread view that human societies usually evolve under some kind of overarching authority, such as a state, which determines their outer boundary. For the English School, the study of international history shows that despite the absence of any authority above them, sovereign states have nonetheless developed meaningful and sustainable social relations between themselves over time. These social relations between sovereign states, the English School argues, show the influence of widely shared and well-established norms and habits of state behaviour. This means that '(i)n the realist view anarchy has one major outcome – the balance of power - whereas for the English School international anarchy can support a wide variety of social forms' (Buzan 2014: 27).

In contrast to realism's rather static view of international politics, in which the only thing that varies significantly is the relative power of states, the English School's claim that relations between states have *societal* qualities introduces a greater degree of dynamism in international politics. This is because societies can change in various ways. We will be further exploring how the idea of an international society introduces a social dynamism to international politics as we explore the English School in more detail.

 THINK CRITICALLY 4.1

Before reading any further, think about what you regard as the essential features of any society, such as those found within states. Then consider the idea of an anarchical international society.

Do you think that it is plausible to bring the two concepts of *anarchy* (i.e., the absence of sovereign power, or government, above the state) and *society* together?

- If your first reaction is scepticism, what are the primary reasons for this? (Hint: Try drawing on realist thinking from Chapter 3 to help you)
- If you think that bringing the two concepts together to describe relations between states seems inherently plausible, what would be the key reasons for this? (Hint: try drawing on liberalism's emphasis on cooperation and international or transnational institutions, as outlined in in Chapter 2, to help you)

Once you have read more about the English School, you might want to revisit your initial response to this question to see if your thinking has shifted.

On what basis did the founding figures of the English School make the claim that it is plausible to speak of an anarchical society of states which, Buzan suggests, both shapes and is shaped by relations between states? Like realists, the English School depicts the behaviour of states as driven by the pursuit of their core national interests (we discuss how realism understands the interests of states in Chapter 3). However, a key difference is that the English School's understanding of the interests that drive states is more social than that of realists. From an English School point of view, the interests of states cannot be reduced simply to the self-interested pursuit of material power and advantage as realism suggests.

The primary goals and common institutions of international society

Although states are clearly different from each other in many ways, the English School depicts them as having a shared interest in a set of what Hedley Bull (1977: 16–19), describes as 'primary goals' that are unique to international society. Bull argues that these primary goals of international society are:

- the preservation of international order
- the maintenance of the independence of states
- peace as the normal condition.

These goals are primary because, Bull argues, it is in the interests of all states that there is some predictability and stability in the international system, just as all states seek to preserve their independence, their sovereignty. Although almost all states prepare for war by maintaining standing armies, for most states most of the time international peace is the condition best suited to the pursuit of their core interests.

Because they share these primary goals in common, Bull argues, states have come to

conceive themselves to be bound by a common set of rules in their relations with one another and share in the working of common institutions. (Bull, 1977: 13)

Common rules and institutions, Bull argues, are core components of any society, and therefore provide the starting point for the claim that it is meaningful to speak of an international society of states. Here, we can see some similarity with the liberal emphasis on the role of international institutions, that we discuss in Chapter 2. There are, nonetheless, significant differences in how liberal IR scholars and English School scholars understand international institutions.

Liberalism depicts the institutionalization of international politics as a comparatively recent and still developing dimension of international politics. We note in Chapter 2, that the liberal thinkers who dominated the establishment of the IR discipline just after the First World War emphasized the importance of institutionalizing international politics in order to avoid a return to world war. This early liberal emphasis on institutions was pretty much side-lined, however, because of the subsequent dominance of realism in the IR discipline, especially after 1945. When liberal IR theorizing regained prominence in the IR discipline in the 1970s, it was centred around a revival of scholarly interest in international institutions. Indeed, the importance of international institutions formed a key component of the claim by liberal IR theorists that relations between states in the post-1945 era were characterized by 'complex interdependence' (Keohane and Nye, 1989).

By institutions, contemporary liberal IR scholars largely mean international and transnational regimes—sets of formal and informal rules and procedures as well as formal international organizations. These are seen to have developed rapidly since the mid-twentieth century in response to the increased complexity of political and economic relations between states and the growing role of a wide range of non-state actors (Keohane and Nye, 1989). You can read more about the liberal concept of complex interdependence in Section 2.4 of Chapter 2.

In contrast to Liberalism's understanding of institutions, the common rules and institutions that Bull refers to are depicted as key historical features of the international society of states since its inception. Their origins are seen to lie in the historical evolution of relations between European states from the fifteenth century onwards. What was originally a predominantly European society of states subsequently and relentlessly expanded across the face of the globe to colonize other countries and by the late nineteenth century had created a single anarchical society of states (Bull and Watson, 1984). It should be noted here that more recent English School scholarship argues that it was more an international society of European empires (alongside the Ottoman, Japanese, and Chinese empires of the nineteenth century) that, as a consequence of decolonization, has only relatively recently become a society of states (Keene, 2002; Buzan, 2004; Suzuki, 2009).

Bull (1977: 74) identifies the 'common institutions' of the anarchical society of states as:

- the balance of power
- international law
- diplomacy
- the great powers
- and, sometimes, war.

You may immediately recognize these as labels for long-standing aspects or practices of international politics that are prominent across the mainstream of IR theory. However, only the English School depicts them as 'institutions' that are constitutive of an international society of states. It is important to note that what Bull means by 'common institutions' or 'the institutions of international society' is not just formal organizations or 'administrative machinery' but also an historically evolved 'set of habits and practices shaped towards the realisation of common goals' (Bull: 1977: 74). These institutions do not detract from the sovereignty of states (they do not add up to any kind of central authority above the state) but are 'an expression of the element of collaboration among states . . . and at the same a means for sustaining this collaboration' (Bull, 1977: 74).

In sum, the English School's conception of an anarchical society of states rests upon a trio of interconnected features: primary goals that all states pursue, common rules, and common institutions.

Buzan usefully brings out the difference between the Liberal and English School's understanding of institutions by distinguishing between 'primary' and 'secondary' institutions. The English school, Buzan (2014: 27) argues, focuses primarily on primary institutions 'which are by definition difficult to manipulate or reform'. It is the primary institutions—those that Bull calls common institutions—that establish the broad rules of the game of the international society as a whole. In contrast, Buzan argues, liberals focus more on secondary institutions which operate within and are constrained by a framework that is already established by the primary institutions. The primary institutions of international society have evolved over a considerable period of time, whereas the secondary institutions are more contemporary creations that have evolved informally, or have been formally established through agreements between states. They are responses to the effects of increasingly complex interdependence between states and the need for greater cooperation in specific areas, such as trade, arms control, fishing rights, control of the airspace, environmental management, and so on.

Pluralists and Solidarists

The idea of an international society forms the conceptual heart of the English School. Within the School there are, however, different interpretations of what its primary purposes are: is international society mainly concerned with maintaining international order or stability, or should it also be concerned with addressing issues of international or global justice?

In his early work Bull (1966) identified two broad historical streams of thought on this, which he labelled *pluralist* and *solidarist*. Bull was referring here to different strands of Western political and philosophical thinking about relations between states since the Enlightenment era of the seventeenth and eighteenth centuries, much of it long prior to the emergence of the modern IR discipline.

What are the key features of the two streams of English School thought, pluralism and solidarism?

- Pluralists lean more closely towards a realist viewpoint. They see the influence of the international society as largely limited to preserving an always fragile international order and peaceful coexistence among states. The pluralist wing of today's English School shares much of realism's scepticism about the prospects for fundamental change in the international system and is therefore broadly oriented towards preserving the status quo. Although pluralism is not indifferent to the question of whether international society can be, or should be more just, it generally sees international order (which, in essence, means international stability) as the essential precursor to the achievement of any greater justice. From the pluralist point of view, the primary function of the international society of states is to 'separate and cushion' states in an anarchical international system (Vincent, 1986: 123). It might be useful to think here of the role of the box in a box of eggs.

- Contemporary solidarists in the English School see the primacy of simply seeking to preserve international order as too limited and coming under increasing challenge from various demands, especially from outside the West, for greater international political and economic justice. Solidarism's emphasis on the pursuit of greater international justice makes it the more obviously *normative* (i.e., value-driven) branch of the English School, although the pluralist commitment to the value of international order also has an inescapably normative dimension to it. This is because it treats order as not merely a condition, but also as a value. International order is seen as a good thing, a preferred condition that any rational state should endeavour to uphold.

For solidarists, however, international order without greater international justice is neither desirable nor sustainable (Buzan, 2014: 16). Today's solidarists depict international society as still developing and having the potential to help bring about a more peaceful and just international order (Dunne, 1998: 11). The progressivism of contemporary solidarists is premised upon what they see as evidence of growing worldwide demand for and recognition of the need for a more just international order. Examples of such recognition include such things as the widespread acceptance of universal human rights as a basis for judging the internal and external conduct of states and the concrete successes of historical international campaigns against such things as slavery and the apartheid regime in South Africa. Additionally, there is widespread recognition of the need for much greater and deeper cooperation between states to address a range of international and global political and moral problems, such as global inequality, poverty, racial injustice, and the environmental crisis.

Some varieties of English School solidarism retain a broadly state-centric perspective, while also emphasizing the implications of the demands for greater justice for the behaviour of states and the role of the institutions of international society. Others place even greater emphasis on the question of justice and explore the need for and possibilities of ultimately evolving beyond a society of states towards the creation of world society. These solidarists also see common ground with Critical Theory's emphasis on global human *emancipation* (which is examined in Chapter 6).

In his early work, Bull appears to see the pluralist perspective as the more plausible of the two and tends to treat the solidarist tradition in rather abstract terms and as a somewhat idealist or utopian alternative reading of the concept of a society of states. Yet, Bull never dismissed entirely a solidarist perspective on international society. Indeed, some see in Bull's later work evidence of a shift towards the solidarist perspective, although quite how much is a matter of debate (Wheeler and Dunne, 1996). It is only since the late 1980s that a new generation of English School theorists began to develop an explicitly solidarist wing of English school scholarship to concretely challenge the hitherto predominantly pluralist tone of the bulk of English School thinking.

We will explore the differences between the pluralist and solidarist wings of the English school more fully later in this chapter. Prior to that we will look at the origins of the English School and explore how its core themes emerged and have been developed through three distinct phases.

4.3 THE FIRST PHASE: THE ORIGINS OF THE ENGLISH SCHOOL

It seems generally agreed that the English School's roots lie in a series of discussions between small group of scholars who met as 'The British Committee on the Theory of International Relations' between the 1950s and 1980s (Dunne, 1998). Who the members of the group were remains a matter of debate, although the key names undoubtedly included Herbert Butterfield, Martin Wight, Adam Watson, and Hedley Bull. It is by no means certain that they all saw themselves at the time as overtly sharing a clearly demarcated and distinctive theoretical perspective on international politics. Furthermore, it would be inaccurate to say that the contemporary English School's origins lay entirely in the discussions of the British Committee, because the influence of scholars outside of that core group can also be detected.

Perhaps surprisingly, the label 'English School' emerged out of a polemical article by Roy Jones that was entitled 'The English School of International Relations: A Case for Closure', published in 1981 (Jones, 1981). The article was highly critical of the some of the work of some of the School's core founding scholars. The somewhat idiosyncratic article itself did not prove to be very influential—what Jones called the English School certainly did not close—but Jones' label has stuck, nonetheless. Indeed, his article stimulated a debate in the 1980s about whether a unique 'English School' actually existed. Since then, it has become widely accepted that there is indeed a distinctive strand of IR thinking centred around the idea of an international society of states.

Prior to the label the 'English School' achieving wide currency, the perspective was often referred to as rationalism and you may see this in some of the early English School scholarly output or references to it. Given that the term rationalism could confusingly be associated with a very wide range of ideas and philosophical standpoints that extend well beyond the confines of the IR field, it is perhaps not surprising that it has fallen largely out of use. Nonetheless it provides a vital clue to the School's intellectual core. To understand why the term rationalism offers insight into the intellectual core of the English School, we need to look at the work of Martin Wight, a legendary name in the emergence and evolution of today's English School.

Martin Wight: the 'Three Traditions' of thinking about international relations

Martin Wight was a British historian and IR scholar much of whose writing was only published after his death in 1972. (You can read more about him and his life in Key Thinker 4.1.) Comparatively little known before 1972, Wight's significance in the development of the English School has subsequently become much more widely recognized. Indeed, the posthumous publication in 1991 of lectures Wight delivered while teaching at the LSE in the 1950s contributed significantly to a revival of interest in the English School (Wight, 1991).

KEY THINKER 4.1 MARTIN WIGHT

Martin Wight (1913–1972) is something of a legendary figure in the history of twentieth-century British IR scholarship. While studying history at Oxford University in the early 1930s, Wight embraced pacifism and subsequently became involved with the pacifist campaigning organization, the Peace Pledge Union. Wight subsequently worked at the Royal Institute of International Affairs and went on to teach history at a private boy's school. He had to give up his position there after being called up for military service in the early stages of the Second World War. As he had registered as a conscientious objector, one of the conditions imposed on him was that he stopped teaching.

During the war, Wight returned to Oxford researching British colonial institutions (about which he published three books), before eventually taking up a position at the London School of Economics (LSE) in 1949. Wight's teaching was both highly regarded and influential. A number of leading English School scholars, notably Hedley Bull, attended Wight's lectures and Wight's influence is very evident throughout Bull's work.

It was while lecturing at the LSE in the 1950s that Wight developed his conception of thinking about international politics as falling into 'Three Traditions'. He was subsequently invited in 1959 to join the British Committee on the Theory of International Politics, widely recognized as one of the key founding sources of the English School perspective.

Wight left the LSE to become Dean of European Studies and Professor of History at the newly established University of Sussex until his death at the age of 58. Wight did not publish a great deal on international politics during his lifetime. Nonetheless, many of his papers delivered to the British Committee, as well as his highly regarded LSE lectures, were published posthumously, further cementing his reputation as a seminal British IR scholar. After his death, Sussex University established the Martin Wight Memorial Lectures which continue to be delivered annually to this day.

Realism, Rationalism, Revolutionism

In his lectures Wight lays out what he called the 'Three Traditions' of thinking about international politics: rationalism, realism, and revolutionism. Apart from the reference to realism, the labelling Wight employed can be a bit confusing at first sight. Wight's presentation of realism (which he also called the 'Machiavellian' tradition) was very much in line with the classical realist tradition that we look at in Sections 3.2–3.4 in Chapter 3. More confusingly, Wight initially used the label 'Revolutionism' (which he also called the 'Kantian tradition') to describe what many of his contemporaries and successors would refer to as liberal idealism. Wight was referring to strands of political thought, notably liberal progressivist thinking but also Marxism, that envisaged the possibility of radical reform of the international system leading ultimately to the creation of a single global human community in which there would be universal justice and peace (Wight, 1991: 8–12 and 15–24). Therefore, in using the two labels of realism and revolutionism, Wight broadly reproduces the key rival ways of thinking about IR we discuss in Chapters 2 and 3 of this book: so-called 'idealism' and realism.

However, it is Wight's use of the third label, rationalism, that provides the clue to the core premise of the English School. Again, Wight's choice of label is confusing as the term rationalism is also widely used in a variety of ways throughout philosophy and the social sciences. Wight uses rationalism to refer to a third tradition—what he called a 'via media' (middle way) between realism and revolutionism. Wight takes the term rationalism initially from the English political philosopher, John Locke, who was one of the most prominent thinkers of the Enlightenment and is often referred to as one of the fathers of modern liberalism.

Marble bust of John Locke

We saw in Section 3.3 in Chapter 3 how some realists drew from Thomas Hobbes' account of an imaginary 'state of nature' in which humans existed without a 'Leviathan' (a sovereign state) to rule over them. For many realists, Hobbes' pessimistic account of such a world provides insight into the anarchical international system of states. In contrast, Locke's depiction of the state of nature points to a less pessimistic account of international anarchy. Locke writes that 'people living together according to reason, without a common superior on earth, with authority to judge between them, is properly the state of nature' (Locke, cited in Wight, 1991: 13–14). Here, Locke is emphasizing a capacity to reason, which he sees as inherent in all humans, regardless of the existence of any higher authority. In other words, our rational capacity as humans exists prior to the creation of any government or society so their absence is not necessarily a barrier to rational dialogue and agreement. Wight takes Locke's description of the state of nature and applies it to the international system. For Wight, dialogue and agreement between states is always possible even in an anarchical international system, because states are comprised of inherently rational people.

Wight also emphasized the existence of international law as a key indicator of the possibility of rational dialogue between states and he has also referred to the rationalist tradition as the 'Grotian tradition'. This reflected the influence of the famous seventeenth-century Dutch legal philosopher, Hugo Grotius, whose wide-ranging scholarly work is particularly noted for his contributions to the development of international law (you can read about Hugo Grotius in Key Thinker 4.2).

Hugo Grotius's most notable and influential work, *De Jure Belli et Pacis* (On the Law of War and Peace), first published in 1625, endeavoured to develop a general theory of international law that would provide the basis for regulating relations between states, even if they resorted to war. He drew upon the idea of natural law (the view that principles of right and justice can be discovered from human rational deduction, rather than religious doctrine or simply the established practices of states), and sometimes Christian theology, to argue that war could and should be regulated according to universally agreed principles. Grotius sought to constrain the propensity of what we would now call states (at the time they were variously described as kingdoms, duchies, principalities, republics, and so on), to go to war to resolve disputes. Additionally, Grotius sought to regulate the conduct of wars should they break out. Grotius was effectively articulating a vision, albeit a rather sketchy one, of an international society bound by law and agreed principles of conduct (Bull, 1977: 26–30).

KEY THINKER 4.2 HUGO GROTIUS

Hugo Grotius (1583–1685) was a Dutch jurist, statesman, and diplomat, widely viewed as a pioneer in the development of international law. A highly intelligent child, Grotius was admitted to university at the age of 11 and started publishing his work only five years later.

By his mid-20s, Grotius was already deeply involved in Dutch politics. Influenced by the often-violent political struggles in his own country (which led to him fleeing the Netherlands for France in 1621), and throughout Europe, Grotius's core objective was to develop a model of law that could serve to reduce the resort to violence in political conflict. His 1625 book *De Jure Belli ac Pacis* (On the Law of War and Peace), written while Grotius was in exile, is widely regarded as his masterpiece.

Grotius's influence in the development of modern international law was undoubtedly very substantial, although his focus was predominantly on relations between European states. For English School scholars he is also seen as an early proponent of the idea of an international society that could be governed not through force or resort to war, but through an enforceable international legal system.

One interesting legacy of Grotius' contribution to the development of the idea that states can and should be bound by international law is the constitution of the Netherlands which, uniquely, was revised in 1953 to include a stipulation requiring all Dutch governments to promote the continuing development of the international legal order.

Wight also described the Three Traditions as a debate between Machiavellians, Grotians, and Kantians, in reflection of three political thinkers who he thought most closely represented their core assumptions. Hedley Bull provides us with a succinct summary of what Wight meant by the Three Traditions:

> The Machiavellians he thought of crudely as the 'blood and iron and immorality men', the Grotians as the 'law and order and keep your word men', and the Kantians as 'the subversion and liberation and missionary men'. (Bull, 1976: 104)

Wight saw the boundaries between the Three Traditions as blurred, with none of them able to offer a complete account of international politics. He thought all of them offered some insight into international political reality, and this commitment to theoretical pluralism arguably remains a prominent feature of English School scholarship (Buzan, 2014: 37).

Wight's legacy is reflected in the fact that what today is now commonly known as the English School is also referred to by other names, especially in the IR literature before the early 1980s. These include 'rationalism', a 'Grotian' perspective, or a 'society of states' perspective. These are all different names for the foundational phase of the English School.

International system or society?

The work of Wight and other early rationalist thinkers, depict relations between sovereign states as displaying the minimal features of an international society, albeit a rather unique form of society.

Compare this to realism's reference to an anarchical international system. System merely suggests patterned interaction between two or more actors, whereas society carries a host of additional implications. Anarchy means the absence of government and also implies the absence of society as we usually understand it. So, as we have already noted, the description of an anarchical society appears almost contradictory. Indeed, Wight, argued that an international society is a society like no other.

The international society of states is a unique form of society in several important ways:

- International society is effectively a society of societies. States are the primary members of the international society, although Wight does note that there is a sense in which its ultimate members are individual humans. In other words, individuals have a dual identity—as members of domestic societies and as members of a wider human community. We are both citizens and humans

- The membership is very small—it has never been more than 200 states

- There is no average state—there are very substantial differences in the size, power, wealth, and influence of states. Nonetheless, all are formally equally sovereign under international law. Wight summarized Points 2 and 3 neatly as 'fewness and heterogeneity' (Wight, 1991: 139).

- A more unusual feature of international society is that its primary members—states—are more or less immortal (Wight, 1979: 107). States do appear and disappear, as a consequence of such things as civil conflict, war, or conquest (Yugoslavia is a relatively recent example), but this is historically infrequent.

Taking these features of international society as a whole, it may seem tenuous to claim the existence of a society in any meaningful sense. But, Wight argues, the clearest evidence of something more than a mere system of states existing is international law. Law suggests that some consensus, some shared understanding, exists between members. Law is central to the idea of a society. A society without law makes little sense in the modern world. Although international laws are clearly breached by some states and such breaches can go effectively unpunished, this is not to say that international law is insignificant. From an English School perspective, the fact that most international law is obeyed most of the time, by most states, reinforces the broad picture of states being meaningfully bound together within a common international legal framework.

Hedley Bull and the anarchical society of states

Wight exhibited a scholarly disdain for drawing out too many practical implications from his historical studies. That was undertaken by his younger colleague the Australian IR scholar Hedley Bull. In the full title of Bull's most famous work, first published in 1977, *The Anarchical Society: A Study of Order in World Politics*, Bull succinctly captures the essence of the foundational or 'classical' phase of the English School. Although Bull shares with many realists a concern with power and the role of the balance of power in particular, he depicts the realist tradition as deficient in a key respect: it fails to sufficiently appreciate the vital role played by shared rules and understandings (such as the 'common goals' we discussed in Section 4.2) in the preservation of international order.

Furthermore, Bull does not develop his claims about international society primarily in the abstract realm of theory, but from an interpretation of the historical behaviour of states. The rules and conventions of international society have evolved out of the dialogues between and shared practices of states, in spite of the evident differences between them. Bull does not suggest that international norms of state behaviour directly control the behaviour of states, but they do provide a social framework within which states act and try to justify and legitimize their actions (Hurrell, 2002: viii).

There are three key themes which thread through Bull's theory of international society:

- the primacy of order in the international system
- the institutions which sustain order
- the threats to order in the contemporary international system.

We will discuss each in turn, starting with the primacy of order in the international system.

The primacy of order in the international system

As the subtitle to his book suggests, the central question for Bull is: how is order maintained in world politics? Bull begins his discussion of order with a definition of order in social life more generally. Order denotes a particular stable pattern of social relations which results from the approximate achievement of what Bull describes as three 'elementary' and 'primary' goals, which, he argues, all forms of societies recognize as essential to their survival. These elementary goals are:

- *Security against violence*

  All societies endeavour to ensure that there is at least some degree of security against violence or harm. In international politics this is reflected in the international norm of non-intervention and the laws of war that govern violent conflict between states.

- *The sanctity of promises and agreements*

  All societies endeavour to ensure that promises are kept, and agreements will be fulfilled. This is a core principle in most legal systems, captured by the Latin expression *pacta sunt servanda* (agreements must be kept). In international politics the equivalent can be found in the creation of legally-binding treaties as well as other forms of less formal agreements between states.

- *The stability of possessions*

  All societies endeavour to ensure that there is at least some degree of stability to the possession of things.

Bull acknowledges that how these primary goals are understood or upheld varies very widely and there are numerous historical instances of them being breached. Again, it is important to emphasize that Bull is not making a purely abstract argument here; he is not suggesting only that in principle these goals should be considered primary. What he is claiming is that all types of society both presently and historically endeavour in some way or other to fulfil them, albeit with varying degrees of consistency or success, to ensure a minimal degree of social stability or order. Without a minimum agreement about the rules of human social life the enjoyment of higher goals is impossible. In other words, without order there can be no justice and no peace.

The primary goals are elementary in that in their absence it would be hard to speak of the existence of anything resembling a society. They are primary in that they are the preconditions for further, higher goals. To these primary goals should be added three elementary, primary goals that are unique to international society:

- the preservation of the system and society of states itself
- the maintenance of the independence or external sovereignty of individual states
- peace (as the absence of war under normal circumstances)

Having laid out the two sets of primary or elementary goals, one set applicable to all societies and the other applicable specifically to a society comprised of sovereign states, Bull goes on to define an international society:

> A *society of states* (or international society) exists when a group of states, conscious of certain common interests and common values, form a society in the sense that they conceive themselves to be bound by a common set of rules in their relations with one another, and share in the working of common institutions. (Bull, 1977: 13)

What did Bull mean by 'common interests and common values'? The key point to understand here is that Bull is not arguing that all the members of an international society share the same beliefs as if there were no significant ideological or cultural differences between them. Rather, the nature of the common values can be found in the consensus between states as to what the primary goals of international order are. It is the fact that, for all their differences, there is a sufficient level of common understanding between states of the rules and values necessary for the preservation of international order, which is key to Bull's argument.

Bull points out that not all historical examples of international systems of states can be described also as international societies. Bull cites the history of relations between Western and non-Western states between the sixteenth and late nineteenth centuries to illustrate this point. If we consider the interaction, say, between European colonial powers seeking to expand their control of foreign territories, and the local rulers of those territories, or the early interactions between imperial Britain and China, we find evidence of an international system but not an international society:

> There may be communication, exchanges of envoys or messengers and agreements – not only about trade but also about war, peace, and alliances. But these forms of interaction do not in themselves demonstrate that there is an international society . . . (they were) outside the framework of any shared conception of an international society of which the parties on both sides were members with like rights and duties. (Bull, 1977: 15)

This is not to say that the international society of states is an entirely modern phenomenon. Like Wight before him, Bull looks to earlier regional systems of states that preceded today's international society of states, such as the ancient Indian states system, the classical Greek city-state system, and the European states system from the sixteenth century through to the early twentieth century. Bull follows Wight in arguing that a common feature of those earlier international systems is that they 'were all founded upon a common culture or civilisation or at least some of the elements of such a civilisation' (Bull, 1977: 16). Bull is referring here to such things as a common language, a common religion, or a common view of the universe. Such shared attributes helped enable these systems to operate not merely as systems of states, but also as societies of states. These attributes helped to facilitate better communication and greater mutual understanding, thereby enabling a shared understanding of common rules and common institutions.

For Wight, an international society required some sense of cultural unity. However, Bull depicts contemporary international society of states as unique in a key respect: the absence of a common culture or civilization. In contrast to earlier societies of states, contemporary international society is composed of all states and is marked by significant variation in cultures and civilizations. For Bull, though, this is not a barrier to the maintenance of an international society. In *The Anarchical Society* Bull describes the contemporary world order as a 'world international society' in which 'there is at least a diplomatic or elite culture comprising the common intellectual culture of modernity' Bull (1977: 317). What Bull means here is that there is a common intellectual culture, such as common languages (notably the increasingly global use of English), common scientific understandings, and some common understandings that arise from the involvement, albeit unevenly and unequally, of most states in the global economy and technological development.

Bull concedes, however, that the shared elite intellectual culture had shallow roots in many parts of the world and that it was 'weighted in favour of the dominant cultures of the West'. This leads Bull to conclude *The Anarchical Society* with a warning:

> Like the world international society, the cosmopolitan culture on which it depends may need to absorb non-Western elements to a much greater degree if it is to be genuinely universal and provide a foundation for a universal international society. (Bull, 1977: 317)

Bull wrote those words more than 40 years ago, when the Global South was raising its voice in various international fora, such as the UN General Assembly. Many decolonized, newly independent states joined together to protest at what they perceived as an international system dominated by the developed Western states that was heavily weighted against their interests (for more on this see Chapters 5 and 9).

By today's standards, Bull's acknowledgement in the *Anarchical Society* of the continuing dominance of the Global North over the Global South even after most colonized countries had achieved their independence seems rather insipid. When he made those remarks however, most of mainstream IR paid comparatively little attention to voices from or the interests of the Global South, or to questions of international justice. Bull was to return to the theme in a somewhat more strident tone a few years later and this helped to stimulate the further development of the English School in a new more solidarist direction. We will return to this in Section 4.5 of this chapter.

The Institutions of World Order

How, then, from an English School perspective is international order maintained? For realists, it is the balance of power between states or groups of states, either regionally or globally, that is the principle source of stability in the international system. The English School sees the balance of power, however, as an incomplete explanation of international order.

We noted in Section 4.1 that Bull's definition of a society of states ended with reference to the working of 'common institutions', by which he meant established habits and practices in state behaviour that served the realization of the 'common goals' that all states pursue. In Bull's analysis, these institutions are the principle underwriters of world order. These institutions do not deprive states of their central role as the principal actors in world politics, but they symbolize the existence of an international society which is more than the sum of its members.

What then are the institutions of international society which sustain international order? Bull identified five:

- The balance of power
- International law
- Diplomacy
- War
- Great Powers

We will look at each one in turn.

The Balance of Power

In common with most realists, Bull emphasizes the importance of the balance of power in maintaining international stability and order. Balances of power can occur at a system-wide level (such as that between the US and the USSR, during the Cold War) or they can emerge at regional levels. There has been a long-running debate about whether balances of power arise by chance, or are the result of deliberate actions by states. Bull acknowledges the ambiguities surrounding the concept of a balance of power, but nonetheless suggests it is hard to analyse international politics without reference to it. Whether or not they are the product of the conscious actions of states, balances of power are important contributors to international order.

The chief function of the balance of power, Bull argues, has been to preserve the states-system itself and this, of course, has worked to the advantage of dominant states, which Bull refers to as the 'Great Powers'. But it is also important to understand that a balance of power is also crucial for the survival of smaller or less powerful states. In helping to prevent the overwhelming dominance of one state, balances of power work to enable the operation of other institutions of international order. In effect, they inhibit the capacity of a state to act with absolute impunity. For all the ambiguities and uncertainties surrounding the balance of power in both theory and practice, Bull sees it as playing a key role in ensuring that the anarchical society of states does not transform into a universal empire controlled by one state.

International Law

The second of the principal institutions of international society is international law, which Bull defines as 'a body of rules which binds states and other agents in world politics in their relations with one another and is considered to have the status of law'. We have already seen in Section 4.2 that Martin Wight saw international law as a key indicator of the existence of an international society. Bull echoes Wight and rejects the common realist contention that international law is not really law because there is no international sovereign power to enforce it.

How does an international society theorist respond to the realist (or someone who is simply cynical about international law) who points to examples of state violations of international law that go unpunished? Bull responds by arguing that the fact that international law exists in the absence of a single global sovereign power does not mean that it does not deserve the name law; enforcement is not a necessary feature of legal rules (Bull, 1977: 130). Particular cases of rule-breaking do not in themselves provide sufficient evidence that international law is a sham, just as the violation of laws in domestic societies are not usually seen to render those laws meaningless. Similarly, most states obey international law most of the time despite the difficulties of enforcing it.

A second response is to examine the historical arguments of the law-breakers. It is surely significant, Bull argues, that states rarely break international law without attempting to justify their acts according to another international legal principle (Bull, 1977: 132–133). The most common example of this is the way in which Article 51 of the UN Charter, which proclaims the right of states to self-defence, is invoked by states to justify their acts of aggression which are judged by others to contravene the spirit of the UN charter. Perhaps the single most transparent example of the substantive impact of law in international relations, however, concerns the progressive outlawing of war. In the last seventy years, international society has seen the emergence of a body of legal rules which place substantial limitations on the right of states to resort to force. In particular, the Charter of the UN established an emphatic prohibition on the use of force, except for unilateral or collective self-defence.

For Bull, international law's importance does not rest on whether states actually have a profound respect for international law. Some may do, but many states may also obey international law out of habit, or because a more powerful state is pushing them to conform. States may also be motivated by the principle of reciprocity. They respect the sovereignty of others, keep agreements and abide by the laws of war because they think it is in their mutual interests to do so. For Bull, in the end, international law is simply a 'social reality'. The importance of international law is ultimately established in the fact that states 'so often judge it in their interests to conform to it' (Bull, 1977: 140).

Diplomacy

The third institution of international society underpinning international order is diplomacy. The historic form of diplomacy has been one of a bilateral relationship between two sovereign states conducted through diplomatic missions (such as embassies and their staff). Bull argues that the fact that the conduct of diplomacy entails the acceptance of various rules and conventions provides evidence of the existence of an international society (Bull, 1977: 167).

During the twentieth century, multilateral diplomacy in forums such as the UN, the EU, and other inter-governmental organizations developed considerably, which some might see as indicating the declining significance of bilateral diplomatic relations conducted by professional diplomats. Additionally, there has been an increase in direct contact between heads of state, and the proliferation of powerful non-state actors in the international system. However, Bull responds by noting that in today's diverse international society marked by multiple cultures, political systems, and identities the diplomat's skills of communication, negotiation, information gathering, and the minimization of friction remain invaluable. In any case, diplomacy is symbolically important. Bull notes that

> The remarkable willingness of states of all regions, cultures persuasions and stages of development to embrace often strange and archaic diplomatic procedures that arose in Europe in another age is today one of the few visible indications of universal acceptance of the idea of international society. (Bull, 1977: 183)

It remains the case today, that such things as the withdrawal of an ambassador or the expulsion of diplomatic representatives by one state in protest against the actions of another continue to have important symbolic and communicative functions in relations between states.

War

The fourth, and perhaps most controversial, of Hedley Bull's institutions of international society is war:

> War and the threat of war are not the only determinants of the shape of the international system; but they are so basic that even the terms we use to describe the system—great powers and small powers, alliances and spheres of influence, balances of power and hegemony—are scarcely intelligible except in relation to war and the threat of war. (Bull, 1977: 187)

124 INTRODUCTION TO INTERNATIONAL RELATIONS THEORIES

In treating war as one of the regulatory institutions of international society, Bull could be seen to be accepting (as many realists do), that the risk of war is a permanent feature of international politics and, further, that it can be a legitimate instrument of foreign policy. Certainly, Bull notes that war has, historically at least, been seen to have positive attributes as a means to not only protect the sovereignty of states, but also to preserve international order. Bull observes, however, that international society has shifted ground regarding the legitimacy and utility of war. Since the early twentieth century, international society has sought to regulate war by restricting the grounds for going to war and establishing limitations on how war is conducted. He also notes that it is more the threat of war rather than war itself that increasingly serves to regulate the conduct of states, especially since the advent of nuclear weapons.

Writing in the 1970s, Bull made two key observations about war. First, that there was a growing reluctance to use war as an instrument of law enforcement; and, secondly, that although wars between sovereign states were declining, other forms of organized violence, involving non-state actors (such as civil wars, violent actions by national liberation groups, and so on), were becoming more prominent (Bull, 1977: 199). Bull's reference to a growing reluctance to use war as an instrument of law enforcement was in reference to controlling the conduct of states. However, the use of war as an instrument of international law enforcement, in the form of armed interventions for example, in response to the emergence of new kinds of organized violence became especially prominent (and controversial) after the end of the Cold War. It also became a subject of concern among a new generation of English School scholars; a point we return to in Section 4.4.

Great Powers

The fifth and final institution of international society for Hedley Bull are what he calls 'the Great Powers'. For Bull, the hallmark of a Great Power was not simply a matter of its comparative military strength or economic power, but also its adherence to 'special rights and duties' (which is captured in Wight's labelling of them as 'Great Responsibles'). Great powers have a right, Bull argues, to play a major role in determining global peace and security issues that affect international society as a whole. However, they should accept the duty also to modify their policies in accordance with the interests of that international society. Bull was often highly critical of the failure of great powers, notably the Cold War superpowers—the US and USSR—to act responsibly, i.e., in the interests of international society as a whole.

Although Bull's reference to great powers has something of an old-fashioned ring to it, the responsibilities and conduct of today's powerful states, such as the US, Russia, and China, undoubtedly remain subjects of widespread academic and public debate.

Threats to the Contemporary International Order

The Anarchical Society appeared in 1977 during a period of *détente*—the relaxation of tensions between the superpowers (see Key events 2.4 in Chapter 2). As we noted earlier, this was a time when states in the Global South (widely referred to at the time as the Third World—see Key concept 5.1 in Chapter 5) were also becoming more vocal about what they perceived to be the inequalities and injustices of the international system. The IR literature was beginning to reflect this and shift its attention away from a long-standing preoccupation with East–West relations to a greater concern with the Global North–South relationship. On the margins of the IR discipline, critical approaches were highlighting the inherently exploitative nature of the international capitalist system and the economic, social, and political injustices that this generated. It is worth noting that some of the key contributors to these radical critiques did not come from the Anglo-American mainstream of the IR discipline, but from the Global South, notably Latin America (we discuss this more fully in Chapter 5, Section 5.3).

Even if *The Anarchical Society* itself does not overtly display any progressivist or reformist zeal, Bull does concede that the order provided by modern international society is precarious and imperfect. In line with this, in the latter parts of the book, Bull turns his attention to challenges to international order as well as various proposals for radical reform of the international system coming from both Liberal and Marxist perspectives. In the main, Bull was sceptical then about the prospects of radical change. He constantly reiterates that much reformist thinking either overstates the significance of increasing interdependence of states, presupposes the imminent demise of the anarchical states system, or requires that it be overthrown comprehensively (see Bull 1977: chapter 11). You can hear realist echoes in Bull's constant reiteration that it is from within the existing system of states that any reform must come. There is order, resting upon a minimum level of consensus between the states in that system, but it is fragile. Significant change will only come when that consensus is deepened substantially because states come to see themselves as having a greater degree of common interests than currently acknowledged.

Only a few years later, however, Bull begins to seemingly shift ground, from the predominantly *pluralist* standpoint of *The Anarchical Society* to one that has more *solidarist* overtones. We will now examine the emergence of a solidarist wing in the English School, starting with a distinct turn in Bull's work.

4.4 **THE SECOND PHASE: ORDER VS JUSTICE**

Many commentators have remarked upon the ambiguities in Bull's work, especially when it comes to the question of order versus justice in world politics. *The Anarchical Society* exhibited an overriding concern with order in world politics, but, as we noted earlier, it also concluded with a warning that the future of international society was in part dependent on the degree to which the still emerging world 'cosmopolitan culture' became less weighted in favour of 'the dominant cultures of the West' and therefore more genuinely universal (Bull, 1977: 317).

Only a few years later, Bull returned to this theme in a more forceful fashion in the 1983 Hagey Lectures entitled 'Justice in International Relations' delivered not long before his untimely death in 1985 (the original lectures are out of print but can now be found as Bull, 2000). In those lectures Bull examined what he called the 'revolt against Western dominance'.

Hedley Bull and the 'Revolt against Western dominance'

Bull was not the first to refer to the concept of a 'Revolt Against the West'. Indeed, it can be found in British scholarly works as far back as the 1950s, when it often carried connotations of 'a sense of dismay and disapproval' at the anti-colonial struggle and the emergence of an anti-Western bloc of post-colonial states (Hall, 2017: 345). Such reactionary connotations are not overtly evident in Bull's analysis, although he stopped short of expressing unequivocal personal sympathy with the rise of anti-Western sentiment in the formerly colonized states. Bull's emphasis was much more on the inescapable significance of the revolt for the future development of international society.

This revolt, Bull argued, centred around grievances that stemmed directly from European colonization and continued to strengthen in the post-colonial era. As Bull saw it, the demands for greater justice coming from what was then widely referred to as The Third World fell into a number of groups:

- The equal right of sovereignty and independence
- The just and equal application of the principle of self-determination
- The right to racial equality
- Greater international economic justice
- The demand for justice 'in matters of the spirit of the mind'—in other words, the protest against the intellectual and cultural dominance of the West (the term Third World is discussed further in Key concept 5.1).

Bull argued that, for all their differences, many formerly colonized states shared a sense of injustice, feeling that the present society of states discriminates against them as states, nations, races, and ethnic groups. In their view, the international society is dominated by a core of Western developed states whose interests and values continue to predominate. Although Bull was quite circumspect about the validity and consistency of many of the Third World's claims against the West, he was clear that nonetheless they constituted a significant challenge to the Western-dominated international order and therefore to the preservation of the international society of states in its present form.

Bull was hardly alone in recognizing the significance of growing Third World resistance to Western domination. Other scholars, mostly outside the IR theory mainstream, were far more strident than Bull in their criticism of Western exploitation and domination of the Third World states (we explore this more fully in Chapters 5 and 9). What makes Bull's analysis significant, though, is that it was coming from within a mainstream IR theoretical perspective, noted for its generally sceptical attitude about the prospects for significant reform of the international system. Not surprisingly then, Bull saw any radical transformation of the international system as neither possible nor desirable. Nonetheless, the Third World put the West on the spot. Bull believed that states in the Global South were not hostile to the idea of an international society itself. By participating in its institutions and abiding by its customs, Bull claimed, they were accepting the broad framework of international society laid down by European states over the last

400 years. Third World states would prefer a stable international order like any other states, but not at the expense of international justice and fairness.

By today's standards, Bull's depiction of challenges to Western dominance written nearly 40 years ago would be seen by many scholars, especially postcolonial IR theorists, as problematic and worryingly indifferent to the complexities of the history, politics of identity, and global political outlooks across the Global South. Bull depicts the present international society as essentially European in origin and design and this is an increasingly questioned claim. Additionally, whether all states in the Global South willingly accept international society in its present form, as Bull seems to suggest, or simply have had little choice but to conform to it, is a matter of debate (Hall, 2017). All these issues are explored further in Chapter 9.

Nonetheless, Bull's depiction of a revolt against the West does touch upon themes that have been developed much more thoroughly in more recent scholarly work on the legacy of colonialism, not least his recognition of resistance to the intellectual and cultural dominance of the West. Here we see the emergence of a more solidarist conception of international society in Bull's work, especially in its analysis of the relationship between order and justice in international politics. Contemporary postcolonialists would emphasize that the West's dominance in cultural and intellectual spheres was not because of any inherent superiority but evidence of the inequalities of power between the Global North and the Global South reinforced by residual colonialist attitudes within the West. These attitudes were expressed in a mix of outright hostility towards non-Western perspectives, ignorance of them, or indifference towards them. The key implication of Bull's analysis was more pragmatically focused: the principles upon which the society of states operates requires the dominant developed states to take the claims of the Global South seriously whatever the West might think of them.

Recall here our examination of the pluralist perspective on international society in Section 4.2. Pluralists see the preservation of international order as necessarily prior to addressing any demands for greater international social justice. Bull's earlier work very much reflected this viewpoint. In the Hagey Lectures, however, Bull seems to have shifted his position in arguing that the preservation of international order may now *require* greater international justice. Bull is not making an overtly normative argument here, in contrast to more contemporary English School solidarists. He is not unequivocally endorsing demands that international society addresses the continued exploitation of the Global South by the Global North. Instead, Bull argues that international society, by its own long established operating principles alone had to respond to demands for greater international justice. If the rules of the contemporary international society were the historical product of consensus and custom among its member states, as English School scholars including Bull had consistently argued, then if the membership of that society changes, as it had because of decolonization, those rules and customs can and should also change. Failure on the part of the developed states to acknowledge the demands for greater justice was not only a strategy that put the fragile consensus underpinning international society at risk, it was also hard to justify in terms of the very operating principles of the society of states.

Bull also highlighted the increasingly widespread view that global justice did not only concern the fair and equitable treatment of states, but also individuals. The second half of the twentieth century was marked by the growing recognition 'that the question of justice concerns what is due not only to states and nations but to all individuals in an imagined community of mankind' (Bull, 2000: 220). This was evidenced by the considerable development of international human rights law since 1945, along with the growth of what Bull called a 'cosmopolitan awareness' within Western developed states. This had led, in Bull's view, to governments of developed states acknowledging, albeit to very varying degrees, that their obligations to promote human development and welfare did not stop at their borders but extended across the globe.

In the nearly four decades since the publication of the Hagey Lectures, it is evident that the issues of economic exploitation, global poverty, racial inequality, and Western cultural dominance have become much more visible in both academic and public debate across the globe. Of course, this is not say that a consensus has been established around them. Nonetheless, the establishment of official Overseas Development Assistance (foreign aid) programmes in most Western states since the 1970s, alongside the considerable growth in Western-based NGOs and private charitable organizations focused on international development, global poverty, and so on could be seen to underscore Bull's claim about heightened awareness in the West around questions of international justice. How effective that greater awareness has been in substantively addressing the key questions of justice confronting today's world is, of course, a matter of considerable debate.

States as agents of 'a world common good'

The need to rethink the relationship between order and justice was reinforced also by the identification of global issues which transcended territorial borders and could only be addressed by the society of states as a whole, such as environmental problems, human rights abuses, and global poverty. To address such dangers, argues Bull, requires us to think in terms of a 'world common good'. This meant moving beyond developing a solidarity among states that is driven primarily by their mutual interest in national self-preservation. Rather, Bull says, 'the world common good to which I refer is the common interest not of states, but of the human species in maintaining itself' (Bull, 2000: 222).

A good dose of pessimism remains in Bull's approach. Even if the concept of a world common good is widely acknowledged, it is another thing to devise policies that might realize it. The world is still organized as a system of states and, in Bull's view, it is likely to remain that way. Nonetheless:

> The Western peoples, who created the global international system of today, have a supreme interest in sustaining a viable international order that will endure . . . It is not credible that such an order can be maintained unless the states of the Third World, representing as they do the majority of states and the greater part of the world's population, believe themselves to have a stake in it. (Bull, 2000: 243)

In concluding that states will increasingly have to act as 'agents for a world common good', Bull is effectively arguing for a society of states *plus*. If a more cooperative world is going to emerge then Western states will have to contribute actively to the development of a feeling of confidence in the society of states among the states in the Global South. Only then are they likely to act fully to preserve order and contribute to the resolution of the various problems that confront us not only as citizens of states but as members of the universal human community. And only then will our Western concerns carry significant weight with them. None of this would be easy, Bull concluded, and at times terrible choices between order and justice will have to be made.

The ascendancy of solidarism in the post-Cold War era

The impact of the apparent shift in Bull's position, suggested by The Hagey Lectures, was not immediate. The lectures were delivered during the Second Cold War, a period of heightened tension between the US and USSR. With the end of the Cold War, however, came a renewed scholarly interest in the English School. In the mid 1990s, a new generation of young IR scholars sought to revisit and revive the English School, starting with a reassessment of Hedley Bull's work.

Scholars such as Nicholas Wheeler and Tim Dunne read Bull's later work as exhibiting a visible shift from a pluralist to a solidarist stance within the broader English School tradition. They saw in Bull's later work 'explorations on the edge of solidarism' (Wheeler and Dunne, 1996: 93). In their view, The Hagey Lectures amount to

> nothing less than an attempt to think through how the advanced industrial states and the poorer states might be drawn into a conversation as to what constitutes the world common good at the end of the twentieth century. (Wheeler and Dunne, 1996: 100)

Wheeler and Dunne acknowledge that Bull's argument was at heart an essentially pragmatic one: the continuation of a stable international order required addressing the demands for equity and justice emanating from the Global South. Nonetheless, they insist that it also had a clear normative dimension to it in that 'Bull was arguing that the Western states had both a long-term interest and a moral obligation in strengthening justice in world politics' (Wheeler and Dunne, 1996: 101).

Once again, shifts in the historical context shed useful light on how theories of international politics evolve in response. In contrast to the international circumstances—the Cold War—in which Bull first explored the question of justice in international politics, the revived interest in the English School occurred in the decade after the end of the Cold War in 1989. The 1990s began with widespread declarations, most notably by the then US President, George Bush, of a 'New World Order' emerging out of the ashes of the Cold War. That decade was also marked by a series of armed humanitarian interventions by Western-led coalitions of states, beginning with Iraq in 1991 (in response to its invasion of Kuwait), followed rapidly by Somalia in 1992, Bosnia in 1992–1995, Haiti in 1994, and Kosovo in 1998. Some of these were explicitly authorized by the UN Security Council whereas others (such as the 1998 NATO-led intervention in Kosovo) were not. Additionally there was the highly controversial failure to intervene in an unfolding genocide in Rwanda in 1994.

Perhaps unsurprisingly, this decade of crises stimulated a rapid escalation of debate in both academic and policy circles about the pros and cons of armed interventions in the name of humanitarian values. There was also debate about the changing nature of war in the post-Cold War era. Scholars such as Mary Kaldor and others were arguing that warfare was decreasingly arising out of conflict between states (Iraq's invasion of Kuwait in 1990, being a rare example) and increasingly out of conflict within states or involving nationalist, ethnic, or religious disputes that straddled state boundaries. These 'new wars' often involved a wide range of actors such as private militias, armed groups claiming specific national, religious, or ethnic allegiances, warlords, and even criminal gangs (Kaldor, 1999). As such they were seen to place unique demands upon the international community to respond appropriately and effectively to prevent large-scale humanitarian crises and disasters. In many cases the conflicts were depicted in terms of states failing to protect their own peoples, or the breakdown of a state resulting in horrific crimes, such as the widespread killing of civilians, ethnic cleansing, or genocide.

The challenges posed by a decade of crises and interventions was a central theme of the UN Secretary General's 1999 annual report to the UN General Assembly (see Key events 4.1). In his speech Kofi Annan recognized that a decade of violent conflicts raised profound questions about the obligations UN member states had regarding large scale violations of human rights within ostensibly sovereign states.

KEY EVENT 4.1 UN SECRETARY GENERAL KOFI ANNAN'S 1999 REPORT TO THE UN GENERAL ASSEMBLY

In his 1999 annual report to the UN General Assembly, UN Secretary General Kofi Annan noted that the UN Charter, drafted 50 years earlier, declared that 'armed force shall not be used, save in the common interest'. A decade of crises and often controversial armed interventions, however, had raised profound questions about the meaning of the common interest: 'Who shall define it? Who will defend it? Under whose authority? And with what means of intervention?', Annan asked.

The international community, Annan argued, was entering a new era in which the traditional notion of sovereignty (a state's absolute right to non-interference in its affairs), 'can no longer do justice to the aspirations of peoples everywhere to attain their fundamental freedoms'. Annan depicted a tension between traditional understandings of state sovereignty and 'individual sovereignty', brought about by a 'renewed consciousness of the right of every individual to control his or her own destiny'.

In Annan's view, the international community urgently needed therefore to reflect on the duties and responsibilities of states, particularly long-standing presumptions about national sovereignty and national interest.

Recognizing that states would continue to put their national interests first, Annan argued that

> A new, more broadly defined, more widely conceived definition of national interest in the new century would, I am convinced, induce States to find far greater unity in the pursuit of such basic (UN) Charter values as democracy, pluralism, human rights, and the rule of law (Annan, 1999).

> In his concluding remarks, Annan referred to a 'developing international norm in favour of intervention to protect civilians from wholesale slaughter'. Any such intervention must, however, be based on 'legitimate and universal principles, if it is to enjoy the sustained support of the world's peoples'. In effect, Annan was questioning the right of states to hide behind the principle of sovereignty when crimes against humanity were perceived to be taking place within their borders.
>
> **Reference**
> Annan, Kofi (1999) 'Secretary General Presents His Annual Report to General Assembly', UN, Press release SG/SM/7136 GA/9596

There are some clear commonalities between the reference in Annan's 1999 report to a 'common interest' and Bull's explorations of the idea of states as 'agents of a world common good', which he made more than a decade before. Around the same time, some English School scholars such as Dunne and Wheeler began to push Bull's somewhat hesitant solidarist turn much further, and argue, like Annan, that states had greater international humanitarian responsibilities than most of them were prepared to acknowledge (Wheeler and Dunne, 1998; Wheeler, 2000).

Nick Wheeler's *Saving Strangers: Humanitarian Intervention in International Society* (2000) offers one of the most comprehensive surveys of humanitarian intervention both before and after the Cold War, viewed through distinctly solidarist English School lenses. Its conclusion starts off by quoting Annan's comments about the need for states to develop greater unity to realize the core values of the UN Charter and goes on to make the case for the further development of 'the solidarist project'. For Wheeler, states were the only actors with the resources to intervene to stop such things as mass murder or genocide, even though historically governments have been 'notoriously unreliable as rescuers'. For Wheeler, the reluctance of states to acknowledge their moral obligations to the political and economic suffering of 'strangers' (i.e., those living outside of their own borders) requires public action. What is needed, Wheeler argues is for scholars, human rights activists, and the media to mobilize public opinion behind a shift in 'moral consciousness' in support of both the promotion and enforcement of human rights. This would not guarantee that states will intervene when morally required to do so. However, Wheeler argues, it will 'heighten awareness on the part of state leaders that they will be held accountable if they decide not to save strangers' (Wheeler, 2000: 310).

Wheeler was making his argument just prior to the US-led invasion of Iraq in 2003. The consequences of that invasion in combination with the US invasion of Afghanistan the year before and the military intervention in Libya eight years later, have undoubtedly severely dampened the willingness of Western states to engage in armed, supposedly humanitarian, interventions. They also severely eroded public support in the West for such actions. Indeed the controversial history of post-Cold War military interventions presented significant challenges for English School solidarist thought and as we shall see influenced its further development.

The English School and 'good international citizenship'

Much of the work by the new generation of English School scholars that followed Bull's 1983 Hagey Lectures focused on the prospects for greater solidarism in Western post-Cold War foreign policies, centred around the idea of the state as 'a good international citizen' (Linklater and Suganami, 2006: chapter 9) or a 'good state' (Lawler, 2005, 2013a). You can read more about the concept of a good international citizen in Key concept 4.1.

⟫⟫ KEY CONCEPT 4.1 GOOD INTERNATIONAL CITIZENSHIP

The idea that states could and should be good international citizens has been a prominent feature in the work of solidarist English School scholars since the 1990s (Linklater, 1992; Wheeler and Dunne, 1998; Linklater and Suganami, 2006). The origins of the concept lie within liberal internationalism, which emerged out of post-1945 European liberal and social democratic schools of political thought. In essence it promotes the view that progressive democratic states should endeavour to see their core principles reflected also in their foreign policy outlooks.

The notion that states should have 'purposes beyond themselves' (Bull, 2000), has also threaded through the foreign policies of a select number of Western states since the 1960s, most notably the Scandinavian states, the Netherlands, and Canada (Lawler, 2005).

The origin of the phrase 'good international citizen' is commonly accredited to Lester Pearson, the Canadian Liberal Prime minister during the 1960s. It was revived by Gareth Evans, the Foreign Minister in Australian Labor governments in the 1980s (Evans, 1990). It clearly also informed the thinking of Robin Cook, Foreign Secretary in the UK Labour government elected in 1997.

Both Pearson (who as Canada's foreign minister received the 1957 Nobel Peace Prize for his contribution to the establishment of UN peace keeping), and Evans deployed the term in reference to highlight what they saw as the humanitarian responsibilities of democratic states to work to reduce global conflict and injustice through such things as the enhancement of the international legal system, the promotion of human rights, and increasing the provision of Overseas Development Assistance (ODA) by developed states.

In the wake of Western-led military interventions in the 1990s and early twenty-first century, however, what some see as the inescapably colonialist and imperialistic undertones of much of Western internationalist intentions and actions has been increasingly subjected to scholarly critique (which is examined further in Chapter 9).

Nicholas Wheeler and Timothy Dunne explicitly locate the idea of the good international citizen within the English School and connect it directly with Bull's considerations of the tension between order and justice. They see Bull's proposition in the Hagey Lectures that states will increasingly have to recognize the multiple demands for greater international and global justice and the responsibilities they generate as providing the basis for a litmus test of good international citizenship. Going on to assess the 'tendencies' of the society of states at the end of the 1990s, however, they detect an 'uneven performance' (Wheeler and Dunne, 1996: 107).

This could to be seen to accord with Bull's own scepticism about the realistic prospects for greater solidarism between states. Dunne and Wheeler see it, however, as a consequence of the limited 'cosmopolitan moral awareness' of Western states. In other words, they do not see the barrier to greater solidarism in international society as simply a consequence of an anarchical society of states, as realists and some pluralist English School scholars tend to argue. Dunne and Wheeler see it more as a failure of national visions and will. States, on this view, need to look beyond their narrow self-interests and the confines of sovereignty and work harder at building an international consensus that will facilitate greater action in addressing the many causes of global human misery. As they interpret it, Bull's own intellectual journey from pluralism to solidarism 'represents an important path down which theorists and practitioners should travel' (Wheeler and Dunne, 1996: 92).

The view of the very purpose of scholarship that underpins Dunne and Wheeler's assessment bears some similarities with that found in Critical Theory (which is the subject of Chapter 6). It rejects a traditional depiction of the IR scholar as purely a dispassionate and objective observer in favour of an academic who is committed to robust scholarly practice but also wears their normative heart—the values driving the analysis—on their sleeve. At the same time, it coheres with the classical English School's objective of offering a middle way or *via media* between realism and idealism, or between pragmatism and an overly abstract idealism. Wheeler and Dunne argue that

> (Bull) saw the role of the liberal intellectual as one which must be both distant enough from the corridors of power to be critical and yet sufficiently close to diplomatic practice to realise that moral progress has to be negotiated in this world of states (Wheeler and Dunne, 1996: 107).

Other scholars have examined the foreign policies of Western states noted for their explicit commitment to internationalism in their foreign policies. Although few if any states could claim to match an ideal-type good international citizen, the foreign policies of countries such as the Scandinavian states, the Netherlands, and Canada, are seen to contain elements that seemingly resonate with the solidarist English School perspective (Dolman, 1979; Verhoeve, 1979; Pratt, 1989 and 1990; Stokke, 1989; Lumsdaine, 1993; Lawler 2005 and 2013a). To greater or lesser degrees, the foreign policies of these states reflects an understanding of their national identity that seemingly corresponds with Bull's notion of states as 'local agents of a world common good'.

THINK CRITICALLY 4.2 STATES AS 'AGENTS OF A WORLD COMMON GOOD'?

Think about states with which you are most familiar.

Do you see evidence of them acting as good international citizens or local agents of a world common good?

- If so, how would you explain this and are there specific issue areas where this is especially evident?
- If you see little or no evidence, do you think this is a country-specific issue, applicable to most or perhaps all states, or a problem with the notions of 'world common good' or 'good international citizenship'?

The English School and Critical Theory

One of the most prominent representatives of Critical IR Theory (which we discuss in Chapter 6), Andrew Linklater, draws upon a synthesis of theoretical approaches, among which the English School figures substantially. In his 1998 book *The Transformation of Political Community*, Linklater detects a need for fundamental reform of international society, in particular its continuing reliance on rigid understandings of sovereignty and the national interest (Linklater, 1998).

The central theme in Linklater's analysis, one which chimes with both the cosmopolitanism of the solidarist perspective and Critical Theory's promotion of human emancipation (which you can read about in Section 6.2 in Chapter 6), is the prevalence of *exclusionary* politics and practices. Exclusionary practices are those that serve to divide communities—national, international, or trans-national—rather than unify them. These lead Linklater to ask what kinds of communities could and, in his view, should emerge that might reduce the exclusionary dimensions of the contemporary international order?

Linklater's argument can be seen as an updated version of Wight's account of the 'Three Traditions', that we examined in Section 4.2 of this chapter. Wight's Three Traditions were realism, rationalism, and revolutionism. Linklater's trilogy is comprised of pluralism, solidarism, and a post-sovereign form of relations between states. Recognizing that profound differences exist between states, Linklater suggests that the development of international society can be viewed through these three analytical lenses. He sees the pluralist conception of international society as an appropriate framework for analysing relations between markedly different states. Its primary purpose would be to ensure peaceful coexistence rather than pursue a moral consensus. For those states which have developed a consensus about key moral principles, however, the solidarist model of international society should be possible to achieve, at least amongst themselves.

Finally, for a number of what Linklater calls 'like-minded societies' a more cosmopolitan model of an international community could evolve. Here, states that are 'keen to establish closer forms of political co-operation' could agree to give up some of their sovereign powers. This third form of an international society echoes what Martin Wight called revolutionism, i.e., what others have labelled a Kantian or idealist perspective. To label it as such, however, would be to suggest that it is an entirely abstract vision disconnected from reality. Yet Linklater sees the development of European integration since the 1950s, which culminated in today's European Union, as offering concrete evidence of the potential for at least some states to contemplate a fundamental revision of the idea of national sovereignty and move beyond the limits of the existing international system of sovereign states.

Linklater's focus on the differences between states and how these differences might impact on the prospects for greater solidarism in relations between them produces a more complex depiction of the potential development of international society. For Linklater, any further development or deepening of the societal dimensions of relations need not occur across the whole of international society at the same time. He clearly wants to acknowledge the dangers inherent in presuming that the solidarist case for the deepening of international society should take its cues solely from Western universalist strands of progressive thinking, which tend to frame the future within a one size fits all Western liberal mindset.

Here we see the clear influence of Critical Theory on Linklater's argument. Linklater draws upon the work of the noted Critical Theorist, Jurgen Habermas, on 'discourse ethics' (which is outlined in Key concept 6.3 in Chapter 6) to argue that the advancement of international society will require authentically open and free dialogue between different worldviews. The outcome of such dialogue cannot be presupposed and what Habermas called the 'unforced force of the better argument' should prevail. In other words, if we want to reduce or eradicate exclusionary politics, then those who have been previously excluded must be included in the dialogue.

Linklater proposes that such dialogue will take different forms and proceed at different speeds according to the relationships between the participants in the dialogue (we discuss Linklater's argument for the transformation of community in more detail in Section 6.4 of Chapter 6). We cannot presume, for example, that the EU provides a model of relations between states that can simply be reproduced elsewhere in the world. The EU emerged out of particular historical circumstances and between states that despite their differences were sufficiently like-minded to deepen their relations with each other because they also shared a lot of cultural, political, and economic commonalities.

In more recent work, Linklater takes a somewhat different tack while continuing to draw upon a mix of theoretical insights from the English School, Critical Theory and historical sociology. Linklater continues to investigate the universalizing and exclusionary assumptions threading through the West's historical rise to international political and intellectual dominance. This is carried out through detailed and thorough examination of how the West has struggled with its participation in causing harm or using violence against others, while also endeavouring to limit both (Linklater 2011 and 2017). It is difficult to capture the complex arguments Linklater puts forward in a few words, but he endeavours to show how people in very different global locales can have remarkably similar views about harm and violence. Linklater also detects in the history of international society signs of successful constraints, through developments in international law for example, on the resort to harm and violence. In essence, the history of international society is depicted as a contestation between 'civilizing' and 'decivilizing' processes, in which Linklater tentatively hopes that a global civilizing process will ultimately prevail. In essence, Linklater is endeavouring to offer a highly nuanced form of solidarism that is much more sensitive to the challenges of improving the human condition in a culturally and politically diverse world.

More recent English School scholarship in the solidarist vein maintains the commitment to explore and promote the pursuit of greater international justice and the growth of a global moral consciousness. It is, however, increasingly sensitive to questions of difference and the complex politics of identity that play out on the global stage. In their comprehensive reassessment of the English School, Linklater and Suganami (2006) depict the pursuit of a more solidaristic international society as still both vital and necessary. However, the realization of such a society will not be easy and they concede that English School solidarism requires a much greater sensitivity to the moral, political, and economic claims of all the various communities that make up the global human community. The rules and moral norms of a more solidaristic international society must be based upon 'sound consensual legitimacy', in other words the genuine agreement of all to whom the rules and norms will apply (Linklater and Suganami, 2006: 271).

Pluralist scepticism about the prospects and virtues of greater solidarism

The solidarist wing of the English School acquired greater prominence against the post-Cold War backdrop of a rise in Western-led interventions carried out in the name of universal humanitarian values. The outcomes of those interventions proved, however, to be very mixed. Kuwait was liberated from Iraqi occupation in 1991, but the Saddam Hussein regime in Iraq initially remained intact for another two decades. A UN-approved international sanctions regime was imposed with the aim of deterring Iraq from developing Weapons of Mass Destruction, but its impact upon civilian life in Iraq generated widespread public and academic disquiet. The 1992–1993 UN-approved and US-led intervention in Somalia ended in abject failure. Although the UN-approved intervention in Bosnia (1992–1995) and the NATO-led intervention in Kosovo (1999) succeeded in halting ethnic cleansing and ending hostilities on the ground, how they were conducted and the degree to which they can be said to have established a stable peace remain matters of debate. This was especially the case with the Kosovo intervention because it proceeded without UN approval. Alongside these interventions was a very controversial failure of the international community to intervene in Rwanda to try to stop the genocide against the Tutsi that unfolded over a three-month period in 1994.

Those interventions in the early post-Cold War era generated widespread public and academic debate. Much of this centred on the fact that the interventions were predominantly initiated by powerful Western states claiming to be upholding universal values. The solidarist wing of the English School, alongside other schools of thought advocating intervention on the basis of humanitarian values, thus became vulnerable to criticism from a range of theoretical standpoints within the academic IR community.

Criticism of the solidarist advocacy of humanitarian intervention also came from within the pluralist wing of the English School. At the end of the 1990s and clearly influenced by the debates around humanitarian intervention, robust restatements of the pluralist interpretation of international society, started to appear, notably James Mayall's *World Politics: Progress and its Limits* and Robert Jackson's *The Global Covenant: Human Conduct in a World of States* (Jackson, 2000; Mayall, 2000). Both of these pluralist retorts to English School solidarists emphasize the centrality of maintaining a fragile world

A tomb for the victims of the genocide in Rwanda in 1994

order resting upon an historically evolved yet fragile consensus around the connected principles of sovereign equality and non-intervention. They emphasize also the vital but limited role of a pluralist international society of states in this. For both authors, however, cultural and ideological differences are hallmarks of a pluralist international society of states and solidarism's universalism is insufficiently sensitive to the dangers of ignoring these differences.

Mayall recognizes that the demands for greater solidarism in relations between states do exist and have substance to them. However, like other pluralists he is sceptical about the possibility that the current international society will develop in a significantly more solidarist direction. Echoing Bull's earlier work, Mayall argues that there are substantial constraints upon the possibility of greater international solidarity stemming from the continuing fragility of international order and thus the need to retain the preservation of international order as a priority. In particular, he emphasizes the continuing influence of nationalism as a constraint upon the emergence of an international society of states centred around a comprehensive set of universally agreed values. 'The pluralists still hold the ascendency', Mayall claims, going on to argue that 'we have no realistic alternative than to approach the future with caution, but also with hope' (Mayall, 2000: 112).

Jackson's pluralism is centred around the claim that the rules of international society emerge out of a limited consensus between states as to how they should conduct themselves procedurally. Jackson sees such rules as not created through reference to universal moral norms of just conduct or some form of higher law above sovereign states, but out of the historical practice of international relations. It is on this basis that very different states can manage to coexist without agreement on principles of justice or fairness. Their principal obligation is to uphold the principles that have been agreed, such as respecting the sovereignty of other states and not interfering in their internal affairs, and therefore contribute to the maintenance of international order. Jackson acknowledges that such things as universal human rights do matter, but the possibility of their realization is constrained by the fact that today's international society is a society of very diverse sovereign states. For Jackson the primary obligations of states as members of an international society are to uphold international order in spite of their evident political and cultural differences (Jackson, 2000).

It is important to note at this point that poststructuralist and postcolonial perspectives were also becoming increasingly influential in the IR field during the post-Cold War era. In different ways both robustly challenge the notion that Western values are self-evidently universal (these challenges are discussed extensively in Chapters 7 and 9). Such criticism has implications not only for English School solidarism but also for the pluralists as well. For example, the poststructuralist IR scholar, Roland Bleiker has questioned the English School's emphasis on 'order' as a core value in world politics. Bleiker argues that the meaning of order is not neutral but highly political:

> Few would question that order is desirable and essential. Without order there can be no rule of law, no protection of human rights, no civilized life in general. But order does not necessarily equate with the good life. (Bleiker, 2004: 187)

The imposition of a particular understanding of world order by dominant states can produce what appear as injustices to others. Thus, what some might call disorder in world politics others would see as necessary to produce progressive change at a global level.

4.5 THE THIRD PHASE: FROM INTERNATIONAL SOCIETY TO WORLD SOCIETY?

We noted at the beginning of this chapter that the evolution of the English School falls roughly into three broad phases. The foundational or classical phase was followed by a period in which the solidarist perspective within the English School became markedly more prominent and generated critical responses from the pluralist wing. Since the early 2000s a third phase in the English School's development has emerged, one which is marked by of reflection on the English School's theoretical underpinnings coupled with explorations conceptual innovation. It is widely recognized that a key figure in this has been the British IR scholar Barry Buzan.

Barry Buzan's reappraisal of the English School

Prior to his interest in the English School, Buzan was probably best known as a leading security specialist with realist leanings who has been widely credited with first putting the now highly developed sub-discipline of Security Studies on the IR intellectual map. In the late 1990s, however, Buzan signalled his interest in the English School. Buzan commends the English School for its long-standing focus on the social dimensions of the international system and sees it as offering concepts (such as international society, primary institutions), and debates (notably between pluralism and solidarism) that are not found in other IR perspectives (Buzan, 2014: 186). Nonetheless, Buzan criticizes the depiction within the English School of pluralism and solidarism in crude either/or terms. Indeed, for Buzan the distinction is questionable since any physical interaction between states entails some level of 'social content' (Buzan, 2004: 99 and Buzan 2014: 171–2).

For example, Buzan criticizes the pluralist English School scholars Mayall and Jackson for continuing 'the English School's long neglect of the economic sector' (Buzan, 2002: 365). For Buzan the global economic market has evolved into an institution of international society, which, to function successfully, requires more from states than merely agreeing to coexist. In other words, it provides evidence of deepening international solidarism around shared values. Buzan argues that similar observations could be made also about 'big science' and the environment, further undermining pluralist scepticism about the possibility of a more solidaristic international society.

Buzan identifies conceptual and theoretical weaknesses that he believes limit the English School's capacity to fully capture the complexities of international politics today. We shall now briefly examine the main elements of Buzan's argument for improving what he sees as the key weaknesses of the English School. Buzan's critical engagement with the English School is, however, both comprehensive and complex and what follows can only be a basic summary of his argument.

Buzan's critique of the English School centres around four overlapping themes. We will briefly examine each of these.

Shifting from normative to structural analysis

Overall Buzan's ambition is to develop a more 'systematically structured' interpretation of the English School. In essence this involves a thorough rethinking of the triad— international system, international society, and world society—that has formed the core of the English School since its inception. In his view, the English School contains both normative and structural elements, neither of which have been clearly delineated to date. Buzan argues both are needed, but his primary concern is with the structural dimensions of English School thinking, notably the conceptual robustness of the English School's analysis of the international social structure. The English School needs, Buzan argues, 'to begin pulling away from its founding fathers' (2004: 11). Nonetheless, Buzan also suggests that a more refined analysis of the three levels of English School enquiry would also bring fresh insight into the normative debate between pluralists and solidarists.

Reconfiguring the system/international society/world society triad

Buzan sees the English School as overly focused on the system/society distinction while insufficiently considering the international society/world society distinction. Although solidarism in the English School is strongly associated with a cosmopolitan normative outlook—i.e., one that focuses on the idea of a potential world society of humankind—in

Buzan's view the English School has paid insufficient attention to reflection on what a world society might mean or look like. Buzan sees this as a consequence of thinking about world society in largely normative terms and on the basis of values which are assumed to be applicable to all of humankind. For Buzan the future evolution of international society and world society is not simply a case of linear progression from one to the other. The emergence of a world society does not require the disappearance of the sovereign state in favour of some distinctive form of universal human community. Rather it is the constant and dynamic interaction between international society and world society that needs closer investigation. Buzan develops this theme further through identifying some other weaknesses in the English School's analysis of international politics.

The problem of levels

Buzan claims that much of English school thinking is focused at the global level, whether this is with reference to international system, international society, or world society. Regarding the concept of an international society in particular, Buzan argues that the English School's depiction of the development of international society as a global phenomenon of European origin has resulted in insufficient attention being paid to developments at the sub-global or regional level and outside Europe. There is clear evidence, Buzan argues, that shows how distinctive regional international societies have emerged within a common global international society, as illustrated not only by Europe, but also by the Islamic world, and Southeast Asia (Buzan 2004: 18).

Buzan sees an urgent need to investigate the development of international society at the regional level, which would reveal more about non-Western or hybrid forms of international society. Regional forms of international society might also be cultural or even religiously resistant to the imposition of universal norms and values that are predominantly Western in origin. At the same time, if the focus is shifted away from a normative focus towards a more empirical enquiry into 'really existing' international society and world society, it becomes readily apparent that regional international societies are actively engaged with global international society and contribute to the development of world society. This becomes especially apparent if the international political economy and the phenomenon of globalization are brought into the picture.

The missing 'sector' — bringing international political economy (IPE) into the picture

A key element of Buzan's overall argument is his view that the English School has paid insufficient attention to the global political economy, in particular the phenomenon of globalization. Buzan is not the first either inside or outside the English School to note this deficiency, Other classical English School thinkers have criticized Bull for paying little attention to the global economy but have not developed the point much further (Buzan, 2004: 19–20). For Buzan,

> . . . the side-lining of the economic sector in representations of international society is surprising given both the enormous development of norms, rules and institutions (including some with powers of collective enforcement) in this sector and the growth of IPE as a major branch of the study of international relations. (Buzan, 2004: 20)

In neglecting the economic dimensions of international society, the English School has failed to appreciate the 'rise of the market as a distinctive institution of international society' (Buzan, 2014: 136). Indeed, Buzan proposes that trade should be considered as a primary institution of international society (one of what Bull in *The Anarchical Society* referred to as the 'common institutions') given its vital role in the construction of both states and international society. More generally, Buzan sees primary institutions in much more dynamic terms than Bull. The significance of primary institutions can rise and fall. For example, Bull depicts war as a primary institution of international society, but Buzan sees this as increasingly questionable given the decline of interstate war coupled with the transnational institutionalization of the market and trade relations in contemporary international society. Similarly, Buzan argues that 'environmental stewardship' can also be seen as an increasingly significant primary institution of international society.

When the globalization of the world economy is factored in, Buzan argues, a more complex picture of the international social structure therefore emerges. Although there is considerable debate about the extent and significance of globalization, it is widely seen to include the creation of new non-state actors and new transnational social networks that sit alongside the states system (Buzan, 2004: 12). The spread of a capitalist market economy across the globe has led to the development of new institutions to manage the global economy which could be seen to constitute a form of collective societal governance. States remain powerful actors in the global economy, and there is still clear variation in their openness to the global market. Nonetheless, the collapse of the Soviet-led communist bloc at the end of the Cold War, Buzan claims, has meant that twentieth-century debates about whether there should be a global market are effectively over. In the twenty-first century there is a global economic market and the building and maintaining of that market involves much more than mere coexistence between states. It is in fact a form of international solidarism, even if it is not based upon shared cosmopolitan values as English School solidarists might have hoped (Buzan, 2014: 1389).

As we noted earlier, Buzan does not see the development of world society as requiring the disappearance of the sovereign state. Nor is the possibility for further development of a world society dependent solely or even primarily on whether all individuals develop a shared universal consciousness of themselves as members of some universal human community, as much of the classical English School seems to suggest. Rather, the development of both international society and world society are inescapably intertwined, not least because even if states remain the dominant actors in a globalizing world, individuals and various kinds of transnational actors must be brought into the picture. They all interact in increasingly complex ways and at all levels of the global social structure and it is out of that dynamic interaction that world society is emerging.

Many English School scholars recognize the impact of Buzan's efforts to reconstruct the English School and welcome the avenues for further investigation that it opens up, even if they are divided about the merits of Buzan's argument overall or certain aspects of it (see, for example: Bellamy, 2005; Dunne, 2005; Linklater, 2005; Wilson, 2016). There can be little doubt, however, that Buzan can take a good deal of credit for revitalizing the English School and bringing it to the attention of an increasingly global audience. The avenues for further development of the School that Buzan opened up are being developed further by a new generation of English School scholars that are not only continuing a process of conceptual revision, but also taking the English School further away from its Western origins (see, for example, Buzan and Gonzalez-Pelaez, 2009; Zhang, X. 2011; Zhang, Y. 2016, 2017; Suzuki, 2005, 2009).

Feminism and the English School

In addition to identifying the absence of economic analysis in classical English School scholarship, Buzan has also noted that there has been relatively little interaction between feminism and the English School (Buzan, 2014: 37; see also Blanchard, 2011: 855, fn.2). This largely remains the case, although some feminist IR scholars have challenged the English School on the absence of gender in its analysis. For example, Jacqui True asks where are the women in international society (True, 2004: 151)? In common with other state-centric IR perspectives, True argues that people are largely absent from the classical English School depiction of international society and women especially so.

International diplomacy, says True, is a case in point. Bull depicted diplomacy as one of the 'common institutions' that form the substance of international society. The account of diplomacy's role in sustaining international society is, however, predominantly depicted in terms of an interaction between states and their human representatives or 'proxies', in which

> Men are more visible than women in international society since the proxies for states have historically been statesmen—either diplomats or other state representatives—and the typical behaviour of states has been deduced from the behaviour of male individuals. (True, 2004: 152)

For True and other feminists in the IR field, gender relations are an integral part of the practice of diplomacy. Historically, international diplomacy has operated within a patriarchal social structure in which women's contributions are largely confined to the private realm and include supporting 'the men who act on behalf of states, both physically and emotionally, and socially and professionally in their public interstate activities' (True, 2004: 153). Other feminists, notably Cynthia Enloe (you can read more about her work in Chapter 10) and Christine Sylvester have also depicted diplomacy as an example of the internationalized operation of the public/private divide. Sylvester describes 'diplomatic wives' as the 'unpaid servants of national interest' (Sylvester, 2002: 197–8). Such observations prompt the question what it might mean for international society if the gender balance and the gendering of roles was different.

Eric Blanchard detects masculinist assumptions throughout the development of the English School, including both its pluralist and solidarist wings. He draws upon feminist critiques of the state and security (which we discuss in Chapter 10, Section 10.4) to question the pluralist account of international society, as well as the universalist assumptions of English School solidarism (Blanchard, 2011).

True also notes the absence of gender analysis in Bull's account of the 'revolt against the West', that was discussed in Section 4.4 of this chapter. Although feminist movements and women's liberation movements were also springing up worldwide at the same time as the revolt against Western dominance of international society, they are absent from Bull's analysis. Again, True argues, this is a consequence of the framing of the struggle between the West and non-West in predominantly state-centric terms. Bringing gender into the picture complicates the issue:

> Bull's conception of a collective revolt against the West, in effect, recounts a struggle among black and white men for political authority. Historically, this struggle has often played out on—and indeed over—non-Western women's bodies. We need only think of the symbolism attributed to women's dress and conduct, and the physical control of women's place and women's movement in anti-Western movements and states. (True, 2004: 157)

Whereas there may be prospects for reconciliation between the West and non-West around formal political issues, such as democracy, that support the idea that international society can progress beyond its Western origins, True argues that there remains considerable differences between the West and the non-Western worlds 'when it comes to aspects of informal politics, specifically attitudes toward gender relations, women, and sexuality' (True, 2004: 158).

For True such differences need to be integrated into analysis of the prospects for sustaining international order and advancing the development of international society. This requires an examination of the connections between attitudes towards gender found within different states and their interaction with international society. Therefore, the English School needs to look inside the state, but it also must examine the contribution transnational feminist movements can make to the development of world society, specifically the evolution of global norms around gender equality and gender justice. These in turn can influence gender relations within states, because they may compel state compliance with evolving gender norms—about domestic violence, for example—at the level of world society. Not that this will be easy. True recalls the problems encountered at the 1995 UN Fourth World Conference on Women in Beijing (which we also discuss in Chapter 10, Section 10.4). There were clear tensions between the formal representatives of states who were 'emblematic of international society' and representatives of various women's NGOs and civil society movements who were 'emblematic of world society' (True, 2004: 160–1).

Ann Towns (2009, 2017) has shown how the expansion of European international society through colonialism and the global spread of European views about 'proper relations of men and women to the state' contributed to the global standardization of gender relations:

> In the seventeenth and eighteenth centuries, the world was filled with an assortment of polities which rested on diverse gender arrangements . . . however, by the late nineteenth and early twentieth centuries, state institutions and political office across the world became populated almost exclusively by men. Formal international relations, needless to say, thus became placed in the hands of men. (Towns, 2017: 380)

The twentieth and twenty-first centuries have witnessed a shift, albeit an uneven one, from the exclusion of women from politics towards their inclusion. It is a complicated

144 INTRODUCTION TO INTERNATIONAL RELATIONS THEORIES

story and much of the credit for this shift, Towns argues, belongs to the development of transnational social movements and activism since women's suffrage activism of the late nineteenth century onwards (which we discuss in Chapter 10, Section 10.2).

In telling the story of the exclusion and subsequent inclusion of women in politics (to which we can add the story of the struggles for the inclusion of people with non-heteronormative gender identities), Towns challenges the notion that the global expansion of international society outwards from Europe is a straightforward story of the globalization of European ideas and values, as suggested in much English School scholarship. When examined closely, the historical struggles for women's political empowerment outside the West show that the struggle for women's suffrage and emancipation and resistance to colonialism and Western domination cut across each other in complex ways. This was sometimes because the notion that gender equality was a European invention became wrapped up in the struggle against the West. Thus, some African and Asian women's suffrage activists turned to their own pre-colonial past, rather than European history, to press their case for the emancipation of women within the anti-colonial movements. The telling of that more complex story, Towns argues, helps 'to unsettle the commonsense account . . . that locates the political empowerment of women to contemporary Europe' (Towns, 2017: 398).

When gender is brought into the English School it raises challenging questions about the history of the evolution of international society, the actual and potential development of world society, and the substantive content of concepts such as solidarism and global justice. Having shown how gender has been consistently absent from the history of English School thinking, the work of Blanchard, Towns, and others illustrates the potential of further constructive engagement between the English School and feminist/gender-focused IR scholarship.

4.6 CONCLUSION

This chapter has depicted the development of the English School as occurring in roughly three phases: a foundational or classical phase; a second phase dominated by a revised debate between its pluralist and solidarist wings; and a third, still unfolding phase. This latest phase is marked by both the development of links with other IR perspectives such as Critical Theory and Feminism, as well as a call for conceptual refinement and innovation, initiated in large part by the work of Barry Buzan.

Since its inception, the English School has revolved around a triad of three concepts: international system, international society, and world society (Buzan, 2014: 12). Beyond that, it is questionable whether it can be described as a singular theory of international politics in the same sense that, say, neorealism can. Indeed, the English School has commonly been seen to be marked above all by theoretical and methodological eclecticism. The contemporary English School, especially its pluralist wing, retains clear links with the early work of Martin Wight, Hedley Bull, and other foundational figures. At the same time, subsequent engagements with constructivism (the subject of Chapter 8), Critical IR

Theory (examined in Chapter 9), and schools of feminist and gender-focused IR theory are producing significant refinements of the more solidarist strands of the English School.

Most recently, Barry Buzan and others have endeavoured to develop more robust theoretical underpinnings for the School, which has also entailed revisiting and revising most of its core conceptual assumptions. English School scholars have come to adopt, therefore a range of approaches each of which requires different research methodologies. Reflecting the core themes of the English School as a whole, some focus primarily on international institutions. Others look at the codes of conduct adopted by states, or examine the development of international law, or they explore the significance of the wider 'environments of action'—international system, international society, or world society (Navari, 2014).

Perhaps it is this conceptual and methodological diversity of the contemporary English School that explains not only why it still resists precise location within the contemporary spectrum of IR theories, but also why it continues to appeal to scholars from a range of other IR perspectives.

SUMMARIZING THE ENGLISH SCHOOL

- The English School (originally known as 'rationalism') emerged out of intellectual debates within the English IR community from the mid-1950s onwards
- In contrast to realist and neorealist depictions of an anarchical *system* of states, the English School argues that sovereign states comprise an anarchical *society* of states, or international society
- At the heart of the English School is the conceptual triad of international system, international society, and world society
- The English School's evolution falls roughly into three phases: a classical foundational phase; a second phase centred around debates between the School's pluralist and solidarist wings; and a third phase marked by theoretical and conceptual renovation
- Bull's *The Anarchical Society of States* (1977) offered the first comprehensive presentation of the English School's key themes. It identifies the 'primary goals' that all states pursue and the 'common institutions' in which they all participate. Together, these are seen to form the minimum basis for an international society of states
- In his early work Bull also identified two historical streams of thought about international society: pluralist and solidarist
- The pluralists depict the primary purpose of international society as the maintenance of international order and is sceptical about the possibility of significantly reforming international society in the pursuit of greater global fairness or justice
- The solidarists see a key purpose of international society as the pursuit of greater global justice and fairness which, some argue, could also lead to the development of a world society binding all humans

- Bull initially seems to locate himself within the pluralist camp. In his later work, however, Bull appears to turn towards solidarism, centred around a depiction of a 'revolt against the West'
- Bull's solidarist turn inspired a new generation of English School scholars to develop the solidarist account of international society further and apply it to analysis of post-Cold War international society, particularly around such issues as humanitarian intervention and human rights
- The solidarist turn subsequently generated some robust defences of the pluralist position and its continuing relevance
- In the third and ongoing phase of the English School's evolution, Barry Buzan and others propose reconfigurations of the English School's core conceptual categories to give it more robust theoretical foundations for analysing an increasingly complex world.

QUESTIONS

1. From an English School perspective, what are the key differences between an international *system* of states and an international *society* of states?
2. According to Hedley Bull, what are the three primary goals that are unique to international society and why would all states have a shared interest in realizing them?
3. What is your assessment of Hedley Bull's claim that a) diplomacy and b) international law provide evidence of the existence of an international society?
4. What are the key distinctions between the pluralist and solidarist wings of the English School?
5. In what ways, if any, do you think that states should be obliged to act 'as local agents of a world common good'?
6. Assess Buzan's claim that a greater focus in English School theorizing on the global economy and globalization in particular, would have significant implications for the concept of a 'world society'.

IR THEORY TODAY ARE TODAY'S 'GREAT POWERS' BEHAVING 'RESPONSIBLY'?

The 'Great Powers' (Martin Wight called them the 'Great Responsibles') are one of five institutions of international society that Hedley Bull identifies as central to sustaining international order. For Bull, the sheer fact of the gross inequality of power in international society means that a great power has a right to play a major role in peace and security issues that could affect all international society, but it also had a duty to exercise this right responsibly. Bull was writing during the Cold War in which the two obvious 'great powers' (then commonly referred to as the 'superpowers') were the United States and the USSR. Bull was often critical of the behaviour of both of the Cold War superpowers, arguing that their acceptance of their special rights and duties was only tentative and rarely explicitly acknowledged.

1. What states in today's world, if any, would you classify as 'great powers' and why? (Hint: might it be their geographical size or location, economic power, military power, moral influence, or some other criterion)

2. Do you think the world's most powerful states have special rights or duties because of their power alone? If so, why; If not, why not?

3. What criteria would you use to assess whether today's great powers are acting responsibly? (Hint: think about how you would define responsibility, and how states are responding to some of the key global issues today, the environmental crisis, terrorism, global economic injustice and poverty, conflicts around race, culture, and religion, and so on).

4. Are there powerful actors on the global stage other than states that you think also have a particular obligation to act responsibly in today's world? (Hint: what about the EU or other regional organizations, Multinational Corporations, NGOs, or the major organized religions?).

TWISTING THE LENS

- Look at Chapter 3 on realism. How might a realist or neorealist assess the behaviour of great powers differently to English School scholars? (Hint: think here about the differences between classical realists and neorealists discussed in Chapter 2).

- Look at Chapter 7 on poststructuralism. What insights might poststructuralism offer to the assessment of the responsibilities of great powers to preserve international order? (Hint: think about the meaning of 'order'—the Bleiker reference will be useful here—or 'responsibility').

USEFUL SOURCES

Bleiker, Roland (2004), 'Order and Disorder in World Politics', in Alex J. Bellamy (ed.), *International Society and its Critics* (Oxford: Oxford University Press).

Bull, Hedley (2002), *The Anarchical Society: A Study of Order in World Politics*, 3rd edition (Houndmills, Basingstoke: Palgrave), Chapter 9.

Morris, Justin (2005), 'Normative Innovation and the Great Powers' in Alex J. Bellamy (ed.), *International Society and its Critics* (Oxford: Oxford University Press).

FURTHER READING

ADDITIONAL INTRODUCTORY READING

Buzan, B. (2014), *An Introduction to the English School of International Relations: The Societal Approach* (Cambridge: Polity Press).
A very comprehensive review of the English School, by a leading British IR scholar noted for his argument that the English School is an important IR perspective but in need of extensive conceptual renovation.

Dunne, T. (2021), 'The English School', in T. Dunne, M. Kurki, and S. Smith, *International Relations Theories: Discipline and Diversity*, 5th edition (Oxford: Oxford University Press).

An accesible and succinct introduction to the key concepts and debates by a prominent contemporary English School scholar.

Navari, C. and Green, D. M. (eds) (2014), *Guide to the English School in International Studies* (Chichester, West Sussex: John Wiley & Sons Ltd).

A collection of essays by leading English School Scholars covering both the historical evolution of the English school as well as its key thematic areas.

MORE IN-DEPTH READING

Bellamy, A. J. (ed.) (2005), *International Society and its Critics* (Oxford: Oxford University Press).

A collection of critical essays on the concept of international society by a wide range of scholars from inside and outside the English School.

Bull, H. (2002), *The Anarchical Society: A Study of Order in World Politics*, 3rd edition (Houndmills, Basingstoke: Palgrave).

First published in 1977, this book by the English School's most noted scholar first put the English School firmly on the IR theory map.

Buzan, B. (2004), *From International to World Society: English School Theory and the Social Structure of Globalisation* (Cambridge: Cambridge University Press).

A comprehensive reconstruction of English School theory that endeavours to bring the idea of world society much more into the foreground of English School theorizing.

Dunne, T. (1998), *Inventing International Society: A History of the English School* (Houndmills, Basingstoke: Macmillan Press Ltd).

Written by a noted English School scholar, this book offers a comprehensive survey of the emergence of the English School, and the core ideas and key scholars in its foundational phase.

Dunne, T. and Reus-Smit, C. (eds) (2017), *The Globalization of International Society* (Oxford: Oxford University Press).

A collection of essays that critically revisit earlier English School accounts of the origins and development of international society.

Murray, R. (ed.) (2015), *System, Society and the World: Exploring the English School of International Relations,* 2nd edition (Bristol E-International Relations).

A collection of essays by key English School scholars that endeavours to illustrate the diversity of thought within the School today. It is an open access publication available at www.e-ir.info/publication/system-society-and-the-world-exploring-the-english-school-of-international-relations/.

Suzuki, S. (2009) *Civilisation and Empire: China and Japan's Encounter with European International Society* (Abingdon, Oxon: Routledge).

An exposition of some of the darker aspects of the drawing of Japan and China into a European-dominated international society, which highlights the need for the English School to take greater account of the role of non-Western states in the development of international society.

Wight, M. (1991) *International Theory: The Three Traditions, edited by Gabriele Wight and Brian Porter* (London: Leicester University Press/Royal Institute of International Affairs).

A foundational English School text, published twenty years after its author's death. Based on a legendary series of lectures at the LSE in the 1950s, you may find the differences in style between Wight's lectures and those you are likely to be attending today rather interesting!

CHAPTER 5

MARXISM AND INTERNATIONAL RELATIONS

LEARNING OBJECTIVES

- Understand the basic elements of Marx's work
- Explain why Marxism was initially seen as irrelevant to the study of IR
- Appreciate the distinctiveness of a Marxist approach to the study of international affairs
- Describe the historical context in which dependency theory and World System's Theory emerged out of, but also departed from Marx's work
- Explain the key aspects of Marxist critiques of globalization.

5.1 INTRODUCTION

Marxism is a vast and complex body of work. It contains numerous competing schools of thought and occupies a prominent place within most of the social sciences today. Yet, within the IR discipline Marxism was almost invisible until the 1970s and after. For most mainstream IR scholars, it was deemed to be largely irrelevant because it was seen to be overly focused on economics and had seemingly little to say about political relations between states in an anarchical international system. Additionally, during much of the Cold War Marxism was strongly associated with the political rhetoric and policies of the Soviet-led communist bloc of states. It was therefore viewed with suspicion by some Western IR scholars, given their focus on actual and potential conflict between the two superpowers. Although still situated on the margins of the disciplinary mainstream, Marxism's influence within the IR discipline is much more evident today.

In this chapter, we will first look at key, recurring themes within Marxism that might help identify what kind of view of international politics it can offer. The chapter goes on to show how Marxism initially appeared in the disciplinary literature in the early 1970s, in conjunction with a growing scholarly interest in the emergence of the so-called Third World as a political force on the world stage, as well as political and economic relations between the developed and developing worlds. We then examine how Marxist and Marxist-influenced scholarship has become increasingly visible, especially in the post-Cold War era. The chapter concludes with an examination of how Marxist scholarship provides a key source of criticism of the widespread notions that globalization is either a novel or a positive development.

5.2 WHAT IS MARXISM?

Marxism is a label used to cover not only the voluminous output of Karl Marx (see Key thinkers 5.1) during the nineteenth century, but also the vast and diverse body of work that has been directly influenced by Marx's writing. It now covers a wide array of schools of thought that vary significantly in their relationship to Marx's original work. Marx's own scholarly writing spans the fields of philosophy, politics, economics, history, and sociology. Indeed, Marx is commonly cited as one of the founding figures of the modern social sciences and his work has had a profound influence across most branches of the social sciences, because of both sympathetic and critical scholarly appreciation of it. It is very difficult to summarize this body of literature succinctly, but our main concern in this chapter is to focus on aspects of the Marxist tradition that have a significant bearing on the analysis of international politics.

KEY THINKER 5.1 KARL MARX

Karl Marx (1818–1883) was born to a middle-class family in the Prussian city of Trier. Marx originally studied law at the Universities of Bonn and Berlin, but during his student years became increasingly interested in philosophy. His earliest writings were both fictional and non-fictional and even included some love poems.

Marx started out as a journalist writing for radical German-language newspapers and moved to Paris, then a key centre for Leftist radical thought. While in Paris, Marx became a revolutionary communist (perhaps surprisingly, ideas of communism preceded Marx) and formed a life-long friendship and collaboration with the German socialist Freidrich Engels. Expelled from Paris, Marx moved to Brussels, renounced his Prussian citizenship, and developed his critiques of capitalism as well as what he saw as weak varieties of socialist thought. Marx and Engels were drawn into the considerable revolutionary activity in Europe that erupted in 1848.

Marx returned to Germany briefly, only to be banished for radical journalism and activism, finally settling in London in 1849, where he remained until his death. Initially Marx and his family often endured considerable poverty, partially alleviated by the financial support of Engels who was working in his father's factory in Manchester.

> While in London, Marx developed his critique of the political economy of capitalism, culminating in the first volume of his magisterial work *Das Kapital* (Capital). A further two volumes were compiled from his notes by Engels and published posthumously. Marx died, a stateless person, in London where he is buried at Highgate Cemetery.
>
> Marx's voluminous journalistic and scholarly output made him a leading intellectual figure of the European Left of the mid-nineteenth century. He is undoubtedly one of the most significant, influential, and criticized thinkers in modern human history.

Prior to looking at some key themes in Marx's work of relevance to the study of international politics, we need firstly to consider its marked absence from the IR discipline until relatively recently. There are a number of reasons why this has been the case.

Firstly, a superficial reading of Marxism's focus on capitalism as a transnational economic system and the vital place of social classes within it, can lead on to the view that, since it is not primarily concerned with the political relations between sovereign states in an anarchical international political system, it is simply largely irrelevant to the concerns of mainstream realist and liberal IR scholarship. While it is true that Marx's writings on the international affairs of his time were mostly journalistic in nature, many scholars today would reject the notion that his scholarly work does not have direct relevance to the study of international politics, especially given the growing recognition of the significance of the *political economy* of the contemporary world.

Secondly, Marxism was for a long time very much associated with the ideology and political systems of communist states, most notably the Soviet Union. After 1945, as the Cold War between the Soviet and Western blocs developed, Marxist scholarship was very much tainted in the West simply by association. Given that for some decades after the beginning of the Cold War the IR discipline was dominated by American scholars and their perspectives, it is perhaps not surprising that Marxism was widely dismissed as a form of political ideology (and a hostile ideology at that) and therefore ill-suited to the pursuit of supposedly objective and balanced scholarly enquiry. Mainstream IR post-1945 was very much focused on superpower political and military relations and Marxism was largely seen as useful only for interpreting Soviet political ideology and, thus, the Soviet Union's foreign policy. Given this, the treatment of Marxism in most key IR texts up until the 1970s was usually astonishingly brief. For example, Hans Morgenthau's landmark text *Politics Among Nations* (discussed in Chapter 2) devotes just two pages to it.

As we shall see, things did begin to change in the 1960s and 1970s and Marxism is much more prominent in the IR field today, not least because of the increasingly widespread recognition that a strict separation of the political and economic dimensions of international relations, as favoured by many classical realist scholars for example, is increasingly implausible. The rise of international political economy (IPE) as a field of enquiry within the IR discipline, the growing recognition of global poverty and economic exploitation as causes of transnational social and political conflict, and, more recently, the prominence of the concept of globalization, have provided key entry points

Karl-Marx-Allee — street sign, Berlin, Germany

for Marxist or Marxist-influenced theoretical enquiry into the IR discipline. Why this is so, should become clearer when we look at some of the key themes within the work of Marx and his successors.

Marxism: key themes

As already noted, Marx's work stretched across most of the academic disciplines that these days we refer to as the social sciences: economics, history, politics, and sociology. This reflects Marx's view that, to be understood properly, the social world had to be studied as a totality. For Marxists, the divisions between the various academic disciplines serve to mask the complex and dynamic interconnections between the different facets of human social life. Marx's work was characterized by an acute attention to history, in particular historical processes of change. This was not just so we might better understand how human societies came into existence and subsequently evolved, but also to help us understand where they might be heading or could be heading if we used our knowledge of their evolution effectively. The latter point is crucial; Marx was very scholarly, but he was never the disinterested or detached scholar. Knowledge, for Marx, is always purposeful. As he famously declared in Thesis XI of his *Theses on Feuerbach*, 'philosophers have only interpreted the world, in various ways; the point, however, is to change it'.

As to what the world might change into, or should change into, Marx was somewhat imprecise. Certainly, Marx was an advocate of achieving what he called 'human emancipation'. Quite what he meant by this remains, however, a matter of considerable debate among Marxist scholars. Marx acknowledged that liberalism offered the prospect of *political* emancipation—achieving greater individual political freedom through the granting of rights to all individuals. *Human* emancipation, however, points towards a more complete conception of freedom from all forms of oppression that emerges out of Marx's emphasis on economic exploitation, not only of individuals but of whole classes of peoples. Additionally, Marx treats humans as inherently social beings and, therefore, complete freedom is to be achieved collectively rather than solely as individuals.

Many of Marx's followers have interpreted his work as an argument for the establishment of a communist political and social system as the concrete expression of the achievement of human emancipation. However, Marx himself was somewhat circumspect about what communism might look like, and many Marxist scholars view established political systems which claim to be communist (such as was found in the Soviet Union and its satellite states, or in China today) as based on crude, partial, or even distorted interpretations of Marx's work.

Historical materialism

Key to understanding Marxism is Marx's philosophical outlook: historical materialism. Again, there is considerable debate around Marx's precise understanding of history, but there are some key features that stand out. In 1852, Marx famously summarized his understanding of history thus:

> Men make their own history, but they do not make it as they please; they do not make it under self-selected circumstances, but under circumstances existing already, given and transmitted from the past. (Marx, *18th Brumaire of Louis Napoleon*)

For Marx, humans, how they live, and the political and economic systems they live within are all historically produced. It is the interaction of humans with the material circumstances they find themselves in that provides the motor of history. In Marxism, this relationship is described as dialectical. Dialectical is a term used to describe the process of juxtaposing opposed or contradictory ideas and attempting to reconcile them. In other words, it is a method of examining and discussing opposing ideas to find the truth of the matter. However, Marx used the term in a particular way. For Marx, it is through the dialectical (i.e., dynamic) interaction of humans with their material circumstances—the social structures and institutions they live within—that the types of society we live in are produced and reproduced. Importantly for Marx, it is also a dynamic relationship which can produce change. It is through greater awareness and analysis of the dialectical relationship between humans, and the historically specific material circumstances they find themselves in, that the possibility of other, better forms of social life can be discerned.

By 'material circumstances', Marx was referring primarily to the prevailing economic system, what he called the *mode of production*, underpinning the totality of social life. The economic system that Marx was most interested in was capitalism. Capitalism, in

Marx's view, was not merely about the emergence of market-based exchange, or the simple pursuit of profit. It was a key stage in human history: a comprehensive form of social life itself, based upon an historically specific set of economic relations, or *relations of production* between humans. For Marx, humans are inherently productive beings; throughout time they have transformed nature—raw materials—to satisfy their needs and wants using tools, constantly evolving technical knowledge, and their labour power. Thus, how humans have gone about producing to fulfil their needs has changed over time. In Marxism, a key distinction is that between the *means of production* and the *relations of production*. The means of production refers to the physical non-human dimensions of production—the raw materials, tools, and infrastructure used to produce goods. As technology advances, the means of production change. This in turn impacts upon the prevailing relations of production.

To help you grasp Marx's argument, imagine a subsistence farmer in a pre-capitalist, feudal economic system working alone to produce sufficient goods to provide for their family. They may well have made their own tools and used these to turn the raw materials of nature—such as crops, trees, and livestock—to provide food, shelter, and so on. In so doing, they develop a direct relationship between their labour power and what it produces. For Marx, labour—the transformation of natural resources into objects with use-value—is key to the development of a person's sense of self, their 'species-being'.

If we compare this to a worker under capitalism, we can see an important change in the relationship between human labour and its product. Capitalism is a mode of production based upon private ownership of the means of production. A worker's labour power is now used to produce commodities to be sold through market-based exchange to produce monetary profit for the owners of the means of production. The worker receives wages for their labour rather than the actual products of their labour. Furthermore, to generate profit for their employers those wages must be less than the value of the commodities they produce. So, as technology advances, the use of labour power changes and new relations of production emerge, workers become dependent upon the wages offered in return for their labour. The competition for profits between the owners of the means of production—the *bourgeoisie*—means that they must extract as much labour from workers—the *proletariat*—as is possible for as little as possible.

From a liberal point of view, capitalism is seen in broadly positive terms, even if liberals disagree as to the degree to which capitalism should be regulated to protect workers from excessive exploitation. Through the earning of wages, a liberal would argue, individual workers can acquire goods or services and enhance their lives materially. If they work harder or endeavour to improve their skill sets in line with technological changes, they can further enhance their material conditions. Furthermore, some of the wealth they generate for the owners of the means of production will be reinvested in enhancing or expanding the means of production so that more profit can be realized, and some will be spent on goods and services for the wealthy. Both processes will generate new employment opportunities. In other words, wealth will ultimately trickle down to benefit the whole of society. The economic system will, of course, remain fundamentally unequal, but if it is able to continue growing then ultimately all will benefit. Inequality is the price we pay for ensuring economic growth and some degree of prosperity for all.

From a Marxist point of view, things look very different, and the language Marxism uses to describe how capitalism functions reflects this. Importantly, Marx's account of industrial capitalism's inherently exploitative nature was not merely the product of abstract theorizing. It was also grounded in the empirical observation of the poverty of industrial workers in the mid-nineteenth century, notably in cities such as Manchester in England where the father of his friend and close collaborator, Freidrich Engels, co-owned a textile mill.

At the time, Manchester was at the heart of the British cotton industry and noted for being both a centre of industrial innovation, as well as a city blighted by poverty and slum conditions for its working class. While working for his father, Engels wrote extensively on the working conditions in Manchester, notably in his first book *The Condition of the Working Class in England*, published in 1845. The concrete living conditions of the working class in the nineteenth century underpinned Engels and Marx's claim that capitalism is inherently exploitative. Workers are effectively dependent for their survival on the owners of the means of production—the bourgeoisie, or ruling class—who pay their wages. As we have already noted, those wages must always be below the value of goods produced. The difference between the cost of labour and the market value of the goods produced—the surplus value—accrues to the owners of the means of production. For Marx, capitalism thus works by extracting surplus value from the worker and the resultant profit is essentially a material expression of the sustained exploitation of the working class. The working class can never receive the full value of their labour and they are kept in a condition of *alienation*—from the goods they produce, from themselves, and from the dominant class that exploits them.

How might a Marxist explain, then, the seeming willingness of many, if not most members of the exploited working class to put up with their own exploitation or even to express political support for the system that exploits them? The answer lies in the capacity of the ruling class to use the dominant social institutions—the legal system, education, mass media, the family, or various forms of cultural activity—to help mask the underlying exploitative nature of the capitalist system by presenting it as somehow natural or commonsensical. Marxism is often described as deploying a *base-superstructure* model of political, economic, and social change to capture the relationship between the economic system and the political and social relations that helped to sustain it. As the economic base—the mode of production and the relations of production—changes, so does the political and social superstructure that rests upon it; in other words, the whole of society changes. As Marx put it, 'the mode of production of material life conditions the social, political, and intellectual life process in general' (Marx cited in McLellan, 2000: 425).

For Marxists, the process of hiding the actuality of relations between the working class and the ruling class is ideological. Through their control of the key institutions of society—the superstructure—the ideology of the ruling class becomes the dominant ideology, which comes to be accepted by many of the working class. Although Marx did not use the term himself, Engels introduced the term 'false consciousness', in a letter written in 1893, after Marx's death, to capture the phenomenon of the working class believing that capitalism worked to their benefit (Engels, 1968: 690). The working

A cotton factory in Manchester, England

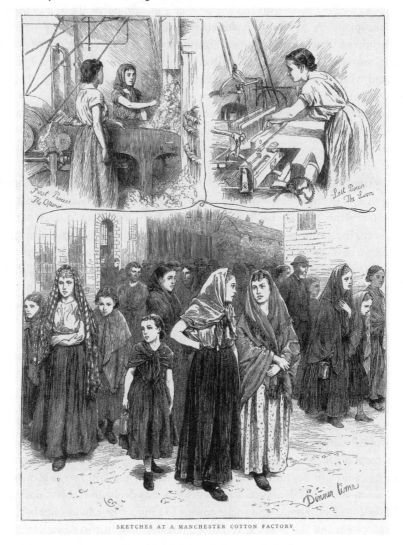

SKETCHES AT A MANCHESTER COTTON FACTORY

class were conscious and active members of the societies they lived in, but in accepting and absorbing the dominant ideology of the ruling class their consciousness of their own circumstances was false because they were actively pursuing goals that were not in their own true class interests. What they are deflected from seeing fully and clearly is the inescapably antagonistic relationship—a class conflict—between the working class and the ruling class, between the proletariat and the bourgeoisie under capitalism.

Class struggle is a vital component of Marx's dialectical view of history. In their famous *Manifesto of the Communist Party* written in 1848, Marx and Engels declared that 'the history of all hitherto existing human society is the history of class struggles' (Marx and Engels in McLellan, 2000: 246). As capitalism matured, Marx believed, the increasing disparity between the working class and the ruling class would lead to a heightening of class consciousness on the part of the working class. They would come to see that the pathway out of their alienated and exploited existence would be through social revolution to bring about the collapse of the capitalist mode of production and its replacement by a superior form of society: 'in the place of the old bourgeois society with its classes and class antagonisms, there will be an association in which the free development of each is the condition of the free development of all' (Marx and Engels in McLellan, 2000: 262). Marx remained unclear, however, as to how this revolutionary change would occur, what form precisely a post-capitalist society might take, whether it would be a national or international process, and so on. Marx himself said relatively little about an alternative economic system to capitalism, other than that it would emerge out of revolutionary class struggle.

Perhaps because Marx and Engels wrote a manifesto for the German Communist Party, the terms Marxism and Communism are often treated in public debate as essentially synonymous. Arguably, this is a simplification for reasons we will now explore a bit further.

Marxism and communism

The historical record of those states who claim or have claimed to be driven by a commitment to Marxist or Marxist-Leninist principles suggests that the relationship between Marxism as a political philosophy and communist states or political parties, past or present, is not straightforward. The end of the Cold War was certainly marked by the overt rejection of all communist governments in the Cold War Soviet bloc by most of their citizens. Most of the few contemporary governments still overtly claiming full or partial allegiance to Marxist principles—such as China, Vietnam, and Laos—are highly engaged in the global capitalist economy and allow market forces to operate inside their borders. Others, such as Cuba and especially North Korea are much less so.

To greater or lesser degrees, moreover, most existing communist states are criticized, especially by the West, for their authoritarian tendencies. Yet, it is important to note here that many contemporary Marxist theorists broadly concur with much of the criticism of former or existing communist states, seeing them as having been based upon distortions or simplifications of Marx's work. Many would argue that Marx believed that any sustainable alternatives to existing national and global political orders must emerge out of authentic popular resistance and debate, the outcome of which should not be predetermined or imposed from above.

Defining communism is not therefore a straightforward matter. Soviet communism is perhaps the most well-known variation, but during the latter half of the twentieth century distinctive variations appeared within the Soviet Bloc (in Yugoslavia and Czechoslovakia for example), in China, as well as between Communist political parties in European liberal democracies, some of whom embraced what became known as Eurocommunism. Broadly speaking, these variations were marked by efforts to distance themselves from Soviet communist doctrine and a willingness to adapt to local political cultures and values. Outside of the states declaring themselves as communist, sizeable communist political parties participating in democratic national elections can still be found worldwide, such as in South Africa, Brazil, Portugal, Cyprus, Nepal, India, Bangladesh, Russia, Spain, and France.

A further reason for questioning the simplistic equating of communism with Marxism is that although its roots lie in the nineteenth-century writings of Marx, Marxism today is a highly evolved and varied body of work. This is in part because much of Marx's voluminous and often dense intellectual output is open to varying interpretations. Additionally, contemporary Marxism contains numerous distinct currents that reflect the influence of Marx's intellectual successors, such as Lenin, Mao Tse Tung, Antonio Gramsci, and various prominent twentieth-century Leftist intellectuals from Europe, Latin America, Africa, and elsewhere. There is undoubtedly significant debate and heated disagreement within the broad Marxist tradition, let alone between Marxism and other political philosophies. Additionally, many contemporary scholars draw from the Marxist tradition whilst also moving intellectually significantly beyond it (this should become clear when reading further in this chapter as well as Chapter 6 on Critical Theory).

Despite the failings of Communist states, Marx's work and that of his numerous successors continues to be highly influential. Indeed, some commentators argue that the influence of Marxism broadly defined is rising again, especially since the 2008 global financial crisis and in reaction to the spread of neoliberal economic and social policies (see for example: Sperber, 2013; Fasenfest, 2018; Tooze, 2018).

In concluding our brief survey of Marxism as a political philosophy, it must be stressed that the account we have given in this chapter is a highly simplified rendition of a very complex body of work. Marxists continue to this day to debate Marx's intellectual legacy, not least because of the evident continuation and further development of global capitalism since the time Marx was writing. Numerous critics, both sympathetic and hostile, have questioned the extent to which the ground-breaking work of Marx and Engels continues to apply to contemporary forms of capitalist societies. Is a two-class model (proletariat and bourgeoisie) adequate to the task of capturing the complexities of contemporary social life under modern capitalism? How does the concept of class intersect with modern preoccupations with other forms of social conflict along, say, racial, religious, cultural, and gender lines? Does Marx and Engel's account of the conditions of the working class in the mid-nineteenth century still resonate with the experiences of workers in contemporary post-industrial societies? These are large and difficult questions with which Marxists and their critics continue to wrestle.

Even if Marx's account of the likely concrete historical trajectory of capitalism is open to considerable critical scrutiny, his intellectual legacy is very substantial indeed. At the very least, it suggests some rather different analytical lenses through which one might view the subject matter of the IR discipline.

THINK CRITICALLY 5.1

Marxism is noted for its emphasis on social class as an analytical category that is key to understanding such issues as inequality, exploitation, and the inherent advantages some people possess.

Consider the following words as prompts:
- Class
- Race
- Ethnicity

- Gender

- Religion

- The personal

- Local

- National

- Global

1) Thinking of your own circumstances, which of these categories, if any, do you think best helps you understand your own life experiences and prospects or those of your family or wider community?

2) Does one of these categories predominate, or do you see intersections between several analytical categories at work?

5.3 **MARXISM AND IR**

As we note in Chapters 2 and 3, mainstream theories of IR are state-centric; they focus on the state as the primary actor in world politics, although they disagree as to whether its significance is unchanging (as realists would claim) or declining because of processes such as interdependence or globalization (as many liberals would argue). That Marxism's understanding of IR starts from a different place is perhaps most succinctly expressed by a famous claim in *The Communist Manifesto*: 'The executive of the modern state is but a committee for managing the common affairs of the whole bourgeoisie' (Marx and Engels in McLellan, 2000: 247). In other words, to understand the role of the modern state you must first analyse class relations under capitalism. Whereas much mainstream IR starts with the state and takes it as a given entity, Marx's understanding of the state is derivative; it emerges out of their understanding of class relations under capitalism.

It is hard to overstate the significance Marx and his successors place on the emergence of the capitalist mode of production and its transformative power. Marx's extensive analysis of the workings of capitalism were primarily aimed at exposing what he saw as its core logics of exploitation and alienation. Nonetheless, Marx often expressed awe at the extent of the changes that capitalism wrought. Capitalism took the human harnessing and control of the natural world to astonishing heights, and in so doing, he thought, held out the promise of overcoming the material scarcities that had hitherto made life precarious for so many humans. Furthermore, the logic of capitalist expansion, driven by the relentless pursuit of profit for the owners of the means of production, meant that it was an international and ultimately a global phenomenon. For Marx, capitalism was gradually unifying the whole human race into 'a single stream of world history' (Linklater, 2013: 118). In the *Manifesto of the Communist Party*, Marx and Engels argue that,

(t)he need of a constantly expanding market for its products chases the bourgeoisie over the entire surface of the globe. It must nestle everywhere, settle everywhere, establish connections everywhere . . . In place of the old wants, satisfied by the production of the country, we find new wants, requiring for their satisfaction the products of distant lands and climes. In place of the old local and national seclusion and self-sufficiency, we have intercourse in every direction, universal inter-dependence of nations. (Marx and Engels in McLellan, 2000: 248–249)

As we will see, this remarkably prescient depiction of capitalism's inexorable expansion across the face of the globe provides the basis for a substantial critical engagement of Marxism with the theorizing of international politics. In its reference to 'distant lands and climes', we can also detect an allusion to a logic of imperial conquest, a theme taken up extensively within Marxist scholarship after Marx. The engagement of Marxist, or Marxist-inspired scholars with the IR field has, however, resulted not only in their rejection of much of orthodox IR's assumptions, but also the significant modification of Marx's original ideas along the way.

Marxism and imperialism

The earliest attempt to develop further the international implications of the pioneering work of Marx and Engels emerges at the beginning of the twentieth century, notably around the issue of imperialism. Perhaps surprisingly, one of the key influences in developing the international dimensions of Marxism further was a path-breaking work by a noted British liberal thinker, John Hobson. In his *Imperialism: A Study,* published in 1902, Hobson argued that a key driver behind the imperialism of prominent Western capitalist states was the inherent weakness of the capitalist system itself. As the owners of the means of production invested their profits into further enhancing industrial output within their home countries, domestic productive capacity would eventually outstrip the demand for the goods produced. This was because the wage poverty of the working class combined with excessive savings by the wealthier members of society, produced under-consumption of the goods that could be produced. Consequently, there were increasingly few investment opportunities for the owners of capital. This prompted the pursuit of new investment opportunities and, therefore, profits overseas.

Echoing some of Marx's observations about the role of ideology in masking the true intent of the ruling class, Hobson argued that key politicians, financiers, and sections of the national press were instrumental in depicting imperial expansion as in the national interest, rather than largely benefiting only a small wealthy section of the national population. Notions of a 'civilizing mission' or manifest destiny in which inherently superior nations would go forth and help distant peoples embrace capitalist modernity were, in his view, spurious arguments intended to generate public support for imperial expansion and the colonization of the non-Western world. Hobson went on to argue that instead of imperial expansion, excess productive capacity could be met by addressing economic inequality at home. In other words, capitalism could be separated from imperialism.

Hobson's thesis influenced several leading Marxist thinkers of the time. The most notable was Vladimir Lenin (see Key thinker 5.2), the Russian communist revolutionary and a leading figure in the 1917 October revolution, which ousted the Russian Tsarist regime and led to the founding of the Soviet Union (the USSR). Lenin disagreed with

Hobson about the possibility of divorcing capitalism from imperialism. Indeed, in his *Imperialism: The Highest Stage of Capitalism*, written in 1916, Lenin argued that capitalism had evolved further since Marx first examined it and imperialist colonialism was now the highest and final stage of capitalism. Indeed, Lenin claimed that 'Capitalism has been transformed into imperialism' (Lenin, 2010: 21). Banks had become key actors in the capitalist system, and they had merged with industrial monopoly companies to produce what Lenin called 'finance capitalism'. In turn, finance capital collaborated with the dominant political classes of the major Western powers to drive forward their imperial expansion. The super-profits that resulted from the export of capital to fund the exploitation of the colonized world, could then be deployed to correct the declining level of profit at home and therefore help blunt working-class discontent arising from falling wages. In effect, it could create a 'labour aristocracy' of sufficiently well-paid workers, who would be disinclined to revolt against their political and economic masters. The working class in the imperial powers (such as Britain, France, and Germany) were materially benefiting from the exploitation of workers in the colonized world.

If correct, Lenin's analysis presented a profound challenge to Marx's notion of a natural affinity between all workers of the world, perhaps most famously expressed in the popular slogan, derived from the *Communist Manifesto*: 'Workers of the world unite! You have nothing to lose but your chains!'.

KEY THINKER 5.2 VLADIMIR LENIN

Vladimir Lenin (1870–1924) was the founder of the Russian Bolshevik Party, leader of the 1917 Bolshevik revolution, and the first head of a new Soviet Russia.

Intending to study law at university, after only a few months Lenin was banished for his political activities. Lenin took the time out to read revolutionary political works, including those of Marx. When finally permitted to take his final exams, Lenin excelled and went on to practise law. His experiences as a lawyer representing poor people in a heavily biased legal system only served to enhance his political radicalism.

Lenin was an active pamphleteer and wrestled particularly with the view held by many on the Russian Left that Marxism was ill-suited to the Russian situation because the industrial proletariat in Russia was tiny, in contrast to its large peasantry. Lenin challenged this view in his *Development of Capitalism in Russia*, published in 1899. Lenin went on to develop his ideas about the role of a revolutionary party as a 'vanguard of the proletariat', thereby establishing a model that was to be subsequently emulated by communist parties worldwide.

Lenin was vehemently critical of Russian involvement in the First World War which he famously viewed as a war between imperialist powers. Somewhat against the odds, given the significant divisions within the Russian revolutionary movements at the time, Lenin managed to persuade the Bolsheviks to start an armed uprising against the provisional government formed after the Tsar's abdication in March 1917. In November 1917, the Bolsheviks seized power and Russia descended into civil war for two years, during which Lenin was wounded in an attempted assassination. By 1922, Lenin had succeeded in establishing the Soviet Union or USSR but died just two years later.

Lenin's scholarly works and revolutionary political activism were enormously influential in the subsequent development of communism as an organized political movement, not only in Russia but worldwide. Arguably, the widely used label Marxism-Leninism, rather than simply Marxism, best captures the ideology of most of the global communist movement after 1917.

From imperialism to dependency theory

Lenin's analysis of imperialism was clearly flawed in one key respect: imperial competition between the great powers in the early twentieth century did not herald the downfall of capitalism worldwide, as Lenin hoped. Nonetheless, Lenin left a considerable intellectual legacy, not least his depiction of the world as consisting of a core of developed states exploiting a periphery of undeveloped states.

This basic core-periphery model of the global political economy was to re-emerge in the late 1940s and 1950s, notably in the work of various American and Latin American scholars, such as Hans Singer, Raúl Prebisch, and Paul Baran. It became considerably more prominent in the 1960s and 1970s when it began to make its presence felt within the IR scholarly community under the guise of dependency theory.

The name dependency theory derives from its focus on the seemingly dependent relationship between the developing world (what today is more usually called the Global South or Majority World) and the developed world (comprised of the advanced industrialized states, including all the major former imperial powers). In contrast to the idea of *interdependence* developed within the liberal perspective, which connotes a relationship of relatively balanced interconnection and benefit between states of a similar level of development (which we discuss in Chapter 2), *dependency* emphasizes the asymmetry between the developed and developing states.

Dependency theory holds that the prospects for the developing states are largely determined by the trade policies and practices of the advanced industrialized states in the world economy. When dependency theory emerged, the developing states were seen as those states in Latin America, Asia, and Africa who had low levels of Gross National Product (GNP), and whose economies were dependent on the export of a few commodities; usually raw materials or agricultural products such as sugar, cocoa, bananas, minerals, and so on. Because it is an approach broadly concerned with the structural features of the world economy, dependency theory and some other broadly similar approaches are also sometimes referred to in IR textbooks as structuralism. With the emergence of structural realism in the early 1980s (as discussed in Chapter 3), however, the use of that name has declined markedly to avoid confusion.

Once again, the wider political and historical context is central to an understanding of why a body of theory acquires greater prominence. Dependency theory came to prominence in the IR field during the era of *détente*, between the late 1960s and late 1970s, when the Cold War between the superpowers was seemingly getting a bit less

5 MARXISM AND INTERNATIONAL RELATIONS **163**

chilly, in some respects at least (for more on this see Key event 2.4 in Chapter 2). The emergence of dependency theory also coincided with the era of extensive US military involvement in SE Asia, as part of its war against the expansion of communism into the developing world, as well as with the continuing and often violent processes of decolonization in Africa.

Additionally, during the 1970s and early 1980s, the UN General Assembly provided some of the most visible illustrations of the rising prominence of the so-called Third World (a term we discuss in Key concept 5.1). As decolonization unfolded in the post-1945 era, many of the newly independent states began to work together as a bloc of states in international fora such as the General Assembly and other UN institutions, notably the United Nations Conference on Trade and Development (UNCTAD). With decolonization, the number of member states in the UN had grown rapidly to the point where the majority were now from the developing world, the Global South.

In 1964, the Group of 77 (G77) was established as a coalition of developing nations aiming to develop common positions on key global social and economic issues. One of their more significant activities was to push for a New International Economic Order (NIEO) in which the world economy would be restructured to improve the terms of trade for developing economies. Consequently, scholarly and public attention became more focused on the developing world and the complex interconnection of the issues of decolonization and economic exploitation. Put differently, the shift in focus was away from East–West conflict towards North–South conflict—from superpower rivalry to the relationship between the developed world located mostly in the Northern hemisphere and the developing world in the Southern hemisphere.

⟫⟫⟫ KEY CONCEPT 5.1 THE 'THIRD WORLD'

The term Third World was introduced by a French Anthropologist, Alfred Sauvy, in the early years of the Cold War, to define those countries that were unaligned with or did not want to be aligned with either the West (led by the US) or First World, and the communist bloc (led by the USSR) or Second World.

Use of the term has always varied and there has never been a consensus as to who should be included. Third World has often been used in reference to any states with a colonial past, or states also variously described as undeveloped, developing, or underdeveloped. Thus, states such as Cuba could be seen as part of the Soviet Bloc, but also Third World because of its development status. Similarly, many former British colonies retained their connection with the UK, through the British Commonwealth, yet could also be classified as Third World in developmental terms. With the end of the Cold War and the effective disappearance of the Second World, the term seemingly became archaic.

Additionally, many have argued that the term is tainted by its association with the caricaturing of the world's poor and the judgemental ranking of supposedly Third World states below the supposedly superior First and Second worlds. The developmental levels of countries associated with the term also vary widely—is it still appropriate to call India and Brazil Third World countries today?

> Alternative terms include the Global South, since most supposedly Third World states are in the Southern Hemisphere, but so too are highly developed countries such as Australia, New Zealand, Singapore, and South Korea. Majority World is used by some (since most of the world's population live in so-called Third World countries) as a preferable alternative. 'Developing world' is also widely used, but the definitions of developed and developing are themselves disputed.
>
> To further confuse matters, there are some who argue that the term Third World should be revived as an overtly political statement to express the condition of those who feel they remain part of the global periphery, including the poor or marginalized in supposedly First World countries (see Dirlik, 2004). It is worth noting here that the leading academic journal covering Global South studies and published since 1978 is still titled the *Third World Quarterly*.

The dependency theory that emerged from the 1950s–1970s was developed both by Marxists and non-Marxists who were critical of liberal economic theory. Indeed, it was two non-Marxist development economists who initially pioneered the concept of dependency in the late 1940s, both working for the then newly established UN: Hans Singer and Raúl Prebisch. Though they worked separately, their work became collectively known as the Prebisch–Singer thesis. This presented one of the first challenges to modernization theory, the dominant explanatory model for the economic and social development of states within the social sciences during the 1950s and 1960s.

Modernization theory depicts the Western, industrialized, developed state as providing a developmental benchmark that the still-developing states should follow. The combination of capitalism, liberal democracy, secular values, technological innovation, individualism, and consumerism is presented as the developmental recipe that propelled the developed states to their position at the top of the global development league. Modernization theory suggests, then, that there is only one viable path to development, and this is to emulate the developmental path taken by the developed states as much as possible. Having achieved independence, former colonial states should therefore be encouraged to adopt the economic, social, and political policies of the Western developed states.

One of the most influential versions of modernization theory was developed by Walt Rostow in the late 1950s and titled 'Stages to Growth'. We discuss this in more detail in Key concept 5.2.

KEY CONCEPT 5.2 ROSTOW'S STAGES TO GROWTH

Drawing largely on European and American history, Walt Rostow famously posited that the developed states had passed through five 'stages of growth'. These went as follows (Rostow, 1959):

- **traditional society**

    economy is mostly agricultural, little surplus to trade in domestic and overseas markets

- **pre-conditions to 'take-off'**

  Agriculture becomes more mechanized, more output traded, some external funding required

- **take off**

  Manufacturing assumes greater importance relative to agriculture, political and social institutions start to develop, savings and investment increase

- **drive to maturity**

  Industry diversifies, technology drives the spread of growth throughout the country, the role of innovation rises to push up real per capita incomes

- **age of mass consumption**

  output rises enabling higher consumer expenditure, tertiary (services) sector grows, and growth is sustained by an expanding middle class of consumers.

Dependency theory became more prominent when some development economists became troubled by growing empirical evidence of the inability of developing countries, notably in Latin America, to emulate the growth patterns of the developed countries as suggested by Rostow. This was despite the fact that they had adopted many of the policies and practices that modernization theory suggested would ensure their economic growth.

In the late 1940s, Prebisch and Singer had shown that the price of primary commodities—which were the mainstay of exports of Latin American developing countries—increased less rapidly than the price of manufactured goods. This meant that the *terms of trade* between the developing and developed states worked decidedly in the favour of the developed industrialized countries. In other words, the ability of developing states to pay for the import of manufactured goods from the developed world was declining, even if they increased exports of their own primary commodities. This in turn inhibited their ability to develop their own technological capacities to reduce their dependence on imported goods. This pointed to the structure of the world economy working to perpetuate the inequality of the international states system.

Subsequent research in the 1960s and 1970s by various Latin-American economists, many of whom were Marxists or strongly influenced by Marxism, developed Prebisch and Singer's initial findings further. Their research suggested that greater economic engagement of Latin American countries with the developed states within the global capitalist system appeared to make inequalities between states worse, rather than better. Indeed, rather than developing, these comparatively new arrivals in the world of independent states were in fact *underdeveloping*. One of the early pioneers of dependency theory, the Marxist scholar Andre Gunder Frank, expressed the research findings of the new dependency theorists succinctly:

> . . . historical research demonstrates that contemporary underdevelopment is in large part the historical product of past and continuing economic and other relations between the satellite undeveloped and the metropolitan developed countries. Furthermore, these relations are an essential part of the capitalist system on a word scale as a whole. (Gunder Frank, 1972: 3)

Gunder Frank's reference to 'satellite' and 'metropolitan' states echoes the structural depiction of the world in Lenin's analysis of imperialism that we discussed previously. Indeed, all the dependency theorists depict the world economy as structured in such a fashion as to benefit a core of developed states at the expense of the underdeveloped states on the global periphery. They challenged depictions of the post-colonial, poorer states in the Global South as somehow lagging, simply because they have failed to adopt the policies and values of the wealthier industrialized democracies in the Global North. Rather, they argued that the experience of the Latin American states showed that the patterns of exploitation established in the colonial era were continuing after decolonization. The underdevelopment of the Latin American states was a consequence of their continuing role as producers of raw materials and cheap labour, primarily for the benefit of their former colonial masters. It was the structural inequality of their relationship with the developed world and their difficulty in escaping from it that was inhibiting their development.

Most dependency theorists were clearly heavily influenced by Marxism, not least in the central place they gave to social classes in their analysis of international political and economic relations. In important respects, however, their work also indicates a decisive development of Marx's own work. For Marx, imperialism was a transformative process that served to extend Western capitalism across the face of the globe. It was seemingly therefore a necessary stage on the path to socialism, since it was under capitalism that class conflict would develop to the level necessary to generate revolutionary change and bring about the transition to socialism. Lenin also took a progressive historical view of capitalist imperialism, which, as we have seen, he depicted as the highest and final stage of capitalism. He believed that the imperial powers would inevitably go to war over the diminishing opportunities for exploitation overseas and bring about their own destruction. Lenin thought, (or, more accurately, hoped), that the penetration of capitalism in the colonized states would also, as in Europe, generate new class antagonisms. Thus, the millions of exploited workers in the colonized world would be crucial, he believed, in bringing about the international revolt against capitalism.

Lenin modified Marx's preliminary analysis through his analysis of imperialism, about which Marx had said relatively little. Similarly, the Marxist dependency theorists were looking at the empirical developments in the post-colonial era, which neither Marx nor Lenin could have anticipated during the high point of the colonial era when they were writing. The dependency theorists' analysis suggested a rather different outcome to that suggested by either Marx or Lenin. Regardless of who colonized them and despite the formal political process of decolonization, the global periphery remained locked into a dependent relationship with the developed world. This perpetuated their relative poverty, thereby sustaining their underdevelopment. Imperialism and colonial rule might have been disappearing in a formal sense, but they were leaving behind a structural legacy. This is captured by the terms neo-colonialism and neo-imperialism, which became increasingly prominent in the vocabulary of the social sciences in the wake of the colonial era.

Dependency and international class relations

As we have seen in Chapters 1 and 2, mainstream IR theory focuses on states as the main agents in the international system and the political dimensions of that system.

Dependency theory is also concerned with states, but its analysis differs from IR orthodoxy in its emphasis on the *political economy* of relations between states, the complex intersection of economics and politics, and not merely their political ties. Dependency theory also emphasizes the significance of international class relations. Dependency theory argues that there is evidence of mutual interest between the bourgeoisie, or ruling classes, in the developed and underdeveloping worlds. However, when it comes to the working classes, any such international class solidarity is much less evident.

How can this difference in class solidarity be explained? Dependency theory argues that within the developed world, this is in part because the economic exploitation of the underdeveloping countries enabled the bourgeoisie in the developed states to offset revolutionary impulses in their own working classes, through the astute use of profits to shore up welfare conditions and also through the cheaper provision of desirable commodities. Furthermore, this relationship of dependency also worked to seemingly set the interests of the working classes in the developed world *against* the interests of workers in the underdeveloping world. The continuing improvement of working-class lives in the developed core states of the world depended in part upon the continuing exploitation of workers in the global periphery.

Within the underdeveloping world, one of the legacies of colonialism is that many of the elites in underdeveloping countries were educated or trained in the former colonial power and absorbed many of the dominant values and ideas there. Therefore, many of the dominant class in underdeveloped states may believe that following the principles and practices of liberal capitalism is in the best interests of the working class in their own states. Additionally, in cases where the development of genuine democracy in an underdeveloping state is still incomplete or even non-existent, elites may use authoritarian policies and practices to constrain or repress dissatisfaction and dissent among their own poor. Working class solidarity in the developed world was also significantly enhanced by large-scale industrialization, something notably absent in most underdeveloped countries. However, dependency theorists have not agreed on the precise nature of class relations in underdeveloping states, not least because many of those states have quite distinctive histories. There is no agreed universal model of the internal nature of underdeveloping states, even if all are seen to suffer in some way from the structure of the global economy.

In the years since Dependency theory emerged, it has also become clear that some of the post-colonial states have fared better than others, at least in terms of their economic development. Latin America offers a mixed picture, African states perhaps even more so, while many post-colonial Southeast Asian states have achieved considerable economic development, Malaysia and Singapore being notable examples. This suggests that the simple binary model of developed and underdeveloped states developed by Dependency Theorists may be increasingly inadequate in capturing the complexities of the contemporary global capitalist system. One of the successors to dependency theory, World System's Theory, addresses this question by proposing three classes of states within the capitalist world economy. We discuss this next.

World Systems Theory

World Systems Theory (WST) emerged in the 1970s, most notably in the work of the American sociologist Immanuel Wallerstein. WST has evolved into a comprehensive and complex body of work, so we can only draw out some key themes here. The influence of Marxism is evident in Wallerstein's depiction of capitalism as the driving force in the evolution of the modern world system, although he also draws on other non-Marxist sources.

Wallerstein's use of the term *world* rather than *international* is significant. For Wallerstein, both orthodox international relations theory and modernization theory are too focused on states as the key unit of analysis. Like the dependency theorists, Wallerstein criticizes orthodox modernization theory, but he also departs from dependency theory in significant ways.

In accordance with the Marxist tradition, Wallerstein depicts capitalism and the imperialism of the major capitalist states as the principal sources of global inequality (Wallerstein, 1974a). Developing Marx's strong emphasis on the historical development of modern forms of social life, Wallerstein depicts capitalism as a system that has evolved out of Europe since the sixteenth century (not a starting date that all Marxists would agree with) and has now expanded across the globe to create a single, highly dynamic 'world economy'. In his view, all social institutions—states, social classes, households— are now shaped by the world economy. Although the world continues to be politically divided between states and is comprised of a variety of cultures, they all exist within a global division of labour, which, echoing Marx, Wallerstein argues is between the owners of capital and those who work for them. The differences between the various political systems found in the modern world system are determined to a significant degree by their location within the capitalist world economy.

In its analysis of the world capitalist system, dependency theory highlights two classes of states: core and periphery. In contrast, Wallerstein draws upon the history of the formation of what he calls the 'European world-economy' from the sixteenth century onwards to identify the roles of three regions or zones within it: core, periphery, and semi-periphery. These different zones effectively form a single division of labour within the European capitalist system (Wallerstein, 1974b). With the subsequent development of the European world economy into a capitalist world economy, a worldwide single division of labour emerges:

- **The core** contains the states that are the principal beneficiaries of the capitalist world system (Europe was the first core region). States within the core tend to import raw materials and convert these into manufactured goods for export, have stable democratic governments, high levels of welfare provision, and so on. Their dominance in the world system enables them to control the terms of trade and ensure their continuing accumulation of capital, derived from various forms of exploitation around the globe.

- **The periphery** is comprised of states that are, as dependency theory has argued, the principal losers in the world system. States within these regions tend to export primary products and import manufactured goods. They do this within terms of trade and unfair trade rules that work against them and suppress the wages of most of their inhabitants. They lack adequate welfare provision and often democratic forms of government as well.

- **The semi-periphery** comprises states that have a mix of peripheral and core features. They may have developed some industrial capacity and thus export manufactured goods as well as raw materials and they play a key 'buffer' role in the world economy. This is because they can be a source of skilled labour, which is still cheaper than in the core zones, and therefore offer new lower-cost locations for industries previously located in core states (Wallerstein, 1974b).

Central to Wallerstein's depiction of the world system is its dynamism. As with Marx, the various stages in human social development are viewed historically: they emerge under certain conditions, which implies that they can also come to an end. As the system develops, the various social and political entities that comprise it, such as states and classes, undergo change. This means that peripheral states may come to acquire semi-peripheral status, for example. Similarly, Wallerstein argues, the total world system itself has a definitive history. Importantly, as a dynamic system, it will go through periods of crisis, which for Wallerstein, as for other Marxists, are also windows of opportunity for change. Only a few years before his death in 2019, Wallerstein maintained that the world capitalist system was slowly disintegrating (Wallerstein, 2013 and 2015). Like many other Marxist scholars, Wallerstein also saw his scholarly work as also a form of political protest and his later work was very much focused on outlining an alternative fairer and more just world system to the present one.

5.4 **MARXISM AND IPE/GPE**

We noted in our discussion of liberalism in Chapter 2 that since the late 1970s a lot of liberal IR scholarship can now be found under the label of International Political Economy (IPE). This is because of the emphasis that some liberal scholars since the 1970s began to place on the influence of economic relations on political relationships between states. The economic dimensions of international relations, they argued, had been traditionally viewed (most notably within the realist tradition) as 'low politics' and, therefore, of less importance in contrast to the 'high politics' of national security issues.

Since then, IPE, increasingly referred to these days as Global Political Economy (GPE), has grown significantly as a field and is continuing to evolve and diversify. Reflecting its origins as a sub-discipline of IR, much of IPE/GPE overlaps substantially with IR and the boundary between the two fields is fuzzy. Although many, perhaps most, IPE/GPE scholars continue to use the term *international* political economy to label their work, the field's main concern these days is arguably with the *global* political economy. This reflects the perception found across most of the different theoretical approaches within the IPE field that the prefix 'international' over-emphasizes the role of states and does not capture the multitude of significant actors or the complex trans-national processes that comprise the intersection of political and economic relations at the global level.

The key concerns of the founding liberal IPE scholars were such things as the role and impact of international economic and financial institutions and the relationship between 'states and markets', as one famous founding IPE scholar, Susan Strange, put it (Strange, 1988). These remain key areas of the IPE research agenda. Importantly, IPE also provides a key site for Marxist and neo-Marxist IR scholars who, following Marx, have always started from a political economy perspective, and found orthodox IR's emphasis on political relations inherently too restrictive. The growth of the Neo-Gramscian perspective on IPE, in particular (which we will go on to discuss in more detail later in this section of the chapter) has led to the emergence of Critical IPE/GPE as an influential counterpoint to liberal and other more mainstream approaches (Cafruny, Talani, and Martin, 2016). In recent years, the perspectives found in IPE/GPE have multiplied considerably with important contributions now also coming from scholars drawing from other critical IR theoretical perspectives such as feminism and environmentalism (for a comprehensive overview of contemporary GPE see O'Brien and Williams, 2020).

One of the key issues in this debate is the concept of globalization. Debates between liberals and Marxists of various kinds around the definition and analysis of globalization form a very large part of contemporary IPE/GPE scholarship.

Marxism and Globalization

The precise definition of 'globalization' is a matter of dispute (we discuss various definitions in Key concept 5.3). The broad thrust of most understandings of the term, however, is that it connotes the transformation of international politics into something better described as *world politics* or *global politics*, with a corresponding decline in the significance of national borders as well as the erosion of distinctions between *domestic* and *international* economic, political, and social relations. Globalization is often presented in terms of a shrinking world or heralding the emergence of a 'borderless' world (Ohmae, 1990). If you look at the use of the term in the public sphere (in the media, everyday political rhetoric, and so on), especially in the West, you might gain the distinct impression that globalization is a relatively new phenomenon that national governments are relatively powerless to affect and must learn to live within.

Much of liberal IR and IPE scholarship, presents globalization in largely positive terms. From a liberal point of view, deepening globalization means the increasing integration, potentially at least, of economic activity across the world. As barriers to trade are eliminated and capital and investment is allowed to flow more freely and globally, the present inequalities between states will begin to decline and the equality of opportunities to grow and develop will increase. If capital is allowed to invest in the underdeveloped parts of the world, it will help bring them up to speed, so to speak. A more integrated world economy presents us then, liberals argue, with a host of new opportunities to transcend the political divisions of old and better cooperate with peoples around the world to address the many global-level problems that confront humanity, such as environmental problems, human rights violations, global poverty, and so on. In key respects, the liberal understanding of globalization can be seen as a radical extension of the idea of *complex interdependence* that emerged within liberal IR scholarship in the 1970s (you can read more about this in Chapter 2, Section 2.4).

> **KEY CONCEPT 5.3** GLOBALIZATION

Globalization is a term used to capture the general idea that the world is becoming increasingly interconnected politically, economically, and even culturally. Scholars disagree as to when globalization started, although there is quite widespread agreement that it has accelerated in the last few decades because of changes in the global political economy (particular the greater mobility of finance, i.e., money, across national borders), the growing influence of multinational corporations, the increased movement of peoples, and revolutions in transport and communications technology.

Globalization continues to generate, often heated, public and scholarly debate. Is it predominantly an economic phenomenon, or are its political social and cultural effects also important? Is it primarily the product of policy decisions from within advanced industrial nations, in reflection of their shared economic and political interests? Or is it somehow an inevitable outcome of human progress and technological innovation, which is inescapably changing most people's lives even at the local level?

Certainly, perceptions of its various effects, exaggerated or not, have also generated a lot of popular opposition. Is it simply a code word for the transformation and deregulation of the whole global economy along neoliberal lines (as many Marxist critics would argue)? Will it accelerate the erosion of local and national cultures and identities, which many people hold dear? Put differently, do ideas, images knowledge and information now increasingly flow across a world space, rather than once distinctive national or local spaces?

Much of globalization is seen to involve the deregulation of transnational economic activity and there is widespread disagreement about the benefits or costs of this, especially for the global poor. Arguably, concerns about some of the consequences of greater global mobility are also stimulating the greater regulation of the movement of peoples. Particularly vulnerable here are political and economic migrants or refugees trying to move from the world's periphery to core countries, where they believe they might have better prospects.

This has in turn generated increasing public hostility within many developed countries from sections of the public who believe that such migration threatens their own livelihoods or poses challenges to dominant cultural and social norms and traditions. In this sense, globalization may entail simultaneous yet contradictory effects: eroding national borders in some respects, while creating political pressures to shore up them up in others.

In Chapter 2 we noted that the wide variety of economic policies that characterized the Western developed states in the post-1945 era have increasingly given way to a single model: neoliberalism. This is not to be confused with the term 'neoliberalism' used in IR theory to refer to the liberal response to the emergence of neorealism (which we discuss in Chapter 3, Section 3.7). Indeed, both enthusiasts and critics of globalization see as one of its key characteristics the acceleration of the spread of neoliberalism worldwide. This is achieved through, for example, the myriad connections between advanced industrial economies states—working with private multinational corporations (MNCs) headquartered within them—and other still developing states.

Neoliberalism is centred around a vision of the world economy that is often also referred to as the 'Washington consensus'. This comprises several policy prescriptions that the developed states have adopted and expect developing states to adopt if they want to ensure their future development and full integration into global markets. Such policies include tight controls on national budget deficits, trade liberalization, greater deregulation of the national economy, eliminating barriers to foreign investment, and carefully controlled public expenditure. In other words, it is markets and not the state that should drive national economic policy and development strategies. In essence, neoliberalism marks the abandonment of the widespread post-1945 consensus that 'governments had a duty to act alongside or against market forces in order to address inequality' (Cammack, 2019: 400).

Underpinning this view is the long-standing notion of 'trickle-down', that was a key part of orthodox modernization theory. If the global very rich are getting richer—and all the evidence suggests they are—then some of this wealth will supposedly ultimately trickle down to the global poor. Indeed, advocates of globalization claim that extreme poverty is falling globally, and social mobility is rising thereby seemingly demonstrating that globalization is making everyone richer. Despite this, however, inequality has been shown to be growing, both between the richest and the poorest states and within most states, including developed states such as the US and the UK (Cammack, 2009).

We have already seen that Marx and Engels, writing in the mid-nineteenth century, showed extraordinary foresight about the future global expansion of capitalism (Pradella, 2015). Echoing this, Marxist critics of neoliberal globalization argue that is an economic and political project with much longer historical roots than popular representations of it suggest. What today is referred to as globalization is in fact the culmination of a long historical process of capitalism's expansion out from its origins in Europe. For contemporary Marxists, globalization is not simply a description of the current world economy, but is, in fact, an ideological construct that is intended to legitimate the further expansion of capitalism and neoliberal policies.

Some Marxists question whether globalization has dramatically transformed the international economy as much as is commonly claimed (Rosenberg, 2000 and 2005; Hirst, Thompson, and Bromley, 2009). They question whether globalization has resulted in a significant decline in national economies or, by extension, the decreasing significance of political borders. In their well-known critique of the globalization thesis, Paul Hirst, Graham Thompson, and Simon Bromley argue that Western Europe offers the only example of a genuinely integrated trading zone. Measuring trade flows is a highly complex and much debated activity, but Hirst, Thompson, and Bromley argue that it is hard to show by any measure that contemporary flows of trade and levels of economic integration are historically exceptional. They also question the level of integrated global *governance* (i.e., coordinated management) of the supposedly globalizing world economy. The key international institutions—the WTO, World Bank, and the IMF—that endeavour to manage and regulate global economic activity remain overwhelmingly dominated by the developed states. Hirst and Thompson argue that the contemporary international economic system is dominated by three major trading blocs, all comprised of developed states: the US-centred North American Free Trade Area, Japan (because of its bloc-sized economy), and the European Union. Most MNCs come from within these blocs and each of the blocs has distinctive policies, institutions, and problems (Hirst, Thompson, and Bromley, 2009).

In sum, some Marxist critics challenge the rather tidy liberal image of a world becoming more integrated and managed along the lines of a single liberal economic model. Instead, they emphasize continuing *national* economic and political rivalry as well as continuing economic disparity between the rich and poor of the world. Trade flows between the developed and developing worlds remain highly asymmetric and political resistance within states on the global periphery (and, it must be said, within developed states as well) to further economic liberalization suggest a much messier picture.

The speed and extent of globalization may be a matter of debate among Marxists but, from a broad Marxist point of view, the further integration of the world economy is neither a natural nor an inevitable process. Rather, it is seen as a project initiated by the major capitalist developed states to serve the interests of their ruling classes.

The major global financial institutions, such as the World Bank and the IMF, now claim that the alleviation or elimination of global poverty is a primary policy goal. One prominent British Marxist IPE scholar, Paul Cammack, argues that in support of this goal these institutions increasingly shifted their focus from the global regulation and integration of trade and finance—their traditional roles—to the promotion of reform along neoliberal lines *within* states. Cammack argues that this even applies to international agencies, such as the United Nations Development Programme (UNDP) and the United Nations Conference on Trade and Development (UNCTAD), that were established in the mid-1960s specifically to address global economic inequality. The UNDP and UNCTAD were once noted for their commitment to state intervention in markets to support more equitable development within and between states, but they are now embracing the market-oriented neoliberal agenda (Cammack, 2009).

Through Marxist lenses, this commitment of the key institutions of global capitalism to the elimination of global poverty is in fact consistent with Marx's original analysis of the historical pattern of capitalist accumulation. The relentless pursuit of profit requires extracting more from the global workforce at the lowest cost. One way to do this is to expand that workforce as much as possible, by bringing into it even the very poorest and unwaged in the global periphery. The creation of new sources of labour also maintains the competition for work and thus keeps downward pressure on wages. This is how, Marxist IPE scholars argue, you can simultaneously appear to be working to reduce absolute poverty while maintaining or even enhancing global inequality.

Cammack develops this line of argument further. He draws upon Marx's original account of the development of capitalism to show how institutions such as the World Bank and the Organisation for Economic Cooperation and Development (OECD) are not merely working to promote the interests of 'The West', or to persuade countries in the Global South to adjust their economies to suit the interests of the industrialized states in the Global North. Rather their ultimate objective is much more expansive than this. It is, Cammack argues, nothing less than 'the management and transformation of social relations on a global scale' in reflection of the interests of global capital. To do this 'they have jointly sought to persuade *all* countries, in the South and North alike, to adjust their economies and societies to the demands of a genuinely competitive capitalist world order' (Cammack, 2022: 15). Here we can see how Marxism is deployed to depict relations between states (the primary focus of most orthodox IR thinking) as ultimately subordinate to the politics of global class relations. Through classical Marxist lenses, then, what is commonly called globalization is not some comparatively recent phenomenon of debatable origin. Rather, it should be understood as the consequence of the long historical evolution of capitalism and global class relations. States may have played their part in this, but they will ultimately be subsumed within it.

THINK CRITICALLY 5.2

Evaluate each of these claims about globalization:
- Globalization will ultimately benefit all because it breaks down barriers and is helping to create a truly global community
- New technologies have revolutionized our awareness of the world beyond our own social and political communities
- Cities across the world are beginning to look more and more like each other
- Cultural trends move far more readily and swiftly across political, social, and cultural boundaries
- Greater awareness of ourselves as members of a wider global community encourages the search for shared solutions to shared problems, such as the global environmental crisis
- Globalization is a highly uneven process which perpetuates global economic exploitation
- Many parts of the world have very limited or no access to new technologies
- The political, social, and cultural values that globalization helps to disseminate flow predominantly in one direction—from the West outwards
- Globalization is marginalizing or even eroding non-Western ideas and lifestyles
- Globalization is generating increased resistance to Western influence, thereby creating new sources of conflict
- Globalization is just the latest stage of Western capitalist imperialism.

1) Which of these claims do you agree or disagree with?
2) Consider your answers to Q1. Do they add up to a positive, negative, or mixed assessment of globalization?

Neo-Gramscianism and the concept of hegemony

A common and long-standing criticism that has been levelled at Marxism is that it is too economistic and deterministic. For some critics, the key deficiency of classical Marxism is an insufficient analysis of the political, particularly the historical evolution of diverse models of the sovereign state. It places too great an emphasis on the prevailing capitalist economic system and tends to depict all other aspects of human social relations as ultimately determined by that system. This is of relevance not only to the analysis of social relations within states but also to the relationship between capitalism and the international system of states (Davenport, 2011). One of the key issues at stake here is whether competition between states can be explained primarily in terms of the logic of capitalist expansion, as Marxism suggests, or whether there is a territorial or security logic to it, as realism proposes (Berki, 1971). In other words, do states compete (or sometimes cooperate) because they are concerned about defending their territorial sovereignty? As is noted in Chapter 3, realists trace inter-state rivalry back to the ancient Greek states system and the Italian states system of the Medieval and Renaissance eras, i.e., prior to the emergence of the capitalist system.

Some varieties of Marxism do accord greater autonomy to the social, cultural, and political realms. One of the most notable examples that has become prominent in both IR and IPE/GPE is neo-Gramscianism, which draws upon and develops the work of the Italian Marxist Antonio Gramsci (1891–1937). In particularly Gramsci's concept of *hegemony*, is deployed to analyse and critique the contemporary global political economy (for more on Gramsci see Key thinker 5.3).

KEY THINKER 5.3 ANTONIO GRAMSCI

Antonio Gramsci (1891–1937) was an Italian philosopher and politician. A brilliant scholar, Gramsci became involved in left-wing politics as a student and went on to establish the Italian Communist Party. When the party was outlawed by the fascist Mussolini government, Gramsci, who had been elected to parliament, was imprisoned. While in prison, Gramsci studied and wrote extensively on a wide range of subjects, including Italian history and politics, fascism, capitalism, and popular culture.

Gramsci was released from prison on health grounds but died shortly afterwards. Because much of it was written during incarceration, Gramsci's scholarly writings are fragmented and sometimes cryptic as they were reviewed by prison censors. Extracts from his prison writings were not published until 1947 (the full set of prison notebooks did not appear until 1975) but they have subsequently had a very significant influence on the development of Western Leftist thinking and politics and the emergence of distinctive Western varieties of Marxism.

Although undoubtedly a Marxist and a founding member of the Communist Party of Italy, Gramsci is also noted for his critique of the economic determinism (seeing economics as the predominant determinant of human social history) of much Marxist scholarship. If we recall that classical Marxism operates with a base-superstructure model, in which the base represents the underlying capitalist economic system and the superstructure represents the political and social institutions that sustain it, then Gramsci was particularly interested in the superstructural dimensions of capitalism. Gramsci wrote extensively on how the ruling class rules and maintains its position of dominance over a working class which it is openly exploiting. Why do not the numerically much larger working class simply revolt against their oppressors? Are they simply coerced into submission, or is the process of domination more complex than that?

Central to Gramsci's analysis is the role of *cultural hegemony*. We note in Chapter 3 how the term hegemony, referring simply to the domination of some states within the international system of states, figures prominently in mainstream IR debates. Gramsci's use of the term is much richer in content. For Gramsci, hegemony is a complex and often subtle process in which consent figures larger than coercion. Under conditions of hegemony, the dominant class develops a social vision which promises to address the needs of all members of society. The values and norms within that social vision permeate the state institutions that make up the superstructure, but they also become dispersed throughout *civil society*—the private or non-state sphere of organized social life—and therefore over time become seemingly commonsensical. Gramsci emphasized the roles of religion, traditional values, and popular culture in helping to develop and sustain such cultural hegemony. In other words, a ruling class cannot dominate by force and coercion alone; it needs also to exercise plausible intellectual and moral leadership, which comes to be accepted by the majority. As James Joll puts it, for Gramsci, 'political leadership must be based on cultural and moral ascendancy as well as on economic predominance' (Joll, 1977: 8). This view can be seen in Gramsci's assessment of how the ruling class rules and, by extension, how the prevailing hegemony was to be challenged.

Gramsci described the various social forces that combined to sustain the cultural hegemony of the ruling class as an 'historical bloc'. The dominant values and norms might be contested to some extent in various arenas, and this can lead to the need for the prevailing historical bloc to make some compromises and concessions, or even adjust key facets of its domination. Cultural hegemony works, however, when the fundamentals of the dominant social vision appear plausible and thus remain uncontested by the majority of those who live within it. Gramsci's account also led to his articulation of a pathway to radical social change—through the development of a counter-hegemonic vision and, the creation of an alternative historical bloc (Gramsci, 1971).

Central to the process of challenging hegemony was the leadership role of 'organic intellectuals'. According to Gramsci these were both established intellectuals within the dominant class who decide to challenge the prevailing hegemonic order and align with the revolutionary class as well as intellectuals who emerged out of the revolutionary class itself. Such intellectuals, moreover, could not be an elite group positioning itself as somehow above the political struggle for change. They had to be 'linked organically to a national-popular mass' (Gramsci, 1971: 204).

It should be noted here that many IR and IPE scholars influenced by Gramsci would see their own intellectual output as contributions, however modest, to the development of a counter-hegemonic *critical* understanding of dominant relations of power in the international system. While retaining a commitment to the principles of robust scholarship, this understanding has, nonetheless, an underlying political purpose to it. It rests on a view that challenges the orthodox depiction of scholars and their theoretical enquiries as offering purely objective analyses, of being somehow outside of or above politics. It is, in other words, a form of Critical International Theory which is premised ultimately on the view that all political analysis is part of politics itself, whether it acknowledges it or not. Gramsci was not the only source of this understanding of intellectuals and their output, but his work is one of the key influences on the idea of Critical International Theory, which we explore more fully in Chapter 6.

Gramsci's influence is particularly prominent within IPE/GPE. Although little of Gramsci's work directly addressed international political economy, his modifications of Marxism have come to influence neo-Gramscian IPE scholarship which has become one of the key counterpoints to liberal IPE. The noted neo-Gramscian IPE scholar, Robert Cox, argues that labels such as IR or international politics are misleading because they over-emphasize the role of states and relations between them. Cox uses the term 'world order' to get around the state-centrism of orthodox IR theories. For Cox, states are an important component of world order, but they are themselves shaped by complex social and economic forces that emerge from both within and outside. Cox draws upon Gramsci's understanding of hegemony to depict world order as the product of specific constellations of historical social, political, economic, and intellectual processes that operate at all levels, from civil societies within states through to the global. The structure of a global order at any given time is, Cox argues, the product of the interaction between material capabilities, ideas, and institutions (Cox, 1981).

As with other varieties of Marxism, the primary focus of neo-Gramscian IPE is on exposing the exploitative structure of the contemporary capitalist global political economy. Neo-Gramscian scholars draw upon Gramsci's understanding of hegemony to capture the way in which the global capitalist system is sustained through the emergence of a *transnational historical bloc*. This bloc—comprised of advanced industrialized states, multinational corporations, international financial institutions, as well as sympathetic think-tanks, intellectuals, social organizations, and so on—works to present globalization as somehow inevitable and necessary. Seen thus, the further standardization of national economies under a single global regulatory regime based on liberal capitalist principles appears as the only sensible or plausible response.

Cox builds upon Gramsci to argue that resisting the current direction of capitalist globalization requires the emergence of a new counter-hegemonic transnational historical bloc to bring about the transformation of the global order into something more just and equitable. In other words, it requires the coming together of social forces—such as social movements, community organizations, non-governmental organizations, and intellectuals—to create a 'counterweight to the hegemonic power structure and ideology' (Cox, 1999: 13). This will be no easy task as any alternative historical bloc would have to emerge in several countries simultaneously to build a critical mass capable of challenging the hegemony of neoliberal globalization.

Cox sees globalization as producing a three-level global social hierarchy among the peoples of the world:

- those who are fully integrated into the world economy
- those who participate within it but in a more precarious and subordinate way
- those who are excluded from it (Cox, 2002: 84).

This social division cuts across national political boundaries and makes the task of resistance even more daunting:

> The challenge to globalization, if it is to become activated, would require the formation of a common will, a vision of an alternative future, and the transcendence of the manifold divisions of ethnicity, religion, gender, and geography that cut across the three-level social hierarchy being created by globalisation. (Cox 2002: 85)

In this observation we can see a shift away from Marxism's traditional emphasis on the struggle between classes defined primarily according to their position in the capitalist economy. For Cox, the understanding of class needs now to incorporate other social identities such as ethnicity, gender, and religion as these are important sites for challenges to the global status quo.

Challenging the 'Washington consensus'

A consistent theme in Marxist IR/IPE scholarship is the depiction of capitalism as undergoing periods of crisis which might provide opportunities for the emergence of widespread popular resistance. There is increasing evidence to suggest that neoliberal globalization is meeting with significant resistance worldwide. Countries like China, India, and Russia have frequently expressed resentment at the Western dominance of global financial institutions. Indeed, China's economic growth model is seen by some as the basis for an alternative to the 'Washington Consensus', the label often used to describe the neoliberal free-market policies supported by the major global financial institutions, such as the World Bank, the IMF, and the US Treasury. In 2004, an American China analyst Joshua Ramo introduced the term 'Beijing Consensus' (which we discuss in more detail in Key concept 5.4). This was intended to capture what he saw as China's rejection of the central assumption of the Washington consensus 'that there was a single prescriptive economic model that would provide reliable growth for all nations were it uniformly followed' (Ramo cited in Elen, 2016). Ramo argued that China's alternative to Western neoliberalism was proving more attractive to many developing nations who wanted to develop independent strategies for growth that did not require them simply to comply with the economic and political demands of dominant Western capitalist states.

KEY CONCEPT 5.4 THE 'BEIJING CONSENSUS'

The collapse of the Soviet bloc in 1989–91 was interpreted by many as demonstrating the failure of any viable communist alternative to the predominant Western model of economic development. The rise of communist China since the end of the Cold War, however, has helped to reignite the debate about alternatives to Western neoliberal development policies.

Joshua Cooper Ramo introduced the term 'Beijing Consensus' in a 2004 paper to describe what he saw as a distinctive Chinese model of national economic development which was proving more attractive to several developing countries than the prescriptions of the Washington consensus. Ramo argues that the Beijing Consensus rests on three broad guidelines:

- a commitment to innovation and constant experimentation reflecting China's economic and political environment (such as China's controversial 'one child' policy), rather than adherence to a single universal model of development

- not measuring economic progress solely by growth in per capita income (a country's economic income divided by its total population) but also by the sustainability of economic growth and the improvement of economic inequality

- The importance of national economic, political, and military self-determination as ways of resisting external pressures to conform to dominant Western economic and political developmental models (i.e., the Washington consensus).

According to Ramo, 'China is writing its own book now. The book represents a fusion of Chinese thinking with lessons learned from the failure of globalisation culture in other places. The rest of the world has begun to study this book' (Ramo, 2004: 5).

The claim that there is a distinctive Chinese model is also widely disputed. For example, The China specialist Arif Dirlik sees the notion of a Beijing Consensus as insufficiently specific to offer a clear alternative model to the Washington Consensus (Dirlik, 2004, 2012). The precise role of Marxism in the concept is also debateable, as is the extent to which it is a product of China's unique circumstances and thus not suitable as a model for other states to emulate.

Nonetheless, even its critics concede that the Beijing Consensus remains a powerful idea that is clearly attractive to several developing states. This is not least because although China is clearly committed to integration into the world economy, it seeks to do so on its own political terms and not those dictated by the dominant Washington consensus.

There are a growing number of national and transnational social movements and Non-Governmental Organizations (NGOs) who also see globalization as a code-word for the promotion of the continuing Western dominance of the global political economy guided by neoliberal economic and social policies. Both Cox and Wallerstein see signs of a potential anti-globalization movement in the growing anti-neoliberal activism of trade unions, peace movements, environmentalists, women's organizations, Indigenous people's movements, and some churches (Cox, 1999; Wallerstein, 2005 and 2013).

The global financial crisis of 2008 appears also to have heightened public discontent with neoliberalism. The emergence in 2011 of the 'Occupy!' protest movement was a notable example of an explosion of popular resistance to the effects of the financial crisis of 2008. The movement emerged out of protests in the US and rapidly spread to more than 80 countries. Its slogan—'we are the 99%'—might be numerically questionable but it expressed the view that while the majority had to suffer the consequences of the failures of key financial institutions, notably because of the adoption by many countries of policies that were widely seen to impose severe economic austerity upon them, the wealthiest continued to prosper. Other examples include the *Los Indignados* (The indignant or outraged) social movement in Spain which also emerged in 2011 and the dramatic rise in Greece of the left-wing political party Syriza (an abbreviation of 'The Coalition of the Radical Left' in Greek) which won the 2015 general election.

The Occupy! movement failed, however, to sustain itself for more than a few years and both Spain and Greece have seen a return to prominence of more mainstream political parties and policies. Nonetheless, anti-neoliberal and anti-globalization movements remain prominent features of many national political landscapes and now intersect with the rise of public concern about the global environmental crisis (which we cover in Chapter 11) and the failure of governments to respond to it. There are also less dramatic but perhaps still significant signs of public questioning of the virtues of neoliberal globalization. In recent years, for example, many social movements in the developed states have attempted to highlight the exploitative underpinnings of cheap commodities, such as clothes, which are so attractive to consumers. Recent initiatives, such as labelling goods as 'fair trade', might suggest growing public and commercial awareness in the developed world of the unequal global terms of trade and their impoverishing effects in the underdeveloped world. An interesting question then, from a neo-Gramscian perspective, is whether and under what conditions might these strands of resistance eventually add up to form a viable alternative transnational historical bloc.

Some parts of the Global South have undoubtedly benefited from better integration into global markets. If, however, dependency theorists, World Systems theorists, and other Marxists or neo-Marxists have been right in their analyses of the fundamental structural features of the global capitalist economy over the last few decades, the bulk of the world's poorest are likely to remain so. The reduction of absolute poverty globally, does not necessarily translate into a lessening of global inequality. Indeed, it may go hand in hand with a growth in the gap between the global rich and poor. Although not a Marxist, the French Economist Thomas Piketty (whose recent best-selling book has, nonetheless, a Marxist-sounding title: *Capital in the Twenty-first Century*) draws upon 250 years of economic data to show that economic inequality is not only an inevitable feature of global capitalism, but that historically it has continued to increase. Piketty proposes a progressive global tax on wealth to combat inequality and bring about a better global distribution of wealth (Piketty, 2014). For Marxists, such solutions are radically insufficient because they only endeavour to address the symptoms of exploitation—such as economic inequality—not the causes. Marxists see human exploitation as the inevitable outcome of a capitalist world economy and the reason why capitalism needs to be replaced with an alternative, more equitable system.

5.5 CONCLUSION

By now it should be clear that as a perspective on international politics, compared to the mainstream IR perspectives, Marxism is distinctive in terms of the central question that it seeks to address. Realism is primarily concerned with state survival in an inherently dangerous anarchic international order which is, moreover, unlikely to change significantly. Liberal IR starts out with a similar recognition of the dangers of international politics in an anarchical system of states. Unlike realism, however, liberals see the possibility of reform and change through greater institutionalization and cooperation in the international system (even if they might disagree about the pace and extent of such reform).

In contrast, Marxism brings to IR an overriding concern with the question of human social and economic inequality, how it came about and how it is sustained globally. Like liberalism, Marxism is a progressive political philosophy (i.e., it promotes the possibility of change at the international level), but it radically parts company with liberalism on how significant change might come about and the extent of the change needed. What liberals see as a pathway to a fairer world in which individual freedom is enhanced—a global, market-based capitalist economy—is for Marxists the principal barrier to realizing a more just and equitable world. The realization of true emancipation (or liberation) for all humans is not to be achieved through the reform of the global capitalist system, but through its eventual elimination and replacement by a radically different system.

As we noted at the outset of this chapter, Marx argued that the point of reflecting on our world is to change it. In this claim we see the germ of the idea of Critical International Theory, the subject of Chapter 6. For Marxists, analysing capitalism is not just a benign, scholarly activity; it is the basis for discerning pathways to a better, more just, and equitable future for all of humanity. If you read the output of most Marxist scholars, it is readily apparent that they are committed to rigorous scholarly enquiry. Because this is underpinned by a commitment to pursing radical economic and social change, however, it is seen by some of its critics as incompatible with orthodox views of social science scholarship as a supposedly dispassionate, objective activity. The relationship between scholarship and politics is a complex and important theme that we also discuss in Chapter 6 and other chapters examining non-mainstream IR theoretical perspectives.

SUMMARIZING MARXISM

- The term Marxism refers not only to the nineteenth-century writings of Karl Marx but also the vast and diverse body of work that has been and continues to be directly influenced by them
- Marx's work was interdisciplinary—drawing from across the whole range of what today are known as the social sciences—in reflection of his view that social reality had to be studied in its totality
- The pursuit of knowledge for Marx was always purposeful and critical, a perspective famously captured in his declaration that 'philosophers have only interpreted the world, in various ways; the point, however, is to change it'
- A central theme in Marx's work was the analysis of historical processes of change. Marx emphasized the need to understand how societies formed and evolved to better discern the prospects for achieving human emancipation from all forms of oppression

- Marx's philosophical outlook was historical materialism. The historical interaction of humans with their material circumstances—a process that Marx described as dialectical—provided the motor of history and determined the prospects for social and political change

- For Marx, 'material circumstances' referred primarily to the prevailing economic system. This led to a sustained critique of capitalism as a mode of production, which he saw as inherently exploitative of the working class, or proletariat

- For Marx, capitalism was nonetheless a necessary stage in societal development because it would ultimately generate class consciousness among the proletariat

- Marx depicted class struggle between the proletariat and the owners of the means of production, the bourgeoisie, as the primary motor of revolutionary change

- Marxism was notably absent from the IR discipline until the late 1960s. Orthodox IR scholars generally saw it as largely irrelevant to the study of political relations between states

- Marx wrote comparatively little on international affairs, but in the early twentieth century, his successors, notably Lenin, began to apply his work to the analysis of imperialism

- Lenin saw European imperialism as the 'highest and final stage of capitalism', which entailed collaboration between banks and dominant political classes in the exploitation of new sources of cheap colonial labour

- Lenin's analysis questioned Marx's assumption of a natural worldwide affinity between workers, because the exploitation of labour overseas could be used to quell working class discontent in the colonizing states, thus creating an international 'labour aristocracy'

- Lenin's depiction of the world as consisting of a core of developed states exploiting a periphery of undeveloped states was developed considerably from the 1960s onwards in the form of dependency theory

- Significantly influenced by Marxism, dependency theory examines the core-periphery relationship between states in the developed world and those in the Global South

- Dependency theory challenges the dominant model of economic modernization, drawing on empirical and historical evidence to show how the structure of the international political economy inhibits the capacity of formerly colonized states to fully develop economically and socially

- Dependency theory was developed and modified further by subsequent Marxist-influenced scholars, notably Immanuel Wallerstein in his World Systems Theory

- Marx is widely seen as a key figure in the development of Political Economy as an analytical perspective. Marxist perspectives have thus become particularly prominent in the field of International Political Economy (IPE), which emerged from the IR discipline in the 1970s

- More recently, Marxists have been particularly prominent in challenging orthodox, liberal understandings of globalization
- From a Marxist perspective globalization is neither new nor natural but the outcome of a long historical process of capitalist expansion. Globalization is depicted as an ideological construction intended to legitimize and make a virtue of the continuing global expansion of capitalism
- Many Marxist IR/IPE scholars are neo-Gramscians who draw upon the work of the Italian Marxist scholar Gramsci
- Gramsci critiqued what he saw as the excessive economic determinism of classical Marxism and developed an understanding of capitalist hegemony which gives greater weight to political, social, and cultural processes.

QUESTIONS

1. What are the key components of Marx's philosophical outlook of historical materialism?
2. Why did Lenin describe imperialist colonialism as the 'highest stage of capitalism'?
3. How useful do you think social class is for the analysis of international politics?
4. What are the main differences between Marxist and Liberal analyses of globalization? Which do you find broadly the more plausible?
5. Do you think Wallerstein is right to depict the capitalist world system as 'disintegrating'? What evidence might you use to support your response?
6. To what extent, if any, should we judge Marxism by the historical record of existing communist states, past and present?

IR THEORY TODAY 'VACCINE APARTHEID': CORONAVIRUS VACCINATIONS AND GLOBAL INEQUALITY

The rapid global spread of the COVID-19 coronavirus during 2020 spurred a race to develop vaccines. By December 2020 several vaccines developed by Western pharmaceutical companies—notably Biontec/Pfizer, AstraZeneca, Moderna, and Johnson & Johnson—were approved worldwide. Some states also decided to approve vaccines developed in Russia, China, and India. Most of the leading vaccines are manufactured in Europe and the US although India is also a major producer of the AstraZeneca vaccine, as well as the Russian Sputnik-V vaccine and some of its own vaccines.

In March 2020, G20 leaders called for the establishment of a framework for global collaboration in the fight to control the global COVID-19 pandemic. Subsequently, under the slogan 'none of us will be safe until all of us are safe', the WHO led the establishment of COVAX. This is a global initiative that works with governments and manufacturers to ensure the equitable distribution of COVID-19 vaccines worldwide. Its initial goal was to distribute 2 billion vaccine doses across almost 200 countries by the end of 2021. It was hoped that this would result in poorer countries ultimately being able to vaccinate at least 20 per cent of their populations.

According to the *New York Times* covid vaccinations tracker, by the end of August 2021 more than 5.3 billion vaccine doses had been administered worldwide, 69 doses for every hundred people. However, the distribution of these vaccines shows significant variation between individual countries as well as between the Global North and Global South. Many states in the Global North, such as the US, UK, Canada, Israel, and the EU member states had fully vaccinated more than 50 per cent of their populations, some considerably more than that. By contrast, some of the world's poorest states and those affected by ongoing violent conflict, such as Chad, Haiti, Congo, Somalia, Mali, Tanzania, and Sudan had achieved full vaccination rates of less than 0.5 per cent. 82 per cent of vaccine shots had been administered in higher- and upper-middle income countries and only 0.3 % in low-income countries (*The New York Times*, 31 August 2021).

A key issue is that of intellectual property (IP) rights, which prevent poorer countries from gaining access to the knowledge required to produce their own vaccines. Vaccine manufacturing, research, and development is very heavily concentrated in a small group of high- and middle-income countries. Companies in these countries hold the IP rights and have sold most vaccine doses to their own governments, or governments of other high-income countries. In stark contrast, Africa imports 99 per cent of its vaccines and most African states lack the purchasing capacity of wealthier countries (Editorial, *Nature*, 27 May 2021). In October 2020, India and South Africa launched a campaign within the WTO to suspend IP rights. In May 2021, China, Russia, and the US agreed to support the campaign, although the pharmaceutical companies who manufacture the vaccines continue to oppose it. However, the capacity of lower-income countries to undertake the complex production of vaccines remained a matter of debate (*BMJ*, 2021).

Some of the wealthier countries, such as New Zealand and Australia, have been less successful in procuring and administering vaccines compared to others, although this is the result of internal political decisions rather than economic factors. Some middle-income countries in the Global South have achieved full vaccination rates comparable to those of many high-income states in the Global North.

Looked at on a continental basis, however, the variation in full vaccination rates by August 2021 was clear:

Vaccination rates by continent
Doses administered per hundred people (global average is 69)

Europe	99
North America	94
South America	83
Asia	76
Oceania	56
Africa	7.4

(*The New York Times*, 31 August 2021)

Vaccine supply became more abundant throughout 2022 with more than two dozen vaccination types used worldwide (although their relative efficacy varies considerably). By early February 2023 much of the global inequality in vaccination rates had been eradicated (72 per cent of the world's population had received at least one dose) and public demand for vaccination dropped markedly. Nonetheless only 35.1 per cent of the total population of Africa had received at least one dose. In Papua New Guinea, Haiti, Yemen, and Burundi less than 5 per cent of the population had received a single vaccine (https://www.nytimes.com/interactive/2021/world/covid-vaccinations-tracker.html, accessed February 5, 2023).

QUESTIONS

Drawing upon this chapter and your own research:

1. How might a Marxist perspective help to explain the inequality of vaccine manufacture, procurement, and administration worldwide? (Hint: where are most vaccines made, by whom, and for whom?) Consider in particular the dependency and World Systems Theory varieties of Marxist thinking, discussed in Section 5.3 here).

2. Do you think the IP rights of vaccine manufacturers should have been suspended? (Hint: think of the Marxist critique of the relentless global pursuit of profit in capitalism, discussed in Section 5.2 here)

3. Thinking beyond the global COVID-19 pandemic, in what other ways might Marxist perpectives help to explain global health inequalities (Hint: think here about inequalities in health services provision in low-income countries as well as the effects of capitalist consumerism on health in both poor and wealthy countries)

TWISTING THE LENS

1. Take a look at Chapter 9 on postcolonialism. In what ways, if any, do you think postcolonialism can offer valuable insights on 'vaccine apartheid'?

USEFUL RESOURCES YOU CAN FIND ONLINE

Gutiérrez, Pablo and Kirk, Ashley (2021), 'Vaccine inequality: how rich countries cut Covid deaths as poorer fall behind', *The Guardian,* 28 June.

Hoder, Josh (2021), 'Tracking coronavirus vaccinations around the world', *The New York Times,* 13 March.

Iacobucci, Gareth (2021), 'Covid-19: How Will a Waiver on Vaccine Patents Affect Global Supply?', *BMJ*, 373:n1182.

Mancini, Donato P (2021), 'Vaccine patent battle intensifies as poor nations struggle in war on coronavirus', *The Financial Times,* 16 August.

Rouw, Anna et al. (2021) 'Global COVID-19 Access: A snapshot of Inequality', *KFF.org,* 17 March.

WHO, 'COVAX Working for global equitable access to COVID-19 Vaccines'. www.who.int

186 INTRODUCTION TO INTERNATIONAL RELATIONS THEORIES

FURTHER READING

ADDITIONAL INTRODUCTORY READING

Horden, S. and Wyn Jones, R. (2020), 'Marxist Theories of International Relations', in John Baylis, Steve Smith, and Patricia Owens, *The Globalization of World Politics: An Introduction to International Relations*, 8th edition (Oxford: Oxford University Press), 115–129.
A highly accessible and brief introductory survey of the main varieties of Marxist approaches to IR.

Kurki, M. (2009), 'Karl Marx' in J. Edkins and N. Vaughan-Williams (eds), *Critical Theorists and International Relations* (London: Routledge), 246–250.
A very succinct assessment of Marx's significance for the critical study of international politics.

Rupert. M. (2021), 'Marxism' in T. Dunne, M. Kurki, and S. Smith, *International Relations Theories: Discipline and Diversity*, 5th edition (Oxford: Oxford University Press).
This offers a more advanced introduction to Marxist perspectives on IR.

MORE IN-DEPTH READING

Anievas, A. (ed.) (2010), *Marxism and World Politics* (London: Routledge).
This book brings together scholars from a number of disciplines who examine some recent developments in Marxist thinking on world politics. It is a challenging read but provides insight into some of the most recent thinking by a diverse body of contemporary Marxist scholars.

Brewer, A. (1990), *Marxist Theories of Imperialism: A Critical Survey*, 2nd edition (London: Routledge).
This comprehensive and clearly written survey of Marxist theories of imperialism covers all the major contributors from Marx himself through to Immanuel Wallerstein.

Cammack, P. (2022), *The Politics of Global Competitiveness* (Oxford: Oxford University Press).
A renowned British Marxist scholar draws upon classical Marxism to examine how key international organizations such as the OECD and the World Bank promote the development of global capitalism to its maximum extent.

Cox, R. (1981), 'Social Forces, States and World Orders: Beyond International Relations Theory', *Millennium: Journal of International Studies*, 10(2), 126–155.
One of the first and most cited examples of a neo-Gramscian perspective on international politics.

Davenport, A. (2018), 'The Marxist Critique of International Political Theory', in C. Brown and R. Eckersley (eds), *The Oxford Handbook of International Political Theory* (Oxford: Oxford University Press), 652–663.

Ferraro, V. (2008), 'Dependency Theory: An Introduction' in Giorgio Secondi (ed.), *The Development Economics Reader* (London: Routledge), 58–64,
A brief and very accessible introduction to dependency theory.

Halliday, F. (1994), 'A Necessary Encounter: Historical Materialism and International Relations' in *Rethinking International Relations* (London: Macmillan).
A leading British Marxist Scholar reflects on the contribution of Marxism to the study of IR.

Hirst, P., Thompson, G., and Bromley, S. (2009), *Globalization in Question*, 3rd edition (Cambridge: Polity Press).
A revised edition of the seminal and highly readable book, first published in 1996, by Hirst and Thompson that questions the claim that globalization is a new and seemingly unstoppable phenomenon.

Marx, K. and Engels, F. (2012), *Manifesto of the Communist Party—A Modern Edition* (London: Verso).
This is a reprint of the first English translation of the Manifesto published in 1888 with a new introduction by the famous British Marxist historian Eric Hobsbawm. It contains Marx and Engels' prescient observations on the future trajectory of capitalism.

Panitch, Leo and Leys, C. (2003), 'The New Imperial Challenge', *Socialist Register 2004*, (London: The Merlin Press).
A series of articles by a range of Leftist scholars and commentators assessing US imperialism in the wake of the 2003 invasion of Iraq.

Villaneuva Lira, J.R. (2022), *Marxism and the Origins of International Relations: A Hidden History* (Cham, Switzerland: Palgrave Macmillan).
A new contribution to the ongoing debate about the origins of the IR discipline, which examines the hitherto neglected influence of Marxism on the so-called 'Idealists' who were prominent in the discipline's early years.

CHAPTER 6

CRITICAL INTERNATIONAL THEORY

LEARNING OBJECTIVES

- Explain the meaning of the term 'critical' when applied to theory
- Identify the historical and political contexts in which Critical Theory emerged
- Define the *epistemological* debate between 'traditional' and Critical Theory
- Identify the disciplinary context from which Critical International Theory emerged
- Evaluate the similarities and differences between the two key strands of Critical International Theory
- Demonstrate how Critical International Theory has been applied to substantive issue areas in the IR field.

6.1 INTRODUCTION

Since the early 1980s, a range of new IR theories that *critique* the fundamental assumptions of the disciplinary mainstream have emerged. To greater or lesser degrees, these various *critical theories* challenge mainstream theorizing in three key respects:

Ontology: The nature of being—what exists, what *is* in the world, and what constitutes international political reality?

Epistemology: the nature of knowledge—what can be known about the world, what are the sources and scope of that knowledge and how do we demonstrate its validity?

Methodology: how do we gain knowledge of the world? What methods of enquiry can we use and how can we justify them?

We discuss these three key terms more fully in Section 1.3, Chapter 1. They are important because in challenging the ontological, epistemological, and methodological dimensions of mainstream theory, critical theories depict the relationship between the theorist, the theories they produce, and the social world they are endeavouring to understand or explain, quite differently to mainstream theorists.

It is important at the outset, however, to note that the emergence of a wide range of critical IR theories within a relatively short period of time can initially seem confusing. In this chapter we are examining the impact of Critical Theory (with a capital 'c' and 't') on the IR discipline. Critical Theory's roots lie in Marxism (which we discuss in Chapter 5), but it also departs from classical Marxism in significant ways. In Chapters 7, 9, and 10, we will look at other forms of critical theory (no capitals) which share many of the key assumptions of Critical Theory, but also depart from it in important ways. These days, the label 'critical theories of IR' is used to cover both Critical Theory and other approaches, that, in various ways, are centred on a multifaceted critique of mainstream IR theory.

Understanding what makes Critical Theory critical requires a basic understanding of some key themes in the philosophy of social sciences (which examines debates around the philosophical foundations of social scientific enquiry). For this reason, the first part of this chapter steps back from IR theory specifically, to consider the meaning of the term Critical Theory, the historical context in which it emerged, and to identify some of its key sources. We then go on to explore the emergence of a distinctive Critical International Theory in the early 1980s and examine how it rapidly triggered a virtual explosion of different kinds of critical approaches to the study of international politics.

6.2 **WHAT IS CRITICAL THEORY?**

In everyday language to criticize is to pass judgement, usually negatively, on something or someone, be it their actions or their point of view. Arguably, most people do not like simply being criticized unless the criticism is received by them as constructive criticism. Usefully, the commonplace idea of constructive criticism points us in the direction of critical theory. In the social sciences, including IR, the term *critical* when attached to a body of theory invokes a somewhat different activity to merely criticizing someone or something and usually invokes the idea of *critique*. To critique something is to offer a careful judgement of something that does not simply entail stating what is wrong with it or expressing a low opinion of it. Critique also usually involves providing an exposition of and careful engagement with an argument or point of view. As such, it may include an appreciation of some merits in an argument or theoretical claim, whilst also identifying weaknesses or silences in it. A good critique of a theoretical claim or point of view generally requires a thorough exposition of that argument's key claims and the assumptions underpinning them, prior to identifying its weaknesses.

Some of the newer perspectives in IR confine themselves to criticizing the mainstream for failing to consider what they perceive to be important aspects of international politics. An example of this would be some varieties of liberal feminism that *criticize* mainstream IR scholarship for largely leaving women out of the international picture. Other varieties of feminism go considerably further and *critique* mainstream scholarship much more comprehensively. They invoke the concept of gender to suggest not only that mainstream theories simply ignore or undervalue the role of women in international politics, but they also offer an inherently biased gendered view of the world. In so doing they are seen to actively contribute to the maintenance of an international order that privileges male-centred perspectives and the interests of men. We explore the diverse varieties of feminist scholarship more fully in Chapter 10, but the key point here is that it is this fuller sense of being critical—of engaging in critique—that we are looking at in this chapter.

The origins of Critical Theory

The roots of Critical Theory can be traced back to the Enlightenment and even classical Greek thought. The principal source, however, is the work of Karl Marx and his successors. Perhaps the most succinct expression of Critical Theory is provided by Marx's famous 'Thesis XI' (the last of eleven short philosophical notes—the 'Theses on Feuerbach'): 'Philosophers have only interpreted the world, in various ways; the point however is to change it'. This simple epigram offers a distinctive view of the relationship between theorists, theories, and the world they are trying to interpret and influence.

As a vast and complex body of work, it was inevitable that Marxism would generate internal theoretical debates some of which led to the emergence of Critical Theory. However, Marxism's fortunes have also been tied to the development of communism. The terms Marxism and communism are not simply synonymous, although they have often been historically treated as such, especially by the media and political commentators. Marxism refers to the body of philosophical writing by Marx and his successors, that we discuss in Chapter 5. Communism refers to a type of political and ideological system based primarily on Marxist principles. In the twentieth century, many states identified their political systems as some form of communism. The most famous was the Soviet Union, but various East European states, Southeast Asian states, North Korea, and, of course, China also depicted themselves or still depict themselves as communist. During the twentieth century, communist political parties emerged also in most Western states, with varying degrees of political success or influence. As the Cold War starkly illustrated, the emergence of communist states or communist parties throughout the twentieth century generated considerable, often very hostile critical reaction from the non-communist world. However, it was critical reaction from within Marxism and Leftist political circles more widely to existing communism that contributed to the emergence of Critical Theory.

An early example of the emergence from within Marxism of a challenge to Marxist orthodoxy came in the early 1930s in the writings of the Italian Marxist, Antonio Gramsci (see Key thinker 5.3). Gramsci questioned the presumed inevitability of revolutionary class conflict that hitherto had characterized most Marxist scholarship. Reflecting on the failure of Marxism as a revolutionary ideology to capture the minds of most workers in industrialized states, notably in his home country, Gramsci wanted to examine how ruling classes exercised their domination, or *hegemony*. In his view, this required analysis not only of the economic base of capitalist societies, but also the political and cultural superstructure contributed to the sustaining ruling class hegemony (we discuss this aspect of Gramsci's work more fully in Chapter 5).

Gramsci's interest in understanding how the ruling class develops and sustains its hegemony clearly pointed Marxism in a different direction to the dominant economistic interpretation of Marx's work at the time. In some Western states, moreover, sections of the working classes had been drawn to the opposite end of the political spectrum and embraced various forms of fascist or right-wing authoritarian dictatorial politics, most notably in Nazi Germany in the 1930s, but also in Italy, Spain, and Portugal.

Additionally, many Marxists outside the Soviet Union became increasingly concerned with what was being done there, supposedly in the name of Marx and Lenin. Exposure of the brutal and oppressive aspects of Joseph Stalin's autocratic premiership of the Soviet Union between 1932 and 1952 and the Soviet imposition of communist rule in Eastern Europe after the Second World War caused considerable disquiet and division within Western Marxist intellectual circles. Particularly notable events such as the crushing of the 1956 Hungarian Uprising by Soviet troops and the invasion of Czechoslovakia by Warsaw Pact troops in 1968 (summarized in Key event 6.1) further stimulated critical reflection by some Marxist scholars.

By the 1960s distinctive variants of Marxism, variously described as Western Marxism, neo-Marxism, or the 'New Left', had emerged. In many respects, they can be seen as further developing themes that had emerged out of the work of Gramsci and others looking to revise Marxism, notably examining how ideology works to give legitimacy to advance capitalist societies and exploring ways of challenging it. For these scholars, the collapse of capitalism no longer seemed inevitable, which raised the question of how the transformation from capitalism to a fairer and more just alternative might still be realized. Being critical of both capitalism as well as key aspects of existing communist states, many of the newer varieties of Marxism were keen not only to take Marxism in a less deterministic and economic direction, but also subject Marxism itself to robust critical scrutiny.

KEY EVENT 6.1 THE 1956 HUNGARIAN UPRISING AND THE 1968 PRAGUE SPRING

By the end of the Second World War, Soviet forces had occupied much of Eastern Europe. Although initially promising to allow for free and open elections, the Soviet Union effectively imposed authoritarian communist rule in most East European states. The East European communist parties were closely tied to Moscow. Nonetheless, there was opposition—much of it clandestine—to Soviet domination in Eastern Europe throughout the Cold War. Two particularly notable expressions of such opposition occurred in Hungary and Czechoslovakia.

In October-November 1956, growing opposition to communist rule in Hungary culminated in a spontaneous uprising across the country which led to the collapse of the Government. However, Soviet troops invaded Hungary and violently crushed all resistance.

The Prague Spring, 1968

Resistance to Soviet domination expressed itself somewhat differently in Czechoslovakia in January 1968 when Alexander Dubček became leader of the Czech Communist Party. In what became known as the *Prague Spring*, over the next few months Dubček initiated a series of radical reforms aimed at liberalizing Czechoslovakian politics and the economy. Moscow was unhappy with this and, after failed negotiations, sent 500,000 Warsaw Pact troops to invade and occupy Czechoslovakia supposedly as an expression of fraternal solidarity. This was followed by eight months of non-violent resistance, but ultimately orthodox soviet-style rule was restored.

Both events had a very significant negative impact upon Western attitudes towards the Soviet Union, especially within Western Left political circles. Many Western communist parties suffered significant losses of members and both events undoubtedly contributed to the subsequent emergence of Eurocommunism in the West.

Many of these critics saw Soviet-style communism as excessively autocratic, bureaucratic, and repressive. Such features seemingly contradicted the claim that Soviet communism was driven by authentically proletarian-led revolutionary politics, as proposed by Marx. Of course, Western conservative and liberal thinkers had long criticized Soviet-style communism in these terms, but the significance of the emergence of Western Marxism was that it came from intellectuals who were themselves drawing, albeit to greater or lesser degrees, from Marx's own writings.

Various European communist parties denounced the 1968 Soviet invasion of Czechoslovakia and increasingly distanced themselves from the doctrines of the Soviet Communist Party, leading to the emergence in the 1970s and 1980s of what became known as Eurocommunism (which we also discuss in Chapter 5). Although there was no singular doctrine uniting the Western Eurocommunist parties, they were all attempting to develop Communism in directions that better reflected the specific conditions and public political appetite in their own countries, whilst moving away from the orthodox Soviet doctrine of a worldwide communist movement headed by the Soviet Union. For some communist parties, notably in Italy, this resulted in some significant electoral successes. Overall, however, the emergence of Eurocommunism coincided with the decline of communism in the West, especially after the collapse of communist governments in the Soviet Union and Eastern Europe which signalled the end of the Cold War. Although many Western communist parties survived the collapse of Soviet communism, they generally have seen their political bases and influence shrink drastically.

Was there a distinctive 'Young' Marx?

It is important to stress that Marxism, as a body of increasingly diverse theoretical ideas, did not simply decline along with communism. Indeed, Marxism continues to be a highly influential body of thought especially in intellectual and cultural circles, both in the West and elsewhere. One reason for this is that the label Marxism now refers to a wide array of intellectual positions that draw to greater or lesser degrees on Marx's work, but also depart significantly from an orthodox interpretation of Marx. The possibility of often strikingly diverse intellectual positions all cleaving to the label Marxism arises, in part at least, from the long-running debate as to whether there are clear distinctions between the work of the young Marx and that produced in the later years of his life.

Some analyses of Marx's work have argued that the younger Marx's work was more overtly *humanist* (Fromm, 1961). In other words, a concern with the human condition—the value and purpose of human life—is more prominent in the young Marx. In contrast, Marx's mature writings emphasize the role of material forces—the modes of production and exchange (see the discussion in Chapter 5, Section 5.2). The claim that the work of the young Marx can be distinguished from that of the older Marx is, however, disputed. There is considerable disagreement, for example as to when the 'young' period might have ended, or whether any clear break in Marx's work can be identified. It is better perhaps to think of the debate as being about the relative prominence of key themes throughout Marx's work. There was a clear shift in emphasis between Marx's earlier and later work, even if whether this was indicative of a decisive philosophical change in direction remains a matter of debate (McLellan, 1980: 207–220). For our purposes this debate is significant because the emergence of Critical Theory from within Marxism displays a clear attempt to resurrect themes associated, rightly or wrongly, with the young Marx.

A particular target for many critics was orthodox Marxism's claim to offer a *scientific* analysis of the human condition. To understand this line of critique, we need to explore the idea of a *social science* a bit further, prior to returning to the specific case of IR theory.

Are the social sciences (such as IR) 'scientific'?

When Critical Theory emerged in the IR discipline in the 1980s it invoked a debate that had already been running for some time in other branches of the social sciences, notably sociology. What is at stake in this debate is the *epistemological* status of theory in the social sciences: to put it bluntly, is it actually *scientific*?

To call a claim to knowledge 'scientific' is a strong statement. We tend to accord knowledge from the natural sciences (which study the material world) a high status because it is ostensibly produced through scientific enquiry. The scientific method aims to produce objective knowledge about the natural world that can be reproduced, i.e., shown repeatedly to be valid and therefore true.

Two key terms used in the philosophy of the social sciences are crucial here: *empiricism* and *positivism*. Let's start by defining what these important terms mean:

- Empiricism refers to the *epistemological* claim that all valid knowledge must be derived from observable and verifiable evidence. This leads on to the *methodological* implication that evidence should be gathered through systematic observation, and hypotheses (theoretical claims) about the significance of that evidence should be tested through some form of controlled and verifiable experimentation.

- Positivism is a philosophical theory of *social* scientific research that states that valid knowledge about the social world is only that which is gained through the acquisition of empirical information, which is then assessed through the scientific method, or something very close to it. Knowledge claims based on speculation, purely philosophical reflection, or appeal to tradition are deemed to be inferior. They may be inherently interesting and thought-provoking and, as such, generate some interesting hypotheses about social phenomena. Positivism argues, however, that if those hypotheses cannot be proved through the scientific method, they cannot be shown to be demonstrably universally valid or true.

As their name suggests, the social sciences have endeavoured to produce knowledge that can plausibly be deemed to be scientific, or at least aspire to be as scientific as possible. Although few social scientists have or would claim to produce scientific knowledge in the strictest sense of the term, the idea of science has, nonetheless, provided an influential benchmark for ascertaining the quality of social scientific research findings.

The nineteenth-century French philosopher, Auguste Comte (introduced to you in Key thinker 6.1), is generally credited as the founder of positivism (as well as the discipline of sociology) and the positivist model of a social science. Positivism in the social sciences rests on four main assumptions:

1. The unity of the natural and social sciences

2. The distinction between facts and values

3. That the social world exhibits regularities which can be discovered through theory

4. An empiricist epistemology—the truth of knowledge claims is demonstrated through appeal to neutral facts.

The overall objective of positivist social science is to *explain* social phenomena; it seeks to develop hypotheses about how the social world works, which can be shown to be demonstrably true. This is seen to require a commitment to objectivity and thus a clear separation between facts and values. The personal values and biases of the researcher must be excluded from research to ensure the scientific status of research findings.

KEY THINKER 6.1 AUGUSTE COMTE

Auguste Comte (1798–1857) was a French philosopher, widely credited as one of the founders of the discipline of Sociology and the positivist approach to social scientific research. Comte argued that society went through three stages:

- a theological stage
- a metaphysical stage
- a 'positive', or scientific stage.

During the first stage our conceptions of ourselves and the social rules we should live by were determined through reference to God. The second stage emerged with the Enlightenment, when the human capacity for purely rational thought prevails. In the third stage societies seek, or should seek, solutions to social problems and the path to progress through evidence-based, scientific research.

Comte's advocacy of positivism was very much a reaction to social problems in France after the French revolution. For Comte, appeal to the will of God or abstract reasoning alone was an insufficient basis for developing a stable social order; a truly scientific analysis of society was both possible and in the best interests of humankind.

Comte's argument for a positivist science of society always contained, however, overtly political elements—Comte was, amongst other things, hostile to democracy and in favour of rule by an intellectual elite—which few social scientists would embrace today. Indeed, the modern understanding of positivism is arguably much more rigorous in its commitment to the separation of fact and value than Comte's foundational vision.

Whether or not mainstream social sciences formally qualify as sciences is not the main issue for the various critical theories we will be examining. What they do challenge is the commitment to seeing the scientific method as the ideal type of knowledge formation about social phenomena. As we will see, in this and later chapters, the critical theorists we are examining in various ways challenge the idea that scientific knowledge of social phenomena is either possible or desirable. For them, there are very important features of social phenomena that the scientific method either cannot capture or even helps to obscure or dismiss.

Traditional versus Critical Theory

We can illustrate Critical Theory's challenge to the positivist idea of social science using Max Horkheimer's distinction between what he calls 'traditional' theories (by which he means those that adopt a positivist model of social theory) and Critical Theory. Horkheimer was a leading member of the *Frankfurt School* (see Key event 6.2), which emerged in Germany in the 1930s. The founding members were a group of loosely connected dissident Marxists who were critical not only of existing liberal-capitalist or fascist political systems (like all Marxists), but also of the Soviet communist system. Their successors further developed their work and, in many respects, took it further away from its Marxist roots.

KEY EVENT 6.2 THE FRANKFURT SCHOOL

The Frankfurt School is an informal school of social theory which has its origins in the Institute for Social Research at the Goethe University in Frankfurt, Germany. Founded in 1923, the institute was initially home to mostly orthodox Marxists.

After Max Horkheimer became director in 1930 it rapidly became a centre for dissident Marxist thinkers who, in various ways, critiqued existing Communist, Capitalist, and Fascist political systems. Although they did not work together particularly closely, the output of the Frankfurt School scholars shared common themes and broadly subscribed to a critique of both orthodox Marxism and positivist social science that evolved into what came to be known as Critical Theory.

The rise of Nazism in Germany led to the institute being moved (most of its members were Jewish), first to Geneva in 1933 and then to New York in 1934 where it became affiliated to Columbia University. It was during the New York period that the most significant work of the Frankfurt School began to emerge, and the location undoubtedly enhanced its influence in the English-speaking world.

The institute relocated back to Frankfurt in 1951. Its subsequent output exercised a significant influence in Leftist intellectual circles and led to the emergence of the 'New Left' in the 1960s, which was both highly critical of capitalist society as well as 'actually existing' communist political systems. Since the late 1960s, the Frankfurt School has come to be predominantly associated with the work of the German political theorist Jürgen Habermas.

Horkheimer depicted the differences between traditional and critical theories as follows:

- *Traditional theories* make a distinction between subject and object. They claim that the subject (the theorist) can stand independently outside of the object (such as the social world) which they are attempting to capture in theoretical terms. There is a world that exists independently of the observer, and the observer can suspend their cultural, linguistic, social, and historical biases when investigating that world. There is a distinction between fact and value and theory must be value-free.
- *Critical theories* deny the possibility of a separation between subject and the social world as an object for investigation. The social scientist (subject) is wholly

embedded and situated in social and political life, in the very thing they are attempting to analyse. As such, their theoretical claims are irreducibly related to that social life. They are not, and cannot be, simple objective descriptions of what there is. Because theories about the social world are inescapably tied up with that world, Critical Theory is concerned with the purposes and functions of social theories—how those theories interact with the world they purport to be analysing. The explicit purpose underlying Critical Theory is the improvement of the human condition through the elimination of injustice. Theory does not simply present an expression of 'the concrete historical situation', it also acts as 'a force within it to stimulate change'.

(Adapted from Horkheimer, 1972: 224–229)

Central to Horkheimer's distinction between traditional and critical theory is the relationship between the researcher (the subject) and the social world (the object) they are attempting to theorize. For critical theorists, any attempt to theorize about the social world must consider that the theorist is the product of the world they are endeavouring to capture. Traditional theories try to address this issue through a commitment to objectivity, wherein a theorist endeavours to step out of that world. For the critical theorist this is simply not possible. Social and political theories (and that would include IR) are inescapably part of social reality; they are the conscious products of socially located human beings. All of us trying to understand or explain the world are socially located within it by virtue of such things as our class position under capitalism, our gender, where we live, as well as our political, cultural, and social values or beliefs.

The critical theorist thus questions the notion that those who endeavour to theorize the world can do so in an authentically objective, i.e., value-free, sense. The issue areas they examine, the questions they ask about social reality, and the theoretical methods chosen to develop answers to those questions are themselves inescapably social products. They are not just generated out of thin air, but are formulated by social beings, inescapably engaged in complex ways with the world that is being examined. The problem with traditional theory, critical theorists argue, is that it does not and cannot take account of its social origins other than try to push them away.

THINKING CRITICALLY 6.1 IS OBJECTIVE KNOWLEDGE OF THE SOCIAL WORLD POSSIBLE?

- Do you think it is possible for a social science researcher to develop objective (value-free) knowledge of the social world?
- If your answer is yes, can you identify kinds of knowledge claims about the social world that can be described as objective? (Hint: some theorists believe we can put aside our personal values or biases through using certain research methodologies such as standardized questionnaires or statistical methods that compensate for subjective bias)

- If your answer is no, what do you think are the main barriers to acquiring knowledge of the social world objectively? (Hint: think about social scientists (or students) being 'socially embedded'.)
- If a researcher openly acknowledges the influence of their political biases or values in choosing their research interests and conducting their research, do you think that invalidates their findings?

Jürgen Habermas: knowledge and human interests

As we have seen, Critical Theory sees an inescapable connection between the pursuit of knowledge and our interests as humans; it cannot be a disinterested pursuit. Indeed, that relationship is a key theme in the work of perhaps the best-known contemporary exponent of Critical Theory, the German philosopher Jürgen Habermas.

According to Habermas, all forms of theory are underpinned by what he calls 'knowledge-constitutive interests' (Habermas, 1971). These define what knowledge we pursue and what we want the knowledge to do for us. Habermas' use of the term interests does not refer to the self-interested motivations of individual natural or social scientists, but to different ways of viewing nature and society as possible objects of knowledge. It poses the question: why do we want to know about nature and society?

At its heart of Habermas' argument is the identification of three types of 'knowledge-constitutive' human interests driving the pursuit of knowledge:

- The technical interest
- The practical interest
- The emancipatory interest (Habermas, 1971: 310–317).

Let's examine each in turn.

The technical interest

This refers to our interest in controlling and mastering the natural world. It is a way of seeing not only the natural world but also society as *objects* of possible knowledge. It is this interest that underpins the natural sciences as well as those forms of social science that embrace the positivist methodology. A positivist model of social scientific enquiry looks for regularities in the social phenomena being studied to develop hypotheses that can be empirically verified (we discuss positivism further in Chapter 1, Section 1.3).

Habermas argues, however, that this understanding of how knowledge should be acquired acts as a kind of ideological mask that hides mainstream social sciences' underlying technical interest in the maintenance and efficient management of capitalist society (remember here that Habermas comes out of the Marxist tradition). It is not interested in, and is in fact methodologically incapable of asking *normative*, i.e., value-driven, questions about the prevailing social world. Is it the best kind of world? Is it a fair or just world? By excluding such questions, the pursuit of technical knowledge of the social world effectively helps to *depoliticize* society and its management.

In various ways, most critical theorists see the mainstream of the social sciences as broadly adopting what Habermas describes as a technical knowledge-constitutive interest. The mainstream social sciences are not interested in posing critical questions about the prevailing social order, but only in developing a technical expertise in managing it.

The practical interest

This sounds confusingly like a 'technical interest', but that is largely a product of translation from German to English. What Habermas is referring to is an interest in developing shared understandings of the social world for inter-personal communication and social interaction to occur. It is these that enable the development of the various types of social consensus that are part and parcel of everyday social life. In other words, the practical knowledge-constitutive interest is in developing an agreed *understanding* of social order and, thus, how to maintain it. For Habermas this knowledge-constitutive interest largely underpins the disciplines that make up the Humanities. Whereas science pursues a definitive *explanation* of things, the humanities are much more focused on developing a rigorous understanding of the meanings we attach to social-cultural phenomena.

The emancipatory interest

Habermas does not dismiss the first two knowledge-constitutive interests that he identifies. Indeed, he sees them as deeply rooted in human existence. The pursuit of technical mastery of the natural and social worlds or of the practical complexities of living and communicating in a social world are legitimate pursuits, in his view.

The problem with such forms of orthodox thinking is that they either cannot, or do not reflect critically on the social status quo, or on their role in sustaining it; they are not *reflexive*. In other words, they are not oriented towards change and the improvement of the human condition. To achieve this, we need to consider a third knowledge-constitutive interest: the *emancipatory* interest. This takes us to the very heart of the idea of Critical Theory.

NB. Habermas' work is often quite dense and can be challenging to read at first sight. You might find the accounts of Habermas' 'knowledge-constitutive interests' by Richard Bernstein and David Held provide more accessible entry points (Bernstein, 1976: 191–200; Held, 1980: 300–329).

THINK CRITICALLY 6.2 WHAT IS THE PURPOSE OF THEORIES OF IR?

- What do you think is the purpose of theories of IR?
- Which, if any, of Habermas' three types of knowledge-constitutive interest best describes the purpose of mainstream IR theories, such as realism, liberalism, or the English School? (You can read brief descriptions of these theories in the introduction and fuller discussions of them in Chapters 2, 3, and 4.)
- From your reading on these theories, do you see any distinctions between them or within them? (Hint: It may help here to think about the difference between *explaining* an authoritative, scientific sense and *understanding* the social world. Additionally, when it comes to the English School, think about the difference between its pluralist and solidarist wings that is explored in Chapter 4)

Critical theory and emancipation

At this point, we should recall Marx's famous assertion in his Thesis XI that the purpose of philosophical enquiry into the world around us is not merely to interpret or understand that world but also to change it. Marx's entire work was aimed at analysing the human social condition to discern how those who were oppressed in a capitalist system could be released from the various 'chains' that prevented them from achieving true freedom and full self-development. As we saw in Chapter 4, Marx saw the purpose of his work as thus contributing to the achievement of *human emancipation* (we also discuss this in Chapter 5, Section 5.2).

For critical theorists, however, Marxism after Marx had lost sight of that goal and they seek to restore it to the heart of critical social enquiry. Such an ambition is inherently *normative*; this means that it is driven by a set of values that enables the identification of unjustified constraints upon human freedom and, by extension, what is meant by freedom itself. For critical theorists, reflecting their roots in Marxism, emancipation refers primarily to the pursuit of freedom from the constraints imposed through the injustices of capitalist society. As Critical Theory has developed, however, so too has its understanding of emancipation evolved to embrace a widening range of injustices. In addition to a focus on the oppressive features of class relations, contemporary Critical Theory (and critical theories more generally) also examine the injustices and exclusionary consequences of such things as gender, race, nationality, the ways in which various forms of democracy work, and sexual identity.

The idea that theory can and should be driven by a normative commitment to emancipation directly confronts the mainstream conception of theory as objective and disinterested enquiry. It is an understanding of theory that emphasizes the need for *reflexivity*: a willingness to reflect critically upon the assumptions and motives underpinning our efforts to theorize about the world around us. It is only through self-reflection that individuals 'can become aware of forces which have exerted a hitherto unacknowledged influence over them' (Held, 1980: 318).

As we have seen, for Habermas all humans have three kinds of knowledge-constitutive interest driving their quest for knowledge. However, the dominance of the technical and practical knowledge-constitutive interests as legitimate forms of knowledge serves to repress the legitimacy of the emancipatory knowledge-constitutive interest. What does this mean for the would-be critical social theorist? It should compel the theorist to reflect upon the deep-seated assumptions they might be bringing to the act of theorizing the social world, and on the effects of their theorizing in that world. The theorist must ask of themselves whether, consciously or otherwise, their theoretical work is effectively part of maintaining the *status quo*, or is it aimed at exposing the injustices in the prevailing social order, with a view to eradicating them?

In his later work, Habermas moved even further away from his Marxist roots. Orthodox Marxism is driven by one preferred goal: the realization of human emancipation through the establishment of a single universal form of social organization: communism. For many critical theorists, including Habermas, this emphasis on a single model of ideal social organization is inherently dogmatic. Any preferred social order should surely be subject to the critical scrutiny of all those who would be participating in it for it be legitimate and not simply another form of domination from above. In other words, it should be grounded in authentic social consensus.

In Habermas' later work he explores this idea, focusing particularly on how humans, perhaps with very different political standpoints, can communicate with each other productively. How might we conceive of communication between humans—*intersubjective* communication—that is not distorted by power and domination? This is a large issue-area and, as we will see, it is a theme that was to emerge within Critical International Theory. After all, if enabling genuinely undistorted communication between different social strata within a particular society is a challenging objective, then realizing this at the international or global level is surely very much more so. Prior to exploring this issue further, we need firstly to look at how Critical Theory emerged within the IR discipline.

6.3 **CRITICAL THEORY AND IR**

Although Critical Theory emerged out of debates within Marxism from the 1930s onwards and became increasingly influential in some social sciences from the early 1960s, it did not impact upon the IR discipline until the early 1980s. Perhaps surprisingly, the origins of a Critical International Theory can be quite precisely dated to the year 1981. This was when two articles emerged, one by Robert Cox in the British IR journal *Millennium* (Cox, 1981) and the other, by Richard Ashley, in the prominent US IR journal *International Studies Quarterly* (Ashley, 1981).

Why did these articles appear in 1981? A clue lies in the publication of Kenneth Waltz's book, *Theory of International Politics*, two years earlier. As we note in Chapter 3, that book laid the foundations of what soon came to be known as neorealism. Both articles are aimed squarely at providing a critique of neorealism and the kind of theorizing it represents. In the next two sections of this chapter, we will look more closely at the seminal arguments of Ashley and Cox to help us discern the key features of Critical International Theory. The arguments of Cox and Ashley are quite complex, so what follows is quite a basic account of them to help you get a grasp on Critical International Theory.

Richard Ashley—realism and human interests

Ashley's principal objective is to offer a critique of the realist tradition (and it might be useful to refer to Chapter 3 on realism while reading this). What is unique about his article was that it was the first time an IR scholar drew upon the Frankfurt School, notably Habermas' typology of knowledge-constitutive interests. We noted at the beginning of Section 6.2 of this chapter that critique is not about simply criticizing a theoretical perspective, but also entails providing a careful exposition of it to bring out its weaknesses and limitations. This is precisely what Ashley does. He does not set out simply to demolish realism but depicts it as a rich tradition with several currents within it. His primary focus is on the differences within realism, particularly between classical realism and Waltz's neorealism. Ashley argues that Habermas' typology provides the means to do this. What Ashley is trying to do is make some sense of the different strands of realist scholarship, and what he sees as the different knowledge-constitutive interests that might lie behind them.

Ashley argues that the sole purpose of Waltz's neorealism is to offer a supposedly value-free, objective analysis of international politics (Ashley, 1981: 215). It is, in other words, an example of what Horkheimer calls traditional theory, or the kind of theory driven by what Habermas calls a *technical knowledge-constitutive interest*. Neorealism commences from the theoretical hypothesis that the international system is comprised of a multiplicity of units (states) within an anarchical system, which leads to a perpetual competition between those units over the means to achieve their competing ends. However, neorealism can only generate hypotheses about the 'general tendencies and potentialities' of the international system (Ashley, 1981: 220). Such a realism, Ashley argues, is inherently blind to the historical origins of the international system; it is simply taken as a given reality. It does not allow for the exercise of moral or political judgement of that system, and it is uninterested in any alternative to it. As Waltz himself acknowledges, neorealism cannot predict or even explain the policies and behaviours of specific states (Ashley, 1981: 220). Because of its commitment to emulating the scientific method, neorealism can only produce a limited body of knowledge about the international system and the likely behaviour of the key actors within it.

Although Ashley thinks all realists have had an element of a technical cognitive interest in their work, classical realist scholarship—that which was developed prior to neorealism—also displayed the features of what Habermas calls a *practical knowledge-constitutive interest*. In contrast to the technical realism developed by Waltz and others, Classical realism is more *interpretive* in its approach, seeking to offer more an *understanding* of the international system than a supposedly scientific *explanation* of it. In our discussion of Morgenthau's work in Chapter 3, for example, we noted it emphasized learning from history by 'looking over the shoulder' of statesmen. For Ashley, classical realism is much more attuned to the human aspect of international politics. It recognizes such things as misunderstanding and misperception as key components of an anarchic international system, as well as the power of shared traditions—the way things have been done over time. The reasons why an anarchical international system was able to display a degree of stability and order, was because there was a degree of shared understanding between states, or, more precisely, the leaders of states. At the very least, they were mutually aware of the dangers inherent in the anarchical international system that they all operated within (Ashley, 1981: 210–215).

Although classical realism emphasizes the centrality of such things as power and the national interest, there is also a recognition that the precise meaning of such things could not be discerned scientifically but had to be *interpreted* from the historical record of relations between states over long periods of time. As we see in Chapter 3, neither of the two most prominent figures associated with the emergence of contemporary realism—E.H. Carr and Hans Morgenthau—dismissed the possibility of fundamental change in international politics. They were highly sceptical about its possibility (this was, after all, the basis on which they criticized the reformist impulses of Liberal scholars), but this scepticism, Ashley argues, should not be confused with outright rejection of, or disinterest in either the need for, or possibility of fundamental change in international politics.

Ashley goes on to argue that, in different ways, the technical and practical varieties of realism serve ultimately the same purpose: to shore up the international status quo. The technical realist claims that a positivist realist theory can provide an explanation of how the anarchical system has reproduced itself over time (you might find the discussion of Waltz in Chapter 3, Section 3.4 useful here). Practical realism does not adopt a positivist theoretical approach, even if it still holds to the view that the theorist can step away from the world and analyse it objectively. It promotes the view that through the study of history and the actions of statespersons over the centuries we can come to understand how a universalized shared practice of international politics has evolved and provides the basis for international order. For the technical realist, such as Waltz, so long as there is an anarchic international system the prospects for significant change are very low. The practical realist would also see efforts to reform the international system as inherently dangerous; they might destabilize a fragile international order and increase the risk of a descent into war.

Ashley turns then to the work of another famous classical realist John Herz. Herz is perhaps most famous for developing the concept of a 'security dilemma' in the early 1950s (Herz, 1950). The dilemma refers to the problem that arises when states endeavour to improve their own security, by acquiring more military power, for example, and in so doing cause other states to feel less secure. What one state claims to be a defensive move can be interpreted by others as an offensive act. Herz developed the concept during the early days of the Cold War, and it provided insight into how the nuclear arms race between the US and the Soviet Union was likely to escalate. The security dilemma highlights problems of perception and communication in an anarchical international political system, and it remains a common theme in realist scholarship. Like other realists of his time, Herz was also highly critical of liberal thinkers who put their hopes primarily in the reform of the international system as the key to international peace. Like most realists, Herz thought liberal thinkers were blind to the problems of power and insecurity—such as the security dilemma—in the international system.

According to Ashley, John Herz nonetheless brings something different to realism, especially in his later work. That difference is reflexivity (Ashley, 1981: 226). In an article published in the same journal issue as Ashley's piece, Herz reflected on key themes within the realist tradition to which he had been a noted contributor for more than three decades (Herz, 1981). He argued that realism's preoccupation with questions of security and the national interest could not provide a response to the mounting evidence of threats to humanity. Herz (1981: 192) identified a 'triad of threats to the survival of mankind': an exploding world population; dwindling finite resources; and threats to the environment. The traditional realist preoccupation with national survival in an anarchical system needed to come to terms with these threats to the survival of the human species. If it did not, Herz argued, then it could no longer claim to be dealing with actual global realities. Realists needed, therefore, to reflect critically upon the assumptions and concepts underpinning their approach and ask if they continued to apply, given mounting evidence of significant social, technological, and environmental changes on a global scale. A focus on human survival was not about abandoning realism's commitment to analysing the world 'out there' in favour of abstract idealism; it was about recognizing that the most pressing real-world problems could no longer be addressed solely at the national level. The 'existing givens' of that world had changed to the extent that we now live in 'a truly interdependent, planetary world where what happens anywhere affects people and events everywhere' (Herz, 1981:192).

For Herz, if realism was to remain true to its name it needed to take account of those changes. It had to recognize that what it has long claimed to be the realities of international politics—states selfishly pursuing their own national interests, the centrality of power-politics and so on—may merely be a set of ahistorical assumptions about the world. These assumptions suited only a very narrowly conceived understanding of national self-interest. In an increasingly interdependent world, in which states and peoples increasingly face a common set of threats, Herz proposed that the pursuit of shared solutions to the principal problems confronting humanity may best serve the long-range interests of all nations and peoples (Herz, 1981: 194–196). For Ashley, the significance of Herz's work does not lie in whether his identification of the world's most pressing problems is accurate or not (although many non-realists would agree with Herz). What is significant for Ashley is that a scholar steeped in the realist tradition is displaying what Habermas would call an *emancipatory cognitive interest* (Ashley, 1981: 227). In asking realists to reflect critically on their own assumptions, Herz is effectively arguing that changes in the world 'out there' need to bear 'right here', on realism itself. At the same time Herz continued to maintain that he was a realist. He still believed that for the foreseeable future we must work with the given realities of a state-centric international system and pursue 'realisable' change (Herz, 1981: 196).

Even though Ashley went on to move beyond Critical Theory and embrace the poststructuralist perspective we examine in Chapter 7, his 1981 article had a significant impact on the IR discipline, especially among young IR scholars (including the author of this book). At the very least, it introduced the IR discipline to Habermas's thought and very rapidly a growing number of IR scholars also began to look for other new sources of theoretical insight from outside the IR discipline.

Robert Cox: traditional IR theory versus Critical International Theory

In contrast to Ashley, the Canadian scholar Robert Cox's explanation of the distinctiveness of Critical Theory has much clearer connections with Marxist political economy, as well as Gramsci's understanding of hegemony. Prior to becoming an academic, Cox had worked for 25 years at the International Labour Organization (ILO). First established under the League of Nations and later a UN agency, the ILO's principal concerns are with the development of international labour standards and the promotion of decent working conditions for men and women worldwide. Thus, Cox already had practical knowledge of key issues in international political economy. His subsequent academic work proved to be a major influence on the development of a critical strand within the International Political Economy (IPE) discipline, which came to be known as the *neo-Gramscian* school of IPE (which you can read about in more detail in Chapter 5, Section 5.4).

Famously, Cox's article contains one of the most quoted lines in contemporary IR theory: 'theory is always *for* someone and *for* some purpose' (Cox, 1981: 128). This sentence succinctly captures the essence of Critical Theory. What Cox is challenging is the idea that IR theory could be politically disengaged from the world, as the positivist model of theorizing suggests it should. He develops the point by postulating two types of IR theory, which clearly echo Horkheimer's juxtaposition of traditional and critical theory that we looked at in Section 6.1 and Habermas' distinction between different knowledge-constitutive interests, although Cox has insisted that he only had a passing familiarity with the Frankfurt School and his work was not influenced by it (Brincat, Lima, and Nunes, 2012: 18).

Cox distinguishes between what he calls 'problem-solving theory' and 'critical theory':

- *Problem-solving theory*

  takes the world as it finds it, with the prevailing social and power relationships and the institutions into which they are organized, as the given framework for action. The general aim of problem-solving is to make these relationships and institutions work smoothly by dealing effectively with sources of trouble.

- *Critical Theory*

  stands apart from the prevailing order of the world and asks how that order came about. Critical Theory, unlike problem-solving theory, does not take institutions and social and power relations for granted but calls them into question by concerning itself with their origins and how and whether they might be in the process of changing (Cox, 1981: 128–129).

For Cox, both neorealism and liberal institutionalism—the two dominant perspectives within mainstream IR theory at the time his article appeared—are examples of problem-solving theory. Neorealism takes prevailing international forces as a given and seeks to work with them, in pursuit of a stable international order. The 'neo-neo' debate between neorealism and neoliberalism (which we discuss in Chapter 3, Section 3.5) emerged just a few years after the publication of Cox's article. The modification of liberalism to produce a neoliberal response to neorealism also conforms to Cox's model of problem-solving theory. Neoliberalism, as its most prominent advocate argues, aims to 'facilitate the smooth operation of decentralised political systems' (Robert Keohane, cited in Devetak, 2022: 123). Neoliberalism seeks to reform the anarchical international system through the promotion of increased international cooperation and institutionalization, thereby reducing the risk of conflict or destabilizing crises emerging. In effect, then, both mainstream perspectives endeavour to show how the stability of the prevailing international system can be maintained. In the case of neoliberalism, its key distinction from neorealism is the need for some incremental reforms in reflection of perceived changing empirical circumstances such as increased cooperation between states and greater institutionalization of inter-state relations.

Cox argues that problem-solving theories generally claim to adhere to the positivist principle of value-neutrality. They do this, firstly, by treating the international system of states as highly resistant to fundamental change. They then investigate the variables that operate within it, such as the fluctuations in the power relations between states, to discern how stability in the international system of states can best be maintained. These variables are treated as objects for investigation, in a similar manner, Cox suggests, to how 'the chemist treats molecules or a physicist force and motion' (Cox, 1981: 130). Such an approach puts aside the history of the prevailing international system—how it developed into its current form. It is therefore an *ahistorical* approach.

For critical theorists (in common with Marxists more generally), the key point is that the international system does have a history. If carefully analysed, this history can help us understand how the international system has evolved to serve the interests of dominant states or classes, through imperialism and colonialism for example. From the perspective of Critical International Theory, then, working simply to preserve the system and ensure its smooth functioning cannot be a value-neutral activity. Rather, it is an inherently political position that seeks to preserve the prevailing international order and therefore the benefits that accrue to those who are dominant within it.

It should hopefully be clear by now that although he gets there by a rather different route, Cox's account of problem-solving theory broadly echoes not only Horkheimer's depiction of traditional theory, but also Habermas' account of a 'technical cognitive interest' (see Section 6.1). Just as Habermas recognized the practical utility of a technical cognitive interest, despite its evident limitations, so too Cox recognizes the appeal of problem-solving theories. They claim to be concerned primarily with providing guides to action for real-world problems. Cox argues that periods of apparent stability or where change in the international system seems improbable—such as during the Cold War, for example—favour problem-solving theory. The prevailing international system is seen as providing a fixed and limited framework for action, within which the problem-solving theorist is concerned with issues surrounding the preservation of international order. This was illustrated by the overriding concern of American IR realist theorists during the Cold War with how to sustain US power, which they argued was crucial to the maintenance of international stability. Like Ashley, Cox recognizes that not all realism fits the model of problem-solving theory perfectly, but he sees Waltz's neorealism as explicitly problem-solving in orientation.

In contrast to neorealism, Critical International Theory adopts an historical perspective on international politics from the outset and is focused on realizing normatively driven change. Cox argues that this does not mean it is therefore impractical, or unconcerned with real world problems:

> (I)t's aims are just as practical as those of problem-solving theory, but it approaches practice from a perspective which transcends that of the existing order, which problem-solving theory takes as its starting point. Critical theory allows for a normative choice in favour of a social and political order different from the prevailing order, but it limits the range of choice to alternative orders which are feasible transformations of the existing world. (Cox, 1981: 130)

6 CRITICAL INTERNATIONAL THEORY **207**

Another way to capture the difference between problem-solving and critical IR theories, Cox suggests, is to see Critical International Theory as a guide to *strategic* (long term) action towards the realization of possible alternative international orders, in contrast to problem solving theory's focus on *tactical* (short term) action to sustain the existing order.

Cox follows Marx in seeing changes in the mode of production (the prevailing economic system) as generating new social forces (we discuss this in Chapter 5, Section 5.2). Such change not only influences the development of the state, but also spills out from the state to influence international politics. In other words, social forces—such as social classes—not only influence the formation of the state but also how that state responds to the external world. Marx emphasized how industrial capitalism in the developed world during the nineteenth century generated the formation of an industrial working class. This influenced the drive towards imperialism because the Western capitalist states sought out new markets overseas to generate profits to placate the demands of their own increasingly organized working classes. This was necessary to shore up the hegemony of the bourgeoisie—the owners of capital. This is, in turn, generated competition (and conflict) between states and in so doing helped structure the prevailing world order (again, we discuss this in more detail in Chapter 5, Section 5.3).

Although Cox sees Marx's historical materialism as a primary source of critical theory, he also draws upon Gramsci's critique of orthodox Marxism's excessive preoccupation with material forces. In contrast to Marx's materialism, Cox presents a picture of Critical International Theory as concerned with the complex intersection of *ideas, material conditions, and institutions* at both the national and international levels. Cox argues that these interact to generate different forms of state (such as the Stalinist Soviet state or the liberal capitalist state). Furthermore, the historical patterns of interaction between these different types of state generate different types of *world order*.

Realism largely sees international politics as arising out of the interaction of states in a largely unchanging anarchical international system. Cox offers a very different and more complex picture in which international politics is depicted as comprising the historical and varying interaction of social forces, forms of states, and types of world order. These are all historical forces that produce specific, relatively stable *historical conjunctures*—configurations of those contributory elements. It is through analysis of the forces at play during any particular historical conjuncture that, Cox argues, the Critical Theorist can better understand how hegemony operates and is sustained at the international level.

Cox illustrates his argument through a comparison of the period of British global hegemony in the nineteenth century, which is often referred to as the *Pax Britannica* (the British peace), and its replacement in the mid-twentieth century with a US-dominated world order—the *Pax Americana*. British supremacy was based upon sea power, the exploitation of its colonial territories, and a trading order inspired by British liberalism and effectively managed by the City of London. By 1945, however, British power had declined, its dominance of the seas was no longer uncontested, and the world had become increasingly organized into two rival power blocs. British dominance was replaced by American hegemony, which was built around the formation of alliances underpinned by an ideological purpose: to constrain the power of the communist Soviet Union (Cox,

1981: 139–141). The international economy also became much more institutionalized with the establishment of the Bretton Woods System (see Chapter 2, Key events 2.2) in which the US acted as the guarantor. It was not simply a case of power shifting from one country to another. This would suggest a cyclical view of international history, as favoured by many realists. Instead, Cox argues that the form of global hegemony itself had changed; shifts in the key historical forces at work had created a new form of world order.

In sum, Cox offers a much more dynamic picture of international politics than that provided by the problem-solving orientation of neorealism. From a problem-solving neorealist perspective, the historical dimensions of the international system matter less since the main concern is how to survive within it. For Cox and other critical theorists, however, history matters very much: theorizing the international system requires first asking how it came about. If it is the product of a particular configuration of historical forces, then carefully analysing those forces may give us insight into the sources of the evident injustices and inequities of the prevailing system and, most importantly, how they might be overcome. The present international order is not something that can be ignored, but it has a history and since history will continue to unfold there is nothing inevitable about it. Critical International Theory accuses mainstream theory of treating the prevailing system unquestioningly and, in so doing, helping to preserve it or, at best, tinker with it.

Cox's account of Critical International Theory wears its normative commitments (the values underpinning it) on its sleeve, rather than trying to exclude them from analysis, as a positivist model of social scientific enquiry would require. It seeks to understand the present configuration of global power with the explicit intent of asking how it might be challenged and changed. Might we, for example, discern the possibility of a new form of hegemonic world order emerging, or even a non-hegemonic world order? Critical International Theory is, then, clearly oriented towards the pursuit of changes in the international system that might bring about a more just and equitable international order. However, critical international theorists, such as Cox, are not saying that we should simply indulge in speculative, utopian thinking. We must start with where we are, so to speak. What they are arguing is that if you envision a different, preferable world order you need to understand the present world order and try and identify the forces within it that might bring about change. This entails identifying the *immanent* (not to be confused with imminent) possibilities for change; in other words, the potential for possible alternative futures that already lie within the present.

We have covered a lot of theoretical ground and it may take a few reads to fully absorb it all. Let us look at how Critical International Theory can be applied to the analysis of international politics, which should help clarify things.

6.4 APPLYING CRITICAL INTERNATIONAL THEORY

We have seen how Critical International Theory emerged out of two strands of critical intellectual thought: a Frankfurt School strand that underpinned Ashley's piece and a Gramscian strand, as represented by Cox's article. Although, broadly speaking, the origins of both strands lie in European Marxism, they each contain distinctive emphases. Broadly speaking, the Gramscian strand remains closer to classical Marxism's core focus on the political economy of capitalism, whereas the Frankfurt School strand departs further from Marxist political economy to embrace the critical analysis of political and cultural phenomena. Thus, those scholars who, following on from Cox, see the principal contribution of Critical International Theory lying in the analysis of the global political economy are generally located these days within the field of IPE, that emerged out of IR in the 1970s and grew rapidly thereafter. The Frankfurt School was comprised of a loose body of scholars who varied markedly in the degree to which they moved beyond Marxist orthodoxy. What they shared, however, was a concern with exploring the barriers to and possibilities for human emancipation in contemporary society. This is what also unites the body of Critical International Theory scholars, who have been significantly influenced by either one or both stands.

There is another way of capturing the different emphases of the two strands of Critical International Theory. The Gramscian strand is focused largely on the uneven distribution of wealth and power in the global economy and developing responses to it. The Frankfurt School, or Habermassian strand, is focused more on the global politics of political exclusion and how this impacts upon the possibilities for the emancipation of all peoples. Both strands, however, have an overtly *normative* dimension to them. They are both informed by an explicit commitment to the rights of all peoples worldwide to realize their full potential through economic, social, and political emancipation. We shall now briefly explore the substantive application of the different strands of critical theory to key global and international issues.

Material power, ideology, and institutions — Neo-Gramscianism and world order

In Chapter 5 we look at how the neo-Gramscians in the IPE field build upon Gramsci's pioneering work in the 1930s to examine the origins and prospects of the contemporary exercise of global hegemony in the present global historical conjuncture. They examine how dominant states, notably the US and its allies, have promoted a set of ideas and institutional structures to create a world order that suits their interests. Echoing Gramsci's analysis of the exercise of hegemony within societies, neo-Gramscian IPE scholars examine how hegemonic power at the global level is sustained not only through coercion, but also by way of consent. They see the current global order as historically constituted; it is, Cox argues, a particular configuration of 'material power, ideology and institutions' (Cox, 1981: 141). This observation provides clear signposts to the research concerns of neo-Gramscianism: the sources of that material power, the ideology that accompanies and helps to legitimate it in the eyes of those who are subjected to it, and the institutional set up that sustains and promotes it. Driving neo-Gramscian enquiry is the normative commitment to identifying actual and potential *counter-hegemonic* forces which might work towards an alternative world order (it might be useful here to look at the discussion of Gramsci and the concept of hegemony in Section 5.4, Chapter 5).

Like most Marxists, neo-Gramscians see capitalism as an inherently unstable system that contains within itself the seeds of its own destruction. However, following Gramsci, they do not see this as an inevitable outcome but something that must be struggled for politically. Such a struggle must consider not only the *economic base* of international capitalism—the material forces at play—but also the political *superstructure* and the social forces that work to sustain it, or, potentially, might oppose it. This is a challenging task, given the degree to which the US and other developed states have exported the politics and economics of neoliberalism world-wide, notably under the guise of globalization (we discuss this further in Chapter 5, Key concept 5.3). This has been achieved, the neo-Gramscians argue, through the formation of a 'transnational historical bloc' comprised not only of powerful capitalist states, but also multinational corporations, think tanks, international financial institutions, and intellectuals. Together they have engineered the spread of neoliberal economic policies worldwide to such an extent that neoliberal policies appear to represent common-sense itself.

As we saw in Chapter 5, the term globalization is used widely to capture this transformation of the global political economy. In contrast to liberal enthusiasm for globalization and in common with Marxist IR scholarship more generally, Cox and his neo-Gramscian successors are highly critical of globalization's impact on world politics. In his later work, Cox argues that the globalization of production challenges the classical Marxian depiction of human society as comprised of a two-class structure. Instead, 'international production is dividing the world's producers into broadly three categories' Cox, 1999: 9).

The proportions of these three parts, or layers, varies from society to society, but the general phenomenon is worldwide:

- The top level, which comprises only a small proportion of humanity, consists of those who manage the world economy as well as relatively privileged workers in stable employment in such sectors as global production and finance.

- The second level is comprised of those whose relationship to the global economy is increasingly more precarious. These are those workers who are increasingly subjected to the risks associated with such developments in employment markets as downsizing, restructuring, outsourcing, and so on. Their employment prospects are increasingly tied to fluctuations in levels of demand and decisions made by those at the top level in the hierarchy.

- At the bottom is a third layer comprised of those who are excluded from the global economy altogether, through permanent unemployment, because their labour skills are no longer required, or because they live in countries that have the poorest prospects in the global economy (Cox, 1999: 9 and 2002: 84–85).

Prior to the global dominance of neoliberalism, political and social forces within capitalist states could put pressure on the state, through political action and the ballot box, to mitigate the exploitative effects of capitalism, at least partially. This could be achieved through such things as welfare policies, progressive taxation, and the erection of national trade barriers to protect local industries. A key ideological component of neoliberal globalization, however, has been the rolling-back and 'internationalization' of the state, in the name of promoting global free trade. The management and regulation of global trade and finance is increasingly conducted at the transnational and global levels, with the main trade and financial Institutions—such as the IMF, World Bank, and WTO—playing a key role. The function of individual states, then, is to act increasingly as agents of globalization and endeavour to integrate themselves as fully as possible into the global economy. This has resulted in a corresponding decline in both their capacity and willingness to reduce the damaging effects of globalizing capitalism within their own societies.

For those states who, for various reasons, resist embracing the neoliberal model of good governance, the coercive powers of neoliberal globalization come into play. The neo-Gramscian scholar Stephen Gill describes this as 'disciplinary neoliberalism' (Gill, 1995). Such states risk losing access to development funding from the major international financial institutions, the imposition of international regulation, and a range of external political pressures, intended to bring them into line with global neoliberal norms or, if necessary, destabilize the state itself.

If Cox and others are right in their depiction of the pervasiveness of neoliberalism and the transnational transformation of social hierarchy, it presents a clear challenge to those Marxists who hold to an orthodox view of revolutionary international class struggle as the engine of capitalism's destruction. The Neo-Gramscian account of contemporary global hegemony presents an altogether more complex picture than that provided in Classical Marxism's depiction of a binary division between the bourgeoise and an industrial proletariat with the potential to form an international revolutionary class. Instead, it paints a picture of an internationalized or even globalized dominant class and a highly fragmented working class. Within the latter, some are benefiting from globalization (especially in developed industrialized states), but many find themselves in increasingly precarious employment, or, worse still, at risk of being excluded altogether from the global economy. This fragmentation is further complicated in many countries because of the intersection of economic insecurity with social tensions arising from the segmentation of peoples along the lines of race, ethnicity, religion, and gender. For neo-Gramscians, then, a key question arises: what are the social forces that have the potential, from the 'bottom-up', to form a transnational counter-hegemonic block that might usher in a different word order?

Most neo-Gramscians adopt a pessimistic view of the prospects of fundamental global social change, given the successes of neoliberal globalization and the corresponding fragmentation of potential opposition to it. Cox has observed that 'the bottom-up forces are many and various but have rarely achieved a degree of coherence that could possibly be considered a basis for hegemony' (Cox, 2002: 91). Nonetheless, if a new form of more equitable and just world economy is ever to be achieved, then those counter-hegemonic forces need not only to be identified, but also mobilized. Gill argues that since neoliberal globalization rests upon a significant degree of consent from those subjected to its effects, then withdrawal of that consent may open spaces for political opposition. Evidence in support for this can be found in the emergence of various kinds of opposition to neoliberal globalization, notably a wide range of 'new social movements' (which are summarized in Key concept 6.1). Although many of these arose initially in specific national settings, they also have strong transnational links. Public opposition to the perceived destructive effects of neoliberal globalization at national and transnational levels, Gill argues, could engender a crisis of capitalism 'that links diverse forces across and within nations—many that oppose neo-liberal globalization in new political forms and moments of struggle'. Such protests against the global status quo could create 'new potentials and forms of global political agency' (Gill, 2008: 163, 244).

KEY CONCEPT 6.1 NEW SOCIAL MOVEMENTS

Since the mid to late 1960s, Western societies have seen a considerable growth in the number of *new social movements* (NSMs). Social movements have been a feature of developed countries since industrialization but have traditionally tended to focus on economic issues (such as the labour movement) or achieving policy change (the suffragette movement, for example).

NSMs are distinctive in the breadth of their concerns, which tend to be post-materialist (i.e., not about economic wellbeing), and in their emphasis on multi-faceted social change. Collectively, they question numerous cultural, social, and lifestyle dimensions of contemporary capitalist societies and tend to operate outside of orthodox institutionalized political settings.

Their emergence has generated a lot of academic debate about their origins and distinctive features. Some see NSMs as predominantly middle-class phenomena; others emphasize their relative lack of formal organization or membership and their greater reliance on social networks of supporters, often with transnational linkages. Key examples include:

- women's movements
- ecology movements
- LBGTQI+ rights movements
- anti-globalization movements
- anti-war movements.

More recent developments include anti-capitalist movements that are distinctive in their lack of a clearly defined shared ideology (exhibiting varying degrees and mixes of ecological thought, Marxism, post-Marxism, and anarchism) and in their disavowal of orthodox party politics.

Analysis of NSMs has tended to focus on left-wing movements, but there has also been a growth in right-wing NSMs. These contest various aspects of contemporary developed societies as well as the homogenizing effects of neoliberal globalization. However, whereas progressive NSM's tend to look to create a different future, right-wing NSMs are more focused on what they think is being lost, often with nostalgic reference to a mythologized 'golden' past. The US-based 'Alt-right' is a notable example. Others include the various right-wing populist movements that have emerged in many European countries in recent years, centred around resistance to increased flows of migrants and refugees, which are seen to threaten traditional national cultures and norms as well as, in some cases, hostility to the liberal social and political demands of EU membership.

There are a range of possible candidates for a *counter-hegemonic bloc*. They range from international activist organizations such as Greenpeace and Amnesty International, coalitions of states in the Global South seeking to cooperatively resist the imposition of 'the Washington Consensus' (see the discussion of the 'Beijing Consensus' in Chapter 5), through to various forms of national and transnational social movements and protest groups centred around a range of issues, such as economic austerity policies, armed intervention in conflict zones, global poverty, environmentalism, anti-racism, sexuality and gender, and so on. An example of how national focused protest can rapidly acquire a transnational dimension, not least in their impact upon public consciousness, was provided by the emergence, in 2011, of the Occupy! Movement in the US (See Key events 6.1).

KEY EVENT 6.3 THE OCCUPY! MOVEMENT

Occupy! emerged in the wake of the international financial crisis that began in 2008. It was influenced by protest movements across the Middle East that came to be known collectively as the 'Arab Spring'. Initially, the movement was predominantly US-based and started with the 2011 Occupy Wall Street protest in New York City. Over the next few months, similar protests erupted in more than 600 US locations in the US and in dozens of other countries, worldwide (such as the *Indignados* movement in Spain, which also started in 2011). In the US, the movement organized around the slogan 'we are the 99%', referring to the disproportionate growth in the wealth of the top 1 per cent over recent decades, even after the onset of the financial crisis.

The Occupy! Movement

> The movement was noted for its broadly anti-capitalist stance but did not adhere to a singular or very clear ideological standpoint. The movement advocated participatory democracy and engaged in a wide range of protest actions—including, as the name suggests, occupation of public spaces, especially those near key financial institutions.
>
> These protests targeted the various unjust and inequitable consequences of a globalizing neoliberal capitalism that is seen to have benefited from increasing deregulation coupled with the declining willingness of states to intervene in the interests of the majority. Arguably, many of the concerns expressed by the movement had been foreshadowed in the critiques of modern capitalist society—the excesses of commercialization, corporatism, consumerism, and materialistic individualism—that came out of the Frankfurt School.

The Occupy! Movement in the US subsequently splintered and along with similar movements in Europe and elsewhere no longer attracts the media attention it once did. This is not to deny that such movements have not left a considerable legacy. Arguably, they stimulated a revival of, predominantly (but not entirely) Leftist, popular activism. This is reflected in more recent protest movements, especially around environmental issues. This is illustrated by the emergence since 2018 of the young Swedish activist Greta Thunberg as a leader of global youth climate activism, as well as organizations such as the UK-based Extinction Rebellion. The limited concrete political successes of such movements reinforce, however, the enormous challenges confronting those who seek to bring about alternative world orders. Additionally, in recent years there has been a growth also in right-wing populist movements worldwide (as noted in Key concept 6.1).

'Praxis' and the role of intellectuals

Importantly, it is the difficulty of changing the present world order that highlights the distinctive role of the critical theorist. The role of intellectuals is a significant component of Gramsci's understanding of hegemony, especially regarding how it is sustained and how it might be overturned. Gramsci distinguished between 'traditional intellectuals' (those whom we might immediately think of as intellectuals, such as scholars, writers, artists, philosophers, theologians, and so on) and 'organic intellectuals'. Organic intellectuals were not necessarily intellectuals in the common understanding of the term, but influential thinkers who emerge 'organically' from within the dominant social class. Organic intellectuals—such as high-ranking bureaucrats, lawyers, doctors, engineers, or teachers—played vital roles in disseminating and applying ideas that serve the interests of the class from which they came and in so doing make those interests seem commonsensical. Many traditional intellectuals might see themselves as independent, as somehow above the fray of politics and they may also be seen as such by the public at large. For Gramsci, however, such independence was an illusion; traditional intellectuals were inescapably intertwined with the interplay of competing political and economic interests. i.e., class struggle. In combination, traditional and organic intellectuals aligned with the interests of the dominant class served to legitimate and shore up the status quo; they were vital to the maintenance of hegemonic power.

It follows that intellectuals are also vital to the development of challenges to hegemonic power—the development of a counter-hegemony. What was needed was for a significant number of traditional intellectuals to discard the illusion of independence and join the struggle against the prevailing hegemonic order, as Marx, Lenin, and Gramsci himself had done, and for subordinate groups to develop their own organic intellectuals. These should not only develop a critique of the present hegemonic order, but also work concretely to help bring about counter-hegemonic transnational solidarities and strategies. In other words, the intellectual who wants to challenge the status quo must not only engage in the creation of inspirational ideas but also act politically to inspire others to embrace those ideas.

In effect, Gramsci was challenging the separation of theory and practice and arguing for what in the Marxist tradition is referred to as 'praxis'. In the spirit of Marx's famous claim that it is not enough merely to think critically about the world but to also seek to change it, praxis refers to the bringing together of theory and practice in revolutionary practical activity. Theory is not seen as something that is perfectly formed prior to political practical action, but as something that develops through its engagement with practice and critical reflection upon that engagement. This means that the relationship between theory and practice is not a one-way street; theory and practice should perpetually inform each other.

Richard Wyn Jones, working in the field of Critical Security Studies (which, as we will see, was itself inspired by Critical International Theory), provides a contemporary example of this understanding of the purpose of theory when he argues that critical scholars should become

> the *organic intellectuals* of critical social movements when they exist, or encourage the creation of the political space necessary for their emergence if they do not . . . by providing a critique of the prevailing order and legitimating alternative views, critical theorists can perform a valuable role in supporting the struggles of social movements. (Wyn Jones, 1999: 76)

What Wyn Jones is presenting here is a rather different image of the IR scholar to that associated with orthodox representations of the politically detached, supposedly objective social scientist. It is a depiction of the researcher as politically engaged and conscious of his location in the wider social world. This very much accords with Horkheimer's description of the distinctiveness of critical theory from traditional theory, as we discussed in Section 6.2.

The Frankfurt School's Critical Theory and IR

We have seen that what binds the different approaches to a Critical Theory of IR is a normative commitment to realizing human emancipation, by which is meant the freeing of individuals and groups from what constrains them from realizing their full potential. An important feature of this commitment is that it is *universalist* in orientation; the objective of Critical Theory is to pursue the emancipation of *all* humans. This is reflective of a commitment to moral *cosmopolitanism*, which we briefly outline in Key concept 6.

KEY CONCEPT 6.2 COSMOPOLITANISM

Cosmopolitanism (from the Greek work *kosmopolitēs*—citizen of the world—refers to the view that all human beings, regardless of location, are, or should be 'citizens' of a single, universal community of humankind. Cosmopolitanism can be thought of in purely political terms (as a basis for arguing for ideas of world citizenship or world government, for example), but it is also one of the key approaches to ethics.

The earliest formulations of cosmopolitanism are found in classical Greek and Roman thought (although, the definition of who qualified as a citizen was often quite restrictive) and political cosmopolitanism, as an abstract ideal at least, is a key element of both modern liberalism (think of the idea of universal human rights) and Marxism (as suggested by the famous slogan 'workers of the world unite'). In both cases, however, the political reality of a world divided into bounded sovereign states has limited their practical adherence to truly cosmopolitan politics.

Modern cosmopolitan moral philosophy is most famously associated with the work of the Enlightenment philosopher Immanuel Kant (who is discussed in Chapter 2). He argued that, as rational beings, we had a *duty* to act morally and those morals we should uphold should be applicable to all. In his formulation of what he called the *Categorical Imperative* (a rule that should be upheld in all circumstances) Kant argued that we should 'act only to that maxim by which you can also will that it would become a universal law'. In essence, Kant is saying that we should only act towards others as we would wish them to act towards us. Furthermore, we should act 'in such a way that you always treat humanity, whether in your own person or in the person of any other, never simply as a means, but always at the same time as an end'. In other words, we should treat all people as of equal moral worth.

Kant's moral cosmopolitanism was deontological (from the Greek for the study of duty): we are duty-bound to act morally, so we should ask what is the *right* thing to do? Some modern cosmopolitan moral philosophers adopt a *consequentialist*, or *utilitarian* standpoint. They argue that we should judge moral actions primarily in terms of their consequences, their utility in realizing the greatest happiness of the greatest number.

This invites the question: what would produce the best universal outcome? Following rules based on principles of duty, or asking what would be the consequences of our actions? Although these two types of cosmopolitan moral thinking are often seen as in tension, in recent years many philosophers have endeavoured to reconcile them.

International politics seemingly presents, however, an immediate challenge to cosmopolitan thinking. This is because most humans exercise whatever rights and duties they have won within the confines of sovereign states. States can use their sovereign power not only to demand the loyalty of their citizens (through such things as military service, for example), but also to set the boundaries of possible political action. In authoritarian forms of state, the rights accorded to citizens and the political space available to them can be highly restricted or almost non-existent.

In contrast, the modern liberal democratic state is often held up as a benchmark of an ideal type of state in which citizens are accorded the greatest amount of individual social and political freedom. However, even though the liberal state is, in principle at least, an expression of universal notions of rights and freedoms, it also demands a degree of loyalty and obligation from its citizens. Additionally, those citizens, to greater or lesser degrees, expect their state to put their interests first. To what extent the state should privilege its own citizens over the rest of humanity has long been a matter of (often heated) debate within liberal democratic states. We can see evidence of this today in debates around the giving of foreign aid, refugee and immigration policies, whether the UK should have stayed in the EU, and so on. Therefore, even citizens of liberal states confront a moral conundrum arising from the tensions between their rights and duties as citizens of their state and those they might claim as members of the whole human community (when they appeal to their human rights, for example, or demand that their state supports those suffering outside its borders).

Whether or not they are supposedly founded upon universal principles, even liberal sovereign states are, by their very nature, an inherently socially and politically *exclusionary* form of community, to some degree or other. These politics of inclusion and exclusion play out within states and at the international and global levels. Think here of the power of national borders as expressions of inclusion and exclusion. Who gets to cross the border from outside to inside the state—and what status they have if they do—are highly political issues, as contemporary debates about the global flows of migrants and refugees so starkly illustrate. Clearly, the possibilities for human emancipation vary considerably according to where people find themselves, both within their national community, or because of the relationship between that community and the wider world.

The various constraints on possibilities for emancipatory politics were a core concern of the Frankfurt School. In the 1930s and 1940s, several of its key figures became interested in the general phenomenon of social domination, analysing the oppressive features of not only Western capitalist societies, but also the still emerging Soviet and Nazi forms of authoritarianism. During the Cold War their focus shifted towards the rise of individualism, consumerism, and 'mass culture' in capitalist societies. They saw this as inducing increasing political and intellectual passivity among the populace, which in turn served to stifle the possibilities of, and desire for, radical political action in pursuit of greater social and economic justice. For some of them, this line of analysis led to a form of intellectual despair. For others such as Herbert Marcuse, the possibilities for escaping the regimentation of thought and behaviour in both capitalist and Communist societies still existed, even if the realization of greater human freedom and happiness presented a considerable challenge (Marcuse, 1964).

Jürgen Habermas came out of the Frankfurt School and shared its interest in analysing contemporary forms of capitalist society while rejecting the pessimistic turn. A notable contribution has been his exploration of discourse ethics—identifying the fairest procedures by which humans can achieve mutual understanding (Discourse ethics is briefly outlined in Key concept 6.3). Following on from the critique of modern society initiated by the Frankfurt School, Habermas argued that a defining feature of modern capitalist democracies was the decline of the *public sphere*, the political space in which citizens actively debated the key questions confronting their own societies. Modern democracies were increasingly democratic in name only. Many citizens exercised their democratic rights, but this was increasingly done in a disengaged, ritualistic fashion.

Habermas' argument is rather complex, but in essence he explores how we might recreate the conditions for open and inclusive public debate so that all citizens can better participate equally in determining the future direction of the societies in which they live. In so doing, he was moving Critical Theory further from its Marxist roots, because he saw authentic public debate as requiring the exclusion of ideology. The model of the ideal society should not be the product of some specific ideological standpoint such as Marxism or liberalism, but of *undistorted communication*. It should emerge out of an authentic consensus arrived at through genuinely public, open, and equitable dialogue. Undistorted communication, for Habermas, is key to the realization of human emancipation.

KEY CONCEPT 6.3 DISCOURSE ETHICS

Discourse ethics (also known as communicative ethics) was developed by Jürgen Habermas. It aims to identify the *ideal speech situation* wherein members of a democratic community can engage in a genuinely free and open debate to arrive at a consensus about the fundamental rules and moral values that should govern their community.

By suggesting this, Habermas (1984 and 1987) was endeavouring to develop Kant's argument that moral principles should be universal and are only legitimate if human beings openly consent to follow them. Kant based his understanding of universal moral principles upon a complex and abstract account of human rationality. In contrast, Habermas seeks to ground ethical principles in a communicative procedure that establishes the conditions for dialogue. Habermas proposes a set of ethical principles that are intended to ensure the procedural fairness of dialogue:

- everyone who is competent to speak should be able to participate
- everyone should be able to question any assertion made in the dialogue
- everyone can introduce any assertion into the dialogue
- no one should be prevented from exercising their rights to participate.

The objective is to achieve consensus based on what one commentator summarizes as 'the unforced force of the better argument' (the title of Allen, 2012). Habermas' intention is to show that the pursuit of authentic communication is itself emancipatory (Rasmussen, 1990: 18).

Habermas also argues that there also needs to be a sense of solidarity between participants, which is a concession to those critics of Kantian ethics who claim that his overly abstracted and universalized accounts of human rationality fail to take sufficient account of the specific circumstances in which people find themselves, such as different community settings and political contexts.

> However, if specific communities, variously defined, can apply the rules of communicative ethics to their own deliberations, this opens up the question of whether those rules could also be utilized to govern discourse between communities, ultimately at the global level. Answering this question guides much of the discussion of Habermas's account of discourse ethics in the IR field, most notably in the work of the Critical IR theorist Andrew Linklater.

Inclusion, Exclusion, and 'The Transformation of Community'

Habermas' work inspired the work of a number of Critical International Theory scholars, most notably the British scholar, Andrew Linklater. In his work, Linklater endeavours to explore the moral and political tensions that arise because of humans' multiple identities as both members of particular communities and members of the human race as a whole. Linklater sees the international system of states as exclusionary because the dominant mode of human community—the state—is itself inherently exclusionary. States can regulate who crosses their borders and who count as citizens. From this point of view, an international system made up of sovereign states can only act as a barrier to the full realization of universal human emancipation. Realism acknowledges the essentially selfish and competitive nature of sovereign states but largely confines itself to exploring how best to live with this (as discussed in Chapter 3). Classical Marxism has a cosmopolitan impulse in its pursuit of the universal freedom of all workers. However, it is analytically constrained by its emphasis on revolutionary class struggle as the pathway to human emancipation (which we discuss in Chapter 5), as well as its failure to adequately consider the impact of *nationalism* upon people's sense of being members of a wider human community.

Despite the challenges arising out of the very nature of an international system of sovereign states, Linklater argues for the possibility of moving further towards the realization of universal human emancipation based on what he sees as the 'triple transformation' of *political community*. The three transformations, according to Linklater, are:

- The growing recognition that moral, political, and legal principles ought to be universalized (in the form of an expanding set of human rights, for example)
- Demands that economic inequality should be reduced, not only within states but in global terms as well
- Greater recognition that respect must be given to differences based on race, class, gender, ethnicity, sexuality, and so on. (Linklater, 1998, 2001)

It is important to emphasize that a key component of Linklater's argument (represented in the third bullet point, above) is that some varieties of cosmopolitan thinking—notably the mainstream of Liberal cosmopolitanism—can be too universalistic. This is because they fail to accord sufficient respect to legitimate differences, especially when it comes

220 INTRODUCTION TO INTERNATIONAL RELATIONS THEORIES

to vulnerable or marginalized groups of people. Although Linklater is keen to challenge the exclusionary effects of the state and the system of states, he takes seriously the importance of various forms of community in people's lives. Liberal cosmopolitanism focuses on individual rights and freedoms, whereas for some peoples, their rights as members of a community with unique shared practices and beliefs, are of primary importance. Accordingly, Linklater, and other critical IR theorists promote what Richard Shapcott describes as a 'thin cosmopolitanism' (Shapcott, 2001: 209–232). This seeks to reconcile universality with legitimate claims for the preservation of difference.

Linklater's thin cosmopolitanism rests upon the claim that the forms of community that humans inhabit are both multiple and overlapping. For example, a British citizen might see themselves simultaneously as British, and as English, or Welsh, or Scottish, or Northern Irish. They may also define themselves as European, or with reference to a particular non-British national identity or religious, ethnic, or cultural group. They might also see themselves as a member of the global human community. Which senses of membership, or belonging, take priority and when is likely to vary from person to person. Such multiple identities can be understood also as multiple moral communities because they each generate different senses of rights and duties. For Linklater, history shows how the complex politics of identity has increasingly been the source of challenges to the widespread idea that the territorially defined sovereign state should constitute the primary moral community. History shows us that dominant conceptions of citizenship have been challenged and subsequently revised to include previously excluded groups, such as the poor, women, people of colour, and sexual and gender minorities. What Linklater wants to do is explore the potential for further expanding the idea of citizenship and political community beyond the boundaries of the sovereign state and out into the international and global levels.

There is significant evidence, Linklater argues, of the potential for our senses of community and belonging to become more inclusive and extend beyond the confines of the sovereign state. As a critical theorist, Linklater sees the international system of states as an historical entity which can and does change. His starting premise is that the relationship between sovereign states has historically displayed a greater sense of belonging to a wider community than realism has conceded. Linklater draws upon the English School's notion that states exist within a pluralist anarchical *society* of states (we examine this claim in Chapter 4). At the very least, the anarchical society of states sets some mutually agreed rules and norms for the conduct of international relations.

In recent decades, as the 'solidarist' wing of the English School argues, many states have begun also to recognize an increasing number of shared moral obligations, such as protecting the global environment, responding to crimes against humanity, regulating the spread of weapons of mass destruction, and so on (you can read more about the solidarist wing of the English School in Chapter 4, Sections 4.2 and 4.4). Could the notion of a transnational community be developed further still, such that states begin to relinquish some of their sovereign powers and develop the transnational institutionalization of their shared norms and values? Writing in 1998, Linklater saw the EU as providing an interesting example of the development of a political community beyond the sovereign state (Linklater, 1998). Of course, the recent troubled history of the EU—with the growth of Euroscepticism, the rise of inward-looking nationalist sentiment within many of its member states, and the UK's decision to leave—reminds us just how difficult the extension of community beyond the state can be. Indeed, for some realists the trials and tribulations of the European integration project provides evidence of the intractable and selfish nature of the anarchical system of states (Mearsheimer, 1990 and 2010).

Linklater's vision rests, nonetheless, on the claim that there is immanent potential within the international system of states for its transformation into a more inclusive community that would extend the prospects of emancipation to an ever-greater portion of humanity. Such developments as the globalization of the world economy, the increasing movement of peoples (willingly or unwillingly) across borders, growing awareness of threats to the global environment, and the growing voices of Indigenous peoples and other sub-national groups, put ever greater pressure on the sovereign state as the primary locus of political debate and decision making.

Realizing such a vision in a world marked by many significant differences and divisions between the multiple forms of community of which it is comprised, is undoubtedly challenging. Linklater's response to that challenge draws directly upon Habermas' work on discourse ethics (as discussed in Key concept 6.3). Rather than pursue a pre-given blueprint for a more politically inclusive world (such as is offered by Marxism, for example), Linklater argues for the need to develop new political spaces for open, inclusive, and unrestricted dialogue between different communities. New political arrangements should emerge out of genuine public deliberation and consensual agreement. This requires the deepening not only of national public spheres, but the development of an international, even global public sphere. What is required are institutional arrangements that facilitate dialogue not just between states, but also enable the inclusion of the various other actors that have a stake in the future direction of global development. The goal would be to fundamentally transform the way in which states and other international actors interact with each other.

Since the emergence of Critical International Theory, several scholars—both inside and outside the IR field—have coalesced around the theme of *cosmopolitan democracy*. They explore how the concept of democratic accountability might be developed at the transnational and global levels. The goal is not the creation of a single world government (an idea that briefly achieved some traction in the early twentieth century) but rather the development of multiple layers of democratic governance ranging from the local, sub-national level through to the global. These would better reflect the complexity of human affiliations and allegiances (Archibugi and Held, 1995; Held, 1995).

Reading this, you might think that the realization of cosmopolitan democracy is a rather grand vision. In contrast, some critical international theorists, such as Deiniol Jones and Mark Hoffman, have explored how Habermassian discourse ethics might be applied on a smaller scale to the resolutions of conflicts between states, or groups of people, which have led to, or could lead to the outbreak of violence. Open dialogue between all the parties to a conflict, perhaps mediated by a third party, is seen as a preferable alternative to the traditional model of negotiation, which rests upon an adversarial mentality of them and us. In contrast, cosmopolitan mediation aims to produce a genuinely shared resolution. Indeed, its advocates believe that authentically open and undistorted dialogue, in which each side is encouraged to understand the other's point of view, can produce more sustainable resolutions because they will be based on more authentic agreement (Jones, 1991 and 2000; Hoffman, 1992). However, they also acknowledge that achieving open and undistorted communication between states and other actors at the international level is very difficult to achieve, given the influence of economic, political, and cultural differences.

Critical Theory and Security

One of the key preoccupations of mainstream IR theories, especially realism, is security. During the Cold War this led to the emergence of the sub-field of Strategic Studies (also known as National Security Studies in the US). Strategic Studies examines the weapons and strategies that states deploy to ensure their security and it has traditionally been predominantly realist in outlook. Not surprisingly then, the primary analytical focus of Strategic Studies, as with mainstream IR theory more widely, has been the security of states. States are the 'referent object' of security; they are, in other words that which is to be secured. From the late 1970s onwards, however, scholars from a range of theoretical positions have endeavoured to broaden the focus of the study of security away from a preoccupation with military threats to state security.

An early seminal example of this challenge was Barry Buzan's 1983 book, *People, States and Fear*. Buzan argued that security was not just a matter for states but for a whole range of human collectivities (hence the reference to 'people' in the book's title). Additionally, Buzan argued that it was entirely inadequate to consider security and threats to security in predominantly military terms. Insecurity can arise in a range of spheres, such as the political, economic, societal, and environmental and each required different forms of analysis and different policy responses. The challenges by Buzan and others led to the establishment of Security Studies as a new sub-field of IR which challenged the predominantly military and statist focus of traditional Strategic Studies.

In the early 1990s, several scholars drew upon Critical International Theory to take the argument for widening and deepening the concept of security further, leading to the subsequent emergence of Critical Security Studies (CSS). CSS scholars such as Richard Wyn Jones argued that Buzan's argument for broadening the study of security did not go far enough and still largely focused on expanding the understanding of challenges to the security of states (Wyn Jones, 1999: 12). The influence of Cox's distinction between problem-solving theory and critical theory (which we discussed in Section 6.3) comes into play here. CSS challenges what it sees as a limited problem-solving approach to the question of security in which the international status quo is simply taken to be unlikely to change fundamentally. Consequently, the state is presumed to be the most significant actor in world politics as well as the primary provider of security, and national security is seen as the principal goal to be pursued.

In contrast, CSS starts by questioning the underlying assumptions of traditional approaches to security. Although the state may be widely seen to be the principal provider of security, especially in developed and highly stable states, other more repressive and authoritarian states can also be the main sources of threats to the physical, economic, and political security of their citizens (Wyn Jones, 1999: 99).

The traditional focus on minimizing the risk of war between states also fails to consider the changing nature of war itself, especially in the post-Cold War era. Mary Kaldor introduced the concept of 'New Wars' to capture the declining likelihood of wars between sovereign states (the traditional understanding of war) and the increased frequency of wars within states, across state borders, or because of the collapse of states (Kaldor, 1999). As illustrated by the conflicts following the breakup of Yugoslavia after the end of the Cold War and in countries such as Rwanda, Somalia, and Sudan, contemporary wars can involve a wide range of actors (including state-sponsored or private militias). These may be fighting over a range of issues such as the politics of ethnic or religious identity, or control of precious resources. From a CSS perspective, orthodox security thinking is simply inadequate for analysing new forms of large-scale conflict between a varying range of human collectivities for a variety of reasons.

Reflecting its roots in Marxism, CSS also locates the question of security within a critique of an exploitative international capitalist economic system. As Richard Wyn Jones puts it, 'the relative security of the inhabitants of the North is purchased at the price of chronic instability for the vast majority of the world population' (Wyn Jones, 1999: 99). This points to the need to investigate the complex linkages between various forms of insecurity and developmental processes in the post-colonial era. Again, a traditional focus on security as primarily concerned with the defence of states and their national interests from external, predominantly military threats is seen as analytically inadequate.

For the advocates of CSS, the meaning of the concept of security is therefore not fixed but *derivative*; it depends on our political and theoretical perspective. If, as many scholars do, we define security simply as the absence of threats this immediately generates further questions:

- what kinds of threat are we referring to?
- who is doing the threatening or being threatened?
- who is seeking freedom from these threats? Is it individuals, groups, nations, states, or a complex mix of some or all of them?

Reflecting their core assumptions about international politics, traditional conceptions of security tend to address the question of threats to security primarily in terms of threats to the national security of states. In contrast, CSS scholars argue that the various kinds of threats to security most directly affect people. In other words, the appropriate referent object of security should not be the state but the individual since it is humans who individually and collectively directly suffer the consequences of multiple forms of insecurity.

In arguing for a shift in the focus of the analysis of security from the state to the individual, CSS draws a direct connection between security and the concept of human emancipation. Indeed, one prominent advocate of CSS, Ken Booth, argues that 'security and emancipation are two sides of the same coin' (Booth, 1991: 319). Along with other CSS scholars, Booth sees the purpose of studying security as the investigation of how individuals can emancipate themselves from the myriad threats, both military and non-military, that prevent them from achieving their full human potential. In this way, security should be understood as more than merely surviving in a dangerous world; it is a condition in which humans can hope to fully develop themselves (i.e., achieve emancipation) in the genuine absence of significant threats.

It is worth noting here that alongside the work of CSS scholars, the idea of a broader, more human-centred understanding of security was also emerging within other fields close to IR, notably development studies and peace research. Since its inception in the early 1960s, for example, peace research has drawn a distinction between 'negative peace'—the mere absence of war—and 'positive peace' which entails the realization of human fulfilment (Lawler, 1995). Similarly, there are debates within the theory and practice of development around the idea of 'human development'. This is a more holistic understanding of development than that of simply achieving economic growth and it led to the emergence of the concept of 'human security' in the 1994 annual report of the United Nations Development Programme (UNDP). Echoing many of the debates within CSS, human security explicitly connects development with security and depicts insecurity as the consequence of both military and non-military processes. The drawing of precise distinctions between these parallel theoretical and conceptual developments is not easy and each has influenced the development of the others.

6.5 **FROM CRITICAL INTERNATIONAL THEORY TO CRITICAL IR THEORIES**

We noted at the beginning of this chapter that the emergence of Critical International Theory opened the doors to a wider and still developing critical turn in the IR field. Within a few years, other types of critical thinking—also influenced by a wide range of theoretical sources outside of the IR field—began to emerge. Many of them shared some of the key epistemological assumptions of Critical International Theory, notably the rejection of a positivist model of the social sciences. However, as we will see over the next chapters, some of the newer forms of critical thinking have also taken issue with key aspects of Critical International Theory.

Arguably, it is Critical International Theory's underlying universalist or cosmopolitan outlook that has been most susceptible to critical challenge. The purpose of Critical Theory is to explore the prospects for universal human emancipation through the extension of freedom from multiple forms of economic, social, and political constraints. The roots of Critical International Theory's understanding of human freedom lie firmly in the European Enlightenment and the subsequent evolution of Western progressive political thinking, within both the Liberal and Marxist traditions.

Critical Theory's universalism can be seen to be vulnerable in significant and connected respects. The contemporary world is still marked by gross inequality and significant socio-cultural differences. Critical Theory's understanding of supposedly universal emancipation could be seen as underpinned by a predominantly Western and, thus, a comparatively privileged outlook. As we have seen, Andrew Linklater and others have endeavoured to take account of the disquiet over Critical Theory's universalism, by arguing for a 'thin' cosmopolitanism centred on open, unconstrained dialogue between people in different circumstances and with different points of view. The intention is that the outcome of such dialogue would not be predetermined but would be the product of an unforced and authentic consensus. However, some of the other forms of critical theorizing raise questions about the very possibility of an 'ideal speech situation' and genuinely undistorted communication, given the complex intersection of various forms of global economic and political inequalities with the politics of identity. Is universal agreement on what human emancipation means achievable, or, some ask, even desirable?

Digging even deeper, other critical theories see Critical International Theory as failing to reflect sufficiently critically upon its underlying assumption that there is a universal understanding of human subjectivity—the 'human' that is to be emancipated. One of the key sources of this line of critique is poststructuralism which we look at in Chapter 7. Another source of criticism of the kind of Western universalist reasoning that underpins Critical International Theory is postcolonialism, which is examined in Chapter 9.

6.6 **CONCLUSION**

As we have seen, Critical Theory of IR emerged out of two, overlapping, intellectual lineages. The first, as illustrated by Ashley's article, is the Critical Theory that came out of the Frankfurt School (and other Western Marxist currents of thought). The Frankfurt School had not addressed international relations specifically; it focused on analysing the constraints upon human emancipation within specific societies. Like other forms of European neo-Marxist or post-Marxist streams of radical thought, it concerned itself with a wide range of injustices emerging out of, but not entirely defined by class relations under capitalism. Ashley must take considerable credit for bringing the Frankfurt School to IR.

The second lineage, represented by Cox's article, has a much more overtly historical and political economy flavour to it and can be traced back to Gramsci's critique of Marxist orthodoxy. As with Ashley and Linklater's deployment of the Frankfurt School, it seeks to extend Critical Theory into the realm of international politics. Therefore, it is focused on the types of world order and the forms of hegemony that emerge within specific historical conjunctures. Given this, it is not surprising that its principal impact has been within the discipline of IPE/GPE, that emerged out of IR since the 1970s.

Whatever their precise intellectual origins, all varieties of Critical International Theory conceive of themselves as not merely endeavouring to understand existing historical circumstances, but also acting as a force for change within them. In this respect, they are all heirs to two powerful themes in Marx's work, even if many Critical Theorists have moved a very long way from classical Marxism. The first is that the point of 'interpreting' the world is surely to change it, given the evident inequities and injustices to be found in that world (Marx's famous Thesis XI). The second is captured in another of Marx's famous observations contained in a pamphlet published in 1852. This was that

> (humans) make their own history but they do not make it just as they please, they do not make it under circumstances chosen by themselves but under circumstances directly encountered, given, and transmitted from the past. (Marx, 2000: 329)

In other words, identifying the prospects for change and transformation requires first an analysis of where we are now and how we got there. Only then, Critical International Theory tells us, will we be able to discern the barriers to and viable prospects for further human emancipation worldwide.

SUMMARIZING CRITICAL INTERNATIONAL THEORY

- Critical Theory criticizes the economic determinism of orthodox Marxism and places comparatively greater emphasis on the political and cultural superstructure that sustains capitalism

- Critical Theory rejects the positivist model of the social sciences, in which the theorist endeavours to stand apart from the world to assess it objectively

- Critical Theory sees all theorists as products of the social world they are studying, and this inescapably influences their work, whether they admit this or not

- Critical Theory is overtly normative, i.e., value driven. Critical theory endeavours to be an agent of social change

- Critical Theory did not appear in IR scholarship until the publication in 1981 of two journal articles by Richard Ashley and Robert W. Cox

- Subsequently, Critical International Theory has largely developed along two overlapping yet distinctive paths, one located primarily in the IPE/GPE field, the other within IR more generally

- Critical International Theory views the international system not as an immutable given, but as an historical construction. As such, it is possible to conceive of it changing, potentially quite radically

- Following Cox, neo-Gramscians focus mainly on critiquing the political economy of global capitalism and exploring the potential for a post-capitalist world order that lies within it

- Critical IR theorists influenced by the Frankfurt School and later Jürgen Habermas focus on the rethinking of political community and the development of more inclusive forms of community and democratic accountability that extend beyond the boundaries of the territorial state

- Critical IR Theorists sees the key agents of change as more varied than an orthodox Marxist account of class struggle suggests. They see potential in a wide range of political actors, such as new social movements, in which people critical of various

aspects of life under capitalism organize themselves for political action around a range of issues and identities
- Critical International Theory embraces moral cosmopolitanism. It is guided by the pursuit of *universal* human *emancipation* from unjustifiable constraints
- Some critical theorists endeavour to reconcile their moral universalism with recognition of the importance of difference for many humans who identify with specific communities, and argue therefore for a 'thin' variety of cosmopolitanism
- Critical International Theory has been a key contributor to the widening and deepening of the concept of security

QUESTIONS

1. Identify and briefly explain the different types of 'knowledge-constitutive' human interest that Habermas claims drive our pursuit of knowledge
2. How does Robert Cox distinguish between 'problem-solving' and 'critical' theories?
3. What does Robert Cox mean by 'theory is always for someone or something'?
4. Why might the emergence of social movements such as the contemporary global environmental movement be significant from the perspective of Critical International Theory?
5. What are the key challenges to developing an 'ideal speech situation' characterized by 'undistorted communication' at the international level (You might want to think here of the challenges of communication between parties to a longstanding conflict such as the Israel-Palestine conflict)?
6. Critical International Theory is generally associated with an understanding of 'human emancipation' that reflects a universalist or 'cosmopolitan' standpoint. Thinking of other critical theories covered in this book, why might this be vulnerable to criticism?

IR THEORY TODAY CRITICAL INTERNATIONAL THEORY AND THE GLOBAL ENVIRONMENTAL MOVEMENT

Consider the following developments:
- In 20–27 September 2019 a series of climate strikes, known as the Global Week for the Future, took place worldwide. Key to the organization of the strikes was the youth-led 'Fridays for Future' movement, inspired by the young Swedish climate activist Greta Thunberg's solo protest every Friday outside the Swedish parliament since the summer of 2018. It has been estimated that more than 6 million people in more than 150 countries participated in the strikes.

INTRODUCTION TO INTERNATIONAL RELATIONS THEORIES

- On Friday September 24, 2021, hundreds of thousands of people in 1,800 towns and cities across 99 countries participated in a coordinated global climate strike, again organized by the Fridays for Future movement. It was the largest global climate protest since the beginning of the COVID-19 pandemic.

- In October 2021, using a NASA database of human population density, 100 people from around the world were chosen by lottery to participate in an online Global Citizens' Assembly to discuss the global climate crisis. The make-up of the assembly is intended to reflect global demographics. This means, for example, that 60 come from Asia, 17 from Africa, 50 per cent are women and 70 are people earning $10 a day or less. The assembly presented its findings to the UN COP26 climate change conference in Glasgow in November 2021. The assembly was organized by *Global Assembly*, a transnational coalition of organizations in 50 countries whose aim is to establish a permanent digital global citizen's assembly with 10 million annual participants by 2030.

Based on what you have learned from this chapter (especially Section 6.4: Applying Critical International Theory) and your own research, answer the following questions:

1. To what extent, if any, do you think developments such as those outlined in the bullet points above support the claim by Andrew Linklater, that there is an immanent potential within the present international system for the 'transformation of community'?

2. To what extent, if any, do you think transnational climate protests support the argument, by David Held and others, for the need to develop more 'cosmopolitan' forms of democracy?

3. What are the key factors that, in your view, challenge the prospects for the transformation of community or the emergence of more cosmopolitan forms of democracy? Do you think they can be overcome? (Hint: think here about such things as the power of the concept of national sovereignty, climate change scepticism, the problems confronting the EU, and the rise of nationalist and right-wing populism worldwide in recent years).

TWISTING THE LENS

1. Look at Chapter 11 on Green IR perspectives. In what ways might the different strands of Green IR thought provide either support or criticism for the transformative potential of the global environmental movement suggested by Critical International Theory?

USEFUL RESOURCES YOU CAN FIND ONLINE

Global Assembly website: https://globalassembly.org/
Fridays for Future website: https://fridaysforfuture.org/
Abnett, Kate (2021), 'World's youth take to the streets again to battle climate change', *Reuters*, September 25.
BBC (2019), 'Climate protests: Marches worldwide against global warming'.
Jarczewska, Daria (2013), 'Critical Assessment of Cosmopolitan Democracy', *E-international relations.* www.e-ir.info

6 CRITICAL INTERNATIONAL THEORY **229**

FURTHER READING

ADDITIONAL INTRODUCTORY READING

Horden, S. and Wyn Jones, R. (2020), 'Marxist Theories of International Relations' in John Baylis, Steve Smith, and Patricia Owens, *The Globalization of World Politics: An Introduction to International Relations*, 8th edition (Oxford: Oxford University Press).
A basic and brief introductory survey of the main varieties of Marxist approaches to IR, including Critical Theory.

Roach, S. C. (2021), 'Critical Theory' in Tim Dunne, Milja Kurki, and Steve Smith, *International Relations Theories: Discipline and Diversity* (Oxford: Oxford University Press).
A more advanced introduction to Critical Theory with a useful case study of the 'Arab Spring'.

Peoples, C. and Vaughan-Williams, N. (2021), 'Critical Theory' in Columba Peoples and Nick Vaughan-Williams, *Critical Security Studies: An Introduction* (London: Routledge), 31–48.
A very accessible overview of Critical Theory's main claims and its contribution to the emergence of the sub-field of Critical Security Studies.

MORE IN-DEPTH READING

Ashley, R. K. (1981), 'Political Realism and Human Interest', *International Studies Quarterly* 25/2: 204–236.
In this pathbreaking article, Ashley uses Habermas' trilogy of 'knowledge-constitutive interests' to critically examine the realist tradition.

Brincat, S., Lima, L., and Nunes, J. (2012), *Critical Theory in International Relations and Security Studies: Interviews and Reflections* (Abingdon: Routledge).
Combines interviews with four leading critical IR theorists with a series of articles reflecting on the origins, limits, and possible future direction of Critical International Theory.

Cox, R. W. (1981), 'Social Forces, States and World Orders: Beyond International Relations Theory', *Millennium: Journal of International Studies*, 10/2: 126–155.
One of the earliest and most cited contributions to the development of Critical International Theory.

Devetak, R. (2018), *Critical International Theory: An Intellectual History* (Oxford: Oxford University Press).
A sophisticated yet accessible account of the emergence and development of Critical International Theory that also endeavours to develop a distinctive account of it.

Diez, T. and Steans, J. (2005), 'A Useful Dialogue? Habermas and International Relations', *Review of International Studies*, 31/1: 127–140.
A useful introduction to a Forum on Habermas in which IR theorists reflect on the utility of Habermas' work for analysing international politics

Kubálková, V. (2016), 'Framing Robert W. Cox, Framing International Relations', *Globalizations*, 13/5: 578–593.
An unusual reading of the work of Robert Cox that argues that describing Cox as a leading figure of Critical International Theory overly 'frames' his work and obscures its unique and eclectic qualities.

Leysens, A. (2008), *The Critical Theory of Robert W. Cox: Fugitive or Guru?* (Basingstoke: Palgrave Macmillan).
A comprehensive survey of Robert Cox's work which suggests that his work is of such significance that it will still be read in many decades time.

Linklater, A. (1998), *The Transformation of Community: Ethical Foundations of the Post-Westphalian Era* (Cambridge: Polity Press).

In this book, the IR fields's most prominent critical international theorist examines the prospects for moving beyond the sovereign states system towards a more cosmopolitan and just world order.

Pusey, M. (1987), *Jürgen Habermas* (London: Tavistock Publications).

A short and accessible introduction to Habermas' work aimed at student readers.

Wyn Jones, R. (1999), *Security, Strategy and Critical Theory* (Boulder: Lynne Rienner).

A seminal text by a key figure in the so-called 'Welsh School' of Critical Security Studies.

Wyn Jones, R. (ed.) (2001), *Critical Theory and World Politics* (Boulder: Lynne Riener Publishers).

A collection of essays by some of the most noted Critical International Theory scholars, including Robert Cox and Andrew Linklater.

CHAPTER 7

POSTSTRUCTURALISM AND INTERNATIONAL RELATIONS

LEARNING OBJECTIVES

- Identify the historical and political contexts from which poststructuralism emerged

- Evaluate key themes within the work of two leading poststructuralist thinkers: Jacques Derrida and Michel Foucault

- Describe the disciplinary context within which poststructuralist IR became prominent

- Explain how key themes in poststructuralism can be applied to the study of international and global politics

- Analyse the similarities and distinctions between poststructuralism and other critical approaches to IR.

7.1 INTRODUCTION

In Chapter 6 we discuss the emergence of Critical International Theory in the early 1980s. Only a few years later, another variety of critical IR thinking emerged: poststructuralism. Like Critical International Theory, poststructuralist IR theory draws from long-running philosophical and theoretical debates from outside the IR discipline and it shares much of Critical Theory's critique of the dominance of mainstream IR theories. In contrast to Critical Theory, however, poststructuralism does not present itself as an alternative theoretical IR perspective. Instead, its advocates present it as more like an interpretive standpoint, or 'critical attitude' (Campbell and Bleiker, 2021: 197).

As we shall see, poststructuralist IR scholarship is certainly highly theoretical, but there is no singular poststructuralist theory of IR to be found. Indeed, most poststructuralist IR theorists are resistant to the idea that anything like a general theory of IR is either possible or desirable. Given this, it is perhaps not surprising that poststructuralism's arrival in the IR discipline initially created considerable hostility. Many scholars viewed it as offering sweeping criticism of orthodox approaches while offering nothing substantial in their place.

Whereas it may be true that poststructuralist IR scholars generally shy away from offering definitive statements about how the world should be or how we should get there, many of them are directly engaging with some of the most pressing issues and problems in today's world. Much of the initial hostility (but not all of it) to poststructuralist IR has subsided and poststructuralism has subsequently become one of the most influential bodies of theoretical scholarship in the contemporary IR discipline. Today poststructuralist perspectives or insights can be found in many if not most sub-fields of the IR discipline—such as feminism and gender, security studies, and IPE—and its emergence has also generated new areas of research that take us a long way from the core concerns of orthodox IR theory.

In this chapter we start by examining the historical and theoretical contexts in which poststructuralism emerged prior to its appearance within the IR discipline. We then explore key themes in poststructuralist scholarship, focusing on the work of two of the most noted poststructuralist scholars: Jacques Derrida and Michel Foucault. Their work is quite challenging at first sight, so we need to spend a bit of time going through the key themes, not least because they have become highly influential in recent IR scholarship. We go on to explore how key ideas drawn from the work of Derrida, Foucault, and other poststructuralist scholars are used by IR scholars to raise profound questions about how other theories *represent* and *interpret* international and global politics. We then consider how poststructuralist IR scholarship also challenges the practices of international politics, in particular the exercise of sovereign statehood.

7.2 **WHAT IS POSTSTRUCTURALISM?**

Summarizing poststructuralism is not easy because it draws from a wide range of theoretical sources and there is no tidy theoretical endpoint to arrive at. Additionally, a lot of the poststructuralist literature can be initially challenging to read and interpret, not least because its intentions include the destabilizing of established ways of thinking. It is meant to throw us off balance intellectually and question some of our most fundamental theoretical assumptions, not least the very idea of theory. It also seeks to question our assumptions about our subjectivity, who *we* as humans actually are.

Nonetheless, there are some recurrent core themes threading through poststructuralist scholarship that do give it a theoretical shape of sorts. In describing the work of one of the most famous of poststructuralist scholars—Michel Foucault—Lynn Fendler suggests that three features stand out: 'provocations, problematization and poetry' (Fendler, 2010: 5). These features could also be said to characterize much of the work of other poststructuralist scholars. Their writing is intended to provoke the reader. They seek also to problematize established assumptions and presumptions about the world, yet generally also refuse to offer definitive solutions or clear-cut alternatives (in contrast to the

Critical Theory we discussed in Chapter 6). It is also often poetic in the sense that many poststructuralists deliberately play with language, conjure up new words and phrases and often write in a style that is markedly different from that of orthodox scholarship.

Let us now consider the name: poststructuralism.

What is 'post' about poststructuralism?

Poststructuralism emerged in France during the 1960s alongside other strands of critical thinking—such as Feminism, varieties of Western Marxism, and environmentalist thinking—that were engaging with the political turbulence of the time (see Key event 7.1)

KEY EVENT 7.1 'THE SIXTIES'

The 1960s, also referred to as the Sixties, has been widely recognized as an era of significant social, cultural, and political turbulence, especially within Western developed states. It was a period marked by the emergence of what is sometimes referred to as the 'counterculture'. This was a multifaceted reaction, especially among younger, often relatively affluent people, to orthodox or mainstream politics, cultural values, and social norms.

Although this was an era in which Western states were experiencing rapidly rising standards of living, there was increasing resistance to what were seen to be the stultifying aspects of social and political life in affluent capitalist societies, notably in North America and Western Europe. A key stimulant to rising levels of political protest was the Vietnam War (1955–1975), which led to civil disobedience campaigns emerging out of US college campuses and widespread protests across the Western world. These were often organized and led by student movements.

1968 is often identified as a key year. It saw widespread student and worker protest on the streets of Paris in May (which undoubtedly influenced radical activism in other countries) and, on the other side of the Iron Curtain, the violent suppression by Soviet troops of the liberalizing 'Prague Spring' in Czechoslovakia. The 'Cultural Revolution' was also underway inside China.

The 1960s was also marked by the emergence of new social movements (NSMs), outside of established political parties. These were organized around such themes as feminism, green political thinking, anti-racism, civil rights, and war resistance. It was an era in which traditional social values were widely challenged, which lead to radical and widespread liberalization of public attitudes, especially regarding sexuality. The 1960s is also still seen as a particularly innovative decade in the areas of design, fashion, and popular music.

It is important to note, however, that the Sixties was very much a Western phenomenon, even if it was in part stimulated by events occurring in the Global South, such as the US military campaigns against communism in S.E. Asia. It was an era in which

> the influence of non-Western philosophical traditions, such as Buddhism, became more influential in the West and affluent Western youth began travelling throughout the Global South, especially in South Asia.
>
> It is a matter of debate, however, as to what extent this greater engagement with the Global South was on authentically equal terms and not tainted by colonialist attitudes (for more on this see Chapter 9).

As the name suggests, poststructuralism is a response to structuralism, an important intellectual movement that originated in early to mid-twentieth-century Western Europe, initially in the field of linguistics and later in the field of anthropology. By the 1950s and 1960s, structuralism's influence was spreading throughout the humanities and much of the social sciences. The prefix 'post' can be a bit confusing here as it suggests that something is definitively after something else. However, the term poststructuralism does not mean that it should be seen as definitively after or against structuralism. It usually refers instead to a critical or questioning stance towards structuralism. To make sense of this, we will first briefly examine structuralism as a theoretical orientation.

In essence, structuralism sees all specific instances of human activity as parts of wider structures which determine their meaning and significance. In linguistics, structuralists argue the meaning of words is not derived from their relationship to actual things but arises from their position within the wider structure of a language system governed by a set of rules. It is this underlining rule-governed structure that determines meaning, although it must be said that linguistic theorists diverge significantly when it comes to precisely defining this process. The meaning of words is constructed through their relationship to other words within a language system and there is no reference point outside of the system to definitively fix their meaning. If we think of the colours green, red, and amber, for example, their meaning and relationship to each other means something quite specific when used in reference, say, to a traffic light and something quite different when used in the context of representing political orientations (where blue is often equated with conservatism and red with leftist politics) or our emotions (such as being 'green with envy').

Structuralism challenges the idea that meanings can be grounded in a 'reality' which is independent of words and language. Instead, we should try to identify the language system or knowledge system that gives meaning to words and actions. If the meanings of words are produced within a language system, might not other aspects of social life also acquire their meaning in a comparable fashion? From an analytical point of view, therefore, structuralism suggests that rather than trying to discern some definitive true origin of meaning, we should investigate the structural conditions that generate and sustain social (i.e., shared) meanings and actions.

The label structuralism can be applied to a very wide range of intellectual currents that vary considerably in their understanding of a structural analysis or the implications they develop from it. Nonetheless, structuralists generally focus on discerning the underlying structures that work to construct and govern aspects of human behaviour. Consequently, the role of individual *agency* is generally side-lined. The behaviour of individual actors and the motivations or meanings that might drive them are seen as largely determined by the various structures within which individuals and their actions are located.

In the IR discipline, for example, we have seen that Waltz's neorealism offers a rather simple version of structuralist analysis in which the behaviour of individual units (i.e., states) is seen to be determined largely by the structure of the international system (which we discuss further in Chapter 3). According to Waltz, once you understand the essential structure of the anarchical system of states you can then explain why most states act in a similar fashion and supposedly have always done so, regardless of what states claim to be the reasons for what they are doing. Their behaviour is largely structured by the system within which they operate. This leads on to claims about the behaviour of states that are seen to be universally applicable. They are deemed to be relevant to analysing state behaviour, pretty much regardless of the characteristics of the state in question (Waltz, 1979).

Numerous critics from a range of IR perspectives have argued that Waltz's structural approach is too deterministic and rigid and fails to consider the differences between the various actors on the international stage or the shifting historical contexts within which states act. The anarchic system of states has a history, as do all states, yet for his critics, Waltz treats the international system and the states of which it is comprised simply as given entities. In its attempt to construct a general theory of IR, neorealism is accused of having to leave out crucial features and much of the complex detail of international politics. It also constructs a singular and simplistic model of the state as a unified actor which, contrary to what individual statespersons may believe or claim, acts in a highly predictable fashion. Indeed, it was the widespread criticism of Waltz's structuralist neorealism that effectively opened the doors to poststructuralist IR perspectives. These perspectives began to ask questions about how the depiction, or representation, of the international system as an anarchical structure that is supposedly the primary determinant of how states behave came to exercise such a dominant influence on the IR discipline. What are the intellectual and political consequences of this dominance? In other words, how might it marginalize or obscure other perhaps vital dimensions of international and global politics? Whose interests does it serve? To what extent might it shut down explorations of other ways of practising global politics, other ways of thinking about our place in the world around us?

The debates around structuralism are undoubtedly complex and vary significantly according to the disciplinary contexts in which they take place. Nonetheless, the debates in the IR discipline between neorealist structuralism and its critics broadly echoes similar earlier critiques of structuralism outside of IR. Structuralism more generally has also been criticized for being too rigid and deterministic. In privileging the role of unobservable structures in the explanation of the observable aspects of human social life, structuralism appears to effectively remove, or at the very least significantly marginalize the role of individual humans and their conscious agency. Furthermore, the various kinds of structures that are so central to structuralist analysis are often presented in ahistorical terms. Critics ask how were these structures constructed and by whom, how are they sustained, and how do they change?

236   INTRODUCTION TO INTERNATIONAL RELATIONS THEORIES

Poststructuralism is one such broad response to the structuralist turn in philosophy (we will be looking at another—social constructivism—in Chapter 8). As we have already seen, it would be wrong to paint a simple picture along the lines of first there was structuralism and then there was poststructuralism. It is all somewhat messier than that. Many of poststructuralism's early leading figures—such as Michel Foucault, Jacques Derrida, and Roland Barthes—were initially strongly associated with structuralism, but became stringent critics of its limitations. Yet, few have ever described themselves as either structuralists or even poststructuralists. They were not part of a unified group of thinkers (they frequently disputed each other's work) and they engaged critically with structuralism in very different ways.

Although the label poststructuralism is used in reference to theoretical developments that emerged in France, it is generally seen to have gained wider currency in 1966 after a colloquium on structuralism (then seen as a very 'continental' or European phenomenon) at Johns Hopkins University in the US. At that meeting, a young French philosopher, Jacques Derrida (see Key thinker 7.1), criticized some key features of structuralism and the idea that this was the beginning of *post*-structuralism emerged.

Poststructuralism's relationship to structuralism should become clearer after we survey the key themes in the work of two leading poststructuralists: Jacques Derrida and Michel Foucault. We will return to it at the end of Section 7.3.

7.3 **POSTSTRUCTURALISM: KEY SOURCES AND THEMES**

The thinkers usually credited with initially developing poststructuralism worked in different intellectual fields, had quite distinct emphases within their work, and did not see themselves as members of a shared or clearly defined intellectual movement. It has only been over several years that recurrent themes have become sufficiently visible to suggest that their work can be (loosely) grouped together under the unifying label of poststructuralism. Given that poststructuralism does not constitute a theory in the usually accepted sense of the term, we shall treat it as a loose collection of ideas and themes that collectively can be best described as a broad critical disposition towards the understanding of social phenomena. What follows are somewhat simplified accounts of some of the most notable ideas and themes in the work of two key poststructuralist scholars who have been enormously influential in the subsequent development of poststructuralist IR scholarship. We will then go on to look at how they have been used by poststructuralist IR scholars.

Jacques Derrida and deconstruction

The work of Jacques Derrida (see Key thinker 7.1) is one of the most important influences upon the development of poststructuralism. Derrida likes to play with language.

His work is deliberately intended to unsettle and challenge the reader's established habits of reading and interpretation; Derrida invites his readers to be inventive even in their reading of his own texts. Central to his work, however, is the idea of *text*. For Derrida the word text does not refer solely to written texts but also to all representations of the world around us. This is because we can only bring that world into being through language; we can only refer to that world through our textual interpretation of it. Derrida famously declared that *'il n'y a pas de hors-texte'*, literally 'there is nothing outside-text' (Derrida, 1997: 158). This is often mistranslated simply as 'there is nothing outside *of* the text', which critics often take to suggest that Derrida (and, by extension, most poststructuralists) is suggesting there is no reality outside of language.

What Derrida is suggesting is not that nothing materially exists outside of text, but rather that nothing material can be made comprehensible to us without textual representation. In effect, we bring things into being by talking and writing about them or representing them as images, such as in paintings, drawings, photographs, or maps (we explore the use of maps further in Section 7.5). These representations of reality are themselves open to multiple interpretations which are the products of distinct contexts. These might include the grammar and vocabulary used, the political, social, and cultural contexts in which the reader and writer or image maker find themselves, and so on. All these multiple contexts serve to shape the meanings we derive from representations of the material world. Derrida pushes the notion that meaning can never be fixed to its limits, something that infuriates and exasperates his critics.

KEY THINKER 7.1 JACQUES DERRIDA

Jacques Derrida (1930–2004) was an Algerian-born French philosopher who is widely recognized as one of the seminal and most influential thinkers behind the emergence of poststructuralism. As a Sephardic Jew, Derrida experienced sometimes violent anti-Semitism in his youth, resulting in him absconding from school for a year and pursuing his dream of becoming a professional footballer.

After moving to France in his late teens, Derrida gained entry to the prestigious *École Normale Supérieure*, where he began to mix with leading lights in French philosophy. Although troubled by ill-health and depression, Derrida's output was substantial from a relatively early age. Three of his most famous books were published in a single year— 1967. He acquired international prominence after a conference presentation in the US in 1966, and he subsequently took several visiting positions at prestigious US universities until his death from pancreatic cancer.

Derrida's work has always been regarded as controversial, especially by the philosophy community, and there was initial resistance to awarding him a university chair (professorship) in France in the early 1980s. In 1992 Cambridge University's offer of an honorary degree was also widely criticized. Derrida's influence extended beyond the academic world, and he was the subject of film, cartoons, and even a pop song.

A political activist throughout his life, Derrida supported dissident intellectuals in communist Czechoslovakia, the anti-apartheid struggle, as well as campaigns against the

> death penalty and aspects of social legislation in France. Although very much the abstract philosopher, an increasingly overtly political tone became particularly evident in his later work, including reflections on issues central to IR, such as *raison d'état* (reasons of state) and sovereignty.
>
> **USEFUL RESOURCE:**
> A short and very accessible open access YouTube video summary of some of Derrida's key ideas, from the School of Life bookshop:
> https://www.youtube.com/watch?v=H0tnHr2dqTs

Derrida is perhaps most famous for his introduction of the strategy of *deconstruction*. These days, this term is often used very loosely to simply mean breaking something down into its constituent parts. Derrida's usage is more complex than this. As one noted Derridean IR scholar, Maja Zehfuss, notes, '(a)s his arguments challenge the categories within which we think—that is, our language—his terms are not easily explained using that language ... Derrida's work is difficult for the best possible reason: it makes you think' (Zehfuss, 2009: 138–139).

At the heart of Derridean deconstruction is the argument that the structure of Western thought rests upon various dichotomies. These are pairs of concepts that are supposedly opposites of each other, such as mind/body, good/bad, reason/passion, equality/inequality, identity/difference, or, in the IR context, domestic/international and sovereignty/anarchy. Seemingly, you cannot use both sides of these dichotomies simultaneously. Furthermore, one side is implicitly seen as superior to the other; there is a hierarchical relationship between them. The source of such hierarchies lies, however, outside of the concepts themselves. There is an assumption that the relative value of either side of the dichotomy can somehow be grounded or given solid foundations. For Derrida, however, the two terms in any such dichotomy cannot be independent of each other; indeed, they depend on each other, whether this is acknowledged or not. Because of the preponderance of binary thinking, however, we can fail to see the insights and virtues that can be gleaned from both sides of a binary dichotomy at the same time as well as the weaknesses of both sides (Zehfuss, 2009: 139–140 and 2002: 197–198).

Derrida explains this by talking about presence and absence. Let us consider, for example, the dichotomy of the domestic/international, which is central to so much orthodox IR thinking. The domestic realm (inside the sovereign state) is seemingly the opposite of the international (outside the state). Additionally, in orthodox IR thinking the domestic is presented both implicitly and explicitly as the superior of the two realms. The domestic realm is usually the more secure and ordered, the more familiar, rule-governed, and knowable. In contrast, the international realm is seen as anarchic and lacking the key features of domestic society inside the state and is thus a realm of potential danger and risk. This is why borders matter so much in conventional thinking about IR. Yet each term makes incomplete sense without the other; in fact, their individual meanings depend on each other. In other words, each side of the supposed dichotomy is immediately implicit within the other. Neither of the concepts that make up the dichotomy can be fully present or fully absent, even if in using such dichotomies we choose to treat them as pure expressions of concepts or things that are in complete opposition.

What Derrida is driving at is that there is always an instability to accepted meanings ascribed to concepts or the representation of things in language. If there is no secure reference point outside of language, no 'outside-text', then any attempt to textually represent an idea, a thing, an institution, a practice is always incomplete and contestable. Derrida does not claim, however, that we can somehow escape this and arrive at some definitive representation of ideas, things, or practices. All text (remember this refers to whatever the use of language is trying to capture) is open to multiple readings and interpretations.

Deconstruction entails closely reading a text in multiple ways to try and bring out not only what any dominant interpretation declares to be present, but also to try and discern what might be absent in the dominant or received interpretation. This is not to say that any alternative reading we attempt is going to provide the unequivocally correct interpretation. From a Derridean point of view, such a goal can never be realized. What Derrida is proposing is that we cannot escape the uncertainties, or, we could say, the inescapable politics of textual interpretation. We need to work and live with those uncertainties.

At this point, you might be tempted to throw your hands up and declare that Derrida is making the analysis of texts—indeed, the analysis of pretty much everything to do with being humans in a social world—virtually impossible. To present meaning and language as never pure and always contestable might seem to be a recipe for despair. Indeed, many critics of Derrida (and other poststructuralists) draw this conclusion. Certainly, a Derridean approach is declaring the interpretation of texts to be an open-ended, always challenging process; to believe we can finally arrive at a definitive end point is to delude ourselves. This presents a challenge to the practice of political analysis and political action. Yet, Derrida also recognizes that decisions must be made, even if we seem to be confronted with competing interpretations which seemingly produce a condition of inescapable undecidability (Derrida, 1992). After all, decisions can have profound moral and political consequences.

If we think about international politics, for example, innumerable decisions must be made, many with very serious consequences for the lives of ourselves and others. For example,

- Should we intervene in a crisis elsewhere? And, if so, should we use violent force?
- Should we help distant others in dire straits and, if we do, will this not mean that resources will inevitably be diverted away from aiding those closer to us (think of the domestic/international dichotomy here)?

From a Derridean point of view, the fact that we can never definitively declare any decision to be unequivocally the morally correct one, since our interpretation of any situation is always incomplete and therefore always contestable, does not absolve us of the responsibility to decide, nonetheless. As Zehfuss succinctly puts it: '(a)cting responsibly therefore does not mean doing good rather than evil. It means negotiating a difficult situation in which no purely good way forward is possible' (Zehfuss, 2009: 146). For Derrida, because of its inherent incompleteness, knowledge is never enough when it comes to making decisions. In contrast to the idea that we can develop abstract general ethical principles to guide us, which is central to most Western moral philosophy, Derrida depicts the ethics and politics of making decisions as inescapably intertwined. Things may seem undecidable, yet we must decide, nonetheless.

It is quite commonplace for critics to dismiss Derrida's work as irrelevant to international politics or politics more generally. Yet, Derrida's work is arguably intensely political. He writes on such things as democracy, justice, the law, and the nation-state. His work may be challenging to read and decipher but political intent threads through it. Derrida endeavours to expose how dominant modes of thinking can repress or exclude ideas and voices that might challenge the established meaning of things and thereby destabilize the political status quo. The Derridean scholar, John Caputo, helps us to identify why Derrida might provide insight into international politics:

> The idea behind deconstruction is to deconstruct the workings of strong nation-states with powerful immigration policies, to deconstruct the rhetoric of nationalism, the politics of place . . . to disarm the bombs of . . . identity that nation-states build to defend themselves against the stranger . . . (Caputo, 1997: 231)

The mainstream theories of IR depict the theory and practice of international politics as centred around borders—between states and peoples and between inside and outside the sovereign state. For some IR scholars, however, Derrida's work offers a powerful basis for questioning the international political order of things, by destabilizing the boundaries that discipline our thinking. If you find Derrida's work challenging to read then you might consider getting to know it first through interviews with Derrida (such as in Derrida, 1995) or biographies (such as Salmon, 2020).

Michel Foucault: Power and knowledge

Alongside Derrida, Michel Foucault (introduced to you in Key thinker 7.2) is arguably the other most influential of the poststructuralist thinkers. Foucault's work has been particularly influential in the development of poststructuralist IR perspectives. Threading through his voluminous output is a range of themes that, like Derrida's work, serve to disrupt many of the core assumptions and presumptions underpinning established thinking across the social sciences, including IR. Foucault's work is too wide-ranging and complex to capture easily in a brief account, so we will focus on bringing out some of the broad themes that have been subsequently applied to the study of international politics.

As with Derrida, we see in Foucault's work an emphasis on language particularly in his focus on *discourse*. In everyday language the term discourse usually refers simply to written or spoken communication and sometimes to suggest that such communication is of a rather formal or authoritative kind. Foucault's use of the term is both different and much richer in content: discourses are systems of thoughts composed of ideas, attitudes,

KEY THINKER 7.2 MICHEL FOUCAULT

The French philosopher and social theorist Michel Foucault (1926–1984) is widely regarded, alongside Jacques Derrida, as one of the two key luminaries of poststructuralist thought. Born into an affluent middle-class family in Poitiers, Foucault rejected his father's wish that he follow in his footsteps and become a surgeon. Attracted to philosophy and history from his teens onwards, Foucault's excellent academic record led to him enrolling in the prestigious *École Normale Supérieure*, the same university that Derrida later attended.

At the *École Normale Supérieure*, Foucault came under the influence of the prominent Marxist theoretician Louis Althusser and briefly joined the French Communist Party. However, Foucault left after 5 years due to philosophical disagreements but also because of what he saw as a bigoted and homophobic culture within the party. During his early career Foucault became interested in psychiatry and this was to become a prominent theme in his work, most notably in his doctoral thesis which became his first book, *Madness and Civilisation* (1961). Derrida criticized the book which led to the two philosophers falling out until reconciling in 1981.

Foucault courted controversy throughout his life, both as a philosopher and as an individual. He had an often-strained relationship with the political and intellectual Left in France, famously quarrelling with leading Marxist scholars, while also participating in leftist politics in the late 1960s. In addition to his voluminous academic output, Foucault was a political activist all his life. He campaigned on prison reform, the penal system was the subject of his book *Discipline and Punish* published in 1975, as well as anti-racism and human rights. Foucault was popular among US intellectuals and taught frequently there in the early 1980s.

Foucault was also very open about his homosexuality, long before it was safe to be so. The first volume of his *The History of Sexuality* was published in 1976, with two further volumes in 1984. He was working on a fourth volume (published posthumously in 2018), when he contracted HIV, eventually developing AIDS, which ultimately led to his death. After Foucault's death his partner, sociologist Daniel Defert, established AIDES, France's first HIV/AIDS awareness organization.

courses of action, beliefs, and practices that systematically construct the subjects and the worlds of which they speak. We can only attempt to comprehend the world within discourse and it is our *discursive practices* that effectively constitute that world, i.e., bring it into being in any meaningful sense.

Discourses produce meanings and, importantly for Foucault, create identities and set the boundaries of social and political relations. Discourses make possible understandings of self and, other, social relationships, and the political options available to us. It is evident, of course, that some discourses become stable over time. They are widely treated as if they were true representations of the social world. In other words, they become powerful and thus can have very material effects. This is because the rules about what is legitimate knowledge and what constitutes truth are created within a specific discourse that emerges within a particular historical and social context. However, over time and through constant reiteration, those rules can come to appear as existing outside of and prior to that discourse; powerful dominant discursive claims thus have the appearance of *ahistorical* truth claims: they seemingly simply represent the way things are.

As we shall see, poststructuralist IR scholars argue that mainstream IR theories reveal this effect. They present the world out there in very particular ways which suggest international politics is highly resistant to fundamental change. They offer a specific starting point for the analysis of international politics. What poststructuralism invites us to do is consider how that starting point came about and how is it sustained. How might the world look if we started from a different vantage point?

What Foucault shares with Derrida and other poststructuralists, then, is a radical questioning of the possibility that we can establish strong foundations—unassailable grounds for establishing the truth—upon which to base our knowledge claims. For this reason, the poststructuralist approach is often described as *anti-foundationalist*. It presents our knowledge of the social world as always, *historical*, *plural*, *incomplete*, *contingent*, and *contextual*. Our claims to know are, therefore, always contestable and, importantly, we should always be willing to contest them. Poststructuralism's inherently critical attitude is often taken by its critics to be purely negative. Two prominent poststructuralist IR scholars, David Campbell and Roland Bleiker argue, however, that it is a positive approach. This is because 'it is about disclosing the assumptions and limits that have made things as they are, so that what appears natural and without alternative can be rethought and reworked' (Campbell and Bleiker, 2021: 207). Thus, poststructuralism shares with Critical Theory a concern with change. As Foucault put it in an interview (one of the easier ways into Foucault's work is to read interviews with him):

> a critique is not a matter of saying that things are not right as they are. It is a matter of pointing out on what kinds of assumptions, what kinds of familiar, unchallenged, unconsidered modes of thought the practices that we accept rest . . . Criticism is a matter of flushing out that thought and trying to change it. (Foucault, 1988: 155)

THINK CRITICALLY 7.1 ARE THERE SECURE FOUNDATIONS FOR OUR KNOWLEDGE CLAIMS ABOUT THE WORLD?

Poststructuralism questions the possibility that we can securely ground our claims to know the world around us.

- Do you think claims to know the social world can be deemed to be unequivocally true or false? If so, why? If not, why not?
- Thinking of other IR theories with which you are familiar, how do they claim that their claims about international politics are securely grounded? (Hint: think about how concepts such as 'observation', 'experience', 'reason', 'facts', and 'objectivity' are deployed).

It must be noted at this point that although Foucault's understanding of critique has, seemingly, much in common with Critical Theory, it also departs from it in significant ways. As is discussed in Chapter 6, Critical Theory aims to contribute to the emancipation of *humanity* from the constraints imposed upon it so that humans can achieve true freedom and thus full self-development. Foucault, along with poststructuralists more generally, questions the understanding of the human subject that underpins this objective. They see any account of a universal human subject or of all humanity as not something that is prior to or comprehensible outside of our representations of it in language. As we shall see, this is a prominent theme in the writings of poststructuralist IR scholars. In other words, the human subject, as with any other social category, is made—brought into being—through representations of it in language that has changed over time. Many of our knowledge claims have, historically, rested upon representations of what it is to be human. Much of Foucault's work concerns itself with how representations of being human, or of humanity, have emerged. In contrast to the common depiction of 'human' as a universal category, Foucault treats it as an historical product that is produced within *discourse*. Thus, for Foucault there is no universal human subject that exists prior to our thinking about it. Rather, there are multiple human *subjectivities* that emerge at different periods and within different social contexts.

Foucault's work has powerful political and moral connotations because it depicts human subjectivity as something that can be manipulated and changed. Here we need to introduce a vital theme in Foucault's work: the relationship between power and knowledge. Power is more usually presented as something that can be possessed and used. If we think of the treatment of power in mainstream theories of IR (such as neorealism), for example, power is seen as something that states struggle constantly to acquire. The more a state has, the freer it is to act as it wishes. Power has traditionally been seen as antithetical to the production of genuine knowledge. Foucault treats power very differently. Power, for Foucault, is a pervasive feature of all relations between people. He captures its intimate connection to knowledge by referring to *power/knowledge*. Foucault's work depicts knowledge as both the creator of power *and* a creation of power. There is no truth outside of power.

It is important to stress that Foucault does not see power as a simply negative force or the coercive expression of the capacity of a single person—a sovereign ruler, for example—or an elite group of people—such as a ruling class—to impose their will upon the majority. For Foucault, power can also be productive. It has far-reaching effects that can be perceived as positive as well as negative. Such productive expressions of power/knowledge permeate social life. They can change over time, from place to place, and context to context, in reflection of changing aims and purposes, increasingly specialized forms of knowledge, or, indeed, resistance to prevailing expressions of power/knowledge.

For example, in some of his best-known work on the institutes of disciplining and punishment—such as prisons—Foucault shows how, since the seventeenth and eighteenth centuries, the human subject has been seen as something that can be classified, disciplined, punished, and reformed. The purposes of institutions such as prisons, the ways their inmates are treated, and the reasons for treating them in specific ways change in reflection of changes in discourses about discipline and punishment. Modern prisons

244 INTRODUCTION TO INTERNATIONAL RELATIONS THEORIES

might be seen as less violent in their treatment of inmates that their predecessors—something Foucault acknowledged—but equally they can be seen as also more effective in their capacity to control prisoners (Foucault, 1991). Modes of surveilling people and ensuring their compliance that were designed for prisons can also be subsequently detected in other social institutions, such as factories, offices, and schools. Perhaps the most famous example of this was Bentham's Panopticon, which is outlined in Key concept 7.1.

> **KEY CONCEPT 7.1** BENTHAM'S PANOPTICON

In the late eighteenth century, the English philosopher, Jeremy Bentham (1748–1832), developed a design for a penitentiary called the Panopticon. The idea behind it was that prison cells would be arranged in circles around a central observation tower so that all the prison inmates could be watched by a single prison officer without any individual prisoner knowing if they were being watched specifically.

The intention was for prisoners to regulate their own behaviour on the assumption that they might be being watched at any time. No true panopticon was ever built, although some prisons and other institutions have been designed to incorporate some of its features. Bentham's design has come to prominence, nonetheless, largely as a metaphor for modern forms of social surveillance and the disciplinary dimensions of modern societies, most notably in Michel Foucault's book *Discipline and Punish*.

The widespread use of CCTV in city centres, which is especially common in the UK, could be seen as an example of what Foucault called 'panopticism'. Similarly, modern 'open plan' office and factory design could be seen to have panoptical dimensions to them.

Parallels have also been drawn between the panopticon and the capacity of internet service providers, social media networks, and national security services to monitor the online activities of individuals and groups. We do not know if we are being monitored, but we can never be certain we are not.

USEFUL REFERENCE:
Foucault, M. (1991), *Discipline and Punish: The Birth of the Prison* (London: Penguin), 201–209.

Foucault's work on such areas as sexuality, medical practice, and the conception of madness endeavours to show how specific conceptions of the human subject emerge and then disappear or are replaced, as a consequence of specific conjunctions of history, claims to knowledge, and changing conceptions of how humans need to be governed and controlled. His earlier work seeks to ask how the dividing lines between such categorizations of individual human subjects as normal/deviant, sane/insane, come to emerge and what effects they have on how people live and are controlled. In other words, power serves to *discipline* people.

By discipline, Foucault is not referring solely to its negative connotations. In his later work, Foucault introduces the notion of *biopower*, which focuses at the level of whole populations. Foucault shows how, especially since the nineteenth century, the need to ensure viable productive societies generated new forms of disciplinary biopower. Examples include public health programmes, mass immunization (of particular relevance to the recent emergence of the COVID-19 virus), the development of public sewerage, the promotion of healthy lifestyle practices, etc. Such developments produced many undeniably positive outcomes while also serving to discipline whole populations in the interests of society as a whole, not least by ensuring they continue to live healthy and therefore more productive lives (Foucault, 1986 and 2004: 239–254).

Whereas power was once widely conceived of as a capacity to decide who lives and who dies—the traditional power of a sovereign—modern forms of power, of biopower, are also about enabling people to live longer. Power is not simply concentrated in the hands of a few who impose it forcefully on the masses; in our daily lives and social practices we also serve to reproduce forms of power/knowledge without always needing to be coerced into doing so. Foucault coined the term *governmentality* to capture the inescapable interconnection between government and individual freedom (Foucault, 2002: 201–222). In effect, we have come to govern ourselves in ways that are beneficial to wider society. However, this is not to say that we are entirely autonomous of government, or simply puppets pulled by the strings of government, or duped into obeying dominant social norms. Foucault's notion of governmentality emphasizes the complex interdependence of freedom and government.

Foucault's work challenges the notion that we can simply locate the ultimate origins of power; he is decentring power. Rather than trying to discern the true intentions that might lie behind those who seemingly wield the most power, a Foucauldian approach studies the sites and effects of power, the detail of power. Power is not seen to flow in one direction; it 'circulates in networks, constituting individuals as both subjects and objects of power' (Neal, 2009: 168). The IR scholar Andrew Neal reads Foucault as inviting us not to 'simply (study) those who act, but also those who are acted upon' and try to 'understand the ways in which their reactions, resistances and their practices of power in turn work to constitute wider relationships and networks' (Neal, 2009: 168).

Much of Foucault's work is historical in orientation. It is motivated by a critical reading of a contemporary issue and a desire to trace the origins of contemporary ways of thinking and being. Foucault does not present a tidy picture of knowledge accumulating over time that leads us into the present. Instead, his historical studies of such things as prisons, madness, and sexuality present a complex picture of disruptions as well as continuities, the intersection of power and knowledge, and the role of sheer chance. Indeed, many orthodox historians are highly critical of Foucault's approach to historical enquiry. Orthodox history endeavours to tell us the truth about the past—what supposedly really happened. Foucault makes no pretence to be offering an objective account of the past. Historical research is necessarily selective; it cannot include everything that happened. Consequently, a lot of historical study leaves a great deal out. Such selectivity is often a product of tradition, custom, and habit and, for Foucault, this rules out the possibility of a truly objective history. Foucault makes explicit his interest in selectively looking for aspects of the past that might help us understand how we have come to think and live as we do today.

In his earlier work, Foucault used the metaphor of *archaeology* to try and capture his historical method and in his later work he sometimes refers to it as a form of *genealogy*. Although Foucault did not always use these terms consistently and the distinction between them is not always clear, together they both do help capture the distinctive nature of not only Foucault's work but also of poststructuralism's orientation more generally. Whereas orthodox historical study tends to be longitudinal, tracing the linear historical development of something over time, archaeologists examine a range of diverse artefacts from the past and try to understand how they collectively might help us understand life in a past historical era (Fendler, 2010: 38). Foucault ranges across different fields of knowledge in a particular historical era to build up a picture of the *regimes of truth* that governed what was deemed to be valid knowledge during particular historical conjunctures.

Foucault's work does not, however, try to definitively show how the past led to the present. The connections between the past and the present are both continuous and discontinuous, visible and also hard to discern. In Foucault's hands, history is a complex repository of different historical interactions between power and knowledge. Which aspects of history one chooses to identify as significant, or insightful for understanding our present, depends on the perspective one brings to historical enquiry. Since our perspectives on history embody our values and reflect our own historical situatedness, they are likely to vary widely. Orthodox historians, in common with much of mainstream social science, requires us to endeavour to remove our biases and try and get to the historical truth of the matter. Foucault, along with other poststructuralists, sees this as an impossibility; our reading of history is inescapably selective.

Summary of key themes in poststructuralism

By now the difference between poststructuralism and structuralism that we discussed at the beginning of this section should be a bit clearer. Our survey of the work of Derrida and Foucault shows that there is much that is seemingly structuralist about their work. Derrida's emphasis on the centrality of language and text and the dichotomies that govern Western interpretation of supposedly reality (good/bad, true/false, etc., etc.) is structuralist in form. Similarly, Foucault's emphasis on how discourses shape meaning is also clearly structuralist in key respects. In different ways, both thinkers explore how meaning is generated within structures of language and text. What is important, however, is that they then go on to raise profound questions about those structures that determine meaning.

Derrida does this through deconstruction and the proposal that multiple readings of texts—of claims to represent reality—are always possible, and none can claim to be the definitive sources of truth. Foucault examines the relationship between power and knowledge to show how the discursive construction of meaning always reflects the effects of power. In other words, they do not take the structures that determine meaning and claims to knowledge about the world as givens. They subject them also to critical scrutiny, and in so doing destabilize them.

How might we best summarize the key themes identified in our brief survey of the work of the two leading poststructuralist thinkers? Three terms are useful here: *interpretation*, *representation,* and *subjectivity*.

- *Interpretation*: in emphasizing the centrality of language and discourse in the construction of meaning, poststructuralism questions whether definitive interpretations of social reality are possible. Poststructuralists do not deny there is a reality outside of our attempts to capture it in language and discourse, but how can we know that reality in any definitive sense? Any interpretation of social reality, poststructuralists would argue, acts immediately upon that reality; it brings it into being in a meaningful way. Our interpretations are produced discursively, and our knowledge of the world is thus inescapably a product of the historical context in which it emerges and the complex relationship between knowledge and power. Other interpretations are always possible, all interpretations are in some way or an other incomplete and they reflect the historical contexts and systems of knowledge production (the discourses) within which they are produced. For poststructuralists, then, there are no absolutely secure foundations upon which to declare one interpretation to be objectively true, or directly correspond with reality.

- *Representation:* It follows that if our interpretations are always only a partial and contestable account of the world then the same must be said of attempts to produce *discursive* representations of that world, be this in speech, the written word, or imagery. Poststructuralism encourages us to ask questions such as *how* do specific representations come about, what relationships between power and knowledge underpin them, and what is excluded from them? It is not a question of specific representations simply being right or wrong, useful or not useful, but of them always being incomplete constructions of reality. As such they should always be looked at critically.

- *Subjectivity*: The idea of the universal human subject has always been at the centre of most varieties of modern social and political thought. Controversially, poststructuralism rejects the idea of a universal, essential human subject that exists prior to or outside of our representations of it. Poststructuralism does not reject the idea of subjectivity itself; indeed, it is a core theme in poststructuralist thinking. For poststructuralists, however, subjectivities (note the use of the plural here) are products of history, discourse, and power. Humans have been discursively constructed in different ways historically, and poststructuralism treats all representations of what it is to be human as inherently problematic and therefore worthy of critical scrutiny. Historically, specific representations of human subjectivity have had very substantial and often violent political consequences. Think here of how colonized peoples were represented during the colonial era (we discuss this also in Chapter 9), or the consequences of deeming someone to be insane or criminal.

The poststructuralist questioning of the possibility of finding secure foundations for our claims to be able to accurately interpret and represent the world in which we live has been widely criticized within the mainstream of social and political enquiry, as well as by other critical theoretical approaches. Critics accuse poststructuralism of being unable and unwilling to offer solutions to some of the world's most pressing problems. When we look at the work of poststructuralist scholars in the IR field, however, we see that much of it is in fact focused on issues that have been central to the IR discipline since its establishment: violence, war, global injustices, and so on. What marks poststructuralist IR scholarship out is the often radically different approach it takes to both defining and examining these issue areas and its reluctance to offer easy answers or straightforward solutions.

7.4 POSTSTRUCTURALISM AND IR

In our discussion of some of the key themes in poststructuralist scholarship in Section 7.3, we see that the politics of interpretation and representation are recurrent themes. Additionally, we explore how key poststructuralist thinkers are noted for their interest in provoking and challenging us to think about things in different ways.

As an introduction to how poststructuralist thinking can cast a different and provocative light on key international issues, let us dive in at the deep end, so to speak. We will look at the treatment of a significant international event—the invasion of Iraq by a US-led coalition in January 1991—by a poststructuralist: the French sociologist, cultural theorist, and photographer Jean Baudrillard.

Representation and IR: Baudrillard's 'The Gulf War Did Not Take Place'

A key theme in Baudrillard's work is the idea of *simulation*. Many critics of modern consumerist capitalist society, notably Marxists, have emphasized the production and consumption of commodities as its defining feature. For Baudrillard, however, it is the play of images, codes, and signs that increasingly determines how people relate to each other. It is the appearance of things, rather than things themselves that increasingly matter. What does buying or driving this or that car, watching this or that form of media output, engaging in any of the constantly multiplying forms of real or *virtual* entertainment and consumer activities say about an individual, be it to themselves or others? Our engagement with the world is increasingly mediated through multiplying forms of communication, information, and entertainment technologies. It is marked by the growing pervasiveness of simulated forms of reality. Baudrillard argues that traditional social, cultural categories and distinctions are collapsing as different realms of life—the political, social, economic, and cultural—implosively mix with each other. In today's highly-consumerist capitalist societies, social relationships are increasingly governed by images, codes, and simulations of the real—what Baudrillard calls the *hyperreal* (Baudrillard, 1994: 1).

For Baudrillard, in technologically advanced societies, reality and hyperreality are increasingly blurred so that the difference between them becomes harder to detect and decreasingly matters. He uses the term *simulacrum* (which refers to an image or representation of something) in a rather distinctive way to refer to simulations of the real without 'origin or reality' (Baudrillard, 1994: 1). In other words, *simulacra* are not simply attempting to copy faithfully something of the real world but offer an alternative *hyperreality*.

One of the realms where Baudrillard detects the significant impact of simulation is warfare. In January–March 1991 he wrote three sequential essays that were published simultaneously in the French newspaper *Libération* and *The Guardian* in the UK. They were published prior to, during, and after 'Operation Desert Storm', the UN-authorized, US-led invasion of Iraq by a multinational coalition of armed forces in response to Iraq's illegal invasion and annexation of Kuwait. The essays were entitled: 'The Gulf War Will Not take Place'; 'The Gulf War Is Not Really Taking Place'; and 'The Gulf War Did Not Take Place' (the three essays can be found in Baudrillard, 1995).

Baudrillard was not saying there was no invasion of Iraq in 1991. There most certainly was. What he argued was that the US fought much of the war *virtually*, using high-technology surveillance and advanced weaponry, thereby avoiding too much direct contact with Iraqi troops (which meant many more Iraqi troops died compared to those of the US). The war was conducted in the full glare of the Western media. Although the media have long reported on wars, the 1991 Gulf War was arguably unique at the time for the extent and speed of media reporting. Journalists were embedded within key elements of the invading forces (which gave the military a high level of control over their output) and there was a great deal of live reporting from small, mobile media teams situated close to or even in the battle zone.

Consequently, the Western public saw most of the war through carefully filtered reports and a media spectacle—a *simulacrum* of what may have occurred on the ground. This effect was enhanced by the public broadcasting of video material taken directly from 'smart' missiles showing them acquiring and striking targets with high accuracy. Even though the bulk of the ordinance used to defeat the Iraqi troops consisted in fact of orthodox explosives dropped from a great height or dispatched from a great distance, what the public saw mostly was a war that seemed to be extraordinarily precise and somehow cleaner or less bloody than previous wars.

For Baudrillard, the issue was one of interpretation: were the events that took place on the ground comparable to how they were presented (and how would the viewing public ever know)? Could these events, as presented, be called a war as we have traditionally understood the term? This war seemingly bore a strong resemblance to interactive video virtual war games, or to a film set using props and actors. Echoing Baudrillard, the poststructuralist IR scholar James Der Derian asked of the Gulf War, 'was this a just war or just a game?' (cited in Debrix, 2009: 60). Der Derian was one of the first IR scholars to analyse extensively the use of simulation by military forces in preparing for war. He argues that the capacity to distinguish between actual war and the representation of war serves to make war more palatable. Simulations of war make 'the killing more efficient, more unreal, more acceptable' (Der Derian, 2009: 200).

Of course, during the Gulf War things would have appeared very differently to people in Iraq or Kuwait who were experiencing the war in a much less technologically-mediated—i.e., a much less virtual and much more brutal fashion. Baudrillard was criticized for presenting a one-eyed view of the influence of the media's representation of the war. There were Western media reports which did reveal the brutality of the war, not least the brutal bombardment of Iraqi troops, most of whom were poorly trained and equipped and many evidently reluctant to fight for Saddam Hussein's regime. Baudrillard could also be accused of embracing a kind of technological determinism by overstating the effects of technological mediation. Nonetheless, Baudrillard's provocative claims arguably do capture some key dimensions of life in a world marked increasingly by the technological mediation of reality.

The undoubted fascination of Western publics with the 1991 Gulf War was followed by numerous other examples of social and political life presented as media spectacle, ranging from the shock of the live images of the 9/11/2001 terror attack on the twin towers in New York to the pervasiveness of 'reality' television shows. The selling point of such shows is that they supposedly offer a window into the real lives of hitherto unknown people. At the same time they immediately and irrevocably change those lives, through the presence of a television crew, editing, and the leading characters becoming public personalities from being in the show. And the viewer most probably knows all of this.

Another development which could be seen as lending support to Baudrillard and Der Derian's claims about the increasing blurring of the line between the virtual and real worlds, is the dramatic growth in the use of unmanned aerial vehicles (UAVs, or drones), especially by the US and the UK, to carry out precision military strikes, notably as part of the 'War on Terror' launched by the US after the 9/11 attacks. Drones are piloted from consoles, often located at military bases a considerable distance from their intended target. The pilot consoles are operated in a manner markedly like sophisticated game consoles. Do such methods help to make fighting wars seem more palatable, less direct, and less bloody for those who use them as well as the audiences who view images of targeted precision drone strikes on television? Are they readily distinguishable from scenes available in myriad virtual war games, many of which are marketed as seemingly offering something ever closer to a 'real' experience of violent conflict? One key difference remains of course: UAVs really do kill people.

Baudrillard and Der Derian's analyses of the 1991 Gulf War highlight the power of representation and interpretation in an age when human communication is increasingly mediated through ever evolving technological lenses. Additionally, the conduct of war is acquiring new technological forms, which also serve to distance people, both observers and participants, from the direct impact and bloody consequences of war. This is not to suggest that the mediation of communication, or the technological evolution of warfare are only recent phenomena. News has long been delivered through the printed press, radio, television, and so on and warfare has been technologically evolving since the invention of long rage weapons and airpower in the early twentieth century. Nonetheless, the Gulf War provided a particularly stark case study of how key international events can be represented and interpreted in multiple ways. Although not entirely invisible to Western observers, the experiences of those on the losing side of the war—the Iraqi soldiers and civilians—played a minor role in the representation of the war to Western audiences.

We might ask how those civilians and soldiers under attack interpreted the war and how was it represented to them?

The US-led invasion of Iraq was more than three decades ago, and the technologies of communication and representation have developed considerably since then. The effects of multiple representations, competing discourses or 'regimes of truth' (see our discussion of Foucault in Section 7.3), and subsequently the dissemination of widely varying interpretations of supposed reality became particularly visible during the COVID-19 pandemic, in debates surrounding such policies as social lockdowns, the compulsory wearing of face masks, and mass vaccination programmes. Social media have also clearly facilitated the global spread of competing interpretations of the threat posed by the global spread of COVID-19 (Choli and Kuss, 2021).

Foucault's conceptions of power/knowledge and biopower (see our discussion of Foucault in Section 7.3) also provide illuminating lenses through which to view the debate between pro- and anti-Covid vaccine positions. The case for mass vaccination was supported and promoted by national governments (with a few exceptions), most of the global medical profession and scientific community, and major international organizations, such as the World Health Organization. In contrast, many of the numerous anti-vaccination groups and organizations presented themselves as anti-elitist opponents of governmental and state power. They articulated a range of countervailing arguments that included the questioning of dominant medical and scientific arguments supporting such things as vaccination and the wearing of masks, the supposed threat to individual and collective freedoms posed by such policies, and suspicions of various possible conspiracies between governments, international organizations, and pharmaceutical companies. What poststructuralism invites us to consider is not so much where the truth might lie, but how the competing discourses emerge, how they are sustained, and disseminated, and what their political effects are.

Mapping the World

The poststructuralist IR scholars David Campbell and Roland Bleiker usefully illustrate the significance of representation and interpretation in international politics through consideration of attempts to map the world (Campbell and Bleiker, 2021: 197–198). We can build upon their brief exploration a bit further.

The need for accurate maps has been a challenge since humans began exploration of the wider world. Maps are a vital navigation aid. Maps are also a representation of the world; they bring the world into being through a visual image. The problem for map makers is that the world is a sphere and representing a sphere on a flat surface is inherently problematic; it requires necessarily some kind of distortion. From a poststructuralist point of view, however, mapping the world is not merely a technical issue but is inherently *interpretive* as well. Maps are a form of discourse, produced within specific historical contexts and the representations of the world they offer are manifestations, intentionally or otherwise, of the contexts in which they are produced.

We can illustrate this by looking at four different maps of the world.

The Mercator Projection

Created by the Flemish cartographer Gerardus Mercator in 1569, the Mercator map (Figure 7.1) is probably the most familiar world map. It was intended to help navigators plot routes across the world's oceans, and it does this by representing lines of longitude and latitude as evenly-spaced straight lines.

The map is based on a cylindrical model of the world and, consequently, distorts the size and shape of land mass increasingly as you approach either of the poles. Thus, the land masses in the Northern hemisphere look significantly larger than those in the southern hemisphere, even though, in fact, the land mass in the Southern Hemisphere is nearly twice that of the Northern Hemisphere. The map makes Europe (excluding Russia) look only a bit smaller than South America, for example, even though South America is twice the size of Europe. Africa appears to be a similar size to Greenland when in fact it is fourteen times bigger. The size of the Scandinavian countries is also vastly exaggerated. The distortion in the southern hemisphere is not so visibly apparent because

FIGURE 7.1 The Mercator Projection of the world

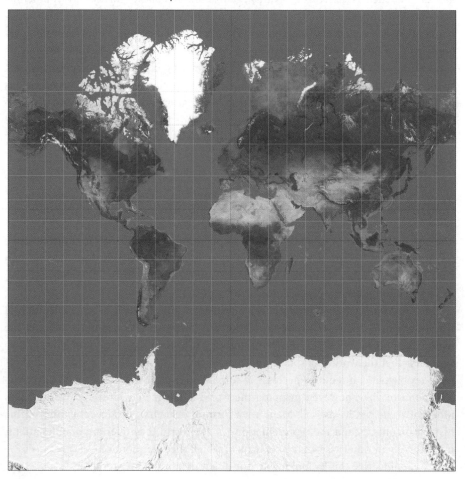

of the large expanses of southern oceans. The size of Antarctica is severely distorted, however, which is why many versions of the Mercator simply leave it out. This has the effect of enhancing the visual centring of the world on Europe rather than the equator.

The creation of this map was driven by the rapid expansion of European exploration and colonial conquest and its representation of the world seemingly visually reinforces the global dominance of Europe during the colonial era and, subsequently, that of the United States and Russia during the Cold War.

The Gall-Peters Projection

The politics of mapping the world came to the fore in 1974 when the German historian Arno Peters presented an alternative projection (which, it turned out, unwittingly closely resembled a map known as the Gall projection invented by a Scottish religious minister in the 1860s). Peter's explicit intention was to challenge the Mercator projection's view of the world. He argued that his projection provided an 'equal-area' map which provided a more accurate representation of the relative size of land masses yet did not reproduce the **Eurocentric** worldview of the Mercator projection.

The publication of Peters' projection coincided with debates within the UN General Assembly and elsewhere about the injustices of the prevailing global economic order, which impacted primarily upon developing countries in the Southern Hemisphere, and the need for a 'New International Economic Order (NIEO)' (which we discuss in Chapter 5). Campbell and Bleiker argue that just as the Mercator projection is a manifestation of specific power–knowledge relations, the Gall-Peters projection is a manifestation of power relations aligned against the dominance of the superpowers at the time of its creation (Campbell and Bleiker 2021: 197–198). You can see that, compared to the Mercator

FIGURE 7.2 The Gall-Peters projection of the world

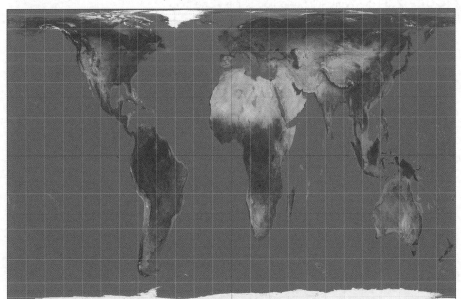

projection, the land mass in the Southern Hemisphere is significantly enlarged, Europe appears to be significantly more marginal, and the North American and Russian land masses are much less dominant.

The Gall-Peters Projection (Figure 7.2) was not well received within the cartography community in part because of its visual distortion of country shapes, even if their relative size is more accurately presented. Nonetheless, it has been adopted by UNICEF, UNESCO, and Oxfam. In 2017, the Boston Public Schools System in the US decided to adopt the Peters projection as the standard for world maps in its schools.

The Winkel III Projection

Designed in 1921 by the German Cartographer Oswald Winkel, the Winkel III projection (Figure 7.3) uses complex mathematics to try and minimize distortions of area, direction, and distance. It does not eliminate distortions—the polar regions are still severely distorted, for example—but it is widely regarded as a reasonable compromise which nonetheless has a familiar look to it, other than the introduction of an element of curvature. Its popularity was significantly boosted in 1998 when the Royal Geographical Society decided to adopt it as their standard world projection.

The AuthaGraph Projection

Looking at Figure 7.4, it is apparent that this map is dramatically different from the preceding projections. Created by Japanese architect, Hajime Narukawa in 1999, the Authagraph map is regarded as the most technically accurate of all projections, even if it is not at all useful as a navigation tool. Through a complex design process, the map produces the relative size and shape of land masses with a high degree of accuracy.

FIGURE 7.3 The Winkel III projection of the world map

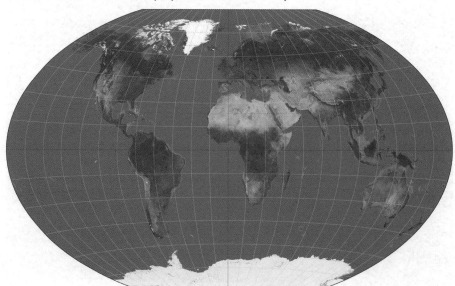

FIGURE 7.4 The AuthaGraph projection of the world map

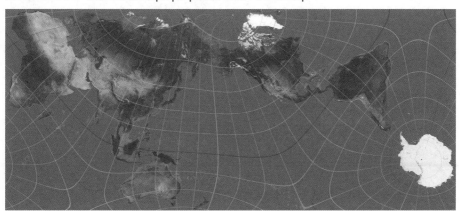

Reflecting its country of origin, the map is centred on the Pacific region with Japan close to the centre and it is used in official Japanese high school textbooks. Because of its design however, the map can be centred on any region of the world.

One key feature is the visual prominence of Antarctica, and the map was designed explicitly to offer a new viewpoint that highlights the importance of environmental concerns, not least the fate of oceans and the polar regions.

The different projections of the world onto a flat surface produce quite different representations of the relative sizes of countries and regions. Yet, there is no singular representation that can be deemed to be unequivocally correct or true to physical geographic reality since all entail some form of distortion. The politics of mapping the world invites a range of questions about how the different maps as representations of the world were produced, by whom, and for what purpose. Similar questions can be asked of all forms of textual or visual representations of international and global politics.

Problematizing the discipline of IR

Like the different map projections of the world's surface, orthodox theories of IR effectively provide maps of world politics. They each offer a representation which purports authoritatively to identify the key actors and processes that constitute international politics. From a poststructuralist point of view, the different mainstream IR theories represent the world and interpret the practice of international politics in different ways. As with maps of the world, poststructuralism depicts mainstream theories of IR as inescapably entailing some form of distortion as they discursively bring the world into being through their differing interpretations and representations of it. The dangers lie in assuming that such representations and interpretations of the world directly correspond with the world 'out there', as positivist approaches to theorizing international politics hope to achieve (if you need a reminder about positivism as a concept, you can read more about it in Section 6.2 in Chapter 6).

This is not to say that poststructuralist IR perspectives depict mainstream theories simply as inherently wrong, or claim to offer a true representation or interpretation in their place. It must be remembered that poststructuralism casts doubt on the very possibility of securely grounding any claims to knowledge. What poststructuralism invites us to do is ask:

- how did mainstream theories of IR come about and what consequences flow from depicting international politics in the way that mainstream theories do?
- What might mainstream IR theories leave out and why?
- What might international politics look like if we started with different assumptions (such as not taking sovereign states and their relations with other as our starting point)?
- What other readings (representations and interpretations) of international politics might be possible?

Of course, as we see in Chapters 5 and 6, Marxist IR perspectives and Critical International Theory also criticize mainstream theories, by emphasizing the underlying interests that mainstream theories serve but do not acknowledge. Both Marxism and Critical International Theory claim, however, to offer a comprehensive alternative theoretical perspective, underpinned by the overt commitment to the pursuit of universal human emancipation (even if they disagree on the precise meaning of emancipation or how it might be achieved).

In contrast, the poststructuralist approach to international politics does not claim to offer an alternative theory or paradigm of international politics. As we have seen, it purports to offers something different:

> Rather than setting out a paradigm through which everything is understood, poststructuralism is a critical attitude, approach, or ethos that calls attention to the importance of representation, the relationship of power and knowledge, and the politics of identity in an understanding of global affairs. (Campbell and Bleiker, 2021: 198)

You will see in this quotation from two prominent poststructuralist IR scholars that they refer to 'global affairs' rather than international politics. Although they are well known scholars in the IR discipline, they do not want to buy into the disciplining effect (the way it regulates thinking) that immediately comes from using the terms 'international politics' or 'international relations'. Those labels immediately serve to privilege relations between states as the essential stuff of politics at the global level. This is not to say that states are not important actors on the world stage or that relations between them are insignificant. What poststructuralist IR scholars resist is the widespread assumption that a focus on states and the relations between them should be the primary frame of reference in the analysis of politics at the global level.

You should also note that Campbell and Bleiker refer to the 'politics of identity'. As we will see, a focus on subjectivity and identity is a vital aspect of poststructuralist analysis of international or global politics (which we discuss in Key event 7.2). By placing states at the centre of their analysis from the outset, mainstream IR theories serve to reinforce a very particular understanding of political identity, which sees it as tightly connected to the territorial state. To put the point differently: what poststructuralist IR scholars challenge is the *sovereignty of the discourse of sovereignty* within mainstream IR perspectives. Let us explore this claim further.

Problematizing the Sovereign State

Given its centrality in mainstream IR theories, the sovereign state exercises a kind of theoretical sovereignty. It is the focal point around which mainstream theories revolve and evolve. The sovereign state is generally taken as a given; it is simply there as the starting point of theorizing international politics.

This unquestioned presence is most starkly apparent in the realist and neorealist depiction of an anarchical system of states as the presupposed context in which states must operate (we discuss various interpretations of an anarchical system of states in Chapters, 2, 3, and 4). In realism, the sovereign state is presented as the source of order and security in a dangerous world marked primarily by the absence of any higher authority above the sovereign state. Key to realist analysis is the difference between inside and outside the sovereign state. Inside the sovereign state, order and security are made possible through the state's sovereign authority over its subjects. Outside the state, however, is a world of ever-present risk because of the absence of sovereign authority. From a poststructuralist standpoint, however, this discursive representation of international politics is not simply a passive reflection of the way things supposedly are. It serves to help constitute that dangerous world, to bring it into being. This is why poststructuralist IR scholars sometimes refer to 'writing' or 'narrativizing' international politics to capture its creation through textual representation. They emphasize that our accounts of the world are inescapably interpretive and, as such, are always open to challenge through infinite other interpretations.

If you recall the discussion of Derrida and deconstruction in Section 7.3 of this chapter, we noted that he highlights the role of dichotomies, or binary pairs, of ideas in Western thought. For poststructuralist IR scholars, the binary juxtaposition of inside and outside the sovereign state is a powerful textual move that serves to discipline our thinking about international politics (see especially Walker, 1993). One side of the binary (inside the state—the secure 'domestic' realm) is depicted as superior to the other—the outside (the international realm, with its inherent dangers and uncertainties). Yet each side of the binary needs the other to make full sense. Furthermore, the inside/outside binary is premised upon giving the state a fixity, an appearance of permanence. From a poststructuralist perspective, however, the state does not exist meaningfully outside the discourses that bring it into being. As we have seen, poststructuralists such as Michel Foucault argue that such discourses, like all discourses, emerge within particular historical moments and particular configurations of knowledge/power. Through the constant reiteration of discourses and the practices that flow from them, a dominant configuration of sovereign power becomes naturalized such that any possible alternatives seem highly improbable or even impossible.

For poststructuralists, IR theories are never simply benign attempts to capture supposed reality, they have very substantial political consequences. They are *performative* discourses (they function as forms of social action which can enact change) and as such help to bring about that of which they speak. If dominant discourses reflect particular relationships between power and knowledge, they are productive; they have effects. This means that through constant reiteration, the emphasis on the difference between inside and outside the state becomes normalized and acquires the appearance of simply reflecting the way things are.

In his pathbreaking poststructuralist analysis of US foreign policy, for example, David Campbell examines how the 'statist discourse of international relations' does not merely reflect a supposed international reality but contributes to both its creation and sustenance. Campbell argues that the identity of the state is produced and sustained through 'discourses of danger'. In contrast to the mainstream depiction of the state as a pre-given entity which must survive in a dangerous world outside of its borders, Campbell argues that the depiction of the world outside the state as inherently dangerous serves to create and sustain a particular understanding of the state. This shores up the legitimacy of its sovereign authority in the eyes of its subjects: the state offers 'the promise of security to its citizens who, it says, would otherwise face manifold dangers' (Campbell, 1992: 56).

Such apparent dangers are not confined to the threat of war (the traditional concern of realism). It is not hard to see how the emphasis on a distinction between inside and outside the state also figures powerfully in contemporary debates about such diverse issues as fears about conflict within one state spilling over into other states, the flows of refugees and migrants, the impact of migration on perceptions of national culture and identity, debates about the positive and negative consequences of globalization, expectations about the loyalty of citizens to their state, and so on. Such issue areas highlight the intersection between the binary of inside/outside with the binary of self/other. How 'we' define ourselves is almost invariably connected to an 'other', or a range of others, from whom we distinguish ourselves. The practices of international politics serve to tie both identity and ideas of legitimate political community strongly to the sovereign state. They reinforce the significance of the national border and, thus, the difference between those who live within the confines of a particular state and those who live outside. Despite the widespread claim that globalization is eroding the boundaries between states, even a cursory survey of some of the key international political issues today reveals that borders still matter.

Many of us may feel we have a range of identities—based on our religious affiliation, ethnicity, gender, place of origin, and so on—that coexist with our formal identity as citizens of a particular state. From a poststructuralist point of view, however, the discourses and practices of international politics invoke a particular understanding—a dominant norm—of identity and political community centred around the sovereign nation-state. This can have exclusionary effects both inside and outside the sovereign state. Most people are citizens of states and, as such, are formally bound by the rules of citizenship of that state. When it comes to the differences between those who reside within a state and those who live outside that state, differences in political identity can lead into the depiction of those outside of a national community as inherently dangerous or threatening in some way. This can also be the case with those who reside within a state but whose origins or allegiances may also lie outside that state. Conceptions of identity and community that transgress (i.e., violate) the equation of identity with the sovereign national state in various ways—such as expressions of allegiance to a transnational religious or ethnic community, immigrant communities who continue to feel a strong connection with a different country of origin, refugee communities who have had to leave a place of origin, or those who simply wish to disavow a strong sense of national identity—may risk being judged as disloyal, unpatriotic, perhaps even a threat to *national* security, and so on. In other words, even within the confines of the state, these other senses of identity can be viewed as somehow inferior to the dominant norm of unalloyed identification with the sovereign state in which one resides.

The politics of difference and identity and their relationship to the inside/outside boundary have been brought sharply into focus in the post-9/11 era. The tragic events of 9/11 are summarized in Key event 7.2, but you can also read about a post-9/11 era response in poststructuralist politics in Key concept 7.2.

KEY EVENT 7.2 THE 9/11 TERROR ATTACKS AND ISLAMOPHOBIA

On September 11, 2001, 19 militants from the Islamic extremist organization *Al Qaeda* hijacked four planes that had taken off from airports on the East Coast of the US with destinations on the West Coast. Two of the planes were flown directly into the twin towers of the World Trade Centre in New York City (which subsequently collapsed), a third struck the Pentagon (headquarters of the US Department of Defense) in Washington DC, and the fourth crashed into a field in Pennsylvania (possibly because of an attempt by passengers to overpower the hijackers). Around 2,750 people were killed in New York, 184 at the Pentagon and 40 in Pennsylvania. All the hijackers also died.

After the 9/11 terror attacks, the phenomenon of *Islamophobia*—hostility, fear, or hatred of Islam and Muslims—became markedly more visible and the number of anti-Islamic hate crimes in the US and other Western states increased sharply. Subsequent terror attacks on public targets in Western states have undoubtedly served to sustain waves of anti-Muslim prejudice. Yet the great majority of terrorist attacks by Islamic extremists since 9/11, along with the vast majority of fatalities, have occurred in the Middle East, Africa, or South Asia.

Additionally, there is little evidence to suggest that terrorist acts in the name of Islam are supported by more than a very small minority of Muslims worldwide and most of the victims of the violence of Al Qaeda, ISIS, and other extremist Islamic groups since 9/11 have been Muslims. Nonetheless, since 9/11 many of the mainstream Western media outlets and leading politicians (especially on the right of the political spectrum) have frequently resorted to highly stereotyped and negative depictions of Muslims and Islam.

Some European countries have also enacted legislation clearly aimed at their Muslim populations, such as bans on the wearing of face veils in public in some EU member states or the Swiss banning of the construction of minarets on mosques. It is important to stress that anti-Muslim hostility is not confined to the West as illustrated by recent events such as the violent crackdown since 2017 on the Muslim Rohingya minority in Burma/

Myanmar, the controversial Citizenship Amendment Bill enacted in 2019 by the Indian government led by the Hindu Nationalist Bharatiya Janata Party, or the repression of the Muslim Uighur minority in China. Collectively, such actions arguably reinforce the tendency to see Muslims as a singular, undiversified community. This bears comparison with the also widespread phenomenon of antisemitism, the most extreme expression of which was the Holocaust, the state persecution and murder of European Jews by Nazi Germany between 1933 and 1945.

USEFUL SOURCES:
- https://ourworldindata.org/terrorism#media-coverage-of-terrorism
- https://news.gallup.com/poll/157082/islamophobia-understanding-anti-muslim-sentiment-west.aspx

In sum, poststructuralist IR scholars generally emphasize the inherently *exclusionary* nature of the discourses surrounding the sovereign state and the inescapably political nature of identity. It is important here to reiterate the point that poststructuralism does not offer a singular alternative perspective that identifies a way to eradicate exclusion. Indeed, poststructuralism emphasizes that the constitution of any account of political subjectivity and identity invokes a binary of self/other and thus entails some form of exclusionary practice. All identities are inherently problematic, but they are also products of historically and culturally framed discourses. They are always in the making and this is what makes change possible. What poststructuralists resist, however, is stating in any ideological or programmatic sense what those changes should be. We can, however, reflect critically on how 'We' understand the 'Other' with whom we are inescapably connected.

KEY CONCEPT 7.2 THE POLITICS OF IDENTITY: CYNTHIA WEBER'S *I AM AN AMERICAN* PROJECT

The poststructuralist IR scholar Cynthia Weber's *I am an American* project was developed in response to a Public Service Announcement (PSA) produced by the American Ad Council (a non-profit organization established by the American advertising industry) shortly after the 9/11 terror attacks.

The PSA consisted of a series of very brief film clips of several US citizens of evidently diverse ethnic, racial, and social backgrounds simply declaring 'I am an American'. It ends with the Latin phrase *E Pluribus Unum* (Out of many, one). While recognizing that the PSA was made with good intentions and sought to foster a spirit of unity amongst all Americans, Weber wanted to question the 'idealised image of the American melting pot' it sought to portray.

Consisting of a series of 14 short films of first-person interviews and subsequently a book that reflects on the experience of making the films, Weber's project endeavoured to capture some of the 'complications and paradoxes' that surround the simple declaration 'I am an American'. Weber argues that in contrast to the image of unity portrayed in the PSA, 9/11 'splintered the US along some very lamentable yet predictable lines'. Weber's intention was not to disparage the celebration of diversity as a facet of American identity, but rather to remind US citizens 'of just how great the gulf between lived realities and principled ideas can be' (Weber, 2011: 8).

The people interviewed represented citizens whose stories throw contrasting lights on the impact of 9/11 and whose lives do not tidily fit into some notion of an average American. They included war veterans, war resisters, and peace activists, an undocumented immigrant, Indigenous rights activists, A Muslim US military chaplain wrongly accused of being a spy, a political refugee, and the founder of the Minuteman Civil Defence Corps, a right-wing volunteer group that patrolled US borders to prevent illegal crossings. Weber drew upon the interviews to produce an alternative PSA. In contrast to the original, however, Weber's ends with the Latin phrase *Ex Unum, Plurus* (From one, many). This is intended to capture 'the always fractured US and the plurality of the citizens who compose it' (Weber, 2007). Although Weber seeks to problematize the dominant narrative of what it might mean to be an American and to provoke critical reflection on conceptions of American identity in the wake of 9/11, she offers neither a definitive reading of the material nor a definitive conclusion.

Weber's project was unusual as a piece of scholarly work not only in its use of a range of textual forms—video, photography, and text—but also in its explicit intention to encourage public commentary on the video material which was later incorporated into the project itself. The project's material now forms part of the permanent collection at the September 11 Memorial Museum in New York.

USEFUL SOURCES:

- Weber, C. (2007), 'I am an American': portraits of post-9/11 US citizens', *Open Democracy*.
- Weber, C. (2011), *I am an American: Filming the Fear of Difference* (Bristol: Intellect).
- Weber, C. (2013), '"I am an American": Protesting Advertised "Americaness"', *Citizenship Studies*, 17(2): 278–292.

Problematizing the liberal sovereign state in international politics

We have seen that poststructuralist IR perspectives critically question the centrality of the state and sovereign statehood. Much of the postructuralist critique is aimed at the Western liberal state model, not least because Western states continue to wield considerable power in the institutions and practice of world politics. They are also the sources of much of the thinking and the theoretical assumptions that underpin mainstream IR theories.

Although liberalism and neoliberalism are often depicted as theoretical counterpoints to realism and neorealism, they all operate from a similar starting premise: the anarchical system of states. There are variations in how liberal and realist perspectives view the inside/outside binary that poststructuralism highlights. As we discuss in Chapter 2, liberal IR theory diverges from realist analysis in its emphasis on the possibility of reforming the anarchical system, thereby seemingly reducing the difference between inside and outside the state. War is arguably the key signifier of the danger that the outside, the international realm, poses for the sanctity of the sovereign state. The key to reducing the risk of war between states, liberals have long argued, lies in enhancing cooperation and greater *interdependence* between states through the creation of a more institutionalized and regulated international order (see the discussion in Chapter 1). In effect, they seek the greater *domestication* of the international. This suggests that on face value liberal approaches to IR seek to challenge the inside/outside binary that poststructuralists highlight.

Few liberal IR scholars suggest, however, that the differences between inside and outside the state can or should be eradicated entirely. Rather they argue only that it can be reduced. Furthermore, the contemporary Western liberal state can be seen as inhabiting something of a paradoxical space marked by a tension between competing discourses. On the one hand, there are the universalist assumptions underpinning liberalism as a political philosophy—as expressed in such things as the promotion of universal human rights, global free trade, and the commitment to the *ontological primacy* of the individual (which you can read about in Chapter 2, Section 2.2). These aspects of liberal political discourse appear to set limits on the liberal state. They suggest that the Liberal state should ultimately give way to the universal rights of individuals, while encouraging the development of a universal community of humankind in which the liberal state plays an increasingly limited role.

On the other hand, there are the more overtly exclusionary discourses that serve to constitute the liberal state as a sovereign state. These would include the discourses that invoke the need to maintain control of rights of entry and exit, or defence and security policies intended to preserve the political and territorial integrity of the state against external threats, or discourses that articulate the view that the state should prioritize the economic and social welfare of its citizens above anyone else. Much of the contemporary political debate within liberal states revolves around the challenges of reconciling these discursive tensions, as illustrated, for example, by widespread public discontent with neoliberal policies that are effectively globalizing national economies or demands that liberal states reinforce their national borders in order to restrict the flow of certain people across them, such as refugees and migrants (both arguments were deployed in the UK to promote Brexit, for example).

When we consider the reform strategies that Liberal IR thought proposes will help make the international system less dangerous and more peaceful, the inside/outside binary continues to figure prominently. For example, many liberals argue that the prospects of international reform will be enhanced through the spread of democracy and other liberal values, such as universal human rights. If non-liberal democratic states evolve in a direction such that they increasingly resemble liberal democratic states the world would, some liberals claim, be a safer and more peaceful place.

Liberal global reformism relies, however, on acceptance of the universal validity of its core assumptions about such things as free trade, the virtue of democracy, the nature and range of universal human rights, as well as the idea of what it is to be human that underpins them. As we see in Chapter 2, such ideas permeate the foreign policies of many Western states. Contrastingly, a poststructuralist approach would emphasize that such ideas are products of history, place, and political debate, yet are frequently presented as self-evident, commonsensical, universal truths. From a poststructuralist perspective, the key issue is not whether core liberal ideas are right or wrong *per se*, but how they frame the world and what effects follow from their deployment in discourses of international politics.

If we consider the history of the efforts of liberal states to reform the world outside of them so that it better accords with core liberal values, for example, it is apparent that they have entailed the forced imposition of liberal values upon others. There is not just the history of colonialism and imperialism to consider here (see Chapter 9 for more on this), but also world history since 1945. Consider here the frequent depiction of some states in the Global South as 'quasi', 'weak', or 'failed' states (in Jackson, 1993; and Rotberg, 2003 and 2004, for example). Or, think about the controversies surrounding Western, or Western-led interventions within what are perceived to be *rogue* or *pariah* states, labels applied to states whom the West, particularly the US, strongly disapproves of for some reason or other. Here, poststructuralists argue, we can see new forms of an inside/ outside binary at work.

A poststructuralist IR perspective invites us to consider questions such as:

- Who decides which states and their exercise of sovereignty are classified as being of an acceptable/unacceptable form, and by what criteria?
- What is the significance of the fact that states that are perceived to be deficient are predominantly located within the Global South and their critics are mostly located in the liberal West (we discuss this in relation to postcolonial thought in Chapter 9, Section 9.7)?

Since the end of the Cold War, for example, there have been a number of military interventions by mostly Western-led coalitions of states. These have been in states that are undergoing various kinds of crisis, such as violent civil unrest or even civil war, or the violent repression by authoritarian governments of dissident sections of their own populations. An early example was the former state of Yugoslavia, which underwent violent upheaval in the aftermath of the Cold War when the Yugoslavian government effectively collapsed, resulting in the emergence of new states seeking sovereign independence such as Serbia, Bosnia, and Kosovo. Additionally, there have been highly controversial military interventions in Afghanistan (2001–2021), Iraq (in 1990/91 and in 2003), Libya (2011), and Syria (since 2014) to name just a few. Each of these interventions have been complex in their genesis and we cannot do them full justice here. Nonetheless, none of them have produced unequivocally successful outcomes, and some are evident failures. This was most recently illustrated by the withdrawal of US and UK forces from Afghanistan in 2021, 20 years after they first intervened and defeated the Taliban regime, which was followed by the return of the Taliban to power. In all these cases, the invocation of liberal humanitarian values has been a key feature of the case made for intervention.

Although these Western-led interventions have been heavily criticized from several theoretical standpoints (we discuss realist critiques, for example, in Chapter 2), poststructuralist IR scholars have been particularly interested in problematizing the discursive assumptions underpinning the interventions.

To illustrate, let us focus on two key assumptions in particular:

- The meaning of 'humanitarianism'
- The meaning of sovereign statehood.

The meaning of 'humanitarianism'

In everyday language humanitarianism is usually taken to refer to a benevolent moral disposition towards all humans by virtue of a shared humanity alone. A humanitarian is someone who believes that our shared humanity obliges us to help alleviate the suffering of others caused by such things as natural disasters, famines, or the consequences of violent conflict.

The classic idea of humanitarianism is usually traced back to the actions of a Swiss businessperson and social activist Henry Dunant who, having witnessed the Battle of Solferino between Austrian and French forces in 1859, organized the provision of assistance to sick and injured soldiers without regard to the side they had taken in the battle. Dunant went on to establish the International Committee of the Red Cross (ICRC) and initiated the Geneva Conventions that govern the conduct of war and the treatment of Prisoners of War. In 1901 Dunant was also the recipient of the first Nobel Peace Prize. The principle of humanitarianism that, in the spirit of Dunant, underpins the work of the ICRC, various UN agencies, and numerous NGOs is marked by a commitment to political neutrality. Furthermore, as Dorothea Hilhorst (2018: 5) argues, 'in classical humanitarianism the recipients of aid—often addressed as the beneficiaries, i.e., those to whom good is done—are typically depicted as victims'. The conceptions of humanity and humanitarianism deployed in support of interventions or the provision of aid to people in conditions of crisis provide a basis for depicting these actions as somehow above politics.

In contrast, the poststructuralist IR scholar Jenny Edkins (2003: 254) argues that 'humanitarianism is not a timeless truth but an ideology that has had particular functions and taken different forms at different times in the contemporary world'. For Edkins and other poststructuralist scholars humanity and humanitarianism are political constructions that are neither self-evident nor unproblematic. These conceptions of a supposedly shared or 'common' understanding of humanity are used to provide moral legitimacy not just for the provision of material forms of aid but also for the criticism of certain states, the imposition of sanctions, or even armed interventions. Yet, they are also inconsistently applied since there are many crises that seemingly warrant intervention on humanitarian grounds, but there is none, or it comes too late to make a difference (the 1994 genocide against the Tutsi community in Rwanda is a frequently cited example).

Many crises elicit expressions of sympathy from states, but the actual provision of aid fails to match up to the humanitarian rhetoric. In the case of armed interventions, the claimed humanitarian motivations are often undermined by the violent consequences of the interventions themselves. This raises several difficult questions, such as who decides when supposedly humanitarian armed intervention is warranted? Cynthia Weber puts this point in a distinctly poststructuralist voice by querying who is the 'interpretive community' (Weber, 1995, chapter 3)? Furthermore, you could ask what amount of material aid or what level of violence, if any, can be legitimated by an appeal to a discourse of common humanity? What are the consequences of reducing complex conflicts or complex emergencies such as famines to a simple binary of good/bad, saints/sinners, saviours/victims?

Edkins argues that trying to establish some common essence, a lowest common denominator, to all humans as the basis for helping others leads to the depiction of human subjects as 'separate, sovereign individuals' (Edkins, 2003: 256). It treats being human as something that is prior to and therefore independent of history and politics. It risks depicting those whom we feel may need our help as 'strangers' whose lives need saving. In other words, it rests ultimately upon a them/us and saviour/victim binary. The key questions then centre around when and how *we* should help *them*. In the case of purely natural disasters, such as earthquakes, the answers may seem to be quite simple and apolitical. However, most large-scale crises have a political dimension to both their causes and the responses to them.

As the history of providing humanitarian assistance in response to such things as famines or helping the victims of violent conflict shows, the situation on the ground is often politically highly ambiguous and the provision of humanitarian aid cannot avoid getting caught up in a host of political and ethical complexities. The provision of aid is not outside international politics but inescapably part of it. For Edkins and others (see also Duffield, 2001a and 2001b; Rieff, 2002; Campbell, 2008), the result is that rather than transcending international relations, supposedly in the name of a universal humanity or abstract principles of humanitarianism, humanitarian assistance ends up effectively being tied to and thereby reinforcing the binary assumptions that underpin international politics—them and us, here and there, and so on. Indeed, Rieff (2002) shows how, especially since the end of the Cold War, humanitarianism in all its forms has become deeply entwined with politics between sovereign states, a point reinforced even by the Director of Operations of the ICRC (Krahenbuhl, 2011).

Poststructuralist IR points towards an alternative understanding of helping others. For example, Edkins proposes that we think of humans as 'as subjects produced always already in and through relations with other subjects' (Edkins, 2003: 256). Our sense of responsibility to help others arises then not because they conform with an abstract conception of being human, but because, like us, they are enmeshed in configurations of power which for many possible reasons they see as inequitable, unfair, or dangerous. Our sense of political solidarity with others arises then out of our understanding of the desire of others to resist domination and oppression. It recognizes that helping others is an inherently political act that occurs within specific political historical contexts, and which inevitably entails making difficult and always political decisions that will not conform tidily to abstract principles. This mitigates against maintaining the illusion of political neutrality or establishing general principles of how and when intervention or assistance is to be offered, in what ways, or by whom.

> **THINK CRITICALLY 7.2** WHAT IS IT TO BE 'HUMAN'?
>
> Arguments for 'humanitarian assistance' or 'humanitarian intervention' imply that there is something that binds us all as human subjects.
>
> - What, if anything, do you think binds us as humans, regardless of where we are in the world?
> - What are the grounds, if any, on which you believe we should help others outside of our own countries facing conditions of emergency or crisis?
>
> **USEFUL REFERENCE:**
> Edkins, Jenny (2003), 'Humanitarianism, Humanity, Human', *Journal of Human Rights*, 2(2): 253–258.

The meaning of sovereign statehood

A key component of the arguments for the legitimacy of many interventions is the claim that they can lead to the construction or reconstruction of stable states out of the ruins of conflict, or the effects of natural disasters and economic crises. The state that needs to be (re)constructed is usually understood in reference to a dominant model of sovereign statehood. However, many interventions show that the very act of intervening often greatly reduces the capacity of states, usually with very different cultural and political histories to those of the intervening states, to recover fully from conflict. Indeed, in cases such as Iraq and Libya the interventions have been followed by still ongoing periods of chronic instability and the lives of much of the local populations in some cases are markedly worse than prior to the intervention. Afghanistan underwent considerable change during 20 years of Western intervention, even if it never became fully stable or free of violent conflict. Yet, with the return of a Taliban government after the withdrawal of Western military forces in 2021, many of the changes that were a direct consequence of intervention (the introduction of democracy, liberalization of the media, improvement in the rights and opportunities of women) have effectively been reversed. Furthermore, many young Afghan citizens have had no experience of a Taliban regime yet will now have to rapidly adjust to some dramatic changes in their lives.

After external armed intervention, states are usually highly dependent on the continuing involvement of the intervening states for their survival. In other words, they struggle to reacquire their own sovereignty in a meaningful sense. At the same time, the states that intervene, which are mostly Western states, are generally very hostile to the idea that they would ever warrant intervention into their own sovereign spaces. This positive self-understanding sits in juxtaposition with a negative perception of other states that the West deems to be incapable of being sovereign according to its own standards, or are effectively rendered incapable through the act of Western-led intervention. Viewed through poststructuralist lenses, a binary of us/them is therefore reinforced. The politics surrounding so-called humanitarian interventions illustrates the broader point that the positive self-understanding of Western sovereign statehood depends in part on the negative representation of other, mostly, non-Western, states as practising, to greater or lesser degrees, inferior forms of sovereign statehood. Therefore, if interventions fail this can be framed in terms of the inadequacies of the states that were intervened in, and not the intervening states.

Representing the non-Western 'other' in the liberal media and entertainment industries

Some poststructuralist IR scholars examine the reproduction of the exclusionary discursive dimensions of liberalism and the binaries that underpin them not just within the confines of theoretical debates in the IR discipline or the concrete foreign and security policies of sovereign states, but in other arenas as well. For example, Western media and the entertainment industries have been shown to be complicit in the reinforcement of the distinction between self/other, or us/them, and connecting this with a range of other binaries such as developed/undeveloped, the West/non-West, or civilized/uncivilized. For example, Campbell and Bleiker illustrate such binary representations through a case study exploring how humanitarian disasters, such as periodic famines in Africa, have been consistently framed in Western media within narratives and images that reproduce a range of simplistic binary distinctions, such as saviour/victim, developed/undeveloped, civilized/uncivilized, modern/premodern, strong/weak, and so on. These effectively erase the complex political and historical contexts within which famines emerge (Campbell and Bleiker 2021: 213–217. See also Edkins, 2000; Bleiker, 2018).

One example has been the widespread tendency to represent Africa, a continent containing 54 very diverse countries as a singular entity marked predominantly by the prevalence of such things as civil wars, inter-ethnic violence, poverty, famine, corruption, and so on. A seemingly innocuous example of this representation of 'Africa' can be found in the song 'Do They Know it's Christmas?' released in December 1984 by Band Aid, a charity supergroup of mostly British musicians, to raise money for victims of famine in Ethiopia. The song went on to sell over 2 million copies worldwide, raising $24 million in the process. Nonetheless, the song's lyrics subsequently attracted a deal of controversy. The song's title seems to reflect unawareness of the fact that nearly two thirds of the Ethiopian population follow various branches of the Christian faith, which made the claim that most Ethiopians might not know when it is Christmas rather implausible. The song contained no direct reference to Ethiopia, but it did refer to 'Africa' where, it declares, 'there won't be snow this Christmastime . . . where nothing ever grows, no rains or rivers flow'. Yet, Africa contains two of the world's longest rivers—the Nile and the Congo—which between them flow through 20 different countries with very widely varying levels of rainfall. Because of its geographical location alone, snow is also a rather rare event in most of Africa. While motivated by humanitarian intentions, the song effectively erased the specific circumstances affecting Ethiopia at the time and in its place offered a wildly inaccurate picture of Africa as a continent.

The reproduction of the inside/outside and self/other binaries in the realms of popular culture such as cinema, television, photography, and gaming is a prominent theme in contemporary poststructuralist IR scholarship (examples include: Lisle and Pepper, 2005; Der Derian, 2009; Kiersey and Neumann, 2013; Weber, 2014; Caso and Hamilton, 2015). Debbie Lisle examines also the complex 'entanglements' between conflict, global dynamics of power, and the tourism and leisure industries. In so doing she questions a number of assumptions about the supposed separateness of everyday activities such as tourism and leisure from the violence of international politics. Patterns of tourism can serve to both reflect and reinforce the contours of global power, just as soldiers can bring a tourist sensibility to conflict, especially in locations that are very different fom their state of origin (Lisle, 2016).

Again, much of this literature reflects poststructuralist IR's critical ethos. It presents critique as being about revealing the often-hidden assumptions threading through dominant discourses about the international, with a view to stimulating critical reflection and opening avenues for thinking differently without laying down definitive alternatives. In so doing, the investigation of international politics arguably becomes wider, more complex, and a lot less certain than mainstream scholarship has traditionally suggested.

7.5 POSTSTRUCTURALISM AND OTHER CRITICAL APPROACHES TO IR

As we see in Chapters 5 and 6, other critical IR perspectives such as Marxism and Critical International Theory resonate with the critical concerns of poststructuralists, even if the language and terms of debate differ markedly. Marxism critiques the state-centric focus of mainstream theories, arguing that it fails to consider the significance of the global capitalist system and excludes consideration of the class-based dimensions of international or global politics (see Chapter 5). Like poststructuralists, Marxists would also see the state and the contemporary international system as products of historical processes and thus not immune to change. Nonetheless there remain important differences.

Alongside liberalism, Marxism is one of the key *metanarratives* (meaning a totalizing, comprehensive discourse based upon a series of claimed universal truths) that have governed progressive political discourse since the nineteenth century, initially in the West, but subsequently far more widely. Furthermore, Marxist analysis is materialist in orientation. It aims to detect the underlying structural forces inherent in a capitalist economic system. These underpin the development of an ideological superstructure that serves to legitimize and sustain the interests of the ruling class (we discuss this further in Chapter 5). Thus, Marxists would reject the poststructuralist claim that nothing can be definitively known outside of discourse. Marxists and poststructuralists might well agree on the need and possibility of social and political change, but Marxism's universalism is a problem for poststructuralists. Marxism pursues the revolutionary emancipation of the working class and, ultimately, of all of humanity. As we have seen, from a poststructuralist perspective this is problematic because it rests upon a specific account of human social development which can never be securely grounded outside of the discourses which claim its significance. This is not to say that poststructuralists would not find much about the Marxist perspective both suggestive and thought-provoking. However, they would see it as always incomplete and potentially dogmatic in its claims to offer a universal account of human social and economic development.

Additionally, Marxism operates with a singular account of the human subject—the person who is to be emancipated from the inequalities inherent in capitalism. As we discussed in Section 7.3, poststructuralism views subjectivity as constantly being formed and reformed in discourse; the human subject has no knowable essence outside of the discourses that bring it in to being. There is no universal person who has existed throughout history. For poststructuralists, political subjects are created in discourses that, because of their inescapable relationship with power, have changed throughout history.

This also puts poststructuralist IR on a collision course with Critical International Theory, even if its critical ethos clearly bears something in common with Critical International Theory's interest in advancing human emancipation by exposing and challenging the multiple constraints on human freedom (as discussed in Chapter 6). However, Critical International Theory holds to a progressive, *cosmopolitan* perspective and follows Kant in depicting all humans as members of a single moral universe. Poststructuralist IR perspectives share with Critical International Theory a critique of realism's presumption of the immutability of the international system of sovereign states (even if it takes a rather different theoretical path) but it also takes issue with Critical International Theory's reliance upon a universal account of humanity and the human subject.

It should be noted that, as we discuss in Chapter 6, some critical international theorists, such as Andrew Linklater, do endeavour to take greater account of difference and the complex politics of identity and develop a 'thin' cosmopolitanism. From a poststructuralist point of view, however, Critical International Theory is insufficiently critical in some key respects. Firstly, Critical International Theory's understanding of emancipation rests on a different view of power. It depicts human emancipation as achieved through freedom from the oppressive constraints of power. In contrast, as Foucault's work powerfully illustrates, poststructuralism sees power as pervasive and perpetual. It is not something to escape from but an ineradicable feature of all discourse. All discourses are exclusionary in some way or other; this is how they express relations of power. But such power is not just repressive and it is not the possession of a single person or class of persons. As we saw in our earlier discussion of Foucault, the relationship between power and knowledge can also be productive; it can bring about change. Yet because all our knowledge claims, whether they are about international politics or any other dimensions of human social and political life, inescapably contain traces of power relations they should be always subjected to critical scrutiny.

Another key difference between poststructuralism and other critical perspectives concerns their conception of the purpose of theory. Marxism and Critical Theory are *teleological* theoretical perspectives. By this is meant that they are driven by the pursuit of an ultimate end, a *telos*. For Marxism, this is the replacement of capitalism by an alternative more just political, social, and international economic order. For Critical IR Theory it is the achievement of complete human emancipation—even if it seems almost impossible to attain. Although poststructuralist IR thinking is clearly driven by a critical ethos, since it seeks to challenge prevailing international political practices and the limits they place upon other possible ways of being, it makes no claim to know authoritatively where we should ultimately end up. Indeed, it sees real dangers in any claim to know definitively what 'humanity' means let alone where it should head. For poststructuralists, we cannot escape the intersection of power and knowledge, just as we cannot eliminate the exclusionary aspects of all forms of political discourse including those that claim to be progressive such as liberalism, Marxism, and Critical Theory. For this reason, poststructuralism presents critique as an always deeply political activity that needs to be conducted in perpetuity.

7.6 **CONCLUSION**

Daniel Levine provides a useful summation of the broad thrust of much poststructuralist IR thinking. He argues that we should resist forgetting 'the distinction between theoretical concepts and the real-world things they mean to describe or to which they refer'. For Levine, such forgetting produces 'unchecked reification'. Reification refers to the presentation of something abstract, such as a concept or idea, as if it was a real, material thing. What we *claim* to be real becomes accepted as reality; it can become 'thingified' (Levine, 2012: 15).

Levine does not claim we can ever fully escape this, but he argues that left unchecked, the reification of our knowledge claims can have dangerous consequences, especially in international politics where bad decisions can produce horrendous outcomes. In other words, we need to constantly scrutinize our assumptions and the relationship between our subject position (who 'we' are) and our claims to know the world and resist the impulse to categorize definitively what goes on 'out there'. There are always other subject positions from which the world can be viewed and other ways of analysing the world. We need to constantly reflect upon the limits to our knowledge claims.

Poststructuralism's standpoint continues to infuriate some critics. Poststructuralist IR scholars have been accused of nihilism, of offering no clear pathway out of the many injustices and inequities of the prevailing social world. Critics see them offering little of value to the world of international policy making. But are these fair criticisms? Poststructuralist IR scholars claim that their critical ethos is driven by the pursuit of concrete alternatives, not least through challenging the stranglehold that the discourse of sovereignty has over our ways of thinking and doing international politics. In its commitment to critique as a perpetual activity, poststructuralism does not deny that different configurations of what Foucault called power/knowledge, while always open to question, can be productive nonetheless in challenging prevailing forms of exclusion and injustice. What poststructuralists refuse to do is to erect new forms of universalizing and totalizing thought in place of the old. This does not preclude the exercise of judgement or the taking of a position on matters of significant political or moral import.

7 POSTSTRUCTURALISM AND INTERNATIONAL RELATIONS

Recall here our discussion of Derrida's work in Section 7.3. We note his claim that there are no secure foundations for our knowledge claims, and this results in a condition of perpetual uncertainty. Nonetheless, Derrida acknowledged that decisions must be made. From a poststructuralist perspective, critical discourses that envisage alternative ways of thinking and doing international politics need, however, to recognize that any discourse always entails the privileging of certain ways of being over others, the marginalization or exclusion of other voices, other points of view, and other ways of doing. From a poststructuralist perspective, then, even the most well-intentioned critical thinking about world politics needs always to recognize its own limitations and exclusionary dimensions. Zehfuss concludes her examination of the political and ethical dilemmas surrounding going to war in the name of the 'good' by proposing that 'there is no heroic resolution; instead we can only resist firm answers, look beyond the obvious context, and try to allow interruptions to challenge our thinking' (Zehfuss, 2018: 208). In many respects this serves as a pithy summary of a poststructuralist sensibility or 'ethos' to bring to the study of world politics.

SUMMARIZING POSTSTRUCTURALISM AND IR

- The various forms of poststructuralist thinking share a common 'anti-foundationalism'. They argue that there are no secure foundations for our knowledge claims and therefore they must always be treated as contingent, contextual, and incomplete.

- As with poststructuralism more generally, poststructuralist IR is focused particularly on questions around interpretation, representation, and subjectivity

- For poststructuralists, the meaning of human subjectivity (what it is to be human) is created through language and therefore alternative understandings of human subjectivity are always possible

- Poststructuralist IR does not see it itself as offering an alternative theory or paradigm to mainstream IR theories. It presents itself instead as offering a 'critical attitude' or ethos

- Poststructuralist IR problematizes mainstream or dominant representations and interpretations of international politics, seeing them as always partial and incomplete.

- It endeavours to show how dominant representations of global politics emerge historically and are sustained, thereby excluding or marginalizing alternative representations and interpretations and therefore other possible forms of international and global social life

- Poststructuralist IR draws extensively on the work of Michel Foucault to use a different understanding of power to other IR theories. Power is seen as pervasive and integral to our knowledge claims about the world. Power is not seen only as negative but also as productive

- In particular, poststructuralist IR interrogates the *sovereignty of the discourse of sovereignty*. It investigates how mainstream IR's emphasis on the sovereign state works

to legitimize dominant practices of international politics and marginalize alternative representations and interpretations of *global* politics
- The discourse of sovereignty's dominance is sustained particularly through mainstream IR theory's reliance on a contestable binary 'inside/outside' distinction between the security found inside and the inherent dangers outside the sovereign state
- In contrast to mainstream IR's primary focus on states and their relations with each other, many poststructuralist IR scholars examine the textual and visual representation and interpretation of international and global politics
- Poststructuralist IR shares many of the concerns of other critical approaches to IR, such as Marxism and Critical Theory, but departs from them in its questioning of the universalized representation of the human or humanity upon which other critical theories are seen to depend
- Poststructuralist IR has been widely criticized for seeming to offer little more than perpetual critique of prevailing theories and practices
- Poststructuralists counter this by arguing that their critical ethos pursues change through critiquing existing exclusionary theories and practices thereby opening the exploration of alternative ways of being.

QUESTIONS

1. Why is poststructuralism described as anti-foundationalist?
2. What do poststructuralist IR scholars mean when they claim not to be offering a new theory of IR but rather a 'critical attitude' or 'ethos'?
3. What did Baudrillard mean when he claimed that 'the Gulf War did not take place'?
4. In what ways can the comparison of different maps of the world's surface show the relationship between knowledge and power?
5. How does poststructuralist IR challenge 'the sovereignty of the discourse of sovereignty'?
6. Thinking of other theories of IR you have studied what, if any, key weaknesses of poststructuralist perspectives on IR do they identify? How do you think a poststructuralist might respond to these critiques?

IR THEORY TODAY 'BREXIT': THE UNITED KINGDOM LEAVES THE EUROPEAN UNION (EU)

On 31 January 2020, the UK formally left the EU, a process widely referred to as 'Brexit'. This was the consequence of a 2016 national referendum in which a narrow majority (just under 52 per cent) of UK voters voted for the UK to leave the EU, thereby ending 33 years of membership. EU Membership required submitting to comprehensive

Activists campaigning for freedom of movement

EU-wide regulations, including a commitment to allowing the free movements of goods and people from other member states across the UK's national borders.

The debate about whether to stay in or leave the EU largely involved three broad lines of argument:

- The mainstream pro-Brexit position depicted the EU as a threat to the UK's national sovereignty by emphasizing the lack of democratic accountability, and the risks and costs associated with allowing free movement of people across the national border. It argued that the UK voted in 1975 to join the then European Economic Community (EEC) on the assumption that it was largely concerned with enhancing free trade between its members. The evolution of the EEC into today's EU was viewed as a project that not only increasingly threatened UK national sovereignty but, some 'brexiteers' argued, could lead ultimately to the end of British sovereignty through the UK's absorption into a future EU federal sovereign state.

- In contrast, 'remainers' (those who did not want the UK to leave the EU) saw the EU as a successful example of how relations between sovereign states can be transformed significantly—most notably by virtually eradicating the likelihood of war between the member states—through institutionalized cooperation and the pooling of some aspects of national sovereignty. EU legislation was credited with having played a sometimes-crucial role in inhibiting some member states from discriminating against certain sections of their community. Additionally, the EU was seen as a powerful trading bloc that could achieve more in global trade negotiations that its member states could hope to achieve acting alone. It was a standpoint that supported, or at least tolerated the free movement of people across national borders.

- There was also a less prominent, but long-standing variety of the pro-Brexit position that came from the British political Left (thus it is sometimes referred to as a 'Lexiteer' viewpoint). Although it shares the mainstream pro-Brexit critique of the lack of democratic accountability in the EU, they also depicted the EU as a club of mostly affluent developed capitalist states which was instrumental in moving the global economy in a distinctly neoliberal direction. This position sometimes invokes the idea of a 'Fortress Europe' whose tariff and trade barriers disadvantage developing states. This depiction of the EU as a fortress also rested on the fact that the free movement within the EU was confined to citizens of other EU member states which did not prevent member states or the EU itself placing strict limits on the movement of non-European peoples within the EU. In terms of global justice then, the EU is seen as a highly exclusionary and elitist club of which a truly progressive UK should not be a part.

QUESTIONS

Drawing from what you have read so far in this chapter as well as your own research, answer the following questions:

1. How significant is the concept of sovereignty in each of the three positions on EU membership? (Hint: think about 'the sovereignty of the discourse of sovereignty' and whether the concept of sovereignty can be applied also to the EU, not just the UK.)

2. In what ways might themes such as *representation* and *interpretation*, provide distinctive lenses through which to problematize each of the various standpoints within the debate around UK membership of the EU? (Hint: think about the representation of the UK *and* the EU in each of the positions.)

3. Poststructuralists recognize that difficult political decisions must be made, even if all the options can be shown to be problematic. Imagine you were a voter in the 2016 EU referendum. In what ways, if any, do you think a poststructuralist analysis might have helped you decide whether the UK should leave the EU?

TWISTING THE LENS

1. Consider the three positions on the UK's membership of the EU described above. Identify and explain why which of these positions, if any, might align with the following IR theoretical perspectives:
- Realism
- Liberalism
- Marxism.

FURTHER READING

ADDITIONAL INTRODUCTORY READING

Campbell, D. and Bleiker, R. (2021), 'Poststructuralism' in T. Dunne, M. Kurki, and S. Smith, *International Relations Theories: Discipline and Diversity*, 5th edition (Oxford: Oxford University Press). *A more advanced introduction that contains a useful case study of visual images of humanitarian crises.*

Hanson, L. (2020), 'Poststructuralism' in J. Baylis, S. Smith, and P. Owens, *The Globalization of World Politics: An Introduction to International Relations*, 8th edition (Oxford: Oxford University Press).

A brief and accessible introduction from a leading Danish poststructuralist IR scholar.

Neal, A. (2009), 'Michel Foucault' in J. Edkins and N. Vaughan-Williams, *Critical Theorists and International Relations* (London: Routledge).

A brief but accessible and IR-focussed introduction to Foucault's work by a Foucauldian IR scholar.

Zehfuss, M. (2009), 'Jacques Derrida' in Jenny Edkins and Nick Vaughan-Williams, *Critical Theorists and International Relations* (London: Routledge).

A brief, accessible, and IR-focussed introduction to Derrida's work by a leading Derridean IR scholar.

MORE IN-DEPTH READING

Bleiker, R. (ed.) (2018), *Visual Global Politics* (Abingdon: Taylor and Francis).

A very wide ranging collection of brief and accessible essays reflecting on the ways in which photographs, television, cinema, and social media visually present global politics and in so doing act as political forces in themsleves.

Bulley, D. (2009), *Ethics as Foreign Policy: Britain, The EU and the Other* (Abingdon, Oxon: Routledge).

This book draws upon Derrida's work to examine the ethical claims of British and EU foreign policies and reveal their ambiguities. Bulley endeavours to show the pursuit of ethical foreign policy to be neither completely impossible nor entirely possible.

Campbell, D. (1998), *Writing Security: United States Foreign Policy and the Politics of Identity*, revised edition (Minneapolis, MN: University of Minnesota Press).

A pathbreaking text by a noted poststructuralist scholar which examines how 'discourses of danger' shape US foreign policy.

Edkins, J. (1999), *Poststructuralism and International Relations: Bringing the Political Back in* (Boulder, CO: Lynne Rienner Publishers).

Written by one the UK's leading poststructuralist IR scholars, this book explores the difference between 'politics' and 'the political' in international relations drawing upon the work of a number of key poststructuralist thinkers.

Foucault, M. and Kritzman, L. D. (1990), *Politics, Philosophy, Culture: Interviews and Other Writings 1977–1984* (London: Routledge).

A useful introduction to the key themes in Foucault's work, not least because it contains a number of interviews with Foucault as well as an illuminating introductory biographical essay.

George, J. (1994), *Discourses of Global Politics: A Critical (Re)introduction to International Relations* (Boulder, CO: Lynne Rienner Publishers).

One of the first books exploring international relations through poststructuralist lenses.

Gutting, G. (2005), *Foucault: A Very Short Introduction* (Oxford: Oxford University Press).

A succinct introduction to Foucault's work, which commences by telling three contrasting but equally plausible brief readings of Foucault's life and work.

Inayatullah, N. and Dauphinee, E. (eds) (2016), *Narrative Global Politics: Theory, History and the Perosonal in International Relations* (Abingdon: Routledge).

A series of essays in which scholars in various ways deploy personal narratives to explore their relationship to academic work about global politics.

Johnson, J. M., Basham, V. M., and Thomas, O. D. (2022), 'Ordering Disorder: The Making of World Politics', *Review of International Studies*, 48/4: 607–625.

> *Reconsiders the concept of 'world order' long central to much IR scholarship, through an examination of how 'disorder' through three 'modes of treatment': tragedy, crisis, and 'scandal'.*

Lisle, D. (2016), *Holidays in the Danger Zone: Entanglements of War and Tourism* (Minneapolis, MN, University of Minnesota Press).

> *Lisle examines the complex 'entanglements' between conflict, global dynamics of power, and the tourism and leisure industries.*

Zehfuss, M. (2018), *War and the Politics of Ethics* (Oxford: Oxford University Press).

> *A comprehensive exploration of the paradox of wars supposedly fought in the name of ethical principles yet which also kill, maim, and destroy in the process. The book expores how the 'seduction of ethics' can serve to legitimize and enable violence.*

CHAPTER 8

CONSTRUCTIVISM AND INTERNATIONAL RELATIONS

LEARNING OBJECTIVES

- Understand the meaning of the term constructivism
- Identify the historical and intellectual contexts in which constructivist IR theory emerged
- Comprehend why constructivism is widely viewed as occupying a 'middle ground' between mainstream and critical approaches
- Explain the differences between the main varieties of constructivist scholarship
- Demonstrate how constructivism can be applied to the analysis and understanding of international politics

8.1 INTRODUCTION

Constructivism emerged in the IR discipline in the late 1980s/early 1990s, not long after Critical International Theory and poststructuralism had begun to make their mark on the discipline. The 1980s were a time of quite sudden and diverse theoretical upheaval. An increasing number of IR scholars were drawing from theoretical perspectives such as Critical International Theory and poststructuralism to challenge the *epistemology* of mainstream IR theories. In other words, they questioned the assumptions of mainstream IR about how we acquire our knowledge of international and global politics.

As we discuss in Chapters 6 and 7, Critical International Theory and poststructuralism challenged what they saw as an underlying *positivism* in much mainstream IR theorizing. The IR discipline is usually seen to be located within the social sciences and positivism is a philosophy of social scientific research. As is discussed in Chapter 1, Section 1.3, positivism holds that we should aim to produce explanatory knowledge of the social world which is demonstrably objective (i.e., value-free), empirically verified, and therefore true. Furthermore, positivism rests upon an epistemology known as empiricism. This is the view that the validity of our theoretical knowledge claims about the world is established through appeal to neutral facts, which are derived from systematic observation of what we are trying to explain.

Although it is debatable how much mainstream IR theorizing adheres strictly to a positivist epistemology, positivism is nonetheless seen by critics of mainstream IR as providing the predominant benchmark—an ideal type—against which knowledge claims about international politics should be judged. For various reasons, non-mainstream IR perspectives like Critical International Theory, poststructuralism, postcolonialism, and most gender-focused and feminist perspectives reject the positivist standpoint. They are therefore commonly referred to as *post-positivist* theories.

So where does constructivism fit in the mainstream vs critical theories, or positivist vs post-positivist story? The answer is not straightforward, because constructivists themselves offer different accounts of constructivism's place in the IR theory field. For some, constructivism is diametrically opposed to mainstream theories (by which they mean neorealism and neoliberalism particularly) and is a distinctive kind of critical approach to IR. For others, constructivism endeavours to find a 'middle ground' or even seeks to build a bridge between mainstream theories and the critical theories. In broad terms then, there do appear to be two distinct wings of constructivist IR theory: one that leans towards positivism and one that leans away from it or rejects it entirely. Constructivism seems therefore to straddle the positivist/post-positivist divide. The division between constructivism's two wings also loosely reflects a geographical divide between constructivists located in the US IR scholarly community, and those located outside of it.

This location of constructivism in the spectrum of IR theories may seem a bit confusing at this stage, but it will become clearer as you work through this chapter. We start by looking at the historical, political, and theoretical contexts in which constructivism emerged. We then go on to explore the key claims of constructivism, followed by a closer examination of the differences between its two main wings. We then look at some illustrative examples of the application of constructivism to the analysis of international politics.

8.2 WHAT IS CONSTRUCTIVISM?

Constructivism emerged as a distinct IR theoretical perspective in parallel with the dramatic end to the Cold War. Therefore, before outlining the key claims of the constructivist perspective in IR, we will first look at the international political context that seems to have played a significant part in its emergence.

Why did constructivism emerge?

The failure of the mainstream IR theories to predict the largely peaceful end of the Cold War (which is summarized for you in Key event 8.1) was a key impetus to the emergence of constructivism. Over a surprisingly short period at the end of the 1980s, the people of the East European states within the Soviet bloc rejected the communist political systems that they had lived under since a few years after the end of the Second World War in 1945. Equally rapid was the establishment of democratic political systems in their place. Ultimately, the transformation of the Soviet Union's allied states led to the collapse of the Soviet Union itself in the early 1990s, resulting ultimately in the ending of the Cold War and the emergence of the post-communist Russia that we know today.

KEY EVENT 8.1 THE END OF THE COLD WAR

After more than four decades, the Cold War ended dramatically between 1989 and 1991. Although the first half of the 1980s saw a marked increase in tensions between the Superpowers, the USA and the USSR, the emergence of Mikhail Gorbachev in 1985 as the Soviet premier saw a rapid shift in the USSR's international outlook, and revision of some of the key aspects of Soviet foreign and security policy. These included a willingness to open arms control negotiations with the US, and the effective abandonment of Soviet control over its East European satellites, many of whom were beginning to experience domestic unrest and increasingly open hostility towards the communist regimes in place.

Although a long-standing anti-communist, the US President, Ronald Reagan, reacted positively to Gorbachev's overtures and things moved very rapidly from that point on.

Mikhail Gorbachev, 1991

> Both sides withdrew medium range mobile missiles from their allies in Europe and commenced comprehensive nuclear arms reduction negotiations.
>
> In 1989 and 1990 all the communist regimes in Eastern Europe collapsed, mostly peacefully, to be replaced by democratically elected non-Communist alternatives. One of the most symbolic events was the tearing down of the Berlin Wall in November 1989. Within a year, East and West Germany were reunified into a single state. In 1991, the Soviet Union also collapsed and broke up into several independent states. After Gorbachev resigned as Soviet President, Boris Yeltsin emerged as the president of a newly independent Russia. In 1999, Yeltsin was succeeded as Russian President by Vladimir Putin.

What these tumultuous events of the Cold War's end signalled, constructivists argued, was that profound change was possible in international politics, as illustrated by the dramatic ending of the bipolar system that had dominated international politics since 1945. This presented an evident challenge to realist and neorealist claims that the international system was inherently resistant to significant change, especially because of developments that took place primarily within some states (such as the Soviet Union and the Eastern European communist states). As we note in Chapter 3, neorealism focuses primarily on the material power of specific states, such as their military capabilities, and treats international politics as an autonomous sphere of political interaction within an anarchical international system.

For constructivists, the key point was that such dramatic change could be brought about through the power of *ideas*. For constructivists, such as Rey Koslowski and Friedrich Kratochwil, the story of the Cold War's end suggested that ideas and values embraced by peoples within states could themselves instigate significant systemic political change at the international level (Koslowski and Kratochwil, 1994). Such change occurred not only within their own states, but in the relations between those states and their former supposed enemies. Within a few years, states that had previously been members of the Soviet-led Warsaw Pact military alliance were queuing up to become members of NATO, the military alliance of Western states led by the US. In effect, the balance of power between the Cold War superpowers (meaning the US and the USSR), and their allies, had seemingly dissolved without a shot being fired or the international system going into systemic crisis. Furthermore, the previously communist states appeared to be undergoing transformations in their very sense of collective *identity*. They were signing up to international rules and norms, such as the obligation to uphold fundamental human rights, without external coercion. As we shall see, identity and norms are central themes in constructivist analysis of international politics.

Constructivists do not claim that material forces played no part in the collapse of the Soviet Union. The last communist leader of the Soviet Union, Mikhail Gorbachev, had clearly recognized that the fundamental weaknesses of the Soviet economy, exacerbated in large part by the costs of endeavouring to maintain military parity with the US for over four decades, necessitated dramatic change. Although his intention was ultimately to preserve Soviet communism, he began to reach out to the West with a view to ending the Cold War. At the same time, he signalled that the Soviet Union was no longer going to try and suppress the growing clamour for political change within its satellite states in Eastern Europe as it had done in the past.

Gorbachev made much of the need to engage in what he called 'new thinking'. What is significant from a constructivist perspective about Gorbachev's domestic reform programmes—known as *perestroika* (restructuring) and *glasnost* (openness)—was that ideas clearly mattered (See Key concept 8.1).

KEY CONCEPT 8.1 GORBACHEV'S 'NEW THINKING': 'GLASNOST' AND 'PERESTROIKA'

In the mid to late 1980s, the Soviet Premier Mikhail Gorbachev introduced 'new thinking' comprised of two key policies that underpinned his efforts to reform (but not eliminate) Soviet communism:

- *Glasnost* (openness)

  Gorbachev promoted genuine openness in public discussion within the Soviet Union, including stringent criticism of both the Stalin and Brezhnev eras. This extended to much greater candidness about the USSR in official dealings with the outside world. Russian journalists and official spokespersons appeared more frequently in Western media and spoke more frankly and in decreasingly ideological terms.

- *Perestroika* (restructuring)

  This was Gorbachev's policy to transform the stagnant, inefficient command economy of the USSR into a decentralized, more market-oriented economy. Industrial managers and local government and party officials were granted greater autonomy, and open elections were introduced to democratize the Communist Party organization.

Gorbachev promoted his ideas in the West about both domestic reform in the USSR and future Soviet foreign policy through a book entitled *Perestroika: New Thinking for Our Country and The World*. In the introduction, Gorbachev declared that 'perestroika is no scientific treatise or propaganda pamphlet . . . it is rather a collection of thoughts and reflections on perestroika and . . . an invitation to dialogue' (Gorbachev, 1987: 9).

Gorbachev's initiatives unleashed forces of change not only within the communist states of Eastern Europe but also the Soviet Union itself, which quickly overran his original objective of reforming but not abandoning the Soviet Union's communist political and economic system. Between mid-1989 and late-1991, the Soviet Bloc effectively disappeared off the world stage and it is no exaggeration to say that the rest of the world looked on in astonishment. The challenge for theorists of international politics was how to explain or understand this.

For constructivists, a better understanding of the end of the Cold War and the subsequent collapse of the Soviet Union requires more than an examination of the material forces at play and their impact on how actors behave, as mainstream theories argue. It also needs to recognize the importance of how actors variously *interpret* the world around them, and how they subsequently act. For constructivists, the *interpretations* of the world by actors (either individuals or states)—how they see the material world and their place within it—helps to shape that world. If you think about neorealism and neoliberalism (discussed in Chapter 3), the emphasis is primarily on the anarchical *structure* of the international system and how it influences state behaviour. Neorealism and neoliberalism recognize that states may have some flexibility and options regarding how they act but argue that they ignore the structure of the international system at their peril. In contrast, constructivists depict states as active *agents* in that international system. The international system is not simply out there; it is made, sustained, and sometimes changed through the social interaction of the actors that exist within it.

The international system is, in other words, *socially constructed*. In contrast to the emphasis on the *structure* of the international system in mainstream IR theories, constructivists give considerable weight to the conscious *agency* of the actors within that structure. We will examine the agency–structure debate further in Section 8.3.

The essence of constructivism

For the early proponents of constructivist IR, the events of the late 1980s and early 1990s highlighted the weaknesses of the IR discipline's theoretical mainstream. In their view, neither neorealism nor neoliberalism had the theoretical tools to explain the peaceful end of the Cold War. Why? The answer, constructivists argued, lay in the failure to adequately consider the power of human consciousness. To put it differently, the mainstream theories' emphasis on material forces as the bases of power, fails to consider the power of *ideas* and values, or the significance of the *meaning* we attribute to things and actions.

The importance of how states see themselves and others and the impact this has on their social relationships is succinctly illustrated by the constructivist IR scholar Alexander Wendt's observation that '500 British nuclear weapons are less threatening to the United States than 5 North Korean nuclear weapons' (Wendt 1995: 73). The material facts about who possesses nuclear weapons, and how many, only tells us so much. The core argument of constructivism is that the reality of the world we find ourselves in is socially constructed rather than simply given. Many facts about the world are *social* facts; they are dependent upon human agreement as to their significance and value.

Karin Fierke offers a simple explanation of the essence of constructivism. Fierke notes that when something is constructed it is brought into being. For example, a piece of wood can be found in nature, but it can then be transformed into a range of possible objects, such as a rifle, a house beam, various kinds of musical instrument, or even a symbolic item of cultural significance such as a totem pole:

> Although these represent material objects in and of themselves, they do not exist in nature but have come about through acts of human creation. Once constructed, each of these objects has a particular meaning and use within a context. They are social constructs insofar as their shape and form is imbued with social values, norms, and assumptions rather than being the product of purely individual thought or meaning. (Fierke, 2021: 164)

Fierke goes on to argue that, in a similar fashion, social phenomena such as states, alliances of states, and international institutions 'take on specific historical, cultural and political forms that are the product of human interaction in a social world' (Fierke, 2021: 164).

'Anarchy is what state's make of it'

Fierke's claim that the international system as a social system is socially *constructed* is also succinctly captured in the title of one of the most famous early statements of constructivist IR thinking, an article by Alexander Wendt, entitled 'Anarchy is What States Make of It' (Wendt, 1992).

Wendt sought to challenge the mainstream depiction of the anarchical international system. As we discussed in Chapter 3, the neorealist Kenneth Waltz argued that it is the anarchic structure of the international system that is the primary determinant of state behaviour (Waltz, 1979). For Wendt, what is missing from Waltz's equation is consideration of how states, or, more precisely, the humans within states—whether that means policy makers, intellectuals, or members of the public—individually or collectively, understand their own identity. For Wendt, individual or collective identities influence states' interpretation of the significance of the formal condition of international anarchy. In other words, it affects what they make of it. Do they all interpret the condition of international anarchy in the same way, or agree on the implications of the international anarchy for them?

Wendt argues that neorealism and realism depict the prevalence of power politics and selfish behaviour by states as the inevitable, logical outcome of the absence of any supreme authority at the international level: the condition of international anarchy. Wendt argues that realism's depiction of international politics as consisting primarily in a struggle for power between selfish states is not simply a logical or causal consequence of an anarchical international system, as Waltz suggests. Rather it arises out of the practices of states:

> There is no 'logic' of anarchy apart from the practices that create and instantiate one structure of identities and interests rather than another; structure has no existence or causal powers apart from process. Self-help and power politics are institutions, not essential features, of anarchy. Anarchy is what states make of it. (Wendt, 1992: 394–395)

In other words, what mainstream IR theories take as the inherent features of the anarchical international system are, in Wendt's account, socially constructed: they are the result of processes—the ongoing social practices and interactions of states—not structure.

The implication of Wendt's argument is that if the processes of interaction between states changes, then the meaning we ascribe to international anarchy can also change. We have already discussed a significant example of this: the end of the Cold War. The Cold War did not end because the formal condition of international anarchy had disappeared; there still was no higher authority above the sovereign state. It ended, constructivists would argue, because key states, notably the USSR and the US shifted their understanding of what international anarchy means for them. Consequently, they changed their behaviour and their practices within that anarchy.

Of course, this also means that states can revert to an interpretation of international politics they may have previously held. Although there is no longer a Cold War, relations today between the US and Russia are undoubtedly very strained again, especially since the onset of Russia's invasion of Ukraine in 2022. This raises a range of interesting research questions from a constructivist point of view: what changes over the last three decades, if any, can be detected in how the US and post-communist Russia understand their own collective identities and how might we explain them? Has their perception of each other changed and if so, what might have brought that about? Has their understanding of the post-Cold War international system changed over time and if so, why?

Another example is the creation of the European Union (EU). Although the wider international system has not changed dramatically, over the last few decades several states have chosen nonetheless to join the EU. In so doing they accept the imposition of rules by a higher authority—the European Commission—and abide by the multiple norms and rules that accompany EU membership. In other words, although all states exist within a single anarchical international system, the 26 member states of the EU have chosen to put aside a substantial portion of their sovereign authority in their relations with each other and abide by a range of collectively agreed rules. Of course, the EU member states are still sovereign states in international law: just as they can join the EU, they can also leave it, as the UK did in 2020.

From a constructivist perspective, events such as the Cold War's end or the creation of the EU suggest that the neorealist claim that relations between sovereign states are primarily determined by the anarchical international system and therefore states will act in largely similar fashion is overly simplistic. As Nicholas Onuf, the IR scholar usually credited with introducing the term constructivism, puts it: we live in a 'world of our making' (Onuf, 1989). This is not to say that any idea that any individual has about the world around them is of social significance. It is to say that shared representations of the world, expressed through language and the development of social norms and rules about how to act in that world, can become powerful in themselves. Individual and shared representations of the world can come to shape how we act and how we see ourselves and others in that world. Most importantly, because such representations of the world are produced through social interaction, they can also change.

So far, we have seen that constructivism focuses in on the way that states variously interpret the social reality of existing within an international anarchical system. Not all states interact with other states in the same way. The key question, then, is why? Another noted constructivist, Emmanuel Adler, helps us here with a helpful analogy. Adler asks us to think about the difference between throwing a rock up into the air and doing the same with a bird. We know that if we throw the rock up into the air it will simply respond to the physical forces it is subjected to: the force with which it is thrown up, the effect of wind speed, gravity, and so on. Ultimately, it will simply fall to the ground. If you throw a bird up in the air, however, it might fly away and take any number of possible directions. This is because the bird is an active *agent* in the process and, having processed what is happening to it, will respond to the force of being thrown in a range of possible ways.

Similarly, when it comes to individuals, a group of individuals, or sovereign states: their reaction to material forces may vary:

> Where they go, how, when and why, is not entirely determined by physical forces and constraints; but neither does it depend solely on individual preferences and rational choices. It is also a matter of their shared knowledge, the collective meaning they attach to their situation, their authority and legitimacy, the rules, institutions and material resources they use to find their way, and their practices or even, sometimes, their joint creativity. (Adler, 1997: 321)

What Adler is highlighting is the significance of who the actors are, how they interpret the world around them, individually or collectively, and how they interact with each other over time. For these reasons, actors—be they individuals, social groups, or sovereign states—may over time come to respond similarly to each other when confronted with comparable circumstances. This means that, if states generally share a similar understanding of the implications of anarchy in international politics, they may well respond to it in rather similar fashion. Indeed, realists interpret the history of the international system as showing that they do just that. The constructivist point, however, is that the reasons why they may respond similarly are much more complex than a simple assumption that anarchy alone is the cause of state behaviour. From a constructivist point of view, it is not the anarchical international system that causes states to act in certain ways, but how those states *interpret* that system and their place in it. Importantly, such interpretations emerge over time because of a host of influencing factors both within and outside of states. Importantly, those factors and the interpretations that flow from them are not pre-given or fixed; they are social phenomena and thus can also change.

From a constructivist viewpoint, then, the dramatic end of the Cold War challenged realism's pessimism about the prospects for significant peaceful change at the international level, a pessimism grounded upon the presumption that international anarchy decisively inhibited such change. Yet, significant change occurred even though the formal condition of international anarchy remained. Therefore, to understand *how* the Cold War came to an end, constructivists argue, we need not only to look at such material things as the balance of power, the military and economic capabilities of the superpowers and so on, but also consider how key actors interpreted the world around them and how they socially interacted in that world. What was significant about the events that led up to the end of the Cold War was that the then leader of the Soviet Union, Mikhail Gorbachev, began to present the identity of the Soviet Union in new terms and began also to act in a manner that genuinely surprised the leadership of other states. Additionally, the then President of the US, Ronald Reagan, also responded positively. A new form of interaction emerged between the two leaders, which changed the nature of the relationship between the two superpowers. This had dramatic consequences not only for the two main protagonists but also for the rest of the international community as well. As Wendt (1992: 397) put it, 'if the United States and Soviet Union decide that they are no longer enemies, the Cold War is over'.

Of course, a realist or neorealist might argue that all that occurred at the end of the Cold War was a very significant change in the balance of power, from the bipolar balance of power of the Cold War to a unipolar system in which one state, the US, was dominant. The consequence of this was simply a realignment of various coalitions of states. For the constructivist, however, what needs explaining is why that dramatic shift occurred without any reversion to war, or any marked shift in the distribution of capabilities between the protagonists.

In the case of the EU, a realist might argue that it simply reflects the fact that states will cooperate if it is their national interest to do. In other words, it does not refute their view that states are ultimately driven by self-interest. For the constructivist, self-interest may indeed provide a part of an explanation of why states join the EU, yet the level of cooperation among the EU states goes well beyond anything comparable elsewhere in the world. After all, EU membership requires states to agree to agree to put aside their sovereign authority regarding a range of key areas, such as trade, fishing rights, food standards, human rights, labour laws, and so on. This does not mean that member states never disagree with each other or protest about EU regulations; they do argue and protest, often vociferously. Remembering that European history up until the mid-twentieth century was marked by frequent recourse to violent conflict between European states, yet the prospects of them going to war with each other now seems highly improbable. This runs counter to the realist view that war is an ever-present possibility in an anarchical international system (we discuss this claim in Chapter 3).

8.3 LOCATING CONSTRUCTIVISM ON THE SPECTRUM OF IR THEORIES

When you read about constructivism in IR you will probably see reference to it as occupying a theoretical middle ground between mainstream and critical theories. Most constructivists focus on aspects of international political interaction—such as ideas, norms, culture, and agency—that they see as inadequately considered or even ignored in mainstream theories.

Some of constructivism's key ideas were emerging on the margins of mainstream theory some time before people began to speak of a distinctive constructivist IR perspective. There are clear commonalities, for example, between contemporary constructivism's depiction of the international system as a social system and the English School's reference to an anarchical *society* of states. The English School argues that although states exist within an anarchical system of states, their behaviour can be constrained by their awareness that the international system of which they are members has some social properties, such as shared rules and norms (for more on this see Chapter 4). The earlier work of English School scholars is not usually seen as particularly radical or critical, but more as offering a correction to mainstream liberal and realist thinking. It does not explicitly reject mainstream theorizing but argues that it fails to capture the full range of influences on state behaviour. As we shall see throughout this chapter, some constructivists take a similar stance. They do not reject mainstream thinking in its entirety but seek to bring something additional to it. However, as we discuss in Chapter 4, the English School evolved a 'solidarist' wing which distanced itself more fully from mainstream IR thinking; similarly, there are constructivist scholars who also depict a greater distance between themselves and mainstream IR thinking.

Some of constructivism's core themes do seem comparable to key aspects of the various critical theories examined in this book. For example, both Critical International Theory (Chapter 6) and poststructuralism (Chapter 7) argue that our theories 'construct' the world. For Critical International Theory the interests that underpin theoretical enquiry help to determine how the international system is viewed, what is deemed to be significant in it, and so on. For poststructuralists, what is seen to be reality is brought into being through text and discourse. On face value then, it could be argued that all 'critical' theories are constructivist in a loose sense of the term. However, this risks brushing over some important distinctions within the constructivist scholarly community and between constructivists and various other types of critical scholar who, although seemingly sharing some of the assumptions of constructivism, are uncomfortable about being lumped in with it. Why is this?

Figure 8.1 represents a spectrum of IR theories and their position on the relationship between social reality and our theoretical accounts of it. On the left-hand side of Figure 8.1 are those mainstream IR theories that view social reality as existing independently of our descriptions of it. These theories endeavour to assess those descriptions according to how accurately they correspond with or truly reflect what they believe are the discernible facts of that reality. The objective is to *explain* the world definitively, i.e., as accurately, objectively, and as authoritatively as possible. On this view, the social theorist needs to step back from the social world they are investigating. This is the *positivist* approach,

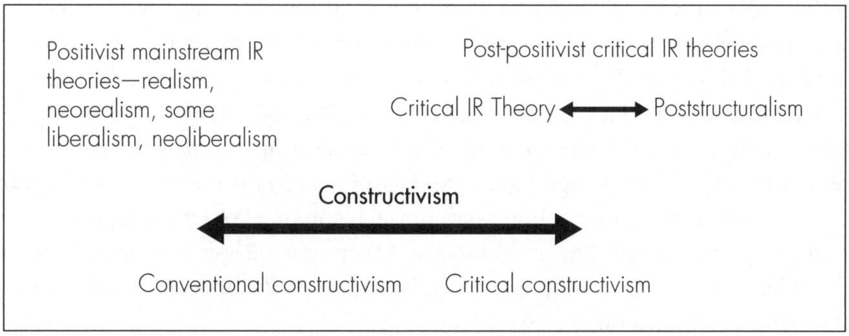

FIGURE 8.1 Locating constructivism on the spectrum of IR theories

derived from the classical scientific method, to which the mainstream theories of IR try to adhere (as discussed in Chapter 6, Section 6.2). In endeavouring to emulate positivism (few mainstream IR theorists claim that they can fully reproduce the scientific model), the key challenge for mainstream IR theorists is therefore to generate hypotheses about the international system which can somehow be objectively tested against reality and be shown to be true or as near as possible to a true and objective account of the world out there.

What all constructivists agree upon is that mainstream theories fail to grasp the *social* dimension of social systems such as the international system. Mainstream theories can tell us some things about the structure of the international system, and they also say something about the individual actors in that system. Where they struggle is in adequately capturing the relationships between those actors and the social system in anything other than rather simple terms. Constructivists usually refer to such mainstream theories as 'rationalist theories'. A leading constructivist, Christian Reus-Smit, argues that mainstream rationalist theories (and he is referring specifically to neorealism and neoliberalism) rest on three key assumptions:

1. They depict political actors, such as individuals or states, as pre-social, i.e., their identities and interests are seen to exist meaningfully prior to their social interaction. Additionally, political actors are depicted as inherently self-interested. They are primarily focused on pursuing their own interests. And such actors are seen as rational in that they endeavour to pursue the most effective and efficient ways to realize their own interests.

2. Actors' interests are also formed prior to social interaction (think here of the realist emphasis on the *national interest* that all rational states supposedly pursue).

3. When states interact, they do so for primarily strategic reasons. They engage in social interaction to maximize the realization of their own interests (Reus-Smit, 2022: 189).

The upshot of these key assumptions is that states as actors are depicted as engaging in international politics as fully formed entities and social interaction at the international level is depicted as being largely driven by strategic imperatives: the realization of actors' primary interests. This leads to an individualist *ontology* (we discuss the term ontology in Chapter 1, Section 1.3). For mainstream IR theories, Reus-Smit argues, 'actors are not therefore inherently social; they are not products of their social environment, merely atomistic rational beings that form social relations to maximize their interests' (Reus-Smit, 2022: 189). This means that mainstream IR theory not only regards states as the key actors in international politics, but also treats them as already fully formed actors who are predominantly concerned with pursuing their interests in an international system which is resistant to significant change. Given these assumptions, the possibility of developing hypotheses about their likely actions and, through empirical observation, testing those hypotheses in a positivist-like fashion to see if they are true seems to be both possible and productive. State behaviour appears to be largely predictable and both neorealism and neoliberalism work on this assumption.

On the right-hand side of the spectrum in Figure 8.1 are the post-positivist, critical IR theories. Of these, poststructuralism is arguably the furthest away from the positivist conception of acquiring knowledge. This is because it argues that social reality cannot be definitively known outside of our representations of it through language and text. The truth or falsity of our claims about social reality, about the inherent qualities of the actors that engage with the social world, and the motivations behind or reasons for their actions can never be definitively established in any positivist or scientific sense. This doesn't mean we can't say anything substantive about the social world, but it does say that our attempts to capture social relations in language are always incomplete in some way or another. This is because language always entails interpretation and other interpretations or representations are always possible (this is discussed more fully in Chapter 7). Additionally, poststructuralists see knowledge claims about the social world as inescapably intertwined with relations of power. We might find such representations useful and productive. They may be widely shared and treated as if they were true accounts of the 'world out there'. This means that they can have very substantial consequences. We cannot, however, establish that they do in fact offer definitive accounts of social reality. Instead, we should ask how certain representations and interpretations of the social world acquire their dominance and what is consequently repressed, obscured, or lost.

Critical International Theory also exists in the space between the positivist mainstream and poststructuralism, but closer to the poststructuralist end of the spectrum (that is why it is also included under 'post-positivist theories' on the right-hand side of Figure 8.1). Critical International Theory decisively rejects positivism because it sees knowledge and distinct human interests as inescapably intertwined (we discuss this further in Chapter 6, Section 6.2). Given this, Critical International Theory challenges the claim that mainstream theory can offer an objective explanation of the world, instead depicting it largely as working to manage and preserve the international status quo. In contrast to this, Critical International Theory explicitly critiques the status quo because it inhibits the pursuit of human emancipation (which we also discuss further in Chapter 6, Section 6.2). Critical International Theory does not claim to be, or pretend to be, a form of disinterested theoretical enquiry. However, Critical International Theory stops short of poststructuralism's wholesale rejection of a decisively knowable material world. Additionally, Critical International Theory holds onto to the idea of a universal human subject, something poststructuralism decisively rejects (we discuss poststructuralism's criticism of the idea of a universal human subject more fully in Chapter 7). After all, Critical International Theory seeks the emancipation of all humans from the chains of social injustice and inequality. For these reasons it sits close to poststructuralism but remains clearly distinct from it.

Somewhere between the positivist mainstream end of the spectrum and Critical International Theory lie the positions favoured by constructivists. They accept there is a real material world out there that exists independently of our representations of it, but they think that the social world—which includes international politics—is made up not only of that physical reality, but also of our collective ideas and interpretations of that reality which help to construct the social world. Additionally, actor's identities are in part constituted by the social structures within which they exist. Whereas mainstream theories of IR tend to depict actors as full-formed entities who operate within a pre-given structure, constructivists see both structure and the agency of actors as *mutually constitutive*: they help give meaning to each other.

Agency and Structure

The agency–structure relationship is central to understanding the constructivist IR perspective. A key source of constructivism's approach to the relationship between agents and structures is the work of the British sociologist Anthony Giddens, notably his theory of structuration (you can read more about Anthony Giddens in Key thinker 8.1).

KEY THINKER 8.1 ANTHONY GIDDENS

Anthony Giddens (born 1938) is one of Britain's best-known sociologists with a prolific output covering a wide range of topics from across the social sciences. One of his most noted contributions to social theory is the concept of *structuration* (Giddens, 1984).

Gidden argues that people (agents) make society (comprised of a complex of social structures) while also being constrained by it. Neither side of the duality of agency and structure can be analysed without reference to the other and there is no clear causal hierarchy between them. Structures (which include such things as institutions, sets of norms, and established expectations) constrain agency, yet they also make it possible by providing common frames of meaning.

Structures can be robust and stable given that social interaction can become routinized, thereby helping to sustain existing structures. They can, however, also change through changes in social interaction which can challenge or reject established structures and lead to their transformation into new structural forms. For Giddens, the impact of social interaction on either structures or agency cannot be predicted since the casual flow goes both ways.

Giddens' treatment of structuration is highly abstract and complex so translating it into empirical research has been a challenge. It has also been extensively criticized from a wide range of theoretical positions. Nonetheless, the core emphasis on the structure–agency relationship has become an enduring feature of modern sociology. It has also had a very significant influence on the development of constructivism in the IR field, much of which draws extensively on Gidden's pioneering work.

For constructivists, an actor's interests can change in significant ways according to their ideas about their self-identity and their understanding of the opportunities provided by the international system as a structured social system (as suggested by the example of Gorbachev's 'new thinking' about the Soviet Union for example). All states might well agree that the structure of the international system is anarchic because there is no authority that sits above the sovereign state. However, not all states necessarily see the anarchical international system in the same way. If actors' ideas about their own identity and how they can and should act in the international system change, then this has significant effects on the both the system and the actors within it.

The key point is that all constructivists want to take issue with what they see as the failure of mainstream IR theories to take sufficient account of the role of ideas and agency. They argue mainstream IR theories do not fully grasp the *social* nature of international reality and the important role that ideas held by agents (such as states) play in it. For constructivists how states interpret the structure of the international system matters. In other words, the meaning attached to the depiction of the international system as anarchic can vary between states. We can illustrate this point by looking at Sweden through constructivist lenses.

Sweden is widely known for its distinctively progressive foreign policy that evolved over several decades in the latter half of the twentieth century. In 1962, it was the first Western state to terminate bilateral relations with apartheid South Africa, 25 years before most other Western states (Sellström, 1999). It is the home of the world's most famous Peace Research Institute, known as SIPRI, founded in 1966. By 1974 Sweden became the first country in the world to reach the UN target of committing 0.7 per cent of Gross National Income to overseas development assistance (ODA or Foreign Aid). Since then, it has never gone below that target and has remained one of the world's most generous providers of ODA (alongside its Scandinavian neighbours and the Netherlands). Until very recently, Sweden always refused to formally join any military alliance such as NATO, even though it is clearly broadly politically aligned with the other Western powers. Sweden is also widely recognized as a key promoter of multilateralism and the rule of law in international politics and has a long history of accepting comparatively large numbers of refugees from active war zones. More recently, Sweden became the first state in the world to declare that it has adopted a feminist foreign policy (we discuss this also in Chapter 10).

These features along with various others have led to Sweden over the last few decades acquiring a reputation as a 'good state' (Lawler, 2005 and 2013a) or a 'good international citizen' (Linklater and Suganami, 2006: chapter 7). Yet in other respects, Sweden is a prototypical Western developed state; it maintains a standing army, it manufactures and exports weapons, it competes in international trade relations, and so on. From a constructivist position, the question arises as to why Sweden chooses nonetheless to act in the anarchic international system in such a comparatively distinctive way? How might we explain Sweden's understanding of its own identity and exercise of its agency in international politics?

Peter Lawler draws upon a constructivist approach to suggest that the answer may be found through investigation of distinctive features of Sweden's evolved sense of national identity. Such features include the evolution of Sweden as a highly developed welfare state, the history of Swedish neutrality, the role of developing government policy through consensus building, the influence of the Swedish Lutheran church, and the influence of the political concept of solidarity in Swedish political thinking (Lawler 1997, see also Lawler, 2005 and 2013a). Lawler suggests that in combination these have contributed to the formation of a distinctive view of the world and Sweden's place within it as well as feeding into Sweden's understanding of its national interest. Lawler does not claim to offer a definitive explanation in the positivist sense of the term, nor does he claim that all Swedes share in this representation of their state in the international system. Lawler is trying to develop a plausible interpretation or understanding of how a specific sense of national identity emerged, was sustained, and subsequently reflected in Sweden's foreign policy outlook—in how Sweden acts in the world.

Importantly, none of the features that suggest Sweden is an atypically progressive Western state are immutable. They are historical, social phenomena and as such they may be modified or even abandoned over time. Over the last few years, for example, Sweden has dramatically revised its immigration policy in response to a widespread domestic backlash against large numbers of refugees. Sweden's recent decision to join NATO (a consequence of Russia's invasion of Ukraine) and to abandon the label 'feminist foreign policy' (after a change in the governing coalition) raise further questions about the prospects for Sweden's progressive reputation. From a constructivist perspective, the key question is whether they are reflections of the hurly-burly of short-term politics in a democracy or symptomatic of a deeper change in Sweden's collective self-understanding and how it views the world.

The significance of the core constructivist claim that state identity and agency matter more than mainstream IR theories admit, should become clearer as we explore constructivism in more detail in the next section.

Conventional and critical constructivism

Like most theoretical approaches in the IR field, constructivism contains distinct strands which, amongst other things, are distinguished by differences in their relationship to mainstream IR thinking. It is because some constructivists endeavour to explore reconciliation with mainstream IR scholarship, and others pursue reconciliation with the critical IR theories that it has become commonplace to describe constructivism as occupying some kind of 'middle ground' between mainstream IR and critical IR.

To explore the theoretical location of constructivism further we will now explore two broad varieties of constructivism: conventional constructivism and critical constructivism (Hopf, 1998). It is important to bear in mind that this requires a bit of a simplification. As with most theoretical schools containing different stands within them, the divisions between them are often somewhat blurred and individual scholars may well work across them.

Conventional constructivism

Conventional constructivists see themselves as closer to the positivist end of our spectrum (the left-hand side of Figure 8.1) than other constructivists. They do not take issue with the basic theoretical assumptions of mainstream approaches, but they do criticize them for failing to sufficiently consider agents (i.e., states) as social phenomena, or the social dimensions of the interaction of agents. In other words, they have a problem with the *ontological* assumptions (about what kind of beings exist in the world) of mainstream or 'rationalist' IR theories but not with their *epistemological* standpoint (how we go about knowing things).

Mainstream IR theory takes both structure and agents (the actors within the structure) as fully formed and unproblematic. For constructivists, however, the ideas that actors hold about their own identities, how they understand their own interests and how these influence their social interaction with other actors should themselves be legitimate objects of enquiry. The objective then is to bring these 'social facts' into the development of a general theory of international politics. The conventional constructivist Jeffrey Checkel argues that constructivists' 'critique of neorealists and neoliberals concerns not what these scholars do and say but what they ignore: the content and sources of state interests and the social fabric of world politics' (Checkel, 1998: 324).

Checkel depicts constructivism as occupying a middle ground between mainstream theories and what he calls 'postmodernism' (what in this book is referred to as poststructuralism). Checkel argues that constructivism shares many of the substantive concerns of poststructuralism, such as the role of identity and discourse, but agrees with mainstream theories that the goal is to produce scientific, causal explanations. He argues that 'constructivists have rescued the exploration of identity from postmodernists' (Checkel, 1998: 325).

Audie Klotz also locates constructivism closer to the positivist end of the spectrum in Figure 8.1. Klotz suggests that there can be a fruitful division of labour between mainstream IR theory and constructivism in which constructivists look at how actors *acquire* their preferences or interests, while mainstream or 'rationalist' theories focus on how actors strategically act to best to *realize* those preferences and interests (Klotz, 1995, Chapter 2). Again, the objective is not to challenge the mainstream commitment to producing rigorous and testable explanations of international politics, but to address their perceived failure to investigate how actors acquire and may subsequently change their understanding of what their interests are.

Critical constructivism

Critical constructivists argue that investigating the social dimensions of structure and agency with positivist methods is unsatisfactory. This places them further along our spectrum towards the Critical International Theory and poststructuralist end (the right-hand side of Figure 8.1). They accept that there is a reality 'out there' that should be systematically and rigorously investigated, but they see positivist methodology as ill-suited to analysing the social dimensions of that reality.

For critical constructivists, however, ideas and the meanings we attach to our actions and the actions of others, are not simply objects or facts that can be investigated like any other. Christian Reus-Smit notes, for example, that early constructivists argued that the study of ideas and meanings requires an *interpretive* analysis, as they are resistant to any quantifiable measurement. The goal is not to offer an explanation, in the positivist sense, but to endeavour to offer a compelling interpretation of the relationship between the *intersubjective* (i.e., consciously shared) meanings that actors attach to their own actions and the actions of others and the social practices they engage in. This is something that he thinks that conventional constructivists not wishing to take issue with mainstream positivistic IR methodologies have forgotten (Reus-Smit, 2022: 199).

Along a similar vein, Karin Fierke, argues that constructivism shares with poststructuralism an emphasis on the significance of language (Fierke, 2021: 172). Fierke's language-based constructivism does not attempt to discern definitive causes of the actions of actors, such as states, but requires that we 'look and see' how social actors use language as they construct their world (Fierke, 2021: 172). Meanings are not a matter of being true or false but are generated through social interaction. Constructivism's task is to interpret the relationship between meanings and social interactions.

Fierke illustrates her point by noting the shift in the understandings of collective identity that occurred with the collapse of communist Yugoslavia after the end of the Cold War and the emergence of violent conflict between its constituent populations of Serbs, Croats, and Muslims. Intersubjective categories of identity can shift, and therefore can significantly affect social relations. In the case of Yugoslavia, the shift in the language of identity from an inclusive understanding of being Yugoslavian to ethnically grounded conceptions of identity—such as being Serbians, Croats, or Bosnian Muslims—produced different, more violent patterns of interaction between ethnic groups. Such violence included 'ethnic cleansing', wherein the armed forces of one group would endeavour to expel member, of another group from a territory over which they claimed control (Fierke, 2021: 172). These changes in domestic discourses of identity also impacted on the relations between those communities formerly within the sovereign state of Yugoslavia and the wider world as they struggled, often violently, to acquire their own sovereign statehood.

Fierke argues that constructivism should not focus on establishing *causality* but look at the *reasons* why things happen. The difference between reasons and causes is significant, Fierke argues, and they should not be conflated. Consider the task of hypothesizing the true cause of the decision by the US to invade Iraq in 2003. Several possible causes suggest themselves. Was it because of oil? Or was it a desire to bring about regime change in Iraq, something that the US administration at the time believed should have been undertaken in the first invasion of Iraq ten years earlier? Or was it because of the belief (later proven to be false) that Saddam Hussein's regime possessed weapons of mass destruction (WMDs), which was a key component of the US's official explanation? Establishing the truth or falsity of causal claims about the invasion is difficult, not least because we cannot get inside the minds of those who made the decision to invade. All these possible explanations are subject to conflicting interpretations. If, however, we ask *how* the invasion was made possible, different lines of enquiry emerge (Fierke, 2021:173).

Language games

Fierke draws here upon an article provocatively entitled 'Why Not Invade North Korea?' by another critical constructivist, Peter Howard, who also adopts a language-based approach (Howard, 2004). The article's title alludes to the fact that Iraq was just one of several states that at the time the US defined as members of an 'Axis of Evil' (which we examine in Key event 8.2). Both Howard and Fierke use the concept of a language game to capture the social relations between groups of actors. Howard writes 'the rules of the language game create possibilities, [which] makes things possible and give meaning to action' (Howard, 2004: 813). As in a board game, the idea of a language game is intended to capture the way language works to establish rules and norms governing social interaction. When we play a board game we interact with other players within a set of shared rules and norms—the rules of the game. Similarly, the idea of a language game is intended to show how through communication actors acquire shared understandings and become socialized into a rule-governed relationship with others. If an actor at some point refuses to follow the rules of the game or disputes their validity, their actions are interpreted, usually critically, by other actors in light of this.

Such language games can intersect in complex ways. For example, the US's identification of an Axis of Evil can be seen as the invocation of a set of rules governing US actions towards a group of states, but within them are subsets of rules governing relations with specific states in that group. To put it differently, there is a family of intersecting games which in some respects resemble each other but in other respects they are unique. This means that, although the US depicted both Iraq and North Korea as members of the Axis of Evil, it responded to them differently (see Key event 8.2).

KEY EVENT 8.2 THE 'AXIS OF EVIL'

Reference to an 'Axis of Evil' was a common trope of the George W. Bush US administration (2000–2009). Bush first referred to it in his inauguration speech and the author of that passage of the speech is commonly thought to have been David Frum, Bush's speech writer at the time. The phrase refers to those states that the US identified as being both 'state sponsors of terrorism' and actual or potential developers of illegal weapons of mass destruction.

The phrase was originally used to refer to North Korea, Iran, and Iraq, but in 2002 the Under-Secretary of State for Arms Control and International Security Affairs, John Bolton, added Cuba, Libya, and Syria. Bolton was noted for his adherence to a *neoconservative* political perspective. The 'neocons' depict the US as an exceptional state which is a bastion of core liberal values, notably freedom, and has a historic mission to defend and promote those values through its foreign policy. It is debateable whether Bush was a true neocon, but he appointed several of them to key positions in his administration.

Although neoconservatives espouse core liberal values, they also criticize liberal approaches to foreign policy for being too dovish on matters of defence and security and too multilateralist in international outlook. Neoconservatism advocates a hawkish US foreign policy, is generally hostile to multilateral institutions such as the UN, and advocates the pursuit of regime change by force, if necessary, in states such as the supposed members of an Axis of Evil.

In the wake of the 9/11 terror attacks, neoconservative foreign policy, centred on directly confronting the Axis of Evil, clearly resonated with a significant section of the American public. However, the inconclusive outcomes of subsequent US military interventions in Afghanistan and Iraq, which failed to transform those states into stable democracies, saw the influence of neoconservatism decline markedly. Perhaps most symbolic of this decline was Barack Obama's victory in the presidential election in 2009, after which reference to an Axis of Evil disappeared from US foreign and security policy rhetoric.

In late 2002 when the US was preparing to invade Iraq, North Korea was known to be developing a covert nuclear weapons programme and had long expressed open hostility towards the US and its allies, South Korea and Japan. Even though North Korea posed a more evident direct threat to the US and certainly to the US ally, South Korea, the US responded with diplomacy rather than invasion. Howard argues that US President Bush's explanation of the reasons for the US decision to invade was based on the claim that although North Korea and Iraq were both developing WMDs in the form of nuclear weapons, Iraq was also developing other forms of WMDs (notably, chemical weapons). Additionally, Iraq was perceived to be more likely to use them. In other words, it was Iraq's perceived *intentions* that mattered.

Both North Korea and Iraq were classed in similar linguistic terms—as members of an Axis of Evil—and this set the broad tone of the relationship between the US and these two states. Nonetheless, each relationship had different historical precedents. The US had engaged with North Korea over its development of nuclear weapons since 1994, when North Korea threatened to withdraw from the Nuclear Non-Proliferation Treaty (which prohibits any states other than existing recognized nuclear powers from developing nuclear weapons). Both sides were engaging in a complex diplomatic process which also involved other actors, notably Japan and South Korea (Howard, 2004: 814–822).

When it came to Iraq, however, the relationship was conducted very differently. Because of the UN-approved invasion in 1990–1991 and a subsequent long-running UN-backed sanctions regime, the relationship between Iraq and the wider international community was already conducted in a language game centred on the application of force and the threat of more of it. However, international support for sanctions eroded throughout the 1990s leaving the US (along with the UK) increasingly alone in seeking to contain and confront Iraq (Howard, 2004: 824). It had become a much more unilateral game, with none of the complex diplomatic interaction of the US–North Korea relationship. In accusing Iraq of possessing WMDs (falsely, as it turned out), President Bush made the invasion possible within a language game that had already established an aggressive, hostile tone to the US–Iraq relationship and in so doing effectively ruled out a diplomatic approach.

For language-based constructivists, a focus on language games can highlight differences in an actor's relationships with other actors which theories looking for general causes are unable to do. On this basis, these kinds of constructivists criticize mainstream general theories of IR which try to identify universal material causal factors—such as military power or wealth—as the principal determinants of relations between states. Other varieties of constructivism emphasize the importance of universal norms in explaining state practices. Although they differ in their treatment of them (we discuss the significance of norms further in Section 8.4).

Constructivism and the 'middle ground' of the IR theory spectrum

It should be clear by now that when the conventional and critical varieties of constructivism are taken into consideration, constructivism occupies a broad part of the *epistemological* spectrum of IR theories. If you look at Figure 8.1 you will see that the line that represents constructivism stretches from the middle of mainstream positivist IR theories on the left-hand side across to the middle of the critical IR theories on the right-hand side. The conventional varieties of constructivism generally can be located on the left-hand side of the constructivist range because they share some of the epistemological characteristics of mainstream IR theory. Nonetheless they are also critical of mainstream IR theory, especially neorealism for neglecting the agency of states and the impact of interpretation on the conduct of international relations. As we note in Chapter 3, neorealism is also known as structural realism and is arguably the most overtly positivist of mainstream IR theories. It therefore occupies the far left-hand side of our IR theoretical spectrum.

The critical constructivists are post-positivist in epistemological orientation so sit on the right-hand side of the constructivist range, overlapping with Critical International Theory but falling short of poststructuralism. Because even critical constructivists generally accept that there is a material reality that exists outside of our interpretations of that reality, poststructuralists argue that constructivism is quite literally not constructivist enough. From a poststructuralist perspective, the constructivist acceptance of the existence of structures, by which they mean forces constraining the agency of states independently of how states interpret them, is problematic (Zehfuss, 2002).

In effect, poststructuralists argue, constructivism shares with mainstream IR the presumption that there is a given international reality out there, even if states as agents might interpret it differently. For poststructuralists the claim to know definitively the structure of international politics is itself also the product of interpretation (we explore the poststructuralist critique of any claim to know reality more fully in Chapter 7). Therefore, the line indicating constructivism's range stops at the edge of poststructuralism.

It must be remembered that Figure 8.1 is intended to offer only an illustrative approximation of the relative location of IR theories. As you become more familiar with the nuances of constructivism as well as other IR theories, you may well form your own distinctive view of their relationship to each other.

8.4 **THE IMPORTANCE OF IDENTITY**

As we have seen, constructivism emphasizes the importance of the identity of states as actors in the international system. Constructivism's interest in identity is in marked contrast to much of mainstream IR theorizing. Outside of IR there is an established tradition within the disciplines of political science and sociology of theorizing the state from a wide range of perspectives. Mainstream IR theory has long been criticized, however, for taking states for granted and failing to investigate them as complex social actors despite the central role they play in mainstream IR theories. Realism is particularly noted for its lack of interest in investigating the state as an actor to any significant extent (although, as we note in Chapter 3, Section 3.8, neoclassical realism does endeavour to take domestic politics into greater account). This is especially the case with neorealism because it's 'outside-in' viewpoint depicts the behaviour of states as largely determined by the structure of the international system (which you can read about in Section 3.4

in Chapter 3). In so doing, it effectively dismisses the significance of variations in the internal nature of states.

In contrast, liberal IR scholarship has accorded comparatively greater significance to the differences between states. As we see in Chapter 2, classical liberalism takes a more 'inside-out' view of international politics and therefore recognizes that the form of the state—whether it is a liberal democracy or not, for example—matters in international politics. The liberal idea of *complex interdependence* that emerged in the 1970s also depicts states as containing a range of sub-state actors that increasingly operate at the international or global level. Nonetheless, liberal and neoliberal IR scholarship have also generally eschewed extensive consideration of the state as a social actor. In constructivism, however, the starting point is the depiction of the international system of states as an international *social* system of states, the analysis of which is seen to require investigation of states as inherently social entities.

Constructivists depict states as operating with a collective sense of themselves and their place in the world which frames how states see the world and other actors within it. This might in fact be a dominant understanding of a state's identity (see our discussion of Sweden in Section 8.3, for example), which not all the people residing within it necessarily share but enough do (or do not actively question it) for it to become stabilized and thus endure over time. It might also be a contested sense of national identity, especially if the state has undergone significant historical change internally, because of external influences, or a complex mix of both. For example, Great Britain was once a major imperial global power, and this undoubtedly influenced the dominant view of the identity of the British state. With the ending of the British Empire, a self-understanding of Britain as a major imperial power inevitably became unsustainable and had to change. This has undoubtedly happened, even if many observers might still detect the residue of an imperial past in British collective self-understanding. Similarly, Britain's recent exit from the EU has undoubtedly generated public debate about what Britain's identity is post-EU.

Another example of how changing historical circumstances impact upon the identity of a state would be today's Germany. Germany's sense of its identity has clearly changed dramatically since the end of the Second World War and the collapse of Nazi Germany. At the beginning of the Cold War there were two Germanies: a German Federal Republic aligned with the West, and a communist German Democratic Republic aligned with the Soviet Union. At the Cold War's end, they merged back into a single state which, moreover, sees itself as a key advocate of European cooperation within the EU. We return to the case of Germany later in this section.

The point that constructivism makes is that a state's sense of its identity contributes to how that state interprets the structure of the international system and its actual or potential agency within it. Rather than seeing sovereign states as merely a set of actors on a global stage pursuing a broadly similar set of objectives (their 'national interest'), constructivism invites the consideration of states as complex social entities.

What constructivists are endeavouring to highlight is the socially dynamic nature of international politics. Wendt argues that a state's identity is made in part through social interaction. Wendt illustrates this through an imaginary interaction between two state actors: Ego and Alter. The interaction goes like this:

- Ego and Alter meet for the first time.
- Ego starts with a gesture, such as an advance, a retreat, a brandishing of arms, a laying down of arms, or an attack.
- Alter then must infer Ego's intentions, and, given that the exchange is taking place within an anarchical system, Alter must decide whether Ego is a threat.
- Alter may wrongly infer Ego's intent, but there is no reason for Alter to assume before the gesture that Ego is threatening. It is only through signalling and interpreting that the costs and probabilities of being wrong can be determined (Wendt, 1992: 404–405).

Wendt concludes that social threats are constructed, not natural. They emerge through social interaction and the interpretations of each other by participants in that interaction. In contrast to the realist tendency to take the preferences and interests of states as largely given, Wendt argues that 'identities are the basis of interests' (Wendt, 1992: 398). From a realist perspective, in an anarchical international system the threat of war is an ever-present possibility, and the prudent state should start from this assumption. Therefore, Alter should start with the presumption that Ego is a potential threat because, like Alter, it is another sovereign state pursuing its selfish national interest until Ego's actions convincingly suggest otherwise.

Wendt counters the realist view by arguing that the form that international anarchy takes, and the international security environment engendered by it depends on how the identities of states are defined. If states consider each other as actual or potential enemies, there will be a self-help system of the worst kind. If, however, they treat each other as friends and partners, then a *security community* might develop (think here of the contemporary relationship between former enemies, such as the UK and Germany today).

In his later work, Wendt proposes three types of anarchical systems that can emerge over time, depending on how states see themselves and each other—as enemies, rivals, or friends—and interact accordingly. Wendt depicts types of international anarchy as the products of distinctive ideas which generate three different forms of an international culture:

- In a *Hobbesian* anarchical system (named after the seventeenth-century English philosopher, Thomas Hobbes, who, as we note in Chapter 3 was highly influential in the emergence of realism) the perception that all other states are actual or potential enemies leads to the emergence of a self-help system. This is the kind of anarchical system that figures prominently in realism and neorealism.
- The *Lockean* culture of anarchy (named after John Locke—a key figure in the emergence of modern liberalism during the *Enlightenment*) emerges around the perception of states engaged in rivalry rather than enmity. States may be in competition but there is a modicum of mutual respect for the principles of sovereignty

and the rights of other states. Consequently, the likelihood of violent interaction is reduced significantly. This depiction of international anarchy accords very much with the English School's conception of an anarchical society of states (which we examine in Chapter 4).

- In a *Kantian* international culture, the relationship between states is conducted primarily in the form of friendship, governed by an extensive range of shared norms (as suggested in Kant's famous eighteenth-century pamphlet *Perpetual Peace*, which was discussed in Chapter 2). Key among these are two rules: that disputes should be settled without recourse to war or the threat of it; and states will respond collectively should one of them be threatened (Wendt, 1999: 246–312).

Wendt's point is that the meaning of international anarchy is not fixed but is a social construction that can change in reflection of different understandings of state identity. His three types of international anarchical culture may co-exist within different regional sub-systems or spread across the whole international system.

If states' perceptions of each other shift over time a tipping point may be reached wherein new representations of self and other may emerge and determine the logic of the overall system (Wendt, 1999: 264). Consequently, the conception of a state's interests will also vary according to how states now view the international anarchy and the opportunities or risks that it presents. This means that states that see themselves as members of a specific community of states—such as the EU or NATO or the UK-US in their so-called 'special relationship'—may understand their interests regarding their relations with other members of the community differently to their relations with other states with whom they may have a more limited or temporary alliance, or with states with whom they have a generally hostile relationship governed by mutual feelings of suspicion or threat.

THINK CRITICALLY 8.1 WENDT'S THREE TYPES OF ANARCHICAL INTERNATIONAL SYSTEM

Wendt (1999) argues that there are three types of international system and culture: Hobbesian, Lockean, and Kantian.

1. Which, if any, of Wendt's three types of international system and culture do you think best captures the contemporary international system (Hint: think about the merits of liberal, realist, or English School depictions of international politics here).

2. To what extent if any, do you think any of Wendt's three types captures the foreign policy outlook of your own home state, or those with which you are particularly familiar?

3. Do you think Wendt is right to suggest that these different conceptions of an anarchical system of states can co-exist at, say, a regional, sub-systemic level? What examples would you draw upon to support your answer? (Hint: think about the relationship between member states of the EU, or other regional organizations such as the Association of Southeast Nations (ASEAN), or the African Union (AU)).

'Systemic' constructivism and 'unit-level' constructivism

Recalling the discussion of the differences between conventional and critical varieties of constructivism in Section 8.3, it should be noted that Wendt follows the widespread constructivist convention of depicting his work as occupying a middle ground between mainstream IR theory and 'postmodernism' (what we refer to as poststructuralism in this book). By his own admission, however, Wendt also sees himself as a 'thin' constructivist (Wendt, 1999: 1–2). By this Wendt means that his focus is primarily pitched at the international level, the systemic interaction between states. Although he sees state identities, and the conceptions of a state's interests that flow from these, as essential components of his 'social theory of international politics', Wendt does not seek to thoroughly investigate the social qualities of states, as Lawler's work on Sweden endeavours to do for example. For this reason, critical constructivists see Wendt's constructivism as an example of conventional constructivism that does not wish to stray too far from the IR mainstream. Reus-Smit describes Wendt's constructivism as 'systemic constructivism' (Reus-Smit, 2022: 194). This is because Wendt shares with neorealism a primary focus on the international system itself and his interest in state identity as a key influence on a state's agency is confined primarily to how this affects a state's understanding of the structure of the international system.

In contrast to Wendt's approach, what Reus-Smit calls 'unit-level' constructivism focuses much more on the origins of norms within states and their impact upon state identity. In arguing that the identity of a state informs its interests and actions, Wendt offers an important challenge to neorealism's account of the international anarchic system. Nonetheless, for Reus-Smit this is a too narrowly focused constructivism. It can tell us something about the implications of changes in state identity for state behaviour in the international system, but it cannot tell us how those changes came about because it does not consider the domestic sources of normative and ideational forces as the factors that drive the creation of a state's sense of identity.

The Construction of National Identities

Peter Katzenstein's work on the role of norms in constructing Japanese and German national identities provides a good example of unit-level constructivism. Katzenstein's comparative study of Germany and Japan is intended to bring out the significance of domestic and international norms in forming and sustaining varying conceptions of national identity which help to determine state behaviour and meet public understandings of national identity (Katzenstein, 2003).

Both Japan and Germany have comparable experiences of military defeat followed by foreign occupation, because of being on the losing side of the Second World War. Both states subsequently underwent a transition from authoritarian forms of government to democracies, and both evolved in the post-1945 era to become powerful economic actors in the world economy. Both states have also experienced periods of heightened domestic terrorism, and both have had to develop policies in response to the threat of international terrorism in the context of the US-led international 'War on Terror' that followed the 9/11/2001 attacks in the US. Nonetheless, the two states have markedly different internal and external security policies. Part of the reason for this, Katzenstein argues is because, 'their conceptions of self and other differ greatly' (Katzenstein, 2003: 737).

When it comes to domestic security—notably counterterrorism policies—Japan has developed an informal, unilateral, low-tech, and largely reactive approach. The Japanese police have relied extensively on close ties with the public, particular regarding collecting intelligence. One of the consequences of their initial success in confronting terrorist groups within Japan in the late 1960s was that these groups relocated overseas, to the Middle East and North Korea. Official responses to incidents of domestic terrorism, such as the 1995 Sarin Gas attack in the Tokyo subway system by the radical religious sect Aum Shinrikyo, were met with a comparatively tepid response and Japan's security services seemed to take little interest in Aum Shinrikyo's very extensive international resources and connections. Despite its violent record. Aum Shinrikyo was never banned by the Japanese state. Similarly, when Japanese citizens have been caught up in overseas terrorist incidents, such as being taken hostage, the Japanese government has tended to prefer to pay ransoms rather than risk the loss of life (Katzenstein, 2003: 745–747). Japan has subsequently agreed to sign up to the principle of no concessions to terrorist demands adopted by most other developed states, but the commitment remains, Katzenstein argues, largely untested.

Regarding external security, it is notable that Japan did not even have a Ministry of Defence until 2007. In the wake of the 9/11 attacks, Japan clearly wanted to dispel the image that had evolved since 1945 of it being a largely passive international actor and offered immediate military support to the US, albeit of a largely symbolic nature. Since the mid 1990s, the Japanese military—known as the Self-Defence Force (SDF)—has attempted to work more actively with the armed forces of other states, especially in responding to international terrorism, thereby helping to shed the widespread image of Japan as having a somewhat-toothless pacifist defence policy (Katzenstein, 2003: 752). Japan's defence budget is now the 6th largest in the world, and yet Japan's deployment of troops overseas has remained very limited and designed to reduce the risk of them being involved in violent contact with armed forces of any other state to an absolute minimum. This is perhaps not surprising given that Japan's foreign and security policy is officially grounded on the idea of 'Japan's orientation as a peace-loving nation' and the SDF's role is defined in reference to Japan's role as a 'proactive contributor to peace' (see the website of the Japanese Ministry of Foreign Affairs at mofa.go.jp). Katzenstein argues that Japan's state behaviour is essentially non-violent and there is widespread public resistance to any dramatic change in this (Katzenstein, 1996).

In the case of both law enforcement and national defence, the post-war Japanese state has displayed a consistent reluctance to deploy physical violence in the name of state security. A common explanation of this is that Japan's pacifistic tendencies are a result of the US imposing a national constitution upon Japan after its defeat in the Second World War. This placed severe constraints on Japan's capacity to develop and deploy armed forces for anything other than self-defence, coupled with a reliance on the US as its security provider. Katzenstein argues, however, that a much richer explanation is provided by investigating the role of pacifist and anti-militarist norms that have become widely diffused and embedded within Japanese society since 1945. These include widespread public resistance to Japan becoming militarily involved overseas, or the Japanese state significantly extending its powers to combat domestic or international terrorism. In his view, Japan has a strong sense of internal community, but in contrast it holds to an essentially 'Hobbesian' view of the international system of states in which Japan prefers, nonetheless, to pursue power and status through economic rather than military strength (Katzenstein, 2003: 737). Although there are clear signs of shifts towards a more muscular security policy, this is likely to always be constrained by embedded public resistance to any fundamental change in Japan's identity. Additionally, Japan's military and security posture is predominantly developed in reference to its bilateral strategic partnership with the US.

In Germany's case, Katzenstein sees the converse of Japan's combination of a strong sense of domestic community and a weak sense of being part of an international community of states (Katzenstein, 2003: 737). When it comes to internal security, Germany also experienced periodic high levels of domestic terrorism—notably from the ultra-leftist Baader-Meinhoff Gang, also known as the Red Army Faction, in the 1970s—but its response has been very different to that of Japan. Germany's police do not enjoy the same close relationship with civil society as seen in Japan. Consequently, it deploys significant resources, uses high-technology, and cooperates extensively with transnational organizations in the fight against both domestic and international terrorism (Katzenstein, 2003: 741–742).

Regarding external security and defence policy, the impact of widespread German public antipathy to militarism and the use of force, as in Japan, has undoubtedly served to influence policy direction. Nonetheless, Germany has been an active member of NATO since 1955 and has also taken a leading role in the formation of international agreements on the prevention of terrorism, notably the 1977 UN Convention on Terrorism and European Convention on the Suppression of Terrorism (Katzenstein, 1996: 175). Katzenstein argues that Germany has adopted a highly multilateralist approach to foreign and security policy with a strong emphasis on the development of international norms. Also consider Germany's central role in the EU and its consistent advocacy of the further development of European Integration.

There are elements of German society that challenge the broad thrust of Germany's foreign and security policies, especially recently. Over the last few years, there has been a significant growth in right-wing populist nationalism and signs of hostility towards membership of the EU, especially in the regions that were part of the former East Germany (Lees, 2018). Additionally, the question of providing military support for Ukraine after Russia's invasion of Eastern Ukraine in 2022 has generated considerable public debate in Germany (Applebaum, 2022). Nonetheless, the identity of Germany as a cooperative, multilaterally oriented state with an aversion to military engagement—except as part of a multilateral operation with clear support from the wider international community—remains firmly in place. The preamble to the German constitution commits Germany to 'promote world peace as an equal partner in a united Europe' and this still accords with a broad public normative consensus.

THINK CRITICALLY 8.2 CONSTRUCTING NATIONAL IDENTITIES

With reference to the state where you reside or a state with which you are particularly familiar or interested in,

1. Do you think it has a national identity or collective sense of self which is widely shared by its residents? If not, why not? If so, how would you explain it?
2. What do you think are key elements in the construction of that collective sense of identity? (Hint: do certain socially embedded norms or values play a key role, have key historical episodes influenced it, has the national identity been imposed from above?)
3. How stable is the dominant sense of national identity? (Hint: think about the degree to which it is or may become contested?)

From the analysis of norms to normative analysis

Despite their different levels of analysis, Wendt's systemic constructivism and the unit constructivism of Katzenstein both fall under the rubric of conventional constructivism. From a critical constructivist perspective, their work is conventional because, like most mainstream IR theory, these authors avoid overtly revealing their political and normative preferences. Their constructivist analyses undoubtedly endeavour to offer a theoretically richer account of international politics, but they step back from engaging in any explicit critique of the prevailing international order. In contrast, Lawler's unit-level analysis of 'good states' such as Sweden, discussed in Section 8.3 is openly normative in that it overtly endeavours to advance a case for progressive, more morally driven Western foreign policies that consider concerns raised by critical IR theories (Lawler, 2005 and 2013a).

Constructivists who see themselves as theoretically situated closer to Critical International Theory and other critical IR theories are less reticent about revealing their normative intentions. Critical constructivists such as Christian Reus-Smit and Richard Price argue that constructivism can add empirical substance to what they see as the overly abstract reflections on alternative forms of international and world order offered by Critical International Theorists (Price and Reus-Smit, 1998). Here we can see a somewhat different conception of constructivism as a 'middle ground'. Whereas conventional constructivism aims primarily to provide a richer theoretical account of international politics to that offered by mainstream IR theories (the left-hand side of Figure 8.1), critical constructivists endeavour to develop a theoretical dialogue with critical IR theories, especially Critical International Theory (the right-hand side of Figure 8.1).

As we note in Chapter 6, Section 6.4, Critical Theorists, such as Andrew Linklater, have explored the potential for new forms of more inclusive community to emerge that overcome the exclusionary dimensions of the sovereign state. Much of this kind of argument rests on the premise that new transnational norms are emerging and, further, that peoples' senses of identity can and do extend above and below their identity as citizens of specific sovereign states. Reus-Smit and Price argue that constructivist research can bridge the sort of rather abstract normative philosophical work of Linklater and others and the empirical study of how norms emerge in the present, and how they might emerge in the future.

This critical constructivist standpoint sees constructivism as engaged not just in the observation and analysis of changes in practices at the international level, but also in helping to bring desired changes about:

> Only by placing our normative contemplations in dialogue with our empirically informed accounts of the limits of possibility can we arrive at practices that will lead to more inclusive, less violent patterns of communal identification and interaction. (Price and Reus-Smit, 1998: 287)

Price and Reus-Smith made these remarks more than 20 years ago. Even a cursory look at today's world shows the rise of nationalist populism not only within Western liberal states, but also in countries such as Russia, India, the US, and Brazil. At the very least, this suggests that the realization of more inclusive forms of communal identity above the national level is likely to be an uphill battle. If Price and Reus-Smit are right, however, then critical constructivist analysis of how more exclusionary norms and understandings of collective identity emerge and are sustained within specific national communities could arguably aid in the understanding and eventual transcendence of the barriers to a more inclusive and less violent world. In other words, understanding how specific states view the international order requires investigation into how norms of social interaction are generated and sustained within those states and then go on to influence their international outlooks and policies.

8.5 **THE IMPORTANCE OF NORMS**

As we note throughout Section 8.3, reference to norms figures prominently in constructivist analysis of international politics. However, constructivists vary in their approach to the analysis of norms. A norm can refer to rules or expectations, principles, social standards of acceptable practice, or dominant social values. These overlapping meanings can be confusing at first sight.

Constructivists do not claim to be the first to recognize the importance of norms. Indeed, reference to norms is a feature of several IR perspectives. When the English School of IR theory (which is the subject of Chapter 4) emerged in the 1960s and 1970s, its distinctive conceptual claim was that states existed within an anarchical *society* of states. By replacing the more usual reference to an international *system* with the term *society*, the English School endeavours to highlight the role of agreed rules or norms in the practice of international politics, particularly in the preservation of international order. The preeminent English School theorist, Hedley Bull, argued that 'states conceive themselves to be bound by a common set of rules in their relations with one another and share in the working of common institutions' (Bull, 1977: 13).

Subsequently, English School scholars have gone on to explore the expansion and evolution of the rule-governed dimensions of international politics, in the form of such things as the development of the international human rights regime. The English School's emphasis on the role of norms, rules, and institutions in the maintenance of international order very much prefigures the concerns of contemporary constructivists. In depicting the international system of states as a form of society, the English School was one of the first schools of IR thought to begin to explore international politics in a more sociological fashion, something that constructivists have sought to develop further.

Even within the mainstream of realist and liberal IR scholarship there has been some acknowledgement of the influence of norms on state behaviour. This has been especially the case within liberal IR thinking, broadly defined. In Chapter 2 we see how the discipline of IR emerged in the aftermath of the First World War out of a liberal concern with exploring the sorts of rules and institutions that might prevent such a war occurring again. Earlier scholarship on such things as the emergence of the project of European integration (which led to the establishment of the EU) and the process of decolonization, wherein former colonies acquired their independent statehood, recognized the impact of norms on state behaviour and state identity. When states became part of the European integration project they signed up to a range of rules and norms governing their relationship with other member states. Similarly, the decolonization process after 1945 reflected increasingly widespread public criticism of colonialism within colonizing states as well as resistance to it within colonized countries. In other words, it impacted on both sides of the debate (Finnemore and Sikkink, 1998: 887). Decolonization constituted a process of change in both domestic and international norms of acceptable state conduct.

However, ideas and norms are largely treated in mainstream IR as peripheral phenomena pertaining primarily to individual actors. For example, a focus on norms and ideas may tell us something about how the foreign policy of a specific state is formulated, as in the case of the foreign policy of a liberal state reflecting the influence of liberal values and principles, for example. Both classical realists and liberal scholars also recognize that states do seek such things as respect and legitimacy in the eyes of other states, and that this can influence their behaviour. Nonetheless, the mainstream emphasis on the material determinants of state behaviour, coupled with the influence of the positivist model of social scientific theoretical enquiry (not least the requirement of objectivity), have served to limit the analysis of norms and the role of ideas in IR more generally.

In the view of some constructivists, their interest in norms is part of a wider 'ideational turn' within the discipline. This entails a return to seeing ideas as significant within the IR discipline, while also opening new lines of theoretical enquiry (Finnemore and Sikkink, 1998: 888). Constructivism examines how international norms emerge and what role they play in the co-constitutive relationship between international actors and the structure of the international system.

Norms, normativity, and constructivism

We return at this point to a consideration of the relationship between norms and normative analysis. For constructivists, norms are expressions of *intersubjective* (shared) understandings about appropriate behaviour. However, it is hard to detach the concept of a norm entirely from the notion that a norm is not merely an agreed rule, practice, or the established way of doing things, but it is also something that *should* be upheld, unless a good reason can be given for not doing so. An interest in norms is often seen to suggest that you are engaging in *normative* enquiry, in other words explicitly advocating what actors *ought* to do, rather than merely describing or explaining what they *are* doing.

The term *normative* is usually applied to scholarship that explicitly seeks to pass judgement on standards of practice or explore the right way to do things. For example, there are moral philosophers who look at notions of international justice, or the moral dimensions of war. As we note in Chapter 6, Critical International Theory has an explicitly normative dimension because it openly pursues the realization of human emancipation. However, from a mainstream IR point of view, normative thinking is inherently problematic. On this view, analysing international politics through a specific moral perspective or passing moral judgement on the conduct of international politics is not sufficiently objective. It breaches the separation of *is* (how things are) and *ought* (how things should be) that is central to a positivist model of social scientific enquiry. For this reason, overtly normative theoretical enquiry is either avoided by mainstream IR theorists entirely or explicitly rejected as a different kind of theoretical activity that does not qualify as properly social scientific research.

This gives us some pointers as to how conventional constructivists deal with the issue of focusing on the role of norms and ideas in international politics without being overtly normative. From a conventional constructivist perspective, norms are legitimate objects for scholarly enquiry because they contribute to the constitution and sustenance of a state's identity, its national sense of collective self. Adherence to norms may reflect a dynamic process of changes in how a state is perceived both by itself and others. Adherence to, or promotion of, specific norms may work also to confirm and uphold an already settled sense of state identity (Katzenstein, 1996: 5). Additionally, norms are seen to form a part of an international social structure comprised of intersubjective knowledge, rules, and beliefs within which actors interact. This *normative structure* not only acts as a constraint upon actors by establishing rules and principles of international social interaction, but also helps to constitute the identity and interests of the actors themselves. A realist would argue that states may uphold international norms because there are perceived material benefits in doing so, but constructivists claim that states adhere to norms also because this becomes connected with their sense of selves: their identity.

It is useful at this point to recall Figure 8.1 in Section 8.3. This shows that conventional constructivists locate themselves closer to the positivist end of the theoretical spectrum. Although they place the role of norms much more firmly in the foreground than mainstream theories, conventional constructivists endeavour to show how the role of norms can be empirically studied in a rigorous and properly social scientific fashion.

One well-known example of this is Martha Finnemore and Kathryn Sikkink's study of what they call 'the life cycle of norms' (Finnemore and Sikkink, 1998: 895).

The life cycle of norms

Finnemore and Sikkink argue that although the evidence of the impact of norms is indirect, it is possible nonetheless to trace the effects of norms systematically. Because norms imply a sense of what Finnemore and Sikkink call a 'shared moral assessment', they 'leave an extensive trail of communication among actors that we can study' (Finnemore and Sikkink, 1998: 892). Such communication may include attempts by states to justify why they are not upholding a norm.

Finnemore and Sikkink argue that the life cycle of norms has three stages:

- Norm emergence
- Norm cascade
- Norm internalization.

Norms emerge in a variety of ways through advocacy by a range of different actors, what Finnemore and Sikkink call 'norm entrepreneurs'. These may be individuals or organizations working at both the international and domestic levels, who for a variety of reasons (such as altruism, empathy, or belief in some specific ideas or values), try to persuade others of the need for a norm to become widely accepted to change the behaviour of actors within a social system. For a norm to have effects at the international level, it needs the endorsement of states. If norm entrepreneurship is successful it will result in the institutionalization of a norm and its effective translation into specific sets of rules; the breach of which may carry sanctions.

At a certain point, the advocacy of a norm reaches a 'tipping point' (Finnemore and Sikkink, 1998: 895). This is when a critical mass of states agrees to adopt the norm. A process of socialization begins where other states transform from norm breakers to norm followers. This is the 'norm cascade' stage when adherence to a norm begins to spread significantly. The speed and intensity of the process may vary significantly, depending on the issue that the proposed norm is intended to address, who the states acting as 'norm leaders' are, the degree of pressure upon states from within due to the actions of domestic norm entrepreneurs, as well as the extent and form of international pressures to comply.

The reasons why states agree to adhere to a norm may also vary, but Finnemore and Sikkink argue that it is connected to their identities. As a norm cascades, non-compliant states will feel a variety of pressures to conform arising from such things as the pursuit of legitimacy, a desire to be seen to conform, and the enhancement of their self-esteem or their esteem in the eyes of others. These pressures may emanate from within a state, if there is widespread support for a norm among the state's population, or from peer pressure applied by other states (Finnemore and Sikkink, 1998: 903). Conformity with a norm may arise from the state's identification with a specific set of states, and the sense of belonging that is attached to this. For example, a liberal state may feel a particular obligation to uphold liberal conceptions of human rights because of its self-understanding as a liberal state. Similarly, a member state of the EU may wish to, or feel obliged to, adhere to emerging norms from within the EU to uphold and legitimize its status as a member state. Likewise, some states may feel that adherence to a norm reinforces their claims to be bona fide members of an international community and avoid the risk of criticism for being 'norm violators' (Finnemore and Sikkink, 1998: 904).

Ultimately a norm may achieve such widespread acceptance that the third stage in the norm life cycle is reached: a norm is internalized by actors to the extent that conformity is effectively taken for granted. Finnemore and Sikkink concede that the precise reasons why states comply with emergent norms is a matter of debate (whether it reflects an authentic commitment to the values implicit in a norm or a more strategic calculation of the costs of non-compliance, for example), as is the question as to what kinds of norms are more likely to attract compliance, or the speed at which the life cycle of norms plays out (Finnemore and Sikkink, 1998: 915).

The work of Finnemore and Sikkink, as well as other conventional constructivists, does not engage in explicitly normative analysis, in the sense of overtly passing judgement on the merits of specific norms. It is instead a form of empirical explanatory analysis which endeavours to study the role of norms in the formation of state identities and their impact on state behaviour. As such, it could be viewed as aiming to comply with the standards of mainstream social scientific research. However, mainstream critics point to the tendency of constructivists to look primarily at norms with a distinctly liberal, progressive flavour, which suggests that they are in fact engaging in a normative analysis, reflecting an underlying Western, liberal political bias.

Finnemore and Sikkink respond to such criticism by arguing that the study of norms does help to bridge the orthodox view that what is in the world and what ought to be in the world should be kept strictly separate in the name of objectivity. They claim that their empirical research on norms is intended to show how 'ought' becomes 'is' (Finnemore and Sikkink, 1998: 916). Nonetheless, there is an air of normativity about their analysis of how certain norms—the illegality of slavery, the right of women to full political participation, and placing of limits and constraints upon the conduct of war (such as banning certain weaponry)—have brought about significant change. Finnemore and Sikkink acknowledge there is a bias in much constructivist enquiry towards 'nice' norms, and they also note that other norms have played a role in the spread of such things as xenophobic nationalism, fascism, and ethnic cleansing which constructivists have tended not to explore. In other words, they see norms *per se* as legitimate objects for social scientific analysis because of their connections with processes of change at the international level (Finnemore and Sikkink, 2001: 403–404).

Critical constructivists such as Reus-Smit and Price see the limited objective of systematically explaining the significance of norms as unsatisfactory. Although critical constructivists share with conventional constructivists a strong commitment to undertaking systematic empirical research and that norms are appropriate subjects for such research, they do not agree that their work should not have explicit normative purpose. Indeed, Reus-Smit and Richard Price see the roots of constructivism as lying in Critical International Theory (Price and Reus-Smit, 1998). Furthermore, they claim that critical constructivism shares some of the core epistemological concerns of poststructuralism: it does not seek to develop a grand theory of IR, nor does it pursue the positivistic search for definitive generalizable statements about the social world that can claim the status of objective truth. In their view, constructivism's theoretical ambitions are more modest. Reus-Smit describes them as 'providing compelling interpretations and explanations of discrete aspects of world politics, going no further than to offer heavily qualified "contingent generalisations"' (Reus-Smith, 2022: 198). From this point of view, the constructivist interest in such things as norms, intersubjective meanings, and social identities align with the purposes of Critical International Theory: the enhancement of human emancipation.

Critical constructivists argue that constructivist analysis can supplement abstract debates about what constitutes a 'morally good norm' by empirically investigating the challenges and constraints that arise in the translation of politically progressive norms into concrete action and change. Therefore, critical constructivists see themselves as 'profoundly engaged as agents of change' (Price and Reus-Smit, 1998: 283).

Constructivism and the nuclear weapons debate

We can illustrate the significance of international norms by looking at the debate about nuclear weapons through constructivist lenses. In Section 8.2 we examined how the end of the Cold War was a key factor in the emergence of constructivist IR theory. A key contextual factor impelling states and their leaders to think differently about international politics was the evidence of widespread public disquiet at the marked increase in tension between the superpowers in the late 1970s and early 1980s, which produced a sharp re-escalation of the nuclear arms race. In the mid-1970s the Soviet Union had begun deploying highly accurate mobile nuclear missiles—SS20s—inside some of its East European allies that bordered on Western Europe, including East Germany. This triggered the NATO decision in 1979 to deploy nuclear-armed, ground-launched Cruise missiles in some of its key European airbases, notably at the joint US/UK airbase at Greenham Common in the United Kingdom.

Because of the actions of both the Soviet Union and the US and its allies, many people throughout Europe feared that if nuclear conflict between the Western and Eastern blocs were to break out, its most likely theatre of nuclear conflict would be Europe. New nuclear weapons were being deployed on both sides of the East–West divide in the name of security yet there was widespread public rejection of the idea that these weapons would in fact make them more secure.

The European Nuclear Disarmament (END) movement was established in 1980 in response to the weapons deployments. A key feature of END's founding statement was a refusal to take sides, with blame being laid squarely at the feet of leaders of both sides of the Cold War divide. Additionally, it called not only for nuclear disarmament across the whole of Europe, but also for an end to the division between East and West Europe itself through a strategy that amounted to détente from below. In other words, pressure for the two superpowers to reconcile their differences had to come from coordinated popular activism on both sides of the 'Iron Curtain' dividing liberal and communist

Europe. END also managed to open dialogues with dissident political figures within East European communist states, even within the Soviet Union itself. END was at the heart of a wave of loosely coordinated very large public protests across Western Europe, perhaps most famously the establishment of a Women's peace camp outside the Greenham Common airbase in 1981 (we discuss this further in Chapter 10, Key event 10.4).

On the other side of the Atlantic, the US Nuclear Weapons Freeze campaign also rapidly gathered pace, leading in 1982 to the largest political demonstration in US history when one million people took part in an anti-nuclear protest in New York. The US campaign's objectives were more modest that those of its European counterparts, arguably reflecting the more conservative tone of American public debate. Nonetheless, the combined volume of public dissent on both sides of the Atlantic was historically remarkable and, constructivists have argued, contributed significantly to the dramatic changes in superpower relations that began to develop in the mid 1980s. The eventual outcome was the removal by both sides of the missiles that had generated public protests, under the 1987 Intermediate-range Nuclear Forces treaty. In 1988, it was widely reported in the Western media that while walking through Moscow's Red Square after a summit meeting with Gorbachev, US President Ronald Reagan was asked about a speech he had made only five years earlier in which he had described the Soviet Union as an 'evil empire'. Reagan replied, 'I was talking about another time, another era'.

Marianne Hanson argues that since the invention of nuclear weapons, the nuclear weapons states (NWS) have worked hard to 'normalize' the possession of nuclear weapons, such that they became widely accepted as a key component of security policy and the armed capability of the states who possess them. Dominant policy elites in the NWS have successfully constructed and sufficiently socially embedded a specific meaning to the possession of nuclear weapons (Hanson, 2018). From a constructivist perspective, what the antinuclear social movements of the early 1980s signified was the construction of different understandings of national identity centred around a challenge to orthodox accounts of what made nations and people secure. Events such as the deployment of nuclear missiles in Europe challenged the established meaning of nuclear weapons and the norms surrounding them because they were widely interpreted as posing a threat to people's security rather than a means of further enhancing it. Therefore, the protests signalled resistance to the established norms governing the acquisition and deployment of nuclear weapons, supposedly in the name of security.

Let's consider those established norms. The international nuclear non-proliferation regime consists of the rules, norms, and institutions that govern the possession and development of nuclear armaments. At its centre is the 1970 Non-Proliferation Treaty (NPT), which requires all signatories to prevent the spread of nuclear weapons beyond the five recognized NWS that currently legally possess them, and for the NWS themselves to work towards complete nuclear disarmament. The NWS countries are France, Britain, China, the US, and Russia. One of the more fractious issues in the debate about the global governance of nuclear weapons, however, is the failure of the five NWS to work actively towards global nuclear disarmament, as they are required to do under Article VI of the NPT. States not possessing nuclear weapons are expected to comply with the non-proliferation norm (and most of the treaty's 190 signatories do), but the

NWS, which happen also to include some of the world's most powerful states, make little or no substantial effort to abide by the norm of nuclear disarmament.

Maria Rost Rublee argues that antinuclear social movements within Western states contributed to the strengthening of non-proliferation as a dominant norm in the global governance of nuclear weapons:

> civil society groups used the international norm to batter their conservative opponents, arguing that acquiring nuclear weapons would pit them against global opinion and make their country out to be aggressive and militaristic. The international norm allowed domestic peace groups to show that opposition to nuclear weapons wasn't simply their quirky or naïve opinion, but rather that the weight of the world was on their side. (cited in Rublee and Cohen, 2018: 330)

There are also a few states known to have developed a nuclear weapons capability, such as Israel, India, Pakistan, and North Korea in clear breach of the NPT. A range of IR scholars, including the neorealist Kenneth Waltz (see the discussion in Chapter 3, Section 3.5), and several postcolonialist scholars, argue that the current nuclear non-proliferation regime effectively constitutes a form of 'nuclear apartheid' (Gusterson, 1999. See also Biswas, 2014). This rests, moreover, upon 'deep seated assumptions and prejudices' left over from the colonial era which underpin the view that only certain states are appropriate and legitimate possessors of nuclear weaponry (Biswas, 2014). Given the failure of the NWS to actively pursue disarmament, does this therefore provide grounds for these illegitimate nuclear weapons states to argue that if the possession of nuclear weapons is acceptable for some states why is it not for others? These sorts of questions, and the surrounding scholarly debate, contribute to what Rublee and Cohen call 'norm contestation' (Rublee and Cohen, 2018: 325). In other words, while most states agree that an international nuclear weapons regime is desirable, they disagree on what its guiding norm should be: non-proliferation or disarmament?

It is worth noting here that when constructivism emerged in the aftermath of the Cold War there was widespread optimism about the possibility of international politics moving in a progressive direction because of the end of a four decade long superpower rivalry. The prospects for progress towards nuclear disarmament was one area of international politics that seemed as if it would benefit from the ending of Cold War superpower rivalry, which, after all, was what stimulated the nuclear arms race in the first place. Significant change is not, however, a one-way street and neither identities nor norms are fixed in stone. The current state of relations between Russia and the Western world (as well as between China and the West) is fraught with tensions, tempting some to suggest a Cold War of sorts has returned (Abrams, 2022; Breuer, 2022; Stent, 2022).

However, the points of disagreement and the issues at stake in the relationship are not entirely the same as during the Cold War. Russia is no longer a communist state and its internal politics have undergone significant change as well. There are evident tensions between states which were once part of the Soviet Union—such as the Baltic States, Georgia, and the Ukraine—and contemporary post-communist Russia. Official invocations of Russian nationalism provide a strong contrast with the pronouncements of internationalist communist solidarity during the Cold War era.

Similarly, Donald Trump, US President 2017–2021, repeatedly articulated an understanding of American identity that was distinct from that of his predecessors, not least in its unusually strong emphasis on nationalism and patriotism. This was coupled with an overt disdain for multilateral international institutions (such as the UN and NATO) and multilateralism as a foreign policy principle. Such sentiments clearly introduced tensions in the relationship between the US and some of its long-standing Western allies, notably in Western Europe. Trump's successor, President Joe Biden attempted to restore a more liberal internationalist perspective in US foreign policy, by re-joining the Paris Climate Agreement for example. Yet there is also evidence of continuing widespread support for Trump's worldview among the US public.

From a constructivist perspective, these changing articulations of national identity and the shifts in foreign policy outlooks and practices that accompany them can provide important insights into contemporary international politics. They highlight vital dynamic aspects that theoretical approaches, centred on a unidirectional causal relationship between structure and agency, such as neorealism and neoliberalism, simply cannot capture. Shifts in conceptions of national identity, and perceptions of how states can and should act internationally, can have significant political effects, even if the structure of the international system seemingly remains relatively constant. On this all constructivists agree, even if conventional and critical constructivists disagree as to the purposes of constructivist scholarship.

8.6 **CONCLUSION**

In this chapter we have seen that constructivism is a label applied to a broad range of scholarship. Although commonly depicted as a middle ground, where precisely constructivism lies in relation to either end of the IR theoretical spectrum is a matter of debate. Neither observers of constructivism nor constructivists themselves agree on its precise theoretical location. Nonetheless, constructivism now occupies a prominent place in the spectrum of IR theories.

The variations in the character and influence of constructivism have something of a geographical dimension to them. In the US particularly, conventional constructivism is widely seen as the principal challenger to the dominance of the neorealist–neoliberal mainstream (the so-called 'neo-neo' debate discussed in Chapter 3). For many mainstream IR theorists, constructivism is effectively the 'acceptable face' of critical scholarship, and this is reflected in many US IR textbooks. Undoubtedly, constructivism in all its varieties has contributed substantially to the development of a more sociological understanding of international politics. The boundary between conventional constructivism and mainstream approaches is, arguably, becoming increasingly blurred. For some, however, the success of constructivism in establishing itself as the primary counterpoint to mainstream theory, in the US at least, has the effect of marginalizing other, more overtly critical theories (Zehfuss, 2002: 60).

It is constructivism's relationship with Critical International Theory that is of more interest to some constructivists, notably those based outside the US. Conventional constructivism focuses on the explanatory study of norms in international politics. These are viewed as 'social facts' and therefore a part of international reality that is amenable to empirical enquiry. In contrast, critical constructivists do not see themselves as bound by the standards of positivistic political enquiry. They favour a more interpretive and more openly normative mode of analysis that has more in common with Critical International Theory than positivist mainstream IR. Critical constructivists also more readily embrace the idea that theory always has political purpose and is not simply a process of endeavouring to explain reality accurately and objectively.

Some constructivists regard poststructuralism as a form of constructivism and see their own work as resonating with some key poststructuralist themes, such as the importance of language as a mediator of meaning and the constructed nature of identity. However, poststructuralists would take issue with both conventional and critical constructivist claims that they are analysing the socially constructed aspects of an international reality—a world 'out there'. As we discuss in Chapter 7, poststructuralists question all definitive claims to know international reality. For poststructuralists, the attribution of meaning to things or practices is always a matter of perpetually contestable interpretation. In contrast, constructivists believe the generation of meanings can be systematically investigated, and for critical constructivists, such investigation can and should provide insight into how we might improve the human condition.

SUMMARIZING CONSTRUCTIVISM

- Constructivism emerged in the late 1980s/early 1990s, partly in response to mainstream IR's failure to anticipate or fully explain the end of the Cold War
- Constructivism is not a singular theory of IR, but a cluster of approaches centred around some core themes
- Constructivism emphasizes the *ideational* aspects of international politics in contrast to the predominantly *materialist* explanations offered by mainstream IR theory
- All constructivists start from the position that the meanings we ascribe to key aspects of international politics and the practices of states in the international system are constructed through social interaction
- Constructivism is widely depicted as occupying a middle ground between mainstream and critical IR theories. Quite where it sits in that middle ground is, however, disputed by both constructivists and critics of constructivism
- All constructivists critique the *ontological* assumptions of mainstream theory, notably the understanding of the state as an actor

- Constructivism challenges overly structuralist explanations of international political behaviour, particularly neorealist structuralism, and sees international politics emerging out of the interaction between structure and *agency*
- Constructivists see the interaction of structure and agents as variable and generally emphasize the possibility of change in the conduct of international politics
- Constructivists differ, however, in their *epistemological* standpoints
- Conventional constructivists broadly endorse the positivistic epistemology of mainstream IR theory. They see the *ideational* aspects of international politics as legitimate objects of social scientific enquiry, which can contribute to developing richer *explanations* of IR
- Critical constructivists dispute the epistemological assumptions of mainstream IR theory, and instead adopt an *interpretive* approach and seek to develop better *understandings* of international politics
- Constructivism emphasizes the significance of norms and identity in analysing the practices of states and the nature of the international system.
- Although constructivists highlight the role of norms, they disagree as to whether constructivism is, or should be, an explicitly normative approach (i.e., one that openly adopts a specific political or moral standpoint)
- Some critical constructivists see constructivism as largely compatible with the emancipatory commitments of Critical International Theory and argue that constructivist research can provide added empirical substance to the claims of Critical International Theory
- Although constructivism shares with poststructuralism an interest in language, meaning, and the politics of identity, poststructuralists reject constructivism's assumption that there is a reality outside of our discursive construction of it.

QUESTIONS

1. Why did constructivist IR scholarship emerge in the aftermath of the Cold War?

2. What does Wendt mean when he says: 'anarchy is what states make of it'?

3. Define the concept of a norm and explain why constructivists would consider norms to be significant.

4. What are the key differences between the 'conventional' and 'critical' varieties of constructivism?

5. Do you think constructivism occupies a 'middle ground' in the spectrum of IR theories? Explain your answer.

6. Consider what you have learned about constructivism, and what you have learned about other critical IR theories. Do you think constructivism qualifies as a critical theory of IR?

IR THEORY TODAY: CONSTRUCTING THE COVID-19 PANDEMIC

Throughout the global Covid-19 pandemic that first emerged in December 2019, numerous national leaders, policy makers, and media platforms referred to the pandemic in terms usually associated with warfare and military combat. We were 'fighting' or 'combatting' the virus, when we succeeded in reducing its spread and impact it was commonly depicted as a victory, and medical personnel were working at the 'frontline', and so on (Caso, 2020; Freedman, 2020). China's President, Xi Jinping, referred to the struggle with the coronavirus as a 'people's war' (Xinhuanet, 2020). French President, Emmanuel Macron, declared that France was 'at war' with the virus (Erlanger, 2020; Momtaz, 2020), and the former US President, Donald Trump, depicted himself as a 'wartime president' (Caso, 2018). Medical personnel in countries that were particularly badly affected in the early stages of the virus's spread, such as Italy, spoke of their experiences as being like in a war.

Many states enacted emergency powers and social restrictions, comparable to those used in wartime. Significant limits were placed on key individual freedoms and the conduct of daily social life. Breaches of new restrictions became criminalized in many states and were met with sometimes brutal responses. New mass surveillance systems were introduced in countries such as China and Germany to assist in the monitoring and tracking of the disease's spread.

The struggle by states to procure enough personal protection equipment, ventilators, or virus testing systems also led to ruthless competition between them. National anti-COVID strategies often entailed closing national borders to all foreign nationals, in

A health worker giving a vaccine against Covid-19 in Mali.

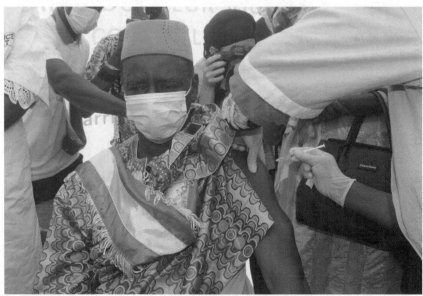

some cases to everyone, and there were expressions of suspicion and enmity from the leaders and prominent media commentators of some states towards other states, notably China, where the virus originated. One prominent realist IR scholar thought the US's handling of the pandemic would lead to long term damage to its international reputation and impact negatively on the US's foreign relations (Walt, 2020b).

The pandemic did stimulate enhanced cooperation between some states in the joint pursuit of decisive responses to the pandemic, such as the development of vaccines. However, again there was considerable rivalry between states trying to procure those vaccines and significant variations in the capacity of states to distribute the vaccines efficiently and equitably (see the 'IR Theory today' feature at the end of Chapter 5). At the global level, many countries in the Global South struggled particularly in the procurement and distribution of vaccines. Media, the World Health Organization, and various NGOs, began referring to the consequences of 'vaccine nationalism' as 'vaccine injustice', 'vaccine inequality', or 'vaccine apartheid' (WHO, 2021, 'Editorial', *The BMJ*, !6 August 2021). The global inequality of vaccine access and distribution arguably further exacerbated existing global health inequalities (Mueller and Robbins, 2021).

Defenders of the use of the rhetoric of war argue that it was an effective short-term strategy to publicly convey the urgency of the situation and legitimize the introduction of temporary emergency measures. It can be used to generate a sense of national unity and camaraderie in what one prominent British media commentator described as 'a cruel, brutal, pitiless war' (Hodges, 2020).

Critics claim, however, that the virus was not an 'enemy' in the conventional sense of the term. Equating a pandemic with a war, moreover, provided opportunities for many states to encroach further on individual freedoms and justify reducing the democratic scrutiny of their actions, some effects of which, critics fear, could remain after the pandemic subsided. Furthermore, it serves to shift the blame for failures to deal adequately with the effects of the virus onto an 'external invisible enemy' thereby deflecting critical analysis of pre-existing national, political, economic, and social weaknesses that were exposed by the pandemic (Caso, 2020).

QUESTIONS

Drawing on this chapter and your own research into the COVID-19 pandemic,

1. a) How do you think a *conventional constructivist* would analyse the use of warfare and military language to describe the COVID-19 pandemic? (Hint: think about the role of norms here.)

b) How do you think a *critical constructivist* would analyse the use of warfare and military language to describe the COVID-19 pandemic? (Hint: think about *normative* analysis here.)

c) What are the key differences between a) and b) and how significant, if at all, are they in your view?

2. What, if any, do you think were the key international consequences of the deployment by several prominent national leaders of the rhetoric of war during the

COVID-19 pandemic? (Hint: think about in what ways war-like rhetoric constructs the meaning of relations between states.)

3. What effects, if any, of constructing the response to the COVID-19 in the language of war, or requiring a military-like response do you think will remain when the pandemic eventually subsides? (Hint: how has it impacted upon people's perceptions of the state in which they reside, or of other states?)

TWISTING THE LENS

Drawing upon what you have learned about Realism (Chapter 3) and Postcolonialism (Chapter 9)

1. How might a realist analyse the national responses to the covid pandemic (Hint: look at the Stephen Walt references listed below)?

2. What key insights, if any, can be gained in your view by examining the COVID-19 pandemic from a postcolonial perspective? (Hint: think about terms such as 'vaccine injustice' and 'vaccine apartheid' here.)

USEFUL REFERENCES

Caso, F. (2020), 'Are We at War? The Rhetoric of War in the Coronavirus Pandemic', *The Disorder of Things* thedisorderofthings.com, 10 April.

Erlanger, S. (2020), 'Macron Declares France "at War" with Virus as E.U. Proposes 30-day Travel Ban', *The New York Times*, 16 March.

Freedman, L. (2020), 'Coronavirus and the language of war', *New Statesman*, 11 April.

Momtaz, R. (2020), 'Inside Macron's coronavirus war', *Politico*, 13 April.

Mueller, Benjamin and Robbins, Rebecca (2021), 'Where a vast global vaccination program went wrong', *The New York Times*, 7 October.

Walt, S. M. (2020a), 'The Realists Guide to the Coronavirus Outbreak', *Foreign Policy*, 9 March.

Walt, S. M. (2020b), 'The Death of American Competence', *Foreign Policy*, 23 March.

Xinhuanet (2021), 'Xi focus: Xi vows to win people's war against novel coronavirus', 11 February.

FURTHER READING

ADDITIONAL INTRODUCTORY READING

Barnett, M. (2020), 'Social Constructivism' in John Baylis, Steve Smith, and Patricia Owens, *The Globalization of World Politics: An Introduction to International Relations*, 8th edition (Oxford: Oxford University Press).
A very accessible introduction from a leading US conventional constructivist IR scholar.

Fierke, K. M. (2021) 'Constructivism' in T. Dunne, M. Kurki, and S. Smith, *International Relations Theories: Discipline and Diversity*, 5th edition (Oxford: Oxford University Press).
A more advanced introduction from a leading exponent of language-based critical constructivism. The chapter also contains a case study of 'the War on Covid-19'.

8 CONSTRUCTIVISM AND INTERNATIONAL RELATIONS **319**

Hurd, I. (2008), 'Constructivism' in C. Reus-Smith and D. Snidal (eds), *The Oxford Handbook of International Relations* (Oxford: Oxford University Press).
A very succinct advanced introduction that outlines constructivism's key features and surveys the key debates within constructivism.

Theys, S. (2018) 'Introducing Constructivism in International Relations Theory', E-International Relations. Available at: www.e-ir.info/2018/02/23/introducing-constructivism-in-international-relations-theory/.
A basic introduction to conventional constructivism that contains an interesting brief constructivist study of the national identity of the Kingdom of Bhutan.

MORE IN-DEPTH READING

Adem, S. (2021), *Postcolonial Constructivism: Mazrui's Theory of Intercultural Relations* (Cham, Switzerland: Palgrave Macmillan).
A study of the work of the Kenyan scholar Ali Mazrui which proposes that it can be interpreted as a synthesis of postcolonialist and social constructivism.

Barkin, J. S. (ed.) (2020), *The Social Construction of State Power: Applying Realist Constructivism* (Bristol: Bristol University Press).
Commonly seen as opposing schools of IR thought, this collection of essays questions the supposed incompatibility of realism and constructivism and endeavours to show how 'realist constructivism' can be applied to concrete issues in international politics.

Finnemore, M. and Sikkink, K. (1998), 'International Norm Dynamics and Political Change', *International Organisation*, 52(4), 887–917.
A key contribution to conventional constructivist analysis of the role of norms in international politics which contains a much cited exposition of the 'norm life cycle'.

Finnemore, M. and Sikkink, K. (2001), 'Taking Stock: The Constructivist Research Programme in International Relations and Comparative Politics', *Annual Review of Political Science*, 4, 391–416.
A wide-ranging overview of constructivism from a conventional constructivist perspective.

Koslowski, R. and Kratochwil, F. V. (1994), 'Understanding Change in International Politics: The Soviet Empire's Demise and the International System', *International Organisation*, 48(2), 215–224.
A constructivist analysis of how the redefinition of Soviet identity and changes in state–society relations contributed to the collapse of the Soviet empire and changes to the norms governing international relations.

Onuf, N. (1989), *World of our Making: Rules and Rule in Social Theory and International Relations* (Columbia, SC: University of South Carolina Press).
The book that introduced the term constructivism into IR theoretical debate.

Price, R. and Reus-Smit, C. (1998), 'Dangerous Liaisons? Critical International Theory and Constructivism', *European Journal of International Relations*, 4(3), 259–294.
Argues that the roots of constructivism lie in critical social theory and constructivism can make a substantive contribution to the further development of Critical International Theory.

Reus-Smit, C. (2002), 'Imagining Society: Constructivism and the English School', *British Journal of Politics and International Relations*, 4(3), 487–509.
A leading critical constructivist explores the differences and commonalities between constructivism and the English School, going on to argue for the possibility of fruitful dialogue between the two perspectives.

Rublee, M. R. and Cohen, A. (2018), 'Nuclear Norms in Global Governance: A Progressive Research Agenda', *Contemporary Security Policy*, 39(3), 317–340.
This article applies a constructivist analysis of norms to the field of global nuclear politics.

Theys, S. and Rietig, K. (2020), 'The Influence of Small States: How Bhutan Succeeds in Influencing Global Sustainability Governance' *International Affairs*, 96(6): 1603–1622.

A conventional constructivist examination of how Bhutan put the norm of 'human happiness' on the global agenda.

Wendt, A. (1992), 'Anarchy Is What States Make of It: The Social Construction of Power Politics', *International Organisation*, 46(2), 391–425.

A famous early contribution to constructivism which argues that both neorealism and neoliberalism fail to theorize identity and its influence on the interpretation of international anarchy.

Wiener, A. (2018), *Contestation and Constitution of Norms in Global International Relations* (Cambridge: Cambridge university Press).

A critical constructivist examination of the constitution, contestation, and re-constitution of norms that focuses on how 'global citizens' contest the always questionable norms that govern them.

Zehfuss, M. (2002), *Constructivism in International Relations: The Politics of Reality* (Cambridge: Cambridge university Press).

A critical exposition of the different varieties of constructivism by a leading poststructuralist IR scholar.

CHAPTER 9

POSTCOLONIALISM AND INTERNATIONAL RELATIONS

LEARNING OBJECTIVES

- Understand the historical contexts of colonialism and anti-colonial struggle out of which postcolonial perspectives emerged
- Explain the key themes in the works of key postcolonial thinkers
- Assess the impact of postcolonial and decolonial approaches upon the IR discipline
- Identify the intersection of colonialism and ideas about race, both historically and presently
- Evaluate the connections between postcolonial thought and contemporary public debates about the continuing impact of colonialism, both locally and globally.

9.1 INTRODUCTION

Postcolonialism is one of the newer critical approaches to IR, emerging in the 1990s. As its name suggests, it is centrally concerned with colonialism and its complex legacy in contemporary global politics. Postcolonial IR thinking not only places colonialism and its consequences more fully at the centre of the IR discipline, but it has also led to some contemporary postcolonial IR scholars offering a rather different story about the founding of the IR discipline and its subsequent evolution. As we shall see later in this chapter, this alternative account shows how colonialism, imperialism, and race were more central to the IR discipline at its inception after the First World War and for some decades after than is commonly supposed.

It must be emphasized from the outset that the issues of imperialism, colonialism, and race are complexly intertwined, and this may lead to some difficult and uncomfortable reading and thinking for you, especially in today's political climate. Much of the postcolonial literature raises a host of difficult questions for IR students to contemplate. However, this chapter starts from the assumption that it is vital nonetheless to explore those questions to develop a thorough and nuanced grasp of the theory and practice of international politics in today's world.

If you are reading this chapter before reading the chapters on mainstream IR approaches, such as liberalism (Chapter 2), realism (Chapter 3), or the English School (Chapter 4), it may give you a somewhat different perspective on those theories than if you had read them first. If you have already read and studied the mainstream theories prior to reading this chapter, you might want to go back and reflect on your previous interpretations of them.

The chapter starts with an outline of the meaning of the term postcolonialism. It then goes on to briefly overview key aspects of the history of imperialism and colonialism to show how the concept of race emerges out of the processes of colonization and how racism becomes endemic to the practices of imperial control and colonization. We then briefly look at the origins and growth of movements against colonialism.

Having established the historical context, we then review how postcolonialism as a body of thought developed outside of IR, focusing on some key thinkers and themes. This is followed by an examination of the emergence of postcolonial approaches in the IR discipline specifically. Here we explore some of the profound questions they raise about the commonly accepted history of the IR discipline as well as many of the most central assumptions of mainstream IR thinking. Finally, the chapter examines decolonial approaches which seek to expose and challenge colonialist assumptions still underpinning much of contemporary IR thinking.

9.2 **WHAT IS POSTCOLONIALISM?**

You may already be familiar with the adjective *postcolonial*. This usually refers to the historical period after the last big wave of decolonization in the 1960s when most territories that were once under the colonial rule of, mostly, European states achieved their formal political independence. However, postcolonial perspectives robustly challenge the depiction of decolonization as a completed process. Postcolonialism focuses on the histories of colonialism and decolonization viewed from the perspectives of those who were colonized, as well as the considerable legacies of colonialism in the contemporary era. Postcolonialism depicts the present as a period that is not *after* colonialism, but '*after the onset* of colonialism' (Krishna, 2018: 22, emphasis in the original). It focuses on 'the continuity and persistence of colonizing practices' in today's world (Chowdhry and Nair, 2002: 11). Even though decolonization may have resulted in the formal transfer of political power from Western imperial powers to formerly colonized territories, postcolonial perspectives depict the institutions and structures of Western global dominance as remaining largely in place (Grovogui, 2006; Bhambra, 2007 and 2011a).

Postcolonial IR perspectives do not constitute a single theory but rather a diverse body of scholarship. In various ways, postcolonialist perspectives challenge the *Eurocentrism* of mainstream (and some critical) IR perspectives. The term Eurocentrism emerged in the 1970s and 'at its core is the assumption of European centrality in the human past and present' (Barkawi and Laffey, 2006: 331). It is a belief that Europeans are the sole 'makers of history' and that Europe, and the West more generally, eternally makes progress, while the rest of the world advances more slowly, if at all (Blaut, 1993: 1). Eurocentrism refers to Europe as not simply a geographical location, but also as a worldview centred around the claim that European civilization is superior to all others. Garminder Bhambra argues that Eurocentrism treats 'European specialness' as a fact (Bhambra, 2007: 5). The European intellectual tradition that evolved out of the Enlightenment era (sixteenth to eighteenth centuries) is seen as the primary source of what is deemed to be worthy of study (our ontological assumptions) and how we should go about studying it (our epistemological assumptions). It has historically provided the benchmark or standard by which the development of all societies has been and still is widely judged (Blaut, 1993; Bhambra, 2007 and 2011b; Hobson, 2012).

Eurocentrism is treated by postcolonial perspectives as having expanded beyond its roots in the European continent and is viewed as broadly synonymous with dominant strands of Western social and political thought. As Bhambra argues, a Eurocentric understanding of the idea of modernity itself and what constitutes the modern world is derived almost exclusively from the Western experience. Yet, it is also assumed to have a validity—a 'world historical significance'—that transcends its European origins (Bhambra, 2007: 4–5).

Postcolonial perspectives endeavour to critically expose two key interrelated facets of Eurocentrism:

- The misrepresentation and/or misunderstanding of non-Eurocentric cultures, forms of knowledge, value systems, and historical experiences or their dismissal as inferior or insignificant.
- The assumption that European or Western superiority is 'self-contained and self-generating' (Barkawi and Laffey, 2006: 331. This point is also made by other postcolonialist scholars such as Blaut, 1993; Chakrabarty, 2000; Hobson, 2004 and 2012; Grovogui, 2006; Bhambra, 2007; Krishna, 2018: 22–24).

For its postcolonial critics, Eurocentrism fails to recognize or acknowledge the vital role of non-Eurocentric perspectives in the development of European ideas, indeed in the formation and sustenance of the very idea of Europe itself. John Hobson describes this as 'the Eurocentric myth of the pristine West' (Hobson, 2004: 1). Eurocentrism marginalizes or excludes consideration of the extent to which European and Western global dominance arose out of complex, often violent, and exploitative entanglements with the wider world beyond Europe, through processes such as exploration, conquest, colonization, and slavery. Siba Grovogui argues that the emergence of the idea of European uniqueness from the seventeenth century onwards not only disavowed 'Europe's connections, debts and relations with other countries', it also 'cast other regions as sites of violent cultures' (Grovogui, 2006: 27). To put the point more starkly, Europe and what is today commonly referred to as The West evolved *out of* international and global politics not independently of it.

In contrast, postcolonialism endeavours to *decentre* Europe, or as Dipesh Chakrabarty puts it, to 'provincialise' it (Chakrabarty, 2000). It does this by drawing upon the experiences, perspectives, and values of those who were colonized, and those whose lives continue to be shaped significantly by colonialism and the consequences of decolonization. In so doing, postcolonialism invites us to consider how the world, both historically and presently, looks very different when viewed from the histories and perspectives of the colonized and those whose lives are still shaped by the legacies of colonialism.

Many of postcolonialism's prominent founding scholars, such as Frantz Fanon and Edward Said (both of whom we examine further in Section 9.5), were also noted political activists. Indeed, much of postcolonial thinking emerges out of the interaction of intellectual currents and concrete political events, such as the various struggles against colonial rule, the political experiences of communities who have migrated from the Global South to the Global North, and resistance to what are seen by many to be the neocolonial and neo-imperial dimensions of the West's interaction with the Global South today. The issues postcolonial thinking centres on—race, imperialism, colonialism, decolonization, identity, culture, and remembering and memorializing the past—have become highly salient in many public debates today. For example, there are increasingly widespread, often student-led calls for the 'decolonization' of Western university curricula, especially in the social sciences and humanities. Western universities are increasingly being pressed to reflect critically on the diversity of their courses and to encourage much greater attention in research and teaching to the legacies and contemporary expressions of colonialism as well as the experiences, cultures, and intellectual traditions of non-Western peoples who have hitherto been misrepresented, marginalized, or excluded entirely from consideration.

9.3 KEY ASPECTS OF EUROPEAN COLONIALISM

The term colonialism refers to the policies and practices of states who imposed their rule over other peoples and territories, usually through the establishment of settlements (colonies). These days it is often used interchangeably with imperialism, although imperialism more usually refers to the general idea of a state exerting its power and control over others outside of its borders. Colonialism and imperialism thus connote a hierarchical relationship between states, peoples, and territories, which sits in direct contrast to the mainstream IR depiction of the international system of states as anarchical (which we discuss in Chapters 2, 3, and 4).

To fully understand postcolonialism we need first to recall the history of European colonialism. This is however, a long, complex and, for many people, an inherently uncomfortable story which we cannot fully do justice to here. For this reason, we will confine ourselves to highlighting some significant aspects of the colonial era that help to illuminate the central concerns of contemporary postcolonial theory. A first aspect of the history of colonialism is that the remembrance of it is surrounded with controversy.

The challenge of remembering difficult histories

The colonial era constitutes a very significant component of world history that is marked throughout by violence and human exploitation. The transatlantic slave trade and the use of slave labour throughout the European colonies was perhaps the starkest example of this, but the formal abolition of the slave trade and subsequently slavery itself from the early nineteenth century onwards did not mean the end of the violent subjugation and exploitation of colonized peoples by all the European imperial powers.

As we shall see throughout this chapter, the legacy of the colonial era remains with us today in various ways. In recent years, however, the telling of the history of European colonialism has become a matter of academic controversy and public debate (Satia, 2020). Additionally, recent controversies around public representations of the colonial era—statues, memorials, and the naming of buildings or prestigious scholarships—also highlight current public sensitivity to the ways in which the colonial era is remembered. Examples include the *#RhodesMustFall* campaign initiated in 2015 by students demanding the removal of a statue of Cecil Rhodes from the University of Cape Town campus in South Africa. Rhodes (1853–1902) was a British diamond magnate, prominent colonial politician, and noted defender of imperialism who firmly believed that the white race was superior to other races.

The campaign spread to other South African Campuses and in 2020 there were also protests about a statue of Cecil Rhodes on the front of Oriel College, Oxford University. The university receives a considerable sum of money from the Rhodes Trust in support of the prestigious Rhodes Scholarships founded by Rhodes. After initially agreeing to remove the statue on the recommendation of an independent commission, the university subsequently backtracked and in 2021 installed a plaque near the statue which describes Rhodes as 'a committed colonialist (who) obtained his fortune through exploitation of minerals, land, and peoples of southern Africa'.

In June 2020, Black Lives Matter protestors demonstrated a different response to the public memorialization of the colonial era by taking down a statue of Edward Colston in Bristol, England. Colston (1636–1721) was a merchant and philanthropist noted for his charitable contributions to the city of Bristol. The bulk of Colston's fortune was, however, acquired through his involvement in the slave trade. Four demonstrators were subsequently arrested and charged with criminal damage, but then found not guilty and acquitted by a trial jury.

These examples raise the question of how we should memorialize the colonial past (which you are asked to consider further in Think critically 9.1). Changing public attitudes in the Global North (or at least parts of it) towards the colonial era are also evidenced by the growing demand for the repatriation of artefacts, pieces of art, and even human remains held in the vaults of Western museums, many, perhaps most of which were simply stolen from colonial territories to indulge the curiosity of European scholars and publics.

THINK CRITICALLY 9.1 HOW SHOULD WE REMEMBER THE COLONIAL AND IMPERIAL PAST?

In recent years, the public memorialization of colonialism has become a very sensitive issue. The debate revolves around three broad positions:

- a conservative view which argues that even if such memorials are seen to reflect now thoroughly discarded attitudes, they should remain part of the visible historical record
- a more conciliatory view that controversial memorials should remain but be accompanied by better and more critical information about their context (as illustrated, for example, by the plaque at Oriel College)
- the view that they should be removed because they normalize the history of intolerance and oppression or, worse, can act as inspiration for those who continue to hold racist or culturally exclusionary views.

Which of these positions do you most agree with and why?

USEFUL REFERENCE

Tyler Steim (2018), 'Statue wars: what should we do with troublesome monuments?', *The Guardian*, 26 September 2018

The expansion of European colonialism

The practice of colonialism stretches back at least to Ancient Greece and the expansion of the Roman Empire in the first to fourth centuries CE. Contemporary debates about colonialism usually refer, however, to the expansion of European settlement and political control over vast swathes of territories outside Europe from the fifteenth century onwards.

European colonialism was not different from earlier forms of imperialism and colonialism solely because of its extent. Randolph Persaud and Alina Sajed argue that it has three distinctive features. Firstly, it was intricately tied up with the introduction and development of the capitalist system, 'which altered—with indelible and long-term consequences—the economic, social, cultural and political dynamics of many societies around the world' (Persaud and Sajed, 2018: 3).

The second distinctive feature was 'the devastating impact of capitalist expansion on the colonies' because of the colonial 'regimes of slavery, systematic violence and ruthless exploitation'. Persaud and Sajed argue that 'what drove the European colonial empire was not simply the desire for profit (capitalism), but also an unquestioned belief in its own superiority and in the inferiority of all those others it encountered (racism)' (Persaud and Sajed, 2018: 4).

A third distinctive feature was 'the systematic production of a body of academic knowledge that underpins and justifies—ethically and "scientifically"—the enterprise of colonialism as a meritorious and worthy enterprise' (Persaud and Sajed, 2018: 4). Persaud and Sajed (along with a host of other postcolonialist scholars) argue that the representation of colonialism as a noble cause and of the colonized as inherently inferior to their colonizers became entrenched not only in scholarly work but also in the formulation of the foreign policies of the colonial powers, the imagination of their publics, and even in the minds of the colonized themselves (Persaud and Sajed, 2018: 4).

During what is widely referred to in Western textbooks as the 'Age of Discovery' in the fifteenth and sixteenth centuries, Portuguese and Spanish exploratory voyages established a European presence in the Americas, Africa, and South Asia. The urge to explore went hand in hand with the search for potentially lucrative sources of spices and precious metals. For voyagers heading East from Europe, exploration led (initially at least) to the establishment of small, fortified trading settlements along key sea trading routes, such as along the southern coasts of India and in Southeast Asia. For westward voyagers, however, exploration and discovery were rapidly followed by conquest and expanding European settlements in the Americas.

The European conquerors saw the 'New World' (the Americas and later Australasia) as under no sovereign authority that they recognized and thus there for the taking. Additionally, newly encountered indigenous peoples were not seen to be living according to European standards of civilization and were variously depicted by their discoverers as mere children, wild, savage, or barbaric (Todorov, 1999). From the outset, European conquest was construed as part of a civilizing process, which included the fulfilment of a Christian evangelical duty to convert Indigenous populations. These were seen to have no meaningful history of their own and 'their equality as human beings, to the extent that it was recognized, depended ultimately on conversion and assimilation' (Inayatullah and Blaney, 2004: 51).

A stark early expression of the European colonial mindset was *El Requerimiento* (The Requirement). Introduced in 1513, this was a declaration of the Spanish monarchy's inherent right to conquer newly discovered territories and subjugate the inhabitants. Upon first contact with native American peoples, it would be read out in Spanish or Latin by Spanish *conquistadores* (conquerors) so they could depict themselves as acting in the service of both the Spanish Crown and God. It invited Indigenous peoples to accept the conquerors as their political and spiritual masters. Should they not agree to subjugation, it declared that 'we shall powerfully enter into your country and shall make war against you in all ways and manners that we can . . . the deaths and losses which shall accrue from this are your fault' (Todorov, 1999: 147). The Requirement's sole purpose was supposedly to relieve the conquerors of legal or moral responsibility for conquering territories and killing or enslaving Indigenous inhabitants should they resist. Use of The Requirement was abolished by the Spanish crown in 1556, but this had little impact on the colonization process.

Spain was the dominant colonial force in Central and South America, but from the early seventeenth century onwards the British and French established trading outposts in North America. By the mid-eighteenth century, more than a million Europeans had emigrated there, mostly as indentured labourers who had committed to working for several years to pay off the costs of their passage. As these labourers, many of whom were violently abused during their servitude, earned their rights to freedom, the growing demand for labour led to the increased use of enslaved African people in their place. These were mostly transported by sea to the Americas in appalling conditions and they could hold out little hope of similarly eventually gaining their freedom.

The eventual abolition of the transatlantic slave trade and, subsequently, slavery from the early nineteenth century onwards did not change the fundamental character of colonialism. Indeed, it was followed by further colonial expansion and competition between the European colonial powers. By the early nineteenth century, Spain and Portugal had lost most of their colonial territories in the Americas, but this was countered by the extension of imperial and colonial control elsewhere in Africa, the Middle East, South, and Southeast Asia. During the latter part of the nineteenth century and the early twentieth century competition increased between the existing European colonial powers along with newer entrants in the race to colonize, such as Italy, Germany, Belgium, the US, and Japan. This led to a rapid increase in colonial acquisitions. By 1914, 85 per cent of the world's surface area was subject to colonial rule. At the top of the colonial hierarchy was the British Empire, which at its peak covered nearly a quarter of the global land mass and exercised control over nearly a quarter of the world's population.

All the European colonial administrations rested ultimately upon a mixture of violent exploitation and expropriation, a presumption of the racial and cultural superiority of the colonial masters, and a belief that colonialism served the higher purpose of civilizing the Indigenous Other. Thinkers from across the European intellectual spectrum during the colonial era generally shared an understanding of human progress as going through various stages towards modernity, as well as a process of cultural evolution (Kohn and Reddy, 2017). Thus, the idea of a civilizing, progressive mission provided a powerful legitimating discourse with which to mask colonial exploitation and violence. With a few notable exceptions, such as the work of the Trinidadian historian, C. L. R. James or the British novelist and historian Edward John Thompson, the depiction of colonialism as a force for progress that was either benign or whose benefits outweighed its costs also threaded through much of the historical literature on the colonial era until comparatively recently (Satia, 2020).

One of the most significant outcomes of early European colonialism in the Americas and the use of slave labour was the emergence of the concept of race and the claim that white race was supposedly inherently superior to all other races.

Colonialism, race, and racism

It is only from the seventeenth century onwards that the term 'race' began to be used to distinguish humans according to their physical differences, such as skin colour or hair type. This usage first appeared during the early period of the English colonization of North America (Allen, 2021). There the term was used both descriptively and judgementally to distinguish between White European settlers, conquered Indigenous peoples, and enslaved Africans. By the eighteenth century usage of race to both identify and rank people had become widespread across Europe and it remains prevalent across the globe today. In short, race is a social construction that emerged within a specific international political context: colonialism.

It is now widely acknowledged that race and the idea of a hierarchy of races did not precede colonialism but were created and rapidly disseminated as part of the global colonizing process. In a 1910 essay 'The Souls of White Folk', the Black American Intellectual W.E.B. Du Bois observed that 'the discovery of personal whiteness among the world's people is a very modern thing – a nineteenth and twentieth century matter, indeed' (Du Bois, 1986: 923). Drawing on Du Bois' extensive writings on race and European colonialism, Reiland Rabaka, argues that 'Whites and non-whites do not exist prior to the imperial expansion that helped to birth, raise and rear European modernity' (Rabaka, 2007: 4). There is now an extensive body of scholarship that shows how the claim that the white race was somehow inherently superior to other races, was a direct product of imperialism and colonization (Bennett, 1993; Doty, 1993; Rabaka, 2007; Gruffydd Jones, 2008; Vitalis, 2015; Saini, 2019; Allen, 2021). For example, in his magisterial survey of the colonization of the Americas, first published in 1994, Theodore Allen offers a predominantly socio-economic argument to show how from the late seventeenth century onwards European colonialism led directly to 'the invention of the white race' (see Key concepts 9.1).

KEY CONCEPT 9.1 THEODORE W ALLEN: *THE INVENTION OF THE WHITE RACE*

The American scholar and activist Theodore W. Allen (1919–2005) captures the kernel of his argument In *The Invention of the White Race* (first published as 2 volumes in 1994 and 1997) thus:

> When the first Africans arrived in Virginia in 1619, there were no 'white' people there. Nor, according to the colonial records, would there be for another sixty years. Others living in the colony at the time were English; they had been English when they left England and, naturally they and their Virginia-born children were English. They were not 'white'. (Allen cited in Perry, 2021: xi)

In 20 years of research into the Virginia colonial records Allen wrote that he found 'no instance of the official use of the word 'white' as a social category prior to its appearance in a 1691 Virginia law. Thus, it was only after 60 years of colonization that 'white' would be used as a synonym for 'European-American' (Allen, 2021, vol. 1: 293, n.76). Indeed, Allen argued that racial slavery, in which Africans alone were condemned to life-long enslavement in the colonies, also only emerged in the late seventeenth century.

Allen saw the invention of the White race as not merely a socially and culturally constructed term, but also as a deliberate mechanism of social control by the colonial ruling class. In his study of European colonization in the Americas and the Caribbean, Allen identifies extensive evidence of deep solidarities emerging between bonded or enslaved labourers of all races. In classifying those labourers by race, Allen argues, the colonial ruling class sought to break down such solidarity, thereby weakening resistance to oppression. Allen cites the historian Lerone Bennett, Jr who argues that a system of racial privileges for propertyless 'whites' was deliberately introduced to encourage them to align themselves with the White plantation owners and against African bonded and enslaved labourers (Allen, 2021, vol.1: 21).

USEFUL REFERENCE

Theodore W. Allen (2021), *The Invention of the White Race: The Origin of Racial Oppression* (London: Verso).

It would seem, therefore, that examining the origins and influence of ideas about race should surely be central to the understanding of both international history and global politics today. As we shall see, in the founding years of the IR discipline this was indeed the case. Yet, by the middle of the twentieth century and until relatively recently at least, race had become only a very marginal concern in the IR discipline. This is a theme we will be considering more fully in Section 9.8.

Race and the Enlightenment

European colonialism and the racial classification of people broadly coincided with the beginning of the European intellectual movement known as the Enlightenment. This was when European philosophers were developing ideas of a supposedly universal community of humankind who were ostensibly equal in their rights and their duties to each other. However, these articulations of a universal human community were for the most part utterly Eurocentric and either implicitly or overtly racist by today's standards (Du Bois, 1986; Mills, 1997; Shilliam, 2011; Allais, 2016). The writings on race by some of the Enlightenment's most notable figures, such as Immanuel Kant, David Hume, and Georg Hegel, 'played a strong role in articulating Europe's sense not only of its cultural but also *racial* superiority'. In their work, Emmanuel Chukwudi Eze, argues, '"reason" and "civilisation" became almost synonymous with "White" people and Northern Europe' (Eze, 1997: 5).

Even the emergence in the early 1800s of campaigns for the formal abolition of slavery, although ultimately successful, arguably helped to reinforce the construction of unequal racial identities. Doty suggests, for example, this is because 'the same system that gave official protection to Black Africans in the form of prohibitions on slavery also constructed particular identities for those same subjects that made other forms of unequal treatment possible' (Doty, 1993: 458). Opposition to slavery did not mean rejecting racism. Gurminder Bhambra argues that opposition was more to the abstract idea of slavery, which after all sat in stark contrast to the core Enlightenment concern with liberty, than with slavery as a concrete practice. Indeed, even prominent abolitionists, such as the eighteenth-century English philosopher John Locke, invested in slavery-dependent commercial ventures (Bhambra, 2007: 40–43). Certainly, the abolition of colonial slavery did little to halt the further development in Europe and the wider West of ideas of white racial supremacy, the superiority of European civilization, or the depiction of people subjected to colonial rule as inherently inferior (Drescher, 1990; Eze, 1997; Grovogui, 2001; Satia, 2020).

During the nineteenth century the political and moral legitimacy of European colonialism became a growing matter of debate within some European intellectual circles. These debates were, however, limited in scope and rarely challenged the racist underpinnings of colonialism. The underlying presumption of much Enlightenment thinking, whether covertly or overtly expressed, was that the benchmark for conceptions of liberty, progress, and the ideal human society was set by Europe and the still developing idea of a distinctive White race. Even among those ostensibly opposed to the colonial slave trade, the widespread perception was that non-white peoples and non-European societies had yet to reach European standards of civilization and their unequal treatment was therefore somehow justifiable (Drescher, 1990; Eze, 1997; Ingold, 2004; Bhambra, 2007).

9.4 RESISTING COLONIALISM

Throughout its history, European colonialism has always met with resistance (Said, 1994: xii). From the early nineteenth century onwards, when the Spanish and Portuguese empires in South America began to decline, resistance and rebellion expanded significantly across the colonized world. By the mid-to-late twentieth century this culminated in the dissolution of the vast bulk of European colonial territorial possessions.

Early Resistance

Prior to then, two early examples of anti-colonial resistance in particular stand out, although their racial dimensions were very different. The first is resistance to British colonial rule by white European settlers in North America in the late seventeenth century and the second, following shortly after, is the slave-led Haitian revolution of 1791–1804.

Anti-colonialism in North America

The American War of Independence (1775–1783) between European settlers in the 'Thirteen Colonies' and their British rulers ultimately led to the foundation of today's US. This anti-colonial struggle was, however, predominantly between White European settlers carving out a distinctive American identity and the governments of their former homelands. The rights and interests of the Indigenous peoples or enslaved Africans figured little in the conflict. Consequently, the hierarchies of race established during colonization largely remained in place after independence and the subsequent legal abolition of slavery. Racialized politics continued within the newly independent US, notably the struggle for equality for people of colour, the wars against Native Americans throughout the eighteenth and nineteenth centuries, and the Civil War of 1861–1865. What European colonialization had started, a newly independent US would continue; Euro-American racial, cultural, economic, and political hegemony became systematically entrenched.

332 INTRODUCTION TO INTERNATIONAL RELATIONS THEORIES

In effect, imperial colonialism was transformed into settler colonialism. This could be seen in the policies of racial segregation of education systems, transport systems, and access to a wide range of public and private amenities and services that persisted into the mid-twentieth century. A notorious example was the so-called 'Jim Crow' laws, enacted by legislatures in the southern US states from the 1870s onwards. These enforced everyday racial segregation and were not formally abolished until the Civil Rights Act of 1964. The legal abolition of segregation did not, however, lead to the total eradication of racial discrimination.

This racist discrimination against people of colour and Indigenous populations after the formal end of colonial rule was subsequently repeated in other former British colonies with large European settler communities, such as South Africa (which we examine further in Key events 9.2), and Australia. These included practices of ethnic cleansing and acts of violence that were at times tantamount to genocide (on the colonization of Australia see Hughes, 1994).

The Haitian Revolution

Haiti's achievement of independence only a few decades after the American revolution was very different in both form and outcome. It resulted from a series of very violent conflicts between 1791 and 1804 in the French Caribbean colony then known as Saint-Domingue. One of the world's major suppliers of sugar, it was France's most profitable colony and the world's richest at the time (Knight, 2000: 107; Bhambra, 2007: n 138) Sugar production relied on slave labour, mostly brought in from West Africa. Enslaved life in the sugar plantations was notoriously brutal which combined with the ravages of yellow fever and malaria meant that many of the enslaved did not survive more than a year.

The colony was also riddled with complex and violent social tensions arising from the colonial caste system used throughout the French Caribbean colonies. This divided the population into white colonists, free people of colour ('*gens de couleur*'), and the enslaved who comprised about 90 per cent of the population. There were tensions and outbreaks of violent conflict within and between all the groups: resentment between relatively poor Whites ('*petits blancs*') and wealthy White plantation owners ('*grands blancs*'), and varying levels of distrust between White colonists as a whole and free people of colour, some of whom were wealthier and better educated than some colonists and owned slaves. Social relations among the enslaved were also complex, because of social stratification and the arming of some of the enslaved to go to war on behalf of different slave owners.

The 1789 French revolution also impacted French Caribbean colonialism as did conflict between the rival European imperial powers. Both Britain and Spain sent troops to Saint-Domingue at various points, thereby adding to a period of violent and chaotic conflict which the new French revolutionary government in Paris struggled to control. The slaves, led by Pierre-Dominque Toussaint Louverture, an ex-slave and ex-slaveowner, mounted a military organized campaign. By 1801 Toussaint had conquered Saint-Domingue, expelled all colonial forces, and appointed himself Governor General. Toussaint proposed a remarkably modern constitution under which equal legal status was granted to all citizens, regardless of race, colour, or individual circumstances (Knight, 2000: 110–112).

When Napoleon Bonaparte seized power in France in 1799, he sent forces to recapture the colony. After a bloody campaign Toussaint agreed to an armistice with the French who promised not to restore slavery and maintain the freedoms the revolt had won. The French subsequently reneged on their promises and Toussaint was seized and shipped to France where he died in prison. The Black community rose again and under the leadership of Jean-Jacques Dessalines (a former lieutenant of Toussaint and a former slave) launched an ultimately successful military campaign against the French forces. Dessalines became Governor General and, on 1 January 1804, declared the independence of Saint-Domingue under the new name of Haiti. Haiti became only the second independent state in the Americas and the first non-European state to be carved out of any of the European colonial territories.

The significance of the Haitian revolution in the history and racialized politics of European colonialism was underscored by Dessaline's introduction in 1805 of a new Haitian constitution. Article 14 declared that all Haitian citizens would 'henceforth be known by the generic appellation of "Blacks"' (1805 Haitian Constitution cited in Girard, 2019: 13). This disrupted the then dominant accounts of race because it made being Black 'a mere implication of being Haitian and thus a political rather than a biological category' (Fischer, 2004: 233). Although Dessalines had allowed the slaughter of white colonialists in retribution for the suffering they had caused, he also recognized that some whites had supported the revolution. These included, for example, Polish legionnaires enlisted in Napoleon's army, many of whom after arriving in Saint-Domingue became uneasy with France's intention to quash the revolution and deserted the French forces to join the revolt. The 1805 constitution guaranteed citizenship to any Polish soldier who had supported the revolution and wished to become Haitian and, therefore, also 'Black'.

The Haitian revolution spawned political unrest in other Caribbean slave communities and alarmed slave owners throughout the Americas (Knight, 2000: 113). Prior to the Haitian revolution, the British assumed that the biggest threat to their colonial holdings came from white European settlers (as was the case in the US), not the enslaved (Drescher, 2001: 12). It also emboldened anti-slavery movements in Europe and arguably contributed significantly to the abolition of the slave trade. However, the use of slave labour continued throughout the colonized world, and, in some respects, the Haitian revolution led to its further expansion in sugar plantations in Jamaica and Brazil (Geggus, 2001b: 249–250).

Historians are divided over the extent to which the Haitian revolution materially impacted upon the slave trade but its symbolic significance is widely recognized as is its influence on the development of political activism by people of colour worldwide in the nineteenth century (Geggus, 2001a). It inspired revolts by the enslaved in the US as well as in other British colonies such as Jamaica, but these were violently suppressed. The newly independent state of Haiti also paid a heavy price. As the Haitian academic Jean Casimir notes, '(t)he State of Haiti was born into a world that considered its very existence inconceivable and undesirable' (Casimir, 2020: 22).

The anticolonial struggles of the twentieth century

In the early twentieth century, intellectuals of colour were becoming increasingly prominent worldwide and many were directly involved in anti-colonial resistance. These included the Indian lawyer and anti-colonial nationalist Mahatma Gandhi (1869–1948), the American intellectual W.E.B. Du Bois (1868–1963), the Jamaican political activist and pan-Africanist Marcus Garvey (1887–1940), the Vietnamese Marxist revolutionary politician Ho Chí Minh (1890–1969), and the Martinique poet and politician Aimé Césaire (1913–2008).

Critiques of the economically exploitative nature of imperialism and colonialism were also emerging, notably from within Marxist schools of thought, such as Lenin's *Imperialism: The Highest Stage of Capitalism* published in 1917 (which we discuss in Chapter 5). Marxist critiques of imperialism would go on to provide a vital intellectual resource for many of those at the forefront of anti-colonial struggles although they did not treat them uncritically. There was a 'rich texture of dissent within the Marxist anti-colonial tradition' (Young, 2016: xi–xii). Young is pointing here to an early sign of a key theme within contemporary postcolonial thought. This is the contestation and sometimes the synthesis between Western and various forms of non-Western thinking and practice to produce hybrid streams of postcolonial intellectual thought.

Many postcolonialist scholars broadly agree with much of the Marxist critique of imperialism and colonialism, but some also argue that it rests nonetheless upon broadly Eurocentric assumptions and pays insufficient attention to the global spread of the complex social and cultural legacies of colonialism. Marxist critiques of the colonial legacy in the contemporary global political and economic order focus primarily on its materialist dimensions: the political economy of imperialism. The postcolonial theorist Robert J. C. Young suggests a different analytical starting point: race and racism. It is a 'simple fact', Young argues, 'that Western imperialism, as it was developed systematically in the nineteenth century, was a race imperialism' (Young, 2016: xi).

Anti-colonialism and decolonization after 1945

Most former colonies gained their independence in the three decades after 1945. How anticolonialism manifested itself in specific cases reflected who the colonial power being challenged was, the balance between Indigenous peoples and settlers from the colonizing country, and the specific characteristics of the colonial territory and its peoples. Again, this is a complex story that we can only briefly touch on.

The post-1945 wave of decolonization started with India. The roots of Indian nationalism lie in the nineteenth century, but it was after the First World War (in which around 50,000 Indian soldiers died supporting Britain) that non-cooperation campaigns began protesting British rule. The decision of the British to bring India (along with their other colonized territories) into the Second World War while failing to respond to demands for greater Indian self-government led to the creation in 1942 of the Quit India civil disobedience movement led by Gandhi. The movement was effectively suppressed by the British through mass detentions, including Gandhi's imprisonment. Nonetheless, it was the most extensive internal uprising the British had experienced in India and 'a decisive moment in India's independence struggle' (Barkawi, 2006: 330).

In the Second World War's aftermath, several factors led to the hasty and chaotic British withdrawal from India. These included growing nationalist anti-colonial sentiment made more complex by tensions between India's Hindu and Muslim communities, disquiet within the Indian armed services which cast doubt on their willingness to continue upholding British rule, and Britain's post-war economic exhaustion. Together these factors made the maintenance of colonial rule in India too burdensome for a new Labour government in Britain keen to focus on post-war recovery and extensive domestic social reform.

Independence was granted in 1947 and British India was immediately partitioned into two new states: India with a Hindu and Sikh majority and a predominantly Muslim Pakistan. This was a poorly planned process that resulted in horrific inter-communal violence as millions of people endeavoured to relocate to either side of the new divide. Apportioning blame for the violence is by no means straightforward, but it was not least a consequence of Britain's frequently brutal use of divide and rule strategies that for decades before had overtly manipulated and exacerbated communal divisions. The trauma of violent partition continues to resonate throughout the politics of the two new states today, as well as their relations with each other.

Anti-colonial struggles were also a key part of post-1945 Southeast Asian history. They were prompted in large part by the defeat of Japan in 1945, which had been the colonial ruler of Korea since 1910 and had occupied various French and British colonial territories in the region during the Second World War. France's attempt to restore control over its colonial territories such as Laos, Vietnam, and Cambodia met with considerable Indigenous resistance. After being defeated by Vietnamese communist nationalists in 1954, France withdrew from the region altogether. The US became militarily embroiled in Southeast Asian nationalist conflicts as part of its campaign against what it saw as the global spread of communism, most notably in Korea and Vietnam. Similarly, after the end of Japan's occupation of the British colony of Malaya (now Malaysia), armed resistance by communist insurgents led, from 1948 onwards, to a decade of often brutal confrontation with British troops prior to the granting of independence in 1957.

In North Africa, French colonialism was first challenged in Algeria and was rendered more complex by the relationship between the settler population, Indigenous communities, and the French state. The French settlers, most of whom were born in Algeria and regarded it and themselves as irrevocably part of France, strenuously opposed decolonization. They played a significant role in the extreme violence of the Algerian War of Independence, the effects of which spilled over into France itself and can still be seen in French politics today, as outlined in Key Events 9.1.

KEY EVENT 9.1 THE ALGERIAN WAR OF INDEPENDENCE

The struggle for Algerian independence began during the First World War and accelerated after 1945 when France failed to fulfil a promise of greater self-rule. In 1954 the National Liberation Front (FLN) began a campaign of guerrilla warfare against France while pursuing diplomatic recognition for an independent Algeria at the UN. Algeria achieved its independence from France in 1962 after eight years of brutally violent conflict which resulted in between 500,000 and 1.5 million deaths. France committed over 500,000 troops to the war and only maintained its control through considerable brutality, including the extensive use of torture and illegal executions. Such brutality included the 1961 massacre of more than 200 Algerians on a single day when the French National Police attacked a peaceful demonstration by Algerian residents in Paris.

The war was rendered more complex by the violent involvement of the large white colonial settler community, around 10 per cent of the population and commonly referred to as *pieds-noirs* ('black feet'). Most of them vehemently opposed independence.

The Algerian war had a considerable impact on politics in France. It was partly responsible for the fall of the Fourth French Republic in 1958, after French military officers sympathetic to the *pieds-noirs* attempted a coup d'état. The election of the legendary wartime leader General Charles de Gaulle to the French presidency in 1959 led to a new national constitution creating France's 'Fifth Republic'.

De Gaulle's subsequent proposals for improving the conditions of Indigenous Muslim Algerians and reducing Algeria's direct integration with France were rejected by the FLN. After another coup attempt by *pieds-noirs* supporters, De Gaulle turned decisively against them. Referenda in France and Algeria in 1962 revealed overwhelming public support for Algerian independence and led to a mass exodus of more than a million *pieds-noirs* to France, with many of them struggling to integrate into their new home.

The Algerian war's legacy resonates in French politics today, through ongoing revelations about the conduct of the war and with the emergence of far-right political movements supported by former *pieds-noirs* and their sympathizers. These led ultimately to the creation in 1972 of the far-right *Front National* (FN) party headed by the infamous Jean-Marie Le Pen, who had served in Algeria as a paratrooper in the French Foreign Legion. He was succeeded as party leader by his daughter Marine le Pen. While broadly sharing her father's views, she toned down the FN's openly antisemitic and racist rhetoric, renamed it the *Rassemblement National* (RN), and achieved much greater electoral success. After elections in 2022, the RN became the largest opposition party in the French Parliament.

India's independence along with anti-colonial resistance in French colonies in Indochina and North Africa contributed to the emergence of anti-colonial movements throughout the British colonies in Africa. Kwame Nkrumah led the way with a campaign of civil disobedience and non-violent resistance in the Gold Coast. This led to the establishment of self-rule after the first general election in colonial Africa in 1951 and in 1957 to the independence of the Gold Coast and Togoland, under the new name of Ghana.

During the 1950s, Nkrumah and other African anti-colonial leaders, such as Julius Nyerere of Tanganyika (now Tanzania) and Leopold Senghor of Senegal, worked on the theoretical and practical development of a distinctive African form of socialism. Nkrumah had spent many years in the US. There he was influenced by the writings of black intellectuals and activists, such as Marcus Garvey and W.E.B. DuBois, exploring ideas of pan-African identity and solidarity that could bring together national and transnational black political activity around the issues of national racial inequalities and the resistance to imperialism and colonialism in Africa. Nkrumah was a vociferous advocate of Pan-Africanism and became an inspirational figure for black activists worldwide.

In such early explorations we can detect the development of postcolonial thinking in which the experiences of colonialism were being threaded into visions of postcolonial life. Becoming independent was seen as not merely a case of joining the international community as supposedly equal sovereign states, but also of developing distinctive senses of national identity alongside international solidarities that were in very large part formed out of the colonial experience.

The decade after Ghana's independence saw most of the British held territories in Africa achieve independence. Like Algeria, the struggles for independence in South Africa and Rhodesia (now Zimbabwe) were complicated by the presence of very entrenched minority white settler communities. South Africa's transition to majority rule was particularly long and complex. Tensions between rival Dutch (Boer) and English settler communities since the mid-nineteenth century culminated in two 'Boer Wars' between 1880 and 1902. Britain's ultimate victory led to the establishment of the Union of South Africa as a self-governing British dominion in 1910 and full sovereignty in 1931. The achievement of independence from colonial rule was, however, only to the benefit of the white settler community. When the whites-only National Party came to power in 1948, the relatively informal segregationist practices developed during the colonial era became strengthened and formalized under the policy of Apartheid (which is briefly outlined in Key event 9.2). After South Africa became a republic in 1961, internal and international opposition to apartheid intensified. Internally, the African National Congress (ANC), began campaigns of protest and international lobbying coupled with guerrilla warfare and urban sabotage against the apartheid regime.

KEY EVENT 9.2 THE APARTHEID SYSTEM IN SOUTH AFRICA

Apartheid (Afrikaans for separateness) was a system of enforced racial segregation, based on a racist ideology of 'separate development'. Introduced in 1948 after the election of a National Party government by a whites-only electorate, it rested upon the classification of the population as either white, Black, or coloured (the latter containing several sub-divisions).

In principle, all the racial groups were entitled to equal development and cultural expression. In practice, apartheid amounted to a brutal and rigid set of policies that radically disadvantaged the non-white population, especially the Black community, and enforced the physical and social separation of the population groups. Apartheid affected every aspect of daily life; interracial sexual relations and marriage were prohibited, and apartheid stringently governed where non-whites could live or work.

From 1960 onwards, the government began to enact a vision of a South Africa containing 10 supposedly self-governing 'Bantustans' or 'tribal homelands' into which the Black population would be forced to relocate based on often highly inaccurate records of their 'origin'. Only 13 per cent of South African territory was set aside for a Black population of 19 million, the remainder being reserved for the 4.5 million whites. The intention was that the Black population would acquire citizenship of their designated homeland and forfeit their South African citizenship.

In 1978 the Minister of Plural Relations, Connie Mulder, told the South African parliament that 'if our policy is taken to its logical conclusion . . . there will not be one single black man with South African citizenship . . . and there will no obligation on this parliament to accommodate these people politically'. The policy was justified on the grounds that it was an 'honourable' approach to separate development that would enable Black self-government. In fact, less than half of the Black population relocated to the homelands prior to the repeal of the apartheid laws in 1991. The majority of Black South Africans continued to live in South Africa, mostly in shanty towns and slums on the periphery of South African cities, where their labour was engaged by white-owned businesses, homes, and industries.

Opposition to apartheid and the long-term incarceration of the ANC leader Nelson Mandela became potent international symbols of what became widely perceived as an indefensible racialized dominance of a majority population by a minority. The combination of militant internal resistance, international trade sanctions, and mounting external pressure led eventually to the opening in 1987 of negotiations between the white minority government and the ANC and, in 1990, the release of Nelson Mandela after more than 27 years of imprisonment. The first election under universal suffrage was held in 1994 resulting in a landslide victory for the ANC with Mandela becoming the first president of post-Apartheid South Africa.

Despite the different timescales and experiences of decolonization, from the mid-1950s onwards the rapidly expanding group of new postcolonial sovereign states found common cause when it came to assessing their place in the international system and the world economy. The early postcolonial era saw the emergence of various formal and informal expressions of shared concerns among the ex-colonial states, despite the variations in their paths to independence, systems of government, religious, racial, and ethnic makeups, and so on.

Early signs of solidarity emerged in 1955 at the *Bandung Conference* in Indonesia where 29 newly independent Asian or African states met to discuss cooperation and resistance to all forms of colonialism and neocolonialism. Between them they represented over 50 per cent of the world's population. This sowed the seeds of *non-alignment*, whereby, despite their generally socialist orientation, the newly independent states would resist taking sides in the Cold War between the Superpowers. This led to the creation of the *Non-Aligned Movement* in 1961, the *Group of 77* (which now has 134 members) in the UN General Assembly in 1964, and the coalition of developing states that during the 1970s pressed for a *New International Economic Order* (you can read more about the NIEO in Chapter 5, Section 5.3). The Organization for African Unity (OAU) was also established in 1963 with 32 signatory African governments, which was succeeded by the African Union (AU) in 2002.

Underpinning the growth of solidarity between very diverse postcolonial states was a shared perception of a significant tension between acquiring formal political and legal equality with other states as newly sovereign states, and the inherent inequalities of the international political and economic systems. Although the end of colonial rule can be plotted quite precisely on a timeline, the international capitalist system was seen to perpetuate the exploitation of the postcolonial states in the Global South for the ultimate benefit of Western economies and societies.

9.5 **KEY SOURCES OF CONTEMPORARY POSTCOLONIAL THOUGHT**

The post-1945 anti-colonial struggles provided a dynamic backdrop to the emergence of postcolonial thought, the roots of which can be traced to several sources. These include the critical writings by anti-colonial intellectuals and activists from the early twentieth century onwards even if the term postcolonialism was not used then. Other sources were literary studies, particularly the work of authors from the former colonies (Darby and Paolini, 1994: 375) and a branch of historical analysis from India known as Subaltern Studies, which we consider more fully later in this section. These sources may be heterogeneous, but the Indian historian Gyan Prakash, argues that collectively they forced 'a radical re-thinking and re-formulation of forms of knowledge and social identities authored and authorized by colonialism and Western domination' (Prakash, cited in Dirlik, 1994: 333). We will now briefly review some of the most notable contributors to the emergence and development of contemporary postcolonial thought.

Frantz Fanon

The work of psychiatrist, philosopher, and revolutionary Frantz Fanon is widely regarded as one of the most influential sources of contemporary postcolonial thinking (see Key thinkers 9.1). In *Black Skin, White Masks*, first published in 1952, Fanon explored the psychological complexities of being a Black person in a colonial setting (Fanon, 2008). Writing in a psychoanalytic tradition, Fanon argues that the material and social conditions of colonialism and racism alienated Black colonial subjects from their own sense of humanity. Colonialism pushes them away from their cultural origins, Fanon argued, and valorizes colonial subjects in terms of their capacities to imitate or try to appropriate the culture and language of the colonizers.

Fanon observes that a few Black colonial subjects might be able to afford to obtain what he calls the 'white masks'—such as education and mastery of the colonizer's language—that might give them enhanced status in their colonizers' eyes. However, this would never be truly sufficient for them to be treated equally in any meaningful sense.

Frantz Fanon

For most, being Black meant being deemed inferior from the outset, and this was reinforced in white representations of Blackness, both formally and through informal everyday language. Furthermore, Black children's exposure to such representations traumatized them, thereby creating a life-long inferiority complex. *Black Skin, White Masks* thus depicts colonialism as a uniquely pernicious form of domination because it effectively demands the complete negation of any sense of self and requires the creation of a new understanding of selfhood that has no connection with the colonized subject's past. It reveals how 'the colonised were repeatedly forced to ask, existentially, who am I in reality?' (Muppidi, 2009: 153).

 KEY THINKER 9.1 FRANTZ FANON

Frantz Fanon was born in 1925 in the French colony of Martinique (currently designated as an 'overseas department' of France) to parents who had African heritage. The family were middle class and sent Fanon to Martinique's best school where he became influenced by Aimé Césaire, the Martinique intellectual, poet, and politician, who, along with other francophone intellectuals, had begun exploring the concept of *negritude*—the affirmation or consciousness of Black African identity.

A vehement critic of European colonial racism, Césaire's influence led Fanon to reorient himself away from a French colonial identity towards an appreciation of his African heritage. During the Second World War, French naval forces sympathetic to the Vichy government in France (who governed part of France in collaboration with Nazi-occupied

France), took over the government in Martinique and Fanon fled the island to fight with the Free French Army in Algeria, later taking part in the liberation of France.

During the war, Fanon experienced racism which had a profound influence upon him. He went on to study medicine and psychiatry in France before working as a psychiatrist at a hospital in the French colony of Algeria. There he found himself treating both French soldiers who had used torture, as well as some of their Algerian victims. His sympathies rapidly shifted to the Algerian anti-colonial movement, and he left his position to work with the FLN, resulting ultimately in his expulsion from Algeria. Fanon relocated to Tunis where he was diagnosed with leukaemia. Having travelled to the US for treatment, Fanon died in 1961.

Fanon's personal experiences of anti-colonial struggle profoundly influenced his intellectual work, which is notable for its emphasis on the psychological consequences of racism and colonialism. The intersection of personal experience and intellectual argument in Fanon's work arguably helped set the tone for much subsequent writing by other critics of colonialism and racism.

Fanon's most influential work *The Wretched of the Earth*, first published in English in 1963, analyses the role of race, class, and culture in colonialism and the emergence of anti-colonial resistance. Its core message is clear: colonialism is inherently and totally violent.

Fanon challenges the depiction of European domination as the rational pursuit of progress through the liberation of the African Other from the supposed savagery of their past. In contrast, Fanon describes colonialism as 'not a thinking machine, nor a body endowed with reasoning faculties. It is violence in its natural state, and it will only yield when confronted with greater violence' (Fanon, 2001: 61). Fanon was not simply justifying violence for its own sake, but as a legitimate, unavoidably necessary response to the violence of an oppressor, who may well only respond if that violence is thrown back at them. Confronting colonial violence with violence is depicted as the forceful rejection of the status of an inferior Other imposed upon the colonized subject, both materially and psychologically.

For Fanon, colonial subjects needed to look beyond Europe and forge their own conception of humanity rooted in solidarity and justice. Arguably, it is this aspect of Fanon's work that proved to be the most influential during the period of intense anti-colonial struggles worldwide. Fanon was urging for those struggling against colonization and other forms of violent European domination to develop no less than a revolutionary philosophy of liberation.

The intellectual influence of Fanon's work can be seen in more contemporary articulations of the continuing need for *decolonization* long after the formal end of the colonial era (we examine contemporary decolonial thought in Section 9.9). However, the limitations of Fanon's work, as well as some of its marked silences, have also been recognized. Fanon's emphasis on violence has generated considerable debate over the years and his vision of a worldwide revolution against European colonial and postcolonial domination clearly failed to materialize as he envisioned. Cooperation among former colonies around the world still finds institutional expression today, in such fora as the Group of 77 at the UN, the African Union, the Association of Southeast Asian Nations, the Arab League, and so on. There is, however, little of the revolutionary fervour of Fanon and his anti-colonial contemporaries within them.

Indeed, much of contemporary postcolonialism endeavours to uncover the more nuanced aspects of colonialism's legacy and the challenges of responding to them in a postcolonial world. Fanon is also criticized for the gendered assumptions underpinning his work, with some arguing that while he praised the role of women, Fanon nonetheless portrayed men as the natural leaders of nationalist struggles against colonialism (Ismail, 1992; Lane and Mahdi, 2012; Ming Wahl, 2021).

Edward Said and Orientalism

Fanon showed how Black subjectivity is constructed as a negative Other, which serves to define and shore up the white European sense of innate racial superiority. This a theme taken up in the Palestinian-American scholar Edward Said's pathbreaking work *Orientalism,* first published in 1978 and widely depicted as the starting point of contemporary postcolonial studies.

The term orientalism has been used widely and often uncritically in art history and literary studies to describe attempts to capture, imitate, or mimic aspects of the Eastern World (most notably the Middle East) in literary, visual, or musical form. Orientalism was also a branch of scholarly research that developed in the nineteenth century, focusing initially on the Middle East and the Islamic world more generally and, subsequently, the Far East as well. Although it presented the Orient as a rich repository of distinctive forms of culture and knowledge, it also was a significant contributor to a depiction of the Orient that Said sets out to critique.

Western representations of the Orient in written or visual form cannot, Said argues, escape the context of colonialism in which they were created. Colonialism was a 'gross political fact' and all representations of the Orient were inescapably political and colonial in some sense, regardless of their authors' stated intentions (Said, 1985: 11). Said draws upon the work of Antonio Gramsci (whom we also discuss in Chapter 5, Section 5.4 and Chapter 6, Section 6.4) to depict dominant representations of the Orient as contributing to the maintenance of Western cultural hegemony and the sense of Europe's innate superiority. Said's examination of Western visual and written representations of the Orient reveals several tropes that collectively add up to a depiction of the Orient as in some ways more fascinating than the West, yet always inferior to it. It was depicted as worth travelling great distances to visit, yet in its distinctiveness from Europe the Orient could never be Europe's equal. In effect, Western orientalism invents the Orient through repeated representations of it by scholars, authors, artists, and travellers. It was seen as fascinating, exotic, and sensuous but also cruel, strange, disturbing, and degenerate (Said, 1985: 40, 49). During the colonial era there was comparatively little interest in what peoples within what the West depicted as the Orient had to say for themselves. Orientalism, as Said describes it, thus offered an inherently unbalanced, partial, and prejudiced depiction of the East.

Orientalist assumptions arguably continue to inform contemporary public understanding of the Middle East and the Islamic world today. Since the 9/11 terror attacks on the US, for example, the depiction of the Arab and the wider Islamic world as fundamentally antithetical to the West and a major threat to its survival has become rife (Jackson, 2005). This is evidenced not only by the tone and language of media reporting, but also by depictions of the 'Arab' in popular culture such as Hollywood movies and television (Alsultany, 2012), as well as innumerable expressions of a widespread Islamophobia across the Western world.

While broadly sympathetic with Said's depiction of the dominant representations of the East, some scholars argue it rests upon overly large generalizations based on a limited number of texts and an overly stark juxtaposition of colonizer and colonized, which understates the two-way flow of power and knowledge, especially if one considers the use of the term Oriental to include the regions further east such as China and Japan (Young, 2016: 389–392). In later work, however, Said extends the argument developed in *Orientalism* to examine Western cultural representations—or misrepresentations—of the wider non-European and colonized world (Said, 1994).

Although not conceived of as a contribution to the IR field specifically, Said's critique of orientalism has direct relevance to it (Biswas, 2007). Said very clearly associates the development of orientalism with the history of Western imperialism and colonialism. *Orientalism*'s influence also stems from the culturally focused range of sources it draws upon—fiction, the arts, travelogues, and so on. This has helped to give the cultural sphere more generally greater prominence in IR scholarship, where considerations of culture have been markedly absent until comparatively recently.

Some authors have followed on from Said to investigate how orientalist assumptions have masked the extent to which Eastern contributions to knowledge formed key components of the supposedly unique Western civilization. John Hobson (2004) argues, for example, that European development has historically relied extensively on the assimilation of Eastern ideas and technologies. Contrary to the widely held view (which we discussed in Section 9.2) that Western development was autonomous and original and is the source of modernity itself, Hobson offers a different picture that pushes the East much more into the foreground. Certainly, European imperialism and colonialism entailed the appropriation of a wide range of economic resources from conquests in the East to help feed Western growth and development. Yet, Hobson argues, Eastern ideas were being diffused across and assimilated by the Western world long prior to the colonial era. Consequently, there are few 'Western' ideas and technologies that don't reveal some Eastern influence. For this reason, Hobson argues, we might more accurately talk of the rise of the 'oriental West' (Hobson, 2004: 2).

Subaltern Studies—excavating unheard voices from below

Since the early 1980s, another significant contribution to postcolonialism has been a body of work by Indian social historians known as Subaltern Studies. This sought to develop a 'history from below'. Rather than examining India's history from the perspective of societal elites—in other words, history viewed from above—Subaltern Studies tries to view it through the experiences of those at the bottom of the Indian social ladder, the roles they played in the struggle against colonialism and their experiences of life during and after colonialism. The term 'subaltern' is taken from Gramsci's famous analysis of how class hegemony works in capitalist societies. It refers to those who are excluded from hegemonic political orders and exist on the margins of society. Thus, Subaltern Studies focuses on people at the lowest levels of society by virtue of their gender, class, race, religion, or, in the case of India, their caste.

Orthodox explanations of Indian nationalist resistance to colonialism generally depict it as largely driven and controlled by a well-educated Indian elite who supposedly inspired the masses to follow them (Prakash, 1994: 1476–1478). Subaltern Studies offers a contrasting picture, which emphasizes subaltern resistance not only to colonial power but also to the power of local landlords, moneylenders, and such like who were often connected to the nationalist movement. One of Subaltern Studies' founders, Ranajit Guha, examined peasant resistance to colonial power and more localized relations of domination in nineteenth-century India. Since the peasants themselves left no written record of their views, Guha chose to read the written historical record, from government sources or independent observers of various revolts, 'against the grain'. By this he meant that a critical reading of colonial authorities' reports of what they originally deemed to be problems of law and order among the peasantry showed the traces of locally organized political revolt (Guha, 1983). Guha argues that seemingly criminal acts by peasants could be shown to have political intent and were expressions of resistance to domination.

Some critics argue that Subaltern Studies underplays the significance and bravery of the Nationalist movement and its leaders and overstates the separation between subalterns and wider Indian society. Indian Marxist scholars have argued that it insufficiently considers the role of class and the political economy of nationalist struggle. British historians from the highly influential 'Cambridge School' of Indian history were also highly critical because Subaltern Studies ran counter to their own 'top-down' analyses of Indian nationalism (Ludden, 2002).

In more recent years, Subaltern Studies has developed several distinct strands (Ludden, 2002: 1–39). One of the most influential voices coming out of debates within Subaltern Studies is Gayatri Spivak. Although supportive of the general thrust of Subaltern Studies, Spivak has also criticized it in key respects. In a famous 1988 article entitled 'Can the Subaltern Speak?' Spivak questions some of the key claims underpinning the earlier work in Subaltern Studies, particularly the very possibility of representing the voices of the subalterns (Spivak, 1994).

Spivak claims that even well-intentioned critical Indian historians, many of whom are in prestigious Western universities, were effectively constructing the subaltern experience from a position of relative power, rather than enabling subalterns to speak of their experiences in any real sense. Spivak does not suggest that scholars should refrain from trying to represent the subaltern but should recognize that such representations cannot be the voice of the subaltern. Indeed, she famously suggests that subalterns may not be able to have a voice, i.e., be heard, at all. In saying this, Spivak raises the possibility that

Subaltern Studies, for all its explicit intentions, is engaging in an exercise of power and dominance which connects them back with the colonial domination that they wish to critique. The category of the subaltern will always have an air of artificiality, of being constructed from outside, about it. To claim to be able to describe the subaltern experience from outside cannot be the same as knowing that experience.

For Spivak, the challenge then is not to place subaltern peoples on a pedestal out of misplaced pity or guilt or give them a collective identity that they themselves have not claimed. Rather, Spivak's more general and radical point is that scholars working from positions of social and political privilege should reflect deeply on how this inhibits their capacity to learn from the marginalized or silenced voices of the Other. As Spivak famously put it, they need to recognize that 'their privilege is also their loss' (Spivak, 1994: 82). This emphasis on the need to recognize the distorting effects of racial, gender, or economic privilege upon one's worldview has subsequently become a very significant theme in debates around postcolonialism and indeed social and political thinking more generally.

Homi K. Bhabha and 'hybridity'

Many of the earlier sources of postcolonial thought rest upon a binary distinction between the colonizer and the colonized. However, some postcolonialist scholars have challenged this, particularly when it comes to questions about identity, notably Homi Bhabha.

Bhabha argues that the relationship between colonizer and colonized was more complex than a simple binary juxtaposition suggests. Colonialism was always ambivalent, Bhabha argues, in its understanding of colonial subjects. On the one hand they were seen as utterly distinctive and inferior to the European/Western 'civilized' subject; on the other hand, they could also be tamed and taught how to become, or least aspire to become European/Western, which was of course also a key theme in Fanon's work. As we have seen, Fanon decried attempts by colonial subjects to acquire 'white masks' in pursuit of status in the colonizer's eyes. Bhabha offers a more nuanced view of such mimicry. He suggests it could sometimes be, if unintentionally, subversive and can serve to expose the artificiality or hollowness of the symbolic expressions of power of the colonial masters (Bhabha, 1994: 121–131). David Huddart argues that Bhabha's work suggests that colonial power only *seems* to be successful in exercising domination over the colonized: 'for Bhabha' colonial power is anxious and never gets what it wants—a stable, final distinction between the colonizers and the colonized' (Huddart, 2006: 4).

Rejecting ideas of an essential 'colonial' subject or identity, Bhabha argues that colonial power led to cultural collisions and exchanges in the attempt to create Westernized colonial subjects and these produced 'hybrid' identities. These have, moreover, become disseminated across the globe as increasing numbers of people from the former colonies settled in the former colonizing states, such as France and the UK. In so doing they challenge notions of the nation-state as a fixed, clearly demarcated entity that is inherently resistant to significant change (which is, of course a core assumption of much orthodox IR thinking). Borders of states may be formally fixed, but one of the key consequences of colonialism is making borders more porous, thereby destabilizing national identities. Bhabha describes this process as *dissemiNation* to capture the impact of hybridity on ideas of national identity (Bhabha, 1994: 199–244).

Bhabha depicts hybridity as opening new 'Third Spaces' for identity formation and is therefore both subversive and transformative (Bhabha, 1994: 303–337). Novel cultural exchanges emerge in these *interstitial* third spaces, the spaces between social structures, established ways of doing or thinking, or categories of identity. In various ways, ranging from the colonial origins of some of their key institutions and laws through to the hybrid character of their postcolonial national cultures after independence, postcolonial states continue to show the imprint of their colonial pasts. Yet, contemporary Western societies also exhibit the imprint of colonialism because of migration. The postcolonial world is characterized then by fluid processes of identity formation and cultural transformations. The anthropologist Arjun Appadurai echoes Bhabha's idea of hybridity in his depiction of globalization as creating a new complex global order out of a series of interrelated 'global cultural flows'. These include the migration of peoples across cultures and borders, the role of transnational media in shaping our imaginations, the effects of technology on the interaction of cultures, the flow of money across borders, and the transnational flow of ideologies (Appadurai, 1996).

Bhabha has been criticized for offering an overly abstracted account of cultures and a too generous account of the relationships between them. He is sometimes accused of idealism for seemingly proposing that a future, more cosmopolitan-minded world is possible because of cultural hybridization and the growing dissolution of clear boundaries between cultures. Marxist critics accuse Bhabha (and some other postcolonial theorists) of overly focusing on culture and language and taking inadequate account of the material realities of global politics within an internationalist capitalist system (Parry, 2004). For such critics, Bhabha's claim that the differences between the First and Third Worlds are being eroded by the hybridization of cultures and identities is undermined by the ongoing realities of neo-colonial economic exploitation and the concrete, everyday experiences of those being exploited (Dirlik, 1994). Masao Miyoshi argues, for example, that capitalist transnational corporations (TNCs) 'travel, communicate and transfer people and plants, information, technology, money, and resources globally . . . and they are welcomed by the leaders of developing nations'. However, in so doing, TNCs actually 'rationalise and execute the objectives of colonialism with greater efficiency and rationalism' (Miyoshi, 1993: 749).

Postcolonial perspectives endeavour in various ways to show how the hierarchies of race, identity, and culture that colonialism rested upon, continue to play out in the contemporary postcolonial world. As our survey of key postcolonial thinkers shows, they do not entirely agree about colonialism's stamp on the contemporary world. Some identify prospects for innovative change and transformation, whereas others emphasize the continuation of inequality and domination, albeit often in different contemporary guises.

9.6 **POSTCOLONIALISM AND THE IR DISCIPLINE**

It should be clear by now that postcolonialism as a body of thinking has always had an inescapably international or global dimension, even if it initially developed largely outside the IR discipline. This invites the question why it has only impacted significantly on the IR discipline comparatively recently? We will explore possible answers to this question later in this section. Prior to this we will look at some of the ways in which postcolonial perspectives generate critical questions about how we study, analyse, and practice international politics.

Postcolonial perspectives offer a profound critique of many of the key assumptions underpinning mainstream IR theoretical perspectives. Postcolonial IR scholars argue that these have been constructed largely around theoretical abstractions derived from the historical and current conduct of states in the Global North, notably the European states since the seventeenth century, with little reference to the Global South in which two thirds of the world resides (Seth, 2013; Krishna 2018: 19–21; Biswas, 2021: 224).

For example, in contrast to realism's emphasis on states as formally equal units interacting within an international anarchy (which we discuss in Chapter 2), postcolonial perspectives depict the international system as, historically and presently, hierarchical and imperial in structure (Krishna, 2001; Grovogui, 2002; Sabaratnam, 2020). Realism acknowledges that states vary significantly in terms of power. However, there is little recognition of the central role of imperialism and colonialism in the development and sustenance of contemporary global inequalities of power as well as the problems encountered by formerly colonized states after their acquisition of independence and sovereignty (Grovogui, 2002; Sabaratnam, 2020).

Grovogui illustrates this point by comparing the histories of weaker and smaller states within Europe compared to that of postcolonial states confronting the inequalities of power in the contemporary world order. The European international order that evolved since the seventeenth century generally worked to protect the sovereignty of weaker states within it to a degree that enabled weaker or smaller states, such as Belgium and Switzerland, to participate in the colonial exploitation of Africa led by the larger European powers (Grovogui, 2002). In short, the formal attribute of sovereignty works quite differently for many states in the postcolonial Global South compared to states in the Global North.

Liberal IR theory emphasizes the increasingly interdependent nature of international politics and the benefits of greater institutionalized cooperation between states even in an anarchical international system (see the discussion in Chapter 2). In contrast, postcolonial perspectives highlight how the contemporary international political and economic order emerged out of the violent expansion of European empires and inter-imperial rivalry. Postcolonial perspectives invite us to ask who is cooperating with whom and whose interests are served by the inter-state cooperation that liberalism argues is a key component of contemporary international order? Postcolonialism highlights the marked inequity of the distribution of any benefits flowing from greater institutionalized international cooperation and expose how this continues to correspond with historical imperial and colonial flows of power (Gruffyd Jones, 2013).

Additionally, liberal IR theory emphasizes the significant role of non-state actors, such as transnational MNCs, in the workings of the contemporary international system. Contrary to the liberal depiction of the contemporary multi-actor international order as a comparatively recent phenomenon (Keohane and Nye, 1989), however, postcolonial analyses show how the intersection of private and state interests was central to the history of imperialism and colonialism from the outset. Postcolonial perspectives show how non-state actors, such as trading companies—like the East India Company, the Royal African Company, the Dutch West India Company, and the Hudson's Bay Company—were significant participants in European imperialism and colonialism from the beginning of the colonial era, usually working hand in glove with the European imperial powers (Gruffyd Jones, 2013; Bhambra, 2021).

These illustrative examples of differences in underlying theoretical assumptions suggest that postcolonial perspectives cast a very different light upon many, if not most of the traditional core concerns of the IR discipline. These include the history of the international system, the bases of international order, the concept of the balance of power, the meaning and substance of sovereignty, the role of international law, and so on. We will now explore what postcolonialism brings to core concerns of the IR discipline a bit further.

Postcolonialism and the Cold War

Postcolonialism casts a very different light on key episodes of international history, from the colonial era through to more recent events. These include the Cold War which framed so much of the IR discipline's focus after 1945 until the fall of the Berlin Wall. Most accounts of the Cold War centre on the relationship between the superpowers, the US and the Soviet Union, and the supposed stability arising from a bipolar balance of power underpinned by the nuclear doctrine of Mutually Assured Destruction.

What postcolonialism brings into the foreground is the 'view from below'—the experiences of those living (suffering and dying) in the many decidedly hot localized conflict zones of the Cold War. Looking at the Cold War through postcolonial lenses, Heonik Kwon argues that

> (t)he history of the global cold war consists of a multitude of . . . locally specific historical realities and variant human experiences and this view conflicts with the dominant image of the cold war as a single encompassing geopolitical order. (Kwon, 2010: 6–7)

The Cold War produced a range of such 'local specific realities' in East and Southeast Asia in the decades after 1945. These were a consequence of the complexities arising from the interaction of several processes. These included the undoing of pre-war Japanese imperialism, anticolonial struggles in countries like Malaysia and Indonesia, and military campaigns—predominantly, but not only by the US—against communist and nationalist movements and insurgencies throughout the region (Shih and Chan, 2020).

Kwon argues that the depiction of the Cold War as a discrete event that began after the end of the Second World War reflects 'the centrality of the European and American experience'. Viewed from the experiences of two countries—Korea and Vietnam—that were at the violent heart of Cold War rivalry in SE Asia however, the Cold War and the long history of colonialism 'were disturbingly entangled and became practically inseparable' (Kwon, 2010: 6). Despite periods of heightened public fear that direct conflict between the superpowers might break out, most people in the US and its allies most of the time enjoyed the benefits and stability of the bipolar superpower nuclear balance of power. Elsewhere, especially where cold war rivalry, anti-colonial struggles, and postcolonial civil conflicts became entangled, 'people had to live the Cold War as part of their everyday lives' (Kwon, 2010: 6).

One of the most significant episodes in the Cold War was the 1962 Cuban Missile Crisis, when the US accused the Soviet Union of trying to install nuclear missile launchers on Cuban soil, just 140kms off the coast of Florida. The subsequent stand-off between the superpowers lasted 13 days and ended with the Soviets ending their Cuba missile programme. The crisis has been subsequently very widely analysed as an example of crisis decision making in foreign policy (Allison, 1971). It is also viewed as one of the key occasions during the Cold War when the two superpowers came closest to the outbreak of nuclear armed conflict. Until comparatively recently however, Cuba and the Cuban people have been largely absent from the bulk of scholarly analyses of the crisis (see Key concept 9.2).

Postcolonialism and international law

Postcolonialism also casts a different critical light on the key practices and institutions central to the operation and sustenance of the contemporary international system, such as the international legal system. In contrast to the commonplace depiction of international law as politically neutral, the *Third World Approaches to International Law* school of critical international legal studies depicts the international legal system as thoroughly Eurocentric and complicit in the historical and continuing subordination of non-European states and peoples (Mutua, 2001; Anghie, 2005).

Antony Anghie argues that the basic doctrines of international law, including the doctrine of state sovereignty that is at its heart, emerged out of the European-led development of an international legal system from the sixteenth century onwards (Anghie, 2005: 3). Contrary to the conventional view that international law was fully formed prior to the colonial era, Anghie depicts the evolution of international law as significantly influenced by the question of its application to relations between the European sovereign states and their colonial territories that were not deemed to be suitable for the granting of sovereign authority. International law was, then, influenced by cultural prejudices towards non-European peoples and thus evolved to manage their subordination and domination. The formulation of the principle of state sovereignty, Anghie argues, reflected the view that the non-European world was different from Europe and if colonial states were ever to acquire sovereignty over their own affairs this would only be possible if they successfully emulated European standards of civilization (Anghie, 2005: 4). Although colonized territories subsequently acquired sovereignty through their resistance to colonialism, Anghie sees this as amounting to an obligation to abide by the rules of international law that the ex-colonies had no part in making.

Similarly, Bhupinder Chimni claims that 'international law is playing a crucial role in helping legitimize and sustain the unequal structures and processes that manifest themselves in the growing north-south divide' (Chimni, 2006: 3). Chimni argues that international legal frameworks regulate the exercise of state sovereignty through rules covering investment, trade, currency controls, property rights, labour market regulations, environmental policies, and so on. These legal frameworks, work primarily to the benefit of the industrialized states in the Global North and the transnational corporate actors based within them. Chimni does not see the increasing regulation of international politics in a globalizing world as a problem *per se*, rather it is their differential impact upon Third World states because of their bias towards the interests of the Global North that is the issue. What Chimni questions is the evolution of 'uniform global standards' which endeavour to standardize the conduct of states, despite the very different development paths of states in the Global South compared to the Global North:

> There is no longer space for recognizing the concerns of states and peoples subjected to long colonial rule. Poor and rich sates are to be treated alike in the new century . . . (e)quality rather than difference is the new norm. (Chimni, 2006: 14)

Chimni and others argue that the international legal order is moving in the direction of enforcing the standardization of state behaviour. However, the legacy of colonialism and imperialism is also detected by postcolonial scholars in the unequal treatment of states within some international legal frameworks.

The Nuclear Non-Proliferation Regime—'nuclear orientalism'?

One example of this is the nuclear non-proliferation regime (NNPR), the legal framework for the management of nuclear weapons, the cornerstone of which is the 1970 Non-Proliferation Treaty (NPT). The ostensible purpose of the NNPR is to prevent the spread of nuclear weapons. In pursuit of this objective, the NPT recognizes five existing (in 1970) Nuclear Weapons States (NWS)—The US, USSR, China, France, and the UK. These are permitted to keep their nuclear weapons capability, although Article Vi of the NPT asks them to 'pursue negotiations in good faith' to achieve nuclear disarmament. All other signatories are permitted to develop nuclear energy technology, but not for the purpose of producing nuclear weapons.

191 states have signed the treaty, but Israel, Pakistan, and India refused, arguing that the NPT constituted a form of 'nuclear apartheid' (Gusterson, 1999: 113). Although the two major NWS—the US and Russia—have drastically reduced their deployed nuclear arsenals in the post-Cold War era, they have shown little interest in working towards the elimination of all nuclear weapons evidently seeing them still as vital components of their defence strategies (Biswas, 2014: 3–4 and 174). It is important to note also that many states in the Global North—such as the members of the US-led NATO alliance, or states who align themselves with Russia—may not possess nuclear weapons but benefit

nonetheless from the nuclear umbrella provided by the two major NWS. The few states who refused to sign the NPT have chosen to develop their own nuclear weapons programmes. Israel, Pakistan, and India are known to be doing so. Iran, a signatory of the NPT, is widely suspected in the West of pursuing a nuclear weapons capability, despite its claims to only be developing the production of nuclear energy. Similarly, North Korea, which signed the NPT only to withdraw from it in 1993, is also widely suspected of developing a nuclear weapons capability.

Drawing upon the work of Edward Said and other postcolonial scholars, Hugh Gusterson depicts the NPT as a form of 'nuclear orientalism' because it is 'the legal anchor for a global nuclear regime that is increasingly legitimated in Western public discourse in racialized terms' (Gusterson, 1999: 113). Gusterson identifies four popular arguments in Western political discourse for denying Third World states the right to develop their own nuclear weapons:

- They are too poor
- Nuclear deterrence will be unstable between Third World states
- Third World states are too technically immature to be trusted with nuclear weapons
- Third World states lack sufficient political maturity.

All four of these arguments are, Gusterson suggests, orientalist in form because they rely upon a binary division between supposedly stable and mature developed states and a generalized negative depiction of Third World states. Gusterson is not arguing for more states to get nuclear weapons or that states do not vary in their reliability as 'custodians of nuclear weapons'. His argument is that the differences between states regarding their suitability for possessing nuclear weapons are much more complex than a binary division between 'a few countries that have nuclear weapons and insist they are safe and those countries that do not have nuclear weapons and are told they cannot safely acquire them' (Gusterson, 1999: 116).

Shampa Biswas acknowledges the central and vital importance of the NPT, but, like Gusterson, draws upon postcolonialism to criticize a simplistic division of states into those who are deemed sufficiently mature and responsible to possess nuclear weapons and those who in many Western eyes are not. Biswas contrasts a postcolonial perspective on the NNPR with realist and liberal perspectives. Liberal IR scholars generally depict the NNPR as an example of the benefits of international cooperation driven by good will (Biswas, 2014: 176). In contrast, realists reject what they perceive to be liberalism's idealism and depict the international inequality of power as a reality that all states and other actors must accept (Biswas, 2014: 179–180). From a realist perspective then, the division between nuclear haves and have nots simply reflects the inequalities of power. However, Biswas also notes that even the neorealist Kenneth Waltz has accused those opposed to Third World states (notably Iran) acquiring nuclear weapons of ethnocentrism (Biswas 2014: 179). (We also discuss this further in Section 3.7, Chapter 3).

Biswas depicts the NPT as playing a crucial role in constraining the spread of nuclear weapons (as liberals argue) while at the same time sustaining 'a colonial nuclear order'.

Here unequal power is at work, as realists claim, but it is underpinned by Eurocentric and colonial prejudices. Certain states, argues Biswas, are perpetually confined to 'the waiting room of history' to be condemned should they ever try to acquire the same nuclear weapons that the 'nuclear five' claim as vital to their security (Biswas, 2014: 177–178). Can we ever feel safe, Biswas asks, in a world when there is so little pressure on the five existing NWS to give up their nuclear arsenals that they continue to update and expand (2014: 178–179)? Western fears about the proliferation of nuclear weapons focus on Third World states, yet the only actual use of nuclear weapons in conflict was by one of the legitimized NWS: the US bombing of Nagasaki and Hiroshima in 1945. Additionally, all the states currently possessing nuclear weapons, legally or illegally, are perfectly capable of, and some have demonstrably engaged in belligerent and dangerous foreign policy behaviour (Biswas, 2014: 20 and 178). 'Irrationality', Biswas proposes, 'is quite evenly distributed across the world' (Biswas, 2014: 20).

Postcolonialism and the state

As emphasized throughout this book, the mainstream of IR theory is statist. It endeavours to explain international politics through analysis of what they see as its primary units: states. Yet it also generally treats the state and state sovereignty in abstract and generalized terms; they 'take the identity of the state as given . . . and deny the processes of state formation in understanding international politics' (Rae, 2002: 15). Mainstream IR traces the origins of the territorially bounded sovereign state back to the 1648 Treaty of Westphalia and depicts the diffusion of the European conception of the sovereign state outwards from Europe across the world to ultimately include the newly decolonized states of Asia and Africa (Biswas, 2021: 224).

Mohammad Ayoob argues mainstream IR has failed to adequately recognize they need to take account of two key developments in post-1945 international politics: the rapid increase in the number of new states because of decolonization; and that these new states are attempting to replicate the European trajectory of state development 'in a vastly different international setting' from that in which European states were formed (Ayoob, 2002: 33). Ayoob observes that neorealism's emphasis on order and stability, the role of the balance of power and so on, is premised largely upon the historical behaviour of European states. In his view, it ignores the fact that 'stability in Europe was achieved at the expense of stability and order in the rest of the world' (Ayoob, 2002: 36).

Turning to neoliberalism's emphasis on international cooperation in an anarchical system, Ayoob notes that this also is premised largely on the behaviour of wealthy industrialized states in the Global North who comprise only a small minority of states today. Additionally, liberal theories of actual and potential political and economic cooperation take little account of the role of colonialism and imperialism in the development of the global capitalist system.

As the European states system was consolidating in the seventeenth century to produce the modern archetype of the sovereign state, European states were establishing new imperial and colonial systems beyond Europe (Keene, 2002). It is out of these imperial and colonial projects that post-colonial sovereign states ultimately emerged. However, their boundaries were determined in large part by inter-imperial rivalries over access to valuable resources, with little regard for long-established cultural and political communities. Makua Mutua notes that colonization divided Africa into 'ahistorical units' which were 'forcibly yanked into the Age of Europe'. 'African states', Mutua argues, are therefore 'distinctly artificial and are not the visible expression of historical struggles by local peoples to achieve political adjustment and balance' (Mutua, 1995: 487).

The emphasis in postcolonial perspectives on the crucial role of imperialism and colonialism in the process of state formation is relevant not only to the transition of former colonies to sovereign statehood, but also to the analysis of the development of European sovereign states as well. As we discussed in Section 9.2, a key dimension of Eurocentric thinking is the presumption that Europe and the states that evolved within it developed uniquely and independently from the wider world. We saw that postcolonialist scholars have challenged this account by emphasizing the role that imperial expansion and colonialism played in the formation and success of the modern European state. That success was, however, acquired on the back of the domination and exploitation of non-European peoples and the extraction of valuable resources from non-European lands to serve European developmental needs and desires.

In the first half of the twentieth century Black intellectuals—such as C.L.R. James, Eric Williams, and W.E.B. Du Bois—had extensively explored the central role of slavery in the development of European capitalism and the European state, but their work has received little consideration within mainstream IR and IPE scholarship (Gruffyd Jones, 2013: 52–54). Yet, this story of violent imperial and colonial exploitation before and after the abolition of the slave trade can be found throughout the histories of the global trade in many if not most of the commodities that played such a crucial role in the development of Europe and its accumulation of wealth: sugar, gold and other precious metals, rubber, cotton, diamonds, tea, coffee, tobacco, spices, and so on. Yet, despite their very different stories of origin, it is against the archetype of the post-Westphalian European sovereign state that the internal and external conduct of postcolonial states are widely judged (Grovogui, 2001).

Consider, for example, concepts such as 'quasi states', 'failed states', 'collapsed states', or 'weak states' often used to describe those ex-colonial states that are widely perceived to be failing to perform properly as sovereign states (Jackson, 1990; Rotberg, 2003 and 2004). The reasons given are some or all of: corrupt or overly repressive governance; ethnic and/or religious rivalries and conflict; bad or incompetent leadership; or an incapacity to maintain law and order throughout their territories. Blame for the perceived chronic inadequacies or complete failure of states such as Haiti, The Sudan, Somalia, or the Democratic Republic of the Congo is thus commonly seen as entirely local. Postcolonial scholars do not deny that many postcolonial states are experiencing varying degrees of social, economic, or political crisis. However, as Branwen Gruffydd Jones argues, the description of states as 'weak, fragile, failing, imploding, disintegrating, failed or collapsed' is used as a substitute for 'historically informed social analysis and explanation'. Such an analysis requires situating the crises confronting postcolonial states 'in the imperial history of global capitalism' (Gruffyd Jones, 2008a: 183–184).

Postcolonialism and human rights

Postcolonial perspectives not only question mainstream IR's treatment of the state, but also question its approach to individuals and peoples, notably concerning the issue of human rights. In 1948 the newly established United Nations adopted the Universal Declaration of Human Rights (UNDHR), the cornerstone of the international human rights regime. Although not a legally binding document, the UNDHR has had an enormous influence. It is referenced in the constitutions of dozens of countries worldwide and has directly influenced the drafting of numerous international treaties as well as national legislation.

Since the mid-twentieth century, the international human rights regime has developed considerably. At it is core is a set of key documents—the UNDHR, the International Covenant on Civil and Political Rights, and the International Covenant on Economic, Social and Cultural Rights—collectively referred to as the International Bill of Human Rights. There are also several other human rights conventions, such as the Genocide Convention, the International Convention on the Elimination of all forms of Racial Discrimination, the Convention Against Torture, the Convention on the Rights of the Child, and the Convention on the Rights of Persons with Disabilities. There are also multiple institutions—both within and outside the UN and at the regional as well as international levels—that are charged with promoting and upholding human rights.

It is widely assumed that the idea of universal human rights is essentially a Western creation. On this view, the origins of modern ideas of universal human rights lie in such things as the English Magna Carta (1215), the United States Declaration of Independence (1776), and the French *Declaration Des Droits de L'Homme et du Citoyen* (1789). Universal human rights are also widely associated with the Enlightenment, liberalism, and Western ideas of natural law (Waltz, 2002; Bonnet, 2015; Mutua, 2016; Slaughter, 2018; Mende, 2021).

There are some problems, however, with depicting human rights as being solely Western in origin. As we discussed in Section 9.4, the first Haitian Constitutions that followed the slave-led revolution abolished slavery and contained references to citizen's rights regardless of colour. As Janne Mende has noted, values that are depicted as central to Western moral philosophy—such as freedom, tolerance, and individual liberty—can be found in several non-Western philosophical and religious traditions, such as Buddhism, Confucianism, Hinduism, Islam, and the Akan conception of personhood from West Africa (Mende, 2021: 41. On Akan philosophy, see Wiredu and Gyeke, 2010). It could be said that ideas of human rights drawn from these non-Western philosophical traditions were often seen as only applicable to certain groups, sexes, castes, or classes and were developed in social settings that were very different from modern societies. Yet, as Mende points out, so too were the much-cited foundational documents of Western ideas of rights (Mende, 2021: 41). The US Declaration of Independence, for example, emerged within an eighteenth-century American colonial setting and was clearly not intended to apply to the enslaved or women.

Although Western states were centrally involved in the development of the international human rights regime after 1945, they were neither consistently nor uniformly enthusiastic about it. In the US, there was considerable conservative opposition, much of it with overtly racist overtones, to the idea of international human rights. This was instrumental in the US effectively withdrawing, after 1953, from direct involvement in the international human rights project. Britain initially opposed the idea of including human rights in the UN charter, fearing that this would fuel unrest in its colonies (Waltz, 2002: 440). The Western campaign for the establishment of international human rights was in fact largely spearheaded by small states, NGOs, and other non-state actors. The drafting of the UNDHR was also more pluralistic than is commonly acknowledged, with several non-Western states—such as India, Egypt, Syria, and several Latin American states—making substantial contributions to the final text (Waltz, 2002: 443–446; Mende, 2021: 42–43). However, some scholars point out that those non-Western contributions came largely from Western educated, elite members of their respective societies (Mutua, 2016: 18; Slaughter, 2018: 739).

Although the intention of the drafters of the UNDHR was to present human rights as universal and therefore above political partisanship, the text was cast in distinctly Eurocentric terms that reflected predominantly liberal values and a Western conception of the individual. Human rights language strongly emphasizes individual freedoms, which, moreover, are presented as best realized within Western-style democratic systems (Mutua, 2001 and 2016). The West was able to impose its liberal philosophy of human rights on the world because it was the dominant force within the UN at the time and it was shaping the post-1945 international order (Mutua, 2016: 168–169). After decolonization, from the 1960s onwards, debates about international human rights texts reflected more diverse non-Western philosophical and political viewpoints. This was because of the expanded UN membership and heightened Third World activism around such issues as national self-determination and the pursuit of global social and economic justice. Since then, the West has been commonly associated with individual and political rights and the Global South with social, economic, and cultural rights. Scholars such as Makau Mutua and Joseph Slaughter have shown, however, that greater Third World involvement in the development of human rights has not fundamentally altered the predominantly Western, liberal tone of most human rights discourse (Mutua, 2016: 168; Slaughter, 2018). From a postcolonial perspective, then, human rights are not neutral but inescapably political. This view is reinforced by the widespread tendency to deploy the supposedly neutral language of human rights to criticize states and governments in the Global South. Since the mid-twentieth century, human rights advocacy has become a central component of the West's self-image as a bastion of progress (Douzinas, 2007).

There is considerable evidence that human rights have had a positive impact globally on such things as women's rights, the protection of children, and the provision of 'an emancipatory vocabulary' (Kennedy, 2004: 3) that can be utilized by those struggling against oppression worldwide. However, postcolonial scholars join other critical scholars in exposing what David Kennedy has called the 'dark side' of the human rights movement and Western humanitarianism more generally (Kennedy, 2004). In its primary focus on civil and political rights understood in Western terms, for example, activism in the name of human rights by Western NGOs and states can fail to appreciate the complex economic, social, and cultural forces at play in non-Western contexts (Kennedy, 2004: 1–35).

The shortcomings of human rights can become particularly stark when they are used to legitimate Western-led armed humanitarian interventions (we discuss this further in Chapter 2, Section 2.5). US foreign policy is especially vulnerable to postcolonial critique because of its history of intervening in Third World states either alone or in coalition with other Western states. During and after the Second World War, the US defined itself as an anti-colonial power (Barkawi and Laffey, 1999: 415). Viewed through postcolonialist lenses, however, US political and military interventions in the Global South, both overt and covert, have had distinctly neo-imperial and neo-colonial overtones. Some interventions have been justified in the name of promoting democracy and a liberal understanding of freedom while others entailed the overthrow of democratically elected governments, such as that of Salvador Allende in Chile in 1973. The US has a long history of supporting authoritarian regimes known for their extensive abuse of human rights in pursuit of its own national political and economic interests (Said, 1994: chapter 4; Barkawi and Laffey, 1999 and 2006; Ohaegbulam, 2004; Burman, 2007). Despite human rights often figuring large in its foreign policy pronouncements, especially when criticizing other countries, the US only ratified the International Covenant on Civil and Political Rights in 1992. Although it signed the Covenant on Economic, Social and Cultural Rights in 1977, it remains today one of only 6 countries that has yet to ratify it and it is the only country in the world that has yet to ratify the convention on the Rights of The Child.

Western, liberal understandings of human rights also clearly underpin the concept of 'good governance' which is now widely presented as a standard against which the conduct of all states can ostensibly be assessed and criticized. The term emerged however largely in reference to problems in Third World states (Anghie, 2005: 249). In its concrete usage, such as by major international financial institutions such as the World Bank and the IMF, international human rights groups, or Western governments, it is evident that the term good governance refers primarily to core liberal concepts such as democracy, free markets, and the rule of law (Anghie, 2005: 249; Mutua, 2016: 169–172).

Postcolonial scholars do not deny that many states in the Global South are poorly governed or that their populations do not suffer from problems, such as corruption, state violence, lack of governmental accountability, the absence of or abuse of the rule of law, and so on (Mutua, 1995: 487). However, postcolonial perspectives do raise several critical questions about the binary depiction of Western states as comparatively stable, democratic, competently governed, and comparatively untroubled by human rights violations, in contrast to states in the Global South which are widely depicted as beset by myriad problems including widespread abuse of human rights. Furthermore, the use of human rights by the West as a means of criticizing Third World states has been historically quite selective. Many of those regimes in postcolonial states most criticized for their human rights abuses, authoritarianism, or even despotism have been and still are supported economically, politically, and militarily by Western powers who were their former colonial masters (Alemazung, 2010; Mahdavi, 2015; Shetty, 2018). Examples include Uganda under Idi Amin, Zaire under Mobuto Sese Seko, the

Central African Republic under Jean Bedel Bokassa, or Rwanda, Egypt, and Saudi Arabia today.

We have already noted the artificiality of the construction of many of today's post-colonial states and that Western democracies evolved over far longer periods of time than most ex-colonies have had to adjust to their acquisition of sovereignty. Additionally, many of the problems that beset postcolonial states have been and still are also present within Western democracies. After all, modern Europe emerged out of centuries of political, economic, and religious conflict, and European states were at the centre of two world wars in the twentieth century. In many Western countries political groups and parties, mostly on the far right of the political spectrum, have become increasingly prominent in recent years. These are openly hostile to key components of Western liberal thought and the human rights and freedoms that flow from them concerning such things as race, gender, religion, and sexuality (Lazaridis, Campani, and Benveniste, 2016; Eatwell and Goodwin, 2018). Even within Western political and moral thought, there is significant disagreement about the nature of and priorities between rights of the individual, economic rights, and the obligations of states towards their citizens. Think here of the differences between many Americans and Europeans about such issues as welfare rights, state health provision, the death penalty, gun rights, abortion, and so on, or debates within and between many Western societies around race and sexuality. Looking from the outside, then, the Global North could be seen to have some significant rights problems of its own.

Rethinking and decolonizing human rights

In 2018 the Secretary General of Amnesty International, one of the world's most prominent human rights NGOs, delivered a speech entitled 'Decolonising human rights'. In it Salil Shetty argues that the international human rights system has been 'misappropriated and instrumentalised in multiple ways', including the 'appropriation and domination of human rights by Western powers, often for neo-colonialist projects' (Shetty, 2018). Shetty offers an open-ended definition of human rights 'as the struggles of ordinary people to hold those in power to account' (Shetty, 2018). To fulfil this mission, Shetty argues, Human rights discourse must move beyond the hierarchical distinction between civil-political rights and economic-social rights and connect with struggles against the abuse of power at the local level.

Makau Mutua argues that the 'grand narrative' of human rights rests upon a depiction of the West as a 'saviour' tasked with rescuing the 'victims' of human rights abuses in the Global South (Mutua, 2001: 201–202. See also Douzinas, 2007). For Mutua and other postcolonial scholars, this understanding of the purpose of human rights should be abandoned along with the presumption that if the Third World is to eliminate the problems it faces it must follow a Western script of development centred around Western conceptions of the rule of law, individual rights, and democracy. Mutua argues instead for a 'cross-contamination' of cultures and a genuine, introspective intra-cultural dialogue that doesn't simply condemn or ostracize other cultures but recognizes that cultural pluralism can provide a basis for finding common ground on some issues (Mutua, 2001: 244–245).

There is a long and rich history of non-Western thought on such things as the relationship and responsibilities between individuals and wider society, rulers and the ruled, the pursuit of social justice and so on (Chakrabarty, 2000; Peetush, 2003; Baxi, 2007; Shilliam, 2013; Bonnet, 2015). Ashwani Peetush argues that the evident differences between human societies and cultures does not mean that there are no shared norms or values. 'Ideals such as compassion, care, trust, loyalty, respect, courage, fairness and so forth', Peetush argues, 'are found in almost all cultures although they may be defined, balanced, and expressed differently' (Peetush, 2003: 5).

> **THINK CRITICALLY 9.2** POSTCOLONIALISM AND HUMAN RIGHTS
>
> Do you think the international human rights regime is inherently Eurocentric? If not, why not? If so, could it be decolonized?
>
> To help you answer this question, consider the following prompts:
>
> - It is more than 70 years since the Universal Declaration of Human Rights (UNDHR) was adopted as a supposedly common standard by which the conduct of all states and peoples was to be judged. Since then, the membership of the UN has more than tripled
>
> - The UNDHR is widely presented as a key indicator of the universal applicability of Western liberal values but clearly many of these values are questioned, not only outside the West but within it as well
>
> - Think about examples of where human rights have been effective in improving people's lives and then about examples of where action in the name of human rights seems to have exacerbated people's suffering
>
> - Think about the relationship between different conceptions of human rights and power
>
> **USEFUL RESOURCES**
>
> 'Decolonizing human rights' Speech by Salil Shetty, Secretary General of Amnesty International at the LSE on 22nd May 2018. www.amnesty.org
>
> Mutua, Makau (2001), 'Savages, Victims, and Saviours: The Metaphor of Human Rights', *Harvard International Law Journal*, 42(1), 201–245.

9.7 EUROCENTRISM AND RACISM IN THE IR DISCIPLINE?

In Section 9.3 we noted how the concept of race emerged during the early colonial era and how much European thought of that era and after has had a distinctly racialized tone. We will now return to the intersection of imperialism, colonialism, and race with specific reference to the development of the IR discipline.

The transformative historical impact of imperialism and colonialism does not figure significantly either in the common story of the IR discipline's origins and early development or in the theories that have dominated the IR discipline for much of its history. As we will see, several postcolonialist IR scholars have sought to expose the reasons for this silence. In so doing, they have raised some uncomfortable questions about the common story of the origins and evolution of the IR discipline and opened some new critical debates about its contemporary state.

As is noted in Chapter 2, the modern academic IR discipline emerged after the First World War, just after European colonialism was at its peak. The common story is that the IR discipline's establishment was underpinned by liberal reformist values and the desire to prevent the recurrence of world war. In recent years, however, postcolonialist IR scholars have been developing a rather different account. Recent work, by Krishna Sankaran (2001); Robbie Shilliam (2011, 2015, 2020a, 2020b); Errol Henderson (2007, 2013, and 2017); Robert Vitalis (2015); John Hobson (2012); Sanjay Seth (2013); Davis, Thakur, and Vale (2020), and others, endeavours to show how the common story obscures the widespread preoccupation of the discipline's founding figures with imperialism and the management of empire. This was undergirded by an implicit and sometimes very explicit concern with maintaining global white supremacy.

Robert Vitalis (2015) traces the preoccupation with race threading through American IR scholarship specifically in the early years of the discipline. He highlights the now largely forgotten efforts of African American scholars that comprised what he calls the Howard School of international relations (named after one of the US's most prominent Black universities), to both expose and challenge the white supremacist assumptions of much early American IR scholarship. For example, in 1925 the African American intellectual W.E.B. Du Bois (who attended Howard University) published an article in the newly established Journal *Foreign Affairs* entitled 'Worlds of Color' (Du Bois, 1925). Here, Du Bois made the claim that what he called the 'color-line', was 'the problem of the Twentieth Century' (Du Bois, 1925: 423). By the color-line DuBois meant 'the relations of the darker to the lighter races of men in Asia, Africa, in America and in the islands of the sea' (Du Bois, 2009: 13–14). In an earlier article for the *Atlantic Monthly*, Du Bois had also described international relations as being effectively 'interracial relations' (cited in Henderson, 2017: 494).

To illustrate Du Bois' point about the centrality of race and the maintenance of white supremacy in the IR discipline's foundational years, Errol Henderson notes that one of the earliest examples of an IR textbook, prosaically entitled *An Introduction to the Study of International Relations*, contained a chapter entitled 'Political Relations between Advanced and Backward Peoples'. It claimed that 'one of the most fundamental facts in human history' is that '(m)ankind is divided into a graduated scale' ranging from civilized to barbarian to savage, and that this justified colonialism. Similar sentiments can be found, moreover, throughout several other early contributions to the new IR discipline (Henderson, 2017: 493–496).

Recent accounts of the establishment of the IR Discipline in the UK in the early twentieth century also highlight a racialized preoccupation among many of its founding figures with the maintenance of the British Empire. This threaded through the establishment of the first institutions of British IR scholarship, such as the Royal Institute of

International Affairs and Chatham House. These became connected in turn with parallel institutions established in key British colonial territories with large white settler communities such as South Africa, Canada, Australia, New Zealand, and later (and less successfully), India. These institutions were comprised of white male scholars and were initially bound together through the *Round Table* think tank, established in 1910, and the journal of the same name (Davis, Thakur, and Vale, 2020).

Only relatively recently has it been acknowledged that many of the leading lights behind the attempts to develop a new less war-prone Liberal international order held overtly white supremacist views. These included the US president Woodrow Wilson (who you can read about in Key Thinkers 2.2) and Jan Smuts, the South African statesman who had a prominent role in the establishment of the League of Nations, the UN, and the British Commonwealth. Their proclaimed liberal internationalism rested in fact upon a racialized, missionary understanding of the pursuit of human advancement led by the white race (Mazower, 2009; Davis, Thakur, and Vale, 2020; Kripp, 2022). Although they conceded that at some point the colonized territories would and should acquire independence, the prospects of independence were determined by where they perceived colonized peoples to be located on a scale of levels of civilization (Henderson, 2017: 494).

Why has it taken so long for such alternative readings of the IR discipline's origin to emerge? Vitalis argues that after 1945 the IR discipline's primary concerns were shaped by the emerging Cold War between the US and the USSR. This contributed to a kind of disciplinary amnesia and the embedding of an 'imagined past' centred around liberal reformism from which colonialism, imperialism, and race were almost completely erased. Realism became the dominant perspective, which shifted the discipline's focus onto the competitive advancement of the national interests of states (principally powerful states in the Global North) in a supposedly anarchic international system. Questions of race or the management of empire faded largely from view or became recoded as a concern, and a rather peripheral one at that, with 'development' or 'nation building' in the former colonial territories (Vitalis, 2015: 173–174. See also Doty, 1993; Krishna, 2001; Davis, Thakur, and Vale, 2020).

John Hobson also depicts the post-1945 IR discipline as marked by the forgetting or 'whitewashing' of earlier overtly racist IR thinking (Hobson, 2012). With the end of the Cold War, however, even if explicitly racist arguments had now disappeared from the IR discipline's scholarly output, Hobson argues that Eurocentric assumptions remained in the foreground in both 'offensive' and 'defensive' forms. The offensive form of Eurocentrism was reflected in a resurgent Western liberal optimism. This meant that much of mainstream IR thinking interpreted 'the end of the Soviet Union as offering up a grand opportunity for the progressive universalisation of Western, and especially, American values' (Hobson, 2012: 258). In contrast, more defensive varieties of Eurocentrism saw the post-Cold War era as posing a series of worrying new threats to the maintenance of Western dominance (Hobson, 2012: 279).

Race, racism, and IR theory

Hobson initially distinguished between the Eurocentrism of mainstream IR theory after 1945 and the overt racism of notable IR scholars prior to then (Hobson, 2012). However, several postcolonial IR scholars have subsequently argued that post-1945 IR scholarship is not merely Eurocentric but continues to be underpinned by racism, even if it is of a less overt form (Sajed, 2016; Sabaratnam, 2020). Hobson has conceded that, even if overtly racist beliefs or terminology are absent, in adhering to the idea that Western civilization self-evidently constitutes a universal benchmark of progress and development, Eurocentric IR perspectives effectively constitute forms of a 'racialised politics' (Hobson, 2016: 226).

Eurocentrism or racism?

Commenting on Hobson's distinction between Eurocentrism and racism, Olivia Rutazibwa asks if it is possible that academic enquiry can be 'miraculously cured' of the sickness of racism when it so clearly continues to permeate everyday life? Rutazibwa is not attacking Hobson personally but questioning the widespread reluctance to use 'the R-word' in examining contemporary IR scholarship (Rutazibwa, 2016: 192).

A vital issue here is the meaning attached to the claim that a body of work is deemed to be racist. The everyday understanding of racism focuses on the overt expression of hostility in words or deeds by people towards other people based on perceived racial differences. The problem with this commonplace restrictive view of racism is that it suggests that if individuals do not express overtly racist views or do not overtly show hostility towards people of another race then racism has been eliminated (Diangelo, 2019: 71–87). A more scholarly understanding depicts racism as a 'structural phenomenon that shapes societies and world politics in multiple ways' (Sabaratnam, 2020: 6–7). In other words, racism can be perpetuated through how the world is defined and how that definition reflects the location of the definer within the structures of political, economic, cultural, and intellectual power even if there is seemingly no explicit racist intent. Eduardo Bonilla-Silva describes the phenomenon of societies in which expressions of overt racism are deemed socially unacceptable yet there is comprehensive evidence of structural racism as 'racism without racists' (Bonillo-Silva, 2021). Racism is not just a product of individual prejudices; it is a system of power. It is mostly in this latter sense, that postcolonial scholars criticize dominant modes of intellectual enquiry, including those found in the IR discipline.

More than 20 years ago, the Indian postcolonialist IR scholar Sankaran Krishna argued that the IR discipline was a 'quintessentially "white" discipline constructed around an amnesia on the question of race' (Krishna, 2001: 406). For Krishna, the whiteness of the IR discipline stems from its epistemological position—its understanding of theory—what other IR scholars have called 'epistemic racism' (Howell and Richter-Montpetit, 2020: 4) or 'methodological whiteness' (Bhambra, 2017; Howell and Richter-Montpetit, 2020). By this Krishna is referring particularly to an emphasis on theoretical and conceptual abstractions which mask the insights that other modes of analysis, particularly historical and descriptive analysis, might offer.

To illustrate the point, Krishna considers how the centrality of the concept of sovereignty and a focus on the balance of power in much mainstream IR led to a depiction of the nineteenth-century 'world' as comparatively peaceful, the so called 'Hundred Years Peace' between 1815 and 1914 (Krishna, 2001: 404). This 'world' experiencing a comparatively peaceful century was, however, predominantly the world of relations between

European sovereign states. If you look at the activities of the British state beyond its relations with other European powers during the same period, argues Krishna, the nineteenth century looks altogether less peaceful. There were, amongst other things, the Opium Wars in China from 1839–42, wars against New Zealand's Māori people in the 1840s and 1871, the Crimean War of 1854–1856, the conquest of Lower Burma in 1854, the suppression of the Indian revolt 1857–1858, the 1874 campaign against the Ashanti people in West Africa, and the conquest of Egypt in 1882 (Krishna, 2001: 404–405).

More recently, Meera Sabaratnam has posed the question: 'Is IR Theory White?' (Sabaratnam, 2020). For Sabaratnam, to say that IR theory is White is not to say that this is the consequence of an IR scholar's skin colour, where they are from, or what their conscious intentions are. Rather, Sabaratnam depicts whiteness in the context of the IR discipline as a conceptual and theoretical standpoint. We have already seen how some IR scholars have identified a preoccupation with race in the early years of the IR discipline and others have noted the absence of discussion of race in the post-1945 IR literature. Sabaratnam argues that these are historically important observations, but they do not directly address the 'theoretical significance of whiteness in IR Theory' (Sabaratnam, 2020: 8).

Sabaratnam draws from the work of one of the pioneers of Critical Race Theory (CRT), Charles W. Mills, to argue that 'interlocking epistemologies' (theories of knowledge) combine to privilege the perspectives of white-racialized people while seemingly leaving race out of the theoretical picture (Sabaratnam, 2020: 12. See also Mills, 1997). The first type of epistemologies are 'epistemologies of ignorance', whereby race is systematically ignored in political theorizing. This ignorance 'is achieved through representations that obscure, exclude, or exceptionalise the central role of racialised dispossession, violence, and discrimination in the making of the modern world' (Sabaratnam, 2020: 12). This resonates with our earlier discussion of how, despite their central role in the formation of the modern international system, imperialism and colonialism have figured very little in most mainstream IR theory since the mid-twentieth century.

Epistemologies of ignorance need nonetheless to be supplemented with some account of how and why white-racialized people became pre-eminent. Here, Sabaratnam introduces 'epistemologies of immanence' (Sabaratnam, 2020: 12–13). Immanence refers to something that is inherent or exclusively existing within something. As we noted in Section 9.2, the idea of the West's innate superiority and by implication the superiority of its historically predominantly White inhabitants is a central component of Eurocentrism. Through Eurocentric theoretical lenses, explanation of Europe's achievements, Western dominance, and even modernity itself does not require reference to the violent and exploitative imperial and colonial historical contexts in which they emerged. Their success is presented as immanent, as coming solely from within.

The final characteristic of whiteness in theory that Sabaratnam identifies is 'innocence'. 'Epistemologies of innocence', Sabaratnam argues, 'seek to emphasise the *inadvertent, unintentional* and *exceptional* character of racist behaviours or practices' (Sabaratnam, 2020: 13, emphasis in the original). They serve to separate out the behaviour and views of contemporary White populations from the errors of the past or from the actions and beliefs of the few who continue to explicitly endorse racist politics and viewpoints. The overt condemnation of the visible racism of others, serves to repress critical engagement with the structural racism that continues to disproportionally confer advantages and benefits to those who are racialized as White. Indeed, it can produce outrage when it is argued that structural racism continues to operate despite legal and social prohibitions on racist expressions or conduct. This is illustrated by recent, heated debates about banning the teaching of CRT in US schools and universities (Fortin, 2021).

Sabaratnam goes on to explore how these epistemologies can be traced through some of the key realist, liberal, and constructivist texts of mainstream IR theory (Sabaratnam, 2020: 16–28). Collectively, these epistemologies effectively marginalize or exclude the history and consequences of imperialism and colonialism from the theorizing of international politics (Sabaratnam, 2020: 26–27).

For Sabaratnam and other postcolonial IR theorists, the IR discipline needs firstly to directly confront and expose the Eurocentric and racialized epistemologies that underpin its conceptual apparatus. But it needs also to go further and explore other accounts of the historical emergence and contemporary practices of international politics that draw from non-Western intellectual sources and recognize the central role that colonial and imperial violence played in the construction of today's hierarchical international order. Additionally, students of IR need to learn how to identify and challenge the racialized underpinnings of IR theory to transcend its limitations, and thereby obtain a much wider, richer picture of world politics historically, presently, and in the future (Rutazibwa, 2016; Sabaratnam, 2020: 27–30).

The challenges confronting the IR discipline identified by Sabaratnam and others effectively add up to a call to decolonize the IR discipline and it is to decolonial perspectives that we now turn.

9.8 **DECOLONIAL APPROACHES**

The term *decolonization* has historically been used primarily to refer to the ending of colonial rule and formerly colonized territories gaining independence. More recently, however, the term has been revivified to refer to contemporary struggles to identify, challenge, and eradicate the residues of colonialism. Decolonial perspectives are very much practice-oriented variants of postcolonialism. Although decolonization in the territorially focused sense appears to be a largely completed process, decolonial approaches emphasize the need to actively resist *coloniality*, to undo the persistence of colonialism in a supposedly post-colonial world. They emphasize the need to resist the dominance of Eurocentric modes of thought and the global political structures and practices that they are seen to still underpin and sustain.

This usage of decolonization has its roots in the works of some of the early anti-colonial intellectuals, such as Frantz Fanon, Aimé Césaire, and W.E.B. Du Bois, who saw the concrete struggle against colonialism as always entailing more than the decolonization of territory. It required also the 'decolonization of the mind'—not just the minds of the colonizers, but of the colonized as well. More recently, a group of Latin American scholars have introduced the concept of decoloniality to refer to a range of intellectual and practical challenges to the dominance of Eurocentrism (Quijano, 2007; Mignolo and Walsh, 2018). A pioneer of decolonial thought, Aníbal Quijano, argues that alongside European colonial domination 'the cultural complex known as European modernity/rationality' was constituted 'as a universal paradigm of knowledge and of the relation between humanity and the rest of the world' (Quijano, 2007: 171–172). Thus, Eurocentrism must be resisted, Walter Mignolo argues, because it is an 'imperial/colonial politics of knowledge production' (Mignolo, 2017: 4). It is not Europe's right to be Eurocentric that is critiqued, says Mignolo, but 'the pretence that Europe has achieved the perfect and happy stage of humanity, and everybody has to bend to it' (Mignolo, 2017: 3). From a decolonial perspective, if Eurocentrism remains dominant, then colonial and imperial structures of exploitation will remain. Decolonial approaches are therefore not just an intellectual orientation but a form of political action: 'decolonial analytics and decolonial enactment are two sides of the same movement' (Mignolo, 2017: 4).

There are several dimensions to decolonial approaches as both an intellectual and practical orientation. The first is confronting the dominance of Eurocentric thought, such as through demands for the *decolonization* of university curricula. This is because university curricula in their present form are seen to actively work to ingrain and thereby sustain colonial attitudes and assumptions. Decolonial approaches push us to ask who decides which 'great minds' or what great pieces of literary or scholarly work should constitute the canon (the essentials that supposedly must be studied) of any academic discipline? Are we sufficiently aware of the colonial contexts in which many canonical texts were produced and, by extension, how those contexts are embedded within the texts themselves?

According to Sabaratnam, decolonization 'calls for scholars to engage, examine, retrieve and cultivate other ways of thinking about and being in the world that can form alternative points of departure to the hegemonic knowledges of empire' (Sabaratnam, 2017: 7). This highlights a second dimension to decolonialize: the exposition of non-Eurocentric sources of intellectual, cultural, and political systems of knowledge, which have been (and still are) marginalized or deemed inferior. For example, Blaney and Tickner argue that the IR discipline adheres to a dominant Eurocentric understanding of a singular world; a universal reality 'out there'. This 'single reality doctrine' effectively renders inferior or simply excludes alternative understandings of the world, i.e., alternative ontologies (accounts of reality) which have meaning for various peoples around the world (Blaney and Tickner, 2017: 297).

Blaney and Tickner cite the work of ethnographers who have long recognized that there are other worldviews that contain, for example, different understandings of the relationship between the human and non-human worlds to the Eurocentric norm: 'many communities do not sharply distinguish humans and other entities, so that animals, plants and spirits are as much "people" (with consciousness, culture and language) as "we" are' (Blaney and Tickner, 2017: 296). Such alternative perspectives underpin different understandings of the relationship between humans and their environment, political and social relations, gender relations, and so on.

It is important to stress that the intention of most of those arguing for the decolonization of the IR discipline is not to replace or reject entirely Eurocentric thought, but to decentre it. One step towards this is the facilitation of the exchange of ideas across cultural divides to enable what Quijano calls 'an interchange of experiences and meanings' (2007: 177). Such an interchange must be equitable and start by rejecting the presumption that other knowledge systems may indeed offer some valuable insights, but they remain, nonetheless, inherently inferior to Eurocentric systems of thought. Mignolo captures what he sees as this colonial attitude towards non-Eurocentric systems of thought succinctly: 'As we know: the first world has knowledge, the third world has culture; Native Americans have wisdom, Anglo Americans have science' (Mignolo, 2009: 160). In other words, decolonization is not about engaging with other non-Eurocentric ways of thinking and reasoning only insofar as they do not disrupt a Eurocentrically-defined 'one-world world'. They should be engaged with because they can show how 'it is not only that people *believe* different things about reality, but that *different realities* are enacted by different practices' (Blaney and Tickner, 2017: 303).

Key concept 9.2 looks at an example of how the dominant account of a significant event in international politics, the 1962 Cuban Missile Crisis, can be challenged when a 'subaltern' perspective is brought into the picture.

KEY CONCEPT 9.2 DECOLONIZING THE 1962 CUBAN MISSILE CRISIS

In their article, 'Decolonizing the Cuban Missile Crisis', Mark Laffey and Jutta Weldes show how most analyses of the crisis almost completely exclude Cuba or its people (Laffey and Weldes, 2008). Laffey and Weldes depict Cuban participants or analysts as 'subaltern' voices that have been largely unheard. Indeed, when shown the movie *Thirteen Days*, in Havana, Fidel Castro (the Cuban leader from 1959 to 2008) famously asked 'where are the Cubans?' (Laffey and Weldes, 2008: 559).

For Laffey and Weldes the virtual silencing of any Cuban perspective on the crisis is a product of the close relationship between power, knowledge, and the international hierarchy. The 'Eurocentric bias' of a predominantly Anglo-American IR discipline produced an account in which

> (t)he Cuban Missile Crisis, and by extension world politics, wasn't about Cuba or Cubans; it was about the United States and the Soviet Union. Here as elsewhere world politics was about great power politics. (Laffey and Weldes, 2008: 558)

The deliberations of ExComm (the Executive Committee of the US National Security Council set up during the crisis) rarely mentioned Cuba or Castro. Cuba was reduced to a place '*in* which Missiles were deployed by the Soviet Union and *from which* they had to be removed by the United States . . . US actions during the crisis were directed against a Soviet threat *in Cuba*' (Laffey and Weldes, 2008: 561, emphasis in the original). The decision by the Soviet Union to withdraw their missiles has conventionally

The Cuban Missile Crisis exhibition in Havana, Cuba

been presented in the form of a heroic narrative in which the US, and President John F. Kennedy particularly, stood firm against Soviet tyranny.

Laffey and Weldes go on to give an account of efforts in the 1990s to bring US, Soviet, and Cuban viewpoints together as part of an oral history project on the crisis. The Cubans argued that their acceptance of the Soviet Union's offer of the missiles was a consequence of their perception that the US wanted to overturn the Castro-led Cuban Revolution that overthrew the US-backed Batista regime only three years before the crisis (as demonstrated by the botched Bay of Pigs invasion). The crisis was, then, not just about the Soviet Union threatening the US, it was also about Cuba responding to a perceived threat from the US.

The project did not result in all parties agreeing on what the Crisis was about. Nonetheless, it constituted a form of postcolonial intervention in which 'subaltern' Cuba could be heard and could no longer be left out of any plausible account of the crisis. However, they conclude that although the oral history project pointed a way forward for decolonizing the IR discipline more widely, 'the heroic myth' of the crisis persists in IR scholarship and textbooks (Laffey and Weldes, 2008: 572).

REFERENCE

Laffey, M. and Weldes, J. (2008), 'Decolonizing the Cuban Missile Crisis', *International Studies Quarterly*, 52(3): 555–577.

A third dimension of decolonial analysis is the exploration of concrete examples of active decolonization worldwide. Decolonialist critiques are not solely aimed at dominant values, social practices, and institutions within the Western world. The influence of Eurocentrism is seen in many of the social, political, cultural, and economic policies adopted by governments of formerly colonized territories as well. From a decolonial perspective these actively aid the perpetuation of colonial and imperial patterns of domination within post-colonial states as well as in their external relations.

Decolonial thinking and activism is developing particularly within former settler colonies in which there were already Indigenous peoples and societies with long established traditions, values, social structures, and ways of living prior to European colonization. Because of mass immigration from Europe (and later from elsewhere) during the colonial era indigenous peoples became minorities in countries where the majority population now generally assumes itself to be a natural part of the developed/modern world—the heartlands of Eurocentrism, so to speak. Notable examples include the ongoing struggles of Indigenous peoples, such as Canada's First Nations, Native Americans, the Indigenous communities of Latin America, the Aboriginal peoples of Australia, and the Māori of Aotearoa/New Zealand. The colonization and repression of indigenous peoples is not only found outside of Europe but also at its margins. The Sámi people of Northern Scandinavia and the Kola Peninsula of Russia—a region they call Sápmi, but which has historically been referred to as Lapland—have also been subjected to overt discrimination and attempts to forcefully assimilate them into the dominant Scandinavian/Russian cultures. Indeed, the Sámi only received formal recognition of their distinct identity as Indigenous peoples in the 1980s and 1990s and they continue to fight for recognition of their land rights, especially over the mineral-rich parts of Sápmi (Bergman-Rosamund, 2020).

Indigenous peoples are not immigrants or settlers; they are the original inhabitants of colonized territories whose sovereignty over their homelands was mostly forcefully expropriated from them. Yet, for most indigenous peoples, achieving full recognition and reparation from the majority population of the significance and consequences of this brute fact remains an ongoing struggle. There are now innumerable examples of decolonial activism worldwide led by Indigenous peoples aimed at challenging the forces that perpetuate the dominant 'modern/colonial matrix of power' (Walsh, 2018: 49). These add up to what Catherine Walsh calls a 'decolonial insurgency' comprised of various forms of resistance by Indigenous peoples and social movements to orthodox models of capitalist development and the assumptions underpinning them about how one should live, think, and be. Notable Latin American examples include the Zapatista movement in Chiapas, southern Mexico and the 'Buen Vivir' movement in the Andean region (Walsh, 2018: 15–33). Walsh argues that such movements are engaged in a *praxis* (the interaction of theory and practice) of confronting the contemporary expressions of colonialism while simultaneously exploring alternatives (Walsh, 2018: 49). This praxis signifies *decoloniality*: the living expression of decolonization.

Some Indigenous scholars and activists have expressed concern about the increasingly widespread use of the term decolonization as a metaphor for social justice and racial equality more generally. Acknowledging the colonial past and endeavouring to eradicate it from school and university curricula may serve to make settler communities feel better about themselves, they argue, but it also risks side-lining the ongoing concrete struggles of Indigenous peoples to have their rights and traditions fully recognized and respected and for the restoration of meaningful forms of Indigenous

368 INTRODUCTION TO INTERNATIONAL RELATIONS THEORIES

sovereignty over dispossessed lands (Tuck and Yang, 2012). Clearly, wealthy and industrialized sovereign states built through settler colonialism, such as Australia, Canada, the US, and New Zealand, will not be going anywhere soon. This leaves the meaningful restoration of Indigenous identity and sovereignty within them a largely unfinished and challenging task.

9.9 **CONCLUSION**

Postcolonial scholars may not agree precisely on how the history of imperialism and colonialism continues to impact upon the lives of peoples worldwide, nor might they come to quite the same judgement as to its positive or negative influences. What they share, however, is an emphasis on the need to examine critically and thoroughly the continuing significance of the colonial era in shaping contemporary social life, from the local to the global sphere.

As the colonial era recedes further in historical memory, the global political picture is also undergoing significant change, as suggested by widespread claims that Western power and influence is in decline because of the growth in wealth and influence of countries in the Global South such as Brazil, China, India, and South Africa. Yet, there also remains considerable evidence of the continuing persistence of imperial and colonial structures of global power. There has been an evident rise of public consciousness throughout much of the Western world about the legacies of colonialism and imperialism and the need to actively work for greater decolonization. However, this must be set against the equally evident continuation of neo-colonial and neo-imperial attitudes towards people outside of the West or of non-Western origin within it. The presence throughout the West of extremist political movements and parties expressing racialized and often explicitly racist political outlooks underscores the persistence of overt racism and racial discrimination. For these reasons, the growth and influence of postcolonial and decolonial perspectives is unlikely to fade anytime soon. Indeed, their emergence in the IR discipline in recent years is arguably one of the most profound developments in its history.

SUMMARIZING POSTCOLONIALISM

- Contemporary postcolonial perspectives emphasize the continuing impact of colonial and imperial attitudes at all levels of social life, from the local to the global

- Key themes central to postcolonial perspectives, include the global significance of race historically and presently, the critical examination of past and present representations of non-Western cultures, and the legacy of colonialism in the formation of personal and collective identities

- The history of European colonialism from the fifteenth century onwards shows how European colonial powers saw themselves as engaged in a 'civilizing mission', underpinned by a view of European civilization and the white race as inherently superior to all others

- The roots of postcolonial thought can be traced back to the work of pioneering Black intellectuals, such as Frantz Fanon, actively engaged in anti-colonial resistance

- Edward Said's pathbreaking 1978 book, *Orientalism,* is widely viewed as a starting point for contemporary postcolonial scholarship. It examines Western representations of the 'Orient' to show how they sustained the claim that European civilization was inherently superior

- Another key source has been Subaltern Studies, which, in contrast to dominant 'top down' accounts of the anti-colonial struggle in India, endeavour to develop 'a view from below'

- Some postcolonialist scholars, notably Homi Bhabha, challenge overly binary distinctions drawn between the colonizer and the colonized, arguing that colonialism has generated hybrid identities

- Postcolonialism emerged as a critical IR theoretical perspective in the 1990s and its influence has grown rapidly since then

- Postcolonial IR scholars argue that the common story of the origins of the IR discipline has been 'whitewashed' and fails to acknowledge the underlying preoccupation of some of the discipline's key founding figures with empire and race

- Postcolonial IR scholars also trace the impact of *Eurocentrism* upon Western thinking about international politics since the eighteenth century. Eurocentrism presents European civilization and its intellectual traditions as universal benchmarks for assessing the legitimacy of all knowledge claims, resulting in the demeaning or exclusion of non-Western thought

- Some postcolonial scholars argue that many prominent schools of IR thought engage in 'methodological whiteness' and 'epistemic racism'

- In various ways, postcolonial perspectives cast a critical light on the core theoretical assumptions and analytical categories of most, perhaps all other IR theoretical perspectives as well as the institutions and concrete practices of contemporary international politics

- The term decolonization, traditionally used in reference to the ending of colonial rule, has been revived to highlight the need to actively challenge coloniality, the continuing dominance of Eurocentrism and the marginalization of non-Western ideas, beliefs, and practices.

QUESTIONS

1. Why was the Haitian Revolution so historically significant?

2. What are the key sources of contemporary postcolonial thought?

3. What do you understand by the term Eurocentrism?

4. Why do you think postcolonial and decolonial perspectives emphasize the importance of identity and culture?
5. Why is race important for the understanding of international politics today?
6. 'Decolonization is an unfinished process'. Do you agree or disagree? Explain your answer.

IR THEORY TODAY VOLUNTOURISM

A widespread practice in recent years has been 'voluntourism'. Many young people from Western states—notably students during vacation periods and gap years—travel to engage in volunteer work, mostly in the Global South. The common rationales for this include notions of 'giving something back' or 'making a difference', engaging in a more ethical form of tourism, seeking a personally transforming experience, or simply looking to enhance a personal CV. Voluntourism has grown into a global industry with thousands of programmes available through governmental agencies, International NGOs, and for-profit operators.

The UK-based *ProjectsAbroad* claims that 'meaningful travel provides a defining experience for young people as they move from adolescence into adulthood, and we know that the work we do transforms communities. We're making the world a better place, one participant at a time' (https://www.projects-abroad.co.uk/about-us/).

Critics ask such questions as:

- who really benefits from voluntourism and what kinds of stereotypes might it reinforce?
- Does it reflect a 'white-saviour' syndrome?
- Is it focused much more on the potential benefits for the volunteers than the developmental needs of the communities they claim to be helping?
- Do participants in short term volunteering programmes have the skills that are desperately needed or not available locally?
- Do such programmes reinforce the representation of communities in poorer countries as largely passive recipients of assistance, incapable of helping themselves?

USEFUL RESOURCES YOU CAN FIND ONLINE

The Norwegian Students and Academic Assistance Fund (SAIH) is a Norwegian student and academics international solidarity organization. Between 2012–2017 they ran an awareness campaign called *Radi-Aid* which included a range of satirical videos highlighting the racial and cultural tropes that surround development fundraising and volunteering. www.radiaid.com

Magrizos, Solon, Kostopoulos, Ioannis, and Powers, Laura (2021), 'Volunteer Tourism as a Transformative Experience: A Mixed Methods Empirical Study', *Journal of Travel Research*, 60(4): 878–895.

Pastran, Sasha (2014), 'Volunteer Tourism: A Postcolonial Approach', *University of Saskatchewan Undergraduate Research Journal*, 1(1): 45–57.

Rosenberg, Tina (2018), 'The Business of voluntourism: do Western do-gooders actually do harm?' *The Guardian*, 13 September.

QUESTIONS

Drawing upon this chapter and your own research:

1. Does voluntourism undermine or reinforce colonialist attitudes and outlooks in your view?

2. Can voluntourism be decolonized? How might this be achieved?

TWISTING THE LENS

1. Look at Chapter 2 on liberalism. In what ways if any do you think a liberal IR perspective can provide a basis for either defending or critiquing Western voluntourism? (Hint: think about liberal claims about the virtues of deepening international cooperation and universalizing Western ideas about individual freedom, democracy, and human rights).

2. Look at Chapter 5 on Marxism. What insights, if any, do you think Marxist IR perspectives bring to the analysis of voluntourism? (Hint: think about Marxist critiques of North–South relations and neoliberal globalization).

FURTHER READING

ADDITIONAL INTRODUCTORY READING

Biswas, S. (2021), 'Postcolonialism' in T. Dunne, M. Kurki, and S. Smith, *International Relations Theories: Discipline and Diversity*, 5th edition (Oxford: Oxford University Press).
A more advanced introduction to postcolonial IR perspectives.

Sabaratnam, M. (2020), 'Postcolonial and Decolonial Approaches' in J. Baylis, S. Smith, and P. Owens (eds), *The Globalization of World Politics: An Introduction to International Relations*, 8th edition (Oxford: Oxford University Press).
An accessible, succinct yet comprehensive introduction to the key sources and themes of contemporary postcolonial and decolonial approaches.

Shilliam, R. (2021), 'International Relations', in R. Shilliam, *Decolonizing Politics: An Introduction* (Cambridge: Polity), 119–149.
Offers an accessible, critical look at the IR discipline through decolonial lenses which explores how the world is seen from outside the centres of global power and influence and the insights that might be drawn from marginalized viewpoints.

MORE IN-DEPTH READING

Anievas, A., Manchanda, N., and Shilliam, R. (2015), *Race and Racism in International Relations* (Abingdon, Oxon: Routledge).
Building upon W.E.B. Dubois concept of 'the color line' that he outlined in the 1920s, this collection of essays addresses the historical silence of the IR discipline regarding the central importance of race and racism in international relations.

Davis, A. E., Thakur, V., and Vale, P. (2020), *The Imperial Discipline: Race and the Founding of International Relations* (London: Pluto Press).

This book explores the early twentieth-century origins of the IR discipline in the UK and its largest colonies. The authors argue that early British IR scholarship was underpinned by colonial and racial thinking to a degree that has been insufficently acknowledged.

Geeta, C. and Nair, S. (2004), *Power, Postcolonialsm and International Relations: Reading Race, Gender and Class* (Abingdon, Oxon: Routledge).

A collection of essays by leading scholars working at the intersection of postcolonial perspectives and IR that add up to a multifaceted critique of the concept of power in both mainstream and critical IR theories.

Grovogui, S. N. (2006), *Beyond Eurocentrism and Anarchy: Memories of International Order and Institutions* (Basingstoke: Palgrave Macmillan).

Takes the reader back to colonial French Africa in the early years of the Cold War. Here the ideas, political reflections and concrete proposals of a small group of African intellectuals are juxtaposed with the parochialism of Eurocentric thinking about world politics at the time.

Henderson, E. A. (2017), 'The Revolution will Not Be Theorized: Du Bois, Locke, and the Howard School's challenge to White Supremacist IR Theory', *Millennium*, 45(3): 492–510.

Examines the largely forgotten or ignored theoretical contributions to IR theory of African American scholars associated with the 'Howard School' of IR thought during the 1920s.

Hobson, J. (2018), *The Eurocentric Conception of World Politics: Western International Theory 1760–2010* (Cambridge: Cambridge University Press).

A survey of Western theorizing of the international centred around a typology of forms of racism and Eurocentrism that have underpinned almost the whole range of IR theoretical perspectives from the eighteenth century up until the present day.

Liboiron, M. (2021), *Pollution is Colonialism* (Durham: NC: Duke University Press).

Written from an Indigenous Canadian perspective and multidisciplinary in focus, this book argues that pollution 'is best understood as the violence of colonial land relations' (pp.6–7). and seeks to develop decolonial research methodologies and scholarly practices.

Muppidi, H. (2012), *The Colonial Signs of International Relations* (London: C. Hurst & Co).

Written in a rather different and personal style from most IR texts, this short book exposes the multiple ways in which the theorists and theories across the IR discipline have served to perpetuate a colonial interpretation of world politics.

Sabaratnam, M. (2020), 'Is IR Theory White? Racialised Subject-Positioning in Three Canonical Texts', *Millennium: Journal of International Studies*, 49(1): 3–31.

Draws upon Critical Race Theory to show how the way IR is theorized can reflect a white subject-position. The argument is developed through a critical reading of three leading IR texts.

Said, E. W. (1985), *Orientalism* (Harmondsworth: Penguin Books).

One of the founding texts of contemporary postcolonial studies first published in 1978, which examines representations of Eastern cultures and beliefs in Western literature and arts that collectively reflect European racist and imperial attitudes towards 'The Orient'.

Shilliam, Robbie (2020), 'Race and Racism in International Relations: Retrieving a Scholarly Inheritance', *International Politics Reviews*, 8: 152–195.

Shilliam engages in a conversation with a diverse range of IR scholars reflecting on how they came to see the significance of race and racism to the study of international politics.

CHAPTER 10

FEMINISMS, GENDER, AND INTERNATIONAL RELATIONS

LEARNING OBJECTIVES

- Identify the historical development of feminist and gender-focused IR perspectives
- Define key concepts, such as *patriarchy*, *intersectionality*, and *hegemonic masculinity*, and understand their place in feminist/gender-focused thinking
- Outline the key similarities and differences between different feminist and gender-focused IR perspectives
- Recognize the key insights feminist and gender-focused perspectives bring to core concerns of the IR discipline
- Compare and contrast different understandings of the meaning of gender and examine their implications for analysing international politics
- Explain the connections between feminist/gender IR perspectives and other critical IR perspectives

10.1 INTRODUCTION

Feminist perspectives became prominent in the IR discipline in the late 1980s and early 1990s, although their intellectual roots can be traced back much further. You may see the terms sex and gender used interchangeably in everyday speech. There is, however, an important basic distinction between the terms. Sex is commonly used to refer to either side of a biologically defined binary distinction between females and males, between 'women' and 'men'. Gender refers, however, to the socially constructed meanings attached to masculinity and femininity. As a social construct, the meaning of gender can and does vary over time, as well as between different cultural and political settings.

It is still commonplace to view gender as simply the product of biological sex differences between females and males. Such 'gender essentialism' underpins the gender stereotypes that are still prevalent worldwide today. These can have profound social, cultural, and political consequences for people who question or transgress dominant social assumptions about gender roles and how to act in the social world (Steans, 2013: 7–12).

Challenging a simplistic equation of sex with gender is a key feature of most feminist and gender-focused scholarship today. Nonetheless, the various strands of contemporary feminist and other types of gender-focused scholarship are also marked by significant differences. That it is why it is important to take note of two features of the title of this chapter:

- The first is that the chapter title refers to *feminisms*, rather than feminism. This is because although the term *feminism* is commonly used as a rather generalized label, especially in everyday speech, this obscures the fact that contemporary feminist thinking ranges across a wide range of theoretical and political perspectives. There is no singular body of theory that can be definitively labelled as feminism, or as feminist IR. Despite their significant differences, however, all feminist IR perspectives start from a simple premise: in international politics, as in any other political or social arena, gender matters.

- The second feature is that the chapter title also refers to gender as well as feminisms. Although feminisms are centrally concerned with gender, by and large they have historically focused on the social, political, and cultural consequences of dominant interpretations and representations of masculinity and femininity for the concrete lives of women. As we shall see, other gender-focused perspectives have emerged which seek to both challenge and look beyond a binary division between masculinity and femininity or male and female.

The similarities and differences between varieties of feminism and between feminisms and other forms of gender-focused IR theorizing will become clearer as you work through the chapter. Viewed as a whole, they have become a very significant part of the contemporary IR field. In common with other critical IR approaches, they all raise profound questions about how, why, and what we think about international politics.

Although they are relatively recent arrivals in the IR discipline, it is vital to emphasize that feminist thinking, and feminist political activism broadly understood has a much longer history. For this reason, this chapter will firstly briefly explore the historical development of contemporary feminisms. Although this preliminary discussion does not deal with the IR discipline directly, it is important nonetheless to take note of the international dimensions throughout the evolution of feminist thinking and activism. We then look at how the development and diversification of feminist thought has flowed into the IR field, focusing on some of the key areas in which feminisms and, subsequently, other approaches to gender have made a significant impact. A key objective of this chapter is to show how the diversification of theorizing about gender has led not only to the emergence of engagements—both critical and creative—with most of the theoretical perspectives discussed in this text, but also to some important debates within gender-focused IR scholarship itself.

10.2 **WHAT ARE FEMINISMS?**

The roots of contemporary theorizing about gender lie in the historical worldwide resistance of women to multiple forms of oppression solely because of their biological sex. The earliest articulations of the idea that men and women should be treated equally fall far short of contemporary feminist ideas, but they show that the presumption of male superiority has long been subjected to challenge. In the fourth century BCE, Plato argued that there was no rational reason to deny women in Ancient Greece the opportunity to advance themselves and participate fully in the creation of the ideal society. Subsequent human history is dotted with other instances of intellectual challenges (by both women and men) to the presumption of women's innate inferiority. However, much of the early history of women's struggle for equality remains little known because the voices and opinions of women were only very rarely acknowledged, valued, or recorded.

The Enlightenment era of the seventeenth and eighteenth centuries emboldened several Western female writers and intellectuals to challenge the exclusion of women from the widespread debates of the time about rights, inequality, and social justice. For example, the *Declaration of the Rights of Man and of the Citizen* that followed the 1789 French revolution made no reference to women at all. So, two years later, the French playwright Olympe de Gouges responded with a pamphlet entitled 'Declaration of the Rights of Women and the Citizen' (the term citizen was written in the female form as *citoyenne*).

A seminal example of early English-language feminist writing was Mary Wollstonecraft's *A Vindication of the Rights of Women* published in 1792. If women experienced the same kind of education as men, Wollstonecraft argued, they would not only be better companions for their husbands but could also develop professional careers in such areas as medicine, business, and even politics. Becoming a better companion for a man hardly sounds feminist today, but in its time Wollstonecraft's work was trailblazing, at least for the White middle class English women at whom it was aimed (Monroe, 1987; Ferguson, 1999).

The voices of Western women predominate in most historical accounts of feminism's evolution, but women outside the West were also challenging male dominance. For example, there is an extensive history of women resisting gendered oppression in India from the mid-nineteenth century onwards, the character of which reflected the complex interaction of gender, class, and the Hindu caste system (Ghosal, 2005; Chaudhuri, 2005; Anagol, 2006; Chaudhuri, 2012). There are numerous other marginalized or long unacknowledged histories of women outside the West challenging male dominance for as long as their counterparts in the West. Several scholars have examined women's roles in various Asian, African, and Caribbean societies to show how women have exercised leadership and developed influential political networks over the centuries.

These histories are distinctive, moreover, because many reflect the colonial context in which the early struggles of women in Asia, Africa, Latin America, and the Caribbean emerged. Women's organizations would also play a key role in many of the twentieth-century nationalist struggles against colonial domination in the Middle East, South America, and Africa (Jayawardena, 1986; Wieringa, 1995; Sudbury, 1998: 3–9; Rosenberg, 2010).

Acknowledging a much richer picture of women's historical struggle for equality worldwide is, however, a comparatively recent development in Western feminism. As Ula Taylor notes, prior to contemporary Western feminist interest in the diversity of women's lives, Western feminist theory suffered from 'White solipsism—to think, imagine, and speak as if whiteness described the world' (Adrienne Rich cited in Taylor, 1998: 234). This was evident in the Western struggle for voting rights for women and it is a theme we will be returning to throughout this chapter.

The fight for women's suffrage

By the end of the nineteenth century, the primary focus for the emerging women's movement in both the US and elsewhere in the West had become women's *suffrage*, i.e., the right to vote. In the UK this led to the emergence of two distinct forms of activism, that of the Suffragists and the Suffragettes (see Key event 10.1)

KEY EVENT 10.1 SUFFRAGISTS AND SUFFRAGETTES

In 1897 British women's suffrage groups merged to create the National Union of Women's Suffrage Societies (NUWSS), led by Millicent Fawcett. The NUWSS adopted a strategy of peaceful campaigning and debate aimed at persuading the solely male UK Parliament to support their cause.

Slow progress led to the formation in 1903 of the Women's Social and Political Union (WSPU) in Manchester led by Emmeline Pankhurst. The WSPU took a much more militant approach to campaigning. They became known as *suffragettes*, in contrast to the more moderate *suffragists* of the NUWSS. The WSPU was in favour of direct and confrontational political action and suffragettes were prepared to go to prison, where they would sometimes go on hunger strikes.

The British suffrage movement developed links with similar organizations across Europe and in the US. In Britain, the vital role played by women during the First World War—working in munitions factories, driving buses, working on farms, and so on—served to strengthen their demands for suffrage after the war ended. In 1918 the British Parliament passed the Representation of the Peoples Act, which granted the right to vote, but only to property-owning women over 30. It was not until 1928 that all British women achieved true equality of suffrage.

The British suffrage activists of the early twentieth century were overwhelmingly White, although there were a few women of colour involved, such as the British born suffrage activist Princess Sophia Duleep Singh, and Indian suffrage activists visiting or studying in the UK (Anand, 2015; Mukherjee, 2018). Some prominent middle-class Indian women resident in the UK also attended suffragist demonstrations.

Sumita Mukherjee argues, however, that their involvement is often overstated and misrepresented. They were invited to attend to 'represent the size of the empire' and 'support the argument that White British women should be granted the vote so they could have a say over imperial matters in parliament' (Mukherjee, 2017).

A key early figure in the US campaign for women's suffrage was Elizabeth Cady Stanton. Although a supporter of the abolition of the slavery still prevalent in the Southern US, Stanton nonetheless thought that white women had to be enfranchised first, prior to any consideration of the voting rights of non-white men, let alone non-white women (Taylor, 1998; 236–237; hooks, 2015: 127).

Nonetheless, African American feminist consciousness had also developed during the abolitionist movement of the early to mid-nineteenth century and Black feminist activists participated extensively throughout the American struggle for suffrage (Taylor, 1998, 235–239). At an 1851 Women's Rights Convention, Sojourner Truth (1797–1883), delivered what is commonly known as the 'Ain't I a Woman?' speech, which is now recognized as one the most important abolitionist and women's rights speeches in American history. Truth had escaped enslavement and, although illiterate, she went on to become an ardent and effective campaigner against slavery and for women's rights. However, Ula Taylor notes that 'in general African American activists were often abandoned by White suffragists' (Taylor, 1998: 238).

The nineteenth amendment to the US Constitution in 1920, granted American men and women equal voting rights. However, many US states used various constitutional loopholes to prevent African Americans, Native Americans, and other marginalized minorities (both male and female) from exercising their right to vote. It was only with the passing of the 1965 Voting Rights Act that all adults in the US became fully enfranchised, in principle at least.

The struggles for women's suffrage in the UK and US are well known but there were earlier successes, notably in New Zealand where women (including Māori women) were no longer denied the right to vote in 1893, and in Australia in 1902 (although Aboriginal and Torres Strait Islander people, male and female were excluded). Sumita Mukherjee has also explored the national and international dimensions of the campaign for suffrage by Indian women in the first half of the twentieth century (Mukherjee, 2018).

Women in many European countries were also no longer denied the right to vote either during or soon after the First World War. There were some notable exceptions, such as France, which disenfranchised women up until 1944, and Switzerland where women were denied the right to vote in national elections until 1971. In the Global South, most women (and men) were denied voting rights until the end of colonialism, or in the case of Black women in South Africa, until the end of the apartheid regime. Women's suffrage has now been formally achieved in all countries worldwide, although women in some countries still confront significant social and cultural political hurdles to exercising their right to vote, which often reveal the complex legacy of the colonial era.

The evolution of contemporary feminisms

It is commonplace to depict the development of contemporary Western feminisms as occurring in distinctive waves or phases. Not all feminist scholars agree on the borderlines between these key waves or the utility of depicting Western feminism's development in such a tidy or linear fashion (Evans and Chamberlain, 2015; Chamberlain, 2017). Equally, the analogy of waves should not be seen as suggesting that each wave entirely superseded a previous wave, as key themes that emerged in all the waves continue still to figure within contemporary feminist debates.

First wave feminism

The term 'first wave' is usually applied to the period of Western feminist writing and activity during the late nineteenth and early twentieth centuries. Because of its emphasis on suffrage and equal rights, first wave feminism is also commonly depicted as the origin of modern liberal feminism, also referred to as equality feminism because its overriding concern is recognition of the equal value of individual women and men (Wendell, 1987: 66).

We now know that there were vigorous contemporaneous campaigns for women's equality outside the West, even if these have only been prominently acknowledged comparatively recently. Certainly, for today's feminists worldwide, a key issue remains the absence or under-representation of women in positions of power, authority, and influence. Many contemporary feminists would reject reducing feminism simply to a struggle to increase women's presence, but they would also concede that in many if not most countries it remains the case that significant barriers to women's participation and advancement remain. Such discrimination becomes especially evident when viewed from an international or global perspective.

In the early twentieth century, Socialist and Marxist varieties of European feminist thought appeared in critical reaction to liberal feminism. These perspectives brought a focus on social class into the equation. Widely memorialized for her commitment to the British suffragette cause, Emmeline Pankhurst also forged connections with European Socialist and Marxist feminists, such as Rosa Luxemburg in Germany, Alexandra Kollontai in Russia, and Emma Goldman in the US. They all criticized 'bourgeois' liberal feminists for focusing exclusively on women's suffrage and failing to take account of the class-based inequalities inherent in capitalism. For Goldman, 'true freedom for both men and women could never be achieved within capitalist society, but only in a socialist society based on co-operation and the elimination of all forms of domination' (Bryson, 2016: 100–101). With the revival of feminism in the early 1960s, the work of many of those early socialist and Marxist feminists acquired renewed prominence.

Second wave feminism

Feminism's second wave was foreshadowed in *The Second Sex,* by the French philosopher Simone de Beauvoir, published in 1949. It contains the famous observation that 'one is not born, but rather becomes, woman' (de Beauvoir, 2011: 330). De Beauvoir argues that although humans can be differentiated in terms of their biological sex, how one lives as a woman is not naturally given but constructed within social and cultural contexts which are,

French philosopher, Simone de Beauvoir's portrait on a postage stamp

moreover, dominated by men. Many feminists credit de Beauvoir with highlighting a crucial distinction between biological sex at birth and gender as a lived social category which remains central to much feminist scholarship today. De Beauvoir went on to argue that man has historically been depicted as the definitive embodiment of human subjectivity—the 'subject'—against whom women were defined, secondarily, as the inferior 'Other'.

The influence of de Beauvoir's pioneering analysis increased markedly in feminism's second wave, the emergence of which is commonly traced to the publication of Betty Friedan's *The Feminine Mystique* in 1963. Acknowledging de Beauvoir's influence, Freidan's starting point was evidence of widespread dissatisfaction among suburban White American women with their lives. The problem was not material deprivation because many were comparatively affluent (Friedan, 2010: 15). Friedan called this 'the problem that has no name'. To explain it Freidan coined the phrase 'feminine mystique' to capture the dominant societal assumption in the US that women could and should be fulfilled in their lives solely through marriage, motherhood, and managing a home successfully (Friedan, 2010: 34–50).

Friedan argued that whereas men were encouraged to discover their identity through personal growth and development in their chosen career, the feminine mystique worked to perpetuate the idea that a woman's identity was determined principally by their capacity to give birth: 'anatomy was her destiny' (Friedan, 2010: 60). She proposed that women reject the feminine mystique and claim for themselves the right to fully develop their own identity through pursuing careers outside of the home.

In the decades following its publication, *The Feminine Mystique* was subjected to often withering critique, perhaps most notably by bell hooks (the pen name of the Black feminist and activist Gloria Jean Watkins). (H)ooks depicted Friedan's book as myopic in its focus on 'college-educated, middle and upper-class married white women'. For hooks, Frieden did not consider the needs of 'women, without men, without children, without homes' and 'ignored the existence of all non-white women and poor white women' (hooks, 2000: 1–2).

The Feminine Mystique struck a chord, nonetheless, with large numbers of Western middle-class women in the US and elsewhere. Second wave feminism developed rapidly from the mid-1960s onwards, especially during the explosion of political dissent and activism in the West that is commonly referred to now simply as 'The Sixties' (you can read more about this in Key Event 7.1). Second-wave Western feminism emerged within this general political turbulence, but also as a critical response to it. In a 1969 *New York Magazine* article entitled 'After Black Power, Women's Liberation', the American journalist and social activist Gloria Steinem expressed the frustration of many feminist activists, who resented the continuing dominance of men even within supposedly progressive political circles. For Steinem, women's liberation was about much more than achieving mere equality with men in what remained a 'man's world'. It was about developing solidarity among all women with a view to fundamentally changing that world and the men who dominated it: '(T)he idea is that women's liberation will be men's liberation, too'.

As both a political and intellectual movement, feminism grew rapidly in the 1970s, albeit primarily (or at least most visibly) among white, educated women in the West. There were tensions, however, between white US feminist activists and their Black counterparts who were engaged also in the wider struggle against racial discrimination and the disempowering effects of poverty upon the Black community. Additionally, because the roots of the American Black community lay in colonial enslavement, many Black feminists saw connections between their struggle and international resistance to imperialism and colonialism (Taylor, 1998). These tensions would subsequently prove to be a significant impetus to the emergence of feminism's third wave.

Patriarchy

In the early 1970s several seminal books established the key terms of debate for markedly more militant feminist thought and action. Key works included Kate Millett's *Sexual Politics*, Germaine Greer's *The Female Eunuch*, and Shulamith Firestone's *The Dialectic of Sex*. It was Millett's book, first published in 1970, that arguably had the most immediate impact. Its title alone introduced a powerful idea: 'that sex is a status category with political implications' (Millett, 2000: 23). By 'politics' Millett was not referring simply to such things as political institutions, or the contestation between political parties or political ideas. Politics for Millett was about 'power-structured relationships . . . whereby one group of persons is controlled by another'. Millett argued that the dominance of the male sex was 'the most pervasive ideology of our culture and provides its most fundamental concept of power' (Millett, 2000: 25).

To explain male dominance Millett introduced the concept of *patriarchy*, which would subsequently provide an intellectual and ideological glue binding the disparate strands of second wave feminist thought and action. Patriarchy literally means 'rule by the father', and traditionally refers to the transference of power within families down the male line. Millett argued that although patriarchy varied in intensity and form it was nonetheless a definitive feature of all societies that was so pervasive that it appeared to be the normal state of things. Patriarchy started with the socialization of children within the patriarchal family setting and was subsequently reinforced through education, politics, culture, and sexual relations. It was not then a product of biology but of culture; patriarchy was socially constructed and thus it could be reduced or even eradicated. Andrea Dworkin later commented that 'Betty Freidan had written about the problem that had no name. Kate Millett named it, illustrated it, exposed it, analysed it' (Dworkin, 2003).

The concept of patriarchy attracted criticism from some feminists, much of which would feed into feminism's third wave. Some saw it as producing an overly simplistic and ahistorical depiction of women's oppression. It painted women as largely passive victims so that 'women's powerlessness, victimisation, and lack of resources . . . constitute women's timeless history' (Lynne Segal, cited in Bryson, 2016: 164). Others recognized that while all women had much in common regarding their exploitation, the nature and depth of gender-based oppression varied from society to society in significant ways. Valerie Bryson argues, however, that, despite its weaknesses, the concept of patriarchy retains a power and utility for many contemporary feminists. This is because at the most general level, 'it provides a handle on the world that connects different areas of experience . . . and enables us to see the extent to which male needs and assumptions are still central to political, cultural and economic life' (Bryson, 2016: 166).

Although clear tensions were emerging within feminist debate, the second wave produced several concrete outcomes. Women's studies began to appear in university programmes. It was an era which also saw the emergence of facilities such as domestic violence shelters, rape crisis centres, women's health clinics, and, especially after the landmark 1973 Roe vs Wade decision by the US Supreme Court, greater access to legal abortions in the US and elsewhere. However, the overturning of *Roe v. Wade* by the US Supreme Court in 2022, challenges a too tidy and linear view of political progress for women's rights.

Third wave feminism

Elizabeth Evans claims that there is more agreement about the origins and content of the first two waves of feminist thought and action than there is about the third. Indeed, 'there is no monolithic third wave feminism' (Evans, 2015: 19–21; see also Bryson, 2016: 271). Third wave feminism continued to address many of the concerns central to previous waves, but it also incorporated a wide range of criticisms of them. These were aimed particularly at their failure to address the diversity of women's experiences and viewpoints when the complex intersections of class, race, culture, gender identity, and sexuality are factored in. The third wave's emergence was tied up also with a resurgence in feminist activism in the US in the early 1990s and a few years later in the UK. Evans argues that this resurgence was stimulated by the interaction of two key developments, both with distinctly international and transnational dimensions: the emergence of *neoliberalism* and the concept of *intersectionality* (Evans, 2015).

Neoliberalism and feminisms

Neoliberalism is a modern variety of liberal socio-economic thinking, promoting a less regulated capitalist economic system built around policies and regimes that prioritize market-based rather than state-based solutions to economic and social policy challenges. However, many scholars view the term neoliberalism as referring also to a distinct set of values intended to shape the behaviour of both individuals and states. For its many critics, neoliberalism is seen to promote selfish individualism and thus a decline in our sense of collective duties or responsibilities, while enhancing and entrenching greater inequality. Because of the multiple dimensions of globalization, moreover, the influence of neoliberalism has spread worldwide (Harvey, 2005).

Some Western feminists, such as Naomi Wolf and Ann Cudd see the feminism that emerged alongside neoliberalism in the 1990s as promoting a highly individualistic feminism which celebrates the increasing freedom of women to live how they please and on their own personal terms (Wolf, 1993; Cudd in Cudd and Holmstrom, 2011: Part I). They argue that this does not mean that contemporary women are less feminist, but that their feminist commitments are expressed differently and acted upon in different ways. It is sometimes said that third wave feminism is more about the diverse everyday personal experiences of young, increasingly savvy, and confident women wishing to express their 'girl power', than academic theorizing about gender (Snyder, 2008: 179).

Others argue that neoliberalism promotes a more consumerist, individualistic feminism that obscures the highly problematic picture of gender relations more generally (Holmstrom, in Cudd and Holmstrom, 2011: Part 2; Snyder, 2008; McRobbie, 2009; Fraser, 2013a and 2013b; Bryson, 2016). The socialist feminist Nancy Fraser even argues that 'feminism has entered a dangerous liaison with neoliberalism'. Fraser sees the seeds of this lying in feminism's second wave. Fraser argues that as the second wave unfolded feminism shifted away from a focus 'on labour and violence', the unjust impact of capitalism on women, to a focus on the politics of 'identity and representation' (Fraser, 2013a: 14. For a summary of her argument see Fraser, 2013b).

Fraser's critics argue that her argument reflects the perspective of a White Western socialist feminism and does not take account of Black feminisms and feminisms in the Global South, which remain very much focused on questions of economic and social justice for women (Sabsay, 2014. See also Aslan and Gambetti, 2011). For many feminists, neoliberalism has hit many women particularly hard. Although women's participation in the workforce has grown substantially, if unevenly, worldwide over the last few decades, women, including many women from minoritized social groups, remain disproportionately represented in lower-paid jobs even in highly developed states (Ortiz-Ospina and Tvzvetkova, 2017). In much of the Global South, in particular, most women's work is also confined to the often largely unregulated informal economy (Ortiz-Ospina, Tzvetkova, and Roser, 2018). This has pushed social justice at both the national and international levels into the foreground of much third wave feminist scholarship and action, especially feminist and gender-focused work on the international and global political economy (Bedford and Rai, 2013; Steans, 2013: 182–208).

Intersectionality and feminisms

The second development Evans highlights is a growing concern about the 'adequate recognition of the multiple inequalities facing women who are not white, middle-class, heterosexual, and able-bodied' (Evans, 2015: 2–3). The term *intersectionality* was coined in

1989 by the American legal scholar Kimberlé Crenshaw to capture specifically the invisibility of Black women in the US legal system (Crenshaw, 1989). This is a consequence, Crenshaw argues, of a tendency in both feminist and legal theoretical discourse 'to treat race and gender as mutually exclusive categories of experience and analysis' (Crensaw, 1989: 139). Intersectionality is now widely used to capture the complex interactions of gender, race, class, culture, and sexuality and the 'multiple and overlapping points of identity' that many women experience (Evans, 2015: 22; see also Snyder, 2008).

Third wave feminist scholarship also emerged alongside the growing influence of *poststructuralism* and *postcolonialism* across many of the social sciences and much of the humanities. As we discuss in Chapter 7, poststructuralism is characterized by a resistance to the pursuit of definitive and generalizable explanations of the social world whereas postcolonialism revolves around analysis of the legacies of colonialism, and how they continue to frame identity in today's postcolonial world (which we discuss in Chapter 9). These critical perspectives challenge political and theoretical analyses that centre around a singular, universalist understanding of human subjectivity: of what it is to be human. Poststructuralism is noted for its resistance to essentialism and this has had an obvious influence on much third wave feminism (Dean, 1989; Snyder, 2008; Budgeon, 2011; Evans, 2015; Bryson, 2016). In various ways, third wave feminists question the idea that there is or should be an essential, singular, or dominant understanding of 'being woman'. In place of narratives centred around a universal conception of 'woman' or 'women' third wave feminism 'foregrounds personal narratives that illustrate an intersectional and multiperspectival version of feminism' (Snyder, 2008: 175).

A concern with the intersections of race, class, and gender was already apparent in critiques of second wave feminism, notably in Black feminist writing or activism and particularly in the US. Sojourner Truth's 'Ain't I a Woman?' speech was arguably an early example of an intersectional standpoint. In her 1981 book *Ain't I A Woman: Black Women and Feminism*, hooks argued that the women's liberation movement of the 1970s was predominantly white and middle class and thus inherently exclusionary. Few Black women actively participated, she argued, despite evidence showing that sympathy among Black women for the broad aims of the movement was in fact markedly higher than among white women. This was because the women's movement had failed to articulate sufficiently the needs of poor and minoritized American women (hooks, 2015).

The landmark black feminist anthology, *All the Women are White, All the Blacks Are Men, But Some of Us Are Brave*, highlighted the complex intersection of race and gender that contextualized the lives of Black women in the US (Hull, Scott, and Smith, 1982). Its title was intended to convey that not only did feminism predominantly reflect the perspectives of white women, but it also tended to stereotype Black men as particularly problematic. This was done without sufficient awareness of the circumstances—racism, dominant cultural representations of black masculinity and sexuality, and comparative economic disadvantage—that most Black men in the US confronted in their daily lives (issues explored extensively in hooks, 2004). In failing to acknowledge or adequately reflect upon their own 'racially privileged position', many white feminists were seen to be reinforcing racialized stereotypes about Black women and men (Bryson, 2016: 240. See also hooks, 2015: chapter 4).

The Black feminist writing that appeared in the early 1980s focused primarily on Black women and other women of colour in the US. Writers such as Audre Lorde and Chandra Mohanty (who is discussed in Key Thinker 10.1) brought in an international and postcolonial dimension. They were pioneers in criticizing what they saw as a colonialist mindset underpinning much of second wave feminism, questioning its overly homogenized depiction of women in the Global South (Lorde, 1984; Mohanty, 1984).

KEY THINKER 10.1 CHANDRA MOHANTY 'UNDER WESTERN EYES'

In a 1984 essay entitled 'Under Western Eyes: Feminist Scholarship and Colonial Discourses', the Indian scholar Chandra Mohanty argued that the representation of 'third world women' in much Western feminist scholarship rested upon the assumption that 'women' were part of 'an already constituted, coherent group with identical interests and desires, regardless of class, ethnic or racial location or contradictions' (Mohanty, 1984: 64). This contributed to the production of an image of 'an average third world woman', who is seen, moreover, to lead a lesser kind of life than her Western counterpart. This is because she is presumed to be 'sexually constrained' and a victim of some or all of poverty, lack of education, tradition, victimization, family obligations, and so on (Mohanty, 1984: 65).

This contrasted with the implicit representation of Western women as 'educated, modern, as having control over their own bodies and sexualities, and the freedom to make their own decisions' (Mohanty, 1984: 65). In effect, Western 'woman' becomes the norm by which a non-Western woman comes to be judged as powerless and exploited and thus a victim that Western feminism is obliged to save in the name of a supposed universal sisterhood.

Mohanty was not suggesting that all Western women were as liberated as much Western feminism suggested. If they were, there would no need for a feminist movement in the West. Nonetheless, Western feminism's self-understanding had relied upon an often-unacknowledged distinction between itself and a representation of non-Western women as an undifferentiated and implicitly lesser Other. This masked the myriad differences between the experiences of women in non-Western contexts while also marginalizing their distinctive voices and histories of resistance to multiple, intersecting forms of oppression.

Mohanty's line of argument has subsequently been further developed in the work of several other feminists, notably from outside of the West (You can read more about this in the discussion of Gayatri Spivak's work in Chapter 9, Section 9.4).

Lourde, Mohanty, and other Black feminist writers highlighted the differences between women's experiences worldwide given the highly varied social, economic, racial, and cultural contexts in which women were situated. In their view, second wave feminism failed to do this and instead incorrectly made assumptions about all women based on their own limited experiences and observations.

Is there a fourth wave?

Several feminist scholars claim that the beginning of the twenty-first century has been accompanied by a distinct, fourth wave of feminism. Although it clearly overlaps with third wave thinking, it also returns to some of the core concerns of second wave feminist activism, such as economic exploitation and violence against women (Bryson, 2016: 278).

Catherine Redfern and Kristin Aune see the new wave of feminism as centred around issues ranging from sexual freedom and choice, violence against women, and economic inequality, to the sexism still permeating the many forms of popular culture (Redfern and Aune, 2013). They detect clear links with the second wave feminism of the 1970s, depicting the resurgence of activism as a process of 'reclaiming the F word' (the title of their book). Kira Cochrane also sees the fourth wave as a response to the impact on women of economic austerity policies introduced after the global financial crisis in 2007–2008, growing anger about the continuing evidence of widespread violence against women, and the persistence of pervasive everyday sexism (Cochrane, 2013). Although Cochrane focuses on the UK, she sees the revival of feminist activism as a worldwide phenomenon. Contemporary fourth wave feminism reflects then the complex influence of greater individualism and a heightened awareness of the implications of intersectionality (key themes in the third wave), and a resurgent, if more nuanced, sense of the global solidarity that was a prominent theme of the second wave (Cochrane, 2013; Chamberlain, 2017).

The fourth wave's distinctiveness stems also from feminism's adaptation to the growth of the internet and the proliferation of social media platforms which have produced new forms of sexual harassment and expressions of misogyny (hatred of women) or misogynoir (hatred directed at Black women). Yet, the internet also opens new spaces for communication and debate between feminist activists worldwide and enables the rapid dissemination of campaigns against sexism and misogynism, such as the *#metoo* campaign. Emerging out of accusations by female Hollywood stars about sexual harassment in the movie industry, *#metoo* rapidly became synonymous with a global campaign of women calling out myriad instances of sexual harassment and assault across most industries, professions, and public institutions.

The #metoo campaign was started in 2006 by the Black feminist and civil rights activist Tarana Burke (Phipps, 2020: 2). Yet, it only went viral after being retweeted by the white actor Alyssa Milano 11 years later. In *Me, Not You: The Trouble with Mainstream Feminism* (the title deliberately plays on 'Me Too'), Alison Phipps argues that mainstream feminist movements in the West often build upon the pioneering work of women of colour only to subsequently decentre their concerns and experiences, as well as other marginalized identities in favour of those of middle-class and cis-gendered white women (Phipps, 2020). In focusing predominantly on the actions of 'bad men', Phipps argues, much of mainstream feminism deflects attention from the deeper causes of gendered inequalities and sexual violence that lie in the global intersections of capitalism, racism, and colonial attitudes.

What Phipps's argument underscores is just how diverse theoretical perspectives and debates around sex and gender have now become. As we shall see, some of the key debates that have developed over the decades within feminist and gender-focused scholarship more generally have now emerged within the IR discipline specifically.

10.3 FEMINISMS, GENDER, AND INTERNATIONAL POLITICS

Our survey of the history of feminisms has shown that feminist theory and action already had an international dimension long before the emergence of feminist perspectives within the IR discipline. This was particularly apparent from the latter part of the second wave onwards when dominant Western perspectives in feminist theory and action were challenged around the themes of race, class, and the legacies of colonialism.

In this section we turn to engagement of feminism with the IR discipline. After considering the question why feminist perspectives are relatively recent arrivals in the IR discipline, we look at early examples of feminist analyses of the international that emerged in Peace Studies and Development Studies. These pioneering efforts developed themes that were subsequently taken up and developed further within the IR discipline. We then go on to look at how feminist perspectives cast a distinctive light on some of the IR discipline's longstanding core concerns, such as war, the state, and security. Finally, we examine how debates around the concept of gender have emerged in the IR discipline.

Why did feminist perspectives take so long to emerge in the IR discipline?

As was noted in the introduction, feminist perspectives only became prominent within the scholarly field of IR from the late 1980s and early 1990s. Given the considerable history of feminist thought and action prior to then, why did it take so long? Answers to this question are suggested by two observations by feminist scholars on the IR discipline in the early 1990s:

- International relations, like many other disciplines, has operated with a relatively narrow conception of what is relevant to its subject matter. Excluded from that conception, quite comprehensively, is the experience of most women. This is not only because women are, with rare exceptions absent from the circle of people— the makers of foreign policy—whose direct experience is the stuff of traditional international relations. It is also because international relations theory has, overwhelmingly been constructed by men working with mental models of human activity and society seen through a male eye and apprehended through a male sensibility (Grant and Newland, 1991: 1).

- As a scholar and teacher of international relations I have frequently asked myself the following questions: why are there so few women in my discipline? If I teach my field as it is conventionally defined why are there so few readings by women to assign to my students? Why is the subject matter of my discipline so distant from women's lived experiences (Tickner, 1992: ix)?

Things have changed to some extent since these observations were made. Firstly, women have become more numerous and more prominent than ever in the upper echelons of political power including diplomatic and foreign policy making circles. Nonetheless, recent UN statistics show that gender parity remains a long way off. As of January 2023, women were serving as Heads of State in only 17 Countries and Head of Government in 19 countries; 119 countries were yet to have a women leader and only 22.8 per cent of government ministers worldwide were women. The majority of these ministers were, moreover, in areas of domestic politics (such as social affairs, employment and labour policy, the environment, or women's affairs/gender equality). (The UN provides a global statistical map of 'Women in Politics' at: https://www.unwomen.org/en/digital-library/publications/2023/03/women-in-politics-map-2023).

A second change is that a focus on a binary distinction between the male and female genders is now subject to considerable academic and public debate. This is because it is seen by many to exclude conceptions of gender, such as LGBTIQA+ (Lesbian, Gay, Bisexual, Transgender, Intersex, Queer or Questioning, Asexual, plus others) that do not conform to a simple gender binary (we discuss this further in the section called 'Queering the Discipline?' later in this chapter). Nonetheless, the key point in both commentaries was that the theory and practice of international politics historically reflected the dominance of men, and a specific understanding of masculinity, and for many feminist IR scholars this remains the case today.

Additionally, for most of its history, the IR discipline has undoubtedly been dominated by White men. In recent years the gender balance within the discipline has improved significantly but it remains mostly male-dominated. A 2011 survey across 20 countries showed that 31 per cent of IR scholars identified as female, with only New Zealand, Sweden, and South Africa achieving gender parity or close to it (Malaniak, Peterson, and Tierney, 2012: 21) The same survey showed also that when IR scholars were asked to name the four most influential IR scholars over the last 20 years, the top 20 names included only two women: the American constructivist, Martha Finnemore, ranked 15th and the British IPE scholar, Susan Strange, ranked 19th (Malaniak, Peterson, and Tierney, 2012: 49). Not surprisingly this gender imbalance has been starkly reflected in the assigned readings for most IR courses and syllabi. For example, in a 2019 survey of the complete IR curriculum across all degree levels and disciplinary subfields in one of the UK's leading IR university departments, it was found that 79.2 per cent of all texts on reading lists were written by men, apart from gender-focused or explicitly feminist course modules and programmes (Phull, Cifliki, and Meibauer, 2019: 383). A 2017 US-wide survey of IR syllabi came to broadly similar conclusions (Coglan, 2017).

The historical absence of women in the academic output of the IR field is perhaps less surprising given that, as Jacqui True (2022: 142) has observed, one of the marked features of most mainstream IR theorizing until comparatively recently is the absence of people, both women and men. History shows how the lives of people can clearly be dramatically affected by international politics; but people's lives have historically not been a very visible concern in the IR theory mainstream. With the emergence of critical perspectives from the 1980s onwards, people became more visible in IR theory. For example, Marxist IR theories bring class relations and processes of global exploitation into the picture (which you can read about in Chapter 5), and the solidarist wing of the English School (discussed in Chapter 4), and Critical Theory (covered in Chapter 6), are marked by a normative commitment to the pursuit of human emancipation worldwide. Poststructuralist and postcolonial IR perspectives highlight in various ways how orthodox theorizing marginalizes or simply excludes the complexities of the politics of individual and collective identities that arise out of encounters with global processes. (You can read more about poststructuralism in Chapter 7, and postcolonialism in Chapter 9.)

In a broadly similar spirit, feminist IR seeks to critically refine our understanding of the impact of international and global politics on people's lives through a particular focus on its gendered dimensions. Cynthia Enloe has remarked that she sees 'the "international" as embedded in the national and the local . . . and the "political" in many other spaces that others imagine are purely economic, cultural, or private' (Enloe cited in Cohn and Enloe, 2003: 1188). Feminist IR scholars often look in places where few other scholars have ventured and ask very different questions. In so doing, not only do they bring people (not just women) into the IR picture, but they also disrupt the discipline's boundaries that have been so central to its claim to be a distinct area of theoretical enquiry.

Early feminist analyses of the international: women, peace, and development

Some of the earliest examples of scholarly work on the gendered dimensions of international politics emerged at the IR discipline's margins, notably in the fields of peace and conflict research and development studies.

Women, peace, and conflict

War has undoubtedly been a central focus of mainstream IR since the discipline's inception. The IR discipline has also generally discounted the possibility of war being fully eradicated from international politics. Since the 1950s, however, the advent of the Cold War and the deployment of nuclear weapons led to challenges to the IR discipline's seeming acceptance of war as a permanent and sometimes necessary dimension of international politics. These challenges emerged principally in the fields of theology, moral philosophy, conflict analysis, and peace research (Lawler 1995: 10–13; Lawler, 2013b). Their emergence also reflected the growth of an international peace movement centred primarily around opposition to nuclear weapons.

There are undoubtedly strong connections between feminism and anti-war thinking and activism. As Jean Bethke Elshtain has suggested, military combat is perhaps the definitive male role, traditionally juxtaposed with a depiction of women as those who must be saved (Elshtain, 1987). The history of women actively campaigning against war and for peace dates to the early twentieth century. For example, the Women's International League for Peace and Freedom (WILPF) was founded in 1919 by feminist activists and writers and remains active today (Ashworth, 2021). It has evolved into a global activist organization that embraces most of the core concerns of contemporary feminist thought and activism. WILPF now depicts 'patriarchy, militarism and neoliberalism as three interrelated causes that push us all towards more conflict' (see WILPF.org).

With the establishment in the mid-1960s of the discipline of Peace Research, a new academic space for the articulation of anti-war feminist thinking emerged. Peace Research has always worn its anti-war sentiments on its sleeves, ensuring that it would be viewed suspiciously by the mainstream of the social sciences. Peace Research was also interdisciplinary in its outlook and none of its founding scholars (the most notable being the Norwegian sociologist, Johan Galtung) came from the IR field. Nonetheless, its primary objective was to challenge the then dominant realist view that war was an ever-present possibility in international politics (Lawler, 1995 and 2013b).

The peace researcher, Berenice Carroll, offered one of the early feminist challenges to predominant notions of power in the IR discipline. Carroll argued that most analysis of the international was governed by a 'cult of power' centred around an understanding of power as 'power over', the dominance of one actor over another or others. Rather than questioning the structure of power in the international system, which was widely accepted as the root source of the perpetual risk of war, most IR scholarship confined itself to explaining or understanding it, thereby serving effectively to perpetuate it (Carroll, 1972). For Carroll, however, power can be also understood as the exercise of autonomous independent action to counter dominant power. Carroll illustrated the difference with reference to debates between feminists. On the one hand there were equality feminists who sought to 'make it in a man's world' and thus pursued the acquisition of 'their fair share of dominance'. On the other hand, there were more radical feminists who believed that 'sisterhood is powerful' and wanted to 'eradicate all systems of dominance and submission from human relations' (Carroll, 1972: 604). If peace research wanted to provide a real alternative to the IR discipline, Carroll argued, it needed to examine the many ways in which the supposedly powerless have historically challenged dominant power. This was through such things as protest, the innovation of alternative strategies, collective resistance, the questioning or disavowal of dominant norms and values, and so on.

Betty Reardon, an early exponent of peace education, sees sexism in domestic societies and the international war system as 'two interdependent manifestations of a common problem: social violence', which cannot be overcome independently of each other (Reardon, 1985: 2). Male oppression of women, Reardon argues, is 'the first and most fundamental form of structural oppression'. Sexist attitudes and values are socially learned from childhood, become deeply embedded in our psyches thereby profoundly influencing how we understand the wider social world. This predisposes individuals and societies to view those that are perceived to be different from themselves, for whatever reason, as a potential threat. This 'gives rise to the notion of enemy and, ultimately, the practice of war' (Reardon, 1985: 7).

Reardon describes the international system as a 'war system' dominated by a small minority of elites, comprised primarily of men from Western industrialized countries who 'run the global economy and conduct the affairs of state' (Reardon, 1985: 3). This war system, permeates every aspect of life within states and perpetuates the fear of an actual or potential external other that threatens our own society. It is thus an important tool for elites wishing to maintain their dominance as it helps to bind people together when internal divisions threaten societal coherence.

Reardon was writing during the latter part of the Cold War, and it is useful to reflect here on how anti-communism in the West or anti-Western sentiment in the Soviet Union and its allies—effectively, two opposing forms of fear—were used to strengthen public support for national security policies. Reardon was not rejecting entirely the realist argument that the structure and processes of international politics are contributing factors to the risk of war. Rather, she argues that there is an interplay between social structures and the psychological forces that arise from the socializing effects of patriarchal societies. If we want to abolish war, we need firstly to unlearn those deeply embedded assumptions that govern our personal relations with other humans within our own societies and with those more distant from us.

Carol Cohn: 'Sex and Death in the Rational World of Defense Intellectuals'

Many feminists see the defence and security policy arenas as particularly prone to highly gendered assumptions that need to be exposed and challenged (Duncanson, 2017). A notable early example was provided by Carol Cohn, who in 1984 was one of several US college teachers attending a summer workshop on nuclear weapons, nuclear strategic doctrine, and arms control. This became the basis for a widely cited article entitled 'Sex and Death in the Rational World of Defense Intellectuals'.

The workshop was taught solely by men who:

> formulate what they call 'rational' systems for dealing with the problems created by nuclear weapons: how to manage the arms race; how to deter the use of nuclear weapons; how to fight a nuclear war if deterrence fails . . . (I)t is their reasoning that is used to explain why it is not safe to live without nuclear weapons. (Cohn 1987: 687–8)

Cohn spent a further year as a participant observer at a defence technology and arms control research centre where she was stunned by the dispassionate language used to describe the lethality of nuclear weapons. Nuclear weapons were described as 'clean bombs' or as a 'damage limitation weapon' that could carry out 'surgically clean strikes' (Cohn, 1987: 691–2). Sexualized imagery was often used to describe what the weapons can do—'bigger bang for your buck'; 'soft lay down'; 'deep penetration'; 'releasing 70–80 per cent of all our megatonnage in one orgasmic whump', and so on (Cohn, 1987: 693). But Cohn also concedes that over time she got drawn into the seductive appeal of 'technostrategic' language, even if she was learning it to critically engage with it. It is a form of discourse that helps enable defence intellectuals to 'think the unthinkable' by glossing over what the weapons are designed to do: kill millions of people (Cohn, 1987: 715).

The power and legitimacy of technostrategic language, Cohn concludes, lies in its claims to be the dispassionate voice of technical rationality and objective professionalism; if you question it, you risk being characterized as too emotional, unrealistic, or irrational. Cohn argues that if, however, you look beneath the language's surface and examine its gendered underpinnings, its claims to be the embodiment of cool-headed rationality appear illusory. The challenge for feminists and other opponents of military solutions to global problems is therefore to learn technostrategic discourse to deconstruct and dismantle it. Cohn concludes that

The dominant voice of militarised masculinity and decontextualized rationality speaks so loudly in our culture, it will remain difficult for any other voices to be heard until that voice loses some of its power to define what we hear and how we name the world—until that voice is delegitimated. (Cohn, 1987: 717)

Feminism and anti-war activism

The work of Carroll, Reardon, Cohn, and other anti-militarist Western feminists coincided with an upsurge in feminist anti-war activism during the late 1970s and early 1980s. One famous example was the Greenham Common Women's Peace Camp set up in England outside a joint US/UK military base in 1981. It remained there for a further 19 years, inspiring other women's peace camps in the US, Australia, and elsewhere. You can read more about the Greenham Common Women's Peace Camp in Key event 10.2.

KEY EVENT 10.2 THE GREENHAM COMMON WOMEN'S PEACE CAMP

In response to the Soviet Union's decision in 1977 to deploy mobile SS20 nuclear ballistic missiles that could target all Western Europe, the US decided to deploy nuclear tipped Pershing II and Cruise missiles at its European bases. These included the joint UK/US base at Greenham Common in Berkshire, England.

In response to the storage of nuclear capable cruise missiles, in 1981 a series of women-only protest camps were set up around the base. The protestors engaged in a range of actions, including chaining themselves to the base's fences, blockading the base's entrance, and breaching its perimeter to go and dance on the missile storage bunkers.

Some of the most famous actions entailed the formation of long human chains. In 1983 one encircled the entire base while another chain of 70,000 women linked the base with the UK's weapons research centre at Aldermaston 14 miles away. When some of the camps were evicted by the police or local authorities, the women rapidly established new camps nearby.

Although the last cruise missile was removed from the base in 1991 because of the 1987 INF Treaty, the camp remained in place in protest at the UK government's new Trident submarine-based nuclear deterrence system.

The camp inspired similar protests around the world, such as the Puget Sound Women's Camp set up in 1983 outside the Boeing Aerospace Center in Seattle where cruise missiles were manufactured, and the 1983 Women's Peace Camp outside the Joint Defence Facility (a key component of the US's global intelligence gathering system) at Pine Gap, Australia.

The Greenham Common camp was finally disbanded in 2000.

USEFUL SOURCE

Suzanne Moore et al., 'How the Greenham common protest changed lives: we danced on top of the nuclear silos', *The Guardian*, 20 March 2017

Feminists have disagreed about the analysis of militarism or how to challenge it. For example, some criticized the 1980s women's peace camps because they were seen to perpetuate gender stereotypes. Much of the rhetoric around peace camps invoked the idea that women universally held unique maternal and nurturing values which provided the basis for opposing a militarism that they believed threatened their children's futures (Shepherd, 2022: 67–69). Some feminists saw this as problematic because it invoked traditional conceptions of women as passive and submissive while also absolving men from their equal responsibility to protect life (Confortini, 2010: 9–10; Steans, 2013: 99–101; Shepherd, 2022: 69). The camps were also vulnerable to the charge that their participants were predominantly white and from the more affluent and educated sections of Western societies. Women outside the West have found and still find themselves in contexts of national militarized violence—such as wars of liberation from colonialism and civil wars—that place complex moral and political demands upon them that defy easy generalizations (Darden, 2015).

Women as warriors?

The simple equation of feminism with anti-war activism and peace as a value is complicated by the history of women undertaking military service or engaging directly in violent conflicts, as participants, for example, in armed national liberation struggles. Women in state militaries have traditionally been confined primarily to non-combat support roles, but the emergence of second wave feminism also saw some feminists, notably those embracing liberal equality feminism, argue that women should also be able to fight for their country (Stiehm, 1989; Carter, 1996; Kennedy-Pipe, 2017). The 1980s saw the beginnings of a considerable growth in the number of women joining the military in various countries around the world and the beginning of campaigns for the widening of opportunities for women to undertake front-line combat duties alongside men.

For some feminists, however, the debate about the right to undertake combat roles cannot be reduced to a question of simple equality of opportunity. Claire Duncanson identifies an extensive feminist literature that depicts 'militarism as a fundamentally anti-feminist system' (Duncanson, 2017: 48–50). If women play a greater role in the military, are they not simply contributing to the perpetuation of the 'war system' that Reardon and others see as reinforcing traditional gender roles?

Cynthia Enloe's *Does Khaki Become You? The Militarisation of Women's Lives* examines the gendered dimensions of life in and around the US military, drawing particularly on the role of US forces in the Vietnam War and the impact of the continuing presence of US bases throughout Asia after the war ended. Enloe argues that women are drawn into the military sphere in seemingly contradictory ways: through sex work near military bases on the one hand and as vital contributors to the provision of nursing care or in supporting roles behind the battlefield on the other (Enloe, 1983). Additionally, modern warfare technology blurs the distinction between the militarized masculinity of the front line and the supposedly more women-friendly support roles. Enloe sees the military as thus presenting a difficult challenge for feminists. If they simply turn their backs on the military and its role in the militarization of society because of its masculinized character they risk leaving it unchallenged. Yet, getting involved with the military or supporting campaigns to improve the lives of servicewomen also carries the risk of collaborating in the sustenance of militarized masculinity, given that militaries remain overwhelmingly male-dominated domains. Enloe concludes that military institutions have a range of contradictory relationships with women both inside its ranks and outside which reveal it to be a 'vulnerable patriarchal institution' (Enloe, 1983: 220). As such, Enloe believes, it can be critically challenged by women on several fronts, inside and outside. It remains a matter of debate amongst contemporary feminists, however, whether the culture, and indeed the very purpose of militaries can be radically transformed or 'regendered' (Duncanson, 2017: 53).

Enloe's emphasis on the personal experiences of women contrasts with the dry abstraction of much mainstream IR theorizing about war and security. In most Western states the impact of violent conflicts these days might be largely indirect, but elsewhere women's lives have been and still are directly impacted by war and other forms of armed violence (Kennedy-Pipe, 2017: 34). Women have also been active participants in numerous armed rebellions and insurgencies around the world, although the form of their participation is often shaped by highly gendered and patriarchal command structures (Marks, 2017). In contrast to feminist explorations that focus on women as peacemakers, feminist IR scholars such as Laura Sjoberg and Caron Gentry explore how women's political violence—as participants in such things as military torture, suicide bombings, or genocides—is usually understood. Conventional reactions to women's political violence, such as shock or incomprehension, effectively deny the women's conscious agency and therefore perpetuate stereotypes of 'appropriate' female behaviour (Sjoberg and Gentry, 2007).

Jessica Trisko Darden argues that because of the different contexts in which women worldwide find themselves 'determining what drives women's participation in war is inherently difficult' (Darden, 2015: 458). The historical social and intersectional contexts in which women are variously situated combined with the nature of a specific conflict arguably shape women's attitudes towards their participation in violent conflicts and war. Thus, Darden concludes, '(e)xamining women as a group and expecting conflict to affect this group in predictable and easily identifiable ways only reinforces existing assumptions about women and conflict' (Darden, 2015: 462).

THINK CRITICALLY 10.1 SHOULD WOMEN FIGHT?

We know that women historically have participated in various forms of armed political violence and that some national armed forces now permit women to join and, in some cases, take up combat roles. Feminist scholars disagree, however, on the question of whether women should join miliary forces or engage in armed political violence. Drawing on what you have read so far, consider the following questions:

1. Thinking about countries with which you are most familiar, are women permitted to a) join the national armed forces and b) undertake combat roles?
2. Do you think women should be able to a) enrol in national armed forces and b) undertake front line combat roles? Explain your answers.

3. Do you think women should be able to participate in other forms of armed political violence such as, for example, armed liberation struggles, rebellions, or resistance to armed incursions?

Hint: when answering these questions think about whether your response is centred around gender specifically or your standpoint on war and armed political violence more generally.

Feminism and International Development

Another area in which feminism made an early impact on international analysis is Development Studies. In the early 1970s several US development practitioners coined the term 'Women in Development' (WID) to highlight their focus on the gendered dimensions of US development assistance to countries in the Global South. That assistance was very much driven by the 'modernization' approach which argued that developing states should be encouraged to mirror the stages of growth experienced by developed states such as the US. WID's founders argued, however, that the impact of modernization strategies in recipient countries was very different for men and women. Influenced by liberal feminism's emphasis on equal opportunity for women, WID's intention was to challenge the then dominant representation of women in the developing world as primarily mothers and wives and recognize their actual and potential role in economic production.

WID was strongly influenced by the pioneering research of the Danish economist Ester Boserup in Sub-Saharan Africa where women had long played a major role in agricultural production. This gave them significant social status and power. Boserup suggested that women often did more than half of the agricultural work, sometimes as much as 80 per cent. She argued, however, that the gendered assumptions of Western development assistance—a primary emphasis on addressing the health and welfare needs of women as wives and mothers, while treating men as the economically productive sector of developing societies—were undermining women's traditional status. Men were being trained to use new agricultural technologies to improve the production of cash crops, whereas women were left to continue using traditional agricultural methods to produce subsistence crops. This meant that women were losing income, status, and power in relation to men (Boserup, 1970). Boserup's work influenced a shift in the focus of Western development assistance policies towards a recognition of the role of women in economic production, and the need to adjust development policies accordingly. This included redefining the notion of 'work' to recognize the vital role of women in subsistence production or unremunerated 'family labour' which was previously treated as merely 'housework'.

The impact of WID was reflected in revisions to the United Nations Development Programme (UNDP), the agendas of many Western development agencies, and the adoption by the UN General Assembly of the Convention on the Elimination of All Forms of Discrimination against Women (CEDAW). However, some feminist critics argued that WID tended to depict women in developing societies as a homogeneous group defined primarily by their biological sex and their place in capitalist economic production. It paid insufficient attention to intersectionality—the impact of race and socio-economic background—on women's lives in the Global South (Connelly et al., 2000: 59). These concerns led to the emergence of 'Gender and Development' (GAD) from the 1980s onwards as a more theoretically diverse and interdisciplinary approach that analyses the gendered roles of both women and men within the complex interaction between local social relationships and increasingly globalized economic processes. The broad intention is to show how gender roles emerge in specific contexts in often quite different ways. This requires a more variable understanding of gender and development which draws more extensively upon localized knowledge and practices (Connelly et al., 2000; Drolet, 2010).

Subsequent feminist work in the field of IPE/GPE not only further developed the theme of gender equality and female empowerment in early feminist development studies but also explored the complex intersection of gender with all aspects of the global economy: production; exchange; consumption; and global economic governance (Bedford and Rai, 2013).

The emergence of feminist perspectives in the fields of peace research and development studies undoubtedly helps to stimulate the rapid growth of feminist approaches within the IR discipline from the late 1980s onwards. It is important to note here that the boundaries between feminist perspectives in peace studies, development studies, and IR have become blurred over the last few decades. The expansion of feminist and gender-focused IR scholarship coincided with the third wave of feminism, which, as we have seen, was marked by a considerable diversification of feminist thought. Certainly, the themes of gender and armed conflict and women's roles in the world economy have been developed further in contemporary gender-focused IR scholarship, although they are now examined through a more diverse range of theoretical lenses.

'Add women and stir'?

It must be stressed that as with feminism generally there is no singular feminist IR theory. Feminist IR scholars draw upon the full spectrum of feminist and gender theorizing to explore in different ways the significance of gender in both the theory and practice of international and global politics. Much of feminist IR is empirical in focus. It investigates previously little explored areas in which the international intersects with the actual lives of women and men to show how gendered assumptions and practices play out. This is not to say that its epistemology (how it theorizes) is necessarily empiricist. Empiricism classifies facts as the products solely of observation and views them as the building blocks for developing and then testing the validity of theoretical hypotheses through adherence to scientific methods. The objective is to produce robust and definitive explanations that can be deemed to be true, regardless of our normative orientation, our values. In the social sciences, this is also commonly referred to as positivism (positivism is discussed in more in Chapter 6, Section 6.2).

Some feminists, notably liberal feminists, do confine themselves to orthodox social scientific methods to show the significance of gender as a variable in the explanation of social phenomena. This kind of liberal feminism tends to focus on the demonstrable value of increasing the number of women in positions of political authority and influence; what is often referred to as an 'add women and stir' perspective. For example, quantitative statistical analysis has been used to test the hypothesis that 'the higher the level of domestic gender equality, the lower the severity of violence in international crises' (Caprioli and Boyer, 2001). The hypothesis is premised upon a general claim that is taken from a cross-section of feminist literature, namely that women are likely to be less belligerent than men.

To test this out Mary Caprioli and Mark Boyer utilized the International Crisis Behaviour (ICB) data set, which codifies data on the sources, processes, and outcomes of all military-security crises since the end of the First World War. Additionally, they classified the level of gender equality within states according to the number of years women had the right to vote and the percentage of women in national legislatures. After cross-analysing the data, the study concluded that there was a correlation between higher levels of gender equality and lower levels of violence in dealing with international crises. Having established this, the authors go on to suggest that their research does have the normative implication that 'the pursuit of gender equality within societies throughout the world may have positive effects for the lessening of violence at national, transnational and international levels' (Caprioli and Boyer, 2001: 515. See also, Caprioli, 2000).

Contemporary feminist IR scholars tend to bring together insights from second and third wave feminism as well as the more critical theoretical schools of IR thought to frame their empirical enquiries. As such, they are critical of the liberal 'add women and stir' viewpoint as well as positivist forms of analysis. Both are seen as inadequate for understanding how gender inequalities are reproduced through international social relations of power which serve to both construct and maintain dominant conceptions of the roles of women and men. Even if there is greater gender equality in a formal sense, as illustrated by the number of women in a national legislature for example, this does not mean that gender inequality has been eradicated (Tickner and Sjoberg, 2016: 183).

Nonetheless, the international historian, Glenda Sluga, defends the utility of an 'add women and stir' perspective when studying the history of international politics:

> recognising the presence of women has the potential to fundamentally shift our perspective on what is important in the past, as well as to illuminate the role of historians in silencing women, their actions, and their ideas . . . This is not an argument for throwing gender aside, but a call to remember the usefulness of adding women, of the recovery and reintegration of women *who were there* as political agents into the stories we tell of the international past. (Sluga, 2014: 66, emphasis in the original)

Sluga's argument is reinforced by a recent collection of interdisciplinary essays on the contributions of 18 leading women thinkers to the study and practice of international history and politics during the first half of the twentieth century (Owens and Rietzler, 2021). The collection is intended to correct 'women's erasure from IR's canon of intellectual "greats" or its disciplinary history' (Owens and Rietzler, 2021: 2). Alongside recent scholarship on the erasure of Black scholars from the IR discipline's history (which we discuss in Chapter 9), such work reminds us that the

IR discipline's history and purview has been much richer and more diverse than the dominant telling of it usually suggests.

Cynthia Enloe—*Bananas, Beaches and Bases*

In *Bananas, Beaches and Bases: Making Feminist Sense of International Politics,* first published in 1990, Cynthia Enloe famously asks: 'where are the women?' (Enloe, 2014: xiv and 1). Of course, women have always been part of international or global politics. They become far more visible, Enloe argues, if you examine international politics from the ground up, rather than from the top-down view of orthodox IR theory which privileges states and their foreign policies as the primary sites for investigation.

Enloe adopts an ethnographic approach by examining the experiences of various differently situated women whose lives intersect with international global political and economic relations of power. Enloe examines how gender has shaped the lives of various women, such as nineteenth-century European and American women who ventured to travel abroad as explorers or colonialists, the contributions of women to the development of the international tourist industry (such as flight attendants or chambermaids in resort hotels), US military wives, Filipino sex workers near US military bases, British diplomatic wives, women working on a Honduran banana plantation, and the Brazilian singer Carmen Miranda, an idealized image of whom was widely used to market those bananas abroad.

Through examining these different lives, Enloe shows how the second wave feminist axiom that 'the personal is political' helps make sense of the international: the personal is also international and the international is personal. In their various roles, be that as mothers, wives, sex workers, secretaries, maids, or poorly remunerated workers, these women's supposedly 'private' or 'personal' relations with men are shown to be vital yet unacknowledged components of global political and economic processes that sustain a heavily masculinized and patriarchal international order. This order also shapes those women's lives and perpetuates the treatment of many women as useful primarily because of male-defined notions of femininity, or as objects for economic exploitation or the gratification of men.

Enloe's book encouraged other feminists to look at international politics from a very different empirical perspective, in which the supposedly private world of women and their everyday experiences are seen as legitimate starting points from which to understand the functioning of international and global politics. It also adopted a multidisciplinary approach which owes more to anthropological and sociological methodology than to IR theory.

The novelty of Enloe's approach can be illustrated through the example of overseas military bases. Orthodox IR thinking suggests we should examine such things as the geopolitics that dictate where such bases are located or the strategic thinking that underpins the decision to maintain a military presence in a certain part of the world. Enloe's feminist analysis of military bases takes a very different approach. It focuses instead on the 'seemingly normal, routine and everyday interactions that go on and around these installations' (Enloe, Lacey, and Gregory, 2016: 538). This would entail looking at the lives of sex workers whose bodies are used by military personnel for sexual gratification, the lives of women (including female members of the military) who are sexually assaulted by soldiers, or the gendered impact of the base on the local economy and culture.

Enloe's work was followed by several other feminist studies of the international politics of foreign domestic workers and transnational migrant workers (see Chin, 1998, for example). Overlapping with the work of feminist development theorists, these examine how globalization has further deepened the intersection of politics and social relations of the household with national and global political and economic processes.

One of the most compelling illustrations of the importance and public impact of looking at international politics from the bottom up can be found in the international garment industry, in which women, mostly very low paid, play such a crucial role. It raises profound questions for people in the industrialized developed world who benefit from cheap clothing that is often manufactured in the Global South under conditions that are highly exploitative. In preparing the second edition of *Bananas, Beaches and Bases*, Enloe noted how she was particularly affected by the tragedies of a fatal fire in 2012 and a building collapse in 2013 in Bangladeshi garment factories (which are discussed in Key event 10.3) producing clothing for export (Enloe, Lacey, and Gregory, 2016: 543). Such episodes, Enloe and many other feminist IR scholars would argue, provide telling illustrations of the gendered impact of international and global politics on people's lives.

KEY EVENT 10.3 THE BANGLADESH GARMENT FACTORY DISASTERS

The ready-made garment (RMG) manufacturing industry economy generates over 80 per cent of Bangladesh's total export revenue. More than 80 per cent of garment workers are women, most earning little more than the legal minimum wage for garment workers. In 2021 this was 8,000 taka per month (c. £74). Many workers are forced to work 12 or more hours per day in often hazardous, cramped, and unsafe conditions.

The Bangladesh RMG industry also has a history of disaster. According to War on Want, between 1990 and 2011, more than 400 workers died and several more thousand were injured in 50 major factory fires. Two garment factory disasters attracted worldwide attention, not least because the garments they produced were for some of the most prominent Western clothing brands. The first, in November 2012, was a fire in the Tazreen Fashions factory outside Dhaka in which more than 120 workers died and 250 were injured. After the fire started, the management told the workers not to evacuate immediately and in any case many of the fire exits were locked.

A second even worse disaster occurred in April 2013 when the shoddily built eight-storey Rana Plaza building in Dhaka, housing five garment factories, collapsed. At least 1100 workers, mostly young women, were killed and 2,500 injured. Deep cracks had appeared in the building on the day before the collapse, but management rebuffed workers pleas to not be sent inside. Local unions described it as 'mass industrial homicide' (*The Guardian*, 24 April 2018).

These disasters resulted in action by Western brands and retailers, in the form of a legally binding Accord on Fire and Building Safety agreed between key Western brands, retailers, local unions, and international labour organizations. This produced dramatic

Bangladeshi people lay floral wreaths in memory of the victims of the Rana Plaza building collapse as they mark the second anniversary of the disaster at the site where the building once stood in Savar, on the outskirts of Dhaka

improvements at the more than 2,000 garment factories that supply the Western clothing market. The accord did not, however, cover conditions at the more than 1,500 factories that do not produce for Western suppliers. These undergo much less rigorous inspection regimes or none. Furthermore, the Accord's term expired in 2018 (subsequently extended to 2020) and since then Bangladesh's RMG factory owners (many of whom are parliamentarians or own newspapers or television stations) have established a Bangladesh-based alternative, the Ready Made Garments Sustainability Council. However, the new council's recommendations are not legally binding, and compliance is entirely voluntary.

Enloe has expressed ambivalence about being referred to as a 'theorist', preferring to think of herself as an 'investigator' or 'analyst' driven by a 'feminist curiosity', and with a particular interest in stories. Nonetheless, Enloe does not think stories 'are the opposite of theory'. Rather stories, such as the stories that *Bananas, Beaches and Bases* tells, are, she claims, 'the building blocks of larger theoretical explanations' (Enloe, Lacey, and Gregory, 2016: 544–545). Stories can paint a much richer and more nuanced picture of the international.

Postpositivist IR feminisms

By bringing in gender as a category of analysis, Enloe certainly poses different questions to those of mainstream IR scholars. Nonetheless, some critics question whether Enloe's empiricism moves much beyond a liberal 'add women and stir' approach. For such critics, Enloe's version of feminist empiricism is inadequate because 'it takes problematic notions of "reality", "men", "women" and "gender" as concrete givens rather than social constructs' (Peoples and Vaughan-Williams, 2021: 55).

We noted in this chapter's introduction that much of feminist IR scholarship, is located within the sphere of critical IR theories. In other words, it rejects the positivist epistemological viewpoint that there is a universal and objective truth that can be arrived at through the politically or culturally neutral analysis of supposed facts. Instead, postpositivist IR feminist theorists recognize that as scholars they are situated social beings trying to understand the social world of which they are inescapably a part (see Chapters 6 and 7 for more on the differences between positivist and postpositivist IR theories). They seek to interpret social phenomena through gender-sensitive theoretical lenses and offer compelling and robust understandings of the social world without claiming these as unquestionable truth claims in which causal relationships are definitively established. In various ways, therefore, postpositivist IR feminist theorists endeavour to be reflective of their positionality in the world and explicit about their wish to question and challenge orthodox explanations of that world. For a postpositivist IR feminist, the problem with orthodox IR theories and some critical theories stems from their unacknowledged gendered assumptions. These assumptions are seen to influence what is being researched, what is regarded as suitable evidence to substantiate theoretical claims, and how the research is carried out.

While never explicitly endorsing a positivist perspective, Enloe does not substantially challenge the positivistic theoretical assumptions of the IR mainstream. She adopts the role of an outside observer of international political reality, albeit one who wants to develop a description of that reality that looks from below—from the perspective of those being exploited. Even Enloe's critics acknowledge that her work constitutes an important 'first stage' in the development of a gender analysis of international politics, because it brings previously neglected women into the picture and thus highlights the gendered nature of the power relationships that underpin practices such as diplomacy and the military (Steans, 2013: 15–17).

J. Ann Tickner on gender in international relations

An early example of postpositivist feminist IR is J. Ann Tickner's 1992 book, *Gender in International Relations*. Tickner describes international politics bluntly as 'a man's world . . . inhabited by diplomats, soldiers, and international civil servants most of whom are men' (Tickner, 1992: 1, see also Tickner, 2001: 1–2). Although there had been some female heads of state, at that time Tickner saw little evidence to suggest that women were playing a significant role in shaping national foreign policies. Tickner identifies a deeply held view in the US and elsewhere that when it comes to the conduct of foreign policy or the defence of the national interest, attributes typically associated with men and masculinity, such as 'strength, power, autonomy, independence, and rationality', are the most valued.

For Tickner, international politics is the realm where it is most apparent that there exists what the Australian sociologist R. W. Connell (now known as Raewyn Connell) has called a 'hegemonic masculinity'. This dominant image of masculinity is a socially constructed ideal stereotype that does not necessarily correspond to the personalities of most men. It constructs the male gender's supposed superiority in opposition to not only lesser valued conceptions of female gender, but also devalued conceptions of masculinity, such as homosexuality (Connell, 1987: chapter 8). Furthermore, it is an account of masculinity that, Tickner argues, is projected onto states 'whose success as international actors is measured in terms of their power capabilities and capacity for self-help and autonomy' (Tickner, 1992: 6–7).

The Western IR discipline's traditional masculinist focus on war and power politics is complicit, Tickner argues, in socializing us into thinking that men are more suited to manage the international conduct of states. Women's traditional roles and their experiences appear simply irrelevant to international affairs (Tickner, 1992: 4–5). Tickner traces the IR discipline's unawareness of its gendered assumptions back to the emergence of realism as the preeminent IR theoretical perspective after 1945. Indeed, Tickner is particularly known for her 'feminist reformulation' of Hans Morgenthau's famous 'Six Principles of Political Realism', which is discussed in Key concept 10.1.

KEY CONCEPT 10.1 J. ANN TICKNER'S CRITIQUE OF MORGENTHAU'S REALISM

'Hans Morgenthau's Principles of Political Realism: A Feminist Reformulation' (Tickner, 1988) is an early example of a postpositivist feminist critique of mainstream IR theory, subsequently developed further in *Gender in International Relations* (Tickner, 1992). Tickner does not say Morgenthau is wrong in his depiction of international politics. Rather, she asserts that he offers only a partial account because it is 'based on assumptions about human nature that are partial and that privilege masculinity' (Tickner, 1988: 431). Tickner is particularly critical of Morgenthau's claim, in the first of his six principles (which we examine more fully in Chapter 3, Section 3.4), that international politics requires a 'rational theory based on objective laws that have their roots in human nature'.

Drawing upon the feminist scientist Evelyn Fox Keller's work, Tickner depicts the idea of objectivity as inherently masculinist in its presumption that a neutral language to describe the social world is possible. Tickner contrasts this account of theory with most feminist thought in which knowledge is seen to be socially constructed (Tickner, 1988: 431–432). Whether Morgenthau was truly a positivist is debatable given his reference to the role of human nature, but Tickner later extended her critique to include Waltz's overtly positivist neorealism (Tickner, 1992: 11–12, 14).

Tickner argues that Morgenthau's realist theory rests upon a deliberate abstraction of 'political man' who is 'a beast completely lacking in moral restraints' (Tickner, 1988: 432). Morgenthau knew that real men and real states are more morally complex than that, but he justified his focus on the amoral 'political' aspect of human nature because of what he saw as the unique qualities of international politics wherein states engage in a perpetual struggle for power. Tickner reads Morgenthau as saying that in such a world 'states may act like beasts, for survival depends on a maximisation of power and a willingness to fight'.

> Tickner proposes that a feminist reformulation of Morgenthau's principles would recognize that objectivity is culturally defined, and that human nature is both masculine and feminine. Furthermore, the realist and masculinist equation of power with domination and control excludes the possibility of 'collective empowerment' which, Tickner (1988: 438) argues, is an 'aspect of power often associated with femininity'.
>
> A feminist perspective would 'seek to find common moral elements in human aspirations' and would view the 'national interest' in today's world as requiring cooperative solutions to a series of global problems such as the threat of nuclear war, economic wellbeing, and environmental degradation (Tickner, 1988: 437–438).

Classical realists draw upon sources—such as Hobbes' imagined 'state of nature', or Rousseau's metaphor of the stag hunt (which is outlined in Key concept 3.5)—which, Tickner argues, reinforce the notion that supposedly masculine attributes such as strength, power, and autonomy are essential to ensuring states' survival in a dangerous world. The value of women (if considered at all) is mostly secondary and lying primarily in the domestic (i.e., national) political realm. In contrast, men are burdened with the ultimate responsibility of being willing to lay down their lives if necessary to protect the homeland. This ultimate responsibility was, until comparatively recently, denied to most women. Therefore, a two-level understanding of citizenship emerges: Women are merely mundane citizens, whereas men are 'citizen-warriors'. Key to this is the depiction of women as passive and in need of protection.

Realism's gendered account of international politics, says Tickner, 'generates a national security discourse that privileges conflict and war and silences other ways of thinking about security' (Tickner, 1992: 51). The challenge for feminists then is to offer alternative accounts of concepts—such as power, sovereignty, and security—that are central to the mainstream or 'malestream' of the IR discipline (see also Youngs, 2004: 82–85). This requires something more than just 'injecting women's experiences' into the discipline. It requires drawing upon feminist theories to critique and reformulate the key assumptions of realism in way 'that might allow us to see new possibilities for solving our current insecurities' (Tickner, 1992: 18).

Tickner notes that alternative accounts to realism could be found at the margins of the IR discipline, in fields such as peace research and development studies where Tickner carried out her own earlier research. For Tickner, these fields' marginal status compared to realism reflect the influence of a 'stereotypical hegemonic masculinity' that offers only a partial account of either human experience or international reality. A more comprehensive understanding needs to consider the experiences of women and of those men who also do not conform to an idealized depiction of masculinity. Tickner draws upon a range of feminist theories to show how conceptions of citizenship, the state, and security could be developed which incorporate a more cooperative, peaceful outlook on resolving disputes and coexisting with those who are different from us.

Tickner views the purpose of theory as seeking not only to critique mainstream theory, but also to contribute to the transformation of international politics through political action. Tickner cites the example of the Greenham Common women who came to see themselves as strong, brave, and creative, qualities more usually associated with men. Tickner was writing during the emergence of third wave feminism, which as we have seen challenged the idea that there is (or should be) a singular feminist perspective which makes claims for all women everywhere. Tickner acknowledges this but argues that the virtuous characteristics that women may exhibit are not natural attributes of the female sex but the products of socialization and the historical roles they have played within patriarchal societies. However, because women have historically developed their distinctive values and outlooks largely within the private sphere, these have been 'de-valued in the public realm, particularly in the world of international politics'. The task then is to bring these values into public life not to claim their inherent superiority, but to inspire and contribute to thinking about how we might build better futures.

Tickner claims her objective is ultimately to develop a 'nongendered' perspective on international politics. Tickner overtly connects this vision to a progressive international political project—the realization of a more peaceful and just world order. In this respect, Tickner's work has many of the hallmarks of Critical International Theory, which explores the barriers to and the possibilities for universal human emancipation (see Chapter 6).

It is doubtful that any feminist IR scholars today would dispute Tickner's observation that the world of international politics is thoroughly gendered (Tickner, 1992: 5–6). For some postpositivist feminists, however, there are several problems with Tickner's brand of international progressivism. Although Tickner rejects the simple equation of feminism with pacifism, Jill Steans thinks Tickner falls into the trap of 'reproducing gender binaries of masculine war and feminine peace' (Steans, 2013: 95). Although Tickner acknowledges the considerable diversity and intersectionality of women's experiences, the extent to which she discards the idea that there are values that bind all women is debateable (Peoples and Vaughan-Williams, 2021: 58).

Additionally, despite her focus on gender, Tickner says comparatively little about how masculine identities are made and reproduced, some of which may also be exposed to violence and repression (Jones, 1996; Hutchings, 2008: 34–31; Carver, 2014). In other words, while Tickner can be lauded for bringing gender into IR theorizing, she is arguably open to criticism for not digging deep enough into the complexities surrounding sex and gender. Certainly, much subsequent feminist IR scholarship has endeavoured to interrogate the categories of sex and gender more thoroughly. There are also reasons to be sceptical about Tickner's vision of the possibility of a 'non-gendered' analysis of security because the gendered dimensions of the theory and practice of international relations remain insufficiently explored or understood.

Poststructuralism, postcolonialism, and gender

The influence of poststructuralism and postcolonialism upon feminist IR thought is extensive, but not easy to capture simply. It is helpful here to recall the differences between schools of critical IR thinking. As is discussed in Chapters 5 and 6, Marxism and Critical Theory are centred around the pursuit of the *emancipation* of humanity. In contrast, postcolonialism and poststructuralism, the subjects of Chapters 7 and 9, in various ways pose the question: *who* is the human that is to be emancipated? They endeavour to show how the meanings attributed to human subjectivity—what it is to be human—emerge within our social and political discourses. In turn, those discourses reflect relations of power and are produced and reproduced within very different political, social, and cultural settings and therefore always open to contestation.

A parallel debate can also be seen within IR feminist scholarship. Second wave feminism was centred around the drawing of a sharp distinction between biological sex and socially constructed gender. Some poststructuralists question this distinction:

> at the broadest level, poststructuralists argue that it is not simply that 'gender' is constructed socially: the category of sex is produced discursively as well. This means there is no 'essence' to being a man or woman and neither shares a particular perspective on the world *per se*. (Peoples and Vaughan-Williams, 2021: 59)

Poststructuralist feminist scholarship focuses on how different conceptions of sex and gender emerge and what effects they have. It endeavours to expose the exclusionary consequences of privileging a particular understanding of either sex or gender: what do such understandings exclude or fail to see?

Poststructuralist feminists endeavour to show how gender is a product of discourses which are themselves tied up in relations of power. Such discourses take many forms, from institutionalized discourses such as philosophy, politics, religion, law, and so on, through to more informal varieties of popular culture as found in film, fiction, television, and such like. Gender does not meaningfully exist, therefore, outside of discourse; discourse brings gender into being. Because of the relationship between power and discourse, however, certain representations of gender and sex and, indeed the relationship between the two, become dominant and can ultimately appear to represent the supposed truth or reality of gender categories.

The influence of poststructuralism and postcolonialism was evident in the third wave's emphasis on *intersectionality*. To greater or lesser degrees, there is a resistance to claiming a definitive essence, including any biological essence of 'man' or 'woman', because

> employing 'women' or 'man' as a category of analysis presupposes that all people of the same gender across classes or cultures are somehow socially constituted as a homogen[e]ous group identifiable prior to the process of analysis. (Steans, 2013: 31)

One of most influential contributions to this debate has been the work of Judith Butler, notably their 1990 book *Gender Trouble: Feminism and the Subversion of Identity*. This begins by asking does feminism need a stable subject: 'women'? Can the gender category of woman be fixed given that it 'intersects with racial, class, ethnic, sexual, and regional modalities of discursively constituted identities' (Butler, 2007: 4)? In other words, the meaning ascribed to the category 'woman' simply cannot be separated out 'from the political and cultural intersections in which it is invariably produced and maintained' (Butler, 2007: 4–5) While recognizing that there are bodily differences that we use as the basis for ascribing a biological sex (male, female, intersex, etc.) to individuals, Butler argues that what we understand by biological sex or gender is a product of the complexities of the knowledge-power relationships within which we are inescapably immersed (Butler, 2007: 2–3).

Butler's argument is controversial for some feminists because 'it challenged the seemingly stable attribute of a biological sex of all women' (Kinsella, 2020: 156). For Butler, both our sexual and gender identities are 'performatively constituted' (Butler, 2007: 34). To understand this, Steans suggests we think of performance in the ordinary sense of the term (like in the theatre for example):

> We perform our identities (characters) and roles (our part in the larger story/stories in which we take part and which play around us). However, it is important to remember . . . that a performance is not the playing out of identities *that are already scripted in the body*— rooted in biology or psychology, for example. The body takes on meaning in and through performances. (Steans, 2013: 32)

Postcolonialism brings a further dimension to the critique of gender essentialism. Postcolonial feminists emphasize the impact and effects of the history and legacy of colonialism on dominant representations or articulations of gender. During the colonial era, women and men in colonized territories were seen to be inferior to their Western counterparts. Arguably, even in the post-colonial era racialized colonial attitudes linger on in the depiction of non-Western women as sexually or culturally oppressed and thus needing Western feminists to come to their rescue. Writing in the mid-1980s, Mohanty had complained of a 'hegemonic white women's movement' effectively colonizing international debates about women's rights (Mohanty, 1984. See also Key thinker 10.1). The experiences of Third World women were being interpreted within a Western discourse of women's emancipation and liberation which did not take account of the intersectional complexities of many women's lives worldwide.

In combination, poststructuralism and postcolonialism question the possibility that there is any singular feminist viewpoint from which to critically analyse the gendered dimensions of international politics, just as there is no incontestable definition of the individual or collective subject positions of 'woman' or 'women'.

10.4 KEY THEMES IN CONTEMPORARY FEMINIST AND GENDER IR PERSPECTIVES

So far, we have seen that feminism has evolved into a broad constellation of perspectives that have moved far beyond a focus on discrimination against women because of their sex, even if the persistence of such discrimination worldwide means it remains a core concern. During feminism's second wave the concept of gender moved into the foreground and subsequently become understood in much more fluid and complex terms.

Although feminist contributions to the analysis of international politics emerged prior to feminism's third wave, this was when feminist IR theorizing grew substantially. Contemporary feminist/gender IR scholars now work within and across diverse theoretical and methodological approaches, but all 'share a focus on understanding gender as an analytical category not simply a descriptive one' (Kinsella, 2020: 158). Because of its diversity, contemporary gender-focused IR scholarship is difficult to summarize in a short space. Nonetheless, it provides distinctive critical contributions to some of the core debates and issue areas in the IR discipline. To illustrate this, in the next section we look at feminist and gender-focused approaches to an issue that has been central to the IR discipline since its inception: security.

Gender and Security

The sovereign state has been at the heart of the mainstream of the IR discipline since its foundation. This has been accompanied by the presumption that security is the concern primarily of sovereign states and that threats to national security, moreover, are primarily military in form. Notably absent from the bulk of mainstream IR theorizing of the sovereign state and security is consideration of gender.

Gendered states

In various ways, feminist IR scholars have endeavoured to expose the 'gendered dynamics' of the state in all its manifestations (Parashar, Tickner, and True, 2018: 1). According to Jacqui True, feminist IR scholars see

> that gender is central, not peripheral to the constitution of the state and to change 'in' and 'of' the interstate system. Western and non-Western patriarchal structures shape and constrain what states are, what they do, and how. (True, 2018: 33)

V. Spike Peterson was one of the first feminist IR scholars to invoke the idea of the 'gendered state'. In her 1992 book *Gendered States: Feminist (Re)Visions of International Theory*, Peterson argues that gendered assumptions flow through the actions of states and our interpretations of those actions (Peterson, 1992). For example, we can ask in what ways might a dominant understanding of national security, that reflects the assumptions of what Tickner calls a 'stereotypical hegemonic masculinity', work to enhance the *insecurity* of a state or some or all the people contained within it? Is the threat of war between states in fact the most significant cause of insecurity for most people in most states in today's contemporary world? Does the primacy given by states to war—how to avoid it or engage in it—hinder the pursuit of other, less militarized or confrontational ways of addressing insecurity? These are just some of the questions, upon which contemporary gender-focused IR endeavours to shed new critical light.

True notes that arguing that states are gendered 'does not imply that gender is the dominant social relation'. Echoing the concept of intersectionality, True argues that patriarchal domination intersects with other forms of domination based on race, ethnicity, class, sexuality, nationality, and age:

> That is why some women, men and states behave to maintain the system of gendered power even when it ensures their subordination. It may advance their status along another axis of power. (True, 2018: 37)

Feminists have long been divided over the role of the state as an actual or potential agent in addressing the gendered dimensions of international politics. Given that the sovereign state remains the dominant actor on the global stage, for some feminists it can and should play a vital role in challenging gender-based discrimination and the patriarchal dimensions of international politics.

There are, however, also long-standing currents of feminist thought that see the state as very much part of the problem, because it has historically been 'a key site of masculinist power that legitimizes . . . patriarchal structures through domestic and foreign policies' (Parashar, Tickner, and True, 2018: 2). For all the evident improvements in gender equality and growing acknowledgement of the gendered aspects of foreign and security policy within some states, there are many others who continue to fail to address gender-based forms of discrimination and violence. Indeed, True argues that

> The unravelling of patriarchal relations in the West has increased the challenges to non-Western patriarchies, as well as prompting a backlash against the West and the norms of gender equality. (True, 2018: 43)

Additionally, the rise of extremism—for example in such forms as Islamic State (ISIS or 'Daesh'), Boko Haram in Nigeria, or far right populist movements in Europe and the US—constitutes a global countercultural movement in favour of maintaining patriarchal social relations (True, 2018: 45. See also Brown, 2018). For True and others, developing transnational feminist networks is key to challenging non-Western forms of patriarchy and the creation of an international normative and cultural consensus around realizing gender justice in all forms.

Feminist Security Studies

Laura Sjoberg suggests that feminist theory and activism has always fundamentally been about security (Sjoberg, 2016: 44). Feminism has long been concerned with analysing and resisting the multiple forms of harm (such as direct violence or because of unequal access to resources) faced by women throughout history. Furthermore, many of the most noted early feminist IR works (such as those by Tickner, Enloe, and Peterson we have already looked at) 'blended security concerns with political economy, human rights, and environmental concerns' (Sjoberg, 2016: 145). Although they came to be recognized within the IR discipline more generally, they were rarely recognized as contributions to the study of security specifically (Sjoberg, 2016: 146).

The mainstream of IR scholarship's narrow understanding of security centred around military threats to national security came under challenge with the emergence of *Security Studies* in the 1980s. One of its founding figures Barry Buzan described security as an 'essentially contested concept'; its precise meaning was debatable (Buzan, 1983: 10). Buzan argued that security should be understood much more broadly to incorporate the insecurities arising not just out of militarized competition between states but also out of the economic, environmental, and societal dimensions of international politics. Security Studies remained, however, predominantly state-centric in focus. Subsequently, from the 1990s onwards several new strands of critical thinking about security emerged to create what is now commonly referred to as *Critical Security Studies* (CSS). The emergence of CSS was initially very much a West European development, but more recently has come to incorporate non-Western and gender-focused perspectives (Peoples and Vaughan-Williams, 2021: 1–14).

A central theme in CSS is challenging the assumption that the *referent object* of security (what needs to be secured) should be the state. Rather than try to fix the meaning of security, CSS tends to focus on the sites of *insecurity* which arguably matter to many people—environmental degradation, health, development, migration, and so on—but have been hitherto marginalized or viewed primarily through state-centric lenses. In moving beyond a narrow state-centric view of security and combining this with the insights of various critical IR perspectives,

> (a) range of otherwise excluded actors and sites—for example, women, people of colour, LGBTQ+ . . . communities, everyday life, and places in the global South have been rendered more visible as intrinsic to understanding the politics of (in)security. (Peoples and Vaughan-Williams, 2021: 3)

Additionally, CSS emerged in conjunction with critical theories of IR, such as Critical International Theory, poststructuralism, and postcolonialism which in various ways also questioned the excessive state-centrism of mainstream IR theory. These critical approaches 'were more conducive to answering the kinds of questions that IR feminists were asking' (Parashar, Tickner, and True, 2018: 4). Not surprisingly then, much of the feminist IR literature that emerged after the publication of Peterson's *Gendered States* in 1992 turned its attention away from the state and focused on such things as human rights, peace and conflict, development, nationalist movements (such as those that emerged following the breakup of Yugoslavia), and the gendered dimensions of economic globalization (Parashar, Tickner, and True, 2018: 3).

At the beginning of the twenty-first century, the 9/11 terrorist attacks on the US and the subsequent declaration by it of a War on Terror saw states and their security concerns return to centre stage across the IR discipline. Similarly, feminist IR scholars also increasingly turned their attention to international security and the term 'feminist security studies' (FSS) began to appear in the work of Laura Sjoberg (2009), Annick Wibben (2011), Laura Shepherd (2009), and others.

It is important to note, however, that FSS scholars differ in their understanding of the relationship between FSS and the orthodox study of security in the IR discipline. Sjoberg sees it as engaging in a conversation with mainstream Security Studies to correct the neglect of feminist work. Others, such as Wibben and Shepherd, depict FSS as a distinctly critical perspective that seeks to expose and question the gendered foundational assumptions of Security Studies and the IR discipline more generally (Sjoberg, 2016: 48). Thus, Shepherd sees FSS as challenging the 'war/peace' dichotomy as a foundational assumption of the IR discipline and offering a more comprehensive understanding of violence in world politics (Shepherd, 2009: 211). For Shepherd, Wibben, and other FSS scholars, gendered violence does not disappear with the supposed cessation of war or the depiction of a period as 'peacetime'. They focus instead on the 'everyday violence' that exists in the spaces between war and peace as a legitimate area of study in the analysis of global politics (Shepherd, 2009: 212).

Wibben locates the origins of FSS in feminist contributions to peace research, hitherto largely ignored in the IR discipline, that drew upon the experiences and perspectives of women to challenge orthodox understandings of security (Wibben, 2011: 5). Wibben revivifies this approach by examining how 'personal narratives' help people make sense of the world around them. Looking at the 9/11 terrorist attacks in New York, for example, Wibben contrasts the different personal stories of ordinary women about their experiences of that event with the official or 'master' narrative of the US Government. This is intended to show how personal narratives can present 'a different version of normality and, consequently, of security influenced by their location in terms of class, gender, and race'. How might listening to the varied personal narratives of women, Wibben asks, 'challenge the way we imagine and study security?' (Wibben, 2011: 3).

'Women, Peace and Security' and UNSCR 1325

The differences between feminist perspectives on security can be illustrated by the debates around UN Security Council Resolution 1325 (UNSCR 1325), adopted in October 2000 by the UN Security Council (UNSC).

UNSCR 1325 is the most prominent of a range of gender-mainstreaming initiatives within the UN's 'Women, Peace, and Security' (WPS) agenda that emerged out of the 1995 UN's Fourth World Conference on Women held in Beijing. Gender mainstreaming is a public policy concept that refers to the process of introducing a gender equality perspective at all levels and all stages of policies, programmes, and projects, and you can read more about its role in UNSCR 1325 in Key concept 10.2.

KEY CONCEPT 10.2 'GENDER MAINSTREAMING' AND UNITED NATIONS SECURITY COUNCIL RESOLUTION 1325

UNSCR 1325 is widely viewed as a cornerstone of the UN's 'Women, Peace and Security' (WPS) agenda. The intention of 1325 is broadly twofold:

- to urge all parties to armed conflict and the negotiations and processes in its aftermath to recognize the disproportionate impact on women and girls, as victims of sexual violence, as refugees, or internally displaced persons. 1325 is intended to strengthen existing legal instruments, such as the 1949 Geneva conventions, the 1951 Refugee Convention, and the 1979 Convention on the Elimination of Discrimination against Women. Additionally, it calls on all parties to take 'special measures' to protect women and girls from all forms of gender-based violence and emphasizes the responsibilities of states to prosecute the perpetrators of such violence

- to promote the equal participation of women in all aspects of peace and security policy. Thus, 1325 calls on states to 'ensure increased representation of women at all decision-making levels in national, regional and international institutions and mechanisms for the prevention, management, and resolution of conflict' (UNSC, 2000: 2).

Some of 1325's proposals are concerned specifically with peace processes. For example, all parties to the negotiation and implementation of peace agreements are urged

> to adopt a 'gender perspective' that recognizes 'the special needs of women and girls during repatriation and resettlement and for rehabilitation, reintegration, and post-conflict reconstruction' (UNSC, 2000: 3). It should also entail 'taking measures that support local women's peace initiatives' and involve women fully in all aspects of the implementation of peace agreements.
>
> Since the adoption of 1325, UN member states have been encouraged to develop National Action Plans (NAPs) for implementing 1325 and more than 100 states have now done so, However only 33 of those include a budget for implementation (see http://1325naps.peacewomen.org/).

For some feminist scholars, 1325 is the culmination of decades of effort by feminists seeking to bring international attention to the impact of armed conflict on women and girls and the roles they can and should play in building peace after conflict (Steans, 2013: 123). The central role played by NGOs in the drafting of the resolution is seen as a particularly commendable feature. Thus, despite its deficiencies, some regard 1325 as a significant positive advance in the struggle for international gender equality (see for example, Cohn, Kinsella, and Gibbings, 2004; Chinkin and Charlesworth, 2006).

Other gender-focused IR scholars criticize both the conception and implementation of 1325. While recognizing the significance of its adoption and the intentions behind it, Shepherd questions whether it can achieve the 'radical reforms' that its proponents seek (Shepherd, 2008: 7). Shephard argues that 1325 reinforces rather than dismantles an orthodox gender binary distinction in which women are seen 'as a homogeneous group whose interests are essentially peaceful and socially beneficial'. 'There is more to gender', Shepherd argues, 'than equal participation of "men" and "women" in formal and informal political forums', such as those engaged in the formulation and implementation of 1325 (Shepherd, 2008: 164).

Shepherd has subsequently detected small 'discursive shifts' in the UN Security Council's language recognizing that women are not just victims but also actors or agents, but there remains insufficient recognition of the structural causes (not least, poverty) which inhibit the capacity of women in post-conflict circumstances to act as agents of change (Shepherd, 2011: 508–509). In essence, Shepherd and others are questioning the benefits of gender mainstreaming as the primary focus of UN policy on addressing gender and armed conflict.

Additionally, there have been significant problems with 1325's implementation. A 2015 UN progress report on 1325 identified several positive impacts, such as an increase in the reference to women in peace agreements from 11 per cent between 1990 and 2000 to 27 per cent after adoption. The number of senior women leaders within the UN was also rising and the level of bilateral aid on gender equality to fragile states had quadrupled, albeit from a very low level at the start.

The report also notes, however, that there had been very few prosecutions for sexual violence and the participation of women in formal peace processes was only 'inching up'. In 31 major peace processes between 1992 and 2011 only 9 per cent of negotiators were women and women comprised only 3 per cent of the military in UN missions.

The report identified 55 states who had developed National Action Plans for implementing 1325 (that number is now over 100) but most of those referred only to process, with no mechanisms for accountability or budgets for implementation (UN Women, 2015: 14).

Shepherd depicts 1325 as reflecting a conception of gender equality framed by a liberal construction of 'the way in which it is legitimate to live' (Shepherd, 2008: 170). This line of critique resonates with that of postcolonialist feminist scholars who argue that liberal calls for the mainstreaming of gender equality or the protection of women's rights can serve to legitimize forms of neocolonial domination (Steans, 2013: 124). Although some women in contexts marked by ongoing conflict, such as Iraq and Palestine, may see some value in 1325 as a tool of empowerment, for many the rigours of everyday life and the inequalities of power (such as that between Israel and Palestine) combine with the impact of local and international patriarchal attitudes to marginalize what they can achieve (Farr, 2011). In difficult contexts, far removed from those found in most liberal developed states, women may not in fact prioritize what the liberal West understands as 'gender issues' in their resistance to the wider political and security environment (Steans, 2013: 125).

Feminist foreign policy

True notes that there have been evident positive changes in gender relations over the last few decades, such as the emergence of national and global feminist movements and greater presence of women in positions of political leadership. The pressures on states to maintain their competitive advantage has led to some powerful states in the Global North actively promoting the cause of gender equality, not least because it is in their national interests to do so. They recognize that drawing upon the talents and potential of their whole population can enhance their economic competitiveness and strengthen their security and defence systems. Additionally, by appearing to support gender equality, powerful states can shore up 'their legitimacy at the top of the international hierarchy' (True, 2018: 38). In other words, overtly supporting gender equality in foreign policy could be seen as a form of Soft Power.

Jennifer Thomson argues that 'gender equality discourse is now commonplace in the work of national, international, and transnational organisations' (Thomson, 2020: 426). For some feminist scholars, the UN's WPS agenda and UNSCR 1325 provides a framework for the idea of a distinctive and overtly feminist foreign policy.

In 2014, Sweden's foreign minister Margot Wahlström announced the introduction of a new 'Feminist foreign policy' (FFP), declaring that Sweden saw 'gender equality (as) an objective in itself'. Sweden's FFP was presented as an extension of its long-standing domestic commitments to gender equality with the then Centre-Left government claiming that gender equality was central to the realization of Sweden's other overall foreign policy objectives such as peace, security, and sustainable development (Ministry for Foreign Affairs, 2015 and 2020). The overall vision—centred around three 'R's—Resources, Representation, and Rights—reflected a broadly liberal feminist international outlook, which views 'global society as predicated on an imbalance between male and female power', a problem that Sweden's feminist foreign policy was intended to address (Thomson, 2020: 429; Bergman-Rosamund,

2020a). Immediately after the 2022 general election, however, the new conservative Swedish governing Centre-Right coalition ditched the FFP label while claiming that gender equality remained a 'fundamental value' for the government.

Sweden's efforts to adopt FFP have subsequently been mirrored elsewhere. In 2017 Canada introduced 'feminist international assistance policy' and since 2019 France, Luxembourg, and Spain have pledged to adopt FFP. In their 2021–2025 Coalition Agreement, the parties making up the German Federal Government also agreed to pursue a feminist foreign policy (Zilla, 2022). Sweden's initiative was also followed by a growing academic literature exploring what FFP could or should look like (see for example, Aggestam and Bergman-Rosamond, 2019; Aggestam, Bergman-Rosamond, and Kronsell, 2019; Thomson, 2020; Zilla, 2022). In 2020 Mexico also claims to have adopted an FFP, the first country in the Global South to do so. However, in contrast to the evident coherence between Sweden's longstanding domestic and international policies, critics argue that Mexico's commitment is undermined by the incongruence between its new foreign policy orientation and the concrete state of gender relations within Mexico itself (Deslandes, 2020). In June 2021 Libya's first female foreign minister, Najla El-Mangoush, announced Libya's intention to adopt an FFP. However, given the ongoing political instability in Libya—at the time of writing there are two rival 'governments' in Libya—the likelihood of the commitment to FFP translating into substantive foreign policy must currently be seen as rather slim.

Innovative though it clearly was, Sweden's FFP model was criticized for broadly accepting much of the international institutional status quo. Some feminist IR scholars detected a neoliberal undertone to Sweden's advocacy of 'empowerment through economic liberalism . . . as a route towards gender equality and women's emancipation' (Achilleos-Sarll, 2018: 41; Bergman-Rosamund, 2020a: 229). Others have noted tensions between Sweden's FFP and its track record as a leading arms exporter, including to countries with poor records on women's rights (Thomson, 2020: 434). Furthermore, in describing its foreign policy as feminist rather than 'gender-sensitive' and in focusing on improving the lives of 'women and girls' Sweden's FFP could be seen as having been insufficiently sensitive to the intersectional complexities of gender identity and gendered discrimination and violence (Achilleos-Sarll, 2018; Bergman Rosamund, 2020: 232). Columba Achilleos-Sarll argues that the challenge for advocates of FFP is to move beyond the simplistic equation of gender with 'women' and integrate insights from postcolonial critiques of the Western liberal assumptions underpinning the foreign policies of Western states (Achilleos-Sarll, 2018).

10.5 GENDER AND THE 'QUEERING' OF THE IR DISCIPLINE

If a general direction can be detected in recent feminist and gender-focused IR thinking, it is greater recognition of the complexity of gender as an analytical category. The centrality of commonly used binaries such as masculine/feminine, man/woman, and male/female has come under increasing critical scrutiny. This has led on to a questioning of the subject position not only of 'woman' but also, if more belatedly, of 'man'. If gender is a social and culturally constructed form of identity that intersects with other forms of identity then it follows that this applies to both masculinity and femininity, as well as conceptions of identity that do not fall tidily on either side of a simple binary gender classification.

Men and masculinities

Scholars such as Adam Jones have criticized some of the earlier feminist IR literature for overly focusing on women and thus failing to acknowledge that men are also victims of the violence of other men (Jones, 1996). Jones uses the term *gendercide*, first coined by Mary Anne Warren to describe 'the deliberate extermination of persons of a particular sex (or gender)' (Warren, 1985: 22). Gendercide targeted against men had attracted comparatively little attention in either scholarship or public policy compared to the gender-selective killing of women. Yet, alongside the violence perpetrated against women, gender-selective mass killings of males have long been a feature of armed conflict (Jones, 2000: 189–190). Recent examples include the wars in Bosnia and Kosovo in the 1990s, which were marked by the deliberate targeting of men, especially those of 'battle age', as a strategy of Serbian forces (Jones, 2000: 185). Perhaps the most infamous instance was the slaughter of more than 8,000 Bosniak (Bosnian Muslim) men and boys by Bosnian Serb forces in Srebrenica, that took place during a campaign of ethnic cleansing in which more than 20,000 civilians were forced to leave the surrounding area.

Feminist IR scholarship has robustly challenged the presumption that masculinity constitutes the superior component of the masculine/feminine binary. Terrell Carver (2014: 114) argues, however, that 'the study of men and masculinities—for arguably very good reasons—often appears as something of an add-on to women-centred studies rather than as central focus for intellectual inquiry or political action'. Carver cites Raewyn Connell's depiction of an 'hegemonic masculinity' (which implies that there are multiple forms of masculinity), to make the point that masculinity

> not only works to confer power on men over women, but also to empower masculinised individuals and groups over feminised ones, and to create power hierarchies of men over men as well as some masculinities over others. (Carver, 2014: 115)

While acknowledging the gains made by women in some key areas of social and political life in some parts of the world, Connell cites a wealth of evidence to suggest that '(p)atriarchy seems decidedly resilient' (Connell, 2008: xi). She goes on to observe, however, that men do not share equally in the multiple benefits of male dominance. Whereas some gain great benefits, others suffer through such things as unemployment, violence, prejudice, exclusion, or injury. In the plethora of civil wars and interventions in the post-Cold War era, 'men from poor, working class, or peasant backgrounds fire most of the guns and stop most of the bullets' (Connell, 2008: xii).

We have already noted that the military as an institution has been long been seen as a key site for an ideal type of masculinity—action-oriented, privileging physical strength and toughness, and so on—which all men should aspire to emulate and against which other conceptions of masculinity are made to appear inferior (Bourke, 1996; Hooper, 2001). Jill Steans depicts the military as a

> key institution in which hegemonic masculinity is exalted to attest to the superiority of 'real' men over 'effeminate' or weak men and to assert the superiority of men/masculinity over women/femininity in general. (Steans, 2013: 40)

Certainly, the reality of military service is messier than any idealized depiction of it. It is widely recognized that many soldiers are only in the military because they have been conscripted, or it was one of the few employment opportunities available to them. The idealization of masculinity also cannot hide the fact that human bodies are vulnerable, even those of ideal-type male soldiers. If they are not killed on the battlefield, soldiers can be maimed for life, or suffer from post-traumatic stress disorders. Christine Masters has suggested that the military forces of powerful countries, such as the US military, are endeavouring to compensate for the bodily weakness of soldiers through a process of integrating them into a technocratic war fighting machine. Using advanced guided weapons systems and Artificial Intelligence, war can be fought at a distance by what Masters calls 'Cyborg soldiers'. 'Techno-militarised' masculinity, Masters argues, 'has come to symbolise the *model* American soldier'. Technology is increasingly deployed to enact idealized notions of masculinity, while 'human soldiers . . . have been feminised and reconstituted within the realms of those needing protection' (Masters, 2008: 96).

LGBT perspectives, Queer Theory, and IR

Debates about gender identity and sexuality have long been a feature of feminist debate. Lesbian feminists figured prominently in feminism's second wave, challenging dominant (heterosexual) notions of womanhood both inside and outside of the women's movement. Since then, the politics of sexual orientation and gender identity have become increasingly prominent in both public and academic debates. In the 1990s, Queer Theory emerged at the margins of the social sciences, arts, and humanities and it is only in recent years that it has become visible within the IR discipline.

Taking its name from the once common and pejorative term for homosexuality (that implied it was abnormal and unnatural), Queer Theory builds upon feminism's emphasis on the social construction of gender and sexuality, but goes much further in questioning the stability of gender identities. Although its origins lie in earlier theoretical work on Lesbian and Gay challenges to 'heteronormativity' (the assumption that heterosexuality is or should be the normal or default mode of sexual orientation), it also departs from it in questioning whether sexual identities such as 'lesbian' or 'gay' can themselves overly restrictive (Steans, 2013: 42; see also Browne and Nash, 2010: 4–7).

Melanie Richter-Montpetit argues that, reflecting developments across a range of academic disciplines, IR scholarship on sexuality and queerness largely falls within two approaches, LGBT and Queer:

> LGBT perspectives tend to focus on LGBT people and/or study norms and struggles around LGBT human rights, often reflecting a liberal stance of advocating for LGBT inclusion in citizenship rights. By contrast Queer Theory is animated by a commitment to the radical contingency of the term queer. (Richter-Montpetit, 2018: 223)

By 'radical contingency', Richter-Montpetit is referring to Queer Theory's refusal to precisely define what is or should be understood as LGBT. LGBT perspectives, on the other hand, 'have tended to question the analytical and political significance of Queer Theory' (Richter-Montpetit, 2018: 223). Many NGOs that campaign globally for LGBT rights, such as the New York based *Outright Action International* do now use more inclusive acronyms, such as LGBTIQ+, but their primary concern is essentially a liberal focus on securing 'empowerment and equality for all people, all genders' (Outright Action International, 2020: 4). In contrast, Queer Theory goes beyond the pursuit of gender equality.

We can illustrate the relevance of LGBT perspectives to the long-standing focus of the IR discipline on relations between sovereign states, by looking at the debates around gender and sexuality at the 1995 Beijing UN Women's Conference. The drafting of the Beijing Platform for Action (BPA) saw concerted action by a coalition of conservative Islamic states, the Vatican, and the US Christian Right challenging those sections of the draft BPA that referred to sexuality and reproductive health, which they claimed reflected a 'homosexual agenda'. They succeeded in removing any reference to 'sexual rights' or 'sexual orientation' from the final document (Steans, 2013: 44). Similar challenges emerged at subsequent five-year reviews of the BPA. Although signed by 189 UN member states and widely recognized as a significant achievement in advancing the rights of women and girls globally, the BPA still contains almost no direct reference to the rights of LGBT communities (OutRight Action International, 2020).

In global terms the debates around a fully inclusive understanding of gender equality have produced countervailing trends. Several states have introduced national legislative protection for a widening range of gender identities and endeavoured to incorporate different forms of sexual orientation and gender identity into their conceptions of human rights. The majority of states in their post-BPA national reviews of their gender equality commitments have, however, either abstained from debate or excluded involvement by LGBT representatives (OutRight Action International, 2020). Public and governmental hostility towards LGBT communities is, moreover, evident across the globe and is not confined to the Global South. Indeed, South Africa has been a leading force in the promotion of gay rights and most Latin American states have signed the 2011 UN Human Rights Council resolution on LGBT rights. Yet, Russia and some countries in Eastern Europe, such as Hungary and Poland are marked by widespread hostility towards LGBT communities. By December 2020 only 28 countries had legalized same-sex marriage, whereas in 69 states consensual same-sex sexual acts remain criminalized and in 11 states they risk the death penalty (ILGA World, 2020: 325–330).

Queer theory reflects the influences of both poststructuralism and postcolonialism in challenging dominant binary classifications such as male/female, West/non-West, rich/poor and a heterosexual/homosexual. Much of queer theory's focus has been on sexual identities and gender expressions that transgress dominant binaries, such as transgender and intersex people:

> The notion of queer asserts the multiplicity and fluidity of sexual subjects . . . and seeks to challenge the processes which normalise and/or homogenise certain sexual and gender practices, relationships, and subjectivities. (Gorman-Murray et al., cited in Browne and Nash, 2010: 5)

It is important to note here that there is no fixed or settled understanding of Queer Theory. Much of the work under the label of Queer Theory has subsequently moved beyond a focus on sexuality and gender to embrace all forms of acting and thinking that challenge or transgress dominant norms and analytical categories. Thus, Kath Browne and Catherine Nash argue that '(q)ueer research can be any form of research positioned within conceptual frameworks that highlight the instability of taken-for-granted meanings and resultant power relations' (Browne and Nash, 2010: 4; see also Weber, 2016: chapter 2).

The queer IR theorist Cynthia Weber argues that there has been a considerable amount of evidently globally focused queer-themed scholarly work dating back for two decades (Weber, 2015). This has not, however, been published in the most prominent IR journals or book series even though it addresses a range of issues that have been central to the IR discipline, such as war, security, sovereignty, intervention, empire, colonialism, and so on (Weber, 2015; Richter-Montpetit and Weber, 2017). This is because the IR disciplinary mainstream continues to only view work that presents itself as a singular and unified theoretical perspective which is, moreover, centrally focused on interstate relations as properly IR theory (Weber, 2015: 40–45).

Queer IR offers a distinctive take on the debate around the struggle for gender and sexual equality worldwide. Progress in advancing LGBT rights is most marked in the West (Theil, 2017: 100). This has arguably produced a 'homonormative' counterpoint to heteronormativity, i.e., a singular, stable (and therefore more widely acceptable) representation of the homosexual subject, which, moreover, has a distinctly Western, liberal character (see also Richter-Monpetit, 2018: 231). Weber explores how a distinction between 'the normal homosexual' and 'the perverse homosexual' has come to operate in international politics. The struggle for LGBT rights in Western developed states, notably the US, has led to LGBT communities being incorporated into depictions of the progressive civilized state, against which other states can be judged and found wanting. To illustrate this, Weber cites a 2011 'Human Rights Day' speech by the then Secretary of State, Hilary Clinton, in which Clinton declares that the US 'defends the human rights of LGBT people as part of our comprehensive human rights policy and as a priority of our foreign policy' (Clinton cited in Weber, 2016: 134). Weber goes on to argue that:

> (t)his is how Clinton divides the world into good gay-friendly states and bad homophobic states. In these bad states, the 'LGBT' needs to be rescued, either by correcting or opposing bad homophobic states and their homophobic policies. (Weber, 2016: 135)

Weber argues that the 'normal' LGBT person can thus be co-opted into the statecraft of dominant and powerful states such as the US, something that Jasbir Puar refers to as 'homonationalism' (Puar, 2007). Even though many LGBT people continue to experience discrimination and exclusion within Western states, they can serve nonetheless to bolster the representation of the Western developed state as the benchmark against which non-Western states can be judged and, if viewed as threatening to Western interests, acted against. This further enhances the already widespread perception in the West of some non-Western states as supposedly problematically different to the Western state (Weber, 2016. See also Puar, 2007).

From a Queer IR perspective then, Western-led global LGBT activism can acquire neocolonial, culturally intrusive, and patronizing overtones. As in other instances of neocolonial international politics (such as military interventions), it risks producing unanticipated and adverse outcomes. It can reinforce a crude binary division of the world into progressive versus intolerant states, which in turn can reinforce neocolonial and highly exclusionary depictions of some states as supposedly backward, underdeveloped, or uncivilized (Richter-Montpetit and Weber, 2017; Puar, 2017). External pressure from states and majority White-led Western NGOs promoting the universalization of Western conceptions of LGBT rights can serve to further marginalize minoritized communities in conservative states, not only in the Global South but in Europe as well (Theil, 2017: 101).

It is important to emphasize that Queer IR Theory does not oppose transnational LGBT advocacy and activism. Rather, it tries to illuminate the complexities and tensions surrounding global sexual and gender politics and the theoretical and practical consequences of trying to stabilize or fix gender identities.

THINK CRITICALLY 10.2 IS WESTERN-LED GLOBAL LGBT ACTIVISM NEOCOLONIALIST?

There is an ongoing debate between those who seek to advance a Western understanding of LGBT rights worldwide and critics of this approach, such as some Queer IR theorists, who identify an underlying neocolonialism to demands for the imposition of Western standards of LGBT rights upon non-Western countries.

For example, Rahul Rao (2015) refers to 'Echoes of Empire in LGBT activism' but goes on to note that such activism increasingly embraces a wide range of political positions, some of which do recognize the complexities around the promotion of Western understandings of LGBT rights in non-Western countries.

1) Do you think Western LGBT activists are right to demand that non-Western states should adopt Western standards of recognition and respect for non-heteronormative sexual orientations and gender identities? (Hint: think about terms like homonationalism.)

2) Given what you know of its influence on the development of feminist/gender thinking, how might the concept of *intersectionality* help navigate a path through this issue?

USEFUL REFERENCES

Rao, R. (2015), 'Echoes of Imperialism in LGBT Activism' in K. Nicolaïdis, B. Sèbe, and G. Maas (eds), *Echoes of Empire: Memory, Identity and Colonial Legacies* (London: IB Taurus).

Richter-Montpetit, M. (2018), 'Everything You always Wanted to Know about Sex in IR but were Afraid to Ask: The "Queer" Turn in International Relations'. *Millennium: Journal of International Studies*, 46(2): 220–240.

Theil, M. (2018), 'Introducing Queer Theory in International Relations'.

10.6 CONCLUSION

Over the last three decades or so the analysis of gender has moved closer to the IR discipline's centre and now figures across much of its subject matter. There is a still expanding body of work examining the whole scope of gendered dimensions of international and global politics. Contemporary feminist and gender-focused IR theoretical scholarship is marked, moreover, by a considerable diversity of perspectives. They range from 'add women and stir' liberal feminist concerns with the insufficient presence of women in both the theory and practice of international and global politics, through to the complexities of Queer IR Theory and the challenges it poses to both preceding varieties of gender-focused scholarship and the IR discipline overall.

For all the evident advances made in the understanding of how international politics is gendered, it remains the case that discrimination because of gender or sexual orientation is a prominent feature of contemporary national and global politics. Violence against women, carried out mostly by men, remains prevalent worldwide (see IR Theory Today at the end of this chapter). Many of the substantial gains made by women in terms of political representation, participation, and rights, remain unevenly spread in both the Global North and the Global South. As the US Supreme Court's striking down in 2022 of the historic 1973 *Roe v. Wade* decision shows, they continue to be subjected to challenge even in one of the heartlands of contemporary feminist/gender thinking and activism.

The picture is even more mixed when it comes to the rights of people of diverse sexual orientation or gender identification. Although LGTBTQI+ peoples have made gains in terms of recognition and rights in some parts of the world, in most of it they continue to face exclusion, discrimination, and a heightened risk of violence.

As feminisms and other varieties of gender-focused IR scholarship comprehensively show, gender has *always* mattered in international politics and it undoubtedly continues to do so.

10 FEMINISMS, GENDER, AND INTERNATIONAL RELATIONS

SUMMARIZING FEMINISMS, GENDER, AND INTERNATIONAL POLITICS

- Feminist perspectives and acknowledgement of the importance of *gender* in the study of international politics emerged in the IR discipline in the late 1980s/early 1990s

- The history of feminist theory and practice is widely depicted as falling into distinct waves, which all continue to influence feminist thinking today

- The first wave encompasses the historic struggle for (predominantly white) women's suffrage—the right to vote—in the late nineteenth and early twentieth centuries. It is also seen as the source of liberal feminism, which emphasizes equality between the sexes

- From the 1960s onwards a second wave emerged alongside the rapid growth of feminist activism, especially in the Global North. Key theoretical developments include the depiction of gender as socially constructed and the concept of *Patriarchy*

- The Third Wave was a reaction to the limitations of the second wave, notably an insufficient appreciation of the differences between women's experiences when viewed worldwide. Key theoretical developments include the concept of *intersectionality*

- Some see a Fourth Wave under way, reflecting the impact of neoliberalism and new communication technologies and marked by a return to the activism of the second wave

- Feminist IR emerged principally during the third wave although influential earlier antecedents can be found in the fields of Peace Research and Development Studies

- Feminist IR comprises a wide range of theoretical perspectives but is inherently critical of mainstream IR because of the absence of gender

- Much of the contemporary gender-focused IR scholarship is located within the sphere of critical approaches to IR. It thus intersects extensively with Critical Theory, poststructuralism, postcolonialism, and, most recently, Queer Theory

- Feminist IR now addresses all aspects of the IR field, including the state, foreign policy, security, and the global economy.

- Much of it is marked by methodological innovation such as the use of the personal everyday experiences and stories of women worldwide to develop 'bottom up' accounts of international politics

- Gender equality now figures prominently in the rhetoric and policy of several states and most major international institutions, but some feminist IR scholars identify significant limitations in the understanding of gender employed. Key sites of debate include UN Security Resolution 1325 and the Beijing Platform for Action

- A notable development in the evolution of feminist and gender-focused IR theory is greater recognition of the complexities of the international politics of people's diverse gender and sexual orientations

- Gender-focused IR today includes analysis of men and masculinities and, most recently, Queer IR Theory, which emphasizes the fluidity of identities and critically explores the international politics surrounding dominant Western conceptions of them.

QUESTIONS

1. The history of feminist theory is commonly depicted as comprised of 3, possibly 4 distinctive waves. What are the key ideas that emerged out of each of these waves?
2. When and around what key themes did feminist and gender-focused IR emerge?
3. What, in your view, are the key strengths and weaknesses of UN Security Council Resolution 1325?
4. Do you think it is possible for a sovereign state to develop an authentically 'feminist foreign policy'? What, in your view, would have to be its key components?
5. What have been the key impacts of the concept of intersectionality on the development of feminist and gender-focused IR?
6. Given the growing recognition of the range and fluidity of sexual orientations and gender identities and the complex global politics surrounding them, do you think it remains meaningful or necessary to refer to *feminist* perspectives on international politics If so, why? If not, why not?

IR THEORY TODAY THE SARAH EVERARD MURDER AND GLOBAL VIOLENCE AGAINST WOMEN

In March 2021, a, 33-year-old white cis woman, Sarah Everard, who worked as a marketing executive, disappeared while walking home in the evening from a friend's house in south London. A serving officer in the Metropolitan Police stopped and falsely arrested her for supposedly breaching Covid regulations. He was subsequently convicted and jailed for life for kidnapping and murder. Ms Everard's disappearance and murder generated a substantial public and media outcry both in the UK and in countries such as the US, Canada, Australia, and India.

Key themes in the debate following the death of Ms Everard included the right of women to be able to walk the streets alone without fear, why the burden of safety fell on women's shoulders rather than on the men who are the source of most violence against them, and the continuing prevalence of violence against women in the UK despite the supposed improvements in gender equality and the impact of such campaigns as #metoo. The UK *Femicide Census* claims that between 2009–2018, on average, a woman was killed by a man in the UK every 3 days and 62 per cent were killed by a current or former partner.

Additionally, some commentators noted that the public and media reaction to Ms Everard's murder was considerably greater than that in response to murders of women of colour, such as Nicole Smallman and Bibaa Henry, stabbed to death in a park in north London in June 2020 or Sabina Nessa murdered while walking home in September 2021 (see for example: Flint, 2021; Hassan, 2021; Manne, 2021). Although their murderers were eventually convicted and jailed for life, questions were raised about the media's handling of their cases.

10 FEMINISMS, GENDER, AND INTERNATIONAL RELATIONS   **421**

There is widespread evidence of discrepancies between the investigation and media coverage of violence against women of colour and white women in many Western countries. Another recent example is the case of Gabby Petito, a young white woman who disappeared in Wyoming in August 2021 while on a cross-country trip with her white male partner and subsequently found to have been murdered. The Petito case attracted such extensive media attention in the US that some commentators queried whether it was not another example of 'missing white woman syndrome', a term coined by the distinguished Black US journalist Gwen Ifill in 2004.

The media coverage of the Petito case starkly contrasted with coverage of the disappearance and murder of women of colour and Native American women (Golden, 2021; Robertson, 2021). 34 Indigenous women were victims of homicide between 2000 and 2020 in Wyoming, yet only 18 per cent of these cases received any newspaper media coverage and this coverage was 'more likely to contain violent language, portray the victim in a negative light, and provide less information as compared to articles about white homicide victims' (Wyoming Survey & Analysis Center, 2021: 2).

A 2018 WHO report based on data from 161 countries between 2000–2018 found that almost 30 per cent of women worldwide have been subjected to physical and/or sexual violence by an intimate partner, non-partner sexual violence, or both.

USEFUL RESOURCES YOU CAN FIND ONLINE

Femicide Census (2018), *UK Femicides 2009–2018*.

Flint, Hannah (2021), 'Why Does the Media Only React When Victims Are Young, Pretty and White?' *Gentleman's Quarterly*, 23 May.

Golden, Hallie (2021), 'Families of missing and murdered Native women ask: where's the attention for ours?', *The Guardian*, Friday 24 September.

Hassan, Jennifer (2021), 'Sabina Nessa was killed walking in London. Women are asking: where is the outrage when the victim isn't White?', *The Washington Post*, 23 September.

Manne, Kate (2021), 'What Sarah Everard's Murder Illuminates—And Might Obscure', *The Atlantic*, 17 March 2021.

Robertson, Katie (2021), 'News media can't shake "missing White woman syndrome" critics say', *The New York Times*, 22 September.

World Health Organisation (2021), *Violence Against Women Prevalence Estimates 2018*.

Wyoming Survey & Analysis Center (2021), *Missing and Murdered Indigenous People: Statewide Report Wyoming* (Laramie, WY: University of Wyoming).

QUESTIONS

Drawing upon this chapter and your own research:

1. Why do you think the disappearance and murder of Sarah Everard in the UK generated such a reaction in the UK *and* worldwide?

2. How would you explain the extensive coverage of the Petito case in the US compared to the coverage of the murders of women of colour and Native American women?

3. In what ways do you think feminist/gender perspectives can help you analyse the continuing prevalence of violence against women worldwide? To answer this question, consider the following key ideas outlined in this chapter:

- patriarchy
- hegemonic masculinity
- intersectionality

4. Do you think violence against LGBQTIA+ people is treated similarly to violence against people who identify as heterosexual in media coverage and public debate in your country? If not, what do you think are key reasons for the difference?

TWISTING THE LENS

1. Look at Chapter 9 on Postcolonialism. In what ways, if any, might a postcolonial perspective provide insight into the prevalence of violence against women, both in countries like the UK, or worldwide?

2. Look at at Chapter 5 on Marxism. To what extent, if any, do you think factors such as class or socio-economic status figured in the public and media reaction to instances of violence against women?

FURTHER READING

ADDITIONAL INTRODUCTORY READING

Kinsella, H. M. (2020), 'Feminism', in John Baylis, Steve Smith, and Patricia Owens (eds), *The Globalization of World Politics: An Introduction to International Relations*, 8th edition (Oxford: Oxford University Press).
A very accessible introduction to feminist and gender-focused perspectives on international politics.

Peoples, C. and Vaughan-Williams, N. (2021), 'Feminist and Gender Approaches' in Columba Peoples and Nick Vaughan-Williams (eds), *Critical Security Studies: An Introduction*, 3rd edition (London: Routledge).
A highly readable yet critical survey of gender-focused critiques of mainstream perspectives on security.

Shepherd, L. J. (ed.) (2015), *Gender Matters in Global Politics: A Feminist Introduction to International Relations*, 2nd edition (London: Routledge).
A more advanced and very wide-ranging introduction to the key debates, theories, and methodological issues, written by many of the most prominent scholars in the field.

Steans, J. (2013), *Gender and International Relations*, 3rd edition (Cambridge: Polity Press).
A very comprehensive yet accessible survey of theoretical perspectives and empirical developments in the field of Gender and IR.

Theil, M. (2018), 'Queer Theory', in Stephen McGlinchey, Rosie Walters, and Christian Scheinpflug (eds), *International Relations Theory* (E-International Relations Publishing).
A very accessible introduction to Queer IR theory.

Tickner, J. A. and Sjoberg, L. (2020), 'Feminism' in T. Dunne, M. Kurki, and S. Smith (eds), *International Relations Theories: Discipline and Diversity*, 5th edition (Oxford: Oxford University Press).

A more advanced and very succinct introduction to feminist perspectives on IR by two leading feminist IR scholars.

MORE IN-DEPTH READING

Achilleos-Sarl, C. (2018), 'Reconceptualising Foreign Policy as Gendered, Sexualised and Racialised: Towards a Postcolonial Feminist Foreign Policy (Analysis)', *Journal of International Women's Studies*, 19(1), 34–49.

A critical assessment of the idea of a feminist foreign policy from a postcolonialist feminist perspective.

Aggestam, K., Bergman-Rosamond, A., and Kronsell, A. (2019), 'Theorizing Feminist Foreign Policy', *International Relations*, 33: 23–39.

An exploration of the concept of a feminist foreign policy by three leading Swedish feminist scholars.

Bedford, K. and Rai, S.M. (2013), 'Feminists Theorise International Political Economy', *Signs*, 36(1): 1–18.

Survey of feminist thinking on the gendered dimensions of the global political economy.

Cohn, C., Kinsella, H., and Gibbings, S. (2004), 'Women, Peace and Security Resolution 1325', *International Feminist Journal of Politics*, 6(1): 130–140.

A dialogue between feminist scholars and representatives of feminist NGOs and the UN around the pros and cons of UNSC Resolution 1325.

Owens, P. and Rietzler, K., (eds) (2021), *Women's International Thought: A New History* (Cambridge: Cambridge University Press).

A collection of essays by historians and IR scholars on the contributions to international thought of 18 leading women thinkers in the first half of the twentieth century whose work has hitherto been effectively erased from the IR discipline's history.

Parashar, S., Tickner, J. A., and True, Jacqui (eds) (2018), *Revisiting Gendered States: Feminist Imaginings of the State in International Relations* (Oxford: Oxford University Press).

Inspired by V. Spike Peterson's legendary 1992 book, Gendered States: Feminist (Re) visions of International Theory, this volume brings together a series of gender-focused analyses of the modern state. It includes a forward by V. Spike Peterson.

Parpart, J. L. and Zalewksi, M. (eds) (2008), *Rethinking the Man Question: Sex, Gender and Violence in International Relations* (London: Zed Books).

The authors of the path-breaking 1998 text, The 'Man' Question . . . in International Relations, return a decade later to address the same question with a new collection of critical essays by some of the most noted contributors to Feminist and gender approaches to IR.

Puar, J. K. (2017), *Terrorist Assemblages: Homonationalism in Queer Times* (Durham, NC: Duke University Press),

An expanded 10th anniversary edition, of a pathbreaking book that explores how the US's supposedly liberal attitude to homosexuality has been co-opted to underpin US global dominance and its self-image as an exceptional state.

Richter-Montpetit, M. (2018), 'Everything You Always Wanted to Know about Sex (in IR) But Were Afraid to Ask: The "Queer Turn" in International Relations', *Millennium: Journal of International Studies*, 46(2): 220–240.

A very useful introduction of Queer IR Theory Centred around a review of 4 key texts.

Shepherd, L. J., (ed.) (2019), *Handbook on Gender and Violence* (Cheltenham: Edward Elgar).

A compendium of succinct articles covering a wide range of conceptual issues, representations, and contexts around the general theme of gender and violence.

Sjoberg, L. (2016), 'What, and Where, is Feminist Security Studies' *Journal of Regional Security*, 11(2): 143–161.
Examines the history of feminist work in security, key debates within it, and where it might be heading.

Weber, C. (2016), *Queer International Relations: Sovereignty, Sexuality and the Will to Knowledge* (Oxford: Oxford University Press).
A comprehensive and engaging investigation of the actual and potential relationship between queer studies and IR centred around the question of sovereignty.

USEFUL RESOURCES YOU CAN FIND ONLINE

Laura Shepherd (2013). 'Why Gender matters in global politics'.
A prominent feminist IR scholar delivers a lively introductory presentation on gender and international politics at the University of New South Wales, Australia. Available online

The Centre for Feminist Foreign Policy (CFFP)
Established in 2016 in the UK and Germany, the CFFP is an NGO that promotes the global adoption of 'an intersectional approach to foreign policy'. Although funded predominantly by Western governments and organizations, its Advisory Council includes Chandra Mohanty (see Key thinker 10.1).

CHAPTER 11

GREEN PERSPECTIVES AND INTERNATIONAL RELATIONS

LEARNING OBJECTIVES

- Identify the key historical philosophical and theoretical roots of contemporary green IR perspectives
- Understand the philosophical differences between *environmentalism* and *ecologism* as well as *anthropocentrism* and *ecocentrism*
- Recognize the interconnections between the development of green political perspectives and phases of environmentalist/green activism
- Evaluate the key differences between the treatment of the global environment in mainstream IR theories and in critical green IR perspectives
- Analyse different critical green IR perspectives on possible alternative and more ecological world orders
- Appraise the debates around the concept of the 'Anthropocene'

11.1 INTRODUCTION

Environmental issues have periodically attracted the attention of IR scholars since 1945 but it is only relatively recently that distinctly 'green' perspectives have emerged within the IR discipline. This reflects the mounting body of robust scientific evidence showing that the sustainability of a healthy global environment is under severe threat. In recent years, it is climate change above all that has moved into the foreground of both public and academic debate. Given that all human activity depends ultimately upon the maintenance of a liveable natural environment, many argue that there is not merely a series of environmental problems and challenges to confront but an environmental *crisis* of global proportions. While the extent and causes of global environmental decay remain disputed, the last decade or so has seen a marked rise in public awareness and activism around environmental issues across the globe. Green politics have moved rapidly from the margins to the centre of public and political debate.

By its very nature the global ecological crisis does not respect national boundaries and as such it seems self-evident that it warrants attention from the IR discipline. It remains a widespread view, however, that solutions to the world's environmental problems can be found within the broadly state-centric parameters of prevailing patterns and practices of international politics. Many of those writing from an overtly environmentalist or ecological perspective do not agree. They see a need for very significant, perhaps very radical changes in how national communities and the human community see themselves and manage their affairs. Thus, most overtly green IR theorizing is inherently critical and normative. The commitment to environmentalist values is overt and the pursuit of substantial socio-economic and political change at both the local and global levels is its priority. Not surprisingly, then, Green IR theory has developed alongside and in interaction with other varieties of critical IR as well as political activism around environmental issues.

Environmental political thought and action covers a wide spectrum from more moderate varieties to the very radical. To help you navigate this spectrum, this chapter commences with an exploration of key philosophical differences between varieties of green thinking. We look then at how debates within environmental philosophy led to a distinctive body of green political thought, which only emerged fully in the late 1980s and early 1990s but within a few years began to turn its attention to the international or global political sphere.

This is followed by a survey of key examples of the early influence of environmentalist thinking and action on international political practice. Dissatisfaction with the intellectual assumptions underlying these early attempts to develop international cooperation in response to the global environmental problem, coupled with the lack of substantive progress in enacting effective global policy and strategies, led to the emergence of a range of more radical green perspectives. Many of these are distinctive because they embrace a more overtly *ecocentric* form of environmental thinking. We then go on to look at some of the key themes of contemporary Green perspectives on international politics, such as green international political economy, global environmental justice, the possibility of a more ecocentric world order, and the significance of the concept of the Anthropocene.

11.2 **WHAT IS GREEN THEORY?**

Because green theoretical perspectives cover a wide spectrum, it is helpful to learn about their philosophical underpinnings. We start in this section by comparing *environmentalism* with *ecologism*, going on to outline *anthropocentrism* and *ecocentrism*. If you are not familiar with these terms, do not worry as we will go through each concept in turn.

Environmentalism versus ecologism

The term 'green' is now widely applied to a range of theoretical perspectives and forms of political action that have *environmental* or *ecological* concerns at their heart. Although these two terms are often used interchangeably in everyday conversation, in fact they also have been used to capture important distinctions between perspectives on the natural environment.

An orthodox view depicts *environmentalism* as a way of thinking and a movement of political activism centred on the protection of the natural environment either from excessive human influence or simply because of its innate beauty and value. *Ecology*, in contrast, is seen to refer to the scientific study of the interrelationship between organisms and their environments, of which the human relationship with the natural environment is but one example. This division preserves the notion that *normative* theorizing (i.e., theorizing explicitly driven by values and an impulse to pursue change in the name of those values) and objective scientific research on the environment should be kept apart.

Most contemporary environmental theorists and activists work across this binary division. They may draw heavily upon scientific ecological evidence, but they also overtly express their normative and political leanings (Naess, 1973: 99). The lines between science, philosophy, politics, and ethics are therefore distinctly blurred in much of contemporary environmentalist theory and practice. This means that in recent environmental philosophy the two terms—environmentalism and ecology—are often used rather differently to their orthodox usage. They are used to refer to distinctive understandings of the relationship between humans and the natural world.

The essence of this difference can be captured by thinking about the differences between reformist and revolutionary perspectives in politics more generally. Reformist positions promote the managed adaptation and preservation of prevailing political and economic systems in response to the demands for change. Revolutionary outlooks tend to seek something altogether more radical, often presenting an overt and intentionally highly disruptive challenge to the political status quo. This may include the abandonment of prevailing thinking and practice and its replacement with something else that is seen to better address the perceived necessity of, or demand for political change.

Something similar can be seen in the range of philosophical outlooks on the human–environment relationship. Here the difference between two broad strands of green thinking is sometimes expressed as that between reformist-minded *environmentalism* and more radical *ecologism* (Dobson, 2007) or between 'shallow ecology' and 'deep ecology' (Naess, 1973). This division also threads through debates within environmentalist activism. Both sides recognize that we need to respond to the degradation of the global environment but differ, often quite markedly, in their interpretations of the extent of the challenge: is it a series of environmental problems requiring some adaptation of human behaviour; or is it better understood as a predominantly human-made environmental crisis, which requires radical changes to the way we humans live?

Varieties of environmentalism tend to argue that we should adapt our existing political and economic systems, perhaps quite substantially, but they retain a predominantly *instrumentalist* view of the natural world. What this means is that the natural, non-human world is viewed primarily through the lens of its usefulness in fulfilling the needs and interests of the human species. Adaptation is not just about preserving or protecting the non-human natural world but also continuing to exploit it for human purposes, albeit in a more sustainable, less-damaging manner. Thus, the natural world could still function as a source of raw materials, a depository for our waste, or a place for recreation. The British environmental theorist, Andrew Dobson, describes environmentalism as a managerial approach to environmental problems, which believes their solution does not require 'fundamental changes in present values or patterns of production and consumption' (Dobson, 2007: 2).

In contrast to environmentalism, Dobson argues that ecologism 'holds that a sustainable and fulfilling existence presupposes radical changes in our relationship with the non-human natural world and in our mode of social and political life' (Dobson, 2007: 3). From the ecologist point of view, then, environmentalist or 'shallow' varieties of green thinking are inadequate or even dangerous because they seek only to alleviate the symptoms of a problem and not address its root causes.

Ecologism generally argues that the natural world is a complex bio-organic system, or biosphere, of which the human species is just one constituent part. One famous early expression of this viewpoint is the Gaia Hypothesis (summarized in Key concept 11.1). Arne Naess argues that for ecologists 'the equal right to live and blossom is an intuitively clear and obvious axiom' (Naess, 1973: 96). The human community is therefore obliged to live in harmony with the biosphere, not just for its own interests but in the interests of the system as a whole. For many ecologists, this requires humanity to consider the comprehensive restructuring and perhaps even the de-industrialization of society to allow the flourishing of the non-human natural world on an equal basis to human society. In its more radical forms, ecologism may even argue for the ethical privileging of the natural world over the human world.

 KEY CONCEPT 11.1 THE GAIA HYPOTHESIS

Named after the Greek Earth goddess and first formulated in the 1960s by the British scientist and inventor James Lovelock, the Gaia Hypothesis (or Gaia Theory) posits that all the organic and inorganic components of planet Earth have evolved together over billions of years to create a single living and self-regulating complex system. This automatically controls such things as global temperature, the make-up of the atmosphere, and ocean salinity resulting in a *homeostatic* (i.e., self-regulating) system which enables life to persist. The human species is but one component of this system.

Gaia theory depicts our planet as analogous to any other living organism, such as the human body, which endeavours to self-regulate to maintain its life. If one element of the complex living system alters for some reason then the other elements endeavour to compensate, through negative feedback loops, to maintain a stable and healthy condition.

From a Gaian perspective, human interaction with other organic and inorganic planetary components, such as using fossil fuels and the production of large amounts of carbon dioxide, may produce compensatory responses, in the form of changes to the climate to restore balance. Such changes may be extreme, with potentially profound implications for human life.

Gaia theory was initially ignored or even ridiculed by other leading scientists, but in recent years it has attracted wider support from across the fields of science and philosophy. Although often described as an environmentalist whose Gaia theory has influenced a lot of radical environmental thinking and activism, Lovelock has frequently expressed a personal ambivalence about contemporary green thinking and politics. In contrast to many ecocentric green thinkers and activists, Lovelock adopts an anthropocentric point of view and has expressed support for such things as nuclear power and shale fracking.

USEFUL SOURCES

Vaughan, Adam (2014), 'James Lovelock: environmentalism has become a religion', *The Guardian*, 30 March.

Johnston, Ian (2016), 'Leading environmentalist James Lovelock: humans should save themselves not the planet', *Independent*, 28 September.

Anthropocentrism or ecocentrism?

Another way to capture the differences between the range of views under the broad umbrella of environmental/ecological theory and practice is to distinguish between *anthropocentric* and *ecocentric* perspectives. Both claim to be concerned primarily with human interaction with and impact upon the environment, but they are differentiated by their understanding of the relationship between the human species and the natural world. To help you distinguish between anthropocentric and ecocentric perspectives, look at Figure 11.1 and notice the position of the human being.

FIGURE 11.1

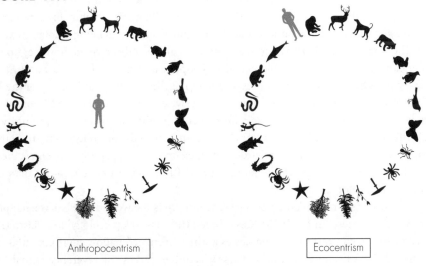

Anthropocentrism   Ecocentrism

Let's discuss these concepts in more detail.

Anthropocentrism

An anthropocentric—literally, human-centred—point of view depicts the human species as distinct from all other species because it is seen to possess several unique qualities. The idea of human exceptionalism has ancient roots. It can be found in various religious texts (such as verse 1:26 in the Old Testament of the Bible) and philosophers have long argued that humans are not merely one species among many, but an apex species because they possess certain characteristics that distinguish them from all other species. These would include such things as self-awareness, the highest level of intelligence of all species, an ability to think conceptually, an ability to accept responsibility for acting, the capacity to use a sophisticated language, and so on.

From an anthropocentric point of view, then, it is entirely legitimate for humans as an exceptional species to use the planet and all its resources in the pursuit of its own well-being. It is important to note that this does not rule out a commitment to environmentalism. This is, firstly, because you might argue that it is ultimately also in the best interests of the human species to maintain a healthy and diverse biosphere. Indeed, a lot of contemporary environmentalist writing embraces a kind of anthropocentrism that strives to recognize the dependency of our species upon the non-human natural world and thus our obligation to respect and protect it. Secondly, anthropocentrism is compatible with the idea of inter-generational obligation or duty, a long-running and powerful theme in environmentally focused thought. This is the recognition of our responsibilities to protect the natural world for future generations of our own species to benefit from and enjoy. This has provided a substantive philosophical basis for many strands of argument for protecting the environment from excessive degradation.

Ecocentrism

From an ecocentric viewpoint, anthropocentrism is a deep-seated and highly problematic feature of most Western traditions of political and moral thinking. Ecocentric thinking can also be traced back through the millennia, notably in a range of non-Western religious and philosophical traditions (Buddhism being a notable example). The origins of modern Western ecocentrism are usually credited, however, to the American philosopher and ecologist Aldo Leopold and his notion of a *Land Ethic*: 'A thing is right when it tends to preserve the integrity, stability, and beauty of the biotic community. It is wrong when it tends otherwise' (Leopold, 1949: 262). For Leopold, humans did not merely exist in a human community but also in a 'community of life' which encompassed 'soils, waters, plants and animals, or collectively: the land'. Leopold's Land Ethic is widely regarded as an example of a properly ecocentric viewpoint because it is centred on the moral worth of the total ecosystem rather than the human species alone.

Another key source of contemporary ecocentrism is the work of the Norwegian philosopher Arne Næss. In the 1970s Næss coined the term 'deep ecology' to refer to true ecocentrism, in contrast to what he saw as anthropocentric 'shallow environmentalism' (Naess, 1973). A keen mountaineer, Naess was influenced by the reverence Himalayan

Sherpa Mountain guides showed towards their natural environment, particularly the mountains within which they lived. Næss's deep ecology was centred on two core norms: biocentric equality and self-realization. He believed that all living things had an equal right to live and reach their full potential. Complete human self-realization would only occur, however, when humans fully grasped that they were part of an ecospheric whole. Echoing Leopold's Land Ethic, Næss saw true human self-realization as requiring that if we did not know how our actions might impact upon other living beings then we should not act.

Since the pioneering work of Leopold, Næss, and others, radical ecological thinking has blossomed significantly. It has drawn also from non-Western philosophical traditions and the historical beliefs and practices of many non-Western and Indigenous communities—such as the Aboriginal peoples of Australia and North America—known for their strong senses of connection with the non-human natural world (Gratani et al., 2016; Liboiron, 2021). Dobson argues that ecocentric Green thinking constitutes a distinctive form of ideology, because it requires us to think deeply critically about our most profound ideas and presuppositions and provides a set of concepts, categories, and ideas that help us make sense of our place in the world and how to act within it (Dobson, 2007: 2–9). More moderate varieties of green thinking do not offer such a comprehensive vision. They consist more of a range of political strategies and policy proposals that seek to ameliorate but not eradicate the human impact on the natural world. As such, moderate varieties of environmentalism can be compatible with a wide range of political ideologies.

So far, we have suggested that environmental philosophy falls roughly into two broad camps that can be captured by the overlapping binaries of environmentalism/ecologism or anthropocentrism/ecocentrism. This is something of a simplification and, as we will see, you can build upon and further nuance those basic binaries. Similarly, if you surveyed contemporary environmental activism across the globe, you would find an almost infinite variety of positions, many of which draw selectively from across the full spectrum of environmental philosophizing. Indeed, the Australian green political theorist, Robyn Eckersley, suggests that most green political theorizing falls somewhere between the two poles of anthropocentrism and ecocentrism (Eckersley, 1992: 33).

THINK CRITICALLY 11.1

After reading Section 11.1 of this chapter, and drawing from your understanding of the distinctions between a) environmentalism and ecologism and b) anthropocentrism and ecocentrism, how would you define your own thinking about the global environment?

Do the binary terms environmentalism/ecologism and anthropocentrism/ecocentrism help to clarify your own thinking? If not, why not?

You might choose to reflect again on these responses after reading the chapter in full. Consider how your views have changed or remained the same.

11.3 **THE EMERGENCE OF GREEN POLITICAL THINKING**

The origins of green political thought lie outside of the IR discipline, and it is only relatively recently that distinctively green perspectives have emerged within it. Initially, this might seem surprising. After all, although there are obvious and significant localized variations in landscape and climate, the environment is an inherently global phenomenon. However, until the emergence of widespread intellectual and public concern about the deterioration of the global environment from the early 1970s onwards, it was simply not seen as a core issue in the study of international politics. Additionally, much early green thinking and environmental activism was itself focused on environmental problems as predominantly local or national issues, with the wider global implications implied rather than directly addressed. As contemporary green thought evolved, however, so did a more explicit focus on the global implications of threats to the environment emerge along with the recognition that the environment was indeed of central concern to the theory and practice of international politics.

Early antecedents

Awareness of the damaging consequences of human interaction with the natural environment is not a recent phenomenon. The first signs of the effects of industrial pollution can be traced back to Ancient Rome, where land sea and air were being contaminated by toxic metals used in the extraction and smelting of metal ores, in the lead pipes used to carry water, and in the manufacture of consumer goods such as cosmetics and salt. Archaeologists have recently discovered that Romano-Britons living in the first to fourth centuries ACE had up to ten times more lead in their bodies than British city dwellers at the height of lead-petrol pollution in the 1960s (Keys, 2003). The Romans were clearly aware of the environmental problems that their manufacturing processes could cause. They famously developed innovative sewerage systems and methods of supplying clean water over great distances. They located manufacturing sites so that in densely populated areas at least some of their citizens were shielded from the effects of air pollution from the burning of coal and wood, while also using slaves and prisoners to carry out much of the dangerous toxic work and suffer the consequences. Lutfallah Gari has also identified an extensive Arabic literature on the dangers to human health because of environmental pollution produced between the ninth and thirteenth centuries (Gari, 2002).

In the fourteenth century, a bubonic plague epidemic, known as the Black Death, spread across most of Europe, the Middle East, and North Africa. It is believed to have killed 30 to 60 per cent of those who were infected. This level of mortality had a devastating effect on social and economic life. Since the plague bacterium was transmitted through contact between humans and plague-infected fleas and other animals, it also starkly illustrated Europe's backwardness compared to other parts of the world, which led to the implementation of new standards of public sanitation and hygiene. The Black Death, along with other smaller outbreaks of plague that followed it, highlighted the connection between environment and human well-being. These early concerns were, however, entirely anthropocentric; they focused mostly on the consequences of such things as pollution and poor hygiene for human communities.

Edmund Burke and our obligations to future generations

It is during the eighteenth century that the first signs of Western philosophical reflections on the importance and value of protecting and sustaining the environment begin to emerge. Contemporary environmental thinking and activism are commonly associated with the politics of the Left. Yet, political conservatism has also been a key source of environmentalist thinking, most notably the general idea of the need to conserve and protect the natural world from the impact of radical change (think here of the literal meaning of the term conservatism). Indeed, a key component of modern ideas of environmental conservation can be traced back to the observations of the eighteenth-century British conservative philosopher, Edmund Burke.

As part of his criticisms of the radical revolution underway in France at the time, in 1790 Burke argued for a politics of continuity between past, present, and future. He wanted to challenge those demanding radical political and social change in the name of achieving greater social equality and justice. Burke argued famously that society is 'a partnership not only between those who are living but between those who are living, those who are dead, and those who are to be born' (Burke, 2000: 80). Those advocating rapid change through revolutionary politics, Burke argued, risked severing the vital connection between their generation and the wisdom and experience of preceding generations, as well as putting the needs of future generations at risk.

Burke was not referring to the environment specifically but to all the material and social resources that any generation inherits from its predecessors. Burke argued that those living in the present are merely 'possessors and life renters' of the resources bequeathed to them from past generations. If they presume instead that they are the entire masters of those resources and thus entitled to squander them, they risk leaving to future generations 'a ruin instead of a habitation' (Burke, 2000: 79). Burke was not speaking in global terms either, but the idea of a global inter-generational obligation—that the present inhabitants of the planet are merely custodians of natural resources which they should feel obliged to pass on intact for future generations to enjoy—remains a consistent theme in contemporary environmentalist debates. This is perhaps most famously illustrated by the young Swedish environmental activist Greta Thunberg who has consistently emphasized how the actions of contemporary human society threaten the prospects of future generations such as her own.

Henry David Thoreau and 'Life in the Woods'

The conservation of the present natural world for those in the future to enjoy and benefit from was also a prominent theme in subsequent examples of more explicitly environmentalist thinking. The nineteenth-century American essayist, philosopher, and naturalist Henry David Thoreau produced a highly influential body of work on ecology and environmental history. The most well-known example is *Walden or Life in the Woods* (1854), which chronicles Thoreau's two-year experiment in living simply in a small cabin near Walden Pond, Massachusetts. Thoreau declared that 'I went to the woods because I wished to live deliberately, to front only the essential facts of life' (Thoreau, 2017: 72). *Walden* is a philosophical, spiritual, and rather romantic reflection on human existence and the experience of living close to nature. Receiving a lukewarm reception when first published, *Walden*'s influence increased markedly through the twentieth century when several prominent figures including Gandhi, John F. Kennedy, Leo Tolstoy, and Martin Luther King Jr. claimed Thoreau as a significant influence.

Thoreau also influenced the emergence of an American conservation movement in the late nineteenth century dedicated to the preservation of the US's extensive natural resources and areas of outstanding natural beauty. One of its founders, the forestry expert Gifford Pinchot, expressed the movement's rationale thus: 'conservation means the greatest good to the greatest number for the longest time' (Pinchot, 2004: 235). Through the establishment of organizations such as the Sierra Club in 1892 (which you can read about in Key event 11.1), the creation of national parks and national forests, as well as the overt support of President Theodore Roosevelt, the US conservation movement developed rapidly.

There were, however, philosophical differences between its members: some advocated a *conservationist* approach to nature while others embrace a more *preservationist* outlook. The conservationists, such as Pinchot, took a utilitarian view of the natural world, emphasizing the need for regulation and management so that the natural world could be enjoyed by as many as possible for as long as possible (Pinchot, 2017: 54–57). At the same time, the natural world could also be exploited (by the forestry industry and the hunting community for example) in a sustainable fashion. In contrast, preservationists sought the preservation of areas of pristine natural environments that would be protected from any human commercial development, because of their natural beauty, their contribution to human pleasure, or their value to the scientific community. Such differences provided a foretaste of some of the philosophical differences within environmentalist thinking and activism today.

KEY EVENT 11.1 THE SIERRA CLUB

The Sierra Club, one of the world's longest running environmental organizations, was founded in California in 1892. It operates mostly in the US although there is now an affiliated Sierra Club Canada established in 1963.

The founding ethos of the Sierra Club was *preservationist*, in that it sought to preserve areas of American wilderness or outstanding natural beauty in their pristine condition. In its early years the Club was very involved in the creation of more US National Parks following the establishment of the Yellowstone National Park in 1872, to ensure that key areas of environmental significance would be preserved for recreational enjoyment and protected from commercial exploitation of their natural resources.

The Club has, however, periodically been embroiled in political controversies. In 1969 it published Paul Ehrlich's controversial book *The Population Bomb* which argued

Students and Sierra Club members protest against climate change in front of Tampa City Hall, US

that population growth was environmentally destructive and coercive population control measures were needed. The club subsequently got entangled in debates about controlling immigration, although it eventually abandoned this position. Despite its long-standing campaign against the coal industry, in 2012 the Club was exposed for accepting more than $25 million in donations from the US natural gas industry although the link has subsequently been severed.

With more than 3 million members, in recent years the Club has become increasingly aligned with environmentalist activism and the pursuit of *environmental justice*. It was explicitly critical of the Trump administration's attitude towards the natural environment and the Club openly supported the Presidential campaign of his successor Joe Biden. They praised Biden for immediately reversing Trump's decision to withdraw the US from the Paris Climate Agreement.

USEFUL RESOURCE
www.sierraclub.org

The other area of controversy concerned the racialized aspects of early conservationism in the US. The relationship between the native peoples of America and their land may have influenced some of the early American pioneers of environmentalism and conservationism, but the creation of national parks and the development of tourism was sometimes at the expense of Indigenous people settled nearby, some of whom were forcefully expelled (Spence, 1999). The question of who benefits most from national conservation projects remains alive today. Some contemporary environmental historians argue that conservation in the US was conceived primarily in reflection of the interests of the more affluent sectors of White society who had the leisure time to enjoy protected natural resources. Even today, many protected areas and the kinds of leisure activities that are pursued within them, such as skiing or backpacking, remain comparatively inaccessible to poorer, minority communities.

Rachel Carson's *Silent Spring* (1962)

A key impetus to the heightening of public concern about the environment emerged in the US in the early 1960s around the use of toxic pesticides, fungicides, and herbicides to improve the production of food crops. The pathbreaking study on this issue was Rachel Carson's, *Silent Spring*, published in 1962 and widely credited with helping to kickstart the global environmental movement. Carson (1907–1964) was a marine biologist working for the US Fish & Wildlife Service. In the 1950s she started to devote herself entirely to researching and writing on conservation and ecology. Her earlier work was on ocean life and her book *The Sea Around Us* (1951) was a bestseller that brought Carson numerous literary awards.

In *Silent Spring*, Carson challenged the widespread use and misuse of synthetic chemical pesticides, especially DDT. Carson described such chemicals as 'biocides' because their effects spread well beyond the pests at which they were targeted. Because pesticides accumulated within and thus poisoned living organisms, including humans, they constituted a threat to the whole biosystem. Furthermore, the various target pests would eventually develop resistance to pesticides: 'among many species only the strong and fit remain to defy our efforts to control them' (Carson, 1962: 229). In other words, the supposed cure would ultimately only worsen the problem. Carson was especially critical of the failure to alert the public to the dangers of pesticides, not only because of their widespread use in agriculture but also in insecticides for household or personal use, domestic gardening, and so on.

Although Carson's extensive research on pesticides was widely supported by the scientific community, the US chemical industry was initially extremely hostile and endeavoured to paint her as an alarmist and fanatic. Nonetheless, *Silent Spring* attracted much public attention; it was serialized in the national press and was the subject of television programmes. It undoubtedly was a major contributor to the banning of DDT in 1972 for agricultural use in the US, something Carson never explicitly advocated. Her goal was primarily to enhance public awareness and promote their right to know what the consequences of pesticide use truly were.

The influence of Carson's work has proved to be far greater than changing attitudes towards the use of pesticides. *Silent Spring* is regarded by many as one of the most, if not the most important Western books on the environment in the twentieth century. This is because it depicted humans as an integral part of a wider ecosystem, but through their own actions humans could also distort that system with consequences they would come to regret. Testifying before a US Senate subcommittee on pesticides in 1963, Carson said

11 GREEN PERSPECTIVES AND INTERNATIONAL RELATIONS **437**

'our heedless and destructive acts enter into the vast cycles of the earth and in time return to bring hazard to ourselves'.

Carson's holistic depiction of an ecosystem of which humans are but one part foreshadowed a core theme of today's environmental movement and undoubtedly inspired a marked increase in environmental activism both in the US and elsewhere. On the other side of the coin, the hostile reaction to the publication of *Silent Spring* also embodied the kinds of criticism of environmentalism—that it is supposedly alarmist, inherently against progress, and fails to appreciate how science and technical innovation can enable humans to both prosper and preserve the natural environment—that continue to be aimed at contemporary environmentalist thought and action.

The growth of environmental awareness

Although these early Western influences were predominantly national in focus, the prominence of environmental issues surged significantly in the late 1960s and early 1970s as intellectual and public concern about global environmental degradation began to emerge and rise. This was also when Western international environmentalist NGOs, such as Greenpeace and Friends of the Earth, appeared on the scene. The emergent environmental activism was further influenced by ideas such as 'small is beautiful', the title of a popular book by the German economist E.F. Schumacher in 1973 (Schumacher, 1993), or 'A Blueprint for Survival' published in 1972 in a new academic journal, *The Ecologist* (summarized in Key concept 11.2)

KEY CONCEPT 11.2 *THE ECOLOGIST* AND THE 'BLUEPRINT FOR SURVIVAL'

The Ecologist was an academic journal established in 1972 by the controversial Anglo-French environmentalist and founding member of the Green Party in the UK, Teddy Goldsmith.

A deep ecologist with a strong antipathy towards industrial modernization, Goldsmith forged links with environmentalists in India, campaigned extensively against large-scale environmentally destructive development projects, such as hydroelectric dams, and sought to popularize the knowledge and insights of Indigenous peoples living in small-scale societies. At the same time, he was closely connected through family and friendships with wealthy and elite social circles and espoused some very conservative social and political views. Nonetheless 'A Blueprint for Survival' attracted the support of a wide range of leading scientists and was turned into a best-selling book that undoubtedly widened public awareness of environmentalism.

The 'Blueprint' argued that to prevent 'the breakdown of society and the irreversible disruption of the life-support systems of this planet' people should follow the example of

> tribal societies and live in small, decentralized and largely de-industrialized communities. This was because it is easier to enforce moral behaviour in small societies, their economic and agricultural practices were less ecologically damaging, and the prospects for greater personal fulfilment were believed to be better.
>
> This line of thought is sometimes referred to as 'bio-environmentalism' because it is centred on the limited capacity of the global biosphere to support the continual growth of the human population and its economic activity. It remains a significant current of thinking in contemporary environmentalist and activist circles.

'A Blueprint for Survival' highlights the localism of much environmental activism. The last few decades have seen a range of activist strategies emerge that effectively entail some form of going 'off grid', to greater or lesser extent, in pursuit of alternative individual and small-scale communal lifestyles. These have embraced a wide variety of ecocentric philosophies and belief systems, both Western and non-Western. In various ways, they can be seen as radical responses to the long-running environmentalist adage 'think globally, act locally'.

The vision of a global network of small communities with low ecological footprints remains a prominent theme in contemporary environmental and ecological thinking. One of the main problems with such visions, however, is that they are evidently very far removed from the concrete reality of today's world. The global population is now more than 8 billion people, many of whom live in enormous urban conurbations with equally enormous ecological footprints. These are located, moreover, within both rich and poor sovereign states, all of whom continue to pursue economic growth as the primary means to address present and future needs. These states exist, moreover, in a world marked by extensive economic, social, and cultural inequality combined with a highly uneven distribution of ecological risks. How might green political thought help us discern a path to a future world in which different less environmentally destructive forms of human community might become possible for more than a comparatively lucky few with the resources to be able to step off the dominant path of growth-led development?

11.4 THE ARRIVAL OF GREEN POLITICAL THEORY

As our survey of the early antecedents of environmental thinking shows, concern about environmental issues has long threaded throughout the social sciences and the humanities. The Australian green theorist Robyn Eckersley argues, however, that it is only since the late 1980s that green political theory has emerged as a distinctive school of political theory to challenge the two leading branches of twentieth-century Western political thought—liberalism and socialism (Eckersley, 2021: 266).

Notable early examples include Robert Goodin's *Green Political Theory*. Here Goodin argues that Green political theory is comprised of two distinct political components.

The first is a 'green theory of value'. Goodin posits this as an alternative to a 'capitalist' theory of value, in which the value of things is ultimately premised upon 'consumer satisfaction', or a 'Marxist' theory of value which values things according to the labour that goes into producing them (we discuss Marxism's emphasis on labour in Chapter 5, Section 5.2). A green theory of value, however, 'links the values of things to some naturally occurring properties of the objects themselves'. It is, Goodin argues a 'natural resource based theory of value' (Goodin, 1992: 24).

The second component of green political theory is a 'green theory of agency' intended to advise us how to act to realize green values and what kind of political agency is acceptable (Goodin, 1992: 15). Importantly, Goodin does not believe that a green theory of value leads straightforwardly into a green theory of agency. Each requires different forms of argument. The green theory of agency may be ultimately guided by the goal of realizing green values, but those values do not straightforwardly tell us what forms of political action or what kinds of political organization and social or political institutions will best serve the realization of green values. Nonetheless, green political activism, influenced notably by the rise and political success of the German green movement in the 1980s, tends to emphasize highly participatory forms of democracy, and decentralized political institutions (Goodin, 1992). At the very least, these are seen to run counter to the orthodox conduct of politics (especially in the industrialized West), which have failed to halt accelerating damage to the environment at both the local and global level.

Eckersley draws upon Critical Theory, particularly its normative commitment to advancing human emancipation (which is discussed in Chapter 6), to draw connections between an ecocentric value system and green political action. In contrast to both the liberal and Marxist traditions, the key distinction of green political theory is that it starts from a fundamental questioning of what our place, as humans, is in nature (Eckersley, 1992: 33).

Green theorizing is divided as to the precise answer to this question, reflecting the wide spectrum of thought between thoroughly anthropocentric and thoroughly ecocentric philosophical standpoints. Nonetheless, attributing a significantly greater value to the environment than most established traditions of political theory does provide some broad pointers as the substance of Green politics. It challenges many of the fundamental assumptions about such things as modernization, industrialization, and a reliance on economic growth, all of which have been central to modern political debate. It introduces new questions about environmental justice, given that the costs and benefits of ecologically destructive economic development are unevenly distributed both locally and globally. These, in turn, raise further questions about accountability, democracy, human rights, and so on.

Eckersley, Goodin, Dobson, and others recognize that green political theory is as divided as it is united in answering these questions precisely because green political thinking does occupy a wide spectrum. It seems fair to say, nonetheless, that an environmentally focused political perspective requires us to 'live with rather than against the natural world' (Dobson, 2000: 26).

Much of earlier green political theory focused on the communal and local levels, in reflection of the enduring idea of thinking globally and acting locally. A key theme was the need to decentralize power radically. On this view, the global nature of environmental and socio-economic problems can only be successfully addressed 'by breaking down the global power structures which generate them through local action and the construction of smaller-scale political communities and self-reliant economies' (Paterson, 2022: 231).

Developing themes that first emerged in the work of Schumacher and 'Blueprint for Survival', John Dryzek argues, for example, that small-scale communities within a highly decentralized policy-making environment are more conducive to environmental responsiveness and responsibility. Describing his position as an 'anthropocentric life-support approach', Dryzek acknowledges that the environment may also be valued for important reasons other than its capacity to provide life-support for the human community. Dryzek's concern, however, is to show how prevailing systems of government, authority, and policy making are ill-suited to the task of developing effective responses to environmental issues. Governments are hampered by political disagreements and rivalries between different interest groups (some of whom would be opposed to more environmental regulation), and large bureaucracies are insufficiently flexible. Dryzek's vision is of communities with highly participatory and open forms of democracy which would be better able to reach consensus about and act upon environmental problems which are close to them. Such communities are also more likely to develop more ecocentric senses of collective selfhood that do not view the environment in purely instrumental terms (Dryzek, 1987).

Dryzek offers a nuanced argument for the virtues of radical decentralization but, as we noted earlier, visions of environmentally preferable futures based upon small self-reliant communities are vulnerable to criticism, even from environmentalist or ecocentric points of view. The green IR scholar Matthew Paterson identifies three key criticisms of the focus on small-scale community development. The first is that small-scale communities might be too parochial to facilitate 'cross-community cooperation' and insufficiently concerned with their impact on the wider ecosystem beyond their borders (Paterson, 2022: 232. See also Paterson, 2000: 155; Carter, 2001: 57). Secondly, they would be ill-suited to developing the capacity to deal with global environmental problems. The historical difficulties of developing coordinated and effective responses within the current international community of states, which we will be looking at shortly, might be only exacerbated if the number of actors involved increased dramatically (Paterson, 2022: 232). Dryzek is also aware of his vision's limits, especially when it comes to the international or global level. 'International problems', he observes, 'constitute perhaps the most intractable class of ecological problems' (Dryzek, 1987: 178).

Paterson's third criticism is somewhat different but also focuses on the global rather than the local. Several critics see an emphasis on small-scale communities as still tied to a 'sovereign model of politics', even if they seemingly entail stepping away from the sovereign state as the primary locus of human socio-political organization (Dalby, 1998, for example). They still address the environment from the spatial perspective of bounded political spaces, albeit smaller ones. In other words, even a highly decentralized and localized politics could exhibit some of the characteristics of an international states system, such as collective selfish and competitive behaviour (Carter, 2001: 57). In contrast, some green theorists argue that ecological problems reflect characteristics of the ecosphere itself and should be understood spatially as about flows and networks that traverse orthodox conceptions of political and territorial boundaries (Dalby, 1998 and 2002).

What these lines of critique add up to is effectively an emphasis on the need to give greater political weight to the global side of the popular environmentalist slogan 'think globally, act locally'. Local action in response to a global problem will be insufficient unless the international and global dimensions of the ecological crisis are addressed. We will return to this theme in Section 11.3.

The impact of green political success

One of the key characteristics of the evolution of green political thought is its interaction with the growing participation of green political parties since the late 1970s as alternatives to established progressive political parties in electoral politics. The Values Party established in 1972 in New Zealand is widely recognized as the first national level environmentalist political party.

The early successes of green political parties certainly were, however, quite limited. This generated a range of pragmatic concerns among some green activists. In essence, the key question was whether green arguments centred around ideas of radical decentralization and alternative forms of human community were politically realistic? Some green political activists began to question the utility of adhering to purist ecocentric alternative politics that sought primarily to disengage with orthodox political practice and institutions and argued for engagement with prevailing political systems and institutions to transform them.

Such divisions were illustrated by the debate in the 1980s between *fundis* (fundamentalists) and *realos* (realists) in one of the world's most successful Green political parties, the German Green Party (see Key event 11.2). Both factions of the party were ostensibly committed to the pursuit of an ecologically preferable future. Nonetheless, such debates pitch two core views about the relationship between the present and future of human society against each other: can greener, more ecocentric forms of human social and political relations, at all levels from the local to the global, emerge from within the old, or will they only be possible outside of or even in full rejection of existing forms of society?

KEY EVENT 11.2 *DIE GRÜNEN*: THE GERMAN GREEN PARTY

Founded in 1980, Die Grünen (literally, The Greens) is arguably the world's most successful green political party. It emerged in what was then West Germany out of environmentalist, peace, and leftist social movements who were campaigning against issues such as nuclear energy, pollution, and the risks of the use of nuclear weapons in the Cold War (in which West Germany was very much the European front line). Its origins were reflected in its foundational 'Four Pillars': social justice, ecological wisdom, grassroots democracy, and nonviolence.

Within only a few years of its establishment, the party gained seats in the lower house of the German Federal government in 1983. Electoral success led initially to disagreements within the party between the 'Fundi' or fundamentalist faction and the 'Realo' or realist faction.

The Fundis wanted the party to retain a commitment to its founding principles, notably a strong environmentalism and preference for grassroots politics outside of established institutional structures and practices. In their view, these commitments sat uncomfortably with the Party's need to engage with other parties because of electoral success.

The Realos took a more pragmatic standpoint that was more open to cooperating with other political parties, something that was hard to avoid given that the German proportional electoral system produces a lot of coalition governments. This led to some radical elements leaving the party and the Realo position ultimately prevailing.

After the reunification of Germany in 1993, the Greens merged with Alliance90, three non-communist political groups that had emerged in East Germany during its collapse as an independent state. Although the Party's electoral successes subsequently waxed and waned, Alliance90/The Greens joined the German Federal Government for the first time in 1998 and the party leader Joschka Fischer was appointed Germany's foreign minister.

The German Greens have repeated their national successes in the 2019 European Union elections, when they secured 20.5 per cent of the national vote. In the 2021 German general election Alliance90/The Greens won 14.8 per cent of the national vote, making it the third largest national party, and subsequently joined the governing coalition led by Olaf Schulz.

If once seen as marginal political players, since the 1990s many of the green parties (especially in Europe) began to have substantial electoral success at the local level. Green parties are now also gaining influence at the national level as well. By 2022, green political parties were participating in governing coalitions in six European states as well as New Zealand and are represented in the national legislatures of more than 20 countries worldwide.

The strategies and arguments green political parties deployed to achieve electoral success have undoubtedly influenced the evolution of green political thought. We will now turn to look at how green political theory interprets the international and global dimensions of the ecological crisis.

11.5 GREEN PERSPECTIVES AND INTERNATIONAL POLITICS I—LOOKING THROUGH STATE-CENTRIC LENSES

We have already seen that some green theorists identify shortcomings to locally focused and overly inward-looking green thinking and action. Although there are obviously distinct and ecologically important localized environmental and climatic regions in the world, their significance and impact flows across political, social, or cultural boundaries. Nonetheless, states matter, not least because they exercise sovereign control over many

Plastic pollution in the ocean

environmentally significant areas, such as the rainforests in Brazil for example. Furthermore, the quality of environmental management at the national level can have profound effects on environmental quality in the wider region as well as globally. Many highly industrialized or heavily populated states contribute disproportionally to the degradation of the planetary environment through such things as their depletion of non-renewable resources, or pollution of the atmosphere, oceans, and river systems. The effects of such damaging activities can extend well beyond the national political boundaries of where they originate.

Although in the last few decades states and international organizations have expressed increasing awareness of and concern for the global environment, substantive change has been slow in coming, as we discuss later in this section. This is one of the reasons that many contemporary environmental activists, such as the prominent Swedish activist Greta Thunberg or the UK-based Extinction Rebellion protest movement have been insisting that in addition to individuals changing their consumption practices and lifestyles, sovereign states and international organizations must also recognize that the world is confronting an environmental crisis and that the time needed to rectify it is fast running out.

Extinction Rebellion describes itself as 'an international movement that uses non-violent civil disobedience in an attempt to halt mass extinction and minimize the risk of social collapse' ('about us' at https://extinctionrebellion.uk/). Much of the environmentalist political action by groups such as Extinction Rebellion can appear quite radical and confrontational at first sight. However, many of their demands are couched in quite anthropocentric terms focusing on the potentially devastating impact of climate change on the future of humanity. Like Thunberg, rather than drawing upon ecocentric philosophy, they focus primarily on the science-based findings of the intergovernmental Panel on Climate Change (IPCC), established by the World Meteorological Society and United Nations Environmental Programme (UNEP) in 1988. What they are effectively demanding is a combination of changes in human consumption patterns and institutional and regulatory reform at both the national and international levels. These are seen to be vital given compelling scientific evidence about such things as the causes and speed of climate change due to carbon pollution, the damage caused by waste materials that are highly resistant to biodegradation, and the consequences of the depletion of the earth's non-renewable resources.

The possibility of and need for international institutional and regulatory reform has in fact been the dominant theme of debates about the global environment within both mainstream IR theory as well as much environmentalist scholarship and activism for more than three decades. The difference between the mainstream and the more critical and radical contributions is in part a matter of degree: what is the appropriate extent and speed of the necessary changes, at both the state and international level, if the global human community is to successfully address the environmental crisis it faces? Additionally, most mainstream IR thinking addresses the environmental crisis in purely anthropocentric terms, focusing on the risks it poses to humanity. Critical green IR perspectives tend to reflect a more ecocentric outlook in that they emphasize the need to protect the whole biosphere.

In this section we will first look at two early influential examples of thinking about environmental challenges at the global level which continue to frame much of the terminology of mainstream debate. We then go on to consider the emergence of what is now known as 'global environmental governance'.

Garrett Hardin and the 'The Tragedy of the Commons' (1968)

An early and controversial exposition of the challenges that environmental degradation presents is Garett Hardin's 1968 essay 'The Tragedy of the Commons'. A microbiologist and human ecologist, Hardin was particularly concerned with the effects of over-population on the environment. It is important to note that although Hardin's work on population and the environment has had a significant influence on debate within environmentalism, some of his other views have been widely condemned because of his openly racist views on restricting non-white immigration to his home country, the US, and his claims about the relationship between race and intelligence. Arguably, Hardin wrote for two audiences. His work on population growth and the environment was clearly aimed at an academic audience and disavowed any overt racist intent. Undermining his academic work, however, was the fact that he was openly a white nationalist who also published articles in far-right publications known for their racist and vehemently anti-immigration sentiments (Mildenberger, 2019). In what follows we look at Hardin's scholarly work on population and the environment only, while acknowledging that other areas of his work are deeply problematic and often thoroughly reprehensible.

Developing ideas first propounded by Thomas Malthus, in the late eighteenth century, Hardin argues that population grows exponentially. Given that food production develops at a much slower rate and many of the earth's resources are finite, Hardin argued that this meant that the per capita share of resources must decline over time. Hardin illustrated his argument through the metaphor of a 'tragedy of the commons'.

The metaphor refers to unregulated grazing of cattle on common land, once a customary practice in many English villages prior to the industrial revolution. From a self-interested point of view, an individual farmer would be rational to graze more and more of their cattle on the common land knowing that this would lead to an increase in yield. Yet in so doing the farmer would also be contributing to the overgrazing of the land. However, the cost of overgrazing is shared by the whole community of grazers, thereby significantly reducing any evident impact in the eyes of the individual farmer. Yet, if all individual grazers acted in the same way this would lead ultimately to the catastrophic overgrazing of that land thereby ultimately rendering it of little value to any of the grazers.

Hardin's tragedy of the commons is an example of a *collective action problem*: individuals and, by extension, states acting solely in their own self-interest ultimately contribute to the disadvantage and even the ruin of all. Hardin saw the metaphor as applicable to all the commons of the Earth—the open seas, the atmosphere, the polar regions, and so on. These are more accurately described as 'open access' resources, since the term commons usually implies spaces governed formally or informally by a specific group of people (Paterson, 2000: 63–64). Many of the earth's key resources are, however, not formally governed by anyone and are thus open to exploitation by anyone who has the capacity to so do.

Hardin's article opens with the claim that 'the population problem has no technical solution; it requires a fundamental extension in morality'. Thus, Hardin argues, we should start by relinquishing the belief that humans have a natural right to breed as much as they wish. Having little faith in merely appealing to human conscience, Hardin concluded that we should agree to 'mutual coercion, mutually agreed upon' (Hardin, 1968: 163). We should agree to enforceable legislation requiring us to comply with policies designed to slow the human birth rate, such as China's recently abandoned one-child policy. In effect, we should agree to having our capacity to deplete the global commons forcibly restricted, just as many societies have restricted their citizens' capacities to accumulate excessively through such things as taxation and property laws.

Hardin has been criticized for failing to consider adequately the relationship between social and economic conditions (such as poverty) and birth rates, which in many developed countries have declined dramatically without any coercion. Nonetheless, Hardin's article helped to stimulate a lot of debate about the problem of international collective action and contributed to the emergence of ideas about environmental security.

This theme can also be seen in two subsequent controversial articles by Hardin: 'Lifeboat Ethics: A Case Against Helping the Poor' and 'Living on a Lifeboat' (Hardin, 1974). As the titles suggest, Hardin uses another metaphor to capture what he sees as the problem of resource distribution in a world of competing and unequal states (a very realist view of international politics). The lifeboat metaphor is intended to illustrate the political and ethical dilemmas produced by a limited national carrying capacity. In Hardin's analogy the lifeboats represent wealthy nations and those swimming around them poorer nations. If a lifeboat designed to take 50 people has room for ten more but the sea around it contains a hundred other people looking to be rescued, how many people should be pulled into the lifeboat and how would you choose between those looking to climb on board?

Hardin was criticizing liberal and other progressive schools of thought that adopt a cosmopolitan standpoint towards the plight of the global disadvantage, in which wealthier states are morally obliged to provide as much aid and assistance to the global poor as they can (a famous example of this view is Singer, 1972). For Hardin, however, complete justice equals complete catastrophe (Hardin, 1974: 562). If liberal-minded, developed states (how Hardin saw the US at the time) endeavour to help as many people as possible this will lead to disaster; the lifeboats will become overloaded and sink. Furthermore, because of the differences in birth rates between rich and poor countries, Hardin argues the problem is going to worsen over time. He concludes that '(f)or the foreseeable future our survival demands that we govern our actions by the ethics of a lifeboat' (Hardin, 1974: 568). Indeed, Hardin also lobbied the US Congress to stop sending food aid to poor nations, since it was their populations who supposedly threatened the planet's carrying capacity (Mildenberger, 2019). However, questions must be asked about the connections between Hardin's supposedly environmentalist argument for stopping food aid to poorer nations and his views on race and non-white immigration.

The political and ethical debates around Hardin's argument for lifeboat ethics have been reproduced more recently in public debate around the efforts of refugees and asylum seekers to enter wealthier developed countries. Although many recognize the moral and legal obligations of states to rescue migrants in danger at sea, critics often utilize versions of Hardin's 'carrying capacity' argument—this country is full up, national resources are under strain, and so on—to criticize rescue efforts. As was the case with Hardin, however, such criticisms also often have cultural and racialized undertones to them which have little to do with the actual economic or environmental capacity of states to absorb migrants and refugees (UNHCR, 2015).

From a liberal IR point of view, Hardin's analysis in 'The Tragedy of the Commons' is unduly pessimistic. The liberal institutionalist focus on international regimes—various combinations of norms, formal or informal rules, and institutionalized practices—such as those that already govern a great deal of international interaction comes into play here (the liberal concept of regimes is discussed in Chapter 3, Section 3.7). The 1959 Antarctic Treaty, which established the Antarctic as a demilitarized zone and restricts its use to scientific research, could be seen as an example of successful international collaboration and regulation of a key global 'commons', one which is thought, moreover, not only to contain a vast amount of valuable natural resources but is also a key component of the global climate system.

What Hardin, as well as many liberal and neoliberal IR scholars share with realists, nonetheless, is a broadly state-centric view of international politics which frames their treatment of environmental issues. Their primary focus is on the creation of international regimes of environmental governance that will provide better management of scarce and shared resources and coordination of states' responses to environmental challenges. There has undoubtedly been a very significant increase in the institutionalized international management and regulation of international politics since 1945. Yet, despite this, we have also seen continued growth in the exploitation of the earth's resources and a corresponding further degradation of the planetary environment. This is one of the reasons that more critical and radical strands of green IR thinking seek to step outside of mainstream understandings of international politics.

The *Limits to Growth* debate (1970s)

Hardin's emphasis on the challenges arising from the finiteness of earth's resources resonated among many of those whom he was in fact critiquing. In his later work, Hardin focuses on the need for 'living within limits' (Hardin, 1993). The key theme here is, again, the incompatibility between the dominant models of economic growth—which rest upon a continuing faith in the possibility of exponential growth—and the inescapable reality of a finite planetary resources. Hardin, it must be said remained primarily focused on what he had long argued was the key problem: the rate of population growth.

The finiteness of the Earth's resources was also the central concern of the report, *The Limits to Growth,* commissioned in 1972 by the Club of Rome think tank, an informal multinational group of individuals concerned with exploring what they called the 'predicament of mankind'. Over 30 million copies of the report in 30 languages have been sold and it remains the best-selling environmental book ever. Using computer simulations, *The Limits to Growth* explored exponential growth in five key areas and its impacts upon the Earth's finite resources:

- world population
- industrialization
- pollution
- food production
- the depletion of non-renewable resources.

A key theme of the report was the speed at which the limits to continual and accelerating growth might be reached. This analysis leads on to a range of possible future scenarios, ranging from a worst-case 'overshoot and collapse' of the global system through to its stabilization. The report concluded with the observation that if present growth trends in the five key areas listed continued unchanged, the planet's limits to growth would be reached sometime within the next hundred years (i.e., before 2072). However, the conclusion goes on to suggest that this need not be the case. If growth trends were altered to establish a condition of ecological and economic stability, a 'global equilibrium', could be reached. If this path was chosen then action to achieve it needed to begin as soon as possible (Meadows et al., 1972: 23–24).

The report was widely criticized for its modelling being overly simplistic and pessimistic. Critics argued, for example, that the report failed to sufficiently account for economic feedback mechanisms wherein resource shortages push prices up and help stimulate the search for alternatives. Others argued that the report took insufficient account of the growth in technological responses to resource depletion and pollution, as well as the discovery of such things as renewable energy sources (Connelly and Smith, 2003: 50–51). Underpinning many of these criticisms was a continuing faith in the possibilities of technological fixes to solve environmental problems, which remains a recurrent theme in many contemporary mainstream responses to environmentalist concerns. Many green thinkers concede that research into such areas as renewable energy and the reduction of energy consumption through technology is of value but see such solutions as radically insufficient to tackle the scale of the global environmental crisis.

Although the findings of *Limits to Growth* were initially largely dismissed as catastrophizing, the scientific community has increasingly come to the view that many of the reports' predictions have proven to be largely accurate. The early twenty-first century has seen several reconsiderations of the report, based on three decades of historical data since it first appeared (Turner, 2012; Jackson and Webster, 2016; Bardi and Pereira, 2022). These analyses have found that rates of growth, production, and consumption have in fact largely conformed to the report's predictions, thereby giving weight to its most pessimistic scenario. Certainly, *Limits to Growth* heralded the emergence of several themes around which much subsequent green political thinking and activism began to coalesce. The report's central claim that infinite growth on a planet with finite resources is simply unsustainable remains a foundation stone of the whole spectrum of contemporary green thinking. It also highlighted the need for greater international cooperation and institutionalization, given the inherently global nature of the environmental crisis.

The evolution of 'global environmental governance'—from Rio 1992 to COP26

As we discuss in Chapter 2, a mainstream liberal institutionalist IR perspective sees virtue in the further development of international organization and cooperation as a response to what are seen as shared problems and challenges. This led to the emergence of the idea of 'global environmental governance'. This was initially cast in terms of a state-centric international regime developing institutionalized norms, rules, and procedures to regulate and protect the global environment.

In the 1970s, this was an outlook shared by many environmentalist scholars and activists, as well as a small group of progressively minded developed countries such as the Scandinavian states and Canada. From their point of view, what was needed was international debate aimed at agreeing key principles as a starting point for cooperatively addressing global environmental problems. The wider international context is significant here. This was also a time of widespread international debate about global inequality and the economic exploitation of developing states. States in the Global South were demanding the creation of a more just New International Economic Order (NIEO – we discuss this further in Chapter 5). The debates around global inequality and those centred on the environment and the limits to growth overlapped in significant respects. Indeed, the challenge of resolving the tension between uneven economic development and the need for international action on the environment has proven to be one of the principal barriers to substantial progress.

This has been apparent throughout a series of major international conferences and summits under the aegis of the UN, the first being held in Stockholm in 1972. Each produced a set of principles that endeavoured to reconcile the complex tensions between demands for action to protect the global environment and calls for greater international economic equality. Additionally, there were disagreements about responsibility and capacity. For many states in the Global South, the industrialized states of the Global North bore far greater responsibility for global environmental damage and had much greater economic and technological capacity to address the problem.

The key broad principle that has emerged out of the various international conferences is that of 'sustainable development'. Introduced in *Our Common World*, the final report of the Bruntland Commission in 1983, it has become a commonplace reference point in mainstream debates about the environment. *Our Common World* defined sustainable development as 'development that meets the needs of the present without compromising the ability of future generations to meet their own needs'. It calls on 'all nations of the world, both jointly and individually, to integrate sustainable development into their goals' (WCED, 1987: 4–5). *Our Common World* found widespread support among many states and international organizations, no doubt because it endorsed economic growth, albeit with an environmentalist twist. For the same reason, however, its reception was more mixed among environmental activists and scholars. Again, many questioned whether it was possible to promote growth-led development on a planet of finite resources without significant and dangerous environmental costs (Sachs, 1993).

Nonetheless, sustainable development was also at the heart of the 'Rio Declaration' that came out of the 1992 Earth Summit in Rio De Janeiro. Again, this was the product of heated debates about such things as the relationship between national sovereignty and a state's obligations to the wider global community, as well as the different degrees of national responsibility for damage to the global environment and therefore the responsibility to do something about it. The final document imposes some stringent demands upon sovereign states, while also reaffirming the presumption that the future management of the global environment is to be achieved primarily through the institutions and established practices of an international system of states. It was accompanied by *Agenda21*, a non-binding action plan to guide the future actions of the UN, individual governments, and multilateral international organizations at local, national, and global levels.

The Rio Declaration and *Agenda21* present an unequivocally *anthropocentric* understanding of the environment. Many of the more fully *ecocentric* voices among academic green theorists and environmental activists criticize the limitations of the arguments underpinning them. Nonetheless, were the Rio Declaration principles and the Agenda21 guidelines fully and meaningfully taken up rapidly and globally, this would arguably amount to a significant move forward.

Unfortunately, more than 25 years of international multilateral negotiations since Rio, have shown that the unwillingness of most states to relinquish any of their national sovereignty, coupled with the competitive impulses and rivalries that are inevitable among states in a global market-based economy, continues to severely inhibit the prospects for substantial international action. The 1997 Kyoto Protocol set targets for limiting the emission of greenhouse gases, but in 2001 the US repudiated the protocol on the grounds that its targets would harm the US economy and, furthermore, other leading countries were failing to try to meet the targets set. China and India, each now a major emitter of greenhouse gases, have also challenged the Kyoto requirements.

The 2015 Paris Climate Change Conference (COP21) took place against a backdrop of mounting scientific evidence of global warming because of carbon pollution. Most of the nearly 200 states that attended have signed and ratified the Paris Agreement that set a target of holding the increase in the global average temperature to 1.5 degrees centigrade by the end of the century. However, it contains little in the way of enforcement or legally binding targets, other than to stipulate those signatories should set themselves increasingly demanding targets, so-called Nationally Determined Commitments (NDCs). However, the UNEP Emissions Gap Report 2020 showed that there remained a very significant gap between the climate emissions pledges of countries and the actual levels of their emissions of global greenhouse gases. More disturbingly, in response to the question 'are we on track to bridging the gap?', the report's answer was a resounding no (UNEP, 2020: xiv).

The Paris Agreement, like its predecessors, has been widely criticized for being undemanding and unambitious. Several subsequent scientific studies argue that although emission levels are falling none of the major industrialized states were meeting their own pledges. Even if they did, this would be insufficient to keep the global temperature increase to below 2 degrees centigrade (Victor, 2017). The prospects of the Paris agreement producing concrete results were weakened further in 2017 when the Trump administration signalled the US's intention to withdraw. One of the first acts by President Joe Biden, when he was sworn in as Trump's successor in January 2021, was to reinstate the US to the Paris climate agreement. However, the fine balance between advocates of stricter environmental legislation and their opponents in the US congress raises questions as to whether Biden's efforts to improve the US's record will be sustained beyond his presidency.

The COP26 agreement reached in Glasgow in November 2021 called on countries to 'revisit and strengthen' their NDCs by the end of 2022. According to the Climatewatch NDC Enhancement tracker, the majority have done so (you can follow their progress at climatewatchdata.org/2020-ndc-tracker). However, the UNEP Emissions Gap Report of 2021 estimates that even if the NDCs are fully implemented and maintained there is still only a 50 per cent chance that global warming will be kept to 2.5 degrees centigrade (UNEP, 2022: 33).

COP27, held in Egypt in 2022 saw a breakthrough insofar as developed industrialized states acknowledged for the first time compensating poorer states for the 'loss and damage' (because of rising sea levels for example) caused by climate change. However, key questions about the financing of such compensation remained unanswered. Additionally, COP27 was notable for the increased number of lobbyists from the oil and gas industries who outnumbered any individual country delegation. Additionally, no further significant steps were taken to curb carbon emissions and address the required cuts to emissions to achieve the goal of limiting global warming to 1.5 degrees centigrade (World Resources Institute, 8 December 2022).

11.6 GREEN PERSPECTIVES AND INTERNATIONAL POLITICS II—CRITICAL GREEN IR PERSPECTIVES

Although few green IR theorists would dismiss entirely the value of the limited amount of international agreement and action achieved since the landmark 1992 Rio summit, most see the current state of multilateral negotiations around climate change as highly problematic. For example, Eckersley argues that the strategy on sustainable development established at the Rio Earth Summit 'continues to serve as the dominant meta-discourse of national and international environmental law and policy, even though it remains deeply contested and only weakly implemented' (Eckersley, 2021: 265). Although on paper there has been progress on agreeing such things as carbon emission targets, international multilateral negotiations since Rio have shown an incapacity for states to transcend their competitive impulses, rivalries, and grievances sufficiently to enable substantial international action. In sum, the international community is clearly struggling to mitigate, let alone halt or reverse the human impact upon the global climate and environment.

Critical green IR theorists are generally highly sceptical of the capacity of the international political system in its present form to adequately address the global ecological crisis. Realism, and especially neorealism, depict the international system as highly resistant to substantial change and offers only limited possibilities for international cooperation or significant change in the broad patterns of international politics. If the realists are right, this does not bode well for addressing the challenge of global warming, which, Eckersley (2021: 267) argues, 'is one of the most complex and challenging collective-action problems facing the international community'.

The contrast between mainstream approaches to environmental problems and critical green analysis of the global ecological crisis mirrors Robert Cox's famous distinction between *problem solving* theory and *critical* social theory (Elliott, 1998: 4). We discuss Cox's distinction further in Chapter 6. One of the ways that attention has been deflected away from the deeper and longer causes of the global ecological crisis is to present global environmental change as made up of a set of discrete environmental problems—climate change, toxic waste, species extinction, and so on—that then seem more manageable and amenable to technological solutions (Saurin, 1995). Much of contemporary environmentalist or ecological scholarship and activism challenges this problem-solving orientation and in so doing is broadly aligned with Critical International Theory.

For critical green IR theorists, however, the starting point is that contemporary forms of human society are ecologically unsustainable and even 'anti-ecological' (Paterson, 2000: 58 and 35–65). Furthermore, they place much greater value on the non-human world than has traditionally been the case with the more established currents of Critical International Theory, coming out of the broad Marxist tradition. These are primarily aimed at realizing greater human emancipation through a critique of the prevailing global socio-political economic order and exploration of the socio-political and economic conditions that will radically improve the lives of the poorest and the most politically excluded of people within the *human* community (we discuss Critical International Theory's emancipatory project in Chapter 6). Adopting a more ecocentric standpoint, however, Critical green International theory is much more focused on the relationship between that human community and the global biosphere. Eckersely argues, for example, that since all living beings are 'embedded in ecological relationships' the emancipatory project should also encompass non-human nature (Eckersley, 1992: 49–53).

Critical green theorists generally view international environmental action as far too limited, because it is so state-centric in focus. Only a few effective environmentally focused international regimes have emerged, such as the Antarctic Treaty or international regimes to protect endangered species. These are the products, moreover, of the complex interplay of values and interests played out through the interactions of a range of actors that include not only states, but also the scientific community and international environmental social movements. Some scholars of international environmental politics have defended international environmental cooperation from a constructivist theoretical outlook. This is because international environmental cooperation does at the very least help to create global environmentalist norms, which places pressure on states to change their behaviour (constructivism's emphasis on the importance of international norms is discussed in Chapter 8, Section 8.4). Such norms have at least helped to place some constraints on the trade in such things as endangered species and the commercially valuable by-products obtained from them, or hazardous waste, as well as stimulating greater cooperation between national scientific research programmes on the environment (Vogler, 2005).

Nonetheless, most critical green IR theorists see a focus solely on what can be achieved in the current state-centric international system as too restrictive. Some recognize that the limited achievements in international environmental institutional and policy development could be seen to indicate a potential of the international system to develop in a more ecocentric direction. In combination, the increasing complexity of international environmental institution building, and the increasing involvement of non-state actors could be interpreted as a challenge to the claim by mainstream IR theorists that we will continue to live in an anarchical international system of sovereign states. At the very least, Paterson notes, 'the potential for what has become known as 'global environmental governance' to create possible post-sovereign politics exists' (Paterson, 2022: 228). Could the global environmental crisis have, then, the potential to move the world beyond the evident limitations of the prevailing system of states?

Green international political economy

Ecocentric green perspectives generally argue that understanding the global ecological crisis requires a different set of questions to those posed by mainstream approaches. For example, Paterson usefully proposes the following three questions:

- Why have ecological problems arisen or how have they been produced?
- What are the impacts of ecological problems on different social groups?
- What should be the responses to these problems? (Paterson, 2001: 3)

Keep these questions in mind as we are going to explore answers to them in the following sections.

To answer the first of these questions requires us to address what Peter Newell calls 'the elephant in the room' in the global environmental debate: the role of capitalism (Newell, 2011).

Mainstream IR analysis generally treats the capitalist global economic system as an immovable backdrop against which responses to environmental problems are formulated. In contrast, critical green IR perspectives broadly share an antipathy or outright hostility towards the global capitalist system. They are sceptical about the capacity of the system in its present form to respond sufficiently to the global ecological crisis. This scepticism has increased markedly in response to the perceived impact of *neoliberal* political and economic thinking at the national and international level over the last few decades. Neoliberalism's promotion of such policies as reduced state intervention, greater deregulation of markets, and the intensification of economic globalization are seen as significant, perhaps insurmountable barriers to the kinds of international reform and global change that most critical green IR theorists see are necessary.

Newell argues that economic analysis is perhaps one of the most developed aspects of green scholarly thinking (Newell, 2020: 74). Critical green thinking has certainly emerged within the field of international political economy/global political economy (IPE/GPE) in response to the mainstream view of global capitalism's largely benign role in the creation of a global ecological crisis. Here green scholars have been bringing together ecocentrism and various strands of Marxist and neo-Marxist thought to develop green IPE/GPE perspectives. These endeavour to expose capitalism's central role in the creation and sustenance of the global ecological crisis. British green theorists such as Paterson and Newell, for example, adopt a broadly *neo-Gramscian* analytical framework (for more on neo-Gramscian approaches see Chapter 5). This examines how the material power of capitalist corporations combined with elements of state power have worked to construct and promote very specific accounts of the human–environment relationship (Paterson, 2001: chapter 3; Newell and Paterson, 2010). These serve to mask capitalism's destructive impact on the environment because economic growth is presented as the inescapably necessary engine of development, while science and technology are seen as capable of addressing all environmental problems that may emerge along the way. The crucial point from a critical green IPE/GPE perspective is that not only do the global logics of economic, political, and ideological power inhibit the development of appropriate responses to environmental problems, they are deeply implicated in the production of those problems in the first place.

Paterson (2000) vividly illustrates how capitalist industrial development has impacted upon the global environment and shaped responses to environmental concerns through his analysis of 'car culture', which is briefly outlined in Key concept 11.3. Highly ecologically destructive aspects of capitalist modernity, such as motor vehicles, have become woven into the production of many peoples' social identities. Along with various other deeply embedded manufactured (and probably environmentally detrimental) symbols of modernity, for many people the car contributes to the definition of who they think they are (see also, Campbell, 2005).

KEY CONCEPT 11.3 MATTHEW PATERSON ON 'CAR CULTURE'

Matthew Paterson, endeavours to show how 'global power structures systematically produce environmental change' through an analysis of what he calls 'car culture'. The car is a significant contributor to environmental degradation in various ways, including atmospheric pollution and the consumption of non-renewable resources, but it also has been central to the development of industrial production in the early twentieth century (which is often referred to as 'Fordism' after the founder of the Ford motor company).

The car industry has also been a central component of many national economic development strategies in the industrialized world, perhaps most famously in the US but also, more recently in newer rapidly expanding economies such as China (Paterson, 2007: 1–4). At the same time, the car industry has generated a range of globally powerful corporate actors who have deployed various marketing and pricing techniques to embed the car in popular cultures all over the world. They also have enormous financial and political resources to deploy to protect their interests in debates about the car's environmental impact.

Paterson shows how the emergence and development of the car industry worldwide can offer analytical insight into the complex global logics of economic, political, and ideological power that have combined to drive forms of capitalist modernization that are highly 'ecologically problematic'. Such modernization has become so deeply socially and culturally embedded into our everyday lives that it becomes normalized as part of the backdrop of modern life and thus seemingly immune to significant change.

USEFUL READING

Campbell, D. (2005) 'The Biopolitics of Security: Oil, Empire and the Sports Utility Vehicle', *American Quarterly*, 57/3: 943–972.

Paterson, M. (2000), 'Car Culture and Global Environmental Politics', *Review of International Studies*, 26: 253–270.

Paterson, M. (2007), *Automobile Politics: Ecology and Cultural Political Economy* (Cambridge: Cambridge University Press).

The poststructuralist IR scholar David Campbell supplements Paterson's examination of car culture through analysis of the economic, social, and cultural politics surrounding the rise in popularity of the Sports Utility Vehicle (SUV) in the US. Campbell shows how commercial promotion of the SUV often draws upon pioneering myths. These depict it as the vehicle that allowed you to fully experience 'the American way of life' by escaping the city to explore the great outdoors, or as a secure refuge from external danger through suggestively connecting it with military vehicles like the Humvee. The SUV's popularity has produced an overall decline in the fuel economy of US vehicles and a per capita fuel consumption rate in the US 20 times higher than in European cities (Campbell, 2005: 966).

One seemingly environmentally conscious response to the concerns of Paterson, Campbell, and others is to promote the comparative virtues of electric cars. Sales of electric vehicles are rising as a proportion of overall car sales globally and evidence suggests that they have a significantly smaller carbon footprint than petrol- or diesel-powered vehicles (Reichmuth, 2020). Nonetheless, they rely still on the generation of electricity which in many parts of the world continues to rely heavily on non-renewable carbon resources. Furthermore, they are expensive to buy and as such can feed into the preservation of social and economic hierarchies. Their cost in the future will arguably depend very much on the play of market forces, i.e., the willingness of manufacturers to shift production from petrol- and diesel-powered vehicles to electric alternatives. Additionally, for electric cars to successfully replace petrol or diesel vehicles requires considerable investment in charging infrastructure. This raises questions about the relative capacities of states to make such an investment.

Environmentalist critics argue that given the powerful economic and political interests at stake, it is not surprising that the predominant mainstream response to questions about the deterioration of the global natural environment has largely been to treat it as a set of discrete environmental problems (such as what to do about cars) and rely on market forces to bring about change, rather than confronting the complex and historically-embedded production of much of today's global ecological crisis.

Environmental justice

The personal and social costs of endeavouring to adopt a more environmentally conscious lifestyle leads into Paterson's second question which asks what are the impacts of environmental problems on different social groups, defined by gender, class, race, and nationality? Critical green IR perspectives share common ground with other critical IR perspectives in their critique of the inequalities and injustices inherent in the present international and global order.

Since the late 1990s green theorists began introducing ecocentric voices into debates about international justice, democracy, and security in a globalizing world (Eckersley, 2021: 267). The question of environmental injustice arises at all levels of human social organization from the local to the global and across the spectrum of development (Adamson, Evans, and Stein, 2002; Martin, 2013). Within both developed and developing states, there is widespread evidence of the unequal environmental impact of growth-led development. Such injustices include the highly uneven environmental impact of industrialization, such as the exposure of workers to hazardous materials in the workplace, or localized instances of significant pollution of the atmosphere, land, and water supply. The poorest or most marginalized communities are often affected disproportionately because of where they must live, the kinds of jobs open to them, and so on.

Critical green IR perspectives emphasize the environmental costs of prevailing forms of growth-led development, not only for human communities but for the global ecosystem as well. There are strong developmental imperatives for many states in the Global South, often aided and abetted by developed world corporate interests, to permit environmentally damaging agricultural methods or large-scale mineral extraction technologies because they will bring in the best income from external markets. However, not only do the poor, ethnic minorities, and Indigenous peoples reap disproportionately less of the material benefits of such development strategies, they also shoulder a disproportionate share of their negative environmental consequences (Chancel, 2020). This can be illustrated through critical analysis of the effects of activities such as land grabbing for large-scale export-led agricultural production, mega-mining, large-scale fishing, use of pesticides, and even renewable energy schemes such as the construction of large dams. Environmental injustices are further exacerbated by such things as political corruption, the impact of outbreaks of civil conflict or violent struggle for control of valuable natural resources, or inadequate systems of legislative control, public accountability, and democratic oversight.

This means that green IR perspectives significantly complicate long-running debates about global justice. Environmental degradation is in large part a transboundary problem. Many of its causes—such as air pollution—have effects that flow across the political boundaries that have traditionally served as powerful determinants of ethical and legal responsibility. From an ecocentric point of view, moreover, the actual and potential victims of growth-led development are not confined only to the human species alone but are found also within all species of flora and fauna that constitute the total biosphere.

We can depict the ethical dilemmas raised in various ways. For example, are wealthy developed states who have already established a very high standard of living now entitled to insist on environmentalist grounds that poorer states should reduce their levels of consumption, or desist from agricultural or manufacturing practices that are ecologically harmful but perhaps vital components of their still developing economies? Similarly, is it fair to demand that poorer and still developing states embrace more sustainable forms of development to mitigate the consequences of highly industrialized developed states historically failing to so do in the process of their own development?

Poorer states are arguably less likely to be able to afford to develop or buy the sophisticated technologies that developed countries are increasingly deploying to mitigate their own ecologically harmful practices and consumption patterns. If the developed states are primarily responsible for the historical depletion of the earth's resources or the pollution of the earth's atmosphere, and most studies suggest they do bear a disproportionate responsibility, are they entitled still to insist that developing countries must now equally share the burden of rectifying the damage? Most critical green theorists insist that the issues of ecological degradation and ecological injustice must be examined jointly. This generally leads to the view that developed states do indeed carry a greater burden of responsibility and are ethically obliged to consider both the interests of the disadvantaged or marginalized within the total human community as well as the obligation to drastically reduce or even halt ecological degradation.

Environmentalism and Indigenous peoples

Another dimension of the tension between environmental issues and the question of social justice emerges out of the impact of efforts to develop greener energy sources by developed states upon their Indigenous peoples. A lot of ecocentric thinking has depicted the relationship between Indigenous peoples and their land as providing key insights into better, more sustainable, and environmentally sensitive ways of living (Nelson and Shilling, 2018; Norgaard and Fenelon, 2021). However, there are also many examples worldwide of Indigenous peoples who claim precolonial ownership rights over dispossessed lands and thus struggle with the consequences of some of the actions of environmentalist organizations. Such actions include the creation of national parks, restrictions on traditional hunting practices, and insufficient consultation with Indigenous peoples over the future use of the lands over which they assert Traditional Ownership (Vincent and Neale, 2016; Pickerill, 2018).

Indigenous peoples have long resisted energy developments, such as oil and gas extraction, that have polluted land they claim as their own (for an examination of Indigenous resistance in Canada see Van Rythoven, 2021). Drawing upon postcolonial perspectives (which we discuss in Chapter 9), some critics also depict green energy development in those states in the Global North with Indigenous peoples as underpinned by a 'settler colonialist' mentality (Maddison, 2013; Crosby, 2021; Össbo, 2023). This refers to the impact of outsiders moving to and settling on land already long occupied by original inhabitants and who subsequently adopt a colonialist attitude towards them.

For example, Canada and Norway are both noted for their investment in renewable energy technology (RET) such as wind power and hydro power. Yet in both countries there is resistance by Indigenous peoples to RET schemes because of such things as the threat to land rights through large scale construction projects and the disruption of traditional Indigenous practices, such as reindeer herding by the Saami community in Norway. Although some argue that Indigenous peoples will ultimately benefit from the growth of RET (for example, Stephens, 2019), others highlight the absence of Indigenous voices in the transition from oil and gas to greater use of RET and the evident insensitivity towards Indigenous culture and practices.

In the case of northern Australia, a region rich in extractable primary resources and with high concentrations of Indigenous peoples (40–50 per cent compared to a national average of 3 per cent), Indigenous–environmentalist relations have long been strained. The geographer, Jenny Pickerill, examines cases of tensions between environmentalists wishing to save or preserve the environment against the exploitation of lucrative extractable mineral and energy resources and Indigenous advocacy for such exploitation of resources in the name of local economic development. Yet Pickerill also identifies examples of collaboration between Indigenous groups and environmentalists. In sum,

Pickerill sees 'Black–Green' relations in Australia as 'messy, negotiated and contingent' (Pickerill, 2018: 1136). On the one hand, there are disagreements between indigenous communities about who has the right to speak 'on behalf of the many different countries ("country" is an Australian Indigenous concept that encapsulates the relationship between place and all the resources and people there) and the region'. On the other, Pickerill found that environmental groups and campaigns often failed to 'advocate for and articulate, a peopled-landscape' relying sometimes on depictions of an 'untouched landscape' (Pickerill, 2018: 1137). Pickering concludes that both sides of the Black–Green debate in Australia need to reflect on their relations with each other to prevent the continuation of simplistic rhetorical dualisms of 'environment or economy' or 'green colonialism versus Indigenous autonomy' (Pickerill, 2018: 1141).

Towards an alternative ecological world order?

Critical green IR theory is made up of a range of perspectives that variously draw from or intersect with the full spectrum of other critical IR perspectives. Not surprisingly, then, there are several key tensions that run through critical green IR theory. These become particularly apparent when it comes to developing answers to Paterson's third question—what should be the response to ecological problems? As we have seen, much of the mainstream debate about the global environment has centred on the development of international norms and institutions through multilateral negotiations. Most green IR theorists are agreed that the concrete outcomes of environmental multilateralism remain radically insufficient considering current knowledge about the rate and extent of global environmental degradation. Significant disagreements emerge within green perspectives, however, when it comes to identifying viable alternative responses to the ecological crisis.

One key division is between what Paterson (2022: 236) usefully describes as *transcendental* and *immanent* critiques of current international strategies for addressing the global ecological crisis. You should now be able to see how the different forms of environmental and ecological thinking that we have already discussed are reflected in these distinctive critical responses to the global ecological crisis.

Transcend the system?

Transcendental perspectives tend to take a pessimistic view of the potential for the current international system to move substantially in a more ecocentric direction. They emphasize the need to transcend it. Rather than try to reform or improve existing institutions and practices—through promoting ideas of sustainable development for example—should we consider abandoning large-scale growth-led development itself? This might entail the creation of small-scale self-reliant forms of community that work to develop small-scale, steady-state, and ecocentric modes of human social existence. We have already seen that this has been a stream of thinking since the emergence of environmental awareness. However, the emergence of ideas such as sustainable development, which invoked the possibility that environmental concern and growth-led development could be reconciled, helped to push those earlier explorations into the background of environmentalist debate. Since the 1990s, however, there has been a revival of critiques of the very idea of development itself, especially as it is currently unfolding in the Global South. These revolve around profound scepticism about the possibility of truly decoupling development from some form of economic growth and, by extension the threat it will continue to pose to a planet with finite resources. Such critiques raise profound questions about the practice of international politics and how we should theorize it.

Examples of transcendental green thought can be found in the work of what Jennifer Clapp and Peter Dauvergne describe as 'social greens' (Clapp and Dauvergne, 2011). Social greens utilize various radical social and economic theories to make the argument that social and environmental problems are inseparable. The damaging effects of 'large-scale industrial life' are being magnified by globalization which drives overconsumption by wealthy elites while further exacerbating global poverty and environmental degradation.

Marxist economic arguments figure prominently in this stream of critical green thinking and the influence of postcolonialism can be seen as well. According to Clapp and Dauvergne, Marxist-influenced social green scholarship argues that

> Capitalism and its global spread via neo-colonial relations between rich and poor countries not only leads to an unequal distribution of global income, power, and environmental problems, but is also a threat to human survival. (Clapp and Dauvergne, 2011: 12)

Other streams of social green thinking also draw upon *ecofeminism* to argue that a Western-led globalizing capitalism not only creates and perpetuates inequalities within and between states, but it also leads to the further marginalization of the poor, Indigenous peoples, and women. Many of those different communal ways of life that are falling victim to the homogenizing effects of globalization are centred, moreover, around a much less destructive relationship with the natural world. This occurs through the erosion of local community values, traditions, and practices and the supplanting of them with new Western and patriarchal forms of domination (Gaard and Gruen, 1993). Ecofeminists 'claim that environmental issues are feminist issues because it is women and children who are the first to suffer the consequences of injustice and environmental destruction' (Gaard and Gruen, 1993: 240).

The upshot of social green analysis is stark. The human community needs to go much further than merely tinkering with international institutions, engaging in international crisis management, or trying to fix production and consumption by making it 'greener'. What is needed is a rejection of the current free-trade global economic system pretty much in its entirety. Globalization is seen to be driven by a complex network of international financial institutions (such as the IMF, World Bank, and WTO), large MNCs, and Western developed states who continue to believe that globalization will ultimately work for the benefit of everyone. What they fail to acknowledge, social greens argue, are the extensive social and potentially devastating ecological costs of a globalizing industrialized capitalism. Social greens argue that we need to dismantle current global economic structures and institutions and move towards a world of local, self-reliant, small-scale economies, a process that Colin Hines calls 'localization'

(Hines, 2000 and 2003). This would also require the abandonment of prevailing understandings of development itself since it entails 'a retreat from the large-scale and capitalist life' (Clapp and Dauvergne, 2011: 14).

For those in the global minority who benefit most substantially from globalized liberal capitalism, this might not be welcome news. From a social green point of view such costs would ultimately be more than compensated for by the growth of communities across the world that in various, perhaps very different, ways would develop collective lifestyles, which would not need global free-market capitalism to survive. Small-scale communities would be capable of fulfilling basic needs and enhancing people's quality of life as defined more by local norms and customs. At the same time these communities could develop new forms of interacting economically, socially, or culturally with other communities that do not simply reproduce the faults of the current international states system. This would require, of course, a radical rethinking of notions of ownership or control of land and other resources as well as the abolition of the notion of absolute sovereignty. The thrust of the argument is that we need to move from using resources primarily for their *exchange value*—i.e., to produce commodities to create wealth—to appreciating them for their *use value*. What this means is that we should ask how would those resources help us, in cooperation with others, fulfil our basic needs and sustain ourselves?

The *immanent* possibility of a greener world?

Other critical green theorists share the social green's claim that radical change is necessary if we are to move towards a greener, more ecocentric world order but are sceptical about the plausibility of the complete abandonment of existing modes of human socio-economic organization, notably the sovereign state. Rather than jumping straight to a vision of a post-statist world, some green theorists explore the prospects for 'greening the state' (Eckersley, 2004; see also Dryzek et al., 2003) and, by extension, the international system of states. In other words, they see an *immanent* potential for significant, even radical change within the current world order.

In continuing to see the state as a vital component of a more ecological global future, Eckersley and others go against the grain of much critical green thinking. In Eckersley's view, states remain the gatekeepers of the global order, therefore greening the state is a vital yet still very challenging step towards the realization of a greener more ecocentric world. Eckersley draws on a diverse range of critical literatures, including critical varieties of constructivism (which we discuss in Chapter 8) and the work of critical theorists such as Andrew Linklater (examined in in Chapter 6), to argue that logics of transformation can be detected within some states and in the current international system. Contrary to the claims of realists and others who emphasize the anarchical nature of the international system, even the limited progress made in the development of environmental multilateralism reveals the potential for further, deeper cooperation and mutual agreement. The fuller realization of that immanent potential requires, however, a radical transformation of at least some key states (notably developed liberal democracies) so that they become more receptive to public expression of ecological concerns and begin a process of social and ecological learning. This requires confronting some key 'liberal dogmas', notably the primacy of individual autonomy, the abiding faith in Western rationality as the key to mastery of an external non-human world, and a recognition of our 'non-instrumental dependency' on the natural world (Eckersley, 2004: 108).

To achieve this, Eckersley argues, would require a transformation from liberal democracy to a far more inclusive form of 'ecological democracy', wherein the state could be more robustly held to account for its anti-ecological domestic and international policies. Like many other critical green theorists, Eckersley sees the emergence of green social movements as already helping to open up a range of 'critical green public spheres'. These suggest a potential for greater public debate and political activism to pressure liberal states to move in a decisively ecocentric direction through modifying their understandings of such concepts as modernization, development, and sovereignty that underpin their policy formulation. Eckersley and others depict some European states (such as Germany and Sweden), and the EU as a whole, leading the way in embedding environmental concerns within their own domestic political debates and policy arenas (Eckersley, 2004. See also Barry and Eckersley, 2005, and Death and Tobin, 2017). They could be seen as acting as greener versions of what the English School theorist Hedley Bull called 'local agents for a world common good' (Eckersley, 2004: 245. See also our discussion of Hedley Bull in Chapter 4, Sections 4.3 and 4.4).

The reconciliation of sovereignty, national interests, and global ethical responsibilities will require the extension of democracy beyond the national sphere. This is a theme that has already been explored extensively in the work of several theorists working within the Critical IR Theory perspective (see the discussion Chapter 6, Section 6.4). One of the key challenges to such ideas, however, has already emerged in the multilateral negotiations since Rio. As we noted in our discussion of environmental justice earlier in this section, these have been marked by fundamental disputes between states in the Global North and those in the Global South who detect strains of neocolonialism in the developed world's approach to combating environmental degradation. Much recent green scholarship has taken on board concerns about imposing Western models of ecocentrism or presuming that the capacity or willingness of states to go green is the same across all states. The influences of both poststructuralism and postcolonialism are increasingly evident in the greater sensitivity shown towards local contexts and the need to listen to the distinctive voices of all communities, especially those most marginalized in or excluded from public and policy debates.

Quite how the immanent potentialities that Eckersley and others identify at the local, national, and global levels will play out is likely, then, to vary widely between states, reflecting not only their diverse social, political, and cultural make-ups but also the consequences of inequalities of wealth and relative weaknesses of domestic political institutions. Eckersley acknowledges that the greening of international politics need not require the complete abandonment of the idea of sovereignty but rather the greening of the concept. Thus, many states that are particularly vulnerable to the negative effects of ecological degradation or who are custodians of particularly ecologically significant resources (such as rainforests) may be legitimately entitled to exercise their sovereign rights to define their environmental protection requirements in specific ways. On the other side of the coin, those states who play a disproportionate role in the creation of transboundary ecological harm and global environmental degradation will have to recognize that appeals to national sovereign rights may no longer be sufficient to set aside their international and global obligations and duties which may be considerably greater than those of other states.

THINK CRITICALLY 11.2 CAN THE CURRENT INTERNATIONAL SYSTEM BE 'GREENED'?

Paterson identifies two broad currents of critical green thought: 'immanent' critiques versus 'transcendental' critiques of the present international system. At the heart of this debate is the role of the sovereign state.

- Do you think it is possible to 'green the state' as Robyn Eckersley and others suggest? If so, why? If not, why not?
- Transcendental Green thinking argues that we need to abandon the state-centric international order altogether and replace globalization with 'localization'. Do you agree? If so, why? If not, why not?

Hint: think about how your answer to the first question connects with your answer to the second.

11.7 IR IN THE 'ANTHROPOCENE'

The current geological epoch is called the Holocene (meaning 'entirely recent'), which is usually dated from the end of the last ice age about 11,700 years ago. In the last few years, however, several scholars from a wide variety of intellectual disciplines across the sciences and social sciences have argued that a new geological era has dawned: *the Anthropocene* (see Box 11.8). However, there is considerable debate surrounding this claim, including what its implications might be for theorizing international politics.

KEY CONCEPT 11.4 THE ANTHROPOCENE

The degree and significance of the human impact upon the Earth's climate and ecosystems has led some scientists and environmentalists to argue that it warrants the declaration of a new geological era: the Anthropocene (from *anthropo*, for 'human' and *cene* for 'new'). This is because humans are seen to have permanently and dangerously changed the planet through such activities as polluting the oceans, changing the geomorphology of parts of the earth's surface (through such activities as deforestation, dam building, and laying of roads), bringing about the mass extinction of a still growing number of animal and plant species, and altering the atmosphere. In so doing, they argue, humans have dramatically reduced or even halted the growth of biodiversity, and their impact will eventually show up in the geological record.

The Anthropocene is a controversial idea that has yet to receive official recognition by the International Union of Geological Sciences that names and defines the epochs making up the geological time scale. The beginning of the Anthropocene is also widely debated. Some trace it back to the nineteenth-century Industrial Revolution, whereas others argue it commenced with the testing of the first atomic bomb in 1945.

Critics argue that, while undoubtedly significant, the impact of humans on the planetary biosphere remains insufficient to warrant the declaration of a new epoch. Despite the controversies surrounding it, the concept of the Anthropocene is having a significant and growing impact upon a wide range of intellectual reflections upon the contemporary condition of, and prospects for humanity's relationship with Planet Earth.

USEFUL RESOURCES

Brannen, Peter (2019), 'The Anthropocene is a Joke', *The Atlantic*, 13 August.

Carrington, Damien (2016), 'The Anthropocene epoch: scientists declare dawn of human-influenced age' *The Guardian*, 29 August.

For some IR scholars, the arrival of the Anthropocene effectively renders orthodox IR thinking and the concept of the 'international' redundant in the face of a planetary crisis. One group of critical IR scholars have produced what they call 'Planet Politics: A Manifesto from the End of IR'. Their manifesto argues that

> The local, national, and global no longer define our only spaces of action. The planet has long been that space which bears the scars of human will: in transforming *the* world into *our* world, we damaged and transformed it to suit our purposes . . . International Relations has failed because the planet does not match and cannot be clearly seen by its institutional and disciplinary frameworks. (Burke et al., 2016: 500–501)

The manifesto's authors claim that 'the Anthropocene issues a profound challenge to politics'. They see the threat of a mass extinction event, in which most species may disappear over the next few centuries, as requiring the near complete abandonment of all existing political institutions and practices. These have been built, the manifesto argues, upon the presumption that 'the Earth is treated as raw material for the creation of a world tailored to human needs' (Burke et al., 2016: 518). Consequently, the discipline needed to rethink its *ontological* categories, i.e., what it considers to be 'real' and significant. Most IR theories focus primarily on relations between states and other actors within an anarchical international system; IR theories variously deem individuals, social classes, states, and the system of states to be ontologically significant. Planet Politics proposes that the primary ontological category should be the planet itself, with which humanity as a whole is 'entangled':

> We are thus challenging IR to reorganise its very foundations around the complex system of processes and interactions that bind society and nature so terribly together and are producing such world-shaking results, rather than around the anthropocentric drama of human cooperation and conflict. (Burke *et. al.* 2016: 520)

In practical terms, the Manifesto asks if it is time to consider granting major ecosystems—such as the Amazon basin, the polar regions, and the Pacific Ocean—the status of nations in the UN assembly and other international bodies. Additionally, it proposes the creation of an 'Earth System Council' comprised of representatives of 'Earth System scientists, major ecosystems, species groups and states' which would function 'much like the current UN Security Council' to both warn and authorize action.

The manifesto does not, however, spell out how such entities as ecosystems or other non-human species would be granted meaningful representation, other than through human agency. Additionally, despite heralding 'the end of IR', it seems ultimately to fall back on revised versions of existing international multilateral institutions, albeit with radically different and expanded memberships. Some critics argue that Planet Politics echoes much of orthodox liberal IR thinking (Chandler, Cudworth, and Hobden, 2018, 194–195). This is because it treats humanity as an undivided whole and proposes what amounts to a top-down, elitist global or planetary regime of governance based upon a supposedly universally held understanding of the value of 'life itself' (Burke et al., 2016: 517). It makes no reference to global inequality or the complex history and politics behind humanity's damaging impact upon the planetary biosphere. Indeed, the manifesto explicitly argues that 'we need not focus on who is responsible, but we do need to learn to adapt to the world we have created' (Burke et al., 2016: 500). This has led critics to accuse the Manifesto of effectively depoliticizing the ecological crisis (Chandler, Cudworth, and Hobden, 2018: 204).

Additionally, various critics argue, Planet Politics treats the concept of the Anthropocene as a self-evident truth rather than a matter of ongoing debate. In key respects, contemporary debates around the concept echo some of the disputes that have marked efforts to forge international agreements about the global environment. For some environmentalists, notably those looking through Marxist and neo-Marxist lenses, describing the current era as the Anthropocene is problematic. As Andreas Malm has put it, 'blaming all of humanity for climate change lets capitalism off the hook' (Malm, 2015). Similarly, Naomi Klein depicts the environmental crisis as in large part a consequence of a carbon-hungry, high-consumption capitalist system (Klein, 2014).

In a similar vein, several green theorists have proposed calling the present era the 'Capitalocene' (the Age of Capital) to highlight the complex connection between the degradation of the planet and the long history of industrial capitalism (Moore, 2016: 5–6). Moore and others argue that we need to critically examine how the global ecological crisis emerged and who is responsible, not least to begin to discern what kind of politics is needed, and at what level to respond to the global ecological crisis. Walking something of a middle path between the 'all of humanity' line of argument and those who emphasize the primary role of capitalism is Dipesh Chakrabarty. Chakrabarty (2017) agrees that climate change is profoundly connected with the history of capitalism but the Anthropocene is nonetheless a crisis for all of humanity: 'left unmitigated, climate change affects us all, rich, and poor. They are not affected in the same way, but they are all affected'. However, Chakrabarty (2017: 35) also notes that the debate about climate change remains 'anchored primarily in the experiences, values and desires of developed nations, that is, in the West'.

Olaf Corry argues that the IR discipline has always had 'a weak grasp of nature', tending to see it as external to its core concerns. Instead, Corry argues, IR theorists should see the environmental crisis as 'something emerging through international dynamics, reciprocally affecting the units, structure and processes of the international system itself' (Corry, 2020: 419). At the same time, Corry criticizes environmental thinking that adopts a planetary perspective, such as the Planet Politics Manifesto, for depicting the world as one space and thereby obscuring the multiplicity of human societies.

If you take the example of climate change—an issue central to the argument that we do now live in the Anthropocene—it is arguably important to recognize that historical responsibility for altering the climate is not evenly spread across the global human community. Malm and Hornberg argue, for example, that the spread outwards from Europe of industrial capitalism, aided and abetted by European imperialism and colonialism, not only shaped the development of the international system, but because of its reliance on fossil fuels also dramatically accelerated the production of climate-altering emissions (Malm and Hornborg, 2014). Although we must acknowledge that the ecological crisis is global, Corry and others highlight how it emerged in the context of a multiplicity of human societies 'each in a metabolic exchange with its environment' (Corry, 2020: 432). Although the whole of humanity suffers the consequences of climate change because emissions accumulate globally, is it fair to assume that responsibility for causing climate change and now doing something about it should be equally shared across humankind?

Humanity remains socially and politically fragmented, which not only continues to make the idea of the international still meaningful, but also presents a significant challenge to those seeking to discern a pathway through the global ecological crisis. For critics, such as Corry, what is needed is not the abandonment of IR, but a much deeper incorporation of the natural world into our understanding of the international.

11.8 **CONCLUSION**

The prominence of the environment as an issue area in the IR discipline has undoubtedly grown significantly, especially since the late 1980s when concerns about the global environment were rising fast. We have seen throughout this chapter, however, that green perspectives on IR vary widely in their scope. They include arguments for 'greening' orthodox IR theories as well as proposals for exploring the *immanent* potential of the current international states system to develop innovative national, international, and transnational responses to the global ecological crisis centred around critical rethinking of the concepts of growth and modernization. For some critical green IR theorists,

466 INTRODUCTION TO INTERNATIONAL RELATIONS THEORIES

nothing less than the thorough transformation of global politics and economics will be sufficient. This might entail the need to explore a post-capitalist world economy, or the replacement of the sovereign state with other forms of, probably smaller, genuinely eco-centric human communities. More recently the concept of the Anthropocene has entered the IR discipline, leading some to claim that the very idea of the international should give way to a planetary theoretical viewpoint.

There is no singular green IR theory, but in the light of scientific evidence about the rate of climate change it is reasonable to conclude that the influence of green perspectives on both mainstream and critical thinking about international politics is likely to increase. Many orthodox IR theorists continue to express a faith in the international system to adapt through developing sufficient political will to agree on common principles and develop solutions to the global ecological crisis, perhaps aided by technological innovations and shifts in human patterns of consumption. At the more critical margins of green IR thinking, however, there is considerable doubt about the human community's capacity to halt let alone reverse its impact on the environment without national and global reforms to an historically unprecedented degree. Although the substantive meaning and value of the concept of an 'Anthropocene' is highly debatable, at the very least it serves as a clarion call regarding the urgency and impact of environmental decay on the future of global politics.

SUMMARIZING GREEN PERSPECTIVES

- Green perspectives are a relatively recent arrival in the IR field, although environmental philosophy and green political thought emerged from the late nineteenth century onwards

- The spectrum of green political theory can be illustrated using two overlapping philosophical binaries: environmentalism vs. ecologism and anthropomorphism vs. ecocentrism

- Environmental awareness has grown significantly since the late 1960s and early 1970s, influenced by publications such as Rachel Carson's *Silent Spring*, the 'Blueprint for Survival', and the *Limits to Growth* report of the Club of Rome

- A distinctive school of green political theory only began to emerge in the late 1980s accompanied by the growing electoral success of green political parties

- The early phase of international summits and conferences led to the emergence of the contested concept of 'sustainable development' in 1983, in the Brundtland Commissions' report *Our Common World*

- The 1992 Rio Declaration was the starting point for a series of international multilateral negotiations in pursuit of what is now known as 'global environmental governance'.

11 GREEN PERSPECTIVES AND INTERNATIONAL RELATIONS · **467**

- International negotiations around the global environment have been marked throughout by disputes between the Global North and South about relative responsibilities for human-induced environmental damage and thus the obligations to act to manage, reduce, or eliminate it

- Mainstream IR theory tends towards either scepticism about the possibility of achieving global environmental reform in an anarchical state system (realism) or seeing continuing and deepening multilateral negotiation and cooperation as providing the best prospects for reducing the human impact on the environment (institutional neoliberalism)

- Most green IR scholars view the outcome of multilateral negotiations to date as radically insufficient to significantly reduce the risk of global environmental catastrophe

- Critical green IR perspectives emerged in the late 1990s bringing more ecocentric philosophical commitments into debates with both mainstream IR theories and other critical IR theoretical perspectives

- Critical green IR/IPE perspectives strongly implicate the global capitalist system and leading developed states in the creation and sustenance of the global ecological crisis and the creation of various forms of environmental injustice

- Explorations of possible more ecocentric world orders fall into two broad camps: *transcendental* alternatives that explore alternatives to the current state-centric international order and those that see *immanent* potential within the prevailing international order to move it in a decisively more ecocentric direction

- A key issue within critical IR perspectives is the present and future role of the state. Is sovereign statehood a hindrance to global environmental reform or can the state be 'greened'?

- The introduction of the concept of the *Anthropocene* into IR debates has led to some to call for the 'End of IR' in favour of a more planetary perspective.

QUESTIONS

1. What are the key differences between a) environmentalism and ecologism and b) anthropocentrism and ecocentrism?

2. What do you think brought about the rise in environmental awareness and activism since the early 1970s?

3. In your view, what are the key reasons why the international environmental agreements since 1972 have only been very weakly implemented?

4. Is environmentalism compatible with growth-led economic development? Explain your answer.

5. Explain and assess the key differences between what Paterson calls *transcendental* and *immanent* critiques of current international strategies for addressing the global ecological crisis.

6. Critically assess the following claim: 'We are concerned that International Relations, as both a field of knowledge and a global system of institutions, is failing the planet' (Anthony Burke et al., 'Planet Politics: A Manifesto from the End of IR', 2016: 504).

IR THEORY TODAY ANALYSING CARBON DIOXIDE (CO_2) EMISSIONS

At the heart of environmental debate today is the issue of global warming caused by the emission of greenhouse gases, notably carbon dioxide (CO_2). According to the UN, greenhouse gas concentrations in the atmosphere are at their highest levels in 2 million years. The last decade (2011–2021) was the warmest on record.

The ten countries that emit the most greenhouse gases together generate 68 per cent of the global total. The 100 countries emitting the least volume of greenhouse gases collectively contribute 3 per cent of the global total (https://www.un.org/en/climatechange/what-is-climate-change).

Look at these 3 tables:

$MtCO_2$=Million tonnes of CO_2 Equivalent tCO_2=tonnes of CO_2 equivalent

TABLE 11.1 Five largest emitters of CO_2 in $MtCO_2$ 2021 (World total: 37,124 $MtCO_2$)

Country	Total Emissions in $MtCO_2$	Population
China	11,472	1.41 billion
USA	5,007	331 million
India	2,710	1.40 billion
Russian Federation	1,756	143.4 million
Japan	1,067	125.7 million

TABLE 11.2 Five largest emitters of CO_2 ranked on a tCO_2 per person basis 2021 (World Average 4.7 tCO_2/person)

Country	tCO_2 per person	Rank (out of 221 countries)
China	8.0	37
USA	15.0	12
India	1.9	137
Russia	12.0	19
Japan	8.6	30

11 GREEN PERSPECTIVES AND INTERNATIONAL RELATIONS 469

TABLE 11.3 Five largest emitters of tCO_2 per person 2021 (World Average 4.7 tCO_2/person)

Country	tCO_2 per person	Total emissions in $MtCO_2$	Population
Qatar	36	96	2.69 million
Bahrain	27	39	1.46 million
Kuwait	25	106	4.25 million
Trinidad & Tobago	24	36	1.53 million
Brunei Darussalam	24	11	445,000

All data is from the *Global Carbon Atlas*, available at: https://globalcarbonatlas.org/

QUESTIONS

Based on what you have learned in this chapter and your own research:

1. What are the key implications for the global environment that you can draw from a comparison of Tables 11.1 and 11.2. (Hint: think about the relationship between emissions and population. Think about green IPE, particularly the concept of environmental justice discussed in Section 11.4 of this chapter)

2. Looking at the 5 largest emitters of CO_2, do you think they are equally obliged to reduce their CO_2 emissions and to the same degree? If so, why? If not, why not? (Hint: think about the comparative levels of development of the five countries, the time scales of their development, and the data in Table 11.2)

3. Look at Table 11.3. How would you explain why the world's highest tCO_2 per person emissions are found in these countries? (Hint: think about where they are located)

TWISTING THE LENS

1. Considering the data in the tables and your own knowledge of the global climate crisis, do you think a liberal IR perspective points towards a viable solution to the problem of global warming. If so, why? If not, why not? (Hint: think about the track record of 'global environmental governance' and putting our faith in technological solutions)

2. Was Greta Thunberg right to tell world leaders in 2019 that they should panic?

FURTHER READING

ADDITIONAL INTRODUCTORY READING

Carson, R. (1962), *Silent Spring* (New York: Fawcett Crest).
This small book on the environmental costs of pesticides has implications that extend far beyond its main subject matter.

Corry, O. and Stevenson, H. (eds) (2017), *Global Environmental Politics: Problems, Policy and Practice* (Cambridge: Cambridge University Press).

A comprehensive collection of essays on global environmental politics written from a wide range of IR theory perspectives.

Eckersley, R. (2021), 'Green Theory' in T. Dunne, M. Kurki, and S. Smith (eds), *International Relations Theories: Discipline and Diversity*, 5th edition (Oxford: Oxford University Press).

A succinct introduction to green IR theory from a leading green IR theorist.

Malm, A. (2015), 'The Anthropocene Myth', *Jacobin Magazine* (available at www.jacobinmag.com/2015/03/anthropocene-capitalism-climate-change/)

In this brief commentary, Malm questions the value of the concept of the Anthropocene because it 'lets capitalism off the hook'.

Vogler, J. (2020), 'Environmental Issues' in J. Baylis, S. Smith, and P. Owens (eds), *The Globalization of World Politics: An Introduction to International Relations*, 8th edition (Oxford: Oxford University Press).

A succinct introduction to the key global environmental issues and the historical development of an international envirnmental agenda.

MORE IN-DEPTH READING

Burke, A. et al. (2016), 'Planet Politics: A Manifesto from the End of IR', *Millennium: Journal of International Studies*, 44(3), 499–523.

Centred around the concept of the Anthropocene, this manifesto argues that the IR discipline is essentially blind to the global ecological crisis that confronts humanity.

Chandler, D. et al. (2018), 'Anthropocene, Capitalocene and Liberal Cosmopolitan IR: A Response to Burke et al.'s 'Planet Politics', *Millennium: Journal of International Studies*, 46(2) 190–208.

A hard-hitting critical response to the Planet Politics Manifesto.

Corry, O. and Stevenson, H. (eds) (2018), *Traditions and Trends in Global Environmental Politics: International Relations and the Earth* (London: Routledge).

Brings together a range of leading green IR thinkers, representing a range of green theoretical perspectives, to consider key aspects of the global ecological crisis.

Eckersely, R. (2004), *The Green State: Rethinking Democracy and Sovereignty* (Cambridge, Mass: The MIT Press).

A seminal contribution to the 'green state' debate by Australia's leading environmental theorist.

Gaard, G. and Gruen, L. (1993), 'Ecofeminism: Toward global justice and planetary health', *Society and Nature*, 2: 1–35.

A useful and sympathetic overview of the ecofeminist perspective that emerged out of the social movements of the 1960s and 1970s

Hardin, G. (1968), 'The Tragedy of the Commons', *Science*, 162 (3859): 1243–1248.

An early, influential but also controversial contribution to debates about the impact of population growth on finite global resources.

Meadows, D. et al. (1972), *Limits to Growth: A Report for the Club of Rome's Project on the Predicament of Mankind* (London: Earth Island).

A landmark publication that used early computer modelling to predict the impact of exponential economic and population growth on the Earth's finite resources. It is the most widely published book on the global environment to date.

Newell, P. (2020), *Global Green Politics* (Cambridge: Cambridge University Press).

A comprehensive and accessible introduction to global environmental politics.

Paterson, M. (2001), *Understanding Global Environmental Politics: Domination, Accumulation, Resistance* (Houndmills, Basingstoke: Palgrave).

A seminal text that critically challenges mainstream IR theories from a green neo-Gramscian perspective which contains two case studies: the global political dynamics of the meat-centred fast-food industry and car culture.

Paterson, M. (2022), 'Green Theory', in R. Devetak and J. True (eds), *Theories of International Relations*, 6th edition (London: Bloomsbury), 224–243.

A nuanced and comprehensive introduction to green IR thinking from a leading British green theorist.

CHAPTER 12

CONCLUSION

The IR discipline has developed considerably since its formal establishment in the US, the UK and its colonies, and Europe in the aftermath of the First World War. We know that thinking about international politics long preceded the founding of IR as an academic discipline and could be found outside the Western world. Nonetheless, for the first five or six decades or so of its existence the IR discipline's theoretical range was dominated by debates among predominantly Anglo-American scholars and between various strands of realist and liberal thinking. Some suggestions of what lay outside of these narrow debates can be found if you dig more deeply into the earlier IR literature or look for some of the more marginalized and, in some cases, subsequently largely forgotten contributions. These include the work of Black US scholars in the early years of the discipline as well as scholarship in countries such as India.

Today, the IR discipline embraces a considerably wider range of theoretical positions which address a far larger range of issue areas than those covered in its foundational years. This expansion has been particularly apparent since the late 1970s and early 1980s. Since then, theoretical approaches such as various strands of Marxism, feminism (which led subsequently to the emergence of a variety of theoretical explorations of gender and IR), Critical IR Theory, constructivism, poststructuralism, postcolonialism, and green theory have become established and very significant components of the contemporary IR theoretical spectrum.

In this conclusion we will briefly recall the theoretical evolution of the IR discipline. Reflecting a key theme throughout this book, we first review the relationship between key episodes in modern international and global politics and the emergence of theoretical debates and new schools of IR thinking. Certain historical contexts or nodal points have seemingly kick-started theoretical developments and innovations within the discipline. In addition to offering a panoramic view of the discipline's evolution, this review will hopefully also serve as a revision source by helping you to recall key moments in the IR discipline's evolution. We then go on to consider some of the key broad trends in the expansion and development of IR theory. Finally, we offer some reflections on the broad future direction of the contemporary IR discipline.

12.1 IR THEORY AND HISTORY—A REVIEW

One notable feature of the evolution of contemporary IR theories is the relationship between theoretical turns or innovations and key episodes and eras in the history of international politics. This is not to say that decisive causal connections between history and theory can be easily identified. For this reason, what follows is only a broad-brush recounting of how major historical episodes or certain historical eras seem to have stimulated critical and innovative reflections on the theoretical state of play in the IR discipline. Such reflections have included:

- identifying significant gaps in our theoretical grasp of international and global politics. Are there issue areas that have been simply ignored historically or have become increasingly recognized as important dimensions of the practice of international and global politics (such as gender, culture, race, and the environment for example)?
- re-examining the utility of existing theoretical assumptions—do they adequately explain or help us understand key aspects of international or global politics considering the continually evolving nature of international and global politics?
- questioning the *epistemological, ontological,* and *methodological* assumptions underpinning dominant theoretical perspectives. What theories of knowledge lie behind them, what are their assumptions about what exists in the world and thus constitutes international political reality, and how do they think we should go about gaining knowledge of the world?
- looking beyond the IR discipline to explore theoretical developments in other fields of social and political enquiry, or the humanities more widely, and bringing them into IR to supplement or challenge existing schools of IR thought.
- re-examining the Eurocentric and racialized origins of the discipline itself and asking how this has shaped thinking about IR. Is the contemporary IR discipline sufficiently open to non-Western perspectives and voices? What might greater attention to these bring to our understanding of international and world politics?

It must be stressed that although the summary of developments in IR theory offered below is linear in historical terms, this is not to suggest that it is also a straightforward story of new theories or theoretical developments emerging to supersede previous theories. Although the increasing diversification of the IR theoretical menu is indisputable, whether this constitutes an advance or improvement in our understanding of international politics is itself a matter of interpretation and debate. In other words, that is for you, the student of international politics, to decide.

The First World War and after

As we saw in Chapter 2, the modern IR discipline was formally established in the immediate aftermath of the First World War (1914–1918), supposedly in direct response to the horrific impact and questionable necessity of that war. It is important, however, to reiterate that this was not the beginning of intellectual reflection on international politics. Indeed, even the theories of IR that dominated the early years of the discipline traced their own intellectual roots back through centuries of human history. As we discuss in Chapter 2, liberal thinking about international politics, the preeminent school of IR thinking at the birth of the modern discipline, drew upon the long tradition of liberal political thought since the seventeenth century, notably the work of the philosopher, Immanuel Kant. Chapter 3 notes that many realists claim even longer historical roots, depicting realism as reflecting 'timeless wisdom' that could be detected, as far back as the classical Greek era, as well as in the Italian states system between the twelfth and sixteenth centuries (Chapter 3).

The widespread common story of the origins of the IR discipline tells us that it was established with an explicit brief to explore the creation of an international order, along distinctly liberal lines, that would significantly mitigate the risk of world war breaking out again. Central to the liberal vision was the expansion of free trade, the spread of democracy, and the creation of international institutions—most notably a League of Nations—that would enhance international dialogue between states while also providing mechanisms for the resolution of conflict. Development of these key ideas remain central to liberal IR theory today.

That commonly told story of the liberal 'idealist' origins of the modern IR discipline has been recently subjected to robust critical review. In particular, as discussed in Chapter 9, scholars of race relations and postcolonialism depict the common story of the IR discipline's origins as highly selective. It is seen to obscure the widespread preoccupation of the IR discipline's founding figures with imperialism and the management of empire after the disruptions of world war. These concerns, critics argue, were underpinned by an implicit and sometimes very explicit concern with maintaining global white racial supremacy. However, the growing influence of realism after 1945 and the discipline's shift in focus towards the emerging Cold War seem to have contributed to a subsequent discipline-wide amnesia and the cementing in place of a sanitized story of the liberal 'idealist' origins of the discipline.

Recent scholarship challenging the common story about the IR discipline's origins reminds us that histories of intellectual development, including the brief one we are embarking on here, may become well established and widely accepted, but this is not to say they should be treated as canonical truth by IR students. They are inescapably the products of interpretation emerging out of specific political, social, and cultural contexts. As such, they are always open to critique, revision, and reassessment.

The Cold War

Just as the First World War impacted upon thinking about international politics so too did the Second World War (1939–1945). Given that it occurred little more than two decades after the war that was supposed to end all wars, it is perhaps not surprising that it damaged the plausibility of liberal aspirations to create and institutionalize a more peaceful world. After 1945, attention rapidly turned to the emerging Cold War between the two superpowers, the US and the Soviet Union. As we discuss in Chapter 3, this formed the backdrop to the emerging prominence of realism within the IR discipline. In contrast to liberalism's emphasis on the possibilities of cooperation and reform of the international system, realist scholars focused on the challenges of maintaining a fragile international order in the context of superpower rivalry and the formation of opposing coalitions of states on each side of the Cold War divide. Whereas liberalism had emphasized both the necessity and possibility of reform of the international system, the failure of the League of Nations to stop the advances of Nazi Germany in Europe or Japanese imperialism in the Far East nurtured a more pessimistic realist account of the limits to reform in an anarchical system of states.

The preoccupation with the Cold War and in particular the development of a nuclear arms race between the superpowers also led to the establishment of Strategic Studies as a key sub-disciplinary area of teaching and research. While more narrowly focused on 'bombs and bullets'—military strategy and weapons development and deployment in a nuclear age—it reflected the predominant realist orientation of the IR discipline more widely. It did not, however, go unchallenged. At the margins of the IR discipline, the emergence of peace and conflict studies and anti-militarist feminist scholarship offered countervailing theoretical viewpoints.

It would, however, be a simplification to simply depict the IR discipline as having undergone a complete shift from liberalism to realism. When concrete developments in international politics are taken into consideration—such as the foundation of the United Nations and the establishment of the Bretton Woods international financial system—it becomes evident that liberal values and principles still held considerable sway, especially in Western foreign policy circles. Indeed, by the late 1960s, liberal IR scholarship was again moving into the foreground against a backdrop of a lessening of Cold War tensions—a *détente*—in superpower relations. This was also when what became known as the English School become more visible. As we see in Chapter 4, in positing the existence of an *anarchical society of states*, in various ways the English School seemingly sat across the theoretical boundary between realism and liberalism.

Détente, the revival of liberal IR and the shift from 'East–West' to 'North–South'

The era of détente in US–USSR relations between the mid to late 1960s and the mid to late 1970s, was exemplified particularly by the onset of one of the most productive periods of negotiations around the control of the nuclear arms race. For some theorists of the time, this improvement seemingly constituted an end to the Cold War. It proved, however, to be only temporary in nature and some historians and IR scholars described the subsequent downturn in superpower relations as the 'Second Cold War'.

Nonetheless, the détente era saw two distinct developments in IR theory, emerging from two broad theoretical orientations. The first, emanating from liberal scholarship, was the claim that the principal concerns of many, if not most states increasingly revolved not around the 'high politics' of security and survival—key themes in Cold War realist scholarship—but much more around the 'low politics' of economic interaction and trade. In contrast to realism's emphasis on inter-state conflict, liberal scholars, such as Keohane and Nye, in the US, introduced the concept of *complex interdependence*.

This depicted international politics as comprised of increasingly formal and informal co-operation between a diverse range of international actors. States remained the primary actors on the world stage, but they were not alone, and their foreign policies needed to adapt to this changing and more complex international environment. The liberal political undertones of this body of scholarship were clear enough: if states responded intelligently to a changing world, and Keohane and Nye were explicitly referring to the US, then a more cooperative and productive future beckoned, in contrast to the more pessimistic assumptions of realists.

The concept of complex interdependence was criticized, however, for being based largely on the interests and concerns of Western industrialized states. Such criticism came particularly from a second parallel development in IR theory. This was centred around the issue of global inequality in all its dimensions, between states in the Global North and those located mostly in the Global South. Resistance to colonialism and the pursuit of independence by colonized states accelerated rapidly in the 1950s and 1960s. As we discuss in Chapter 5, it is around this time that Marxist and neo-Marxist scholarship became more visible within the IR discipline, much of it coming out of formerly colonized states in Latin America and elsewhere. A key early theoretical contribution was the concept of *dependency*. This presented a highly critical depiction of an exploitative relationship between the Global North and South, which was in stark contrast to the more benign liberal notions of growing interdependence.

In combination, the shift in focus towards global economic relations from both liberal and Marxist or neo-Marxist directions led to the emergence in the 1970s of the subfield of International Political Economy (IPE) which went on to develop into a significant discipline in its own right.

The Second Cold War and after

The late 1970s and early 1980s saw relations between the Superpowers decline rapidly and the return of a Cold War between them. In 1980, the liberal US president, Jimmy Carter lost his bid for re-election and handed over to the markedly more conservative and hawkish Ronald Reagan. Reagan's challenge to Carter's liberal foreign policy coincided with the emergence of a new challenge to liberal IR theory: Kenneth Waltz's neo-realism. As we discuss in Chapter 3, Waltz's reformulation of core realist assumptions into what he presented as a simpler yet more robust realist theory had a substantial impact on the IR discipline in two distinct ways:

- it induced a response from liberal scholars in the form of 'neoliberal institutionalism', which conceded ground to neorealism's emphasis on the anarchical international system as the key determinant of states' foreign policies, while retaining the view that enhancing interstate cooperation was both desirable and possible. The so-called 'neo-neo' debate between the revised versions of realism and liberalism effectively constituted the mainstream of a still very US-centric IR discipline in the 1980s and continues to form a substantial component of the disciplinary mainstream today.

- Additionally, neorealism kicked off a response from some new theoretical schools of thought, notably Critical IR Theory and, shortly after, poststructuralism. Influenced by European social and political theory, these critical theories took issue with the kind of theorizing that neorealism and neoliberalism engaged in. As we discuss in Chapters 6 and 7, they posited a radically different understanding of the purposes of IR theory and the role of the IR theorist.

The return to a full-blown Cold War between the superpowers also produced an increasingly loud critical response from the public, mostly but not only within states that were on the Western side of the Iron Curtain. One of the key issues was the ramping-up of the nuclear arms race in Europe. The early 1980s witnessed the largest peace demonstrations that the world had ever seen and the emergence of a range of transnational social movements around the overlapping issues of peace, development, and the environment. After the arrival of Mikhail Gorbachev as the USSR's Premier, superpower relations underwent rapid change. By the end of the decade, the Soviet-led Eastern Bloc had disappeared. The Cold War had ended.

In parallel with the unfolding of these dramatic changes on the global political stage, the IR discipline underwent some significant developments. It is not an exaggeration to say that there was an explosion of theoretical activity, especially outside of the liberal-realist mainstream of IR theorizing. Much of this drew upon European schools of social and political thought that hitherto had largely been ignored by the IR discipline.

As we note in Chapter 6, Critical IR Theory had already raised profound questions about the epistemological underpinnings of mainstream IR theory. This was followed rapidly by the growing influence of poststructuralism. Like Critical IR Theory, its intellectual roots lay mostly in European social and political thought, but it pressed the epistemological and ontological critique of mainstream IR even further to the extent that it was initially greeted with considerable intellectual hostility from all quarters. In Chapter 7 we explore how poststructuralist IR scholars presented themselves not as proponents of a new theoretical perspective on IR, but as advocates of a critical attitude or ethos which questioned the universalizing assumptions of other theories and emphasized the inescapable intertwining of power and knowledge. Intersecting with these theoretical currents and reflecting developments within wider public political debates was a rapidly expanding body of feminist IR scholarship. This also posed a range of critical questions about the hitherto largely unacknowledged gendered dimensions of mainstream IR theory, the subject of Chapter 10.

Thus, by the time the Berlin Wall came down in late 1989, the IR discipline had become markedly more theoretically diverse, certainly more than was the case when the wall was erected nearly three decades earlier.

The post-Cold War era

The theoretical diversification of the IR discipline continued at a pace in the post-Cold War era, especially outside of the mainstream debates. A key stimulant was the controversy surrounding the widespread claim, made notably within Western academic and policy-making circles, that the liberal West had effectively won the Cold War. This was mostly famously expressed in Frances Fukuyama's declaration that we had reached the 'end of history' (Fukuyama, 1989 and 1992). By this was meant that the Cold War had ended with the ideological victory of liberalism, even if the global spread of liberalism as a political system remained incomplete. The idea that a 'New World Order' had emerged from the ashes of Cold War rapidly became prominent in Western media, policy, and intellectual arenas. For both its advocates and critics, moreover, this new world order was decidedly liberal in character.

This was also the era when the concept of globalization was acquiring significantly greater currency. Although its precise meaning was and still is a matter of debate, it was widely taken to refer to the global spread of liberal capitalism and with it, albeit to varying degrees, Western liberal values, consumption patterns, and so on. Put differently, it was a process that some saw as heralding an increasingly homogenized world.

A key issue was whether globalization was an inevitable, perhaps unstoppable development, or an ideological construction that had, moreover, imperialist and colonialist undertones. In other words, did globalization authentically demonstrate the universal appeal of liberal values and norms, as Fukuyama and others suggested, or was it more about the consolidation of Western liberal capitalist dominance in the wake of communism's apparent failure to establish itself as an alternative?

Throughout the 1990s, there was also a series of mostly Western-led armed 'humanitarian interventions', in countries such as Afghanistan, Iraq, Somalia, the former Yugoslavia, East Timor, and Sierra Leone. Producing few unequivocally successful outcomes, these interventions generated considerable intellectual and public debate from the outset. Within the IR discipline's theoretical mainstream there was clear disagreement. Realists were generally highly sceptical about and sometimes sharply critical of interventions in the name of Western humanitarian values. This contrasted with the arguments being put by a revivified and overtly normative body of liberal IR scholarship, along with some adherents to the English School of IR theory. While sometimes critical of the specific conduct and rationales of the various post-Cold War interventions, they endeavoured nonetheless to see progressive virtue in the broad pursuit of a predominantly Western-led international reformist agenda. This was seen to sometimes necessitate the use of military force, centred around the advancement of core liberal values of democracy, human rights, and gender equality, themes we discuss in Chapters 2 and 4.

Outside of the disciplinary mainstream an increasingly prominent range of critical theoretical viewpoints saw accelerating globalization and the rise of liberal interventionist internationalism as deeply problematic in various ways. Marxist and neo-Marxist perspectives, which are examined in Chapters 5 and 6, depicted globalization and liberal interventionism as connected phenomena, consistent with a long historical process of consolidating a global liberal capitalist economic and political order. As is shown in Chapter 7, poststructuralist IR scholars robustly questioned the universalism threading through the liberal discourses of human rights and humanitarianism. From poststructuralist viewpoints, liberal globalization and interventionism provided revealing examples of how 'discourses' (dominant representations and interpretations) of international politics reflecting and reinforcing social relations of power emerge historically and are sustained. A key consequence of this is seen to be the marginalization or exclusion of alternative representations and interpretations of international and global politics and thus other possible forms of international and global social life.

This latter line of critique was developed in key respects by another emergent stream of critical IR thought: postcolonialism. Postcolonial IR scholarship highlights the legacies of colonialism and imperialism and their impact, both historically and presently, not only on the conduct of international and global politics but also the analysis of it. Chapter 9 explores how postcolonial perspectives have been central in exposing the predominantly Eurocentric orientation of much IR theorizing as well as its largely unacknowledged racialized underpinnings.

This is not to say that all the theoretical developments from the 1980s onwards were taking place outside of the mainstream of the IR discipline. The rapid expansion and diversification of critical IR theorizing is indisputable, but there were also significant developments within the mainstream as well as at the intersection of orthodox and newer schools of critical IR thought.

Within realism, for example, neoclassical realism endeavoured to reconcile neorealism with earlier classical realist thinking, as is noted in Chapter 3.

The intersection between mainstream and critical streams of IR theory can be seen in the arrival of constructivism on the IR theoretical scene in the early 1990s. As is discussed in Chapter 8, constructivists endeavour to reconcile the materialism of much mainstream IR theory with the emphasis on ideas, interpretation, and identity that were the hallmarks of some of the newer critical theorists. Whether constructivism can therefore be said to occupy a 'middle ground' between mainstream and critical IR theories is a matter of debate, not least among constructivists themselves. Similarly, scholars within the English School, once seen as a middle way between realism and liberalism, took divergent paths. Some on the 'solidarist' wing of the English School began exploring commonalities with constructivism and Critical Theory.

At the very least, such developments should remind us that the impact of theoretical shifts flows in several directions.

The twenty-first century—from 9/11 to the Anthropocene

By the beginning of the twenty-first century, the IR discipline had expanded in two interconnected ways. Theoretical diversification went hand in hand with a widening of the discipline's purview—its subject matter. The discipline had traditionally focused primarily on the political, military, and economic dimensions of relations between sovereign states, centred around a broad debate about the extent to which international politics was primarily about conflict or cooperation. Now, issues such as the rise of a host of non-state and transnational actors, new understandings of the concept of security, gender, race, the environment, class relations, the flow of refugees, and the phenomenon of globalization—especially the global spread of neoliberal economic and social policies—were attracting the attention of many IR theorists.

Additionally, the critical theories that emerged in the 1980s and 1990s had raised profound questions about what was 'out there' and deemed important to theorize about (our ontological assumptions) and how we theorize international politics (our epistemological assumptions), as well as the very purpose of theorizing. Should IR theory be primarily concerned with developing objective general *explanations* of international politics as neorealists and others argued? Or was it in the business of developing compelling *interpretations* of the complex world in which we live, so that we might better *understand* it? Should IR theory aim to offer a dispassionate account of world politics, or should it be openly normative and explore such things as the enhancement of global social justice and human emancipation, as Critical IR Theorists claim?

For some of the newer schools of critical thought, such as poststructuralism and postcolonialism, however, both sides of this debate are problematic because they both tend to adopt universalizing assumptions about either how international politics works or how the world should be. Emphasizing the complex intersections of knowledge, power, and identity, poststructuralism, postcolonialism, and gender-focused theorizing depict our knowledge claims about the world as always highly contingent, exclusionary, and incomplete. This is not to say we should give up scholarly enquiry into international or world politics, far from it. Rather, it is about recognizing the limits to what we can know, and the need to reflect on ourselves as students of IR—where we are situated, the effects our claims to know have, and the need therefore to constantly subject them to critical scrutiny.

Just as previous historical eras had confronted the IR theorist with several challenges, so too has the twenty-first century. '9/11'—the terrorist attacks on the World Trade Centre in New York in September 2001—generated considerable debate across the whole spectrum of IR theories. For mainstream theories it raised a host of questions about the kinds of threats states were facing and their implications for national foreign and security policies as well as inter-state security cooperation. The subsequent declaration of a War on Terror by the US and the US-led invasions of Afghanistan in late 2001 and Iraq in 2003 provided the backdrop to some very robust theoretical disputes which at times cut across the mainstream/critical divide. Neorealists provided some of the most robust criticisms of the war in Iraq, while some support for a hawkish Western response to the perceived threat posed by militant Islamic fundamentalists came from within liberal IR and even some Marxist and feminist circles.

In the main however, it was the newer critical IR perspectives that robustly interrogated the assumptions lying behind the War on Terror and a host of related developments. These included such things as the growth in national and international surveillance, the colonial and imperial overtones of the War on Terror, the long-term local and regional destabilizing consequences of the invasions of Afghanistan, Iraq, and, later, Libya. In various and often intersecting ways, feminist, poststructuralist, and postcolonial IR scholarship critically examined how the War on Terror served to construct and represent an enemy Other, the effects of which spread far beyond any strategic need to counter the perceived threat of terrorism. It was seen to feed into and nurture not only the rise of anti-Muslim sentiment, but also the growth of often openly xenophobic nationalisms worldwide.

This century has also seen several other developments which are being reflected in the work of many critical IR theorists today. These include growing concern about the global environmental crisis, the emergence of activism and scholarship around LGBQTI+ issues and the continuing complex legacies of colonialism, themes which we examine in Chapters 11, 10, and 9 respectively. Many of these concerns also strongly connect academic activity and public social, cultural, and political activism. Additionally, they also all have strong transnational dimensions to them. In combination they could be seen to be pushing the traditional emphasis on relations between states even further away from the centre of the IR discipline's attention.

One of the newest and perhaps boldest arguments for decentring the state within theorizing world politics has emerged around the concept of *the Anthropocene*. As we note in Chapter 11, some scholars writing from green IR perspectives claim that the Anthropocene constitutes a profound challenge to very idea of international politics. They argue that our primary ontological categories should no longer be states, the system of states, or the myriad communities that make up humanity, but planet Earth itself.

Is the IR discipline going 'critical'?

It is tempting to simply answer, 'Yes'. The twenty-first century has undoubtedly seen considerable growth in both the variety and influence of critical theoretical IR perspectives to the extent that the idea of, or indeed the desirability of a predominantly state-centric, clearly demarcated discipline of IR has increasingly come under challenge. However, going against the grain of theoretically decentring the state or *international politics* more generally are a host of factors that in combination serve to remind us that the world is still divided, both territorially and in human terms. After all, many of the newer critical theories endeavour to show how in complex ways the state and the exercise of sovereign power impacts upon the everyday lives of peoples and communities. The boundaries of states—their borders—continue to play a crucial role in the control and management of the flow of people and ideas across the globe. The recent rise of highly exclusionary, sometimes xenophobic forms of nationalism around the world suggests also that significant numbers of people worldwide are resistant to the erosion of the state and national borders.

Through more orthodox IR lenses, today's sovereign states continue to behave in predictable ways; great power rivalries remain a prominent feature of international politics, as does violent conflict, both within states and between them. Most states continue to maintain powerful national defence systems and most engage, individually or collectively, in trade competition and disputes. Fewer nuclear weapons may be deployed today than during the height of the Cold War, but these are still sufficient to threaten the future of humanity or the planet on which it resides. The environmental crisis reminds us that developing meaningful and effective international cooperation remains an uphill struggle against the forces of selfish national interest and the pursuit of financial profit. Not surprisingly then, mainstream IR theories still focus primarily on cooperation and conflict between sovereign states. They continue also to figure large in academic research and teaching and their influence can still be seen in foreign ministries worldwide. Whether this is a good or bad thing is, again, for you to decide.

12.2 SUMMARIZING BROAD THEORETICAL TRENDS OVER THE LIFE OF THE IR DISCIPLINE

Having roughly mapped the development of IR theory historically, we now consider what might be the key trends in the development of IR theorizing since the discipline was first established. This is only a suggestive listing; other IR scholars or readers of this text may identify other broad directions of theoretical travel.

From simplicity to complexity

It is perhaps inevitable that the growth in the variety of theoretical starting points and the accompanying expansion of the IR discipline's purview would make studying international and global politics seemingly more complex today than in the past. This raises an interesting question: has international politics itself become more complex or has theoretical diversification served to expose hitherto unrecognized or unacknowledged complexities? As we note in Chapter 3, for some IR theorists, most famously the neorealist Kenneth Waltz, keeping theories 'parsimonious' (i.e., simple) and focused on a few important things was a virtue. For many other theorists, keeping it simple comes at the price of leaving a lot out, which risks excluding what may be important explanatory factors or insights to enhance our understanding. This leads on to the question of how the criteria for deciding what to include or exclude are to be determined. The answer to that question depends of course on your theoretical starting point.

Additionally, we must ask what does our theorizing hope to achieve: a general theory of international politics (which was arguably Waltz's goal) or, given the perceived complexity of international politics, something altogether less ambitious? At the risk of over-generalization, mainstream theories, along with some varieties of Marxism, tend to aim towards explaining international politics (or, in the case of Marxism, international political economy) as a whole. Arguably, this pushes the theorist towards focusing on what they believe really matters about international politics generally and across historical time. The more recent critical theories tend, however, to disavow general or 'grand' theorizing (metanarratives), preferring to offer much more contingent accounts of what they see as key aspects or dimensions of world politics.

Of course, exceptions to these rules of thumb can be found across the whole range of theories. Some mainstream theorizing can be very nuanced and aware of its limitations, whereas some critical theories can be read as implying some underlying general assumptions, perhaps more so than some of their advocates are willing to concede.

From explanation to understanding

At various points throughout this book, we have noted disputes about the *epistemological* assumptions of theory. In Chapter 6, we examine how Critical IR Theory takes issue with mainstream theories over the very purpose of theory. Critical IR Theory emphasizes the social dimensions of IR. It challenges the idea that the IR theorist, as a social being, can stand outside the world they are attempting to theorize because they are inescapably a part of that world. Mainstream IR theories are depicted as overly preoccupied with providing definitive and objective explanations of international politics that accord as much as possible with a scientific model of theory. In so doing, Critical IR theory argues, they obscure the specific human interests that lie behind the gloss of a scientistic objectivity. In contrast, Critical IR Theory posits the idea that our knowledge of the world should be aimed at developing a shared understanding of our world in order, ultimately, to improve it. Subsequent chapters went on to show how other critical theories have developed this alternative understanding of the purpose of theory much further, challenging not only mainstream IR theory, but also Critical IR Theory because it is seen to presume there was or could be a universally agreed understanding of how the world should be.

Most mainstream IR theorists are more cautious these days about depicting their theories as offering thoroughly objective or scientific-like explanations that constitute truth-claims. Nonetheless, the mainstream view of critical IR theories is that they are too subjective and normative, or not really theory at all. To complicate things, some critical theorists—such as poststructuralists, postcolonial theorists, and some gender theorists—also reject overtly normative theorizing, albeit for rather different reasons. They agree that IR theory cannot stand outside of the world it is attempting to theorize, but they also do not wish to privilege a particular set of universal values or ways of being. Rather they are more focused on showing how orthodox IR theories (and some critical theories), overtly or covertly, espouse or reinforce dominant value systems, relations of power, and social orders, which marginalize other theoretical voices invoking alternative understandings of social life.

Decentring the state and the international system of states

One of the most visible features of much mainstream IR theory is that it is *state-centric*. As the discipline's name reminds us, states and relations between them have always been the central focus of most orthodox IR theorizing. Realism and neorealism's emphasis on the anarchical structure of the international system—the absence of any authority above the state—necessarily places the state at centre stage. In various ways, the bulk of liberal IR thinking has endeavoured to modify or moderate the discipline's state-centrism. This is shown in its emphasis on such things as the virtues of greater cooperation between states, the development of a more institutionalized international system to mitigate the risks of conflict, the virtues of the global spread of democracy, the need to bring non-state actors into the theoretical mix, and, of course, the importance of individual human rights. Underpinning these theoretical commitments, if not always very visible, is the classical liberal emphasis on individual freedom within a single universal human community (even if, its critics argue, much early liberal thought implicitly or explicitly effectively confined that community to the white race). Although liberal individualism seems to invoke the idea of a universal world community, most liberal and neoliberal IR theory nonetheless takes the international system as a given and, thus, remains essentially state centric.

Most critical theories are to varying degrees hostile to the state-centrism of mainstream IR. This is not to say they deny the importance of the state, but they critique the state's central place in IR thinking for a variety of reasons. For Marxists and neo-Marxists, state-centrism masks the role of a global capitalist system. It is this, they argue, that determines much of the behaviour of states, depending upon where they are positioned in the global pecking order. Critical IR Theorists depict the state as an inherently exclusionary institution that not only reflects the interests of the dominant class (reflecting Critical IR Theory's roots in Marxism) but from a global point of view also serves to divide peoples, variously defined, from each other. Like liberalism, Critical IR Theory is cosmopolitan in outlook: it sees all humans as members of a universal community with a shared interest in advancing human emancipation, although its cosmopolitanism has become more sensitive to differences between people in recent years. Feminist and gender-focused perspectives endeavour to expose the gendered dimensions of state conduct while highlighting the transnational dimensions of the politics of gender.

Poststructuralists depict the state's primacy as constructed and sustained (or 'performed') through language to the exclusion of other possible forms of community. They interrogate the effects of the dominance of the discourse of sovereignty, which constructs IR around a fundamental binary distinction between inside and outside of the state. This binary also ties human identity very closely to the state, thereby marginalizing or excluding other representations of human identity which transgress national boundaries.

Postcolonialism also looks beyond contemporary relations between states to emphasize the impact of the history and legacy of European colonialism in the creation of today's postcolonial world. It endeavours to show how the legacies of imperialism and colonialism continue to frame the behaviour of states and the social relations between them as well as within them.

For many green IR theorists, the selfish conduct of states is a principal barrier to international cooperation to address the global environmental crisis. As the slogan 'think locally and act globally' suggests, green IR theory looks both beyond and below the state to explore more ecocentric forms of human community. While some green IR theorists argue for the development of the green state willing to compromise its sovereignty to protect the planetary ecosphere, other green IR theorists argue that the state-centrism of IR needs to be abandoned entirely and urgently in favour of a perspective that privileges the interests of the planet as a whole.

The growing recognition of the coloniality of the IR discipline

A long overdue and still developing theme in much critical IR thinking is the need to reflect critically on the IR discipline's intellectual Eurocentrism and the significance of race in both its origins and subsequent development. Chapter 9 shows how several scholars offer a different story of the IR discipline's origins by exposing the influence of imperial and colonial attitudes at the time of its establishment. The liberal sentiments that are widely assumed to have driven the founding of the discipline are revealed as having had racialized underpinnings. However, within many, perhaps most schools of IR theory there still is only a limited acknowledgement of this alternative account. Thus, some post-colonial theorists accuse the discipline of effectively 'whitewashing' its story of origin.

The bulk of contemporary IR theory across most of the theoretical range is still produced in the Global North, and especially from within the English-speaking world, including this textbook it must be said. Not surprisingly then, this is where most of the discipline's best-known theorists, be they mainstream or critical, come from. Many of the comparatively few who do not nonetheless hold positions in universities within the Global North. For critics, this raises the question of whether the discipline is truly benefiting from the range of actual and possible conceptual and theoretical viewpoints that the world has to offer. For postcolonial theorists and a growing number of scholars from other streams of IR theory, the answer remains, 'No', leading some to ask if the contemporary IR discipline remains quintessentially 'White'.

Things are changing. New academic IR journals are providing publishing outlets for once marginalized or simply ignored non-Western theoretical perspectives. Some Western IR scholars do now engage in critical reflections on the racialized underpinnings and Eurocentrism of their own theoretical assumptions and those of their peers. Albeit to varying degrees, some universities in the Global North are also endeavouring to diversify their academic staff and offer students access to a wider range of non-Western, non-Eurocentric intellectual voices and perspectives. Additionally, there is a growing push, in many cases driven by student demand, to decolonize teaching curricula across the range of university scholarly disciplines. The question is, of course, whether these changes are going to be sufficient or sufficiently fast. Whatever your answer to that question is, it seems reasonable to suggest that, given its global subject matter, the IR discipline needs to be at the heart of that necessary and perhaps inescapable journey.

12.3 CONCLUDING THOUGHTS: DISCIPLINE, INTERDISCIPLINE, OR ANTI-DISCIPLINE?

If we look across the history of the IR discipline it could read as suggesting different conceptions of the possible future trajectory of the IR discipline. As a final encouragement, or perhaps a provocation for further critical reflection, it is proposed that these can be captured by a suggestive trilogy: discipline, interdiscipline, and anti-discipline.

Discipline

One conception is that the study of the theory and practice of international politics still properly belongs within a distinctive academic discipline that has clear intellectual and empirical boundaries. On this view, IR has a unique subject matter that requires its own distinctive theoretical tools. This is a view that can be found in much of the mainstream of IR theory, most notably realism and neorealism. This is not to say that advocates of a distinctive IR discipline do not draw from closely related disciplines such as history—they have long done so—but their primary aim is to enhance the IR discipline as a still distinctive field of enquiry.

Interdiscipline

A second conception sees the study of IR as increasingly a multi-disciplinary or even interdisciplinary activity. Multi-disciplinarity sees intellectual virtue in looking at something from different disciplinary viewpoints. Interdisciplinarity pursues the acquisition of new forms of knowledge and understanding through the interaction and synthesizing of ideas from diverse disciplinary sources. Knowledge that emerges at the interstices of multiple disciplines but has not developed or, in the view of some, should not develop into some new clearly bounded discipline can be captured by a recently arrived conceptual term: interdiscipline.

Arguably, these views have become increasingly prominent over the last few decades, notably within the new critical approaches. It is especially apparent within the many sub-disciplinary areas of teaching and research within the broad IR field that have sprung up over the years, such as critical security studies, gender and IR, peace and conflict studies, migration studies, Green IR theory, and so on.

Certainly, the boundaries between IR and a range of other branches of the social sciences such as geography, politics, sociology, history, anthropology, and so on, while never completely rigid, have become ever more blurred over the last few decades. Indeed, the intellectual conversations between IR and other fields of enquiry now extend well beyond the confines of the social sciences, to embrace much of the humanities as well. Arguably this flow of ideas and debates across traditional intellectual boundaries tells us something important about the complexity of the world in which we now live.

Anti-discipline

Finally, within some strands of IR theory can be found arguments which suggest that the idea of a distinct IR discipline has reached its sell by date, which raises the question of whether it should simply be dissolved. From a poststructuralist perspective for example, it could be argued that a distinct IR discipline is inherently problematic because it disciplines thought itself. It sets boundaries around what should be legitimately part of the discipline's subject matter and around how we should think about it. Postcolonial perspectives suggest that such boundaries reflect deeply embedded and insufficiently acknowledged racialized assumptions about what matters in international and global politics today. Gender-focused theoretical viewpoints raised further questions about what constrains or shapes theoretical enquiry into contemporary world politics. And from within green IR theorizing have emerged arguments that the arrival of the Anthropocene renders the very idea of an IR discipline redundant in the face of a planetary ecological crisis.

Of course, all the boundaries between these three conceptions of the IR discipline are fuzzy at best and they all could continue to coexist for some time to come. If so, then it is to be hoped that through their critical and creative interaction our understanding of world politics will be further deepened and enriched.

BIBLIOGRAPHY

Abrams, E. (2022), 'The New Cold War', *National Review Magazine*, 21 March, available at: https://www.nationalreview.com/magazine/2022/03/21/the-new-cold-war/. Accessed 13 March 2023.

Achilleos-Sarll, C. (2018), 'Reconceptualising Foreign Policy as Gendered, Sexualised and Racialised: Towards a Postcolonial Feminist Foreign Policy (Analysis)', *Journal of International Women's Studies*, 19/1, 34–4.

Adamson, J., Evans, M., and Stein, R. (eds) (2002), *The Environmental Justice Reader: Politics, Poetics & Pedagogy* (Tucson, AZ: University of Arizona Press).

Adler, E. (1997), 'Seizing the Middle Ground: Constructivism in World Politics', *European Journal of International Relations*, 3/3: 319–63.

Aggestam, K. and Bergman-Rosamund, A. (2019), 'Feminist Foreign Policy 3.0: Advancing Ethics and Gender Equality in Global Politics', *SAIS Review of International Affairs*, 39/1:37–48.

Aggestam, K, Bergman-Rosamond, A., and Kronsell, A. (2019). 'Theorising Feminist Foreign Policy'. *International Relations* 33/1: 23–39.

Alemazung, J. A. (2010), 'Post-Colonial Colonialism: An Analysis of International Factors and Actors Marring African Socio-Economic and Political Development', *The Journal of Pan-African Studies*, 3/10: 62–84.

Allais, L. (2016), 'Kant's Racism', *Philosophical Papers*, 45/1–2:1–36.

Allen, A. (2012), 'The Unforced Force of the Better Argument: Reason and Power in Habermas' Political Theory', *Constellations*, 19/3: 353–368.

Allen, T.W. (2021), *The Invention of the White Race: The Origin of Racial Oppression*, introduction by J.B. Perry (London: Verso).

Allison, G. T. (1971), *Essence of Decision: Explaining the Cuban Missile Crisis* (Boston, MA: Little, Brown and Company).

Alsultany, E. (2012), 'Arabs and Muslims in the Media after 9/11: Representational Strategies for a "Postrace" Era', *American Quarterly*, 65/1: 161–169.

Anagol, P. (2006), *The Emergence of Feminism in India 1850–1920* (Aldershot: Ashgate).

Anand, A. (2015), *Sophia: Princess, Suffragette, Revolutionary* (London: Bloomsbury).

Anghie, A. (2005), *Imperialism, Sovereignty, and the Making of International Law* (NewYork: Cambridge University Press).

Annan, K. (1999), 'Secretary General Presents His Annual Report to General Assembly', UN Press release SG/SM/7136 GA/9596 (New York: United Nations).

Appadurai, A. (1996), *Modernity at Large: Cultural Dimensions of Globalization* (Minneapolis, MN: University of Minnesota Press).

Applebaum, A. (2022), 'Germany is Arguing with Itself Over Ukraine', *The Atlantic*, 20 October. Available at: https://www.theatlantic.com/ideas/archive/2022/10/germany-military-aid-ukraine-tanks-debate/671804/. Accessed 12 March 2023.

Archibugi, D. and Held, D. (eds) (1995), *Cosmopolitan Democracy: An Agenda for a New World Order* (Cambridge: Polity Press).

Ashley, R. K. (1981), 'Political Realism and Human Interests', *International Studies Quarterly*, 25/2: 204–236.

Ashworth, L. M. (2006), 'Where Are the Idealists in Interwar International Relations?', *Review of International Studies*, 32: 291–308.

Ashworth, L.M. (2021), 'Women of the Twenty years Crisis: The Women's International League for Peace and Freedom and the Problem of Collective Security" in P. Owens and K. Rietzler (eds), *Women's International Thought: A New History* (Cambridge: Cambridge University Press).

Aslan, Ö. and Gambetti, Z. (2009), 'Provincializing Fraser's History: Feminism and Neoliberalism Revisited', *History of the Present*, 1(1), 130–147.

Ayoob, M. (2002), 'Inequality and Theorising in International Relations: The Case for Subaltern Realism', *International Studies Review*, 4/3: 27–48.

Bardi U. and Pereira, C. A. (eds) (2022), *Limits and Beyond: 50 Years on from the Limits to Growth, What Did We Learn and What's Next? A Report to the Club of Rome* (Exapt Press).

Barkawi, T. (2006), 'Culture and Combat in the Colonies: The Indian Army in the Second World War', *Journal of Contemporary History*, 41/2: 325–355.

Barkawi, T. and Laffey, M. (1999), 'The Imperial Peace: Democracy, Force and Globalization',

European Journal of International Relations, 5/4: 403–434.

Barkawi, T. and Laffey, M. (2006), 'The Postcolonial Moment in Security Studies', *Review of International Studies*, 32/2: 329–352.

Barry, J. and Eckersley, R. (eds) (2005), *The State and the Global Ecological Crisis* (Cambridge, MA: MIT Press).

Baudrillard, J. (1994), *Simulacra and Simulation*, translated by Sheila Faria Glaser (Ann Arbour, MI: The University of Michigan Press).

Baudrillard, J. (1995), *The Gulf War Did Not Take Place* (Bloomington, IL: Indiana University Press).

Baxi, U. (2007), *The Future of Human Rights*, 3rd edition (Delhi: OUP India).

Beauvoir, S. de (2011), *The Second Sex*, translated by C. Borde and S. Malovany-Chevalier (New York: Vintage Books).

Bellamy, A. J. (ed) (2005), *International Society and Its Critics* (Oxford: Oxford University Press).

Bellamy, A. J. (2019), *World Peace (and How We Can Achieve It)* (Oxford: Oxford University Press).

Bellamy, A. and Wheeler, N. J. (2020), 'Humanitarian Intervention in World Politics' in J. Baylis, S. Smith, and P. Owens, (eds) (2020), *The Globalization of World Politics*, 8th edn (Oxford: Oxford University Press), 514–529.

Bedford, K. and Rai, S.M. (2013), 'Feminists Theorise International Political Economy', *Signs*, 36/1: 1–18.

Bennett, L., Jr (1993), *The Shaping of Black America: The Struggles and Triumphs of African-Americans 1619 to the 1990s*, revised edn (New York: Penguin Books).

Bergman-Rosamond (2020a), 'Swedish Feminist Foreign Policy and "Gender Cosmopolitanism"', *Foreign Policy Analysis*, 16: 217–235.

Bergman-Rosamund, A. (2020b), 'Music, Mining and Colonisation: Sámi Contestations of Sweden's Self-Narrative', *Politik*, 23/1: 70–86.

Berki, R.N. (1971), 'On Marxian Thought and the Problem of International Relations', *World Politics*, 24/1: 80–105.

Bernstein, R. J. (1976), *The Restructuring of Social and Political Theory* (Oxford: Basil Blackwell).

Bhabha, H. K. (1994), *The Location of Culture*, (London: Routledge).

Bhambra, G. K. (2007), *Rethinking Modernity: Postcolonialism and the Sociological Imagination* (Basingstoke: Palgrave Macmillan).

Bhambra, G. K. (2011a), 'Talking among Themselves? Weberian and Marxist Historical Sociologies as Dialogues without "Others"', *Millennium: Journal of International Studies*, 39/3: 667–681.

Bhambra, G. K. (2011b), 'Historical Sociology, Modernity, and Postcolonial Critique', *The American Historical Review*, 116/3: 653–662.

Bhambra, G. K. (2017), 'Brexit, Trump and "Methodological Whiteness": On the Misrecognition of Race and Class', *The British Journal of Sociology*, 68/S1: S214–S232.

Bhambra, G. K. (2021), 'Colonial Global Economy: Towards a Theoretical Reorientation of Political Economy', *Review of International Political Economy*, 28/2: 307–322.

Biswas, S. (2007), 'Empire and Global Public Intellectuals: Reading Edward Said as an International Relations Theorist', *Millennium: Journal of International Studies*, 36(1): 117–133.

Biswas, S. (2014), *Nuclear Desire: Power and the Postcolonial Nuclear Order* (Minneapolis, MN: University of Minnesota Press).

Biswas, S. (2021), 'Postcolonialism' in T. Dunne, M. Kurki, and S. Smith (eds), *International Relations Theories: Discipline and Diversity*, 5th edn (Oxford: Oxford University Press), 220–236.

Blanchard, E. M. (2011), 'Why Is There No Gender in the English School?', *Review of International Studies*, 37/2: 855–879.

Blaney, D. L. and Tickner, A.B (2017), 'Worlding, Ontological Politics and the Possibility of a Decolonial IR', *Millennium: Journal of International Studies*, 45/3: 293–311.

Blatt, J. (2018), *Race and the Making of American Political Science* (Philadelphia: University of Pennsylvania Press).

Blaut, J. M. (1993), *The Colonizer's Model of the World: Geographical Diffusionism and Eurocentric History* (New York: The Guilford Press).

Bleiker, R. (2004), 'Order and Disorder in World Politics', in A. J. Bellamy (ed.), *International Society and Its Critics*, (Oxford: Oxford University Press), 179–194.

Bleiker, R. (2018), *Visual Global Politics* (London: Routledge).

Bonilla-Silva, E. (2021), *Racism without Racists: Color-Blind Racism and the Persistence of Racial Inequality in America*, 6th edition (Lanham, MD: Rowman and Littlefield).

Bonnet, S. (2015), 'Overcoming Eurocentrism in Human Rights: Postcolonial Critiques—Islamic Answers?', *Muslim World Journal of Human Rights*, 12/1: 1–24.

Booth, K. (1991), 'Security and Emancipation', *Review of International Studies*, 17/4: 313–326.

Boserup, E. (1970), *Women's Role in Economic Development* (New York: St Martin's Press).

Bourke, J. (1996), *Dismembering the Male: Men's Bodies, Britain, and the Great War* (London: Reaktion Books).

Breuer, C. (2022), 'The New Cold War and the Return of History', Editorial, *Intereconomics: Review of European Economic Policy*, 57: 202–203.

Brincat, S., Lima, L., and Nunes, J. (2012), 'For Someone and for Some Purpose: an interview with Robert W. Cox' in S. Brincat, L. Lima, and J. Nunes, *Critical Theory in International Relations and Security Studies: Interviews and Reflections* (Abingdon: Routledge).

Brown, K. E. (2018), 'Violence and Gender Politics in the Proto-State "Islamic State"', in S. Parashar, J. A. Tickner, and J. True (eds) (2018) *Revisiting Gendered States: Feminist Imaginings of the State in International Relations* (Oxford: Oxford University Press).

Browne, K. and Nash, C.J. (eds) (2010), *Queer Methods and Methodologies: Intersecting Queer Theories and Social Science Research* (Abingdon: Routledge).

Bryson. V. (2016), *Feminist Political Theory*, 3rd edn (London: Palgrave).

Budgeon, S. (2011), *Third-Wave Feminism and the Politics of Gender in Late Modernity* (Basingstoke: Palgrave Macmillan).

Bull, H. (1966), 'Society and Anarchy in International Relations' in H. Butterfield and M. Wight (eds), *Diplomatic Investigations* (London: George Allen & Unwin), 35–60.

Bull, H. (1976), 'Martin Wight and the Theory of International Relations: The Second Martin Wight Memorial Lecture', *British Journal of International Studies*, 2/2: 101–116.

Bull, H. (1977), *The Anarchical Society: A Study of Order in World Politics* (London: Macmillan).

Bull, H. (2000), 'Justice in International Relations: The 1983 Hagey Lectures' in K. Alderson and A. Hurrell (eds), *Hedley Bull on International Society* (Basingstoke: Macmillan Press), 206–245.

Bull, H. and Watson A. (eds) (1984), The *Expansion of International Society* (Oxford: Oxford University Press).

Bulley, D. (2009), *Ethics as Foreign Policy: Britain, the EU and the Other* (London: Routledge).

Burke, A., Fishel, S., Mitchell, A., Dalby, S., and Levine, D. (2016), 'Planet Politics: A Manifesto for the End of IR', *Millennium: Journal of International Studies*, 44/3: 499–523.

Burke, E. (2000), *Reflections on the Revolution in France* (Kitchener, ONT: Batoche Books).

Burman, S. (2007), *The State of the American Empire: How the USA Shapes the World* (Abingdon: Earthscan/Routledge).

Burton, J. (1972), *World Society* (Cambridge: Cambridge University Press).

Butler, J. (2007), *Gender Trouble: Feminism and the Subversion of Identity*, with an introduction by the author (Abingdon: Routledge Classics).

Buzan, B. (1983), *People, States, and Fear: The National Security Problem in International Relations* (Brighton: Wheatsheaf Books).

Buzan, B. (2002), Special Book Review: Review of James Mayall, *World Politics: Progress and its Limits* (Cambridge: Polity Press), 2000 and Robert Jackson (2000), *The Global Covenant: Human Conduct in a World of States* (Oxford: Oxford University Press), 2000, in 'Special Book Reviews', *Millennium: Review of International Studies*, 31/2: 363–366.

Buzan, B. (2004), *From International to World Society* (Cambridge: Cambridge University Press).

Buzan, B. (2014), *An Introduction to the English School of International Relations* (Cambridge: Polity Press).

Buzan, B. and Gonzalez-Pelaez, A. (2009), *International Society and the Middle East: English School Theory at the Regional Level* (Basingstoke: Palgrave).

Cafruny, A., Talani, L.S., and Martin, G. P. (eds) (2016), *The Palgrave Handbook of Critical International Political Economy* (London: Palgrave Macmillan).

Campbell, D. (1992), *Writing Security: United States Foreign Policy and the Politics of Identity* (Manchester: Manchester University Press).

Campbell, D. (2005), 'The Biopolitics of Security: Oil, Empire and the Sports Utility Vehicle', *American Quarterly*, 57/3: 943–972.

Campbell, D. (2008), 'Why Fight: Humanitarianism, Principles and Post-Structuralism', *Millennium: Journal of International Studies*, 27/3: 497–521.

Campbell, D. and Bleiker, R. (2021), 'Poststructuralism', in T. Dunne, M. Kurki, and S. Smith, *International Relations Theories: Discipline and Diversity*, 5th edn (Oxford: Oxford University Press), 197–219.

Cammack, P. (2009), 'Poverty Reduction and Universal Competitiveness', *Labour, Capital and Society*, 42/1 and 2: 32–54.

Cammack, P. (2019), 'Why Are Some People Better Off Than Others?', in J. Edkins and M. Zehfuss (eds), *Global Politics: A New Introduction*, 3rd edn (Abingdon, Oxon: Routledge), 386–407.

Cammack, P. (2022), *The Politics of Global Competitiveness* (Oxford: Oxford University Press).

Caprioli, M. (2000), 'Gendered Conflict', *Journal of Peace Research*, 37/1: 51–68.

Caprioli, M. and Boyer, M. A. (2001), 'Gender, Violence and International Crisis', *The Journal of Conflict Resolution*, 45(4): 503–518.

Caputo, J. D. (1997), *The Prayers and Tears of Jacques Derrida: Religion without Religion* (Bloomington, IN: Indiana University Press).

Carr, E. H. (2016), *The Twenty Years Crisis, 1919–1939*, reissued with a new preface by Michael Cox (London: Palgrave Macmillan).

Carroll, B. A. (1972), 'Peace Research: The Cult of Power', *Journal of Conflict Resolution*, 16/4: 585–616.

Carson, R. (1962), *Silent Spring*, Introduction by Lord Shackleton, Preface by Julian Huxley (Harmondsworth: Penguin Books).

Carter, A. (1996), 'Should Women be Soldiers or Pacifists?', *Peace Review*, 8/3: 331–335.

Carter, N. (2001), *The Politics of the Environment: Ideas, Activism, Policy* (Cambridge: Cambridge University Press).

Carver, T. (2014), 'Men and Masculinities in International Relations Research', *The Brown Journal of World Affairs*, 21/1: 113–126.

Casimir, J. (2020), *The Haitians: A Decolonial History*, Translated by L. Dubois, with a foreword by W.D. Mignolo (Chapel Hill, NC: The University of North Carolina Press).

Caso, F. (2020), 'Are We at War? The Rhetoric of War in the Coronavirus Pandemic', *The Disorder of Things*, 10 April. Available at thedisorderofthings.com/2020/04/10/are-we-at-war-the-rhetoric-of-war-in-the-coronavirus-pandemic/#more-17670.

Caso, F. and Hamilton C. (eds) (2015), *Popular Culture and World Politics: Theories, Methods, Pedagogies* (Bristol: E-International Relations).

Chakrabarty, D. (2017), 'The Politics of Climate Change is More than the Politics of Capitalism', *Theory, Culture and Society*, 34/2–3: 25–37.

Chakrabarty, D. (2000), *Provincializing Europe: Postcolonial Thought and Historical Difference* (Princeton, NJ: Princeton University Press).

Chalmers, A. F. (2013), *What is This Thing Called Science?*, 4th edn (Maidenhead, Berks: Open University Press).

Chamberlain, P. (2017), *The Feminist Fourth Wave: Affective Temporality* (Cham: Palgrave Macmillan).

Chancel, L. (2020), *Unsustainable Inequalities: Social Justice and the Environment* (Cambridge, MA: Harvard University Press).

Chandler, D., Cudworth, E., and Hobden, S. (2018), 'Anthropocence, Capitalocene and Liberal Cosmopolitan IR: A Response to Burke et al's "Planet Politics"', *Millennium: Journal of International Studies*, 46/2: 190–208.

Chaudhuri, M. (ed.) (2005), *Feminism in India* (London: Zed Books).

Chaudhuri, M. (2012), 'Feminism in India: The Tale and its Telling', *Revue Tiers Monde*, 209: 19–36.

Checkel, J. T. (1998), 'The Constructivist Turn in International Relations Theory', *World Politics*, 50: 324–48.

Chimni, B. S. (2006), 'Third World Approaches to International Law: A Manifesto', *International Community Law Review*, 8: 3–27.

Chin, C. B. N. (1998), *In Service and Servitude: Foreign Female Domestic Workers and the Malaysian Modernity Project* (New York: Columbia University Press).

Chinkin, C. and Charlesworth, H. (2006), 'Building Women into Peace: The International Legal Framework', *Third World Quarterly*, 27/5: 937–957.

Choli, M. and Kuss, D.J. (2021), 'Perceptions of Blame on Social Media During the Coronavirus Pandemic', *Computers in Human Behaviour*, 124: 106895. Available at: https://www.sciencedirect.com/science/article/pii/S0747563221002181?via%3Dihub.

Chowdhry, G. and Nair, S. (2002), 'Introduction: Power in a Postcolonial World: Race, Gender, and Class in International Relations' in Chowdhry, G. and Nair, S. (eds), *Power, Postcolonialism, and International Relations: Reading Race, Gender, and Class* (New York: Routledge).

Clapp, J. and Dauvergne, P. (2011), *Paths to a Green World: The Political Economy of the Global Environment*, 2nd edition, (Cambridge, MA: MIT Press).

Cochrane, K. (2013), *All the Rebel Women: The Rise of the Fourth Wave of Feminism* (London: Guardianshorts ebook).

Coglan, J. (2017), 'Gender Bias in International Relations Graduate Education? New Evidence from Syllabi', *PS: Political Science and Politics*, 50/2: 456–460.

Cohn, C. (1987), 'Sex and Death in the Rational World of Defense Intellectuals', *Signs*, 12/4: 687–718.

Cohn, C. and Enloe, C. (2003), 'A Conversation with Cynthia Enloe: Feminist Look at Masculinity and the Men who Wage War', *Signs*, 28/4: 1187–1107.

Cohn, C., Kinsella, H., and Gibbings, S. (2004), 'Women, Peace and Security Resolution 1325', *International Feminist Politics*, 6/1: 130–140.

Confortini, (2010), 'Feminist Contributions and Challenges to Peace Studies', *Oxford Research Encyclopedia: International Studies*, 29 pp. Available at: https://doi.org/10.1093/acrefore/9780190846626.013.47. Accessed 20 April 2023.

Connell, R. W. (1987), *Gender and Power: Society, the Person, and Sexual Politics* (Cambridge: Polity Press).

Connell, R. (2008), 'Preface' in J.L. Parpart and M. Zalewski (eds), *Rethinking the Man Question: Sex, Gender and Violence in International Relations* (London: Zed Books), viii–xiv.

Connelly, J. and Smith G. (2003), *Politics and the Environment: From Theory to Practice* (London: Routledge).

Connelly, M. P., Li, T. M., MacDonald, M., and Parpart, J. L. (2000), 'Feminism and Development: Theoretical Perspectives' in J. Parpart, M. P. Connelly, and V. E. Barriteau (eds), *Theoretical Perspectives on Gender and Development* (Ottawa: IDRC).

Corry, O. (2020), 'Nature and the International: Towards a Materialist Understanding of Societal Multiplicity', *Globalizations*, 17/3: 419–435.

Cox, R. W. (1981), 'Social Forces, States and World Orders: Beyond International Relations Theory', *Millennium: Journal of International Studies*, 10/2: 126–155.

Cox, R. W. (1999), 'Civil Society at the Turn of the Millennium: Prospects for an Alternative World Order', *Review of International Studies*, 25: 3–28.

Cox, R. W. (2002), The *Political Economy of a Plural World: Critical Reflections on Power, Morals and Civilization*, with M.G. Schechter (Abingdon, Oxon: Routledge).

Crenshaw, K. (1989), 'Demarginalizing the Intersection of Race and Sex: A Black Feminist Critique of Antidiscrimination Doctrine, Feminist Theory and Antiracist Politics', *University of Chicago Legal Forum*, Iss.1, Article 8: 139–167.

Crosby, A. (2021), 'The Racialized Logics of Settler Colonial Policing: Indigenous "Communities of Concern" and Critical Infrastructure in Canada', *Settler Colonial Studies*, 11/4: 411–430.

Cudd A. E. and Holmstrom N. (2011), *Capitalism, For and Against: A Feminist Debate* (Cambridge: Cambridge University Press).

Dalby, S. (1998) 'Ecological Metaphors of Security: World Politics in the Biosphere', *Alternatives*, 23/3: 291–319.

Dalby, S. (2002), *Environmental Security* (Minneapolis, MN: University of Minnesota Press).

Darby, P. and Paolini, A. J. (1994), 'Bridging International Relations and Postcolonialism', *Alternatives*, 19: 371–397.

Darden, J. T. (2015), 'Assessing the Significance of Women in Combat Roles', *International Journal*, 70/3: 454–462.

Davenport, A. (2011), 'Marxism in IR: Condemned to a Realist Fate?', *European Journal of International Relations*, 19/1: 27–48.

Davis, A. E., Thakur, V., and Vale, P. (2020) The *Imperial Discipline: Race and the Founding of International Relations* (London: Pluto Press).

Dean, J. (1989), 'Who's Afraid of Third Wave Feminism?', *International Feminist Journal*, 11/3: 334–352.

Death, C. and Tobin, R. (2017), 'Green States and Global Environmental Politics: Beyond Western IR?' in O. Corry and H. Stevenson (eds), *Traditions and Trends in Global Environmental Politics: International Relations and the Earth* (London: Routledge).

de Beauvoir, S. (2011), *The Second Sex* (New York: Vintage Books).

Debrix, F. (2009), 'Baudrillard', in J. Edkins and N. Vaughan-Williams, *Critical Theorists and International Relations* (London: Routledge), 54–65.

Der Derian, J. (2009), *Virtuous Wars: Mapping the Military-Industrial-Media-Entertainment Network* (Abingdon: Routledge).

Derrida, J. (1992), 'Force of Law: The "Mystical Foundation of Authority"' in D. Cornell, M. Rosenfeld, and D.G. Carlson (eds), *Deconstruction and the Possibility of Justice* (London: Routledge), 3–67.

Derrida, J. (1997), *Of Grammatology*, translated by Guyatri Chakravorty Spivak, corrected ed. (Baltimore, MD: John Hopkins University Press).

Deslandes, A. (2020), 'Checking in on Mexico's Feminist Foreign Policy'. Available at: foreignpolicy.com/2020/12/30/mexico-feminist-foreign-policy-one-year-in/

Devetak, R. (2022), 'Critical Theory' in R. Devetak and J. True (eds), *Theories of International Relations*, 6th edn (London: Bloomsbury), 119–140.

Diangelo, R. (2019), *White Fragility: Why It's So Hard for White People to Talk About Racism* (London: Penguin).

Dirlik, A. (1994), 'The Postcolonial Aura: Third World Criticism in the Age of Global Capitalism', *Critical Enquiry*, 20/2: 328–356.

Dirlik, A. (2004), 'Spectres of the Third World: Global Modernity and the End of the Three Worlds', *Third World Quarterly*, 25/1: 131–148.

Dirlik, A. (2012), 'The Idea of a "Chinese Model": A Critical Discussion', *China Information*, 26/3: 277–302.

Dobson, A. (2007), *Green Political Thought*, 4th edn (London: Routledge).

Dolman, A. J. (1979), 'The Like-Minded Countries and the New International Order: Past, Present and Future Prospects', *Cooperation and Conflict*, XIV: 57–85.

Doty, R. (1993), 'The Bounds of Race in International Relations', *Millennium: Journal of International Studies*, 22/3: 443–461.

Douzinas, C. (2007), *Human Rights and Empire: The Political Philosophy of Cosmopolitanism* (Abingdon: Routledge-Cavendish).

Doyle, M. W. (1983), 'Kant: Liberal Legacies and Foreign Affairs', *Philosophy and Public Affairs*, 12/3: 205–235.

Drescher, S. (1990), 'The Ending of the Slave Trade and the Evolution of European Scientific Racism', *Social Science History*, 14/3: 415–450.

Drescher, S. (2001), 'The Limits of Example' in D.P. Geggus (ed.), *The Impact of the Haitian Revolution in the Atlantic World* (Columbia, SC: University of South Carolina Press).

Drolet (2010), 'Feminist Perspectives in Development: Implications for Women and Microcredit', *Affilia: Journal of Women and Social Work*, 25/3: 212–223.

Dryzek, J. S. (1987), *Rational Ecology: Environment and Political Economy* (Oxford: Basil Balckwell).

Dryzek, J.S., Downes, D., Hunold, C., Scholsberg, D., and Hernes H-K. (2003), *Green States and Social Movements in the United States, United Kingdom, Germany and Norway* (Oxford: Oxford University Press).

Du Bois, W. E. B. (1925), 'Worlds of Color', *Foreign Affairs*, 3/3: 423–444.

Du Bois, W. E. B. (1986), 'The Souls of White Folk' in W.E.B. Du Bois, *Writings* (New York: The Library of America), 923–938.

Du Bois W. E. B. (2009), *Of the Dawn of Freedom* (London: Penguin Books).

Duffield, M. (2001a), 'Governing the Borderlands: Decoding the Power of Aid', *Disasters*, 25/4: 308–320.

Duffield, M. (2001b), *Global Governance and the New Wars: The Merging of Development and Security*, (London: Zed Books).

Duncanson, C. (2017), 'Anti-Militarist Feminist Approaches to Researching Gender and the Military' in R. Woodward and C. Duncanson (eds), *The Palgrave Handbook on Gender and the Military* (London: Palgrave Macmillan), 39–58.

Dunne, T. (1998), *Inventing International Society: A History of the English School* (Basingstoke: Macmillan).

Dunne, T. (2005), 'System, State and Society: How Does it All Hang Together?', *Millennium: Journal of International Studies*, 34/1: 157–170.

Dworkin, A. (2003), 'Andrea Dworkin on Kate Millett: sexual politics', *The New Statesman*, 14 July. Available at: https://www.newstatesman.com/long-reads/2003/07/andrea-dworkin-on-kate-millett-sexual-politics. Accessed 19 April 2023.

Eatwell, R. and Goodwin, M. (2018), *National Populism: The Revolt Against Liberal Democracy* (London: Pelican).

Eckersley, R. (1992), *Environmentalism and Political Theory: Toward an Ecocentric Approach* (New York: SUNY Press).

Eckersley, R. (2004), *The Green State: Rethinking Democracy and Sovereignty* (Cambridge, MA: MIT Press).

Eckersley, R. (2021), 'Green Theory' in T. Dunne, M. Kurki, and S. Smith (eds), *International Relations Theories: Discipline and Diversity*, 5th edn (Oxford: Oxford University Press), 263–284.

Eckersley, R. and Barry, J. (eds) (2005), *The State and the Global Ecological Crisis* (Cambridge, MA: The MIT Press).

Edkins, J. (2000), *Whose Hunger? Concepts of Famine, Practices of Aid* (Minneapolis. MN: University of Minnesota Press).

Edkins, J. (2003), 'Humanitarianism, Humanity, Human', *Journal of Human Rights*, 2/2: 253–258.

Elen, M. (2016), 'Interview: Joshua Cooper Ramo', *The Diplomat*, 10 August. Available at: https://thediplomat.com/2016/08/interview-joshua-cooper-ramo/. Accessed 2 April 2023.

Elliott, L. (1998), *The Global Politics of the Environment* (London: Macmillan).

Elshtain, J. B. (1987), *Women and War* (Chicago, IL: University of Chicago Press).

Engels, F. (1968), 'Engels to F. Mehring in Berlin', in K. Marx and F. Engels, *Karl Marx and Frederick Engels: Selected Works in One Volume*, (London: Lawrence and Wishart), 689–693.

Enloe, C. (1983), *Does Khaki Become You? The Militarization of Women's Lives* (Boston, MA: South End Press).

Enloe, C. (2014), *Bananas, Beaches and Bases: Making Feminist Sense of International Politics*, 2nd edn (Berkely, CA: University of California Press).

Enloe, C., Lacey, A., and Gregory, T. (2016), 'Twenty-Five Years of *Bananas, Beaches and Bases*: A Conversation with Cynthia Enloe', *Journal of Sociology*, 52/3: 537–550.

Erlanger, S. (2020), 'Macron Declares France "at War" with Virus as E.U. Proposes 30-day Travel Ban', *The New York Times*. 16 March.

Evans, E. (2015), *The Politics of Third Wave Feminisms: Neoliberalism, Intersectionality, and the State in Britain and the US* (Basingstoke: Palgrave Macmillan).

Evans, E. and Chamberlain, P. (2015), 'Critical Waves: Exploring Feminist Identity, Discourse and Praxis in Western Feminism', *Social Movement Studies*, 14/4: 396–409.

Evans, G. (1990), 'Foreign Policy and Good International Citizenship', Address by the Minister for Foreign Affairs, Senator Gareth Evans, Canberra, 6 March. Available at: http://www.gevans.org/speeches/old/1990/060390_fm_fpandgoodinternationalcitizen.pdf. Accessed 23 March 2023.

Eze, E. C. (1997), 'Introduction' in E. C. Eze (ed.), *Race and the Enlightenment: A Reader* (Oxford: Blackwell Publishing).

Fanon, F. (2001), *The Wretched of the Earth* (London: Penguin Books).

Fanon, F. (2008), *Black Skin, White Masks*, translated by R. Philcox (New York: Grove Press).

Farr, V. (2011), 'UNSCR 1325 and Women's Peace Activism in the Occupied Palestinian Territory',

International Feminist Journal of Politics, 13/4: 539–556.

Fasenfest, D. (2018), 'Is Marx Still Relevant?', Editorial, *Critical Sociology*, 44/6: 851–855.

Femicide Census (2018), *UK Femicides 2009–2018*. Available online at: https://www.femicidecensus.org/wp-content/uploads/2020/11/Femicide-Census-10-year-report.pdf

Fendler, L. (2010), *Michel Foucault* (London: Bloomsbury Academic).

Ferguson, S. (1999), 'The Radical Ideas of Mary Wollstonecraft', *Canadian Journal of Political Science*, 32/3: 427–450.

Ferraro, V. (2008), 'Dependency Theory: An Introduction' in Giorgio Secondi (ed.), *The Development Economics Reader* (London: Routledge), 58–64.

Fierke, K. (2021), 'Constructivism' in T. Dunne, M. Kurki, and S. Smith (eds), *International Relations Theories: Discipline and Diversity*, 5th edn (Oxford: Oxford University Press), 163–181.

Finnemore, M. and Sikkink, K. (1998), 'International Norm Dynamics and Political Change', *International Organization*, 52: 887–918.

Finnemore, M. and Sikkink, K. (2001), 'Taking Stock: The Constructivist Research Program in International Relations and Comparative Politics', *Annual Review of Political Science*, 4, 391–416.

Fischer, S. (2004), *Modernity Disavowed: Haiti and the Cultures of Slavery in the Age of Revolution* (Durham, NC: Duke University Press).

Flint, H. (2021), 'Why Does the Media Only React When Victims Are Young, Pretty and White?' *Gentleman's Quarterly,* 23 May.

Fortin, J. (2021), 'Critical Race Theory: A Brief History', *The New York Times*, 8 November. Available at: https://www.nytimes.com/article/what-is-critical-race-theory.html. Accessed 17 April 2023.

Foucault, M. (1986), 'Right of Death and Power over Life', in P.D. Rabinow (ed.), *The Foucault Reader: An Introduction to Foucault's Thought, with Major New Unpublished Material* (Harmondsworth Penguin Books/Peregrine), 258–272.

Foucault, M. (1988), *Politics, Philosophy, Culture: Interviews and Other Writings*, edited with an Introduction by L.D. Kritzman, translated by Alan Sheridan and others (London: Routledge).

Foucault, M. (1991), *Discipline and Punish: The Birth of The Prison*, Translated by Alan Sheridan (London: Penguin).

Foucault, M. (2002), 'Govermentality', in M. Foucault, *Power: Essential Works of Foucault 1954–1984 Volume 3*, edited by J. D. Faubion (London: Penguin Books), 201–222.

Foucault, M. (2004), *'Society Must be Defended' Lectures at the Collège de France, 1975–1976*, translated by D. Macey (London: Penguin Books).

Fraser, N. (2013a), *Fortunes of Feminism: From State-Managed Capitalism to Neoliberal Crisis* (London: Verso).

Fraser, N. (2013b), 14 October. Available at: https://www.theguardian.com/commentisfree/2013/oct/14/feminism-capitalist-handmaiden-neoliberal Accessed 14 September 2023.

Freedman, L. (2020), 'Coronavirus and the language of war', *New Statesman*, 11 April Available at www.newstatesman.com/science-tech/2020/04/coronavirus-and-language-war.

Friedan, B. (2010), *The Feminine Mystique*, with an introduction by Lionel Shriver (London: Penguin Classics).

Fromm, E. (1961), *Marx's Concept of Man* (New York: Frederick Ungar).

Fukuyama, F. (1989), 'The End of History?', *The National Interest*, 16: 3–18.

Fukuyama, F. (1992), *The End of History and the Last Man* (London: Hamish Hamilton).

Gaard, G. and Gruen, L. (1993), 'Ecofeminism: Toward Global Justice and Planetary Health', *Society and Nature*, 2: 1–35.

Gari, L. (2002), 'Arabic Treatises on Environmental Pollution up to the End of the Thirteenth Century', *Environment and History*, 8/4: 475–488.

Geggus, D. P. (ed.) (2001a), *The Impact of the Haitian Revolution in the Atlantic World* (Columbia, SC: University of South Carolina Press).

Geggus, D. P. (2001b), 'Epilogue' in David P. Geggus (ed.), *The Impact of the Haitian Revolution in the Atlantic World* (Columbia, SC: University of South Carolina Press).

Ghosal, S.G. (2005), 'Major Trends of Feminism in India', *The Indian Journal of Political Science*, 66/4: 793–812.

Giddens, A. (1984), *The Constitution of Society: Outline of the Theory of Structuration* (Berkeley, CA, and Cambridge: University of California Press and Polity).

Gill, S. (1995), 'Globalisation, Market Civilisation, and Disciplinary Neoliberalism', *Millennium: Journal of International Studies*, 24/3: 399–423.

Gill, S. (2008), *Power and Resistance in the New World Order*, 2nd edn (Basingstoke: Palgrave Macmillan).

Gilpin, R. (1981), *War and Change in International Politics* (Cambridge: Cambridge University Press).

Girard, P. (2019), 'The Leclerc Expedition to Saint-Domingue and the Independence of Haiti, 1802–1804', *Oxford Research Encyclopedia of Latin American History*, 23 May. 20pp. Available at: https://

doi.org/10.1093/acrefore/9780199366439.013.743. Accessed 14 April 2023.

Golden, H. (2021), 'Families of missing and murdered Native women ask: where's the attention for ours?', *The Guardian*, Friday 24 September. Available online at: https://www.theguardian.com/us-news/2021/sep/24/native-american-women-missing-murdered-media.

Goodin R. E. (1992), *Green Political Theory* (Cambridge: Polity Press).

Gorbachev, M. (1987), *Perestroika: New Thinking for Our Country and the World* (New York: Harper and Row).

Gramsci, A. (1971), *Selections from the Prison Notebooks of Antonio Gramsci*, edited and translated by Quentin Hoare and Geoffrey Nowell Smith (London: Lawrence Wishart).

Grant, R. and Newland, K. (eds) (1991), *Gender and International Relations* (Bloomington, IN: Indiana University Press).

Gratani, M., Sutton, S.G., Butler, J. R. A., Bohensky, E.L., and Foale, S. (2016), 'Indigenous Environmental Values as Human Values', *Cogent Social Sciences*, 2/1.

Grovogui, S. N. (2001), 'Come to Africa: A Hermeneutics of Race in International Theory', *Alternatives: Global, Local, Political*, 26/4: 425–448.

Grovogui, S. N. (2002), 'Regimes of Sovereignty: International Morality and the African Condition, *European Journal of International Relations*, 8/3: 315–338.

Grovogui, S. N. (2006), *Beyond Eurocentrism and Anarchy: Memories of International Order and Institutions* (Basingstoke: Palgrave Macmillan).

Gruffyd Jones, B. (2008a), 'The Global Political Economy of Social Crisis: Towards a Critique of the "Failed State" Thesis', *Review of International Political Economy*, 15/2: 180–205.

Gruffydd Jones, B. (2008b), 'Race in the Ontology of International Order', *Political Studies*, 56: 907–927.

Gruffyd Jones, B. (2013), 'Slavery, Finance and International Political Economy: Postcolonial Reflections' in S. Seth (ed.), *Postcolonial Theory and International Relations: A Critical Introduction* (New York: Routledge), 49–69.

Guha, R. (1983), *Elementary Aspects of Peasant Insurgency in Colonial India* (Oxford: Oxford University Press).

Gunder Frank, A. (1967), *Capitalism and Underdevelopment in Latin America: Historical Studies of Chile and Brazil* (New York: Monthly Review Press).

Gunder Frank, A. (1972), 'The Development of Underdevelopment', in J. D. Cockcroft, A. Gunder Frank, and D. Johnson, (eds), *Dependence and Underdevelopment* (Garden City, New York: Anchor Books), 3–17.

Gusterson, H. (1999), 'Nuclear Weapons and the Other in the Western Imagination', *Cultural Anthropology*, 14/1: 111–143.

Habermas, J. (1971), *Knowledge and Human Interests* (Boston, MA: Beacon Press).

Habermas, J. (1984), *The Theory of Communicative Action Volume 1, Reason and the Rationalization of Society*, translated by Thomas McCarthy (Oxford: Polity Press).

Habermas, J. (1987), *The Theory of Communicative Action Volume 2, Lifeworld and Systems: A Critique of Functionalist Reason*, translated by Thomas McCarthy (Oxford: Polity Press).

Hall, I. (2017), 'The "Revolt Against the West" Revisited' in T. Dunne and C. Reus-Smit (eds), *The Globalization of International Society* (Oxford: Oxford University Press), 354–361.

Halliday, F. (1983), *The Making of the Second Cold War* (London: Verso).

Hanson, M. (2018), 'Normalizing Zero Nuclear Weapons: The Humanitarian Road to the Prohibition Treaty', *Contemporary Security Policy*, 39/3: 464–486.

Hardin, G. (1968), 'The Tragedy of the Commons', *Science*, 162/3859: 1243–1248.

Hardin, G. (1974), 'Living on a Lifeboat', *Bioscience*, 24/10: 561–568.

Hardin, G. (1993), *Living within Limits: Ecology, Economics and Population Taboos* (New York: Oxford University Press).

Harvey, D. (2005), *A Brief History of Neoliberalism* (Oxford: Oxford University Press).

Hassan, Jennifer (2021), 'Sabina Nessa was killed walking in London. Women are asking: where is the outrage when the victim isn't White?', *The Washington Post*, 23 September. Available online at: https://www.washingtonpost.com/world/2021/09/23/sabina-nessa-teacher-murder-uk/

Held, D. (1980), *Introduction to Critical Theory: Horkheimer to Habermas* (London: Hutchinson).

Held, D. (1995), 'Cosmopolitan Democracy and the Global Order: Reflections on the 200th Anniversary of Kant's "Perpetual Peace"', *Alternatives*, 20: 415–429.

Henderson, E. A. (2007), 'Navigating the Muddy Waters of the Mainstream: Tracing the Mystification of Racism in International Relations' in W. Rich (ed.), *The State of the Political Science Discipline: An African-American Perspective*, (Philadelphia: Temple University Press).

Henderson, E. A. (2013), 'Hidden in Plain Sight: Racism in International Relations Theory', *Cambridge Review of International Affairs*, 26/1: 71–92.

Henderson, E. A. (2017), 'The Revolution Will Not Be Theorised: Du Bois, Locke, and the Howard School's Challenge to White Supremacist IR Theory', *Millennium: Journal of International Studies*, 45/3: 492–510.

Henley, J. (2020), 'Support for Eurosceptic parties doubles in two decades across EU', *The Guardian*, 2 March on 20 March 2023, at https://www.theguardian.com/world/2020/mar/02/support-for-eurosceptic-parties-doubles-two-decades-across-eu.

Herz, J. H. (1950), 'International Idealism and the Security Dilemma', *World Politics*, 2/2: 157–180.

Herz, J. H. (1981), 'Political Realism Revisited', *International Studies Quarterly*, 25/2: 182–197.

Hilhorst, D. (2018), 'Classical Humanitarianism and Resilience Humanitarianism: Making Sense of Two Brands of Humanitarian Action', *Journal of Humanitarian Action*, 3/15: 12pp. Available at: https://jhumanitarianaction.springeropen.com/articles/10.1186/s41018-018-0043-6%20. Accessed 14 September 2023.

Hill Jr, T. E. and Boxhill, B. (2001), 'Kant and Race', in B. Boxhill (ed.), *Race and Racism* (Oxford: Oxford University Press), 448–472.

Hines C. (2000), *Localization: A Global Manifesto* (Abingdon: Earthscan).

Hines C. (2003), 'Time to Replace Globalization with Localization', *Global Environmental Politics*, 3/3: 1–7.

Hirst, P., Thompson, G., and Bromley, S. (2009), *Globalization in Question*, 3rd edn (Cambridge: Polity).

Hobbes, T. (2005), *Leviathan*, A Critical Edition by G.A.J. Rogers and Karl Schumann, Vol. 2 (London: Continuum).

Hobson, J. M. (2004), *The Eastern Origins of Western Civilisation* (Cambridge: Cambridge University Press).

Hobson, J. M. (2012), *The Eurocentric Conception of World Politics: Western International Theory, 1760–2010* (Cambridge: Cambridge University Press).

Hobson, J.M. (2016), 'The "R-Word" and "E-Word" Definitional Controversies: A Dialogue with my Five Interlocutors', *Postcolonial Studies*, 19/2: 210–226.

Hoffman, M. (1992), 'Third Party Mediation and Conflict Resolution in the Post-Cold War World' in J. Baylis and N. J. Rengger (eds), *Dilemmas of World Politics* (Oxford: Clarendon Press).

Hoffman, S. (1977), 'An American Social Science: International Relations', *Daedalus*, 106/3: 41–60.

hooks, b. (2000), *Feminist Theory: From Margin to Center*, 2nd edn (London: Pluto Press).

hooks, b. (2004), *The Will to Change: Men, Masculinity, and Love* (New York: Washington Square Press).

hooks, b. (2015), *Ain't I a Woman: Black Women and Feminism*, new edition (New York: Routledge).

Hooper, C. (2001), *Manly States: Masculinities, International Relations and Gender Politics* (New York: Columbia University Press).

Hopf, T. (1998), 'The Promise of Constructivism in International Relations Theory', *International Security*, 23/1: 171–200.

Horkheimer, M. (1972), *Critical Theory: Selected Essays*, translated by M. J. O'Connell and others (New York: Continuum).

Howard, P. (2004), 'Why Not Invade North Korea? Threats, Language Games and US Foreign Policy', *International Studies Quarterly*, 48/4: 805–828.

Howell, A. and Richter-Montpetit, M. (2020), Is Securitization Theory Racist? Civilizationism, Methodological Whiteness, and Antiblack Thought in the Copenhagen School', *Security Dialogue*, 51/1: 3–22.

Huddart, D. (2006), *Homi K. Bhabha* (London: Routledge).

Hughes, R. (1994), *The Fatal Shore: The Epic of Australia's Founding* (New York: Alfred A. Knopf).

Hull, G.T., Scott, P.B, and Smith, B. (eds) (1982), *All the Women are White, All the Blacks are Men, but some of Us are Brave: Black Women's Studies* (Old Westbury, NY: Feminist Press).

Hurrell, A. (2002), 'Foreword to The Third Edition: *The Anarchical Society* 25 Years On' in H. Bull, *The Anarchical Society: A Study of Order in World Politics*, 3rd edn, with forewords by Andrew Hurrell and Stanley Hoffman (Basingstoke: Palgrave).

Hutchings, K. (2008), 'Making Sense of Masculinity and War', *Men and Masculinities*, 10/4: 389–404.

ILGA World (2020), *State Sponsored Homophobia: Global Legislation Update*, December (Geneva: ILGA.org). Available at: https://ilga.org/downloads/ILGA_World_State_Sponsored_Homophobia_report_global_legislation_overview_update_December_2020.pdf Accessed 25 April 2023.

Inayatullah, N. and Blaney, D. L. (2004), *International Relations and the Problem of Difference* (New York: Routledge).

Ingold, T. (2004), 'Beyond Biology and Culture. The Meaning of Evolution in a Relational World', *Social Anthropology*, 12/2: 209–221.

Ismail, Q. (1992), 'Boys will be Boys: Gender and National Agency in Frantz Fanon and LTTE', *Economic and Political Weekly*, 27/31–32: 1677–1679.

Jackson, R. H. (1993), *Quasi-States: Sovereignty, International Relations, and the Third World*, (Cambridge: Cambridge University Press).

Jackson, R. H. (2000), *The Global Covenant: Human Conduct in a World of States* (Oxford: Oxford University Press).

Jackson, R. (2005), *Writing the War on Terrorism: Language, Politics and Counter-Terrorism* (Manchester: Manchester University Press).

Jackson, T. and Webster, R. (2016), *Limits Revisited: A Review of the Limits to Growth Debate*, (CUSP, University of Surrey: APPG on Limits to Growth). Available at: https://limits2growth.org.uk/wp-content/uploads/Jackson-and-Webster-2016-Limits-Revisited.pdf. Accessed 27 April 2023.

Jayawardena, K. (1986), *Feminism and Nationalism in the Third World* (London: Zed Books).

Joll, J. (1977), *Gramsci* (Fontana Paperbacks).

Jones, A. (1996), 'Does Gender Make the World Go Round? Feminist Critiques of International Relations', *Review of International Studies*, 22/4: 405–429.

Jones, A. (2000), 'Gendercide and Genocide', *Journal of Genocide Research*, 2/2: 185–211.

Jones, D. L. (1991), *Cosmopolitan Mediation: Conflict Resolution and the Oslo Accords* (Manchester: Manchester University Press).

Jones, D. L. (1996), *Cultural Norms and National Security: Police and Military in Postwar Japan* (Ithaca: Cornell University Press).

Jones, D. L. (2000), 'Mediation, Conflict Resolution and Critical Theory', *Review of International Studies*, 26: 647–662.

Jones, R. E. (1981), 'The English School of International Relations: A Case for Closure', *Review of International Studies*, 7/1: 1–13.

Kaeding, M., Pollak, J., and Schmidt, P. (eds) (2019), *The Future of Europe: Views from the Capitals* (Cham: Palgrave Macmillan).

Kaldor, M. (1999), *New and Old Wars: Organized Violence in a Global Era* (Cambridge: Polity).

Katzenstein, P. (2003), 'Same War—Different Views: Germany, Japan and Counter-Terrorism', *International Organization*, 57/4: 731–760.

Keene, E. (2002), *Beyond the Anarchical Society: Grotius, Colonialism and Order in World Politics* (Cambridge: Cambridge University Press).

Kegley, Jr C. W. (1993), 'The Neoidealist Moment in International Studies? Realist Myths and the New International Realities', *International Studies Quarterly*, 37: 131–146.

Kennan, G. F. (1981), 'Two views of the Soviet problem', *The New Yorker*, 2 November: 54–62.

Kennedy, D. (2004), *The Dark Side of Virtue: Reassessing International Humanitarianism* (Princeton, NJ: Princeton University Press).

Kennedy-Pipe, C. (2017), 'Liberal Feminists, Militaries and War in Rachel Woodward and Claire Duncanson (eds), *The Palgrave Handbook of Gender and the Military* (London: Palgrave Macmillan), 23–37.

Keohane, R. O. (1984), *After Hegemony: Cooperation and Discord in the World Political Economy* (Princeton, NJ: Princeton University Press).

Keohane, R. O. (1989), *International Institutions and State Power: Essays in International Relations Theory* (Boulder; London: Westview Press).

Keohane, R. and Nye, J. S. (1989), *Power and Interdependence*, 2nd edn (Glenview, IL: Scott, Foresman and Company).

Keys, D (2003), 'How Rome Polluted the World', *Geographical*, December: 45–48.

Kiersey, N. J. and Neumann, I. B. (eds) (2013), *Battlestar Galactica and International Relations* (Abingdon: Routledge).

Kindleberger, C. (1973), *The World in Depression 1929–1939* (Berkeley, CA: University of California Press).

Kinsella, H. M. (2020), 'Feminism' in J. Baylis, S. Smith, and P. Owens (eds), *The Globalization of World Politics*, 8th edn (Oxford: Oxford University Press), 287–302.

Klein, N. (2014), *This Changes Everything: Capitalism versus the Climate* (London: Allen Lane).

Kleingeld, P. (2007), 'Kant's Second Thoughts on Race', *The Philosophical Quarterly*, 57/229: 573–592.

Klotz, A. (1995) *Norms in International Relations: The Struggle Against Apartheid*, (Ithaca and London: Cornell University Press).

Knight, F. W. (2000), 'The Haitian Revolution', *The American Historical Review*, 105/1: 103–115.

Kohn, M. and Reddy, K. (2017), 'Colonialism' in E. N. Zalta (ed.), *The Stanford Encyclopedia of Philosophy* (Fall 2017 Edition), Available at: https://plato.stanford.edu/archives/fall2017/entries/colonialism/. Accessed 13 April 2023.

Koslowski, R. and Kratochwil, F. V. (1994), 'Understanding Change in International Politics: The Soviet Empire's Demise and the International System', *International Organization*, 48/2: 215–247.

Krahenbuhl, P. (2011), 'The Militarization of Aid and Its Perils', *International Committee of the Red Cross*, 22 February. Available at: https://www.icrc.org/en/doc/resources/documents/article/editorial/humanitarians-danger-article-2011-02-01.htm. Accessed 10 April 2023.

Kreisler, H. (2002), 'John Mearsheimer: Through the Realist Lens', interview with John J. Mearsheimer, 7 April 2002. Available at: https://iis.berkeley.edu/publications/john-mearsheimer-through-realist-lens

Kripp, J. (2022), 'The Creative Advance Must be Defended: Miscegenation, Metaphysics, and Race War in Jan Smut's Vision of the League of Nations', *American Political Science Review*, 116/3: 940–953.

Krishna, S. (2001), 'Race, Amnesia and the Education of International Relations', *Alternatives*, 26: 401–424.

Krishna, S. (2018), 'Postcolonialism and Its Relevance for International Relations in a Globalized World' in R. B. Persaud and A. Sajed (eds), *Race, Gender and Culture in International Relations: Postcolonial Perspectives* (London: Routledge), 19–34.

Kwon, H. (2010), *The Other Cold War* (New York: Columbia University Press).

Laffey and Weldes, J. (2008), 'Decolonizing the Cuban Missile Crisis', *International Studies Quarterly*, 52(3): 555–577.

Lane, L. and Mahdi, H. (2012), 'Fanon Revisited: Race, Gender and Coloniality Vis-à-Vis Skin Colour' in R. E. Hall (ed.) *The Melanin Millennium: Skin Color as 21st Century International Discourse* (New York: Springer).

Lawler, P. (1995), *A Question of Values: Johan Galtung's Peace Research* (Boulder, CO: Lynne Rienner).

Lawler, P. (1997), 'Scandinavian Exceptionalism and European Union', *Journal of Common Market Studies*, 35/4: 565–594.

Lawler, P. (2005), 'The Good State: In Praise of "Classical" Internationalism', *Review of International Studies*, 31/3: 427–449.

Lawler, P. (2013a), 'The "Good State" Debate in International Relations', *International Politics*, 50/1: 18–37.

Lawler, P. (2013b), 'Peace Studies' in P.D. Williams (ed.), *Security Studies: An Introduction* (Abingdon: Routledge), 77–89.

Layne, C. (1994), 'Kant or Cant: The Myth of the Democratic Peace', *International Security*, 19/2: 5–49.

Lazaridis, G., Campani, G., and Benveniste, A. (eds) (2016), *The Rise of the Far Right in Europe: Populist Shifts and 'Othering'* (London: Palgrave Macmillan).

Lebow, R. N. (2003), *The Tragic Vision of Politics: Ethics, Interests and Orders* (Cambridge: Cambridge University Press).

Lebow, R. N. (2020), 'Classical Realism' in T. Dunne, M. Kurki, and S. Smith (eds), *International Relations Theories: Discipline and Diversity*, 5th edn (Oxford: Oxford University Press), 33–51.

Lees, C. (2018), 'The "Alternative for Germany": the Rise of Right-Wing Populism at the Heart of Europe', *Politics*, 38/3: 295–310.

Lenin, V. I. (2010), *Imperialism: The Highest Stage of Capitalism* (London: Penguin Books).

Leopold, A. (1949), *A Sand County Almanac and Sketches Here and There* (Oxford: Oxford University Press).

Levine, D. J. (2012), *Recovering International Relations: The Promise of Sustainable Critique* (Oxford: Oxford University Press).

Levy, J. S. (1988), 'Domestic Politics and War', *Journal of Interdisciplinary History*, XVIII/4: 653–673.

Liboiron, M. (2021), *Pollution is Colonialism* (Durham, NC: Duke University Press).

Linklater, A. (1992), 'What Is a Good International Citizen?' in Paul Keal, ed. *Ethics and Foreign Policy* (Canberra: Allen & Unwin).

Linklater, A. (1998), *The Transformation of Community: Ethical Foundations of the Post-Westphalian Era* (Cambridge: Polity Press).

Linklater, A. (2001), 'Citizenship, Humanity, and Cosmopolitan Harm Conventions', *International Political Science Review*, 22/3: 261–277.

Linklater, A. (2005), Book review of B. Buzan, *From International Society to World Society? English School Theory and the Social Structure of Globalisation*, *Perspectives on Politics*, 3/1: 196–197.

Linklater, A. (2011), *The Problem of Harm in World Politics: Theoretical Investigations* (Cambridge: Cambridge University Press).

Linklater, A. (2013), 'Marx and Marxism' in S. Burchill and A. Linklater (eds), *Theories of International Relations*, 5th edn (London: Palgrave Macmillan), 113–137.

Linklater, A. (2017), *Violence and Civilisation in the Western States-Systems* (Cambridge: Cambridge University Press).

Linklater, A. and Suganami, H. (2006), *The English School of International Relations: A Contemporary Reassessment* (Cambridge: Cambridge University Press).

Lisle, D. (2016), *Holidays in the Danger Zone: Entanglements of War and Tourism* (Minneapolis, MN: University of Minnesota Press).

Lisle, D. and Pepper, A. (2005), 'The New Face of Global Hollywood: Black Hawk Down and the Politics of Meta-Sovereignty', *Cultural Politics*, 1/2: 165–92.

Lorde, A. (1984), *Sister, Outsider: Essays and Speeches* (Trumansburg, NY: The Crossing Press).

Ludden, D. (2002), 'Introduction: A Brief History of Subalternity' in D. Ludden (ed)., *Reading Subaltern Studies: Critical History, Contested Meaning and the Globalization of South Asia* (London: Anthem Press).

Lumsdaine, D. (1993), *Moral Vision in International Politics: The Foreign Aid Regime 1949–89* (Princeton, NJ: Princeton University Press).

McLellan, D. (ed.) (2000), *Karl Marx: Selected Writings*, 2nd edn (Oxford: Oxford University Press).

Mac Ginty, R. (2010), 'Hybrid Peace: The Interaction Between Top-Down and Bottom-Up Peace', *Security Dialogue*, 41/4: 391–412.

Machiavelli, N. (1975), *The Prince*, translated with an introduction by George Bull (Harmondsworth: Penguin Books).

McRobbie, A. (2009), *The Aftermath of Feminism: Gender, Culture and Social Change* (London: Sage).

Maddison, S. (2013), 'Indigenous Identity, "Authenticity" and the Structural Violence of Settler Colonialism', *Identities*, 20/3: 288–303.

Mahdavi, M (2015), 'A Postcolonial Critique of Responsibility to Protect in the Middle East', *Perceptions*, XX/1: 7–36.

Malaniak, D., Peterson, S., and Tierney, M.J. (2012), *TRIP around the World: Teaching Research and Policy Views of International Relations Faculty in 20 Countries* (Williamsburg, VA: The College of William and Mary).

Malm, A. (2015), 'The Anthropocene Myth' *Jacobin Magazine*, 30 March. Available at: https://jacobin.com/2015/03/anthropocene-capitalism-climate-change/. Accessed 29 April 2023.

Malm, A. and Hornborg, A. (2014) 'The Geology of Mankind? A Critique of the Anthropocene Narrative', *Anthropocene Review* 1(1): 62–69.

Manne, K. (2021), 'What Sarah Everard's Murder Illuminates—And Might Obscure', *The Atlantic*, 17 March 2021. Available online at: https://www.theatlantic.com/ideas/archive/2021/03/what-sarah-everards-murder-illuminatesand-might-obscure/618302/.

Marcuse, H. (1964), *One-Dimensional Man* (Boston, MA: Beacon Press).

Marks, Z. (2017), 'Gender Dynamics in Rebel Groups' in R. Woodward and C. Duncanson (eds), *The Palgrave Handbook on Gender and the Military* (London: Palgrave Macmillan), 437–454.

Martin, A. (2013), 'Global Environmental In/Justice, in Practice: Introduction', *The Geographical Journal*, 179/2: 98–104.

Marx, K. (2000), 'The Eighteenth Brumaire of Louis Napoleon' in D. McLellan (ed.), *Karl Marx: Selected Writings*, 2nd edition (Oxford: Oxford University Press), 329–354.

Masters, C. (2008), 'Bodies of Technology and the Politics of the Flesh' in J.L. Parpart and M. Zalewski (eds), *Rethinking the Man Question: Sex, Gender and Violence in International Relations* (London: Zed Books), 87–107.

Mayall, J. (2000), *World Politics: Progress and its Limits* (Cambridge: Polity).

Mazower, M. (2006), 'An International Civilization? Empire, Internationalism, and the Crisis of the Mid-Twentieth Century', *International Affairs*, 82/3: 553–566.

Mazower, M. (2009), *No Enchanted Palace: The End of Empire and the Ideological Origins of the United Nations* (Princeton, NJ: Princeton University Press).

Meadows, D.H., Meadows, D. L., Randers, J., and Behrens III, W.W. (1972), *The Limits to Growth: A Report for THE CLUB OF ROME's Project on the Predicament of Mankind* (New York: Universe Books).

Mearsheimer, J.J. (1990), 'Why We Will Soon Miss the Cold War', *The Atlantic Monthly*, 266/2: 35–50.

Mearsheimer, J.J. (1994–5), 'The False Promise of International Institutions', *International Security*, 19/3: 5–49.

Mearsheimer, J.J. (2002), 'Through the Realist Lens: John Mearsheimer', an interview with Harry Kreisler, *Conversations with History* interview series, Institute of International Studies at the University of California, Berkeley, 7 April. Available at: https://iis.berkeley.edu/publications/john-mearsheimer-through-realist-lens. Accessed 14 September 2023.

Mearsheimer, J.J. (2010), 'Why is Europe Peaceful Today', ECPR Keynote Lecture, *European Political Science*, 9: 387–397.

Mearsheimer, J.J. (2020), 'Structural Realism' in T. Dunne, M. Kurki, and S. Smith (eds), *International Relations Theories: Discipline and Diversity*, 5th edn (Oxford: Oxford University Press), 51–67.

Mearsheimer, J.J. and Walt, S. M. (2003), 'An Unnecessary War', *Foreign Policy*, January–February: 51–59.

Mende, J. (2021), 'Are Human Rights Western—And Why Does It Matter? A Perspective From International Political Theory', *Journal of International Political Theory*, 17/1: 38–57.

Mignolo, W.D. (2009), 'Epistemic Disobedience, Independent Thought and Decolonial Freedom', *Theory, Culture and Society*, 26/7–8: 159–181.

Mignolo, W.D. (2017), 'Interview—Walter Mignolo/Part 2: Key Concepts', *E-International Relations*, 21 January. Available at: https://www.e-ir.info/2017/01/21/interview-walter-mignolopart-2-key-concepts/. Accessed 14 September 2023.

Mignolo, W. D. and Walsh, C. E. (2018), *On Decoloniality: Concepts, Analytics, Praxis* (Durham, NC: Duke University Press).

Mildenberger, M. (2019), 'The Tragedy of The Tragedy of the Commons', *Scientific American*, 23 April. Available at: https://blogs.scientificamerican.com/voices/the-tragedy-of-the-tragedy-of-the-commons/. Accessed 25 April 2023.

Millett, K. (2000), *Sexual Politics*, First Illinois Paperback (Urbana, IL: University of Illinois Press).

Mills, C. W. (1997), *The Racial Contract* (Ithaca, NY: Cornell University Press).

Mills, C. W. (2017), *Black Rights/White Wrongs: The Critique of Racial Liberalism* (Oxford: Oxford University Press).

Milne, D. (2015), 'Woodrow Wilson Was More Racist than Wilsonianism', *Foreign Policy*, 3 December. Available at: https://foreignpolicy.com/2015/12/03/woodrow-wilson-was-not-a-racist-in-foreign-policy/. Accessed 14 September 2023.

Ming Wahl, E. (2021), 'Black Women in Fanon's Black Skin, White Masks: The Intersection of Race, Gender, and Oppression', *Stance*, 14/1: 41–51.

Ministry for Foreign Affairs (Sweden) (2015), *Swedish Foreign Service Action Plan for Feminist Foreign Policy 2015–2018* including focus areas for 2016 (Stockholm: Government Office of Sweden).

Ministry for Foreign Affairs (Sweden) (2020), *The Swedish Foreign Service Action Plan for Feminist Foreign Policy 2019–2022*, including direction and measures for 2021 (Stockholm: Government Office of Sweden).

Miyoshi, M. (1993), 'A Borderless World? From Colonialism to Transnationalism and the Decline of the Nation-State', *Critical Enquiry*, 19/4: 726–751.

Mohanty, C. T. (1984), 'Under Western Eyes: Feminist Scholarship and Colonialist Discourses', *Feminist Review*, 30/3: 61–88.

Momtaz, R. (2020), 'Inside Macron's coronavirus war' *Politico*, 13 April. Available at www.politico.eu/interactive/inside-emmanuel-macron-coronavirus-war/

Monroe, J. A. (1987), 'A Feminist Vindication of Mary Wollstonecraft', *Iowa Journal of Literary Studies*, 8/1: 143–152.

Moore, J. W. (2016), 'Introduction' in J. W. Moore (ed.), *Anthropocene or Capitalocene? Nature, History and the Crisis of Capitalism* (Oakland, CA: PM Press).

Morgenthau, H. J. (1961), 'Death in the Nuclear Age', *Commentary*, September, available at: https://www.commentary.org/articles/hans-morgenthau/death-in-the-nuclear-age/, accessed 20 March, 2023.

Morgenthau, H. J. (1962), *The Restoration of American Politics* (Chicago, IL: Chicago University Press).

Morgenthau, H. J. (1978), *Politics Among Nations: The Struggle for Power and Peace*, 5th edition, revised (New York: Alfred A. Knopf).

Mudde, C. (2019), 'European governments are fuelling Euroscepticism', *The Guardian*, 15 July on 20 March 2023, at: https://www.theguardian.com/commentisfree/2019/jul/15/european-council-fuel-euroscepticism-governments-eu.

Mueller, Benjamin and Robbins, Rebecca (2021), 'Where A vast global vaccination program went wrong', *The New York Times,* 7 October. Available at: www.nytimes.com/2021/08/02/world/europe/covax-covid-vaccine-problems-africa.html.

Mukherjee, S. (2016), *Human Rights Standards: Hegemony, Law, Politics* (Albany, NY: SUNYPress).

Mukherjee, S. (2017), 'Black History Month: Diversity and the British Female Suffrage Movement', *The Fawcett Society*. Available at: https://www.fawcettsociety.org.uk/blog/diversity-british-female-suffrage-movement. Accessed 19 April 2023.

Mukherjee, S. (2018), *Indian Suffragettes: Female Identities and Transnational Networks* (New Delhi: Oxford University Press).

Muppidi, H. (2009), 'Frantz Fanon', in J. Edkins and N. Vaughan-Williams, *Critical Theorists and International Relations* (London: Routledge), 150–160.

Mutua, M. (1995), 'Conflicting Conceptions of Human rights: Rethinking the Post-Colonial State', *Proceedings of the Annual Meeting (American Society of International Law)*, 89: 487–490.

Mutua, M. (2001), 'Savages, Victims, and Saviours: The Metaphor of Human Rights', *Harvard International Law Journal*, 42/1: 201–245.

Naess, A. (1973), 'The Shallow and the Deep, Long-Range Ecology Movement. A Summary', *Inquiry*, 16/1–4: 95–100.

Navari, C. (2014), 'English School Methodology' in C. Navari and D.M. Green (eds), *Guide to the English School in International Studies* (Chichester: Wiley Blackwell), 205–222.

Neal, A. (2009), 'Michel Foucault' in J. Edkins and N. Vaughan-Williams, *Critical Theorists and International Relations* (London: Routledge), 161–170.

Nelson, M. K. and Shilling, D. (2018), *Traditional Ecological Knowledge: Learning from Indigenous Practices for Environmental Sustainability* (Cambridge: Cambridge University Press).

Newell, P. (2011), 'The Elephant in the Room: Capitalism and Global Environmental Change', Editorial, *Global Environmental Change*, 21: 4–6.

Newell, P. (2020), *Global Green Politics* (Cambridge: Cambridge University Press).

Newell, P. and Paterson, M. (2010), *Climate Capitalism: Global Warming and the Transformation of the Global Economy* (Cambridge: Cambridge University Press).

Nobel, J. W. (1995), 'Morgenthau's Struggle with Power: The Theory of Politics and the Cold War', *Review of International Studies*, 21/1: 61–85.

Norgaard, K.M. and Fenelon, J.V. (2021), 'Towards an Indigenous Environmental Sociology' in C. B. Schaefer, A. Jorgenson, S.A. Malin, L. Peek,

D.N. Pellow, and X. Huang (eds), *Handbook of Environmental Sociology* (Cham, Switzerland; Springer).

O'Brien, R. and Williams, M. (2020), *Global Political Economy: Evolution and Dynamics*, 6th edn (London: Bloomsbury).

Ohaegbulam, F. U. (2004), *US Policy in Postcolonial Africa: Four Case Studies in Conflict Resolution* (New York: Peter Lang).

Ohmae, (1990), *The Borderless World: Power and Strategy in the Interlinked Economy* (New York: Harper Business).

Olsen, W.C. and Groom, A.J.R. (1991), *International Relations Then and Now: Origins and Trends in Interpretation* (London: Routledge).

Onuf, N. (1989), *World of Our Making: Rules and Rule in Social Theory and International Relations* (Columbia, SC: University of South Carolina Press).

Orbán, V. (2014), 'Speech at the XXV. Bálványos Free Summer University and Camp', available at: https://budapestbeacon.com/full-text-of-viktor-orbans-speech-at-baile-tusnad-tusnadfurdo-of-26-july-2014/

Orford, A. (1999), 'Muscular Humanitarianism: Reading the Narratives of the New Interventionism,' *European Journal of International Law* 10/4: 679–712.

Orsi, D., Avgustin, J.R., and Nurnus, M (2018), *Realism in Practice: an Appraisal* (Bristol: E-International Relations Publishing), available at: https://www.e-ir.info/publication/realism-in-practice-an-appraisal/. Aaccessed 19 March 2023.

Ortiz-Ospina, E. and Tvzvetkova, S. (2017), 'Working Women: Key Facts and Trends in Female Labor Force Participation', *Our World in Data*, 16 October. Available at: https://ourworldindata.org/female-labor-force-participation-key-facts. Accessed 19 April 2023.

Ortiz-Ospina, E., Tzvetkova, S., and Roser, M. (2018), 'Women's Employment', Our World in Data, March. Available at: https://ourworldin-data.org/female-labor-supply. Accessed 19 April 2023.

Össbo, A. (2022), 'Hydropower company sites: a study of Swedish settler colonialism', *Settler Colonial Studies*, 13/1: 115–132.

Outright Action International (2020), *Beijing+25: 25 Years After the Global Platform for Action on Gender Equality* (New York: Outright Action International).

Owens, P. and Rietzler, K. (eds) (2021), *Women's International Thought: A New History* (Cambridge: Cambridge University Press).

Oye, K. A. (ed.) (1986), *Cooperation Under Anarchy* (Princeton, NJ: Princeton University Press).

Parashar, S., Tickner, J.A., and True, J. (2018), 'Introduction: Feminist Imaginings of 21st Century Gendered States' in S. Parashar, J. A. Tickner, and

J. True (eds), *Revisiting Gendered States: Feminist Imaginings of the State in International Relations* (Oxford: Oxford University Press), 1–16.

Paris, R. (2010), 'Saving Liberal Peacebuilding', *Review of International Studies*, 36/2: 337–365.

Parry, B. (2004), *Postcolonial Studies: A Materialist Critique* (London: Routledge).

Paterson, M. (2000), 'Car Culture and Global Environmental Politics', *Review of International Studies*, 26: 253–270.

Paterson, M. (2001), *Understanding Global Environmental Politics: Domination, Accumulation, Resistance* (London: Palgrave).

Paterson, M. (2007), *Automobile Politics: Ecology and Cultural Political Economy* (Cambridge: Cambridge University Press).

Paterson, M. (2022), 'Green Theory' in R. Devetak and J. True (eds), *Theories of International Relations*, 6th edn (London: Bloomsbury), 224–243.

Peetush, A. (2003), 'Cultural Diversity, Non-Western Communities, and Human Rights', *The Philosophical Forum*, XXXIV/1: 1–19.

Peoples, C. and Vaughan-Williams, N. (2021), *Critical Security Studies: An Introduction*, 3rd edn (Abingdon: Routledge).

Perry, J.B. (2021), 'Introduction to the 2021 Edition' in T.W. Allen, *The Invention of the White Race: The Origin of Racial Oppression*, introduction by J.B. Perry (London: Verso).

Persaud, R. B. and Sajed, A. (2018), 'Introduction, Race Gender and Culture in International Relations' in R. B. Persaud and A. Sajed (eds), *Race, Gender and Culture in International Relations: Postcolonial Perspectives* (London: Routledge).

Peterson, V.S. (1992), 'Security and Sovereign States: What is at Stake in Taking Feminism Seriously?', in V. S. Peterson, (ed.), *Gendered States: Feminist (Re)Visions of International Theory* (Boulder, CO: Lynne Rienner), 31–64.

Phipps, A. (2020), *Me, Not You: The Trouble with Mainstream Feminism* (Manchester: Manchester University Press).

Phull, K., Cifliki, G., and Meibauer, G. (2019), 'Gender and Bias in the International Relations Curriculum: Insights from Reading Lists', *European Journal of International Relations*, 25/2: 383–407.

Pickerill, J. (2018), 'Black and Green: The Future of Indigenous–Environmentalist Relations in Australia', *Environmental Politics*, 27/6, 1122–1145.

Piketty, T. (2014), *Capital in the Twenty-First Century*, translated by Arthur Goldhammer (Cambridge, MA: Harvard University Press).

Pinchot, G. (2004), 'Excerpts from *The Fight for Conservation* (1910)', *Organization and Environment*, 17/2: 232–243.

Pinchot, G. (2017), *Gifford Pinchot: Selected Writings*, edited by Char Miller (University Park, PA: Pennsylvania University Press).

Pradella, L. (2015), *Globalisation and the Critique of Political Economy: New Insights from Marx's Writings* (London: Routledge).

Prakash, G. (1994), 'Subaltern Studies as Postcolonial Criticism', *The American Historical Review*, 99/5: 1475–1490.

Pratt, C. (ed.) (1989), *Internationalism Under Strain: The North-South Policies of Canada, Norway, The Netherlands, Norway and Sweden* (Toronto: The University of Toronto).

Pratt, C. (ed.) (1990), *Middle Power Internationalism* (Montreal: McGill-Queens University Press).

Price, R. and Reus-Smit, C. (1998), 'Dangerous Liaisons: Critical International Theory and Constructivism', *European Journal of International Relations*, 4/3: 259–294.

Puar, J. K. (2017), *Terrorist Assemblages: Homonationalism in Queer Times* (Durham, NC: Duke University Press).

Pugh, M. (2013), 'Peace Operations' in P.D. Williams (ed.), *Security Studies: An Introduction*, 2nd edn (Abingdon, Oxon: Routledge).

Quijano, A. (2007), 'Coloniality and Modernity/Rationality', *Cultural Studies*, 21/2–3: 168–178.

Rabaka, R. (2007), 'The Souls of White Folk: W.E.B. du Bois's Critique of White Supremacy and Contribution to Critical White Studies', *Journal of African American Studies*, 11/1: 1–15.

Rae, H. (2002), *State Identities and the Homogenisation of Peoples* (Cambridge: Cambridge University Press).

Ramo, J.C. (2004), *The Beijing Consensus*, (London: The Foreign Policy Centre). Available at: https://fpc.org.uk/publications/the-beijing-consensus/. Accessed 3 April 2023.

Rao, R. (2015), 'Echoes of Imperialism in LGBT Activism' in K. Nicolaïdis, B. Sèbe, and G. Maas (eds), *Echoes of Empire: Memory, Identity and Colonial Legacies* (London: IB Taurus).

Rasmussen, D. M. (1990) *Reading Habermas* (Cambridge, MA: Basil Blackwell).

Reardon, B. A. (1985), *Sexism and the War System* (New York: Teachers College Press).

Redfern, C. and Aune, K. (2013), *Reclaiming the F Word: Feminism Today* (London: Zed Books).

Reichmuth, D. (2020), 'Are Electric Vehicles Really Better for the Climate? Yes. Here's Why', *The Equation* (Union of Concerned Scientists). Available at: https://blog.ucsusa.org/dave-reichmuth/are-electric-vehicles-really-better-for-the-climate-yes-heres-why/. Accessed 28 April 2023.

Reus-Smit, C. (2022), 'Constructivism' in R. Devetak and J. True (eds), *Theories of International Relations*, 6th edn (London: Bloomsbury), 188–206.

Richmond, O. (2006), 'The Problem of Peace: Understanding the "liberal peace"', *Conflict, Security and Development*, 6/3: 291–314.

Richmond, O. and Mitchell, A. (eds) (2011), *Hybrid Forms of Peace: From Everyday Agency to Post-Liberalism* (Basingstoke, Hants: Palgrave Macmillan).

Richter-Montpetit, M. (2018), 'Everything You always Wanted to Know about Sex in IR but Were Afraid to Ask: The "Queer" Turn in International Relations' *Millennium: Journal of International Studies*, 46(2): 220–240.

Richter-Montpetit, M. and Weber, C. (2017), 'Queer International Relations', *Oxford Research Encyclopedia of Politics*, 24 May. 33pp. Available at: https://oxfordre.com/politics/display/10.1093/acrefore/9780190228637.001.0001/acrefore-9780190228637-e-265. Accessed 25 April 20203.

Rieff, D. (2002), 'Humanitarianism in Crisis', *Foreign Affairs*, 81/6: 111–121.

Robertson, K. (2021), 'News media can't shake "missing white woman syndrome" critics say', *The New York Times*, 22 September. Available online at: https://www.nytimes.com/2021/09/22/business/media/gabby-petito-missing-white-woman-syndrome.html?searchResultPosition=2.

Rösch, F. and Lebow, R. N. (2018), 'A Contemporary Perspective on Realism', *E-International Relations*, 17 February. Available at: https://www.e-ir.info/2018/02/17/a-contemporary-perspective-on-realism/, accessed 19 March 2023.

Rose, G. (1998), 'Neoclassical Realism and Theories of Foreign Policy', *World Politics*, 51/1: 144–172.

Rosenberg, J. (2000), *The Follies of Globalisation Theory: Polemical Essays* (London: Verso).

Rosenberg, J. (2005), 'Globalization Theory: A Post Mortem', *International Politics*, 42: 2–74.

Rosenberg, L. (2010), 'The New Woman and the "Dusky Strand": The Place of Feminism and Women's Literature in Early Jamaican Nationalism', *Feminist Review*, 95: 45–63.

Rosenthal, J. H. (1991), *Righteous Realists: Political Realism, Responsible Power, and American Culture in the Nuclear Age* (Baton Rouge: Louisiana State University Press).

Rostow, W. W. (1959), 'The Stages of Economic Growth', *Economic History Review*, XII/1, 1–16.

Rotberg, R.I. (ed.) (2003), *State Failure and Weakness in a Time of Terror* (Washington, DC: The World Peace Foundation/Brookings Institution Press).

Rotberg, R.I. (ed.) (2004), *When States Fail: Causes and Consequences* (Princeton and Oxford: Princeton University Press).

Rublee, M. R. and Cohen, A. (2018), 'Nuclear Norms in Global Governance: A Progressive Research Agenda', *Contemporary Security Policy*, 39/3: 317–340.

Ruggie, J. G. (1992), 'Multilateralism: The Anatomy of an Institution', *International Organisation*, 46/3: 561–598.

Rutazibwa, O. U. (2016), 'From the Everyday to IR: In Defence of the Strategic Use of the R-Word', *Postcolonial Studies*, 19/2: 191–200.

Sabaratnam, M. (2017), *Intervention: International Statebuilding in Mozambique* (London: Rowman & Littlefield).

Sabaratnam, M. (2020), 'Is IR Theory White? Racialised Subject-Positioning in Three Canonical Texts', *Millennium: Journal of International Studies*, 49/1: 3–31.

Sabsay, L. (2014), 'Nancy Fraser: Fortunes of Feminism: From State-Managed Capitalism to Neoliberal Crisis', *Feminist Legal Studies*, 22: 323–329.

Sachs, W. (ed.) (1993), *Global Ecology: A New Arena of Political Conflict* (London: Zed Books).

Said, E. W. (1985), *Orientalism* (Harmondsworth: Penguin Books).

Said, E. W. (1994), *Culture and Imperialism* (London: Vintage Books).

Saini, A. (2019), *Superior: The Return of Race in Science* (London: 4th Estate).

Sajed, A. (2016), 'Race and International Relations - What's in a Word? A Debate Around John Hobson's *The Eurocentric Conception of World Politics*', *Postcolonial Studies*, 19/2: 168–172.

Salmon, P. (2020), *An Event, Perhaps: A Biography of Jacques Derrida* (London: Verso).

Sankaran, K. (2001), 'Race, Amnesia and the Education of International Relations', *Alternatives: Global, Local, Political*, 26/4: 401–424.

Satia, P. (2020), *Time's Monster: How History Makes History* (Cambridge, MA: Belknap Press of Harvard University Press).

Saurin, J. (1995), 'International Relations, Social Ecology and the Globalization of Environmental Change' in M. Imber and J. Vogler (eds), *Environment and International Relations: Theories and Processes* (London: Routledge), 84–107.

Schweller, R.L. (1996), 'Neorealism's Status-Quo Bias: What Security Dilemma?', *Security Studies*, 5/3: 90–121.

Schweller, R.L. (2008), *Unanswered Threats: Political Constraints on the Balance of Power* (Princeton: Princeton University Press).

Schumacher, E. F. (1993), *Small is Beautiful: A Study of Economics as if People Mattered* (London: Vintage Books).

Schumacher, E. F. (2006), *Unanswered Threats: Political Constraints on the Balance of Power* (Princeton, NJ: Princeton University Press).

Sellström, T. (1999), *Sweden and National Liberation in Southern Africa. Vol 1: Formation of a Popular Opinion* (Copenhagen: NIAS).

Seth, S. (2013), 'Postcolonial Theory and the Critique of International Relations' in S. Seth (ed.), *Postcolonial Theory and International Relations: A Critical Introduction* (New York: Routledge), 15–31.

Shapcott, R. (2001), *Justice, Community and Dialogue in International Relations* (Cambridge: Cambridge University Press).

Shepherd, L. J. (2008), *Gender, Violence, and Security: Discourse as Practice* (London: Zed Books).

Shepherd, L. J. (2009), 'Gender, Violence and Global Politics: Contemporary Debates in Feminist Security Studies', *Political Studies Review*, 7: 208–219.

Shepherd, L. J. (2011), 'Sex, Security and Superhero(in)es: From 1325 to 1820 and Beyond', *International Feminist Journal of Politics*, 13/4: 504–521.

Shepherd, L. J. (ed.) (2015), *Gender Matters in Global Politics: A Feminist Introduction to International Politics*, 2nd edn (New York: Routledge).

Shepherd, L. J. (2022), '(Why) Gender Matters in Global Politics' in L. J. Shepherd and C. Hamilton (eds), *Gender Matters in Global Politics: A Feminist Introduction to International Relations*, 3rd edn (London: Routledge), 60–74.

Shetty, S. (2018) 'Decolonising Human Rights', Speech delivered by Salil Shetty, Secretary General Amnesty International at the London School of Economics, 22 May. Available at: https://www.amnesty.org/en/documents/doc10/8463/2018/en/. Accessed 17 April 2023.

Shih, C. and Chan, H.Y. (2020), 'Introduction: The Cold War and Decolonization in East Asia', *Asian Perspective*, 44/2: 171–177.

Shilliam, R. (2011), 'Decolonising the Grounds of Ethical Inquiry: A Dialogue between Kant, Foucault and Glissant', *Millennium: Journal of International Studies*, 39/3: 649–665.

Shilliam, R. (2013), 'The Spirit of Exchange' in S. Seth (ed.), *Postcolonial Theory and International Relations: A Critical Introduction* (New York: Routledge), 15–31.

Shilliam, R. (2015), *The Black Pacific: Anti-Colonial Struggles and Oceanic Connections* (London: Bloomsbury Academic).

Shilliam, R. (2020a), 'Race and Racism in International Relations: Retrieving a Scholarly Inheritance', *International Politics Reviews*, 8: 152–195.

Shilliam, R. (2020b), 'Race in World Politics' in J. Baylis, S. Smith, and P. Owens (eds), *The Globalization of World Politics*, 8th edn (Oxford: Oxford University Press), 287–302.

Singer, P. (1972), 'Famine, Affluence and Morality', *Philosophy and Public Affairs*, 1/3: 229–243.

Sjoberg, L. (ed.) (2009), *Gender and International Security: Feminist Perspectives* (New York: Routledge).

Sjoberg, L. (2016), 'What, and Where, is Feminist Security Studies?', *Journal of Regional Security*, 11/2: 143–161.

Sjoberg, L. and Gentry, C. E. (2007), *Mothers, Monsters, Whores: Women's Violence in Global Politics* (London: Zed Books).

Slaughter, J. R. (2018), 'Hijacking Human Rights: Neoliberalism, the New Historiography, and the end of the Third World', *Human Rights Quarterly*, 40/4: 735–775.

Sluga, G. (2014), 'Add Women and stir: Gender and the History of International Politics', *Humanities Australia*, 5: 65–72.

Smith, B. (2009), 'Realists Warn on Afghan War', *Politico*, 15 September. Available at: www .politico.com/blogs/ben-smith/2009/09/ realists-warn-on-afghan-war-021401

Snyder, R. C. (2008), 'What Is Third-Wave Feminism: A New Directions Essay', *Signs*, 34/1: 175–196.

Spence, M. D. (1999), *Dispossessing the Wilderness: Indian Removal and the Making of the National Parks* (Oxford: Oxford University Press).

Sperber, J. (2013), 'Is Marx still relevant?', *The Guardian*, 16 May. Available at: https://www. theguardian.com/books/2013/may/16/karl-marx-ideas-resonate-today, accessed 30 March 2023.

Spiro, D. E. (1994), 'The Insignificance of the Liberal Peace', *International Security*, 19/2: 50–86.

Spivak, G. (1994), 'Can the Subaltern Speak?' in P. Williams and L. Chisman (eds), *Colonial Discourse and Post-Colonial Theory: A Reader* (London: Routledge).

Steans, J. (2013), *Gender and International Relations*, 3rd edn (Cambridge: Polity).

Stent, A. (2022), 'The New Cold War is Here', *Foreign Policy*, 245: 8–12.

Stephens, J.C. (2019), 'Energy Democracy: Redistributing Power to the People Through Renewable Transformation', *Environment: Science and Policy for Sustainable Development*, 61/2: 4–13.

Sterling-Folker, J. (2015), 'All Hail to the Chief: Liberal IR Theory in the New World Order', *International Studies Perspectives*, 16: 40–49.

Stiehm, J. H. (1989), *Arms and the Enlisted Woman* (Philadelphia, PA: Temple University Press).

Stokke, O. (ed.) (1989), *Western Middle Powers and Global Poverty* (Uppsala: The Scandinavian Institute of African Studies/Norwegian Institute of International Affairs).

Strange, S. (1988), *States and Markets* (London: Pinter Publishers).

Sudbury, J. (1998), *'Other Kinds of Dreams': Black Women's Organisations and the Politics of Transformation* (London: Routledge).

Suzuki, S. (2005), 'Japan's Socialization into Janus-Faced European International Society', *European Journal of International Relations*, 11/1: 137–164.

Suzuki, S. (2009), *Civilisation and Empire: China and Japan's Encounter with European International Society* (London: Routledge).

Sylvester, C. (2002), *Feminist International Relations: An Unfinished Journey* (Cambridge: Cambridge University Press).

Taylor, U. (1998), 'The Historical Evolution of Black Feminist Theory and Praxis', *Journal of Black Studies*, 29/2: 234–253.

Theil, M. (2017), 'Queer Theory' in S. McGlinchey, R. Waters, and C. Scheinpflug (eds), *International Relations Theory* (Bristol: E-international Relations Publishing), 97–103.

Thomson, J. (2020), 'What's Feminist About Feminist Foreign Policy? Sweden's and Canada's Foreign Policy Agendas', *International Studies Perspectives*, 21: 424–437.

Thoreau, H.D. (2017), *Walden or Life in the Woods*, with an introduction by Benjamin Markovits (London: Vintage Classics).

Thucydides (2009), *The Peloponnesian War*, a new translation by Martin Hammond (Oxford: Oxford University Press).

Tickner, J. A. (1988), 'Hans Morgenthau's Principles of Political Realism: A Feminist Reformulation', *Millennium: Journal of International Studies*, 17/3: 429–440.

Tickner, J. A. (1992), *Gender in International Relations: Feminist Perspectives on Achieving Global Security* (New York: Columbia University Press).

Tickner, J. A. (2001), *Gendering World Politics: Issues and Approaches in the Post-Cold War Era* (New York: Columbia University Press).

Tickner, J. A. and Sjoberg, L. (2016), 'Feminism' in T. Dunne, M. Kurki, and S. Smith (eds), *International Relations Theories: Discipline and Diversity*, 4th edn (Oxford: Oxford University Press), 179–195.

Todorov, T. (1999), *The Conquest of America: The Question of the Other*, with a Foreword by Anthony Pagden (Norman, OK: University of Oklahoma Press).

Tooze, A. (2018), 'Why Karl Marx is more relevant than ever', *Financial Times*, 4 May, at https:// www.ft.com/content/cf6532dc-4c67-11e8-97e4-13afc22d86d4. Accessed 30 March 2023.

Towns, A. E. (2009), 'The Status of Women as a Standard of "Civilization"', *European Journal of International Relations*, 15/4: 681–706.

Towns, A. E. (2017), 'Gender, Power and International Society' in T. Dunne and C. Reus-Smit (eds), *The Globalization of International Society* (Oxford: Oxford University Press), 380–398.

True, J. (2004), 'Feminism' in A. J. Bellamy (ed.), *International Society and its Critics* (Oxford: Oxford University Press), 151–162.

True, J. (2018), 'Bringing Back Gendered States: Feminist Second Image Theorizing of International Relations', in S. Parashar, J. A. Tickner, and J. True (eds), *Revisiting Gendered States: Feminist Imaginings of the State in International Relations* (Oxford: Oxford University Press), 33–48.

True, J. (2022), 'Feminism(s)', in R. Devetak and J. True (eds), *Theories of International Relations*, 6th edn (London: Bloomsbury).

Tuck, E. and Yang, K. W (2012), 'Decolonization is not a metaphor', *Decolonization, Indigeneity, Education & Society*, 1/1: 1–40.

Turner, G. M. (2012) 'On the Cusp of Global Collapse? Updated Comparison of the Limits to Growth with Historical Data', *GAIA: Ecological Perspectives for Science & Society*, 21/2: 116–124.

UN Women (2015), *Preventing Conflict Transforming Justice Securing the Peace: A Global Study on the Implementation of United Nations Security Council resolution 1325* (New York: UN Women). Available at: https://wps.unwomen.org/

UNEP (2020), *Emissions Gap Report 2020* (Nairobi: United Nations Environment Programme).

UNEP (2022), *Emissions Gap Report 2022* (Nairobi: United Nations Environment Programme).

UNHCR (2015), *Press Coverage of the Refugee and Migrant Crisis in the EU: A Content Analysis of Five European Countries*, Report prepared for the United Nations High Commission for Refugees, Report authors: M. Berry, I. Garcia-Blanco, K. Moore, December. Available at: https://www.unhcr.org/media/press-coverage-refugee-and-migrant-crisis-eu-content-analysis-five-european-countries. Accessed 27 April 2023.

UNSC (2000), *Resolution 1325 Adopted by the Security Council at its 4213th Meeting on 31st October, 2000.* (New York: United Nations). Available at: https://peacemaker.un.org/sites/peacemaker.un.org/files/SC_ResolutionWomenPeaceSecurity_SRES1325%282000%29%28english_0.pdf. Accessed 22 April 2023.

Van Rythoven, E. (2021), 'A Feeling of Unease: Distance, Emotion, and Securitizing Indigenous Protest in Canada', *International Political Sociology*, 15/2: 251–271.

Verhoeve, J.J.C. (1979), *Peace, Profits and Principles: A Study of Dutch Foreign Policy* (The Hague: Martinus Nijhoff).

Victor, D. G. (2017), 'Prove Paris Was More Than Paper Promises', 3 August *Nature*, 548: 25–27.

Vincent, R. J. (1986), *Human Rights in International Relations* (Cambridge: Cambridge University Press).

Vincent, E. and Neale, T. (2016), *Unstable Relations: Indigenous People and Environmentalism In Contemporary Australia* (Crawley, WA: UWA Publishing).

Vitalis, R. (2015), *White World Order, Black Power Politics: The Birth of American International Relations* (Ithaca, NY: Cornell University Press).

Vogler, J. (2005), 'The European Contribution to Global Environmental Governance', *International Affairs*, 81/4: 835–850.

Walker, R. B. J. (1993), *Inside/Outside: International Relations as Political Theory* (Cambridge: Cambridge University Press).

Wallerstein, I. (1974a), 'The Rise and Future Demise of the World Capitalist System: Concepts for Comparative Analysis', *Comparative Studies in Society and History*, 16/4: 387–415.

Wallerstein, I. (1974b), *The Modern World System, Vol. 1: Capitalist Agriculture and the Origins of the European World-Economy in the Sixteenth Century* (Cambridge, MA: Academic Press).

Wallerstein, I. (2005), 'After Developmentalism and Globalization, What?', *Social Forces*, 83/3: 1263–1278.

Wallerstein, I. (2013), 'Structural Crisis, or Why Capitalists May No Longer Find Capitalism Rewarding' in I. Wallerstein, R. Collins, G. Derluguian, and C. Calhoun, *Does Capitalism Have a Future?* (Oxford: Oxford University Press), 9–36.

Wallerstein, I. (2015), 'The Global Systemic Crisis and the Struggle for a Post-Capitalist world', Interview with Immanuel Wallerstein, Kontext TV, 20 May. Available at http://www.kontext-tv.de/en/broadcasts/immanuel-wallerstein-global-systemic-crisis-and-struggle-post-capitalist-world#. Accessed 23 March 2023.

Walsh, C. E. (2018), 'Decoloniality in/as Praxis' in W. D. Mignolo and C.E. Walsh, *On Decoloniality: Concepts, Analytics, Praxis* (Durham, NC: Duke University Press), 15–102.

Walt S. M. (2020a), 'The Realists Guide to the Coronavirus Outbreak' *Foreign Policy*, 9 March. Available at: https://foreignpolicy.com/2020/03/09/coronavirus-economy-globalization-virus-icu-realism/.

Walt, S. M. (2020b), 'The Death of American Competence', *Foreign Policy*, 23 March. Available at foreignpolicy.com/2020/03/23/death-american-competence-reputation-coronavirus/

Waltz, K.N. (1959), *Man, The State and War: A Theoretical Analysis* (New York: Columbia University Press).

Waltz, K.N. (1979), *Theory of International Politics* (London: McGraw-Hill; New York: Random House; Reading, MA: Addison-Wesley).

Waltz, K.N. (1981), 'The Spread of Nuclear Weapons: More May Be Better', *The Adelphi Papers*, 21/171: 1–32.

Waltz, S. (2002), 'Reclaiming and Rebuilding the History of the Universal Declaration of Human Rights', *Third World Quarterly*, 23/3: 437–448.

Warren, M. A. (1985), *Gendercide: The Implications of Sex Selection* (Totowa, NJ: Rowman & Allanheld).

WCED (1987), *Our Common Future* (Oxford: Oxford University Press).

Weber, C. (1995), *Simulating Sovereignty: Intervention, the State, and Symbolic Exchange* (Cambridge: Cambridge University Press).

Weber, C. (2011), *I am an American: Filming the Fear of Difference* (Bristol: Intellect).

Weber, C. (2014), 'Encountering violence: terrorism and horrorism in war and citizenship', *International Political Sociology*, 8/3: 237–255.

Weber, C. (2015), 'Why Is There No Queer International Theory?', *European Journal of International Relations*, 21/1: 27–51.

Weber, C. (2016), *Queer International Relations: Sovereignty, Sexuality, and the Will to Knowledge* (Oxford: Oxford University Press).

Wendell, S. (1987), 'A (Qualified) Defense of Liberal Feminism', *Hypatia*, 2/2: 65–93.

Wendt, A. (1992), 'Anarchy is What States Make of It: The Social Construction of Power Politics', *International Organization*, 46/2: 391–425.

Wendt, A. (1995), 'Constructing International Politics', *International Security*, 20/1: 71–81.

Wendt, A. (1999), *Social Theory of International Politics* (Cambridge and New York: Cambridge University Press).

Wheeler, N. J. (2000), *Saving Strangers: Humanitarian Intervention in International Society* (Oxford: Oxford University Press).

Wheeler, N. J. and Dunne, T. (1996) 'Hedley Bull's pluralism of the Intellect and Solidarism of the Will', *International Affairs*, 72/1: 91–107.

Wheeler, N. J. and Dunne, T. (1998), 'Good International Citizenship: A Third Way for British Foreign Policy', *International Affairs*, 74/4: 847–870.

Whitman, J. (2005), 'Humanitarian Intervention in an Era of Pre-emptive Self-Defence', *Security Dialogue*, 36/3: 259–274.

WHO (2021), 'Vaccine inequity undermining global economic recovery', 21 July. Available at: https://www.who.int/news/item/22-07-2021-vaccine-inequity-undermining-global-economic-recovery

Wibben, A. (2011), *Feminist Security Studies: A Narrative Approach* (New York: Routledge).

Wieringa, S. (1995), *Subversive Women: Historical Experiences of Gender and Resistance* (London: Zed Books),

Wight, M. (1960), 'Why is There no International Theory?, *International Relations*, 2/1: 35–48.

Wight, M. (1979), *Power Politics,* edited by H. Bull and C. Holbraad (Harmondsworth: Penguin Books).

Wight, M. (1991), *International Theory: The Three Traditions*, edited by Gabriele Wight and Brian Porter (London: Leicester University Press/RIIA).

Williams, M. (2005), *The Realist Tradition and the Limits of International Relations* (Cambridge: Cambridge University Press).

Wilson, P. (ed.) (2016), 'The English School in Retrospect and Prospect: Barry Buzan's *An Introduction to the English School of International Relations: The Societal Approach*', Review Symposium, *Cooperation and Conflict*, 51/1: 95–102.

Wiredu, K. and Gyeke, G. (eds) (2010), *Person and Community: Ghanaian Philosophical Studies I* (Washington, DC: The Council for Research in Values and Philosophy).

Wolf, N. (1993), *Fire with Fire: New Female Power and How It Will Change the Twenty-First Century* (New York: Random House).

World Resources Institute (2022), 'COP27: Key Takeaways and What's Next', 8 December. Available at: https://www.wri.org/insights/cop27-key-outcomes-un-climate-talks-sharm-el-sheikh?_gl=1*1lze9pe*_up*MQ..&gclid=CjwKCAjwuqiiBhBtEiwATgvixEBSg8w3z-S2P8V-dLeNXLOO-vSsfAnQk8pzOYh__a6Iw0ycIfQW0hoCBq4QAvD_BwE. Accessed 27 April 2023.

Wyn Jones, R. (1999), *Security, Strategy and Critical Theory* (Boulder, CO: Lynne Rienner).

Xinhuanet (2021), 'Xi focus: Xi vows to win people's war against novel coronavirus', 11 February. Available at: www.xinhuanet.com/english/2020-02/11/c_138771934.htm.

Young, R. J. C. (2016), *Postcolonialism: An Historical Introduction*, 15th Anniversary Edition (Chichester: Wiley Blackwell).

Youngs, G. (2004),'Feminist International Relations: A Contradiction in Terms? Or Why Women and Gender Are Essential To Understanding The World "We" Live in, *International Affairs*, 80/1: 75–87.

Zehfuss, M. (2002), *Constructivism in International Relations: The Politics of Reality* (Cambridge: Cambridge University Press).

Zehfuss, M. (2009), 'Jacques Derrida', in J. Edkins and N. Vaughan-Williams, *Critical Theorists and International Relations* (London: Routledge), 137–149.

Zehfuss, M. (2018), *War and the Politics of Ethics* (Oxford: Oxford University Press).

Zhang, X. (2011), 'China in the Conception of International Society: The English School's Engagements with China', *Review of International Studies*, 37: 763–786.

Zhang, Y. (2016), 'Pluralism, Solidarism and the Yin-Yang of International Society' in P. Wilson (ed.), 'The English School in Retrospect and Prospect: Barry Buzan's *an Introduction to the English School of International Relations: The Societal Approach*', Review Symposium, *Cooperation and Conflict*, 51/1: 95–102.

Zhang, Y. (2017), 'Worlding China' in T. Dunne and C. Reus-Smit (eds), *The Globalization of International Society* (Oxford: Oxford University Press), 204–224.

Zilla, C. (2022), 'Feminist Foreign Policy', *SWP Comment*, 48 (Berlin: Stiftung Wissenschaft und Politik) 8pp. Available at: https://www.swp-berlin.org/publications/products/comments/2022C48_FeministForeignPolicy.pdf. Accessed 24 April 2023.

SUBJECT INDEX

Notes:
Tables, figures, and boxes are indicated by an italic *t*, *f*, or *b* following the page number.

Aberystwyth narrative 38
ABM (Anti-Ballistic Missile Treaty) 47*b*
absence, Derrida 238
absolute gains, relative gains *vs.* 89
Acheson, Dean 80
Adler, Emmanuel 285
Afghanistan
  humanitarian interventions 478
  military action in 52, 101–3, 263, 266
Africa
  assistance to 267–8
  ependency theory 162
  feminism and 376
African National Congress (ANC) 337–8
African Union 342
Age of Discovery 327
Agenda21 449
agents of a world common good 133–4*b*
agreements, sanctity of 119
ahistorical truth 242
Ain't I A Woman: Black Woman and Feminism
  (hook) 383
Algerian War of Independence 335–6*b*
alienation 155
*All the Women Are White, All the Blacks are Men, But
  Some of Us Are Brave* 383
Allen, Theodore W. 329–30, 329–30*b*
Allende, Salvador 356
Alter 299
America *see* United States of America (US)
Amin, Idi 356–7
Amnesty International 213
*The Anarchical Society: A Study of Order in World
  Politics* (Bull) 107, 118, 120, 124–5, 141
anarchical society of states 106, 107–11, 118–25, 235,
  300*b*, 475
  English School 14, 118–25, 286–7
anarchy 283–6
  implications of 285
  international politics (Waltz) 84–5
  realism 13
'Anarchy is What States Make of it' (Wendt) 283
Ancient Rome, industrial pollution 432
Angell, Norman 37
Anghie, Anthony 349–50
Annan, Kofi 130–1, 130–1*b*

Anthropocene 19, 429*f*, 462–3*b*, 462–5, 479–81
  ecocentrism *vs.* 426
anthropomorphism 430
Anti-Ballistic Missile Treaty (ABM) 47*b*
anti-colonialism, post-1945 334–9
anti-discipline 486
anti-foundationalist 242
anti-war activity, feminism and 391–2
apartheid system
    opposition to 338
    South Africa 337–8*b*
Appadurai, Arjun 346
Arab League 342
archaeology, metaphor as 246
Aron, Raymond 82
Ashley, Richard 201–4, 208, 225
Ashworth, Lucian 37
Asia
    dependency theory 162
    feminism and 376
    see also Southeast Asia
Association of Southeast Asian Nations 342
Aune, Kristen 385
Australia
    indigenous people resistance 457
    opinions of 327
AuthaGraph projection 254–5, 255*f*
autonomous independence 389
'Axis of Evil' 295*b*
Ayoob, Mohammad 352

Baader-Meinhof Gang (Red Army) 303
Baker, Noel 38
balance of power
    international power and 80–1
    World Order and 121–2
Baltic States 312–13
*Bananas, Beaches and Bases: Making Feminist Sense of
    International Politics* (Enloe) 397–9
Band Aid (1984) 267
Bandung Conference (1955) 338
Bangladesh garment factory disasters 398–9*b*
Barthes, Roland 236
base-superstructure model 155
Baylis, J. 5
Beijing Consensus 178–9*b*, 213

SUBJECT INDEX

Beijing Platform for Action (BPA) 414
Bellamy, Alex 54–6
Bentham's Panopticon 244b
Berlin Wall 477
Bhabha, Homi K. 345–6
Biden, Joe 313
biopower 244–5
Biswas, Shampa 351–2
Black Death (14th century) 432–3
Black Lives Matter (2020) 325
Black Skin, White Masks (Fanon) 339
Black–Green relations 458
Blanchard, Eric 142
Blaney, D. L. 364
Blatt, Jessica 39
Bleiker, Roland 242, 256–7, 267
Bokassa, Jean-Bedel 357
Bolton, John 295b
Boserup, Ester 394
Bosnia 52
  independence 263
bourgeoisie 154
Boyer, Mark 396
BPA (Beijing Platform for Action) 414
Brailsford, H. N. 37
Bretton Woods System 42, 43b, 44, 46, 208, 475
Brexit 50, 92–3, 272–4
'The British Committee on the Theory of International
  Relations' 112
British Empire, ending of 298
Bromley, Simon 172
Browne, Kath 416
Brundtland Commission 449
bubonic plague epidemic (14th century) 432–3
Bull, Hedley 107, 110, 112, 116, 118–25, 126–9,
  141, 306
Burke, Edmund 433
Burton, John 47
Bush, George W. 129, 295b, 296
Butler, Judith 404
Butterfield, Herbert 112
Buzan, Barry 138–42, 222, 406–7

Cambodia, anti-colonial struggles 335
Cammack, Paul 173–4
Campbell, David 242, 256–7, 267, 455
Canada
  foreign policy 133
  renewable energy technology 457
Capital in the Twenty-First Century (Piketty) 180
capitalism
  definition 154
  liberalism and 50–1
  Marxism and 151, 153–4
  neo-Gramscianism 210
Capitalocene 464
Caprioli, Mary 396
Caputo, John 240
'Car Culture' 454b
carbon dioxide emissions 468–9

Caribbean, feminism and 376
Carr, E. H. 36, 72–3b, 72–4, 202–3
Carroll, Berenice 389
Carson, Rachel 436–7
Carter, Jimmy 476
Casimir, Jean 333
Castro, Fidel 365b
CDAW (Convention on the Elimination of All Forms
  of Discrimination against Women) 394–5
Central African Republic 357
Césaire, Aimé 334, 363
Chakrabarty, Dipesh 324, 464–5
Chatham House 360
Checkel, Jeffrey 293
Chimni, Bhupinder 350
China
  carbon dioxide emissions 468t
  rise of 4, 49
Chinese Empire 110
Christian Right, anti-LGBT 414
civil society 176
civilizing missions 160, 328
Clapp, Jennifer 459
class solidarity
  differences in 167
  green policy 455
class struggle 156
class theory, dependency theory and 166–7
classical Greek thought, Critical International Theory
  and 190
classical liberalism 26, 298
classical realism
  contemporary 71–8
  core assumptions 78–82
  definition 64
clean bombs 390
climate change, anthropocene 465
Clinton, Hilary 416
Coalition Agreement (2021–2025), Germany 412
Cohn, Carol 390–1
Cold War (1945–1989) 3, 474–5
  classical realism 66
  end of 25, 48–51, 93b, 223, 263, 279–80b, 282, 285,
    286, 310, 477
  liberalism 30
  local specific realities and 348
  neorealism and 93b
  postcolonialism 348–9
  realism 13
  security and 203, 222
  stability during 96
  superpowers 86
collapsed states 353
collective action problem 445
collective defence 45
collective identity 280
collective security 45
  League of Nations 34, 35b
colonialism 38
  dependent countries 167

Marxist critique 334
racism and 328–31
see also decolonization; postcolonialism
colonialism resistance 331–9
early resistance 331–3
twentieth century 334–9
coloniality 484–5
Colston, Edward 325
common institutions, international society 107–11
communal level, green theory and 439–40
communication technology, liberalism 31
Communism
definition of 157, 190
Marxism and 151, 157–8
rejection of 157
Communist states, failure of 158
competition 85
complex interdependence 47, 82, 89, 298, 475–6
globalization 171
liberalism 47–8
Comte, Auguste 194, 195*b*
The Condition of the Working Class in England
(Engels) 155
conflict of interests, Carr 73
conflicts, feminisms 388–93
Connell, R. W. 400–1
conservationist approach 434
Constructivism 17, 277–320
agency 290–2
analysis 310
definition 278–86
development 278–82
essence of 282–6
middle ground as 296–7
nuclear weapons 310–13
position in spectrum of theories 286–97
structure 290–2
types 292–6
constructivism, conventional constructivism 292–3
consumerist feminism 382
contemporary liberalism 51–4
contingent generalisations 310
Convention against Torture 354
Convention on the Elimination of All Forms of
Discrimination against Women (CDAW) 394–5
Convention on the Rights of Persons with
Disabilities 354
Convention on the Rights of the Child 354
conventional constructivism 292–3
cooperation under anarchy 90–1
COP26 448–51
COP27 451
Cornell, D. 413
Corry, Olaf 465
cosmopolitan awareness 128
cosmopolitan democracy 221
cosmopolitan moral awareness 133
cosmopolitan perspectives, Critical International
Theory 269
cosmopolitanism 216*b*

Frankfurt School 215–16
Linklater 220
Council of Foreign Relations (USA) 31
counter-hegemonic bloc 209, 213
COVID vaccines 183–5
COVID-19 pandemic 245, 250, 316–18
vaccine apartheid 183–5
Cox, Robert 177–8, 201, 204–8
Crenshaw, Kimberlé 383
Crimean War (1854–1856) 362
critical constructivism 293–6
Critical International Theory 12, 15–16, 112, 133,
135, 188–230
applications of 208–24
definition 189–201
development 224–5
emancipation and 200–1
English School and 134–6
Frankfurt School 215–18
global environment movement and 227–8
mainstream theories *vs.* 10–12
normative analysis 304
origins of 190–3
roots of 189
security 222–4
theoretical perspective 256
traditional theories *vs.* 195–8
see also Poststructuralism
Critical Race Theory (CRT) 362
banning of teaching of 363
Critical Security Studies (CSS) 222, 223, 408
Critical Theory 205, 482–3
Critical Security Studies 408
emancipation and 403–4
feminism 387–8
green theory and 439
Horkheimer 196–7
CRT *see* Critical Race Theory (CRT)
CSS (Critical Security Studies) 222, 223, 408
Cuba 295*b*
Cuban Missile Crisis (1962) 349
decolonization and 365–6*b*
Cudd, Elizabeth 382
cultural hegemony, Gramsci 176
cultures 2
differences between 358
Curtis, Lionel 38

damage limitation weapons 390
Darden, Jessica Trisko 393
Das Kapital (Marx) 151*b*
Dauvergne, Peter 459
de Beauvoir, Simone 378–9, 379*f*
de Gaulle, Charles 336*b*
de Gouges, Olympe 375
De Jure Belli et Pacis (On the Law of War and Peace)
(Grotius) 115–16, 116*b*
Declaration Des Droites de l'Homme et du Citoyen
(1789) 354
Declaration of the Rights of Man and of the Citizen 375

510 SUBJECT INDEX

decolonization 51, 306, 363–8
  continuing need 341–2
  human rights 357–8
  post-1945 334–9
  university curricula 364
  see also colonialism
deconstruction, Derrida 238
defensive neorealism, offensive neorealism *vs.* 87–8
democracy, liberalism 25
democratic peace theory 29–30
dependency 476
  international class relations 166–7
dependency theory
  class theory and 166–7
  classes of states 168
  definition 162
  emergence of 164
  Marxism and 162–7
depoliticization 198–9
Der Derian, James 249
Derrida, Jacques 232, 236–40, 246, 257
  biography 237–8*b*
  see also Poststructuralism
Dessalines, Jean-Jacques 333
détente 46, 46–7*b*, 48, 82, 162–3, 475–6
developing states, economic exploitation of 449
development economists 165
Development of Capitalism in Russia (Lenin) 161*b*
The Dialectic of Sex (Firestone) 380
dichotomies 257
diplomacy, World Order 123
discipline 485
Discipline and Punish (Foucault) 244*b*
discourse ethics 218–19*b*, 243
  Foucault 241
Discourse on the Origins of Inequality (Rousseau) 79*b*
discursive practices 241
dissemiNation 346
distribution of capabilities 86
'Do They Know It's Christmas' 267
Dobson, Andrew 428
Does Khaki Become You? The Militarization of Women's Lives (Enloe) 392–3
domestic security 302
domestication 262
dominant relations, critical understanding of 177
Dryzek, John 440
Dubček, Alexandre 192*b*
DuBois, W. E. B. 329, 334, 337, 353, 363
Duncan, Henry 264
Duncanson, Claire 392
Dunne, Tim 129, 132–3
Dutch West India Company 348
Dworkin, Andrea 381

Earth Systems Council 464
East Timor
  conflict in 53
  humanitarian interventions 478
East–West rivalry 3

East–West shift 475–6
Eckersley, Robyn 438, 451, 460
ecocentrism 429*f*, 430–1
  anthropocene *vs.* 426
ecofeminism 459
ecological democracy, liberalism 461
ecologism 428
  environmentalism *vs.* 426
ecology, environmentalism *vs.* 427–9
economics
  inequalities 385
  injustices 80
  international society 141
  Marxism and 154
ECOWAS 53
Edkins, Jenny 264–5
education programmes, liberalism 31
Ego 299
Egypt 357
Ehrlich, Paul 434–5*b*
El Requerimento (The Requirement) 327
electric cars 455
Elshtain, Jean Bethke 388
emancipation 112
  cognitive interest 204
  Critical International Theory 269
  Critical Theory and 200–1
  Frankfurt School 217
  Habermas 199
  humanity of 243
empiricism, social sciences 194
END (European Nuclear Disarmament) 310–11
energy developments, indigenous people resistance 457
Engels, Friedreich 155, 156–7
English School 12, 14, 105–48, 478
  anarchical society of states 286–7
  critical theory and 134–6
  definition 106–12
  feminism and 142–4
  good international citizenship and 132–4
  international politics 306
  liberalism *vs.* 110–11
  origins of 112–25
  pluralists and solidarists 111–12
  realism *vs.* 107–8
  reappraisal of 138–42
  reconstruction of 141–2
  solidarist wing 136, 220–1
'The English School of International Relations: A Case for Closure' (Jones) 113
The Enlightenment
  Critical International Theory and 190
  feminisms 375
  race and 330–1
Enloe, Cynthia 142, 388, 392–3, 397–9
environmental degradation 456
environmentalism
  ecologism *vs.* 426
  ecology *vs.* 427–9
  orthodox view 427

SUBJECT INDEX 511

epistemology 9–10, 188, 473
  assumptions 473
  Critical International Relations theory 15
  realism 66
ethnic cleansing 52, 309
ethnic minorities, green policy 456
ethnicity 2
Eurocentrism 322–3, 358–63, 473, 484
  Mercator projection 253
  offensive form 360
  racism *vs.* 361–3
  replacement of 365
Eurocommunism 193
Europe
  state system consolidation 352–3
  women's right to vote 377
European Coal and Steel Community (ECSC) 44
European colonization 324–31
  expansion of 326–8
  Global South 126–7
  memories of 325
  North America 327
  racialism and 333
European Commission 284
European Convention on the Suppression of
    Terrorism 303
European Empires 110
European integration 44, 221
  neoliberalism and 92–3
European Nuclear Disarmament (END) 310–11
European Union (EU)
  emergence of 92
  establishment of 44, 284
  inclusivity 221
  state cooperation 92
Euroscepticism 93
Evans, Elizabeth 132*b*, 381
Everard, Sarah 420–2
exclusion 219–22
  realism and nuclear weapons 97
exclusionary politics 134
explanation to understanding 482–3
exponential population growth 445
external security 302
Extinction Rebellion 443–4

failed states 353
fairness, abstract ideal as 68
false consciousness 155–6
'The False Promise of International Institutions'
    (Mearsheimer) 91
Fanon, Franz 324, 339–42, 340*f*, 363
  biography 340–1
fascism 191, 309
favoured positions, Constructivism 289–90
Fawcett, Millicent 376*b*
The Female Eunuch (Greer) 380
female gender, male gender *vs.* 387
The Feminine Mystique (Friedan) 379–80
Feminism and Gender 18–19

feminisms 373–424
  consumerist feminism 382
  definition 374, 375–85
  ecofeminism 459
  emergence of 386–8
  English School and 142–4
  evolution of 378–85
  first wave feminism 378
  foreign policy 411–12
  fourth wave feminism 385
  individualistic feminism 382
  International Development 394–5
  intersectionality and 382–4
  key themes 405–12
  neoliberalism and 381–2
  peace and conflict 388–93
  second wave feminism *see* second wave
      feminism
  third wave feminism 381–4, 396
  see also gender; women's suffrage
Feminist Foreign Policy (FFP) (Sweden) 411–12
feminist security studies (FSS) 407–11
Fendler, Lynn 232
FFP (Feminist Foreign Policy) (Sweden) 411–12
Fierke, Karin 282–3, 293–4
Finnemore, Martha 308
Firestone, Shulamith 380
first wave feminism 378
First World War 359, 473–4
  afterwards *see* post-First World War
Foreign Affairs 39
foreign policies
  neoclassical realism 94
  states, influence of 80
former Yugoslavia 52, 294
  conflicts in 223
  humanitarian interventions 478
Foucault, Michel 232, 236, 240–6
  biography 240–1*b*
  see also Poststructuralism
14 Points Speech (Wilson) 33, 50
fourth wave feminism 385
Frank, André Gunder 51, 166
Frankfurt School 196*b*, 208, 225
  Critical International Relations theory 15
  Critical International Theory 215–18
Fraser, Nancy 382
free trade
  global economic systems 459
  liberalism 24–5
Friedan, Betty 379–80
FSS (feminist security studies) 407–11
Fukuyama, Frances 48, 478
functionally specialized, international politics
    (Waltz) 84–5

Gaia hypothesis 428, 428–9*b*
Gall–Peters projection 253–4, 253*f*
Gari, Lutfallah 432
Garvey, Marcus 334, 337

SUBJECT INDEX

gas extraction, indigenous people resistance 457
gender 2, 357, 373–424
  analytical category as 399–400, 412
  definition 373–4
  equality 411
  green policy 455
  key themes 405–12
  mainstreaming 409–10b
  poststructuralism and postcolonialism 403–5
  security and 406–12
  theorists 483
  see also feminisms
Gender and Development (GAD) 394–5
gender essentialism 374
  critique of 405
Gender in International Relations (Tickner) 400–3,
    401–2b
Gender Trouble: Feminism and the Subversion of
    Identity (Butler) 404
gendercide 413
gendered states 406–7
Gendered States: Feminist (Re) Visions of International
    Theory (Peterson) 405, 408
gendering, states 405–6
gender-focused theories 486
general theory of international politics 482
generalizations, Orientalism 343
Geneva Convention 264
Genocide Convention 354
Gentry, Caron 393
Georgia 312–13
Germany
  Coalition Agreement (2021–2025) 412
  security policies 303
  sense of identity 298
Ghana, independence 337
Ghandi, Mahatma 334
Giddens, Anthony 290b
Gill, Stephen 211
Gilpin, Robert 47, 66, 86–7
glasnost 281b
global dominance, neoliberalism 210–11
global ecological crisis 451
global environment movement, Critical International
    Theory and 227–8
global financial crisis (2008) 179
global governance 173
global hegemony, neo-Gramscianism 211
global inequality/injustice 4–5
  COVID vaccines 183–5
Global North
  gender equality 411
  Global South and 4, 125
  Global South, migration from 324
  IR theory 485
  public attitudes towards 325
  racist states 347
Global Political Economy (GPE) see international
    political economy (IPE)/Global Political
    Economy (GPE)

Global South 124–5
  depiction of 263
  development problems 459
  global market integration 180
  Global North and 4, 125
  Global North, migration to 324
  importance of 121
  postcolonialism 166
global violence against women 420–2
Globalization 171–2b, 210
  definition 170
  inevitability of 478
  Marxism 15, 170–4
  world economy 141
GNP (Gross National Product) 162
Golan Heights (1967) 42
Goldman, Emma 378
good international citizenship 132b
  English School and 132–4
Goodin, Robert 438–9
Gorbachev, Mikhail 279–80b, 280–1, 281b, 285–6,
    290, 311, 477
governmentality, Foucault 245
Gramsci, Antonio 175b, 190–1, 215, 225, 342
Great Powers 146–7
  neorealism and 86–7
  World Order 124
Greek city-states 120
Green perspectives 19–20, 425–71
  alternative ecological world order 458–62
  anthropomorphism vs. ecocentrism 429–31
  awareness growth 437–8
  definition 426–31
  emergence of 432–7
  environmental justice 455–8
  environmentalism vs. ecology 427–9
  global environmental governance 448–51
  impact of 441–2
  international political economy 453–5
  internet perspectives 451–62
  state-censured status 442–51
Green Political Theory (Goodin) 438–9
Greenham Common Women's Peace Camp 391,
    391b, 403
Greenpeace 213
Greer, Germaine 380
Gross National Product (GNP) 162
Grotius, Hugo 115f, 116b
Group of 77 (G77) 163, 338, 342
Grovogui, S. N. 347
Die Grünen (German Green Party) 441, 441–2b
Guha, Ranajit 344
Gulf War (1991) 247–8, 250–1
Gusterson, Hugh 97, 351

Habermas, Jürgen 198–9, 217–18, 218b, 219
Hagey Lectures (1983) 125, 127
Haitian Revolution (1791–1804) 331, 332–3
Hanson, Marianne 311
Haram, Boko 406

SUBJECT INDEX 513

Hardin, Garrett 444–7
Hegel, Georg 330
Hegemonic Stability Theory 87, 87*b*
hegemony concept, non-Gramscianism 175–8
Henderson, Errol 359
Herz, John 82, 203–4
hierarchy, international politics (Waltz) 84–5
Hilhorst, Dorothea 264
Hindu caste system 375
Hines, Colin 459–60
Hiroshima (1945) 95, 352
Hirst, Paul 172
historical context 3–5
historical materialism, Marxism 153–7
The History of Sexuality (Foucault) 241*b*
The History of the Peloponnesian War (Thucydides)
    67–8, 67*b*
Ho Chi Minh 334
Hobbes, Thomas 70–1, 115*f*, 299, 402
Hobbesian anarchical system 299
Hobson, John 160, 343, 359, 360
Hoffman, Mark 221
homonormativity 416
horizontal proliferation, nuclear weapons 95
Horkheimer, Nax 196*b*
Hornborg, A. 465
Howard, Peter 294, 296
Huddart, David 345
Hudson's Bay Company 348
human emancipation, Marxism 153
human nature 77–8*b*
    Morgenthau 75
human rights
    global impact of 355–6
    postcolonialism and 354–8, 358*b*
    rethinking and decolonizing 357–8
    shortcomings of 356
human socio-political organization 440
humanitarian assistance 265
humanitarian interventions 51–2, 53–4, 478
humanitarianism 264–6
humanity, emancipation of 243
Hume, David 330
Humvee 455
Hungary
    post-Cold war liberalism 59–60
    uprising (1956) 191–2*b*
Hussein, Saddam 294
hybridity 345–6
hyperreality, Poststructuralism 247

I am an American (Weber) 260*b*
ICRC (International Committee of the Red Cross) 264
idealism 34*b*
    liberalism 37–8
    realism *vs.* 36
identity
    conception of 258–9
    formation, Third Spaces 346
    importance of 297–305

ideology, Critical International Theory 209–15
ignorance, epistemology of 362
ILO (International Labour Organization) 31, 204–5
IMF (International Monetary Fund) 43*b*, 173, 178, 211
imperialism 38–40, 324, 326*b*
    crucial role of 353
    Marxism and 160–2, 166
    Marxist critique 334
    violent expansion of 347–8
Imperialism: A Study (Hobson) 160
Imperialism: The Highest Stage of Capitalism
    (Lenin) 83, 161, 334
implementation 410–11, 410*b*
inclusion 219–22
India
    carbon dioxide emissions 468*t*
    decolonialism 334–5
    Marxism and 344
    Non-Proliferation Treaty breach 311, 350
    resistance to colonialism 344
    revolt (1857–1858) 362
    rise of 4
Indigenous peoples
    civilization excuse 328
    environmentalism 431, 457–8
    green policy 456
    modern-day struggles 367
    scholars 367–8
individual freedoms 355
    liberalism 50
individualism
    feminism 382
    liberalism 24
industrial capitalism, Marx 207
industrial pollution 432
Institut Universitaire des Hautes Études Internationales
    (Graduate Institute of International Affairs,
    Switzerland) 31
institutionalized environments, neoliberalism 90
instrumentalist view of natural world 427–8
intellectual currents identification 234–5
interdependence 162
    states 262
interdiscipline 486
    essays on 396–7
interest definition, power and 76
Intergovernmental Panel on Climate Change
    (IPCC) 444
Intermediate-Range Nuclear Forces treaty (1987) 311
international anarchy 65, 94
International Bank for Reconstruction and
    Development 43*b*
international class relations, dependency 166–7
International Committee of th Red Cross (ICRC) 264
International Convenant on Civil and Political
    Rights 354
International Convention on the Elimination of all
    forms of Racial Discrimination 354
International Covenant on Economic, Social and
    Cultural Rights 354

International Crisis (ICB) data set 396
international environmental action 452
International Labour Organization (ILO) 31, 204–5
international law 115*f*
 postcolonialism 349–52
 World Order and 122–3
International Monetary Fund (IMF) 43*b*, 173,
  178, 211
international order
 prospects of 143
 threats to 124–5
international organizations 2
 green awareness 443*f*
international political economy (IPE)/Global Political
  Economy (GPE) 47, 140–2
 green politics 453
 Marxism and 151–2, 169–80
international politics 256
 definitions 6
 English School 306
 institutions, liberalism 41–5, 109
 realism and 66–71
international power, balance of power and 80–1
international regimes 90
International Relations (IR) 256
 definitions 6
 origins challenges 37–40
 spectrum of theories 287–8, 287*f*
international societies 107
 economics 141
 international systems *vs.* 117–18
 primary goals and common institutions 107–11
 reconfiguration 139–40
 regulatory institutions and 124
 rules of 137–8
 world society to 138–44
international society of states 107, 483–4
 historical features 109–10
international systems
 international societies *vs.* 117–18
 primacy of order 118–21
interpretation, Poststructuralism 247
interpretive analysis 293
intersectionality 382–3, 404
 feminism and 382–4
 Feminism and Gender 18–19
interstitial third spaces 346
intersubjective (shared) understanding 307
inter-state relations 47
*An Introduction to the Study of International
  Relations* 359
The Invention of the White Race (Allen) 329–30*b*
IPCC (Intergovernmental Panel on Climate
  Change) 444
Iran 295*b*
Iraq 295*b*
 2003 invasion 131
 humanitarian interventions 478
 invasion (1990–1991) 296
 military action in 263, 266

UN-led invasion 250
 weapons of mass destruction 296
Islamic State, anti-LGBT 414
Islamophobia 259–60*b*
Israel, Non-Proliferation Treaty breach 95, 312, 350

Jackson, Robert 136–7, 139
James, C. L. R. 328, 353
Japan
 carbon dioxide emissions 468*t*
 post-war 302–3
Japanese Empire 110
'Jim Crow' Laws 332
Joll, James 176
Jones, Adam 413
Jones, Branwen Gruffydd 353
Jones, Deiniol 221
Jones, Richard Wyn 215, 222, 223
Jones, Roy 113
Journal of International Relations 39
Journal of Race Development 39
justice
 abstract ideal as 68
 order *vs.* 125–38

Kant, Immanuel 27–30, 28*f*, 44, 54–6, 216*b*, 218*b*,
  300, 330, 474
Kantian international culture 300
Katzenstein, Peter 301, 302, 303
Kegley, Charles 49–50
Kennan, George 80
Keohane, Robert 47, 51, 54–5, 89, 475
Kerr, Philip 38
Kindleberger, Charles 87*b*
Klotz, Audie 293
knowledge, acquisition of 198
knowledge claims 242
knowledge-constitutive interests 200
Kollontai, Alexandra 378
Koslowski, Rey 280
Kosovo 52
 independence 263
 NATO-led interventions 136
Krasner, Stephen 86–7
Kratochwil, Friedrich 280
Krishna, Sankaran 361–2
Kyoto Protocol (1997) 450

Laffey, Mark 365*b*
Land Ethics 430
language-based constructivism 294–6
Laos, anti-colonial struggles 335
Latin America
 Dependency Theory 162
 development 165
 economic development 167
 feminism and 376
law enforcement 302
law-breakers, historical arguments 122
Le Pen, Jean-Marie 336*b*

League of Nations 34, 204, 474
  advocates for 38
  collapse of 40, 73
  creation of 33*b*
  missing members 35
Lenin, Vladimir 83, 160–1, 161–2*b*, 334
  modification of Marxism 166
Leopold, Aldo 430
Lesbian feminists 414
levels, problems of 140
The Leviathan (Hobbes) 70–1
LGBT perspectives 414–17, 417–18*b*, 481
  relevance of 414
  Western-led activism 417, 417–18*b*
liberal feminists 395–6
liberal institutionalism, Cox 205
liberal sovereign states 217, 262
  problematizing of 261–7
liberalism 12–13, 22–62, 261–2
  application of 32–6
  capitalism and 50–1
  classical liberalism 26, 298
  complex interdependence 47–8
  contemporary liberalism 51–4
  core tenets of 24–5
  definition 23–5
  ecological democracy 461
  English School *vs.* 110–11
  foundational phase 26–36
  global reform 263
  idealism 37–8, 40–51
  imperialism and 51–4
  International Political Economy 170
  international politics institutionalization 41–5, 109
  origins of 30–2
  post-1945 45–7
Libya 295*b*
  conflict in 52
  military action in 266
'Lifeboat Ethics: A Case Against Helping the Poor'
    (Hardin) 446
The Limits to Growth 447–8
Linklater, Andrew 134–5, 136, 219, 225, 304–5, 460
Lippman, Walter 80
Lisle, Debbie 268
Locke, John 114–15, 115*f*, 299–300, 330–1
Lockean structure of anarchy 299–300
Lovelock, James 428*b*
Lower Burma, conquest of 362
Luxemburg, Rosa 378

McCarthy Era 93*b*
Machiavelli, Niccolo 69–70, 69*f*
Magna Carta (1215) 354
mainstream theories, critical theories *vs.* 10–12
male gender, female gender *vs.* 387
Malm, A. 465
Malthus, Thomas 445
Man, the State and War (Waltz) 83
Manchester, Marx and 155, 156*f*

Mandela, Nelson 338
The Manifesto of the Communist Party (Marx and
    Engels) 156–7, 159–60
Māori people, wars against 362
Marx, Karl 150–1*b*
  Critical International Theory and 190
  industrial capitalism 207
  philosophical inquiry, views on 200
Marxism 4, 14–15, 149–87, 478, 484
  classical definition 175
  Communism and 151, 157–8
  Critical International Theory and 189
  Critical Security Studies and 223
  definition 150–9
  dependency theory and 162–7
  emancipation and 403–4
  feminism 387–8
  First wave feminism 378
  globalization and 170–4
  green theory 439, 459
  historical materialism 153–7
  imperialism and 160–2
  India 344
  international political economy 169–80
  key themes 152–9
  political economy 209
  theoretical perspective 256
  'young' type 193
masculinism 413–14
material power, Critical International Theory 209–15
materialism 479
Mayall, James 136–7, 139
Me, Not You: The Trouble with Mainstream Feminism
    (Phipps) 385
means of production, Marxism and 154
Mearsheimer, John 87, 88, 91, 93*b*
Melian Dialogues 68
Mende, Janne 354
Mercator Projection 252–3, 252*f*
metanarratives 268–9
methodology 10, 188
  assumptions 473
#metoo campaign 385
Mignolo, Walter 364
military service
  institution as 414
  women 392–3, 393–4*b*
Millennium (Cox) 201
Millett, Kate 380, 381
Milne, David 40
Minuteman Civil Defences Corps 261*b*
Mitrany, David 37
Miyoshi, Masao 346
mode of production, Marxism 153
modernization theory 164
modernization, trickle-down politics 172
Mohanty, Chandra 384*b*
moral development, Kant 2
moral significance, political realism of 76–7
morality, Carr 73–4

SUBJECT INDEX

Morgenthau, Hans 74–8, 80, 82, 106, 151, 202–3, 401, 401–2*b*
  biography 74–5*b*
  nuclear weapons 95–6
Mukherjee, Sumita 377*b*
Mulder, Connie 338*b*
multinational corporations (MNCs) 8
  transnational 348
multinational organizations 2
Mutua, Makua 353, 355
Mutually Assured Destruction (MAD) 47*b*, 96, 348

Næss, Arne 430–1
Nagasaki (1945) 95, 352
Narukawa, Hajime 254–5
Nash, Catherine 416
National Action Plans (NAPs) 410*b*
national defence 302
national economic rivalry 173
national identities 2, 301–3, 304*b*
The National Interest 81*b*
national political rivalry 173
National Union of Women's Suffrage Societies (NUWSS) 376*b*
nationalism, impact of 219
nationality, green policy 455
Nationally Determined Commitments (NDCs) 450
NATO *see* North Atlantic Treaty Organization (NATO)
Navari, Cornelia 106
Nazism, rise of 196*b*
NDCs (Nationally Determined Commitments) 450
Neal, Andrew 245
neglect of power, Carr 72
neoclassical realism 94–5
  definition 64, 94
'The Neoidealist Moment in International Studies? Realist Myths and the New International Realities' (Kegley) 49–50
neoliberalism 25, 88–93, 261–2
  Cox 205
  definition 88–9
  European integration and 92–3
  feminism and 381–2
  global dominance 210–11
  globalization 171–2
  Green economy 453
  institutionalism 90–1, 476
  neorealism *vs.* 89
  postcolonialism and 352
  relative *vs.* absolute gains 89
neorealism 48, 55, 63–104, 235, 480, 483
  definition 64, 82
  development of 82–8
  end of Cold War 93*b*, 286
  English School 106
  great powers and 86–7
  neoliberalism *vs.* 89
  offensive *vs.* defensive 87–8
neo-colonialism 52

neo-Gramscianism 170
  analytical framework 453
  Critical International Theory 209–15
  global change and 211
  global hegemony 211
  hegemony and 175–8
neo-imperialism 52
neo-Marxism 478, 484
Netherlands, foreign policy 133
New International Economic Order (NIEO) 163, 253, 338
new social movements (NSMs) 211–12, 212*b*, 233*b*
New Wars 223
'New World Order' (Bush) 93*b*, 129, 478
  opinions of 327
New Zealand 377
Newell, Peter 453
NGOs (Non-Governmental Organizations) 2, 8, 128, 179
Niebuhr, Reinhold 80
NIEO (New International Economic Order) 163, 253, 338
Nigeria, right populist movements 406
9/11 terror attacks 250, 259*b*, 261*b*, 295*b*, 301–2, 409, 479–81
Nkrumah, Kwame 336
NNPR (nuclear non-proliferation regime) 351
Noel-Baker, Philip 37
nongendered perspectives 403
Non-aligned Movement (1961) 338
Non-Governmental Organizations (NGOs) 2, 8, 128, 179
Non-Proliferation Treaty (NPT, 1970) 311, 350
  importance of 351–2
non-renewable carbon resources 455
non-Western world, Poststructuralism 267–8
norm entrepreneurs 308
norm violators 309
normative 307
  conventional constructivism 307
normative analysis 304–5
  structural analysis from 139
normative structure 307
normative (value-driven) conception of theory, Critical International Relations theory 16
normativity 307–10
norms 307–10
  adherents to 308–9
  analysis of 304–5
  Constructivism 306, 309
  importance of 305–13
  life cycle of 308–10
North America, anti-colonialism 331–2
North Atlantic Treaty (1949) 35*b*
North Atlantic Treaty Organization (NATO) 44–5
  Sweden membership 292
North Korea 295*b*
  Non-Proliferation Treaty breach 312
  nuclear weapons 282, 295–6
  weapons of mass destruction 296

SUBJECT INDEX 517

North–South shift 475–6
Norway, renewable energy technology 457
NPT *see* Non-Proliferation Treaty (NPT, 1970)
nuclear arms race 475
    Cold War 79–80
Nuclear Non-Proliferation Regime (NNPR) 350–2
nuclear weapons
    clean bombs as 390
    Constructivism 310–13
    horizontal proliferation 95
    North Korea 282
    reduction in 481
    vertical proliferation 95
    Waltz 96–7
Nuclear Weapons Freeze campaign 311
Nuclear Weapons States (NWS) 350
NUWSS (National Union of Women's Suffrage
    Societies) 376*b*
Nye, Joseph 47, 51, 54–5, 475
Nyerere, Julius 336

OAU (Organization for African Unity) 338–9
objective laws, politics and 75–6
objectivity
    positivism and 11
    social world and 197–8*b*
'Occupy' protest movement 179–80, 213, 213–14*b*
OECD (Organisation for Economic Cooperation and
    Development) 173–4
offensive neorealism, defensive neorealism *vs.* 87–8
oil extraction, indigenous people resistance 457
ontology 8–9, 188, 473
    anthropocene 463–4
    conventional constructivism 292–3
    realism 65–6
Onuf, Nicholas 284
Opium Wars (1839–1842) 362
order, justice *vs.* 125–38
organic intellectuals 215
    traditional intellectuals *vs.* 214
Organisation for Economic Cooperation and
    Development (OECD) 173–4
Organization for African Unity (OAU) 338–9
Orientalism 342–3
Oslo Accords (1993) 42
Oslo Accords (1995) 42
Ottoman empire 110
Our Common World 449
Outright Action International 414
overseas development aid (ODA) 291
Overseas Development Assistance programme
    128, 132*b*
overseas military bases 397–8
Owens, P. 5

Pakistan, Non-Proliferation Treaty breach 311, 350
Palestinian Liberation Organization (PLO) 42
Pankhurst, Emmeline 376*b*, 378
Paris, Roland 53
Paris Climate Change Conference (2015, COP21) 450

parsimonious theory, realism 84
participation, realism and nuclear weapons 97–8
Paterson, Matthew 440, 454, 454*b*
patriarchy 380–1
    resilience 413
Pax Americana 207
peace, feminisms 388–93
Peace Research Institute (PIRI) 291, 389
Pearson, Lester 132*b*
Peetush, Ashwani 357–8
People States and Fear (Buzan) 222
perestroika 281, 281*b*
performing discourses 257–8
Perpetual Peace: A Philosophical Sketch (Kant) 27, 28,
    29, 44, 55, 300
Persaud, Randolph 326
'personal is political', second wave feminism 397
Peters, Arno 253
Peterson, V. Spike 405, 408
Phipps, Alison 385
pieds-noir (black feet) 336*b*
Piketty, Thomas 180
Pinchot, Gifford 434
PIRI (Peace Research Institute) 291, 389
Planet Politics, anthropocene 464
plastic pollution 443*f*
PLO (Palestinian Liberation Organization) 42
pluralism
    English School 111–12, 139
    solidarism and scepticism 136–8
politics
    autonomy of 77
    economy 167
    emancipation and Marxism 153
    identity of 54, 256–7, 260–1*b*
    moral significance of realism 76–7
    objective laws and 75–6
    parity 387
    women's inclusion 144
*Politics Among Nations: The Struggle for Power and
    Peace* (Morgenthau) 74, 151
The Population Bomb (Ehrlich) 434–5*b*
positivism 277
    definitions 11–12
    objectivity and 11
    social sciences 194, 195–6
possessions, stability of 119
postcolonialism 17–18, 321–72, 479, 480, 483, 484
    Cold War 348–9
    contemporary thought 339–46
    definition 322–4
    gender 403–5
    human rights 356–7, 358*b*
    human rights and 354–8
    international law 349–52
    state and 352–3
    see also colonialism; subaltern studies
postpositivist feminists 399–405
postpositivist theories 278, 289
    definition 12

SUBJECT INDEX

Poststructuralism 16, 231–76, 478–9, 480, 483, 484
   definition 232–6
   discipline 255–6
   feminisms 404
   gender 403–5
   helping others 265–6
   mapping the World 251–5
   non-Western world 267–8
   representation 248–51
   sources and themes 236–48
   sovereign states 257–67
   see also Critical International Theory
post-Cold War 477–9
   Hungary liberalism 59–60
   Non-Proliferation Treaty 350–1
   solidarism 129–36
post-First World War 109
   liberalism 30–1
post-war Japan 302–3
power, balance of *see* balance of power
power, interest definition and 76
power acquisition, states and 79–80
Power and Interdependence (Keohane and Nye) 47
power of the people 50
practical issues, Habermas 199
practical knowledge-constitutive interest 202
Prague Spring (1968) 191–2*b*
Prakash, Gyan 339
praxis 214–15
Prebisch, Raùl 164, 165
presence, Derrida 238
Price, Richard 305, 309
primacy of order, international systems 118–21
primary goals, international society 107–11
The Prince (Machiavelli) 69–70
prisons 243–4
private charitable organizations 128
problem-solving theories 205, 206
proletariat 154
promises, sanctity of 119
public health programmes 245
punishment institutes 243–4
Putin, Vladimir 280*b*

qualitative research 10
quasi states 353
Queer Theory 414–17
queering of discipline 412–18
Quijano, Anibal 364

race 2, 357
   Enlightenment and 330–1
   green policy 455
   hierarchy of 329
racism 38–40, 332, 358–63, 473
   colonialism and 328–31
   Eurocentrism *vs.* 361–3
radical contingency 414
radical decentralization 440
Ramo, Joshua Cooper 178–9
Rassemblement National (RN) 336*b*

rationalism, Wright 114–17
Reagan, Ronald 279–80*b*, 286, 311, 476
realism 13–14, 63–104, 479, 483
   classical realism *see* classical realism
   definition 64–6
   early sources of 67–71
   end of Cold War 286
   English School *vs.* 106, 107–8
   idealism *vs.* 36
   international politics and 66–71
   neoclassical realism *see* neoclassical realism
   nomenclature 65–6
   nuclear weapons and 95–8
   see also nuclear weapons
   political realism 76–7
   United Nations 42
   Wight 114–17
reality representation *see* representations of reality
realpolitik 64
Reardon, Betty 389
Redfern, Catherine 385
reductionist theories, realism 84
reform limitations 81
reformist-minded environmentalism 427
regional organizations 2
regulatory institutions, international society and 124
relations of production, Marxism and 154
relative capability 85–6
relative gains
   absolute gains *vs.*, neoliberalism 89
   states and 91
relative power 86
religion 2, 357
   postcolonialism 354–5
renewable energy technology (RET) 457
renunciation, realism and nuclear weapons 98
representations of reality
   Derrida 237
   Poststructuralism 247
republics, liberalism 28–9
research programmes, liberalism 31
Reus-Smit, Christian 293, 301, 305, 309
'Revolt against Western dominance' (Bull) 126–9
revolutionism 114–17
Rhodes, Cecil 325
RhodesMustFall 325
Richter-Montpetit, Melanie 415
right populist movements 406
Rio De Janeiro Earth Summit (1992) 448–51
role of law, Carr 73–4
Rosenthal, Joel 80
Rostow, Walt 164–5*b*
The Round Table 38
Royal African Company 348
Royal Institute for International Affairs (UK)
   31, 359–60
Rublee, Maria Rost 312
ruling classes, ideology of 155
Russian Federation, carbon dioxide emissions 468*t*
Russia's invasion of Ukraine (2022) 284, 303
Rutazibwa, Olivia 361

SUBJECT INDEX 519

Rwanda 357
  conflicts in 223
  Tutsi community 264–5

Sabaratnam, Meera 362, 364
Said, Edward 342–3, 351
Sajed, Alina 326
Sankaran, Krishna 359
Saudi Arabia 357
*Saving Strangers: Humanitarian Interventions in
    International Society* (Wheeler) 131
Scandinavia, foreign policy 133
Schumacher, E. F. 437, 440
Schweller, Randall 94–5
SDF (Self-Defence Force) 302
The Sea Around Us (Carson) 434–5b
Second Cold War 129, 476–7
second wave feminism 378–81, 396, 404
  personal is political 397
security
  Critical International Theory 222–4
  gender and 406–12
  traditional approaches 222–3
  violence against 118
security community 299
Security Council, United Nations 42
security dilemmas 203
Security Studies 222
Segal, Lynne 381
Seko, Mobuto Sese 356–7
Self-Defence Force (SDF) 302
self-help system 78
self-interest, states and 78–9
self-reliance 65
self-reliant economics 440
Senghor, Leopold 336
Serbia, independence 263
settler colonization 332
*Sex and Death in the Rational World of Defense
    Intellectuals* (Cohn) 390–1
sexual freedom 385
sexual orientation 2
Sexual Politics (Millett) 380
sexuality 357
sexualized imagery 390
Shepherd, L. J. 408, 410
Shilliam, Robbie 359
Shinriko, Aum 302
The Sierra Club 434–5b
Sierra Leone, humanitarian interventions 478
Sikkink, Kathryn 308
The Silent Spring (Carson) 436–7
simplicity to complexity 482
simulacrum, Baudrillard 249
simulation, Baudrillard 248
Singer, Hans 164
Singer, P. 165
Singh, Sophia Duleep 376b
'Six Principles of Political Realism' (Morgenthau)
    75, 401–2b
'The Sixties' 233–4b

Sjoberg, Laura 393, 406
Slaughter, Joseph 355
slavery, prohibitions on 330
Sluga, Glenda 396–7
Smith, B. 5
Smuts, Jan 39, 360
social classes, Marxism 15
social conservatism 236
social constructs 282
social reality, interpretation of 284–5
social sciences 193, 194–5
social scientific research 11
social systems 298
  green policy 455
social threats, construction of 299
social world, objective knowledge of 197–8b
Socialism, First wave feminism 378
socialization 85
societies
  collective security *see* collective security
  differences between 358
  domestic security 302
  external security 302
  feminist security studies 407–11
  states of 108
society of states 119
society of states plus 128–9
solidarism
  English School 111–12, 136, 139
  pluralist scepticism and 136–8
  post-Cold War 129–36
Somalia
  conflicts in 223
  humanitarian interventions 478
  US-led interventions 136
'The Souls of White Folk' (Du Bois) 329
South Africa
  apartheid system 337–8b
  British dominion of 38
  republic as 337–8
  white supremacy 39
Southeast Asia
  anti-colonial struggles 335
  economic development 167
sovereignty 78, 257, 266–7
  liberal states as 262
  Poststructuralism 257–67
  reconciliation of 461
Soviet Union
  collapse of 282
  constraints on 207–8
  economic weakness 280–1
Spanish colonialism 327–8
Spanish *conquistadores* 327
Spivak, Gayatri 344–5
Sports Utility Vehicle (SUV) 455
The Stag Hunt 79b
Stages to Growth (Rostow) 164–5b
Stalin, Joseph 191
Stanton, Elizabeth Cady 377
state of Nature 70–1

SUBJECT INDEX

state power, variations in 76
state-centred terms 6
    definitions 7
state-centric international system 452
states
    actors as 288
    anarchical society of *see* anarchical society of
        states
    Baltic States 312–13
    boundaries of 481
    collapsed states 353
    decentring 483–4
    developing states 449
    failed states 353
    foreign policies, influence of 80
    gendered states 406–7
    gendering 405–6
    Greek city-states 120
    identity of 258
    interaction between 284
    interdependence 13, 262
    international society of *see* international societies
    liberal sovereign states *see* liberal sovereign states
    liberalism 13
    postcolonialism and 352–3
    power acquisition and 79–80
    quasi states 353
    relative gains and 91
    Scandinavian states 133
    self-interest and 78–9
    society of 108, 119
    sovereign states *see* sovereignty
    Third World States 356
    weak states 353
    world common good and 128–9
statism 65
Steans, Jill 403, 405
Steinem, Gloria 380
stereotypical hegemonic masculinity 402
Strange, Susan 170, 387
Strategic Arms Limitation Treaty (SALT, 1972) 46–7*b*
Strategic Studies 222
structural analysis, normative analysis to 139
structuralism 234, 235
structuration 290*b*
subaltern studies 343–5
subjectivity, Poststructuralism 247
Sudan, conflicts in 223
Suffragettes 376–7, 376–7*b*
Suganami, H. 136
superpowers 86
    conflict between 349
survival 65
    threats to 203–4
Sweden 291
    Feminist Foreign Policy (FFP) 411–12
    NATO membership 292
    welfare state development 291–2
Sylvester, Christine 142
Syria 295*b*
    military action in 263

system reconfiguration 139–40
system units, international politics (Waltz) 85–6
systemic constructivism 301–5

tactical action, problem solving 207
Taliban regime 263–4
Taylor, Ula 376
technical knowledge-constitutive interest 202
technology, Baudrillard 248–9
technostrategic language 390–1
teleological theoretical perspectives 269–70
terror attacks 259–60*b*
terrorist groups 302
text analysis 239
Theory of International Politics (Waltz) 82–3, 84, 201
Theses on Feuerbach (Marx) 152–3
Third Spaces, identity formation 346
third wave feminism 381–4, 396
Third World 163–4*b*
    approaches to International Law school 349
    rising prominence of 163
    states 356
    see also Global South
Thompson, Graham 172
Thoreau, Henry David 433–6
Thucydides 66, 67–8, 67*b*, 84
Thunberg, Greta 443
Tickner, J. Ann 364, 400–3
TNCs (transnational corporations) 346
Toussaint, Pierre-Dominique 332–3
Towns, Ann 143
traditional intellectuals, organic intellectuals *vs.* 214
traditional theories 196, 197
'The Tragedy of the Commons' (Hardin) 444–7
transatlantic slave trade 325
    abolition of 328
'The Transformation of Community' 219–22
The Transformation of Political Community
    (Linklater) 134
transnational corporations (TNCs) 346
transnational historical bloc 177
transnational multinational corporations 348
transnational relations 47
trans-governmental relations 47
trickle-down politics, modernization 172
True, Jacqui 142
Trump, Donald 313
Truth, Sojurner 377, 383
The Twenty Years Crisis, 1919–1939 (Carr) 36, 72

Ukraine 312–13
UN Convention on Terror (1977) 303
underdeveloping countries 165–6
    green politics 456–7
undistorted communication 218
United Nations (UN) 41–2
    headquarters 43*f*
United Nations Conference on Trade and Development
    (UNCTAD) 173
United Nations Development Programme
    (UNDP) 173, 224, 394

SUBJECT INDEX **521**

United Nations Environmental Programme
  (UNEP) 444
  Emissions Gap Report (2020) 450
United States of America (US)
  anti-colonial power definition 356
  Civil War (1861–1865) 331
  conservation movement emergence 434
  Constitution 377
  Declaration of Independence 26
  foreign policy 258
  War of Independence (1775–1783) 331
  War on Terror (2001) 250, 480
United States of America–Russia relations 284
  carbon dioxide emissions 468*t*
  see also Cold War (1945–1989)
unit-level constructivism 301–5
Universal Declaration of Human Rights
  (UNDHR) 354
  drafting of 355
universality
  Critical Theory 224–5
  Frankfurt School 215
  liberalism 26
university curricula, decolonization 364
unmanned aerial vehicles (UAVs) 250
UNSCR 409–11
US *see* United States of America (US)
US Declaration of Independence (1776) 354
utopianism, Carr 73

Values Party 440
Vatican, anti-LGBT attitudes 414
Versailles Peace Conference (1919) 31, 32*b*
vertical proliferation, nuclear weapons 95
Vietnam War (1955–1975) 233*b*
  anti-colonial struggles 335
A Vindication of the Rights of Women
  (Wollstonecraft) 375
violence, security and 118
violence against women 385
Vitalis, Robert 39, 359
voluntourism 370–1

wa Mutua, Makau 357–8
Wahlstrom, Margot 411
Walden or Life in the Woods (Thoreau) 434
Wallerstein, Immanuel 51, 168
  see also World Systems Theory (WST)
Walsh, Catherine 367
Waltz, Kenneth 82–3, 201, 235, 283, 312, 351, 476
  international politics and 84–6
  nuclear weapons 96–7
war
  Poststructuralism 247
  World Order 123–4
War on Terror (US, 2001) 250, 480
Warren, Mary Anne 413
Washington consensus 172
  challenges to 178–80
Watson, Adam 112
weak states 353

weapons of mass destruction (WMDs) 294
  development of 296
Weber, Cynthia 260–1*b*, 416–17
Weldes, Jutta 365*b*
Wendt, Alexander 282, 283, 299, 300, 301
West, dominance of 127
Wheeler, Nicholas 129, 131, 132–3
white supremacy 360
  South Africa 39
WHO (World Health Organization) 250
Wibben, Annick 408
WID (Women in Development) 394
Wight, Martin 112, 113–14*b*, 113–18, 122
WILPF (Women's International League for Peace and
  Freedom) 388
Wilson, Woodrow 32–6, 49, 50
  biography 33*b*
  white supremacist views 360
Winkel III projection 254, 254*f*
WMDs *see* weapons of mass destruction (WMDs)
Wolf, Naomi 382
Wollstonecraft, Mary 375
women as warriors 392–3, 393–4*b*
Women in Development (WID) 394
Women, Peace and Security (WPS) agenda 409,
  409–10*b*
Women's International League for Peace and Freedom
  (WILPF) 388
Women's Social and Political Union (WSPU) 376*b*
women's suffrage 376–7
Woolf, Leonard 37
World Bank 173, 178
world economy, globalization 141
World (Global) Politics, definitions 6–8
World Health Organization (WHO) 250
The World in Depression 1929–39 (Kindleberger) 87*b*
World Order 207
  institutions of 121–4
World Peace (and How we can Achieve it)
  (Bellamy) 54–6
World Politics: Progress and its Limits (Mayall) 136
world society
  international society from 138–44
  reconfiguration 139–40
World Systems Theory (WST) 168–9
World Trade Organization (WTO) 173
World War I *see* First World War
WPS (Women, Peace and Security) agenda 409,
  409–10*b*
The Wretched of the Earth (Fanon) 341
WSPU (Women's Social and Political Union) 376*b*
WST (World Systems Theory) 168–9
WTO (World Trade Organization) 173

xenophobic nationalism 309

Yeltsin, Boris 280*b*
Yugoslavia *see* former Yugoslavia

Zapatista movement 367
Zehfuss, Maja 238–40